THE W~~I~~ RABASH

ESSAYS

Volume Four

LAITMAN
KABBALAH
PUBLISHERS

Rav Baruch Shalom Halevi Ashlag

The Writings of RABASH
Volume Four—Essays

Contact Information
E-mail: info@kabbalah.info
Web site: www.kabbalah.info
Toll free in USA and Canada: 1-866-LAITMAN

1057 Steeles Avenue West, Suite 532, Toronto,
ON, M2R 3X1, Canada
Tel. 1-416-274-7287

2009 85th Street #51, Brooklyn, New York, 11214, USA
Tel. 1-800-540-3234

Printed in the USA

ISBN: 978-1-9864-9453-3

Library of Congress Control Number: 2016938484

Translation: Rinah Shalom, Chaim Ratz
Translation Assistance: Mickey Cohen, Moshe Eisenberg
Content Editing: Noga Bar Noye
Editing and Proofreading: Mary Pennock, Mary Miesem
Internal Design: Gill Zahavi
Cover Design: Baruch Khovov/Inna Smirnova
Executive Editor: Chaim Ratz
Printing and Post Production: Uri Laitman

FIRST EDITION: MAY 2018
Second printing

Table of Contents

Tav-Shin-Nun (1989 - 1990)

Tav-Shin-Mem-Tet

(1988 - 1989)

What Is the Measure of Repentance?

Article No. 1, Tav-Shin-Mem-Tet, 1988/89

It is written (Hosea 14), "Return, O Israel, unto the Lord your God, for you have failed in your iniquity." We should understand the following: 1) What does "unto the Lord your God" mean? It appears as though if the repentance did not reach "the Lord your God," it is still not regarded as repentance. Thus, how can we know if the repentance has reached "the Lord your God?" Who can climb up and see if it has reached or not? 2) We should understand the words, "for you have failed in your iniquity." It appears as though this is the reason why repentance must rise "unto the Lord your God." We should understand how they are related to each other. 3) We should understand the meaning of "for you have failed in your iniquity." What does "your iniquity" mean? It appears as though there could be failure from something other than man's iniquity. This is why the verse says to us, "for you have failed," meaning that your failure came from your iniquity and not from something else. Thus, what is that other thing that one might think that it did not come to him from his iniquities?

Failure means that a person calculated that now he can make good business, but then lost in the deal because some failure happened to him. It is like a person walking on a road and stumbling on a rock he did not see. In spirituality, we should understand that he suffered a fall and must have stumbled on some rock along the way.

Therefore, we must know what is the rock on which he stumbled and which caused him to fall midway. The writing comes and says that the failure was because of your iniquity, which is the stone on which you stumbled and fell. We need to know this in order to be wary of the stumbling block. Thus, we should understand why one's iniquity is a stumbling block for which he cannot walk in the path of the Creator and observe Torah and Mitzvot [commandments/good deeds].

The thing is that the first iniquity begins with the sin of the tree of knowledge. Adam HaRishon was born circumcised (Avot de Rabbi Natan, 2nd ed., 5). But afterward, because of the sin, he pulled on his foreskin (Sanhedrin 38). As he interprets in the "Introduction to Panim Masbirot," pulling on his foreskin refers to the foreskin of the three impure Klipot [shells/peels]. When he was born, he did not have this foreskin since the external body of Adam HaRishon, says the ARI, was of Malchut that rose to Bina of Malchut de Assiya, called "Malchut that is sweetened in Bina." This is considered being born circumcised.

Through the sin of the tree of knowledge, he drew on himself the Malchut from the quality of judgment, which is the form of Gadlut [greatness/adulthood] from the vacant space. This is regarded as pulling on his foreskin. That is, he drew on himself the three impure Klipot, from which come all the sins that one commits. That is, the Gadlut of the reception that Adam HaRishon elicited by himself through the sin causes all the sins, for the root of the sins extends from the mind and heart.

By this we can interpret what we asked, What does it mean that "you have failed in your iniquity"? This refers to your iniquity, which extends from the sin of the tree of knowledge. This is called "your iniquity," meaning that stone, on which all created beings stumble, is that a person comes and says, "I want to understand if this is worthwhile, if it pays off to observe Torah and Mitzvot," meaning what the reception for oneself—which extends from the Gadlut of the reception that Adam HaRishon extended to himself due to the sin of the tree of knowledge—will gain out of it.

As in corporeality, when a person walks along the way and stumbles on a rock on the road, he does not see the rock. This is why he stumbles on it. Similarly, in the work, when a person wants to walk on the path of the Creator, he does not see that the rock, which is the will to receive, for Even [stone] comes from the [Hebrew] word Avin [I will understand], when he wants to understand everything—what pleasure will come from this to the receiver for himself.

When a person is told he must believe above reason that Providence is good and does good, he says, "I want to see that this is so." But to believe is against the understanding. The understanding says that what you see is true, and what you do not see, how can you tell if it is true? When he is told he must believe, he says, "How do you know that what you believe is true?" This is the stumbling block on which people fail.

It follows that the stone on which we fail is only the lack of faith. When a person begins to walk on the path of the work of bestowal, he complains to the Creator, "Why have You made the concealment of Your face to the point that we cannot overcome the concealment that the Creator has placed, so we can overcome those two things— mind and heart?"

Indeed, the question is, Why did the Creator make it so we must believe, and did not do this otherwise, meaning that anyone who begins to work immediately sees the greatness of the Creator? The fact that the Creator made it that we must work with faith causes many people to move away from the work. It is as though the Creator made working with faith a stumbling block for all those who are failing. Why did He do this?

Baal HaSulam said about this that we must believe that the Creator made it this way, that our work will be in the form of

"And they believed in the Lord and in his servant, Moses," is the best way in order to achieve the complete goal, which is to do good to His creations. It is specifically through faith that the creatures can achieve the completion of the goal, which is to receive the delight and pleasure that the Creator contemplated giving to the created beings.

However, we must not say that the Creator could not have done it otherwise, meaning through knowing. Certainly, the Creator is almighty and can do anything He wants. However, as we must believe in the purpose of creation, that it is to do good to His creations, we should also believe about the way to achieve the goal, that faith is the best and most successful way. Therefore, the Creator chose the path of faith, for only by faith will man be able to achieve the completion of the goal.

Accordingly, the clarification, "for you have failed in your iniquity," is the *Gadlut* of the vessels of reception, which *Adam HaRishon* extended on himself due to the sin of the tree of knowledge. We should interpret what we asked, What is the connection between "You have failed in your iniquity" and "Return, O Israel, unto the Lord your God"?

We asked, Can one ascend and see if the repentance has reached "the Lord your God"? According to the above, we should interpret that since all the failures that a person cannot achieve wholeness and fails midway are only because the first iniquity is the stumbling block for which the person falls. Therefore, when a person wants to repent and does not know what is repentance, the prophet says, "Return, O Israel, unto the Lord your God."

This means that everything a person does will be for "the Lord your God." It follows that "unto" means "until you clearly know that everything you do is for the Lord your God." That is, he has reached a degree where he feels that for himself, it is not worth living, and he lives for the sake of the Creator. This is called "repentance."

But if he has not achieved this degree, it is still not regarded as "repentance." The reason is that "you have failed in your iniquity," which is self-reception. That is, the only failure is that a person cannot achieve Dvekut [adhesion] with the Creator. Naturally, correcting it is by reaching "unto the Lord your God," where all his actions are only to bestow. This is called "repentance."

For this, a person does not need to ascend and see if his repentance has reached "the Lord your God." Rather, the person himself sees and feels if he has no other aim in life other than what pertains to the benefit of the Creator, and he says that it is not worth living for his own sake.

However, a person might deceive himself in this. That is, he might agree to work for the sake of the Creator because he thinks that it will yield great pleasure for his own benefit.

Still, a person can see the truth about this, too, since according to the rule, if a person really wants to adhere to the Creator and he already has equivalence of form then he needs to be rewarded with opening the eyes in the Torah. According to the rule, "He who learns Torah *Lishma* [for Her sake] is shown the secrets of Torah," if he has still not been rewarded with the secrets of Torah, it is a sign that he is still far from aiming only to benefit the Creator.

It is written in the "Introduction to The Book of Zohar" (Item 33): "This is the work in Torah and *Mitzvot Lishma*, in order to bestow and to not receive reward. This work cleanses the will to receive for oneself in him, and replaces it with a will to bestow. To the extent that one purifies the will to receive, he becomes worthy of receiving the five parts of the soul called NRNHY, for they stand in the will to bestow and cannot clothe one's body as long as the will to receive controls it, since dressing and equivalence of form go hand in hand. And when one is rewarded with being entirely in the will to bestow and not at all for oneself, he will be rewarded with obtaining equivalence of form with his upper NRNHY."

Accordingly, we see that if a person walks on the path of bestowal, he must be rewarded with the secrets of Torah. If he has not been rewarded, it is a sign that he is still in self-love, although he feels that he wants to work only in order to bestow. For this reason, at that time he must seek more counsels and tactics to be rewarded with love of the Creator and not with self-love. However, we must remember that in order to be rewarded with love of the Creator and not for one's own benefit is not within man's power. Rather, it is a gift of God.

However, we should know that when a person wants to emerge from merely performing actions, without the aim, and wants to begin the work of acting with the aim to bestow, there is much work in this, since when the body begins to hear about the aim to bestow, it immediately begins to resist and does not let one continue this work, showing him dark colors in this work.

In that state, a person should believe that only the Creator can help. Here is where a person can make a true prayer. It is called "true" because it is really the truth. That is, the Creator has made man unable to help himself, and the reason is that "There is no light without a *Kli*," as we have said several times. As Baal HaSulam says, the Creator made man unable to exit self-love by himself in order for man to need the Creator's help. How does the Creator help? With a holy soul, as it is written in *The Zohar*. Otherwise, a person does not have the need to receive the light of the Torah, and will settle for observing Torah and *Mitzvot* and not needing to receive the *NRNHY* of *Neshama* that have been prepared for him.

But when he sees that he cannot exit self-love and be rewarded with equivalence of form, he needs the Creator's help. How does He help a person? Through a holy soul, called "upper light" that is revealed within man, so he will feel that there is a soul within him that is "a part of God above." It follows that according to man's ability to overcome, he increases the disclosure of the light of the Creator. For this reason, the Creator has made the hardening of the heart, so that man will be unable to overcome the evil in him and will need the Creator. By this, man will need to be rewarded with the *NRNHY* of *Neshama*.

However, this order of hardening of the heart comes precisely when one wants to work in order to bestow and makes efforts to achieve *Lishma* [for Her sake]. Then begins the hardening of the heart.

This is similar to a mother wanting to teach her child to walk on his own. She kneels and lets the child approach her. When she sees that the child is near, she moves farther from the child so the child will become accustomed to walking on his own more than before. But the child begins to cry, since he has strained to approach the mother, and he is crying because his mother moved away. He thinks that his mother hates him, and this is why she moved away from him. He cannot judge his mother to the side of merit, that her distancing is to the child's best.

Conversely, as long as the child did not begin to walk, the mother did not move away from him. Instead, he saw that wherever he walked, she held him by her hand and led him.

It is likewise in the work. Before a person begins to walk alone, meaning before he emerges from the general public, whose work is only in the practical part, without the aim to bestow, it is considered that the mother is holding the child by her hand and leads him. That is, he does not feel remoteness on the part of the upper one. On the contrary, he sees no flaws in his work. Naturally, he cannot say that He is moving away from him, since he feels that He is close.

The reason is that he is following the path of the general public, whose reward is self-benefit. Hence, this view is close to the body. Therefore, the body does not resist his work, and he feels whole. It follows that he is in a state as though his mother is leading him by the hand.

But when he emerges from the general public and wants to work in order to bestow, he is regarded as a child who has begun to walk alone. Then the mother moves away from him. Each time he thinks that he has achieved the work of bestowal, he is shown from above that he is still far from the work of bestowal. How is he shown that he is far? By showing him each time what is "in order to bestow." At that time, these thoughts bring him foreign thoughts until sometimes he wants to escape the campaign.

Afterward, he is given another nearing and he begins to think that now he is close to the mother. But once again, he is shown that He is moving away from him. This is the meaning of "Do not go far from us." It is also written, "Do not hide Your face from us." There are two meanings to this: 1) Your moving away from us causes us to want to escape the campaign. 2) Do not move far from us, let us understand that it is not moving away, but that You are doing this for our sake, so we may know that everything You do is all for our sake.

What Is a Great or a Small Sin in the Work?

Article No. 2, Tav-Shin-Mem-Tet, 1988/89

First, we need to know what is regarded as "work." That is, what is the meaning of the word "work" that we use? We should know that we were given the 613 Mitzvot [commandments/good deeds] of the Torah to observe, and the seven Mitzvot of our great sages [De Rabanan]. We should also observe the customs of Israel that the sages of Israel established, each place according to its custom. They determined for us what is a great Mitzva [singular of Mitzvot] and what is a great transgression.

For example, our sages said, "Great is respect of the father and mother, for the Creator was more strict about it than about His own glory" (Jerusalem Talmud, Chapter 1, 5:1). Or, "Almsgiving is greater than charity" (Sukkah 49), and many others like it by our sages. The same applies to transgressions. Our sages said, "The punishment for slander is worse than the punishment for idolatry" (Midrash Gadol and Gedolah, Chapter 18).

It follows that they determined what is a great Mitzva and what is a small Mitzva by comparing one to the other. Also, concerning transgressions, they determined which is a grave transgression, and opposite it, which is a small transgression. We must believe that what they determined is really so. This is the meaning of "faith in the sages," that we must believe what they said and we must not doubt them. All this is called "Torah," meaning that man's hand has no connection to it.

"Work" is named after man, after what he does, since a person who works makes the measures, how to keep them. That is, the intention over the act is not in one's hand to change in any way. Rather, this pertains to the reason, meaning that the worker has measures of the reason for which he observes Torah and *Mitzvot*.

This is as Maimonides said (*Hilchot Teshuva*, Chapter 11), "Therefore, when teaching little ones, women, and uneducated people, they are taught to work only out of fear and in order to receive reward. Until they gain much knowledge and acquire much wisdom, they are taught that secret little-by-little."

We see that Maimonides says that there are measures in the reason, meaning that "women," "little ones," and "uneducated people" have the reason of *Lo Lishma* [not for Her sake]. But those who have already gained much knowledge and acquired much wisdom are given a different reason, which is the *Lishma* [for Her sake], which is that they must work in order to bestow contentment upon their Maker, and not for their own sake.

It follows that in terms of the act, there is no difference between small and great. But in the intention, meaning in the reason for observing Torah and *Mitzvot*, there are differences between types of people. Some people belong to the general public, or as Maimonides says, "uneducated people." There is a difference between the general public and the individual. That is, some individuals do not want to walk in the path of the general public and work for their own sake, but a passion has awakened in their heart to work in order to bestow.

We should know that the work of bestowal means that the person is the giver, while in the work in order to receive reward, the

Creator is the giver. There is a big difference between them because the reason for the work is what one receives for it. Thus, a person evaluates the Mitzvot according to the reward. If there is a great and important reward for the work, a person regards it as a great Mitzva, since he is examining the reward.

Conversely, in the work of bestowal, where man is the giver, the consideration is the greatness of the receiver, meaning to whom a person gives. The greater the receiver, the greater and more important is the giving. It is as our sages said, "With an important person, if she gives and he says, 'You are hereby dedicated [wedded],' it is as though he has given, since she enjoyed his receiving from her."

Thus, we see that the greatness of the giving depends on whom we give. By this we measure the greatness of the act. That is, if we give to a great person, it is considered "great giving." If we give to a small person, it is "small giving."

From this we can gauge the measure of the work of bestowal. If a person bestows upon a small king, it is small work, since the giver is not so impressed while giving to a small king. But if the person bestows upon a great king, the act of giving is great because "she enjoyed his receiving from her." It is a great pleasure because he is bestowing upon a great king.

Thus, we see that the greatness or smallness of the giving depends on the worker himself. One who works in Torah and Mitzvot determines to which type he belongs. If he is still in the education called "commandments taught by people," it means he is still working in Torah and Mitzvot for his own sake, as mentioned in the words of Maimonides, who says, "When teaching little ones, women, and uneducated people, they are taught to work in order to receive reward," called Lo Lishma.

"Taught" means that as he has been used to working thus far, which was the time of Lo Lishma, that person measures smallness and greatness according to the measure of the reward. But those who work in order to bestow, measure according to the greatness of the receiver of the work.

Accordingly, we can understand that there might be two people performing the same *Mitzva*. To one, it will be considered a great *Mitzva*, since he gives his work to a great king. Thus, he feels that he is serving a great king, which makes him delighted and elated that he has been given the great privilege of entering and serving a great king, and there is no end to his joy.

Conversely, the other one does not think that in everything he does, he is serving a great king, but rather a small king. That is, he sees that no one appreciates observing his commandments. But since he feels sorry for this king, he observes his commandments. In that state, a person understands that the king should be considerate of him because he feels sorry for the king when no else wants to look at the king. In that state, a person measures what the king pays him for his work.

If the reward that the king gives him does not shine for him, although he does everything that the king commanded him, then he does it lazily, without vitality, since the reward that the king will give him for his work does not shine for him.

It follows that those two people, who are doing the same, to one it is regarded as performing a great commandment because he receives much vitality and elation in serving a great king, while the other has no elation and he does it by force, since the reward he will receive later does not shine for him as important.

Hence, there is a great difference between them: One thinks that the *Mitzva* he is observing is a small *Mitzva*, meaning of little importance, and the other considers it a great *Mitzva*, meaning he says that he cannot grasp the importance and greatness of the *Mitzva*, and feels that he does not need to be given any reward for it later.

Rather, he feels right now the reward in that he derives great pleasure in the privilege of serving a great king. It follows that he is delighted because he has already received the reward. He does not have to believe he will receive reward, and he has no doubts about the reward, that we can say that he is unhappy since he doubts the matter of reward and punishment because he has received the reward right on the spot, and he does not expect any other reward.

Rather, he believes that in serving a great king, this gives him pleasure, and for this, it is worthwhile to be born, to have the privilege of serving a great king. It follows that the person himself determines what is regarded as a great Mitzva or a small Mitzva.

However, sometimes it might be to the contrary, meaning that he is walking on one line, where all his actions are only to aim that the act will be in order in its every detail and subtlety. He engages in Torah and Mitzvot in order to later receive reward in this world or in the next world, and he believes in reward and punishment when he performs the Mitzva, and is meticulous in doing the most important Mitzvot that our sages determined which is a great Mitzva and which is a less important one.

When he performs the Mitzva that he has chosen as a great Mitzva, he is happy and feels that he is the most important person, since he has a greater reward than the rest of the people. Naturally, he performs the Mitzva with great enthusiasm.

But his friend, who is doing the same great Mitzva as he, does not want to work in order to receive reward. Rather, he wants to work in order to bestow. And in order to work in order to bestow he must believe that he is serving a great and important king, worth serving without anything in return. If the faith he has in the Creator cannot make him feel that he is serving a great King then he has no power to work joyfully.

Instead, at that time he works compulsively, overcoming resistance, since the body makes him see that it is not worthwhile to work in order to bestow upon a small king. It tells him, "I can understand your friend, who is working in order to receive reward, so it does not matter if he is serving a great king or a small one, since he looks mainly at the reward."

Thus, it makes no difference whether he is a great or a small king, since what makes him a great king is mainly the reward. If he gives a small reward, he is a small king. It follows that here there is a different order than in bestowing contentment upon his Maker, which is the only reason obligating him to engage in Torah and *Mitzvot*, compared to the reason obliging him to engage in Torah and *Mitzvot* being to receive reward.

We see that it is impossible to determine the truth according to man's feelings. When a person sees that he is working gladly and enthusiastically, it still does not mean that he is on the right path. This is why our sages said, "Make for yourself a rav [great one/teacher]," for only the rav can guide him and determine which way he is going.

But a working person, although he feels which is good and which is bad, he still cannot know the truth because he still can understand only one scrutiny—the scrutiny of "bitter and sweet." This is so because when he is happy and works with enthusiasm, he feels a sweet taste. Therefore, he says that he is on the right path. But when a person has to work coercively, he tastes a bitter flavor. Then, a person understands that he is in a state of descent, and a person takes this discernment to know that this is a true scrutiny.

However, the scrutiny of "bitter and sweet" was before the sin of the tree of knowledge. After the sin of the tree of knowledge we were given a different scrutiny called "true and false." That is, a person might taste sweetness in a state but it is a lie, and he might taste bitterness but it is true.

This is similar to what is written in the "Introduction to *Panim Masbirot*" (Item 16): We should thoroughly know the two types of scrutiny applied in us: The first scrutiny is called "scrutinies of good and bad," and the second scrutiny is called "scrutinies of true and false."

The first scrutiny is a physical active force, which works through the sensation of bitter and sweet. It loathes and rejects the form of bitterness because it feels bad, and loves and attracts the form of sweetness because it feels good.

In addition to them there is the human species, in whom the Creator has imprinted an intellectual active power, which works in the second scrutiny: rejecting falsehood and vanity by loathing to the point of nausea, and attracts true matters and any benefit with great love. This scrutiny is called "the scrutiny of true and false." This applies only to the human species, each according to his own extent.

Know that this second active force was created and came to man because of the serpent. By creation, he had only the first active force from the scrutinies of good and bad, which was enough to serve him at that time.

Accordingly, we see that when a person wants to go by "bitter and sweet," that scrutiny is no longer true after the sin of the tree of knowledge. Instead, it might be that a person feels sweetness in the work, while he is immersed in falsehood, or the other way around. For this reason, they said, "Make for yourself a rav and depart from doubt" (Avot, Chapter 1:16).

Although the person himself determines how he feels, he might still feel sweetness though it is not on the path of truth that enables us to achieve Dvekut [adhesion] with the Creator, since he might be walking in the opposite direction than the track that leads to Dvekut with the Creator, where all his labor is in order to achieve equivalence of form, which applies to all the degrees, as this is the meaning of the Masach [screen] that is on the Aviut [thickness], where specifically by placing the Masach, the delight and pleasure are revealed.

By this we should interpret what our sages said (Avot, Chapter 2:1), "Be careful with a light Mitzva as with a grave one, for you do not know the reward for the Mitzvot." There is seemingly a contradiction in the words of our sages, who said, "Great is respect of the father and mother, for the Creator was more strict about it than about His own glory," or "Almsgiving is greater than charity," and many others like them. If they said, "Be careful with a light Mitzva as with a grave one," what does it mean that it is great, how is it expressed that one Mitzva is greater than another?

While performing the Mitzvot, it is impossible to know whose Mitzvot he is observing. Certainly, one who observes the Mitzvot of a great king, who commanded us to observe, is certainly more important than one who observes the Torah and *Mitzvot* of a small king. It follows that a light *Mitzva*, but one that a great king commanded to do, is certainly more important than one who observes a grave *Mitzva* of a small king.

Man is always in ascents and descents, meaning that sometimes he believes that he is serving a great king, and sometimes to the contrary. Therefore, our sages instructed us that we should know that greatness or smallness do not depend on the commandment, but on the greatness of the one who gives the commandments. This is what a person should mind, that he believes each time that there is a great king. In other words, a person should try to obtain the greatness of the Creator. This is the most important thing, and not other things.

What Is the Difference between the Gate of Tears and the Rest of the Gates?

Article No. 3, Tav-Shin-Mem-Tet, 1988/89

Our sages said (*Berachot* 59), "Rabbi Elazar said, 'Since the day of the ruin of the Temple, the gates of prayer have been locked. Although the gates of prayer have been locked, the gates of tears have not been locked.'" People ask, If the gates of tears were not locked, why are gates needed, if they are not locked?

We see that when little children cry when they want something, or when a person sees children playing with games and one child snatches something from another and the child cries, when people pass by them, who pays attention to this? Everyone knows that although now they are squabbling, later they will make up. Therefore, no one pays attention to the weeping of children.

But when a grownup walks on the street and people see that he is crying, it captures the attention of those who pass by him to know why he is crying, because certainly, a grownup does not cry over nothing. Therefore, the crying of a grownup causes interest; perhaps he can help him.

It is likewise in the work. There are people who observe Torah and *Mitzvot* [commandments/good deeds] with all the details and consider themselves complete and with fear. But since we must observe what our sages said, "Be very, very humble," this causes them a lot of work since they must search within them for some flaw that will enable them to say that they are lowly.

For example, I heard of a person who asked a wise disciple how come he says that he is lowly and has transgressions, when he sees for himself that not many people in the world are as wise and God fearing as he. It follows that by saying that he is lowly, he is lying. He replied to him that he believes in our sages who said, "No person is saved from the dust of slander." Therefore, he already has a flaw. A person like him, who knows about himself that he is a complete person, when he cries for the Creator to give him strength to engage in Torah and *Mitzvot*, is not crying over an essential matter—that the Creator will bring him closer to Torah and *Mitzvot*. Rather, he lacks some supplement to the completeness that he has. Although he cries bitterly, no one looks at his cries since he is crying over luxuries.

It follows that there are gates of tears before this person, but they are closed and do not let his prayer enter for the same reason as in corporeality, one does not cry over luxuries, but over necessities.

This is similar to the allegory about a person who came from abroad and went to a certain town or a small settlement. The secretariat of the settlement wanted to charge him, say, $10,000 in order to give him a place to stay at the settlement. But that Jew did not have the required amount. He went to the rabbi and poured his heart out. The rabbi promised him that on Shabbat [Sabbath], before the reading of the Torah [the highlight of the Shabbat service], he would speak to the congregants and they will certainly donate.

So it was. The rabbi raised his voice wailing about how a man tending to children came from Russia and suffered a great deal, now he has no place to live and no job, and we can save this person. The rabbi's wailing impressed the congregants and they gave him the required sum.

Six months later, the rabbi came to the congregants once more and started wailing and crying out once more: "Compassionate Jews, now, too, I need $10,000. My wife was at a wedding and another rabbi's wife came from America, and wore a diamond ring worth $10,000. Now my wife wants me to buy her such a ring, as well. The rabbi raised his voice weeping, but no one in the crowd would donate for the rabbi's wife's ring. As the rabbi began to wail more loudly, the crowd began to laugh at his weeping. He complained to the congregants, "Why when I came to collect money for an ordinary person, each gave according to his heart's desire, and now that I am asking for money for a wise disciple, who is a rabbi, too, you are not helping me? Where is the glory of the Torah?"

The lesson is that when a person cries and his tears are over necessities, meaning that he cries out and wails to the Creator to help him be a simple person, not even a wise disciple, but simply a Jew who believes in the Creator, and to be able to observe "And you shall love the Lord your God with all your heart and with all you soul," and that he will not be immersed in self-love, but wants to be a simple person, meaning to always want to love the Creator and not work for his own sake, yet he sees that he has no power to overcome the self-love, and everything he does is for his own sake, so what makes him be regarded as a Jew when he cannot even observe the *Shema* reading [a key section in every Jewish prayer], and when he says, "And you shall love the Lord your God," he sees how far he is from it. He cries over this and sees that he has already done everything in order to be rewarded with anything that is true, and he has already been to all the gates with his prayer, but saw that all the gates are locked. Then, in his anguish, he begins to cry.

When these tears come to the gate of tears, he sees that this gate was not locked, since he is not asking for luxuries, for supplements to the possession of Torah and *Mitzvot* that he already has. Rather, he is asking only to be a simple Jew, to believe in the Creator and to love Him, and not be immersed in self-love. But since he cannot do anything for the sake of the Creator, he feels that he is simply not a Jew.

That is, he asks himself, "I believe in the Creator, and He is very great, yet He sees that I cannot relinquish my self-benefit before the benefit of the Creator." Therefore, he yells and cries simply that he lacks faith, to truly believe in the Creator, and not as lip-service. This is similar to a person whispering that he is taking upon himself faith in the Creator, when in fact, he is not impressed when he says, "I hereby take upon myself the burden of the kingdom of heaven," and he does everything for his own sake, and has no strength to work for the sake of the Creator. It is said that before such a person, the gates of tears were not locked, since he is asking for necessity and not for luxury, as in the above allegory about the wise disciple rabbi who asked to be given money for a diamond for his wife.

It follows that saying that the gates of tears were not locked, and we asked, "If they were not locked, why is a gate required in the first place?" The answer is that the gate of tears was locked before those who cry over luxuries. Their tears are as the tears of a child crying over nothing, or as in the allegory about the rabbi. This is not so for those who cry over necessity, which are things that concern every person who sees that he is standing between life and death, since he believes what our sages said, "The wicked in their lives are called 'dead,'" since they have no *Dvekut* [adhesion] with the Creator and are immersed in self-love, which is considered separation from the Life of Lives, and this is why they are called dead. It follows that he is crying simply to be given life. Certainly, one who prays for life, who is afraid of death, cries from the bottom of the heart, and his prayer is not mere weeping.

But on the surface, a person cannot tell if one is crying over nothing, the way children cry, or like the rabbi allegory. However, above, it is known what a person is asking for so that his request will be answered, since luxuries are not given from above, as he is certain not to keep what he is given and the *Sitra Achra* [other side] will receive it all. Therefore, if a person sees that his prayer was not accepted, he must go over the request that he is making and see whether he really needs heaven's mercy, or if what he is lacking is a mere luxury. A person should believe that when he prays for necessity, his prayer will be answered, as was said, "The gates of tears were not locked," when a person asks for his life to be saved and not to remain in a state of "The wicked are called 'dead.'" Instead, he will be rewarded with *Dvekut* with the Creator.

This is similar to what Baal HaSulam explained about the words, "When the gates of prayer were locked, the gates of tears were not locked." That is, when were the gates of tears not locked? It is when a person has been to all the gates and saw that they were all locked before him. In that state, the wailing and the tears burst from his heart, when he sees that all the gates were locked and he has no hope of approaching the Creator. These tears cause the gates of tears not to be locked.

But mere tears, before a person sees that all the gates were locked, these tears cannot be accepted at the gate of tears. For this reason, before him, the gate of tears is locked, since he still does not have a real desire for the Creator to bring him closer. Rather, he thinks that he can approach the *Kedusha* by himself, as well. As a result, his prayer is incomplete, so he really needs the Creator to help him.

Accordingly, we can interpret what we ask (at the *Yom Kippur* closing prayer), "Open a gate for us, when a gate is locked." We should understand why specifically when a gate is locked, we need a gate to open up to us. After all, we have been praying all day, so why is it not enough for our plea to be accepted, and we ask that only now, when a gate is locked, it will open for us, as though only now we can pray and before, our prayers were not enough?

The thing is that we should pray two kinds of prayers: 1) When a person comes to pray to the Creator for his needs, he still does not know what he needs. He might be crying bitterly to the Creator to grant his wish, but he is praying for trivialities, such as in the allegory about the children or the allegory about the wise disciple rabbi. Therefore, a person's first prayer is that the Creator will let him know what he really needs, so he will know what to ask.

In the *Rosh Hashanah* [beginning of the year] prayer, and in the *Musaf* [supplemental] prayer on *Yom Kippur* [Day of Atonement], we say, "Be the mouths of Your people, the house of Israel, who are poised to ask for prayer and litany before You for Your people, the house of Israel. Instruct them what to say; make them understand what they will say; answer what they will ask; make them know how to glorify."

It is known that in terms of the work, every person is a small world. Therefore, "Your people, the house of Israel," means the person himself. "The messenger of Your people, the house of Israel" means that the person prays and asks that the Creator will save him. The one who prays is called a "messenger" for the person himself, and the person himself is regarded as "Your people, the house of Israel." We must pray that our messenger will know what to pray for, since one does not know what he really needs. Rather, the Creator should notify a person what is important and what is unimportant, meaning what is regarded as necessity, and what is considered luxury.

This is why we are told to pray for those who pray, "Instruct them what to say; make them understand what they will say; answer what they will ask." We pray that the Creator will let us know what to pray. At the time of the locking of a gate, we believe that we already have the knowledge, meaning we already understand what to pray for because we already know how to pray for the main thing we need.

2) At that time begins the second kind of prayer, where He sheds real tears, meaning for a real need. It is about this that we pray, "Open a gate for us when a gate is locked." When a gate is locked, we believe that we already received the knowledge from above what to pray for. For this reason, we say, "Do not close the gate," as though now, at the end of the day of all the prayers, we can ask on a real prayer.

By this we can interpret what we say on *Rosh Hashanah* and *Yom Kippur*, "And all believe that He answers the anxious, opens a gate to those who knock in repentance." We should understand why we need to pray to open the gate if the gate is open. That is, why do we need to pray that He will open the gate if there is a very simple way—to shed tears in the prayer he is praying? It is known that the gate of tears was not locked, so a person has the option of crying and he does not need to ask for a favor, that the gate will be opened for him. Thus, why does one need to believe this, as it is written, "And all believe that He answers the anxious, opens a gate to those who knock in repentance"? After all, he has a good solution—that the person making repentance will cry with tears and that gate will not be locked.

However, a person must pray first, in order to know what he really needs. Then, he is notified from above that he does not need luxuries, but as *The Zohar* says about the verse "Or make his sin known to him," the Creator makes him know the sin. At that time he knows on what he needs to repent, meaning to restore what he is lacking.

It follows that when a person knows that he is wicked, as in "the wicked in their lives are called 'dead,'" when he has come to realize that the fact that he is placed under the control of the will to receive separates him from the Life of Lives, he knocks about this and wants to repent. That is, he wants to be given help from above so he can emerge from self-love and be able to love the Creator with all his heart. Thus, he feels that he is wicked, since where he should love the Creator, he loves himself.

It follows that his knocks, we understand that he does what he can to make the Creator bring him closer and take him out of the control of his own evil. This is called "real tears." This is the meaning of what we explained, "Open a gate for us, when a gate is locked." That is, since he sees that all the gates are closed, he begins to knock. It follows that at the time of the locking of the gate, when he has already prayed and was notified the reason for the sin, he begins to shed the real tears, meaning at that time he simply wants to be a Jew. At that time, his knocks are regarded as tears, and this is the meaning of "Who opens a gate to those who knock in repentance."

What Is a Flood of Water in the Work?

Article No. 4, Tav-Shin-Mem-Tet, 1988/89

*T*he *Zohar*, Noah (Item 148), interprets the verse, "Behold, I bring the flood of water on the earth." These are its words: "Rabbi Yehuda opened: 'These are the waters of Merivah [Hebrew: quarreling], where the children of Israel quarreled.' He asks, 'Did the children of Israel not quarrel with the Creator elsewhere?' He answers, 'These were the waters of quarreling, which gave power and might to the accuser to grow stronger because there is sweet water, and there is bitter water, *Kedusha* [holiness] and the opposite of the right line. There is clear water and there is murky water, the *Kedusha* and the opposite of the left line. There is water of peace and water of quarreling, *Kedusha* and the opposite of the middle line. Hence, the verse says, 'These are the waters of Merivah, where the children of Israel quarreled with the Creator,' indicating that it is the opposite of the middle line, for they extended on themselves what they should not have extended—the opposite, called 'waters of quarreling'—and were defiled in it, as it is written, 'And He sanctified in them.'"

We should understand the meaning of the three types of water, which he says correspond to three lines. What is it in the work? *The*

Zohar certainly speaks from high degrees, where there is the matter of three types of abundance that manifest in three manners, but what can we learn from this in the work?

First, we must know what is "a flood of water" in the work. This flood was the saboteur who "obliterated every living thing." It is known that when a person begins to work in the work of bestowal, the body complains, "What is this work for you?" "What point is there in it, that you do not want to work for your own benefit? since you must see that you will enjoy life, and bestowing means that you will not work for yourself. What benefit will you derive from working to delight the Creator by observing His Torah and *Mitzvot* [commandments/good deeds], which He has commanded us through Moses? Will He reward you for your work, that you labor in Torah and *Mitzvot*?"

"To this, you tell me that you want to work without reward. How is it possible to understand such a thing as working for no reward? It makes no sense! Our inherent nature is a desire to receive delight and pleasure, and if we exert in something, it must be that we are receiving delight and pleasure in return for our efforts. Thus, it is against our nature!" This is called the "What" argument.

However, there is another argument by which the body resists the work of the Creator when a person tells the body, "We must believe in the Creator, that He is the overseer who leads the world as The Good Who Does Good." At that time, the body comes to the person and makes the Pharaoh argument, who said, "Who is the Lord that I should obey His voice?" That is, it is hard for him to believe in the Creator. He says he can work for the sake of the Creator, but on condition: If he felt the greatness of the Creator, he would understand that it is worthwhile to work for Him.

It is as we see in corporeality: If a great person comes and many people determine that he is great, and common sense agrees with those who say that he is great, then just as in corporeality, a person can work and serve the great one. Clearly, if he could feel this greatness about the Creator he would also be able to work and serve the Creator. Yet, we do not have this feeling with regard to the Creator. Rather, as we see, the *Shechina* [Divinity] is in exile and there is no sensation whatsoever of the greatness of the Creator. Thus, how can he annul his self-benefit before the benefit of the Creator?

When those two—*Mi* and *MA* ["Who" and "What" respectively]—connect, it creates the combination *Mayim* [in Hebrew]. This is the meaning of the words "a flood of water on the earth," by which they died. That is, all the spirituality, which is called "life," was lost due to these waters, which are the two questions, "Who" and "What." The spirit of life of *Kedusha* departed from them and they remained dead, as it is written, "The wicked in their lives are called 'dead.'" This is called "the waters of the flood" in the work. Because of these waters, they died in the work and could not continue the work of the Creator due to the arguments, "Who" and "What."

This is the meaning of what is written in *The Zohar* (Item 200): "Rabbi Yosi said, 'He saw the angel of death coming with the floodwater and therefore went into the ark.'" This means that the saboteur, who is the angel of death, is within the arguments, "Who" and "What."

The salvation of the ark from the flood in the work means that there is the matter of above reason. This is regarded as wanting to walk with his eyes shut, meaning that although reason and the senses do not understand what our sages tell us, they assume upon them faith in the sages and say that we must take upon ourselves faith in the sages, as it is written, "And they believed in the Lord and in His servant, Moses." Without faith, nothing can be achieved in spirituality.

This discernment is called *Bina*, which is covered *Hassadim* and is called "desiring mercy." This means that he does not want to understand anything, and says about everything that it is certainly God's *Hesed* [grace/mercy] that He does with him. Although he does not see the *Hassadim* [plural of *Hesed*] that the Creator does with him and with the entire world, he still believes that the Creator leads His world with private Providence of benevolence, as it is written, "And all believe that He is good to all, the good who does good to the bad and to the good."

This is covered *Hassadim*, meaning that although he does not see that it is *Hassadim*, he still believes above reason and says, "They have eyes and see not." This is also called an "ark," for one who enters covered *Hassadim* and accepts everything above reason, in that place there is no control to the *Sitra Achra* [other side]. This is so because all the questions that the *Sitra Achra* asks can control only within reason, but above reason, that territory belongs to the *Kedusha*, for all the questions are only according to the external mind.

Conversely, the internal mind comes after a person has been rewarded with equivalence of form. At that time he understands within the internal mind and sees that everything that the external mind thought that it was right, once he is rewarded with the internal mind, he sees that everything that the external mind argues is untrue, as Baal HaSulam wrote in an essay in *Tav-Shin-Gimel* [1942-43].

Accordingly, "the saboteur being inside the floodwater and puts a person to death" means that within the water, which is the "Who" and "What," meaning with these arguments, he kills people. This is the meaning of what *The Zohar* says, "Rabbi Yosi said, 'He saw the angel of death coming with the floodwater and therefore went into the ark.'"

In other words, he saw that with these arguments he would lose his spirit of life. At that time, he went into the quality of above reason, which is *Bina*, which desires mercy, meaning that he wants only to bestow and not receive a thing. Instead, he is happy with his share and regards whatever understanding and feeling about the work of the Creator that he has as a great reward. He is also happy about all the arguments he heard from the "Who" and "What" because now he can go above reason. By this he is saved from the flood of water.

According to the above, we can interpret what *The Zohar* says (Noah, Item 196), "A person should certainly hide himself so as not to be seen by the saboteur when he is in the world, so he will not look at him, for he has permission to destroy all those seen by him."

(And in Item 200) "This is why the Creator sought to cover Noah and hide him from sight. And Noah came to hide from the eye, from the water of the flood, for the water pressed him into the ark. He saw the water of the flood and feared it, hence he came to the ark."

We should understand how it can be said about a sabotaging angel that if Noah enters the ark, the angel cannot see him because he is in the ark. How can we understand this if the Creator advised Noah to enter the ark so the sabotaging angel would not see him? Clearly, when he saw the ark, what would he think, that this is an empty ark without people? Even if the saboteur were corporeal, he would certainly want to see what is in the ark, all the more so with an angel, does he not see what is in the ark? Is this possible?

In the work, we should interpret that the sabotaging angel sees those people who walk within reason. With them, he can argue with arguments of "Who" and "What." But when the Creator told him to go into *Bina*, which is called "the covered world," meaning it is covered from external ones, who are those who go with the external mind, the saboteur can see them because they have a common language, meaning externality.

But those who go above reason, who do everything because of faith in the Creator and through faith in the sages, who give them guidance how to go and achieve *Dvekut* [adhesion] with the Creator, and be rewarded with the internal mind, called "the mind of the Torah," in that place it is regarded that the sabotaging angel has no means to see because his vision is in vessels of reception.

For this reason, our sages said, "Once the saboteur is given permission, it does not distinguish between good and bad." We interpreted that this means that when the saboteur is given permission, even people who engage in reception in order to bestow, who are considered good, since they engage in reception, there can be slandering by him. Hence, they, too, enter *Bina*, which is vessels of bestowal, where the *Sitra Achra* has no grip. This is regarded as the sabotaging angel not being able to see who is in the ark, since his grip is only on vessels of reception, where he can slander and accuse.

But one who walks into the ark, which is *Bina*, a vessel of bestowal, the *Sitra Achra* does not see them. That is, they have no common language making it possible to understand what the *Sitra Achra* argues against the work.

When a person walks on the path of bestowal, which is regarded as above reason, faith, until the point of faith the *Sitra Achra* can argue with a person. But as soon as a person has entered the ark of faith, above reason, the *Sitra Achra* remains standing by the gate of faith and cannot continue.

It is as it is written in *The Study of the Ten Sefirot* (Part 14), "This *Bina* is still not regarded as devoid of *Rosh* [head] (meaning wholeness) because *Bina* does not suffer from any force of *Tzimtzum* [restriction]." This means that since *Bina* is regarded as desiring mercy, which is a vessel of bestowal, she does not need anything for herself, and anything that she can do above reason, she feels that she has something to give. That is, *Tzimtzum* is called "lack," and the lack always comes by one's desire to receive something. If he needs to receive and someone interferes, meaning that the giver says, "Yes, I will give you, but only on my terms. If you agree to my terms, you will receive. Otherwise, you will not." Here there is room for interferences.

That is, if the receiver is unfit to meet the terms that the giver requires then the giver is deficient. That is, the conditions that the giver requires are called "limitations and restrictions," and the receiver is not always willing to meet these terms.

But if he does not want to receive anything from the giver, he does not mind that the giver wants to give only according to restrictions, since he has no business with the giving of the giver. This is called *Bina*, a vessel of bestowal. She wants to give and not receive anything.

However, there is great depth here in *Bina* wanting to give and not receive anything. Here, there is already a condition on the part of the lower one, the giver. That is, the fact that the lower one wants to bestow, the lower one says, "Only according to the term

I will present to You, I am willing to bestow upon You. Otherwise, I cannot give You anything." What is the condition? "I want to see if You are really important. And not simply important, but in order for me to be able to give You everything and leave nothing for myself, but observe 'with all your heart and with all your soul,' I can give You this only on condition that I feel Your greatness and importance. Then I will be ready for anything. Otherwise, I cannot give You what You ask of me."

It follows that when a person does not feel the greatness of the Creator, the body cannot annul before Him "with all your heart and with all your soul." However, in truth, by presenting a condition that says, "I agree to work for You only on condition that I see Your importance and greatness," he already wants to receive from the Creator—the greatness of the Creator—or he will not want to work with all his heart. Thus, a person is already limited and placed under the governance of concealment, and he is not free to say that he wants nothing but to bestow. This is not true since he does want something before he observes "that all your works will be for the sake of the Creator." That is, he first wants to receive the greatness of the Creator, and then say that he will annul before the Creator. Certainly, this is not regarded as *Bina* because *Bina* desires mercy and wants nothing, for she does want.

It follows that *Bina*, whose quality is desiring mercy, meaning that she does not need to receive anything, is therefore free, since only one who needs to receive is limited and dependent on the view of others. But one who goes with his eyes shut and does not need any greatness or anything else, this is called "freedom."

However, we must know that it is a lot of work before we attain the quality of *Bina*. That is, to be content with little with his feeling and his mind, and be happy with his share, with what he has. That person can always be in wholeness because he is happy with his share.

But what can one do if he has not yet obtained this quality, and he sees that he cannot overcome his will to receive. At that time, he must pray to the Creator to help him so he can go in the work with his eyes shut, and will not need anything, and will be able to do everything for the sake of the Creator despite the resistance of the body to this.

That is, he does not tell the Creator how He should help him. Rather, he must subjugate himself and annul before the Creator unconditionally. But since he cannot overcome his body, he asks the Creator to help him win the war against the inclination, since he understands his lowliness.

For this reason, he asks the Creator to have mercy on him because he is worse than other people, who can be servants of the Creator, whereas he is worse than them. He sees that he has a desire to receive in self-love more than all of them. Therefore, he is ashamed of himself that he can be so lowly. For this reason, he asks the Creator to have mercy on him and deliver him from the governance of the evil inclination.

Yet, he does not ask for help because he is more important than other people. Rather, he is worse than the rest of the people because his will to receive is more developed and works within him more vigorously.

However, he is not asking to be given more knowledge about the greatness of the Creator, and then he will be able to emerge from the governance of evil. Although this is true, he does not want to tell the Creator that he wants to present Him with conditions and only then he will annul before the Creator. Rather, he agrees to remain with little understanding and little feeling, not more than he has now. But since he does not have the power to overcome, he asks the Creator to give him the power to overcome, and not brains, mind, or feeling.

Any advice that a person gives to the Creator seems as though he is setting conditions, as though he has a status and a view. But this is insolence of a person to present the Creator with conditions and say, "If You give me, for example, good taste in the work, I will be able to work for You. Otherwise, I cannot." Instead, one should say, "I want to annul myself and surrender unconditionally, just give me the strength to really be able to emerge from self-love and love the Lord 'with all your heart.'"

If a person presents conditions, it does not point to one's lowliness. On the contrary, it shows that this person considers himself worthy and proud. It is as though he says, "The rest of the people are mindless; they can work for You. But I am not like other people; I know better what it means to be Jewish and what is the work of the Creator." Therefore, he says to the Creator that He should treat him as he understands it, and not as the Creator understands it.

Accordingly, we can understand the matter of three lines, where *The Zohar* introduces three discernments: 1) Sweet water, and the opposite of *Kedusha*, which is bitter water. It is known that "right" means wholeness, as it is written in Baal HaSulam's essay from *Tav-Shin-Gimel* [1942-43], that one must believe above reason that he is complete. The opposite of complete is that the *Sitra Achra* comes and shows him all the deficiencies, how he is not following the path of the Creator, thus dropping a person into a state of sadness to the point that the person wishes to escape the campaign. At that time he only wishes to kill time and sees everything as black.

2) The "left line" is when a person wants to introspect within reason to see what he is truly like according to his eyes, whether he is whole or lacking. Since he has prepared himself for this scrutiny and shifted to the left line because now he wants to pray to the Creator to help him love the Lord with heart and soul, this is called "clear water," since there is no waste or mixture here. Rather, he wants to find a place where he can pray to the Creator.

Conversely, the opposite of *Kedusha* comes with complaints and makes him see that he is just fine and has nothing to pray for. This is called "murky water," for "clear" means that there are no mixtures there. That is, he sees the truth, as he sees according to his view and mind. He sees that he is wrong and has the power and desire to pray to the Creator to help him be rewarded with loving the Creator "with all your heart." At that time comes the opposite of *Kedusha* and mixes falsehood there, telling him that he is fine and has nothing to pray for. This is murky water, where falsehood is intermingled in that they say that he is fine and has nothing to pray for.

We should also interpret what *The Zohar* says, "There is water of peace and water of quarreling, *Kedusha* and the opposite of the middle line." The law is that the middle line is a merger of the two lines. Since the right line of *Kedusha* is wholeness, with respect to above reason, and the left line means that he sees within reason that he is incomplete, but quite the contrary, he is full of deficiencies.

For this reason, the middle line consists of two lines. That is, it is impossible to go above reason before he has reason that shows him the situation, how it seems to him within reason. Then it can be said that he is not looking at what the mind obligates him to do. Rather, he goes above the intellect and believes in the sages, in what the sages tell him, and does not use his own mind.

But if he has no mind and reason to tell him something, it cannot be said that he is going above reason. This is why the middle line is called "peace," since he needs the two lines. That is, by having two opposite lines and needing both.

But why is it called "peace"? We should interpret that when he has two lines together, he must raise the right line over the left line, as it is written in *The Zohar*. It means that the line of wholeness is built on the above reason, on the left line, and by this we acquire the desire to love the Creator. This is the *Segula* [virtue/remedy/quality] of above reason.

It is as Baal HaSulam said, that the fact that the Creator wants us to serve Him above reason, the Creator chose this way since this is the most successful way for the created beings to be rewarded with *Dvekut*, and then they are rewarded with peace. It is as it is written (Psalms 85), "I will hear what the Lord God shall speak, for He shall speak peace unto His people and unto His followers, and let them not turn back to folly." It follows that the merging of two lines is called "peace," and this is the middle line in *Kedusha*.

Conversely, the opposite of *Kedusha* is called "waters of quarreling," since they extended upon themselves that which they should not have extended, called "waters of quarreling," and were defiled in it. This means that the opposite of *Kedusha* raised the left line over the right line, meaning said the exact opposite of *Kedusha*.

The path of *Kedusha* is that we need the "within reason," which resists what the "above reason" says. The reason why they need to use and engage in the left line is not that they want to walk in the left line and listen to it. On the contrary, they need to use and engage with the reason so as to have room to go above reason. But what did the opposite of *Kedusha* do? They extended the left line so as to control the right line, meaning go within reason.

This is real *Tuma'a* [impurity], for *Tuma'a* in the work is called "the denseness of the heart." That is, the will to receive blocks the heart so the *Kedusha* cannot enter the heart due to disparity of form. Thus, a quarrel with the Creator ensued over why the Creator is not giving them delight and pleasure, which is the opposite of peace. For this reason, we must try to go with faith above reason.

What Does It Mean that the Creation of the World Was by Largess?

Article No. 5, Tav-Shin-Mem-Tet, 1988/89

The first ones explained that the creation of the world was not because of lack, for it cannot be said about the Creator that He is deficient. Rather, the creation of the world was out of largess. That is, as it is said (in *Midrash Rabbah, Beresheet*), "The Creator said to the angels when He wanted to create *Adam HaRishon*, and they said, 'What is man that You should remember him?'"

The Creator replied to them, "What is this like? It is like a king who has a tower filled abundantly but he has no guests." This is not a lack; it is simply that He wants to give with largess so the created beings will enjoy. A lack is what a person must receive, but cannot receive it. This is regarded as a lack. But to bestow is not considered a lack. Therefore, we learn that the creation of the world because of His desire to do good to His creations was out of largess and not out of a lack.

But one who receives something must have a deficiency. That is, if the receiver wants to enjoy what he is receiving, the receiver must choose only those things he wants. Otherwise, he will derive no pleasure from this. He wants to enjoy but it is impossible. This is what we see in our nature. Moreover, the extent of the pleasure he receives depends on the extent of the yearning. Thus, the yearning for something determines the extent of the pleasure from it, whether a lot or a little.

In order for His desire to do good, meaning for the creatures to enjoy the delight and pleasures, He created in the creatures a desire and yearning to always crave to receive pleasure. If they cannot satisfy the lack for the thing they want, they suffer, and the extent of the suffering from not being able to satisfy the lack also depends on the extent of the yearning for it.

Sometimes, the suffering becomes such that a person says, "I'd rather die than live," if I cannot satisfy my deficiency. But this is because of the suffering he suffers from his lack. Naturally, when he receives the satisfaction of his need, of which he said "I'd rather die than live," what pleasure he feels when he receives the filling!

When speaking of the work, a person must come to such a lack at not having *Dvekut* [adhesion] with the Creator that he says, "If I cannot achieve *Dvekut* with the Creator, this absence causes me such torments that I say, 'I'd rather die than live.'"

This is called a "real desire," and this desire is worthy of satisfaction. The order of the work is that each time, a yearning for *Dvekut* awakens in a person, and when he walks on the path toward *Dvekut* with the Creator, he always checks if he has been granted nearing the Creator. That is, when it says, "And you shall love the Lord your God with all your heart," does he really love the Creator or does he love himself, as well?

This is as our sages said (*Sukkah* 45), "Anyone who joins for the sake of the Creator with another thing is uprooted from the world." This means that he prays to the Creator to help him be able to do everything for the sake of the Creator, meaning that his only aim will be to bestow. However, he also adds a little bit of the aim for himself, as well, which is another thing from "for the sake of the Creator." "For the sake of the Creator" is to bestow, while he, during the prayer that the Creator will help him, wants also for his own sake, which is another thing from the desire to bestow, the complete opposite.

This is why he is "uprooted from the world." That is, the Creator created the world in order to do good to His creations, and from this world he is uprooted due to lack of equivalence of form. Hence, each time, he criticizes himself to see if he is walking on the right path. If he sees that he is not, it pains him. But the suffering must be to a great extent, meaning that the suffering is the result of the need.

That is, it does not mean that he should suffer, but he must have a need, and the need causes suffering. In other words, the suffering he suffers testifies to the extent of his need.

It follows that the birth of the created beings with a desire to receive was necessary, for without a desire and yearning to receive pleasure, we would not have the concept of pleasure. Thus, why are we not feeling pleasure when we already have a desire and yearning for the pleasure, and we must labor or we will not be given pleasures in corporeality or spirituality?

The answer pertains to the above-mentioned intention to do good to His creations, as it is written (in the book *Tree of Life*), in its beginning: "The *Tzimtzum* [restriction] was in order to bring to light the perfection of His deeds." It explains there (*The Study of the Ten Sefirot*, Part 1) that it means that "Since there is the matter that every branch wants to resemble the root, when the created beings receive the delight and pleasure from the Creator, there will be shame in them. Hence, there was a correction in favor of the creatures, that if they receive in order to bestow, there will be no shame during the reception of the pleasures."

Accordingly, we should understand that if we say that the Creator desires to do good to His creations out of largess, from where do the wicked come? This implies that one who does not want to receive the delight and pleasure is called "wicked," but why is he called "wicked" if he does not want to receive the abundance, and one who does receive the delight and pleasure is called "righteous"?

The matter of observing Torah and Mitzvot [commandments/good deeds] is as our sages said, "I have created the evil inclination; I have created the Torah as a spice." Through Torah and Mitzvot, the evil will be corrected. But what is the evil? It is that we cannot receive delight and pleasure because of the disparity, which causes us the shame. Because of the shame, we cannot be given, since the shame prevents the completeness of the delight and pleasure. This is why we are not given the delight and pleasure. Hence, they are told, not only are they not given delight and pleasure, but they are also given a name, "wicked."

We should understand why they are called "wicked" if they cannot receive delight and pleasure. Since the Creator created the world out of largess, it is like a rich man who has everything and does not need a thing. He wishes to give almsgiving to the poor, and since he wants the poor to feel elated when they receive the almsgiving, and not feel any unpleasantness, the rich person said, "I will give the almsgiving, great or small, but on one condition." That is, the almsgiving, great or small, does not depend on the giver, but on the receiver.

This is so because from the perspective of the Giver, He can give much more than the receiver can attain. That is, the receiver cannot know how much delight and pleasure the Giver can give him, since the receiver does not know what is the possession of the Giver. Instead, to the extent that the receiver tries to demand delight and pleasure, according to what he evaluates and understands that the Giver can give him. And indeed, what the Giver has to give to him is also above man's intellect, and he cannot evaluate anything above his intellect.

Therefore, he must believe that there are things that are more precious and important than what the receiver can imagine, since all the attainments of the lower one are built on a corporeal, external mind, whereas spirituality is built on an internal mind. It is written about it in the introductions: "Each lower world, with respect to the world above it, is like a seed of mustard compared to an entire world." For this reason, all the giving of the upper one, which we say is a great or small giving, does not depend on the upper one, but on the ability of the lower one to meet the conditions of the Giver. Only to the extent that the lower one tries to meet the conditions, to that extent the lower one receives. That is, if the lower one can place an aim on great giving, he receives great giving.

And what are the conditions that the Giver wants to give, which the lower one should meet? since the Creator created the world out of largess! That is, He is not deficient, so why does He need the lower one to follow His will? It seems as though the Giver does not want to give to him unless He receives from the receiver something in return.

The answer is that the Creator placed conditions at the time of the giving, that the receiver would not receive the almsgiving because of the yearning of the receiver, although the yearning for the giving that the Giver wants to give is very strong. Still, the Giver wants that on this reason, he should relinquish the reception and receive the almsgiving only because of the pleasure this gives to the Giver, who bestows upon the receiver. Our sages called this, "All your works will be for the sake of heaven and not for your own sake."

However, we must know that this condition, that the Creator wants everyone to work only for Him, and not for one's own sake is not in order to benefit the Creator, as though He needs this. Rather, the fact that the creatures work for the sake of the Creator is for the benefit of the creatures! That is, it is so that the creatures will not feel unpleasantness when they receive the almsgiving from the Giver. This is why the Giver placed this condition that they must do everything for the sake of the Creator and not for their own sake.

Now we can understand what we asked, Why are those who do not want to observe Torah and *Mitzvot* called "wicked"? After all, the Torah and *Mitzvot* were given in order to cleanse Israel with it, as Rabbi Hanania Ben Akashia says. It follows that one who does not observe Torah and *Mitzvot* will not receive delight and pleasure.

But, why are they called "wicked"? This is like a great doctor who comes to a hospital where cancer patients, which is a terminal illness, are operated. He says that he has a cure, and if they take the cure, they will all survive. Moreover, everyone will say that now they are enjoying life. That is, they will say that now they see that it was worthwhile to be born in order to receive these pleasures. And afterward, everyone will say wholeheartedly, "Blessed is He who said, 'Let there be the world,'" since they will be in a world that is all good.

However, there is a group of people who are not letting the doctor come into the hospital. And when the doctor finally enters, after several pleas, and gives his cure to the patients, this group interferes and insists that they should not take the doctor's cure. The question is, What name should be given to this group, which does not let these patients heal, since the patients are under their control? And it is so because as long as they are sick, this group has provision, but if they were cured from their illness, this group would have no provision. Certainly, they are regarded as wicked!

From aside, each one understands that if the doctor can punish them for not letting the patients heal, the doctor should certainly do so. No one will even think of saying that the doctor is angry at these wicked ones because they are disobeying him, but the doctor is punishing them for the sake of the patients. That is, the doctor wants to heal the patients out of largess and does not need any reward, since the doctor does not need anything that the patients should give him, but he comes to heal the patients only so the patients will feel good and be able to enjoy life. Certainly, one who sees what the doctor does will not say about him that he is doing something for his own sake.

For this reason, when the doctor says that this group, which does not let the patients take the cure, is wicked and deserves punishment, so that through the punishments they will suffer, these sufferings that the wicked will feel will cause them to stop interfering with the patients so that they can take the cure, as everyone understands that this is for the sake of the patients and not for the sake of the doctor.

By this we should interpret that although the Creator created the world out of largess, and the Creator has no lacks that the creatures can give Him something to complement it, since the Creator is complete and has no lacks in Him, still, because He wants the creatures to enjoy life, He sets a condition that the creatures will receive everything because the Creator wants them to receive delight and pleasure, for by this the delight and pleasure will be without any shame. This is called "the completeness of His actions."

This is the cure that the doctor wants to give to the patients, who are near death, called "the wicked in their lives are called 'dead.'" Through the cure, called "desire to bestow," they will achieve *Dvekut*, and will adhere to the Life of Lives. It therefore follows that those who do not want the patients to receive, do not let them engage in Torah and *Mitzvot*, by which they can be rewarded with the cure called "desire to bestow." In these *Kelim* [vessels], the Creator can place the delight and pleasure, since when they receive the delight and pleasure in these *Kelim*, they will not lose the *Dvekut* called "equivalence of form." *Dvekut* means that they emerge from the state of "the wicked are called 'dead,'" and are rewarded with life.

Thus, what does it mean that this group does not want and interfere with the reception of the cure? With what do they interfere? By not letting them observe Torah and *Mitzvot*, for by this they receive the cure, which is the aim to bestow. Naturally, it is clear why they are considered wicked for interfering with the reception of the cure. That is, the cure by which they will be rewarded with life is called "desire to bestow." The forces that interfere do not let them take the cure, called "Torah and *Mitzvot*," as our sages said, "I have created the evil inclination; I have created the Torah as a spice."

For this reason, those who interfere, who are considered wicked, deserve punishments. Through the suffering they will feel, they will stop interfering with the reception of the cure. It follows that everything that the Creator does, meaning the punishments, is all for the sake of the created beings.

What Is Above Reason in the Work?

Article No. 6, Tav-Shin-Mem-Tet, 1988/89

It is written in the *Musaf* [supplemental] prayer of *Rosh Hashanah* [Hebrew New Year], "Thus said the Lord, King of Israel and his redeemer, the Lord of Hosts: 'I am the first, and I am the last, and there is no God besides Me.'" We should understand the words "King of Israel." Is He not the king of the nations of the world? After all, He is the king of the world.

The thing is that we should know that all that we say about the Creator is not about the Creator Himself, as was said about this, "There is no thought or perception in Him whatsoever." Rather, all the appellations we attribute to the Creator are how the creatures attained Him according to these names, as it is written, "By Your actions, we know You."

Therefore, although the Creator is the king of the world, even if the created beings do not want to recognize His kingship, He does not need their consent in order to be king over them. He rules without asking them and does what He wants. No one has any say in the world, but He does what He wants and He does not need the consent of the created beings, as it is written, "I believe in whole faith, and He alone does, is doing, and will do all the deeds,"

Yet, we could ask, If He is king over us without asking us, why must we take upon ourselves the burden of His kingship, if He rules over us in any case? The answer is that we must know that He rules over us, and before a person takes upon himself the burden of the kingdom of heaven above reason, meaning that we cannot understand this within reason, and a person cannot see that His guidance is in the form of good and doing good. Instead, every person feels lack in pleasure, in enjoyment in his life. Each one thinks that if he could see that he immediately receives what he prays for and asks of the Creator, which is called "within reason," he would not have to believe that the Creator hears the prayer, since he would see with his own eyes that the Creator helped him.

But when he prays to the Creator several times and thinks that the Creator does not grant his prayer, as evidenced by the fact that he did not receive anything he prayed for, then a person must strengthen himself and say that he believes what is written, "For You hear the prayer of every mouth." Since this is against reason, because reason shows him that the Creator does not answer him, when he overcomes and says that what the intellect and reason oblige him to believe, he says, "I am not looking, but I believe in the sages who told us that the Creator does hear the prayer of every mouth," this is called "faith above reason."

By assuming the burden of the kingdom of heaven in this way, we are later rewarded with "And you will love the Lord your God with all your heart," and with equivalence of form, called "vessels of bestowal," the *Kelim* [vessels] in which the Creator bestows the delight and pleasure that He wanted to give.

Now we understand what we must attain by crowning the Creator over us, since by this we acquire *Kelim* with which we can enjoy the Creator. Therefore, while we have no connection with the Creator, He does not give us anything, meaning that we cannot enjoy something that is not in us, meaning we cannot enjoy the Creator.

Only to the extent that a person believes in the Creator, he can say that he is receiving from the Creator. However, one who does not believe in the Creator cannot receive from Him. Only to the extent of the faith in Him can one receive from Him what He wants to give to the created beings.

However, it takes a lot of work to achieve the degree of assuming the burden of the kingdom of heaven. 1) A person must know that if he has no faith in the Creator, how can he ask anything of Him? 2) What will it give him if he has fear of heaven? That is, for whose sake should he assume the burden of the kingdom of heaven? Is it for his own sake or for the Creator's sake? If we say that it is for the sake of the Creator, the question is, What will this give to the Creator if we believe that He is the king? What does this add to Him? We can understand that a flesh and blood king needs respect, but does the Creator need the creatures to respect Him? Is He needy of His created beings?

This is as it is written in the "Introduction of the Book of Zohar" (Item 191): "Fear, which is the most important, is when one fears the Creator because He is great and rules over everything. He is great because He is the root from which all the worlds expand, and His greatness is seen by His actions. And He rules over everything because all the worlds He has created, upper and lower, are regarded as nothing compared to Him for they add nothing to His essence." In other words, all the creatures do not add anything to Him.

Thus, why do we need to work for the sake of the Creator, as it is written, "All your works will be for the sake of heaven, and not for your own sake"? After all, the Creator does not get anything from our work for Him because He has no lacks. Why then do we need to work in order to bestow?

Indeed, this is only for the sake of the created beings, for by this they will be saved from disparity of form from the Creator and will be rewarded with equivalence of form, called "As He is merciful, so you are merciful." It is not that He needs them to work for Him, as though He needs the respect of the creatures. Rather, by working for the sake of the Creator, called "only for the sake of heaven," the creatures will benefit from this and will enjoy. This is called that the *Tzimtzum* [restriction] and the concealment were in order to bring to light the perfection of His deeds, meaning for the creatures to be able to enjoy without feeling any shame. This is the meaning of equivalence of form and *Dvekut* [adhesion] with the Creator.

By this we will understand what we asked about the words, "King of Israel." Is He not the king of the nations of the world? The answer is that in the work, every person is a whole world, as it is written in *The Zohar*. For this reason, man consists of the nations of the world, and of Israel. Therefore, the meaning of "king of Israel" is that when a person takes upon himself the kingdom of heaven, He is called "king of Israel."

In other words, "Israel" means *Yashar-El* [straight to the Creator], when a person says that He is his king. In other words, he does not say that the Creator is the king of the world from His perspective, meaning without the created beings accepting His kingship over them of their own volition. Rather, "king of Israel" means that the person consciously takes upon himself the burden of the kingdom of heaven.

The "nations of the world" means that He rules over them unconsciously. That is, the Creator is the king of the world although they have no idea about faith in the Creator, and do not even want to think about the matter of the kingdom of heaven. This is considered that the Creator is the king of the nations of the world, meaning rules over them and does what He wants without their awareness that He is doing and will do all the deeds. This is why when it says, "king of Israel," it refers to those who have taken upon themselves the kingdom of heaven consciously and willingly. This is called "king of Israel."

This is as it is written (*Avot* 3:20), "A person repays consciously and unconsciously." "Consciously" means "king of Israel," and "unconsciously" means the nations of the world, whom He rules although a person is unconscious, and does not even give one thought to faith. This aspect of man is called "the nations of the world within a person."

Accordingly, "Thus said the Lord, King of Israel" means that to those who have taken upon themselves the burden of His kingship, it says, "his redeemer, the Lord of hosts." That is, they feel that the Creator has redeemed them from the nations of the world, whose control is in the mind and heart. "In the mind" means that the nations of the world say that only what reason confirms is true, and they do not give a person permission to go by the way of believing above reason. "In the heart" means that they do not let a person emerge from self-love. Rather, they say that what the heart wants and feels that it is for one's own sake, these actions they permit. But if a person wants to work in order to bestow, they resist with all their might and a person cannot emerge from their control. Instead, the Creator Himself redeems him from their governance.

This is the meaning of the words, "king of Israel and his redeemer." That is, once they have taken upon themselves the kingdom of heaven, called "king of Israel," they attain that the Creator is his redeemer, meaning that only the Creator redeemed them from the control of the evil, and they themselves were powerless to do so.

In this way, we should interpret the words "Lord of hosts." This name means, as Baal HaSulam interpreted, that as he said, *Tzevaot* [hosts] are two words: *Tze* [leave/go out] and *Ba* [comes]. That is, *Tzava* [army] are men of war. These are people who go each day to fight the evil inclination. They are called "army." Therefore, after they have been rewarded with redemption, meaning after they conquer the evil inclination and emerge from the control of the evil, their conduct in the work is by way of ascents and descents, which is called *Tzevaot* [plural of *Tzava* (army)]. Meaning, at times they emerge from their control, and then are under their control again. Thus, the name for ascents and descents is *Tzevaot*.

During the work, a person should say, "If I am not for me, who is for me?" At that time in the work, they think that they themselves are doing the ascents and descents, that they are men of war, called

Tzava, "mighty men." Afterward, when they are redeemed, they attain that the Lord is of hosts [*Tzevaot*], meaning that the Creator made all the ups and downs they had.

In other words, even the descents come from the Creator. A person does not get so many ups and downs for no reason. Rather, the Creator caused all those exits. We can interpret "exit" as "exit from *Kedusha* [holiness]," and *Ba* [comes] as "coming to *Kedusha*. The Creator does everything. Hence, after the redemption, the Creator is called "Lord of Hosts." And who is He? "The king of Israel and his redeemer."

Accordingly, we should interpret what is written, "The deliverers will ascend Mount Zion to judge the mountain of Esau." *Har* [mountain] means *Hirhurim* [thoughts/contemplations], which are thoughts that lead to the state of Zion, from the word *Yetziot* [exits]. Mount Zion means contemplations and thoughts that bring descents upon a person, meaning that he ejects himself from *Kedusha*. These thoughts—it will later be revealed—are where the deliverers ascended from, "to judge the mountain of Esau."

The "mountain of Esau" means thoughts and contemplations pertaining to wicked Esau. "To judge" means to conquer and subdue the contemplations of wicked Esau. And what is the meaning of "The deliverers will ascend"? Who delivered them to conquer the mountain of Esau? It is Mount Zion. That is, the thoughts that caused them to exit the *Kedusha*, meaning the descents, are themselves what helped them conquer the mountain of Esau.

This is as it is written, "From the blow itself he makes a bandage." The fact that they had descents, which is called "a blow," since at that time he fell from the *Kedusha* into the authority of the *Sitra Achra* [other side], from this itself came only good. This is also called as it is written, "He brings down to the netherworld, and He lifts us." By seeing that one is worse than everyone else, it makes him do what he can, and not rest until he sees that the Creator took him out and delivered him from the control of wicked Esau. This is the meaning of the words, "The deliverers will ascend Mount Zion to judge the mountain of Esau."

It is written, "And the kingship will be the Lord's." This means that specifically then, the kingship will be the Creator's, meaning during the redemption, as it is written, "The king of Israel and his redeemer."

And before this, is the kingship not the Lord's? Who else governs the world? We should interpret that *Malchut* has two names: 1) Zion, 2) Jerusalem. In the work, we should say that Zion is when she is still not revealed in and of herself. This is called *Malchut* that is inside, meaning it is still not evident to the creatures that *Malchut* is the ruler of the world, and there is no other force in the world, and only the Creator is the king. This discernment is still hidden from the creatures. This aspect of *Malchut* is called "Zion," meaning *Yetziot* [exits] from *Kedusha*.

At that time, a person thinks that the *Sitra Achra* governs him because he feels that he has no need for spirituality. This means that faith in the greatness of the Creator is in concealment. Sometimes, he exits the work to such an extent that he forgets altogether about the existence of the work of the Creator. This is regarded as having fallen from his state, when he worked enthusiastically and thought that from this day forward he will remain permanently in the holy work.

Yet, after some time, he suddenly sees that he has been completely ejected from *Kedusha*. That is, he does not remember the zero point, meaning he cannot recall the moment he was ejected from *Kedusha* and fell to the corporeal world, since during the fall, a person is unconscious and remembers nothing. As in corporeality, when a person falls from a high place, he does not remember having fallen. Only when he comes to, he sees that he is in the hospital. So it is in the work.

This is regarded as "Zion." That is, at the time of redemption, when he sees the kingdom of heaven openly, he attains that the Creator has delivered him from wicked Esau. Then *Malchut* is called "Jerusalem," whose governance is revealed. This is the time to see that all those descents came from the king, as well. That is, all the foreign contemplations and thoughts they had, no other force was there, but the Creator sent them. In other words, the Creator sent them the descents, as well, so that through them they would need the help of the Creator.

It follows that Mount Zion—as was said, that "The deliverers will ascend to judge the mountain of Esau"—now they say that Mount Zion was also *Malchut*, called "Zion." In other words, her power was concealed, and she helped judge the mountain of Esau. That is, they conquered the quality of wicked Esau, meaning corrected the quality of Esau, and now they attain that there is no other force in the world.

This is the meaning of "And the kingship will be the Lord's," meaning that now they see that the kingship was the Lord's then, too, and not only now, but before, as well, since there is none else besides Him. Now that they have been redeemed, they attain that this was so before, as well.

However, during the concealment, we also must believe that the Creator does everything. But this is above reason. Conversely, now they attain that this is so. However, afterward, they will need to come to the end of correction, which is called "in the future," and at that time, "The Lord will be king over all the earth," meaning even over the nations of the world. This means that the Creator will be revealed among the nations of the world, as well, as it is written, "For they shall all know Me, from the least of them unto the greatest of them."

This is called, "The Lord is king over all the earth." That is, even before the end of correction, the Creator is the king over all the earth, but this is called "unconsciously." That is, they do not know that the Creator is the leader of the world, as it is written (in the Morning Prayer, in the *Shema de Korbanot* section), "Who in all Your works in the upper ones and in the lower ones will tell You what to do and what to work?" Only He does everything, and there is no other force in the world but Him.

However, this pertains to the people of Israel, who believe in the Creator. With respect to them, it can be said that the Creator is the king. That is, consciously, meaning that they, too, know that the Creator rules over them. It is not necessarily that the Creator Himself knows that He is the king, which is called "unconsciously." Rather, they took upon themselves the burden of the kingdom of heaven as faith above reason, and they regard it as though it were within reason.

This is called "consciously," meaning that in the work, "faith above reason" means we must believe although the mind does not see that this is so, and it has several proofs that it is not as he wants to believe. This is called "faith above reason," meaning he says that he believes as though he sees it within reason. This is called "faith above reason" in the work.

In other words, it is a lot of work for a person to take this upon himself; it is against reason. This means that the body does not agree to this, yet he accepts it nonetheless as though it were within reason. Such faith requires help from the Creator. For this reason, for such faith, a person needs to pray that He will give him the power to be similar to Him as though he had attained it within reason.

In other words, a person should not pray to the Creator to help him understand everything within reason. Instead, he should pray to the Creator to give him the strength to assume faith above reason as though it were within reason.

But before this, he must have faith in the sages that such is the will of the Creator—that we will take upon ourselves faith in the Creator above reason. And here, in this order, begins the ascents and descents. Sometimes he grows stronger in faith, and sometimes he falls from his degree and must believe, while he is praying to the Creator, that He will help him. Yet, he does not see that he received the help he needs.

Then, too, he must believe above reason that everything comes from the Creator, and at the same time say "If I am not for me, who is for me?" Then he comes to the state of "Mount Zion," and then to the state of the "mountain of Esau," for all the work at that time—before we are rewarded with redemption—to emerge from their control.

At that time, we come to know the work, as it is written, "Thus said the Lord, King of Israel and his redeemer, the Lord of Hosts: 'I am the first, and I am the last, and there is no God besides Me,' and the kingship will be the Lord's, and the Lord will be king over all the earth." It is as it is written, "All who are of flesh shall call in Your name, to turn to you all the wicked of the earth; all the dwellers of the world will know and recognize." That is, at that time, everyone will know that the Creator is the king, and before this, only the people of Israel know that He is the king.

What Is "He Who Did Not Toil on the Eve of Shabbat, What Will He Eat on Shabbat" in the Work?

Article No. 7, Tav-Shin-Mem-Tet, 1988/89

Our sages said (*Avoda Zara* 3), "They said to Him, 'Lord of the world, give us in advance and we will do it' (give us the Torah now and we will observe it). The Creator said to them: 'Fools, he who toiled on the eve of Shabbat [Sabbath] will eat on Shabbat. He who did not toil on the eve of Shabbat, from where will he eat on Shabbat?'"

We should understand this in the work: 1) What is the "toil on the eve of Shabbat"? 2) What is "Shabbat" in the work? 3) Why must we toil in order to obtain the quality of "Shabbat"?

It is known that Shabbat is called "the conclusion of the making of heaven and earth." That is, the purpose of the creation of heaven and earth was for Shabbat. In other words, the revelation of His desire to do good to His creations, when it is revealed to all, is called "Shabbat." It follows that He "*Shabbat* [rested/ceased] from all His work" because there is great work to reveal to all that His guidance is in the form of good and doing good.

At that time, there is no more work to do in the quality of weekdays, since work means turning *Hol* [unholy/weekday] into *Kodesh* [holy]. *Kedusha* [holiness] means *Kodesh*, when he separates himself from any vessel of reception and does all this work with the aim to bestow, as it is written, "You will be holy, for I am holy." This means that as the Creator is the giver, the creatures, too, should achieve equivalence of form.

In corporeality, we see that a person works only for sustenance. Sustenance means foods on which the body nourishes. This means that the foods are what he gives to the body, both corporeal life, called eating, drinking, and so forth, and spiritual nourishment, called honor, knowledge, power, governance, etc.

In order to acquire these nourishments, a person must toil. Otherwise, he will not get it. This means that the nourishments one yearns to receive in return for his work are like a meal, and the toil is like the preparation for the meal. Clearly, one who is unfit to toil does not receive corporeal nourishments or emotional nourishments. In other words, if someone wants to be given something, the giver will not give unless the conditions that the giver requires are met.

For this reason, in *Kedusha*, called "in order to bestow," man was created with a will to receive for himself, but the Giver demands that he will work for Him, regarded as "All your works will be for the sake of heaven." Otherwise, if the Giver gives to the receiver into vessels of self-love, everything will go to the *Sitra Achra* [other side], who robs the abundance from the *Kedusha*. *Kedusha* means that what he does is for the sake of the Creator. If the intention is for himself, it is called "disparity of form," and it is the opposite of *Kedusha*.

However, since it is against nature, both in mind and in heart, it is called "labor," and this is the preparation for the meal. In other words, the fact that a person must aim to benefit the Creator and not himself in order to obtain the *Kli* [vessel] called "in order to bestow" is great labor and toil. This is called the "preparation for the meal," and the "meal" is called "Shabbat."

It follows that the work is considered "weekdays," when we must toil in order to remove the secularity in man's heart, and place *Kedusha* there instead. *Kedusha* means *Dvekut* [adhesion] with the Creator, and "secular" means separation from the Creator. All the work is to place over the will to receive the intention to bestow. At that time, a person adheres to the Creator, as was said, "You will be holy for I the Lord am holy." For this, he obtains *Kelim* [vessels] that can receive what the Creator wants to give: the delight and pleasure called "the meal." This is the Shabbat meal, and this is the meaning of "He who did not toil on the eve of Shabbat [before Shabbat], what will he eat on Shabbat?"

Baal HaSulam gave an allegory about working for the sake of the Creator and not working in order to obtain self-benefit, but to do everything for the sake of the Creator, or all the abundance will go to the *Klipot*. This is brought in the book *A Sage's Fruit* (Part 1, p 158): "A great, benevolent king, who did not need any work to be done for him, wished only to delight his countryfolk. He sent out a decree to all the people in the country, none excluded, and dedicated a place in his palace for that purpose.

"He stipulated explicitly that it is forbidden to work outside the designated place, and their reward was with them in the place where they worked, where he prepared for them lush meals. When the work began, they thought that the king had prepared overseers to examine their work so as to know who worked for him and who did not. Yet, the king hid, and there was no supervision. But they did not know about the wondrous invention: He placed a sort of foul powder in the delicacies and confections, and as an antidote, he placed a healing powder in the workplace.

"By this, supervision happened by itself. Those who loved him kept the king's commandments meticulously, as well as worked precisely in the designated place, and thereby inhaled the healing powder. When mealtime came, the taste of the confections was such that they had never before tasted. Naturally, they praised the king.

"But the lowly ones, who did not understand the king's merit, for which they should love him, once they saw that there was no supervision, they did not observe the king's commandments properly. When mealtime came and they tasted the confections, their mouths filled with a foul taste due to the abovementioned powder, and they cursed and vilified the king."

Accordingly, it is impossible to feel the delight and pleasure found in Torah and Mitzvot [commandments/good deeds] because of the Tzimtzum [restriction] and judgment that were set up, so it is impossible to feel any light in vessels of reception. In vessels of reception there are only darkness and death, due to the disparity of form between the light and the Kli [vessel]. Therefore, when we want to feel taste in Torah and Mitzvot with vessels of reception, there is no taste there. In vessels of reception we can only feel taste in corporeal pleasures, where the sweetness is revealed when a person obtains the corporeal pleasures.

This was done on purpose, so that creation would exist, so there would be something to enjoy even before a person obtains vessels of bestowal, which are called "Kelim for unification with the Creator," meaning that a person does not become removed from the Creator when receiving the pleasures. And in order to have something from which man receives vitality and pleasure, we learned that because of the breaking of the vessels, a thin illumination shines, a tiny illumination of Kedusha that shines within the Klipot [shells/peels], on which all of the corporeal pleasures feed.

Therefore, in corporeal pleasures, a person can have pleasure and high spirits. But as for feeling real pleasures, which is the primary intention in the desire to do good to His creations, there, there is the powder of concealment, and hiding, and darkness and bitterness, and there is no flavor in Torah and *Mitzvot*. That is, the hiding and concealment are the bitter powder that is placed there by the correction of the *Tzimtzum*.

He placed the healing powder in the labor in Torah and *Mitzvot*. That is, you find the healing powder precisely in labor in Torah and *Mitzvot*. And why specifically in the labor, and mere engagement in Torah and *Mitzvot* is not enough to receive the healing powder to cure a person from the bitter powder in the meal? To understand this, we must first know what is the powder that heals the bitter powder that the Creator placed in the meal, and what is the labor in Torah and *Mitzvot* by which we can find a place to obtain the healing powder.

It is known that the main labor is when we work against reason. That is, when a person does not know why he must work and he must work against his reason. This is very difficult, and it is called "labor in Torah and *Mitzvot*." However, we should understand why a person must work in Torah and *Mitzvot* against reason, which is very difficult and not every person is capable of this, and why we cannot work in Torah and *Mitzvot* within reason, something that everyone can do.

The thing is that we must know what is above reason, which is called "labor," that we must labor in engagement in Torah and *Mitzvot*. The point is that man was created with a desire to receive for himself. Since there was a correction on this will to receive so there would not be disparity of form upon the reception of the abundance but that even during the reception of the abundance he will remain in *Dvekut*, called "equivalence of form," hence, a *Tzimtzum* and restriction were made.

This means that when a person wants to receive the delight and pleasure in vessels of reception, he sees no light at all, but only darkness, called "a space devoid of light." However, one must fashion for himself vessels of bestowal, regarded as "as He is merciful, so you are merciful."

How can we obtain these *Kelim*? It is done by labor in Torah and *Mitzvot*, when we engage in Torah and *Mitzvot* in order to obtain vessels of bestowal. This means that a person does not want to receive any reward for his work in Torah and Mitzvot, but his reward and payment will be that he will have the strength to do everything for the sake of the Creator and not for his own sake.

This means that if a person observes Torah and Mitzvot in order to receive reward, to obtain delight and pleasure for his own sake, this is called "observing Torah and Mitzvot within reason." That is, the body does not object to this, since to the extent that he believes he will receive from this pleasure for his own sake, this is called "within reason."

Maimonides says about this quality, "When teaching little ones, women, and uneducated people, they are taught to work only out of fear and in order to receive reward. Until they gain knowledge and acquire much wisdom, they are taught that secret little-by-little" (*Hilchot Teshuva*, p 60b).

From the words of Maimonides, we see that there are two aspects to observing Torah and Mitzvot: 1) For one's own sake, which is in order to receive reward and not work above reason. To the extent that he believes in reward and punishment, since he takes everything for his own benefit, this work is called "the work of uneducated people," which is within reason. In the work, this is not considered labor (although the general public does regard this as labor).

2) Labor in Torah and Mitzvot. That is, he engages in Torah and Mitzvot not in order to receive any reward for this. Rather, he works completely for the sake of the Creator. This is against reason, since reason obligates that the person will work for his own sake. Therefore, when he says he is observing Torah and Mitzvot in order to thereby receive power to work only for the sake of the Creator and not for his own sake, the body begins to resist with all its might, and yells, "What?!! Are you crazy??? Are you trying to revoke yourself before the Creator? You tell me, what will you get out of it??"

This aspect is considered "great labor" because he must fight against his own body, when justice and common sense side with the body, as this is its nature. It follows that this is called "labor," since it is above reason and the body does not agree to work for the sake of the Creator.

This is regarded as engaging in Torah and *Mitzvot* as labor. That is, by his engagement in Torah and *Mitzvot*, he wants to be rewarded with the quality of bestowal, which can be obtained precisely by learning in the form of labor—when he engages in Torah and *Mitzvot* with the intention that our sages said, "I have created the evil inclination; I have created the Torah as a spice, because the light in it reforms him."

This means that he sees that he has no love for the Creator, but rather self-love. He cannot do a single movement for the sake of the Creator because the body objects to it. Each time he overcomes, yet he is not progressing. Rather, it is to the contrary: After all his labor to overcome, he sees that he is regressing rather than progressing.

This labor gives him room to pray that the Creator will help him. It follows that each time he sees he is regressing, he is actually progressing in his prayer because as he sees it, he is far from the goal, and can therefore pray more wholeheartedly because he sees the place of danger.

This means that he is afraid that the bad might overcome him and make him think he should escape the campaign. That is, the body makes him think that this work was given to people with strong characters and not for the general public. Although now he has taken upon himself to walk on the path of truth, meaning for the sake of the Creator and not for his own sake, but since he is not succeeding and is regressing, he is afraid that the bad will overcome him and make him think within reason that the body is right, as he sees the reality, that he does not doubt what the body tells him, that this work is for a chosen few.

Hence, this makes him pray to the Creator from the bottom of the heart to save him from this danger of having to escape the campaign. He says, "Lord of the world, please help me now while I still have the strength to pray to You, since I don't know what will happen later; there may be no one to ask You for help."

For this reason, he says, "Lord of the world, help me while the soul is still within me, since I'm afraid that I might die later and decline to a place of separation," which is despair, and there is no faith in the Creator there, not even a tiny measure, so as to make it possible to pray to the Creator.

A person who falls into a place of despair no longer asks for any help. As long as one has confidence that he will emerge from his state, he still works, as in, "Everything that is in the power of your hand to do, that do."

It follows that the labor, the fact that he wants to work in bestowal, causes him labor. This, in turn, causes him to pray that the Creator will help him, and to believe in the sages, who said, "He who comes to purify is aided."

It follows that the healing powder is found in the labor. That is, his labor in Torah and Mitzvot in order to achieve Lishma [for Her sake], the Lishma that he later obtains causes him to have the ability to enjoy the meal, called "delight and pleasure." Since he already has vessels of bestowal, which remove the concealment and hiding that are on the meal, that concealment pushes away anyone who wants to taste the food, and he says about the meal that it tastes bitter.

By this we can interpret what our sages said, "Fools, he who toiled on the eve of Shabbat will eat on Shabbat." We asked, What is the "Shabbat meal" in the work? We should interpret as our sages said, that while creating Adam HaRishon, the Creator said, "What is this like? It is like a king who has a tower filled with abundance but no guests." The meal is called "a tower filled with abundance."

This is called the "Shabbat meal." This is after the completion of the work, which is obtainment of the vessels of bestowal, which is all the labor during the weekdays [Hebrew: also, "secular days"]. The week [secular] days are called "six days of action," which is the making of Kelim that are capable of receiving the general meal for the whole of Israel. This will be at the end of correction, which our sages called "Israel," as they said, that the creation of the world was for Israel, as it is written, "In the beginning [God] created, and there is no beginning but Israel," as it is written, "the beginning of Israel." In other words, the tower filled with abundance is for the whole collective.

Individually, the meal is when a person corrects his actions and comes into a state of "Israel," called *Yashar-El* [straight to the Creator]. This means that all his actions are for the sake of the Creator, called *El* [God]. At that time he is rewarded with the "meal" individually. At the end of correction, all the individuals will come with *Kelim* that are suitable to receive the meal, as the Creator said, "He who toiled on the eve of Shabbat will eat on Shabbat," as mentioned in the allegory about the healing powder. In other words, through labor in Torah and *Mitzvot*, there, in the labor, they will find the cure that revokes the *Tzimtzum* and concealment lying over the meal.

Accordingly, we should interpret what was presented in *Masechet Shabbat* (p 119): "The emperor said to Rabbi Joshua ben Hananiah, 'Why has the Shabbat dish such a fragrant scent?' 'We have a certain spice,' said he, 'called Shabbat, which we put into it, and that gives it a fragrant scent.' He asked, 'Give us some of it.' And he replied, 'To him who observes the Shabbat, it is beneficial, and to him who does not observe the Shabbat, it is of no use.'"

Although the literal meaning concerns he who observes Shabbat, but in the work, we should interpret "observing Shabbat" through the words, "And his father kept the matter." That is, he sits and waits and says, "When will I be able to obtain the *Kelim* that can receive the Shabbat meal, whose scent is fragrant, since the Shabbat meal is called "delight and pleasure clothed in the 613 *Mitzvot* in the form of 613 deposits."

As it is written in the *Sulam* [commentary on *The Zohar*] (Part 1), "In each and every *Mitzva*, a special light is deposited. This is regarded as the Shabbat meal. We can receive this specifically after the work and labor, as it comes by observing the 613 *Mitzvot* as counsels, meaning tips how to achieve the quality of 'The light in it reforms him.'"

For this reason, the meaning of "one who observes" is observing the 613 Mitzvot in the form of counsels how to achieve bestowal, for precisely in vessels of bestowal can we enjoy the Shabbat meal, for then the *Tzimtzum* and concealment have been removed from the delight and pleasure. This is like the above-said allegory about the healing powder: The powder found in observing the 613 Mitzvot as counsels heals the bitter powder that lies over the delight and pleasure. For this reason, if we do not obtain the vessels of bestowal, found in Torah and Mitzvot, through the labor, the concealment over the delight and pleasure remains.

By this we can interpret what our sages said (*Avot* 2:21), "You can trust your landlord to pay you for your work, and know that the reward of the righteous is given in the future." This is perplexing, since we must work not in order to receive reward. Thus, why do they say, "know that the reward of the righteous is given in the future"? Accordingly, we should interpret that our sages explain to us what is the reward of the righteous in the future.

That is, all the labor they give in order to receive reward, we are told what is their reward. It is in the future, meaning that they will be rewarded with working only so that "all your works will be for the sake of heaven," which is vessels of bestowal. For this, they give all the labor, in order to obtain "in the future" in different *Kelim* than the ones they have now, which are vessels of reception. In the future, they will be rewarded with vessels of bestowal, and this is the meaning of "The reward of the righteous is in the future."

What It Means, in the Work, that If the Good Grows, So Grows the Bad

Article No. 8, Tav-Shin-Mem-Tet, 1988/89

The verse says (Genesis 25:22), "And the sons were running within her, and she said, 'If this is so, why me?' and she went to seek the Lord." RASHI brings the words of our sages, "The word 'running,' when she was passing by the doors of the Torah of Shem and Ever. Jacob was running and pressing to come out, passing by the doors of idol-worship, Esau was pressing to come out. Another interpretation: Struggling with each other and quarreling about the inheritance of two worlds."

We see that during pregnancy, one turned toward *Kedusha* [holiness], and one turned toward idol-worship. Thus, what is the novelty that the Torah tells us later, that "The boys grew, and Esau became a hunter, a man of the field, and Jacob was an honest man, dwelling in tents"? Presumably, when they were born, so they continued according to their qualities.

RASHI explains this and says, "'The boys grew,' as long as they were little, they were not recognized by their actions and a person is not meticulous about their nature. When they turned thirteen years of age, one turned toward seminaries, and one turned to idol-worship."

In order to understand this in the work, how we learn Jacob and Esau in one person, we must first understand the qualities of Jacob and Esau in the work.

It is known that all the evil that we learn, which is against *Kedusha*, is called in the work, "desire to receive for oneself," while *Kedusha* is called "a desire to bestow upon the Creator," as it is written, "You will be holy, for the Lord am holy." "Holy" means that he retires from receiving for himself, but only to bestow, since the Creator bestows upon the creatures, and the creatures must bestow upon the Creator, as our sages said, "As He is merciful, so you are merciful."

For this reason, we call the will to receive for oneself by the name Esau, and the desire to bestow upon the Creator by the name Jacob. Now we can understand the meaning of Esau, as RASHI interprets, "They all called him this because he was complete [made] and fully developed with hair, like one many years old." This implies the will to receive for oneself, on which there is no need to work because the Creator had already made it, in that the desire to do good to His creations created the will to receive. For this reason, the evil inclination is called "a foolish old king," as it is written in *The Zohar*.

But the desire to bestow, which is called Jacob, requires much work before one obtains this desire. It is the complete opposite of Esau, who was done by itself by the Creator. Conversely, the desire to bestow pertains to man's work, as it extends from the correction of the *Tzimtzum* [restriction], when *Malchut*, called "will to receive," yearned to be a giver like the Emanator. Hence, she made the correction of the *Tzimtzum* to receive only in order to bestow, and by this she acquires equivalence of form.

This is called the quality of Esau, as RASHI interprets about Esau, "They all called him this because he was complete [made] and

71

fully developed." In other words, a person does not need to work in order to obtain vessels of reception. Rather, as soon as one is born, he already has the evil inclination, as The Zohar says, that as soon as he is born he has the evil inclination, as it is written, "Sin crouches at the door." It interprets that the "door" is the opening of the womb. The evil inclination, called "sin," promptly comes to him, as David said, "My sin is ever before me."

Conversely, Jacob is vessels of bestowal. For them to control the man comes by deceit, as it is written (Genesis 27:35), "And he said, 'Your brother came deceitfully and took away your blessing.'" Concerning this deceit, Baal HaSulam said that since the beginning of engagement in Torah and *Mitzvot* [commandments/good deeds] is in *Lo Lishma* [not for Her sake], as for this the will to receive can agree, but later, by this, we are rewarded with *Lishma* [for Her sake]. Then Esau yells, "You deceived me!" as it is written, "And he said, 'Is he not rightly named Jacob, for he has supplanted me twice!'" We should interpret that "twice" means in mind and in heart. We begin in *Lo Lishma*, hence the body does not object so much, since he makes it believe him that he is working only for the sake of the body, which is called "self-love."

However, to later emerge from this governance of self-love and be rewarded with the love of the Creator, here begins the real work, and here begins the order of the work, regarded as a person wanting to step on the track that leads to *Dvekut* [adhesion] with the Creator.

The work begins with *Ibur* [conception/impregnation], when we want to shift from the will to receive for oneself and come into the desire to bestow. This is the meaning of the words, "And the boys were running within her." RASHI interpreted the word "running," that when she passed over the doors of Torah of Shem and Ever, Jacob was running and pressing to come out, and when she was passing by the doors of idol-worship, Esau was pressing to come out.

Baal HaSulam interpreted that when a person begins the work, this is the time when contradicting thoughts come to him. That is, before he begins the work of bestowal, he cannot really notice the subtle discernments in the order of the work, but when he wants to begin the work of bestowal, he can feel every state that he is in.

He said that when a person passes by the doors of Torah, he awakens and thoughts that he should enter a place of Torah—which is regarded as "for they are our life and the length of our days"—come to him. This is regarded as the awakening of the quality of Jacob. At that time, he thinks he will remain in such thoughts forever, since he feels that this is life's purpose, and it is not worthwhile to pay attention to corporeality, as this is not what matters in life and not what one should live for.

But later, when he passes by the doors of idol-worship, meaning when he goes out to the street and sees that all the people are immersed in self-love and are not interested in bestowal whatsoever, he immediately gets thoughts that he should follow their path, and forgets all the work he has done in the matter of *Lishma*, that this is what matters in life. Now, he thinks completely differently. This is called "idol-worship," when he serves himself and not the Creator.

In the work, this is called "idol-worship," which means that a person sees that the Esau in him is pressing to come out and partake with them. However, we see this only during the *Ibur*, when a person wants to shift from self-love to love of the Creator, which is in order to bestow. But when he is still working like the general public, he cannot notice all these sensations although they are in him.

The reason for this is simple. It is as our sages said, "A matter of no interest about a person I do not know." It means that something that is of little interest to a person, he does not think about it. For this reason, specifically those who want to walk on the path of individuals, called "in order to bestow," because they want to know if they are advancing in the work, their sense of criticism is developed so as to notice every little thing. They see every little thing to know if they are fine or not. Hence, the above-mentioned running between Jacob and Esau begins in the *Ibur*.

It is written, "And the sons were running within her, and she said, 'If this is so, why me?'" That is, when a person begins to see

73

that once he yearns for love of the Creator, and once he yearns for self-love, and then he says, "If this is so, why me?" meaning why do I need all this work, if I see that my ups and downs are endless, and I feel that since I have begun to work on the path of bestowal, I have been left empty handed from here and from here?

That is, while I was working like the general public, I knew that each day I was advancing in the work of the Creator, since each day I could introspect and see how long I prayed, how much I learned, and I had what to look at. I was happy and high spirited, since I was looking only at the actions, and saw that thank God, I was successful in the work.

But now that I have begun to work on the aim to bestow, and I was told that the acts I do with the aim that it is because the Creator commanded us to do and to observe the Torah and *Mitzvot* are not enough, and I must also aim to bestow, meaning for the sake of the Creator. Yet, I see that as much as I exert, I cannot prevail. Even though I think I did all that I could, I am not moving one step forward. So what is the purpose? If this is so, why me? Why did I leave the work in the manner of the general public?

This is the meaning of the words, "and she went to seek the Lord." That is, he saw that now there was no choice, since he could no longer return to the general public because once he saw that there was a path of truth, he could no longer work only in practice. Therefore, he had no choice but to seek the Lord, that He will help him, as our sages said, "He who comes to purify is aided."

He says, "Now I see what our sages said, 'Man's inclination overcomes him every day. And were it not for the help of the Creator, he would not overcome it.'" He does not need to believe that he cannot overcome it, since he sees it within reason.

But those who work within reason must believe that the Creator helps them since within reason they see that they are engaging in Torah and *Mitzvot*, and see that when the body wants to be a little lazy, they immediately overcome the body's idleness and do not see that there is a flaw in their work. Although they see that there are greater people than they, in quantity and quality, it is known that there is no end to greatness, and thank God, he sees that he is considered among the important people, and he never gets bad thoughts, to think that there is bad in him. Rather, he is almost fine, since "There is not a righteous man on earth who does good and does not sin." Hence, he believes above reason that he has faults, but it is only because he is looking for lowliness, though in truth, his state in spirituality is not so bad.

Conversely, those who want to shift to working in bestowal, it is within reason that they have no progress in Torah and Mitzvot, so as to be able to aim in order to bestow. Therefore, they see that they have no other choice but to demand of the Creator to help them. Also, it is difficult for them to pray for the help of the Creator because they fall into doubt that the Creator will hear their prayer.

This comes to them because they have already prevailed many times and asked the Creator to help them be able to engage in the work of bestowal, but they received no progress in the work of bestowal. Thus, they need great strengthening in order to be able to pray to the Creator to help them. That is, they must believe above reason that the Creator will help them, while within reason they see that they are bare and destitute with respect to the work of bestowal. This is the complete opposite of how they were while they worked like the general public.

Now we will explain what we asked, Why is it written, "The boys grew, and Esau became a hunter, a man of the field, and Jacob was an honest man, dwelling in tents"? We asked, What is the novelty? Certainly, as they were during the *Ibur*, so they would be when they grow up. RASHI explains this and says, "As long as they were little, they were not recognized by their actions and a person is not meticulous about their nature. When they turned thirteen years of age, one turned toward seminaries, and one turned to idol-worship."

We should interpret this in the manner that our sages said (*Kidushin* 40), "Our sages said, 'One should always see oneself as half guilty, half innocent. If he performs one *Mitzva*, happy is he, for he has sentenced himself to the side of merit." The question is, After he has performed one Mitzva and has sentenced himself to the side of merit, how can he still say that he should see himself as half guilty, half innocent? After all, he has already sentenced himself to the side of merit.

We should explain as our sages said (Sukkah 52), "That old man taught him: 'Anyone who is greater than his friend, his inclination is greater than him.'" We should also understand this: Why if he becomes great, his evil inclination grows in him, as well? As was said above, it is because they must be half and half, or it will be impossible to choose, to make a decision. Once he has performed one Mitzva, he has already sentenced to the side of merit, or vice versa. Hence, when evil is added to him, when he becomes great, after he has performed one Mitzva, it follows that each time he grows, evil is added to him. This is why he is always in a state of half good and half bad. This is why it says, "One should always see oneself as half guilty, half innocent."

By this we can interpret what RASHI explains, "And the boys grew." "As long as they were little, they were not recognized by their actions, and a person is not meticulous about their nature." That is, when one is small, he does not have much good. Naturally, he also does not have much bad, so that the bad in him becomes apparent. This is why RASHI interprets, "They were not recognized by their actions and a person is not meticulous about their nature."

But when they grow, both grow, and then there is a distinction between the good inclination and the evil inclination. This comes to teach us that in the beginning of the work, during the Ibur, meaning when a person begins to shift from the work of the general public to the work of individuals, the bad immediately begins to appear in him. However, it is not so apparent. Yet, when he begins to ascend in the work and begins to grow, as it is written, "The boys grew," to the extent and order of the growth, so grows the evil. According to the measure of the good that he does, so grows the measure of the evil in him, as was said, so he will be half guilty, half innocent.

Now we can understand what RASHI explained, "Another interpretation: Struggling with each other and quarreling about the inheritance of two worlds." We should understand for what purpose there needs to be a quarrel between them. It is as our sages said (*Berachot* 5), "Rabbi Levi said, 'One should always vex the good inclination over the evil inclination.'" RASHI explains that he should wage war against the evil inclination. We need to understand what is the purpose of this war. Would it not be better if a person saw that the bad in him did not awaken? Why does he need to awaken it and fight it? It would be better if he did not risk himself, for he might not be able to defeat it, as our sages said, "One must not put oneself in danger."

In the work, when we want to achieve bestowal, we must say when we perform *Mitzvot* or engage in Torah, that we want to do everything with the aim to bestow. This is called vexing the good inclination over the evil inclination, since when a person says to his body, "We must work for the sake of the Creator and not for our own sake," the body immediately becomes angry and resists with all its might. It tells him, "You can do anything, but for the sake of the Creator and not for our own sake? This is out of the question." It follows that if he does not vex it, he will never be able to achieve the truth.

What Is, "Calamity that Comes upon the Wicked Begins with the Righteous," in the Work?

Article No. 9, Tav-Shin-Mem-Tet, 1988/89

Our sages said (*Baba Kama* 60), "No calamity comes to the world unless when there are wicked in the world, but it begins with the righteous."

We should understand why the righteous deserve calamity if the calamity should come to the wicked. Why is it the fault of the righteous?

In the work, we must first interpret what is calamity, what are "wicked" in the work, and what are "righteous" in the work. To understand all this, we must know what is "work." Also, we should understand why we need to work in the first place, meaning what do we gain by having to work? After all, who created all the things that exist in the world? It was all done by the Creator. Thus, for what purpose did He create this world, where we must work for everything we want to acquire, whether corporeal needs or spiritual needs?

To understand all this, we first need to understand the meaning of the whole of creation, meaning for what purpose the Creator created the world. The answer to this is as our sages said, "to do good to His creations." For this reason, He created creatures and imprinted in them a desire and yearning to receive delight and pleasure. This is called the "purpose of creation." Since this is not in equivalence of form with the Creator, the creatures will feel shame in the delight and pleasure.

Hence, a correction was made, called "*Tzimtzum* [restriction] and concealment," so as to receive only with the aim to bestow. Since the lower one must make this *Kli* [vessel], and this is against nature, since the Creator created the creatures with a desire to receive delight and pleasure, for this reason, everything that is not natural is hard for one to do. This is called "labor."

It therefore follows that labor does not mean that a person must exert himself. Rather, it is a result. Since it is against nature, it is hard to do this act, and this is the labor. This is so between man and the Creator, but there is the same correction between man and man, in order not to have shame, for man is afraid to eat the bread of shame.

For this reason, we were given the matter of negotiation, where the employee gives the landlord the work, and for the work, he gives him money. Naturally, there is no shame here.

Also, between man and man, the landlord's wish is not that we would labor for him, but that we would work for him. This pertains to the product, which is the matter of swapping—the employee gives the host the produce, and in return, the host gives him money.

With a buyer and seller it is to the contrary. The seller gives the buyer the product, and the buyer gives the seller money. One way or the other, both must give. Otherwise, if one gives and the other only receives and gives nothing back, then there is disparity of form here, and the receiver feels shame.

It follows that the purpose of the labor is not the labor, but rather that in order to prevent shame, both must give. Since by nature, man is created only to receive, this is the labor. Thus, the labor is only a result and not the aim, meaning the purpose. It follows that it is not the labor that we need, but the equivalence of form. The labor comes because we do not have this by nature.

Now we can understand what are "wicked" and what are "righteous," and why "No calamity comes to the world unless when there are wicked in the world." In the work, "calamity" means that the delight and pleasure are not revealed, meaning that it cannot be revealed to the created beings that His desire is to do good to His creations due to the disparity of form. As long as man has no vessels of bestowal, which is called "equivalence of form," this is the reason that detains the abundance from descending to the creatures. It follows that "wicked" is one who is remote from the Creator. Thus, in the work, "wicked" is one who is in disparity of form from the Creator, who is not in the form of "As He is merciful, so you are merciful."

It follows that the upper abundance cannot descend to the lower ones because of the quality of "wicked" in a person, since in the work, it is considered that the person himself consists of the wicked, which are the sparks of reception. This is the meaning of "No calamity comes to the world unless when there are wicked in the world." This means that the fact that the abundance is not coming to the world, this is considered a calamity that comes to the world due to the will to receive in man, which detains the delight and pleasure.

By this we can interpret the whole matter of the wicked who do not obey the Creator. He commanded us through Moses that we must obey the Creator, or He will punish us. We should ask about this, We can understand that a flesh and blood king, who demands respect, would punish anyone who did not obey him, but why does the Creator punish for disobeying Him? Does He need honors and to receive respect from the created beings? And if He is not respected, is He offended?

It is like a person walking into a henhouse and giving them orders, and they do not obey him. Can it be said that the person is offended by them? It is much more so with regard to the creatures and the Creator. How can it be said that the Creator is offended by the creatures when they do not obey Him, and that for this reason, He sends them calamities?

However, we should believe that the whole matter of the Creator's vengeance is not for the sake of the Creator, but for the sake of the creatures. That is, the punishments they suffer bring them to be rewarded with the delight and pleasure, which is the will of the Creator that the creatures will receive from Him.

This means that the suffering brings the creatures to take upon themselves the matter of bestowal, for only they are the real *Kelim* [vessels] that can receive the upper abundance that the Creator wants to give them. This is the meaning of what is written, "No calamity comes to the world unless when there are wicked in the world." For this reason, they suffer. That is, everything they do in the work gives them a bitter taste, since they have no vessels of bestowal, for only in them do the delight and pleasure shine. It follows that the wicked, who are the reception within man, prevent the reception of the good.

It is as Nahmanides said (presented in *The Study of the Ten Sefirot*, Part 1, Item 1), "There is a difference between 'One,' 'Unique,' and 'Unified.' Interpretation: 'Uniting to act with One Force,' when He works to bestow, as is fitting of His Oneness. When He divides to do His work, and His operations are different from one another, and He seems to be doing good and bad, then He is called 'Unique,' since all His different operations have a single outcome: to do good. It follows that He is unique in every single act."

It is as we interpreted, that the matter of "calamity that comes" is not a matter of vengeance by the Creator for not obeying Him. Rather, it is that He wants us to obey Him and observe the Torah and *Mitzvot* for the sake of the creatures, and not for the sake of the Creator, since He has no deficiency whatsoever for which He needs something for Himself.

All He wants from the lower ones is that they will receive delight and pleasure without any unpleasantness, but that the pleasure will be utterly complete. If there were shame while receiving the pleasure, there would be no wholeness in the pleasure. It follows that the calamity that the wicked feel is for their own good, as this will induce the correction of their actions.

However, we must know the meaning of correcting the actions in the work. It is that on each and every act we do we must place an intention. The intention is that with this act, we want to bring contentment to our Maker. By this we will achieve *Dvekut* [adhesion] with the Creator. When doing the act, it must not have an aim to benefit himself, but all of his concerns should be how to please the Creator.

These people, who want to walk on the path of bestowal, are called "righteous." That is, although they still have not achieved the degree where their whole intention is to bestow, they want to achieve it. They are regarded as "walking on the path of the righteous," meaning to achieve the degree of "righteous." They are named after its end.

But those who work like the general public, who are not concerned with the intention, to achieve the degree of "righteous," we do not speak of them in the work on the path of truth. Rather, they belong to the work on actions. Their intention in Torah and *Mitzvot* is as Maimonides wrote, that "they are taught in order to receive reward." Only those who have already understood that we must work for the sake of the Creator are regarded in the work as walking toward achieving the path of truth.

Although they have not reached it, Maimonides says to them, "They are shown that secret bit by bit." And what is the secret that is forbidden to reveal "to little ones, women, and uneducated people"? The secret that the act alone is not enough, but there must also be an intention to bestow and not receive reward. Rather, his whole pleasure is in his ability to serve the Creator. This is his reward, and to him, it is worth a fortune. This is why they do not need anything else in return for their work, but the fact that they are serving the King is their entire pleasure, and this is what they expect.

Now we can interpret what we asked, If the calamity comes to the world because of the wicked, why does it begin with the righteous? The answer is that the righteous in the work are those who want to walk on the path of truth. Although they have not reached it, they are walking on that line. Hence, we must know that this calamity is that they feel the taste of dust in Torah and *Mitzvot*. Where they should have felt that "They are our lives and the length of our days," they feel a bitter taste.

They ask themselves, But the purpose of the creation of the world was to do good to His creations, so where is it? We see the opposite! We should feel sweetness in the work when we are serving the King without asking for any return, but we see that the body objects to it. This causes them to understand that this entire lack is because the King is a lowly king, and has no importance.

Otherwise, they should have felt the importance of the King and would have annulled before Him, since we see that inherently, it is a great privilege for the small one to serve the great, and we have no work annulling before the great. Why, then, do we not see this with regard to the Creator? We must say about this that the Creator, who is the King of the world, we do not believe in His greatness. On the contrary! In *The Zohar*, this is called "*Shechina* [Divinity] in exile" or "*Shechina* in the dust."

Thus, all we need is faith that the Creator is a great and important King. It follows that specifically among those people who are called "righteous," who want to be righteous and serve the Creator without any return, they see and feel the bad in them. That is, they feel the calamity that they are unable to receive delight and pleasure because of the wicked within them. It is simply that they feel that they are wicked, that they are lacking faith that the Creator is a great and important King, and you have no greater wicked than this. They simply see that they are lacking faith in the Creator. It follows that when are the wicked in a person revealed? Precisely when one wants to be righteous.

By this we should interpret what is written, "but it begins with the righteous." "Begins with the righteous" means that the calamity begins to be apparent and felt from the beginning, meaning as soon as one begins to shift from the work of the general public to the work of individuals, for the work of individuals is called "the path of the righteous."

For this reason, our sages imply that immediately, as soon as one wants to work in order to bestow, the calamity appears in a person—that he feels that he is far from faith in the Creator, and therefore far from receiving the delight and pleasure that He wishes to impart upon His creations. In such states, a person sees in himself descents and ascents. Thus, the meaning of "but it begins with the righteous," is that "begins" means when he begins to enter the path of the righteous.

But those who work like the general public do not feel that they are placed under the control of the evil. They do not see that they are lacking faith in the Creator. On the contrary, they know that they have so much faith that they could give to others. They even preach to others why they are not walking on the upright path, so they would understand that what matters is spirituality and not corporeality.

When these people hear their words, they think that the admonition they are giving them, that we must do everything for the sake of the Creator, they must know what "for the sake of the Creator" means, for otherwise they would not preach. But in truth, they do not even know what is to bestow, for bestowal is against nature, and when a person sees how difficult it is to prevail and engage in the work of bestowal, how can he rebuke another? He sees that he is lacking faith, to believe that the Creator is a great King, since by nature, the small can serve the great without any reward.

But when people from the general public say that we must work for the sake of the Creator, they do not even know the meaning of the words, except what they heard when they were taught. They did not understand what they had heard, but they continue this slogan because in them, the evil is only as a hairsbreadth, as our sages said,

"To the wicked, it seems like a hairsbreadth, and to the righteous, like a high mountain."

This is so because there is a correction that a person will not see more bad than he can correct. For this reason, "wicked" in the work are those who have no need to work for the sake of the Creator, but engage in Torah and *Mitzvot* for their own sake. Therefore, the bad in them, which is the will to receive for oneself, is apparent in them as bad. This is regarded as the evil inclination being as a hairsbreadth.

But the righteous—who want to walk on the path of bestowal and begin to correct the will to receive—see each time that the bad in them appears to a greater extent until it becomes in them like "a high mountain." Therefore, they cannot lecture others because they are busy asking for faith in the Creator for themselves. This explains what our sages said, "No calamity comes to the world unless when there are wicked in the world, but it begins with the righteous."

What Does It Mean that the Ladder Is Diagonal, in the Work?

Article No. 10, Tav-Shin-Mem-Tet, 1988/89

The verse says (Genesis 28:12), "He had a dream, and behold, a ladder was set on the earth with its top reaching to heaven. And behold, the angels of God were ascending and descending on it." We should understand what it implies that the ladder must stand diagonally, for we see that if a ladder stands upright, it is impossible to climb it. RASHI brings the explanation of our sages in the following words, "Rabbi Elazar said in the name of Rabbi Yosi Ben Zimra, 'This ladder stands in Beer Sheba, and the middle of its slant reaches opposite the Temple.'" This means that the ladder had to stand diagonally. What does this tell us in the work? Also, we should understand the question of the interpreters, "Why does it say, 'Angels of God ascending' and then 'descending'? It should have been written the other way around."

To understand all this, we must first understand what is work in creation, which we are given in the observance of Torah and *Mitzvot* [commandments/good deeds]. After all, the purpose of creation was to do good to His creations. Thus, why do we need this work, as it is written, "I labored and found, believe; I did not labor but found, do not believe." Why this labor and what does it add to us in the purpose of creation, which is to do good to His creations?

According to what is written in (the beginning of) the book *Tree of Life*, in order to "bring to light the perfection of His deeds," there was the correction of the *Tzimtzum* [restriction]. That is, concealment and hiding were placed in the place of *Malchut*, who is called "receiving in order to receive," and in the place of the will to receive, called *Aviut* [thickness], there was the correction of the *Masach* [screen]. This means that one will not receive more than one can receive with the aim to bestow. This is what causes us work, and why our sages said specifically, "I labored and found, believe."

But what is labor? By nature, man is born with a will to receive for his own sake. Since there was a *Tzimtzum* and concealment on that *Kli* [vessel], and one needs to work in order to bestow, because this contradicts nature, it is labor, since it is hard work. Therefore, if someone says that he is working for the Creator but feels no effort, it must be that he is working for his own sake and not for the sake of the Creator. When someone works for the sake of the Creator, the sign is that the body, called "will to receive," resists it. This is why it is so difficult to work in order to bestow by ourselves, to the point that we must have the Creator's help. It was said about this, "Man's inclination overcomes him every day. Were it not for the help of the Creator, he would not be able to overcome it." It follows that this work is considered that we must work for the sake of the Creator.

But we need to work for the sake of the Creator not really for His sake, as though the Creator needs man's work. Rather, this fits into the perfection of His deeds, for by a person working for the sake of the Creator and not for one's own sake, he becomes fit to receive the delight and pleasure without any shame, which is called "bread of shame," since he receives with the intention to bestow, and not to receive for his own sake.

However, in the order of the work, when a person must achieve the degree of Dvekut [adhesion], as it is written, "and to cling unto Him," a person cannot ascend on one leg, but needs two legs—right and left. It is as our sages said (Sotah 47), "The left should always push away and the right pull near." We should interpret that on one hand, a person should see that he is being pushed away from the Creator, meaning see how far he is from Dvekut with the Creator, called "to bestow," and that he is immersed in self-love.

And the more he wants to increase the work of bestowal, the more he sees that he is retreating, meaning that the evil within him is intensifying with each day. Finally, he decides that it is impossible that he will be able to be freed from self-love, and says that unless the Creator helps him, he is lost. He says, "Now I do not need to believe that the Creator helps." Rather, now, when he is rewarded with Dvekut with the Creator, he will say that he sees within reason that the Creator helped him.

This is as it is written (Psalms 127), "Unless the Lord builds a house, its builders labor in it in vain." There is nothing he can do but ask the Creator to help him emerge from the control of the will to receive.

Sometimes, he does not even have the strength to ask of the Creator to help him. This is called the "left leg," when he is walking on the path of seeing how full of faults and corruptions he is. As it is known, "Left," in the work, means something that requires correction. This is called "The left should always push away."

The other leg is called "right," since something that does not require correction in the work is called "right." That is, a person must know that he has a great privilege in being among the servants of the King. That is, he must believe that the little time that he can give of his work that he does for his own needs, to engage in Torah and Mitzvot, which is called "the work of the Creator," he does not say that this is out of his own strength that he wants to work in the holy work. Rather, the Creator gave him a thought and desire to have some grip on Torah and Mitzvot, and he is happy that he has been rewarded with the privilege of doing some service for the King.

He thanks the Creator for this because he sees that many people in the world do not have such a privilege, and he feels that he is close to the Creator. This is the meaning of "and the right pulls near," meaning that the right leg is that he feels himself close to the Creator.

Precisely on two legs can we go up and up, and reach the King's palace. By this we can interpret what is written, "and behold, a ladder was set on the earth with its top reaching to heaven." That is, the ladder, by which we climb up to the King's palace, has two ends. 1) "A ladder was set on the earth." This is the left line, called "earth." One should see that he is placed in worldliness, immersed in self-love, as in, "the left pushes away." Then there is room to pray from the bottom of the heart, for then one looks within one's reason at how he cannot do anything for the sake of the Creator, and only He can deliver him from the governance of the evil in him. It is said about this, "Were it not for the help of the Creator, he would not be able to overcome it." 2) It is written, "its top reaching to heaven." The other end of the ladder is in "heaven," as though he has complete wholeness because he is content with his lot, in the little bit of contact that he has with the work of the Creator. He feels that he is happy with this, since it is a great privilege to be rewarded with serving the King and speaking with Him even one moment a day; this is enough for him to be in high spirits, and he thanks the King for this and praises Him.

It follows that this ladder, on which we climb up to the King's palace, stands diagonally. That is, the bottom of the ladder, which is "a ladder set on the earth," is not really down, like a ladder standing upright, or it would be impossible to climb it, as we see in corporeality. This shows that even in corporeality the ladder must stand diagonally, and the slant indicates that "above" is not really above.

And likewise, "below" is not really "below." Rather, as was said, when "its top reaches to heaven," when one walks on the right line, which is wholeness, it is not the end. Rather, he must also walk "on the earth," meaning to see that he is still on the earth. And when he is walking "on the earth," which is the left, he must also know that he needs to walk on the right, as well, which is called "its top reaching to heaven." That is, although both states are contradictory and opposite, they are not that far off from one another, creating a long distance to walk from one end to the other. That is, we must walk on both lines, and this is called "a slant," meaning it shows that we must walk on two lines.

This extends from the correction called *Tzimtzum Bet* [Second Restriction], which is the association of the quality of mercy with judgment, as our sages said, "First, He created the world with the quality of judgment," called "straight line, where there is above and below, called 'high importance,' which is the purest, and is considered the *Sefira Keter*, the purest, where there are no lacks. Below means of low importance, the thickest, considered the *Sefira Malchut*, which is the will to receive. He saw that the world could not exist, so He associated with it the quality of judgment." Since *Malchut* of the quality of judgment, called "will to receive," is the root of the created beings, it was difficult to invert her into working in order to bestow. This is called "the world could not exist."

As he says in the "Preface to the Wisdom of Kabbalah" (Item 58), "'He saw that the world cannot exist' means that in this way, it was impossible for Adam, who was to be created from this *Behina Dalet* [Fourth Phase], to acquire acts of bestowal. This is why He 'put *Midat Ha Rachamim* [quality of mercy] first and associated it with the *Midat Ha Din* [quality of judgment].' The Emanator raised *Midat Ha Din*, which is the concluding force made in the *Sefira Malchut*, and elevated it to *Bina–Midat Ha Rachamim*. He associated them with one another, and thereby enabled Adam's *Guf* [body], which emerged from *Behina Dalet*, to be integrated with the quality of bestowal, too."

It follows that specifically by the ascent of *Malchut* to *Bina*, the world can exist. The ARI calls the ascent of *Malchut* to *Bina*, "a diagonal line." He says that this is the meaning of what is written (in *The Study of the Ten Sefirot*, Part 6), "After the *Tzimtzum* itself placed one *Parsa* [partition], which is the meaning of 'Let there be a firmament in the midst of the water, and let it divide between water and water.'"

This is the meaning of the [letter] *Aleph* [], for the line of the *Aleph* is diagonal, as he says (in *The Study of the Ten Sefirot*, Part 6), "The connection of two points in the *Tzimtzum* is the line of the *Aleph*, like this []. And the first quality of each degree is a *Yod* [], over the line from above, which includes *Keter* and *Hochma* of the degree, as in "upper water," like this *Yod* []." Thus, the association of the quality of mercy with judgment is called "a diagonal."

This is the root, and why in the corporeal branch, too, we climb up a ladder only when it stands diagonally, regarded as *Tzimtzum Bet*. When the ladder stands upright, regarded as "the quality of judgment," it cannot exist.

However, we should know that the two extremes are regarded as "two writings that deny one another until the third writing comes and decides between them." That is, the two lines are needed, for by both, we achieve the middle line, for there cannot be a middle line unless there are two lines before it. Therefore, when there is a dispute, it can be said that "the third one comes and decides between them and makes peace." But if there is no dispute, there is no need to make peace. That is, if we want to have peace, we must first produce a dispute, or there is no room for peace.

Yet, the question is, Why do we need peace? It would be better, so we understand, if there were no dispute and no need for peace. This is common sense.

The answer is that since we have these two opposites in our nature, it follows that this dispute is the reality, for nature has made us this way. That is, from the perspective of the purpose of creation, we have a nature that the Creator gave a desire to receive delight and pleasure. And from the perspective of the correction of creation, we must go in the opposite direction, namely to bestow, like the Creator, "As He is merciful, so you are merciful."

It follows that those two extremes are in us. And what we say is that a dispute is required, as our sages said, "One should always vex the good inclination over the evil inclination." As RASHI interpreted, "He should make war with it." This means that one should reveal the evil in him. He does not produce evil through the dispute. Rather, the evil within us is concealed, and if light of *Kedusha* [holiness] enters there, the will to receive in us promptly awakens and receives everything for itself. This will immediately go to the side of *Tuma'a* [impurity] and *Klipot* [shells/peels].

For this reason, we must wage war, by which the evil will come out of its hiding and fight with the good inclination.

It follows that specifically through war it becomes revealed, since it wants to fight with the good inclination. When it shows its real face, the person sees what a "high mountain" it is and realizes that the only way is to ask the Creator to help him subdue the evil and to be able to work only with the aim to bestow.

By this we will understand the meaning of "two writings that deny one another until the third writing comes and decides between them." The two ends of the ladder shows that they are opposite from one another. On one hand, it is "set on the earth," indicating the lowliness, when he sees within reason how far he is from the Creator because he is immersed in self-love, which is disparity of form. On the other hand, "its top reaches to heaven," as though he has complete wholeness and he is happy with his lot and is delighted as though he is in heaven and has no connection to worldliness. This is regarded as the ladder standing diagonally. This is the meaning of the words, "two writings that deny one another until the third writing comes and decides between them."

This is the middle line. That is, those two lines engender a third writing, which is the Creator, called "middle line." This is as our sages said (*Nida* 31a), "There are three partners in man: The Creator, his father, and his mother. His father sows the white; his mother sows the red; and the Creator places within him a spirit and a soul."

We should interpret "his father gives the white." His father is the first discernment in the work, the right line, which is wholeness. The second is the left line, meaning a lack. This is called "gives the red," which is a lack. At that time, the Creator gives the soul and the spirit, for then the Creator gives him the required assistance, as said in *The Zohar*, "He is assisted by a holy soul." This is called "the Creator gives the spirit and the soul." This interprets what RASHI says, "This ladder stands in Beer Sheba, and the middle of its slant reaches opposite the Temple." That is, the middle line is opposite the Temple, which is the Creator.

Now we should interpret why it is written, "And behold, angels of God were ascending" and then "descending." It should have been written "descending" first, and then "ascending." We should explain this in the work: Those people who want to work for the sake of the Creator and not for their own sake are called "angels of God," meaning they came to this world as God's messengers, meaning to serve God.

It is as our sages said (*Sukkah* 72), "They are messengers of a *Mitzva* [commandment/good deed]." And RASHI interpreted there, since they went to greet the head of the congregation, and one must greet one's rav [great teacher] on foot, meaning that when we engage in *Mitzvot* [plural of *Mitzva*], we are "messengers of a *Mitzva*," meaning messengers of the Commander. In other words, they came to the world to be the Creator's messengers, and all of them must do and observe everything that the Creator has commanded to do, as it is written, "Which God has created to do." It is explained in the *Sulam* [Ladder Commentary on *The Zohar*] (In "The Introduction of The Book of Zohar"), that "created" means existence from absence. This refers to the will to receive, which comes from the Creator. "To do" pertains to the created beings, meaning that they must work for the sake of the Creator. It follows that those who work for the sake of the Creator are called "angels of the Creator," as was said, "messengers of the Creator."

By this we should interpret what is written (*Moed Katan* 17a), "If the Rav is similar to an angel of the Creator, let them seek to learn from him. If he is not, let them not seek to learn from him. They ask about it, Must one who wants to learn from a rav first see the angel of the Creator and then, after he has seen the form of the angel of the Creator, this is the time to go seek a rav who is similar to an angel of the Creator?"

According to the above, we should interpret that if the rav teaches the disciples the work that must be done in order to bestow, meaning why a person comes into this world, to do God's mission, to work for the sake of the Creator, that person is a messenger of the Creator and not a landlord in this world, but is a servant of the Creator. The meaning of "messenger of the Creator" is "angel of the Creator." This is the meaning of "If the rav is similar to an angel of the Creator, let them seek to learn from him."

Now we can understand why it is written, "and behold, angels of God were ascending" first. The reason is that in the work, being an angel of the Creator means to work for the sake of the Creator, which requires that we first ascend the ladder, called "right," and called "its head reaches to heaven," and then descend, which is the left, called "set on the earth," and then again. This is called "ascending and descending." Afterward, they are rewarded with the middle line, meaning that the Creator gives the soul, and then they are rewarded with *Dvekut* with the Creator.

What Are the Forces Required in the Work?

Article No. 11, Tav-Shin-Mem-Tet, 1988/89

Our sages said (*Megillah* 6b), "Rabbi Yitzhak said, 'Should one tell you, 'I labored but did not find,' do not believe; 'I did not labor but did find,' do not believe; 'I labored and found,' believe.'" We should understand the meaning of "believe." Are we speaking of people telling lies? We are speaking here of people who engage in Torah; certainly, they are decent people. Why should we think that they are lying? Thus, why does he say, "believe" or "do not believe"?

To understand this, we must first know the meaning of labor. We already said many times that labor is when a person has to do things against nature. That is, since we are born with a desire to receive for ourselves, in order to have *Dvekut* [adhesion] and equivalence of form—since specifically by this it is possible to receive delight and pleasure without shame—there was a correction that we must do everything in order to bestow. Otherwise, we are left in a vacant space devoid of light, which is called "concealment and hiding," where we do not feel any *Kedusha* [holiness] while engaging in self-love.

For this reason, when beginning to work in order to bestow, which is against nature, it is called "labor" because the body resists it. The body resists with all its might to any movement that it sees that it will not be for its own benefit, and it requires great strength to overcome it. This is where the main work begins, of which it was said, "I labored" or "I did not labor."

We asked about this, How can it be said that if people come and say, "I did not labor but found, do not believe"? After all, we are speaking of people who have already "found." Certainly, these are decent people. It cannot be said that they are lying! So, why does it say, "Do not believe" them, as though they are lying? But in truth, they did labor, so why are they saying that they did not labor when they say, "I did not labor but found"?

The answer is that when a person begins the work of bestowal, the body begins to resist. Then, a person begins to use the *Segula* [remedy/power] of Torah and *Mitzvot* [commandments/good deeds] in order to have the strength to overcome the evil in him. With the assistance he should receive from the Torah and *Mitzvot*, he sees the opposite. He thought that each time, he would march forward and feel that it is not worthwhile to work for self-love and that it is time for the evil to surrender before, him and he believed that he was given this feeling from above and henceforth he would no longer have any contact with the evil. But suddenly, he sees that he is once again in utter lowliness, immersed in self-love and feeling the concealment and hiding from the purpose of creation, which is to do good to His creations. Although he believes that in order to be rewarded with it we must first be rewarded with the love of the Creator, he sees that he only loves himself and cannot accept that he will annul before the Creator and say that there is no other authority in the world, everything belongs to the Creator, and the lower one does not merit a name.

Therefore, when a thought about annulling before the Creator comes to him, the body stands against him and makes him think, "How do you want to annul yourself before the Creator and have no reality of your own, so there is only the single authority of the Creator and you do not want to merit a name?" This is against nature, since as long as one is alive, he wants to exist and feel his being. So how is he told that he must annul before the Creator and lose his being?

At that time the body says that it does not agree to this. This is called "exile," meaning that the "nations of the world" in a person control the "Israel" in him. It is known that "Israel" means *Yashar-El* [straight to the Creator]. That is, a person does not want to have a reality of his own, but wants to annul directly before the Creator. As it was in the exile in Egypt, the Egyptians controlled the people of Israel and they could not emerge from their governance. Rather, as it is written, "I am the Lord your God, who brought you out from the land of Egypt." This means that a person cannot have the power to overcome and emerge from the control of the body by himself. Rather, the Creator Himself can redeem them from this exile.

Now there is a question: A person made great efforts and went through many states of ascents and descents, and many times despaired, meaning came to the conclusion that the verse "All your works will be for the sake of heaven" is not for him, but belongs to people with exceptional skills, and who are strong and brave. But he himself cannot achieve this, and he has already decided that he must leave this campaign. But then he received another awakening from above, to the point that he has forgotten his decision prior to the current state. He says, "Now I see that I am back on the horse and I, too, can achieve a state of bestowal and emerge from self-love." But then, he suddenly declines from his degree once more.

Also, there is the matter of forgetfulness. That is, he forgets what he said earlier, that he could come to work in order to bestow, and it did not occur to him that there could be a time when he would fall from his degree once more. Rather, he was certain that now he would move forward. But now he sees that it is not as he thought. Such thoughts and states come upon him ceaselessly.

It therefore follows that when the Creator Himself helps him and delivers him from exile, he does not know what to say, but sees that on one hand, all the efforts he had made bore no fruit. He sees within reason that had the Creator not helped him, he would have left the campaign, since many times he had such thoughts. Thus, he cannot say, "I labored and found"? since he sees that the labor earned him nothing. The fact that he was rewarded with finding was only by the Creator's salvation, which is why he comes and says, "I did not labor but found." That is, the labor he had given made no difference.

Now we will understand the question, How can we suspect that he is lying? According to the above, this is simple: He says what he sees, and he sees that all his labor did not help him whatsoever. Therefore, he makes an honest statement: "I did not labor." That is, with regard to attaining the goal, he did nothing. That is, for all the labor he had given, he remained in a state of lowliness that is even lower than he felt in the beginning of the work, since when he started the work of bestowal, he thought he had a little bit of evil, and he would certainly have the power to overcome it and be able to work in bestowal and not receive for himself.

But what did he earn from the work and the labor he had put? It is that he has reached the worst lowliness. Thus, how can he say, "I labored and found," since the labor caused him to perceive more evil, and not to find the Kedusha and enter it. Therefore, he knows that he is making a true statement, meaning that the labor is worthless. Thus, he is certain that the labor is not the reason for the finding. This is why he says, "I did not labor but found." In his eyes, he is not lying.

Now we should ask, Why do they say, "Do not believe"? since he is telling the truth. Thus, what do we find in his words that is untrue, for which our sages said, "Do not believe"?

The thing is that there is a rule: "There is no light without a Kli [vessel]." That is, there cannot be a filling without a lack. Therefore, when a person makes an effort to come to bestow upon the Creator, the more he exerts, the more the need for the filling awakens in him. That is, to the extent of his effort to achieve the degree of bestowing, so he sees that he is far from it.

And who makes him see that he is far from being a giver? It is the work itself. It is like a person who catches a thief, and the thief wants to run away from him. Therefore, if the person is holding the thief and the thief does not show much resistance, the person does not need to make great efforts to hold the thief. But if the thief begins to show more resistance, the person, too, must make greater efforts to prevent the thief from escaping him. And if the thief is more powerful than the person, and he sees that soon he will escape from him, the person begins to yell for help and cries, "Help!"

Thus, when does one yell for help? Precisely when he cannot save himself by himself. Then he begins to yell, "Help!" But if the thief is but a small child and the person caught him in his hands, he would not normally yell, "Help me keep the boy from running away because I haven't the strength to keep him, since he wants to run away from me!"

Certainly, everyone would laugh at him because we do not normally ask for help where we can do what needs to be done without anyone's assistance. This is because the conduct is that "there is no filling without a lack." Therefore, since he has no need for help, when he asks for help needlessly, everyone laughs at him because this does not match the order of correction of creation.

It follows from this that when a person does not need people and has sustenance, yet asks for help and support for his sustenance, those who see him laugh at him, even though he is standing and asking for help. We see that to the extent that he pleads for mercy, people who know him—that he is not in need—laugh at him and do not give him anything.

Now we can understand why when he says, "I did not labor but found," our sages say, "Do not believe." As we explained, he makes an honest statement. But as we explained, a filling is not given without a lack. Therefore, a person must work and exert and do all that is required to achieve the degree that "all your works will be for the sake of heaven." To the extent of the labor he put into the work, so he becomes more needy of the Creator's help. Then, when he has a *Kli*, meaning a need for the Creator's help, when he sees no way that he can achieve the degree of bestowal, this is when he receives help from above.

It therefore follows that both are true. He must say, "I did not labor," meaning that his labor was worthless, since he sees that he did not gain from the effort he had made. Quite the contrary, through his efforts, he came to realize that the labor is worthless, meaning that nothing can be obtained through the labor. He sees this within reason, and there is no issue of believing above reason here that the labor did not help him and only the Creator helped him, since he sees it with his own eyes.

Then he can say, "I did not labor but found." This is why he says to everyone that the labor is worthless. In his opinion, he is telling the truth. But our sages said about him, "Do not believe" that he did not toil, since "There is no light without a *Kli*, no filling without a lack." This is why we need the labor, as it increases his lack so as to need the Creator's help more each time, until he acquires a real lack. The Creator knows when is the completion of the lack so it fits the filling, and then the Creator gives him the filling.

It follows that if a person does not labor, there is no place for the Creator to give him the filling. Thus, we see that the labor does have value, so much so that without labor there is no finding, as said above, "There is no filling without a lack." This is why they said, "I did not labor but found, do not believe." Indeed, there must be labor, as this gives us the need for the salvation of the Creator.

Therefore, when a person comes and says, "I labored but did not find," they say, "Do not believe." That is, if a person truly did exert, and received the need for the Creator to give him the filling, the Creator would certainly give him the filling. Rather, it must be that he did not labor sufficiently to receive the filling. But when is the need completed? This, the Creator knows. Therefore, a person must increase the efforts and not escape the campaign until the Creator helps him.

By this we will understand the question we asked, Which forces does one need in order to be able to achieve the degree that "All your works will be for the sake of heaven"? Does one need great skills, a strong desire, and a brave heart and so forth? That is, does it require having great powers in all those things we find among people, which make them be considered superior to others? Because it is written, "I labored and found, believe," it implies that we need great powers.

They said about this, "I did not labor but found, do not believe." That is, it does not require great strength or great skills, but only a desire—to want to adhere to the Creator. Then the Creator brings him closer without any labor or great powers. As said above, when a person is granted with "finding," he says, "I did not labor," as he sees that all the labor does not merit a name, for even if one had the greatest powers in the world, it would not help him.

In order to achieve *Dvekut* with the Creator and emerge from the control of self-love, only the Creator can deliver him from the control of man's vessels of reception. It is as it is written, "I am the Lord your God, who brought you out from the land of Egypt, to be your God." No powers within a person will help in this.

By this we can explain what is written (in the [Hanukkah] song, *Mighty Rock of My Salvation*), "Greeks gathered around me, then in the days of the Hasmoneans, and broke the walls of my towers and defiled all the oils." Since we need the labor in order to reveal the lack in us, and only then is it possible to satisfy the lack, in order to know exactly what we need, we can see this specifically when a person wants to approach *Kedusha*, meaning to do everything for the sake of heaven. This is regarded as the quality of "Hasmoneans," whose role was to bring out the *Kedusha* from the governance of the *Klipot*, which are called "Greeks."

Precisely when a person wants to draw near the *Kedusha*, which is done through faith above reason, the "views of the Greeks" appear in a person. This is a *Klipa* [singular of *Klipot*] against faith. At that time we see that before he began the work of bestowal, the Greeks were not revealed in the person, and he thought that he had sufficient faith in the Creator and had the strength to observe Torah and *Mitzvot*, and all that he needed was to do more Torah and *Mitzvot*.

But when one wants to be a Hasmonean, meaning that only *Kedusha* will govern the world, the "Greeks," which is the *Klipa* opposite faith, appears more vigorously every time and wants specifically to break "the walls of my towers." Faith is the "wall," and all the greatness depends on the measure of faith that a person has in the Creator, as it is written in *The Zohar* about the verse "Her husband is known at the gates," that each one according to what he assumes in his heart. That is, each person has a different measure of faith in the Creator, as it is written in the "Introduction to The Study of the Ten Sefirot" (Item 14).

Now we can understand when the walls of my towers were broken, meaning that they saw they had no faith, that they could not go above reason. It is precisely when they wanted to come into the work that is all to bestow upon the Creator; this is when the "Greeks gathered around me" and the thoughts of the Greeks began to come, which let us go only where the intellect asserts that it was worth doing.

But that which is against the intellect, they insist on resisting and do not let one move one bit. This is when the labor begins. That is, precisely when we begin to walk in the work of bestowal, only then do we see that a person cannot do anything against his nature, which is the will to receive for oneself.

Therefore, when the Creator made a miracle for them, meaning helped them, everyone saw that all the work did nothing for them, meaning that all the work was in vain, since they could not conquer them, as it is written (in "For the Miracles"), "You delivered mighty into the hands of the weak, and many into the hands of the few."

That is, naturally, there was no way for them to win because they were weak and few there. Thus, they saw within reason that the Creator helped them. This comes to teach us that when the Creator helps, it cannot be said that He can help specifically a mighty man, and cannot help a weak person.

Now we can see what great forces and good qualities must be in a person so the Creator will help him approach Him. In the work, we should interpret "You delivered mighty into the hands of the weak," meaning the strong thoughts and the strong desires of the Greeks in a person into the hands of the "Israel" in a person, who are weak in thoughts and are not skillful. They do not have the strong desire and the ability to overcome the desires of the nations of the world in a person. And yet, You delivered these mighty ones into the hands of the weak. This is called a "miracle" because it is not natural that a person will be able to overcome them.

This teaches us that one cannot say that he is unfit to be a worker for the Creator in order to bestow, since he sees that he does not meet the requirements that make him capable of this. Therefore, we are shown that a person cannot overcome nature, even if a person is the mightiest of the mighty. Rather, the Creator is the one who helps, as our sages said, "I did not labor but found, do not believe." That is, finding means finding the vessels of bestowal, and this the Creator gives.

This is as it is written (Psalms 33), "The king is not saved by a mighty army; a mighty man is not delivered by great strength. Behold, the eye of the Lord is on those who fear Him, who hope for His mercy [Hesed], to deliver their souls from death." The meaning of "Behold, the eye of the Lord" is that the Creator looks at those people "who hope for His Hesed," who await the Creator to give them the quality of Hesed, meaning give them the vessels of bestowal.

What Is
a Groom's Meal?

Article No. 12, Tav-Shin-Mem-Tet, 1988/89

Our sages said (*Berachot* 6), "Anyone who enjoys the meal of a groom and does not delight him breaches in five voices." We should understand why this meal is called "the groom's meal" and not "the bride's meal." In the Torah we find in regard to Jacob, that Lavan [Laban] made the meal and not Jacob, as it is written (Genesis 29:22), "And Lavan gathered all the men of the place and made a feast."

Concerning the dances at the wedding, we see the opposite: Our sages did not say, "How does one dance before the groom?" but "How does one dance before the bride?" (*Ketubot* 16b). These are their words: "How does one dance before the bride? Beit Shammai say, 'The bride as she is.' And Beit Hillel say, 'Beautiful and graceful bride'! Beit Shammai said to Beit Hillel: 'If she were lame or blind, does one say of her, 'Beautiful and graceful bride'? But the Torah said, 'Keep far from a false matter.'" Said Beit Hillel to Beit Shammai: 'According to your words, if one has made a bad purchase in the market, should one praise it in his eyes or criticize it? Surely, one should praise it in his eyes. Therefore, the Sages said, 'Always should the disposition of man be pleasant with people.'"

To understand these two phrases, we should interpret this in the work. The bride means the time of the exile, a time of working in concealment of the face, when the love of the Creator and the glory of the greatness of the Creator do not shine for him and are ever before him, and he will not fall from his degree but always ascend ever higher. Instead, the person is in concealment of the face, called "the time of exile." This means that he is still under the control of the "nations of the world," which is the will to receive for himself.

This means that as long as he did not emerge from the authority of the will to receive, the *Tzimtzum* [restriction] and concealment are still over him. Each time he must overcome the concealment, see the Creator's guidance, say that He is really good and does good, and everything he receives from the Creator is only good. Naturally, he should be thankful and praise the Creator from the bottom of the heart for giving him abundance.

In this respect, sometimes he has the power to overcome what he sees and say as it is written, "They have eyes and see not." But this is only during the ascent.

But afterward, thoughts of the will to receive come to him and demand to see and agree above reason that this is really so, that all that he is receiving from the Creator is good. The body does not let him believe this and he falls from his degree.

Although he knows that the way to emerge from a state of descent is through prayer, at that time he does not have the strength to pray. Although there is a rule that for anything that a person needs he should pray to the Creator, so he should also pray for his inability to pray. But sometimes, he does not have the strength to pray even for this. Hence, in that state, a person is in utter decline.

However, sometimes a person deteriorates to the point where he forgets and does not feel that he is in decline. As we have said several times, a person falls so low that he remains unconscious. That is, at that time he is unaware that he is at the "netherworld." Only once he recovers, he sees that he is at the lowest point and does not even have the power to pray.

At that time, a person must brace himself and say, "Now I can say wholeheartedly, 'The song of ascents; from the depths I have called upon You, Lord,' since it is impossible to be lower in the ground than I am. " Certainly, if he asks from a state of truth, and at that time sees that unless the Creator helps him, he is lost, he will see that he cannot do anything by himself. Therefore, then he should tell the Creator, "I cannot even pray for You to save me. Therefore, only You can save me." Then he says, "From the narrow place, I have called on the Lord; answer me in the wide expanse, Lord." Through the descents and ascents, a need and lack for the Creator's help form in a person. Then, each time, *Kelim* [vessels] manifest in man for the Creator to fill.

It is written in the *Sulam* [commentary on *The Zohar*] ("Introduction of The Book of Zohar," Item 125): "The days of the exile are called 'night,' since this is the time of the concealment of His face from the children of Israel. At that time, all the powers of separation control the servants of the Creator. Yet, precisely at that time, the bride bonds with her husband—through Torah and *Mitzvot* [commandments/good deeds] of the righteous, who at that time are regarded as the 'supporters of the Torah.' All the sublime degrees called, 'secrets of the Torah,' are revealed by them, since this is why they are called those who make them, for they seemingly make the Torah."

We see that "bride" is the name of the work during the exile, when there is concealment of His face. At that time, all the powers of separation control a person, meaning that thoughts come to him that cause him to feel separated from the Creator. At that time, he faces a dilemma: 1) Either he runs from the work and becomes completely separated from the *Kedusha* [holiness/sanctity], or 2) He does all that he can in order for the Creator to help him be saved from these thoughts. That is, the Creator will illuminate His face, and then there will be no place for the control of the powers of separation.

This means that he need not pray that these thoughts will depart from him. Instead, he should ask the Creator will shine His face to him, that He will not hide His face from him. That is, if he prays to the Creator that these thoughts will depart from him, then he has gained nothing from the powers of separation, and he will return to the state he was in before the thoughts of the powers of separation came to him. Thus, he has not gained a thing. This is regarded as suffering in vain. But if he asks the Creator to shine His face to him so that the powers of separation will surrender, then he has risen in degree by being rewarded with the nearness of the Creator.

It follows that "bride" is the work of "accepting the burden of the kingdom of heaven," regarded as "faith in the Creator." Opposite this are forces of separation, which do not let a person believe in the Creator above reason. Rather, according to how the external mind mandates, so the forces of separation separate a person from the Creator. Hence, there are ascents and descents in these states, since the whole basis of the faith is above reason. In consequence, the powers of separation have room, meaning they do not allow a person to go against reason.

By this we should interpret what we asked, why concerning a bride our sages said, "How does one dance before the bride?" Concerning dancing, we see that when we dance, a person goes up and down, and sometimes falls to the east, to the west, to the north, and to the south. That is, the falls during the dance are to all six directions. The falls come so that the person will feel the need for the Creator's help. That is, it was done on purpose, so that the person will not be able to emerge from the control of the nations of the world within him by himself, without the Creator's help.

But why does the Creator want a person to ask for His help? It is as Baal HaSulam said, since a person does not have the need and urgency to obtain *Nefesh-Ruach-Neshama* (NRN), which the Creator wants to give to a person, and since man is content with little, by asking for help, the help that the Creator gives him is *NRN*, as it is written in *The Zohar*, "He who comes to purify is aided. And it says, 'With what is he aided? With a holy soul.'"

This means that each time he wants to be more cleansed, he is given help through a higher soul. It follows that according to the request for help from above, this is the cause that he will receive a higher degree each time, and by this he will receive his *NRN*. For this reason, the Creator wanting that we ask for His help causes us to have to extend a higher degree each time.

Now we can understand why they asked about the bride, "How does one dance before the bride?" and not before the groom. This is because dancing means ascents and descents that apply during the exile, called "concealment of His face," when the powers of separation govern. However, the question is, What causes the existence of ascents and descents? In this there is a dispute between Beit Shammai and Beit Hillel.

Beit Shammai say "the bride as she is." That is, to the extent of the flavor that he feels in the work, he should overcome and say, "Even if I do not feel its importance, I still take upon myself the kingdom of heaven with faith above reason." And to say, "Since I want to work and serve the King, it does not matter to me what flavor I feel in this work." Rather, it should all be above reason. That is, a person should say that he agrees to do the holy work "Even if I remain with this flavor my entire life." This is called "the bride as she is."

As Baal HaSulam said (in the essay, "Order of the Work"), we should believe only with faith that the Creator is the guide. That is, although faith has lower importance than his understanding within reason, he chooses to walk in this path.

Moreover, he is not going above reason because he has no choice. Rather, even if he is given knowledge, he chooses to go above reason. This is called "the bride as she is." In other words, he takes upon himself the kingdom of heaven even though he has no feeling of importance, as one should feel when serving a great and important King. Yet, he does not mind what he is feeling, but takes upon himself everything with great joy.

Yet, since everything is above reason, there are ascents and descents in this work. Therefore, during the work in a state of a bride, there are ascents and descents, which are called "dances."

Beit Hillel say that the dance is not necessarily as is the view of Beit Shammai, who say that we must say, "the bride as she is," meaning that he takes it upon himself although she is of little importance to him, and that only in this way are there ascents and descents, called "dances." Rather, in our view, we need not be so strict about those workers who want to take upon themselves faith in a way that it is of such little importance.

Instead, we should accept the faith in a way that he will not regard what he is feeling, but he should say that the bride is indeed beautiful and graceful ("graceful" means that a thread of *Hesed* [grace, but also mercy] is extended on her). What he does not feel is because he is still unworthy of feeling, but afterward he will really see her beauty, how beautiful and graceful she is. And yet, since now he does not have this feeling, there is the matter of ascents and descents, which is called "dances" in the work.

It follows that this applies only when the work is in a state of "bride." This is why our sages said "How does one dance before the bride?" and did not say "How does one dance before the groom?" But when speaking of a meal, it is called "a groom's meal" and not "a bride's meal" because a meal is as our sages said (*Avoda Zarah*, p3), "He who labors on the eve of Shabbat [Sabbath], eats on Shabbat. But he who did not labor on the eve of Shabbat, from where will he eat on Shabbat?" since the Shabbat is "the conclusion of the making of heaven and earth."

Shabbat is a time of reception of delight and pleasure, which is the final purpose of creation. For this reason, Shabbat is called "the conclusion of the making of heaven and earth." The giving of delight and pleasure pertains to the groom, which refers to the Creator, who gives delight and pleasure to the creatures. The Creator is called "groom" after what our sages said (*Yevamot* 63), "descend in degree and choose a wife." A "groom" means he must descend to a lower degree and receive a wife, as it is written in the book *Matan Torah* [The Giving of the Torah], "And the Lord descended to the top of the mountain." With respect to the descent, the Creator was a groom, from the word, "descending in degree."

We should interpret the meaning of descent with regard to the Creator. As is explained in the words of the ARI, in order for the created beings to be able to receive His light, there were many restrictions and diminutions of the light until it was suitable for the attainment of the lower ones. If the light is too big, the lower ones will not be able to receive His abundance because "they annul before the light as a candle before a torch."

For the Creator, this is called "descended," as in descending from His greatness. In other words, the lower ones are unfit to see His greatness. Rather, each according to his ability, to that extent the Tzimtzum [restriction] is lifted from him and the light appears. In this respect, the Creator is called "groom," when He takes the people of Israel as a bride, to give her everything she needs, as it is written in the Ketubah [a formal letter outlining the groom's responsibilities to the bride] that the groom gives to the bride: "I will labor and respect and feed and provide and sustain and clothe you."

In other words, when the Creator takes the people of Israel as a bride, He will give her everything she needs. This is called "a groom's meal," when the Creator, who is the groom, from the words, "of inferior degree," nourishes and provides for the created beings. That is, He must lower Himself so as to give each one according to his attainment, as because of this, all the restrictions took place, and from this comes the whole matter of multiplicity of names.

Clearly, when a person receives delight and pleasure from the Creator, it cannot be said that in that state, during the reception of the abundance, there will be ascents and descents. This is only when a person is in a state of concealment of the face, when he must overcome what he feels and say that the Creator is good and does good, and one cannot always do so.

But during the reception of the delight and pleasure, it is impossible to have states of descent, which are called "dances." This is why they did not say, "How does one dance before the groom?" since the Creator is called a "groom" when He takes the "bride," when there is union between the groom and the bride, and union means "equivalence of form."

That is, when the people of Israel as a whole, or a single individual, achieves equivalence of form, this is called "union." At that time, the concealment of the face departs and each one receives the revelation of the face of the Creator. This is called "a groom's meal." This is why they said that there, with the groom, the work is received in a different way at that time, meaning that we must delight the groom.

However, we should understand what our sages said (*Berachot* 7), "Anyone who enjoys the meal of a groom and does not delight him breaches in five voices. But if he delights him, what is his reward? Rabbi Yehoshua Ben Levi said, 'He is rewarded with the Torah, which was given in five voices.'" We should understand what the groom's meal symbolizes in the work, that anyone who enjoys a groom's meal must delight him. In corporeality, it is difficult to understand why we need to delight the groom. Is he not already happy? Who forced him to be a groom? Of course he is happy, as it is written, "As the joy of a groom with a bride." In corporeality, there are certainly answers to this, but what does this imply to us in the work?

The thing is that it is known that all of our work is to achieve equivalence of form through observing Torah and *Mitzvot*. That is, we must come to a state where all of our work should be in order to bring contentment to the Maker, and not to ourselves. The state of this work is called "bride," meaning that there are ascents and descents there, called "dances."

Afterward, when he completes this work on the part of the lower one, it is regarded as "Everything that is in your hand and in your strength to do, do." At that time it is called "the conclusion of the work." This is the meaning of "bride," as it is written, "When Moses concluded," which is the conclusion of the work from the perspective of the lower one. At that time a person is rewarded with permanent faith. That is, he has come to a degree where "All your work is for the sake of the Creator." For this reason, the abundance he receives at that time from above, which is called "the King's meal," he must receive the abundance in order to bestow and not for his own sake.

In other words, at that time he must be willing to say that this pleasure he receives is not because he wants to delight himself, but because he wants to delight the Creator, because the Creator created the world in order to do good to His creations. If he does not receive the delight and pleasure, His intention will not be carried out. By his enjoyment now, the Creator is enjoying from His purpose being revealed in practice. It follows that by this he observes what our sages said, "Anyone who enjoys the meal of a groom and does not delight him," but he does delight Him.

Indeed, we should understand the following: 1) How can we delight the groom? 2) Why do we need to delight the groom?

In the work, how can it be said that the people of Israel should delight the Creator? Can such a thing be said about the Creator, that He needs our joy, that we will delight Him?

3) Why does he breach in five voices if he does not delight him? Why specifically the five voices? 4) Anyone who delights him is rewarded. What is his reward? Rabbi Yehoshua Ben Levi said, "He is rewarded with the Torah, which was given in five voices." We should understand this, too. Every person knows that the reward is in the next world. Why does he say that the Torah is the reward? It appears to mean the opposite, as it is written in *Tanna Devei Eliyahu*: "Anyone who recites rules each day is guaranteed to have the next world." It follows that the reward we receive for the Torah is the next world. But here, Rabbi Yehoshua Ben Levi says that the reward is the Torah.

As was said, all of our work is that through observing Torah and *Mitzvot*, a person should aim that by this, he will achieve equivalence of form, as it is written, "As He is merciful, so you are merciful." That state is called a "bride."

Everything we receive from the Creator, whether corporeality or spirituality, but rather any pleasure we receive from the Creator, is called "a groom's meal." That is, everything that a person enjoys is called "a meal." For this reason, all the pleasures that a person receives from the Creator are called "a groom's meal."

By receiving, a person comes into disparity of form, which causes separation, and on this discernment there were *Tzimtzum* and concealment so the light of His face is not revealed in a place of separation. The Creator gives him something to enjoy, and by the Creator giving him something, he should receive from this an ascent in degree. That is, he should be closer to *Kedusha*, since now he is better qualified to believe that the Creator is good and does good. Because of it, he had to take upon himself to love the Creator, since He nourishes and provides.

The evidence to this is that now he received nourishment. The body exists and leads a happy life not necessarily from eating and drinking. Rather, a person also needs nourishments that pertain to man's spirit, meaning respect, knowledge, and service of the Creator. Each one, according to his own spirit, needs things that will lift his spirit. All this is called "nourishments." For this reason, any pleasure that a person receives from the Creator will reasonably bring a person nearer to *Kedusha*. But in fact, by this one grows farther due to the disparity of form resulting from the reception of the pleasure.

For this reason, if a person, while receiving the pleasure from the Creator, tries to delight the King by receiving in order to bestow upon the Creator, and his joy is from trying to aim to bestow contentment upon his Maker, by this he obtains a *Kli* [vessel] of bestowal with which he delights the Creator because the purpose of creation is to do good.

This delights the Creator, since now the Creator can give delight and pleasure to man, since man is now able to receive in order to bestow. Then the verse "The Lord delights in His works" comes true, meaning with the work of creation, for His will is to do good to His creations.

Because of the *Tzimtzum*, the Creator had to hide Himself from His creations. But when a person aims while receiving the pleasure to receive it for the sake of the Creator, this gives pleasure to the Creator from giving to the creatures.

It follows that from every pleasure he receives with the aim to benefit the Creator, it creates within him a *Kli* called "receiving in order to bestow." When that *Kli* grows in him, after each giving, what will be his reward from the growth of the *Kelim* [vessels]? That they will be in order to bestow. His reward will be that he will later be rewarded with the Torah, called "the names of the Creator," since now what he receives will be in order to bestow.

It follows that the reward will be the Torah, as Rabbi Yehoshua Ben Levi said. That is, what will happen once a person has been rewarded with a degree where he can delight the King? When he wants only to bring contentment to his Maker? And what is his reward? It does not mean that the person should receive reward for delighting the Creator. Rather, he says that his reward is that he can please the King.

How does he please the King? By receiving the Torah. Doing good to His creations is the benefit that the Creator wants to give to the created beings; it is the revelation of His Godliness to the creatures. This is called "Torah," meaning "Torah, as in the names of the Creator." It follows that his reward is that the Creator can give him the Torah, as the Creator enjoys this giving and it pleases Him.

It follows that "Anyone who enjoys the meal of a groom and does not delight him" means that he is still immersed in self-love and cannot say that everything he does is only for the sake of the Creator. Then, the Creator cannot give the Torah, as it will all go to the *Sitra Achra* [other side]. This is why they said that he "breaches in five voices." It is known that five *Behinot* [discernments] contain all the worlds and all the degrees, which appear as the names of the Creator. These are the tip of the *Yod*, and the four letters, *Yod-Hey-Vav-Hey*. In the worlds, they are called *AK* and *ABYA*, and in the souls they are called *Nefesh*, *Ruach*, *Neshama*, *Haya*, and *Yechida*.

Thus, the meaning of "breaches in five voices" is that he causes the five abovementioned *Behinot* not to manifest because they are not trying to achieve the intention that all the actions are only for the sake of the Creator and not for self-benefit. This is considered that where he should work to delight the Creator, he is concerned only with delighting himself. By this, he prevents the upper abundance from manifesting.

It follows that man causes the prevention of abundance below. This is considered that where man should have exerted to make the glory of heaven revealed—which is called "the revelation of His Godliness to His creations," which is the purpose of creation—man is doing things that cause the glory of the Creator not to be revealed. Instead, the glory of the *Sitra Achra* is revealed and the *Shechina* [Divinity] is in the dust.

This is called "the *Shechina* in exile under the nations of the world" within each person. That is, instead of trying to make The Good Who Does Good be revealed, and the concealment to be removed by aiming to bestow, he causes the nations of the world in him to rise ever higher.

The nations of the world is the will to receive for oneself. When we work for it, it gains strength and its quality manifests. Then, Israel in man descends below it, and this is called "breaching in five voices."

But if we work in order to bestow, *Kedusha* gains power and controls. "One who enjoys the meals of a groom and his intention is to delight him, it means that his reward is that he was given the privilege of delighting the Creator. The sign of the reward, meaning the way to know that his aim is truly to delight the Creator, is as Rabbi Yehoshua Ben Levi said, that "his reward is the Torah." If he is rewarded with the Torah, meaning if his aim is really only to please the King, and this is his only reward, the *Tzimtzum* and concealment are naturally removed from him, and he must be rewarded with the revelation of the light of His face. This is called "the Torah of His names," called "the revelation of His Godliness to His creatures."

It follows that "bride" means work of faith, meaning acceptance of the burden of the kingdom of heaven. But here there is a matter of ascents and descents, meaning what a person should give to the

Creator, which is unconditional surrender. In other words, a person should accept faith above reason even though he has no feeling and no excitement over taking upon himself the burden of the kingdom of heaven. Nevertheless, he should agree with that state and say that this must be the will of the Creator that he will work and serve Him in this lowliness, so he does not mind what elation he feels about this faith because about himself, meaning his own benefit, he has no concern, but only about the benefit of the Creator. If He wants him to remain in that state, he accepts this unconditionally. This is called "unconditional surrender."

In that regard, faith is called "below," meaning that it is of inferior importance for man. It is as it is written in the book *A Sage's Fruit*: "Faith means below, since it is of low importance. For this reason, when faith is thrown to the ground, meaning when the greatness of faith is not valued, it becomes a serpent. In other words, in that state, a person becomes worse than when he began the work on faith. Prior to this, he was regarded as sacred still and did not lack faith. But now that he has begun to take upon himself faith above reason, his faith is unimportant because his reason does not let him believe without reason. Therefore, he falls into the *Klipa* [shells/peels] of the serpent. Hence, when he wishes to enter *Kedusha*, he grabs it by the tail, where "tail" is the last discernment in everything. In other words, he accepts faith with all its lowliness, meaning above reason. At that time it becomes a scepter. He interprets there that in the hands of the redeemer was a scepter. This is the meaning of the "faithful shepherd," who has a scepter in his hand to direct the hearts of Israel to their father in heaven.

Conversely, the groom is the giver. Considering what the Creator does, His quality is to do good to His creations. This is why it is called "the groom's meal," as they said, "Anyone who enjoys the meal of a groom."

What Is the "Bread of an Evil-Eyed Man" in the Work?

Article No. 13, Tav-Shin-Mem-Tet, 1988/89

It is written in *The Zohar, Shemot* [Exodus] (Item 21): "Rabbi Hiya started, 'Do not eat the bread of an evil-eyed man,' since it is not good to eat and enjoy the bread or the pleasure from that evil-eyed man. And had Israel not tasted the bread of the Egyptians when they went down to Egypt, they would not have been left in the exile in Egypt and they would not be able to harm them." (In Item 23) It says, "There is no evil bread in the world but the bread of an evil-eyed man. What does it say? 'Because the Egyptians could not eat bread with the Hebrews, for that is an abomination unto the Egyptians.' This means that they could not look at the Hebrews eating. Thus, an evil-eyed bread."

We should understand the prohibition of the "bread of an evil-eyed man," to such an extent that had Israel not tasted the bread of the Egyptians, they would not have remained in exile. This is very perplexing. What is the connection between the "bread of an evil-eyed man" and the exile? Why does it cause them to be in exile, implying this is a grave prohibition? Is it included in the negative

Mitzvot [prohibitions on certain actions] from the Torah or by our great sages, that it warrants exile?

To understand this in the work, we must always remember these two things before us: 1) The purpose of creation is to do good to His creations. This reminds us that we must achieve wholeness and merit receiving the delight and pleasure found in the purpose of creation. Prior to this, a person is regarded as deficient because he has not achieved the purpose of creation and is still in the middle of the work. In Kabbalah, this is considered that a person should be rewarded with attaining the *NRNHY* in the root of his soul. 2) The correction of creation. Since disparity of form creates separation, and since man was created in order to be able to receive the delight and pleasure, he must have a desire and yearning to receive pleasure, and that will to receive separates him from the root. Since the Creator wants to bestow, but the created beings have a desire to receive, this causes separation that removes the creatures from the Creator. Therefore, a correction took place, called *Tzimtzum* [restriction] and concealment, whereby the creatures cannot feel their root—meaning who created them—before they correct the separation.

It is written (in the "Preface to the Wisdom of Kabbalah," Item 10), "Thus, you find that this *Nefesh*, the light of life that is dressed in the body, extends from His essence, existence from existence. As it traverses the four worlds ABYA, it becomes increasingly distant from the light of His face until it comes into its designated *Kli* [vessel], called *Guf* [body]. And even if the light in it has so diminished that its origin becomes undetectable, through engagement in Torah and *Mitzvot* [commandments/good deeds] in order to bring contentment upon his Maker, he purifies his *Kli*, called *Guf*, until it becomes worthy of receiving the great abundance in the full measure included in the thought of creation, when He created it."

Accordingly, we can understand that our work is to emerge from self-love, meaning that our sustenance should be from sustaining the body so it has life and can enjoy life not because the will to receive for oneself is enjoying, for it is called "evil-eyed," meaning that it does not want to be a giver but wants only to receive for itself.

This is called "evil-eyed," when it does not want to give anything to others and is immersed in self-love.

This is called "evil-eyed." Therefore, the nourishments that a person eats, which is called "bread," are forbidden for a person to enjoy, as it is the "bread of an evil-eyed man." That is, a person is enjoying and satiating himself on the bread of an evil-eyed man. That is, that which the evil-eyed man enjoys gives pleasure to the person. In other words, the will to receive, which is called "evil-eyed," enjoys, and from this comes all the joy and high spirits that a person receives. This, he does not agree to receive because this pleasure causes him to part from the Kedusha [holiness] due to disparity of form.

Now we can understand what we asked, Why is the grave prohibition of "Do not eat the bread of an evil-eyed man," for which Israel remained in exile? It is as it says, "Had Israel not tasted the bread of the Egyptians when they went down to Egypt, they would not have been left in the exile in Egypt." "Exile" means that the people of Israel could not work in order to bestow upon the Creator, but only in order to receive for themselves. This is called the "exile in Egypt," when they could not emerge from their control and the will to receive for oneself dominated. This is why The Zohar says that if, when they descended to exile in Egypt, they had been cautious not to eat—meaning not to enjoy what the Egyptians enjoy, meaning the evil-eye, which is the will to receive for oneself—they would not have come under their control in the exile.

It follows that the gravity of the prohibition of an evil-eyed man is because his bread is entirely in order to receive, and this causes all the separation from Kedusha. This is the prohibition of "Do not eat the bread of an evil-eyed man." That is, all our work in Torah and Mitzvot is in order to emerge from the exile of the will to receive for ourselves. In other words, we must aim—while engaging in Torah and Mitzvot—that our reward will be that by this we will be rewarded with emerging from the exile and enslavement in the will to receive for ourselves, and we will be able to work only in order to bring contentment to the Creator, and we will not demand any other reward for our work in Torah and Mitzvot.

In other words, we want to be rewarded with feeling—while engaging in Torah and *Mitzvot*—that we are serving a great and important king, and that by this there will be love of the Creator within us, from feeling His exaltedness. However, all of our pleasure will come from serving the Creator; this will be our reward, and not that He will somehow reward us for the work. Instead, we will feel that the work itself is the reward, and there is no greater reward in the world than the privilege of serving the Creator.

Conversely, the bread of the Egyptians in the work is the complete opposite, as it is written, "Because the Egyptians could not eat bread with the Hebrews, for that is an abomination unto the Egyptians." "Abomination" comes from the verse, "for every shepherd is an abomination to the Egyptians," meaning that they despised the shepherds. For this reason, the meaning is that the Egyptians despised the food of the Hebrews, since all the bread of the Hebrews, meaning their nourishment, was in order to bestow, and to the Egyptians, all the bread is evil-eyed, namely to receive. When they heard that the Hebrews' bread is to bestow, and bestowal is loathsome and despicable, since when they must work in order to bestow and not receive for their own sake, they regard this work as despicable and they do not feel any taste in it.

Therefore, as soon as the Egyptians heard that we must work in order to bestow, they came to feel that they must lower themselves, meaning that all their reason, which mandates that a person should see to his own benefit and they cannot do anything that does not yield self-benefit.

Therefore, when the body is under the governance of Egypt, as soon as it hears the slightest hint that we must work in order to bestow, it immediately despises this work and claims that it is still with all its wits and will not surrender and eat the Hebrews' bread, as for them this bread is abomination because this bread is against reason.

What Is the Meaning of "Reply unto Your Heart"?

Article No. 14, Tav-Shin-Mem-Tet, 1988/89

It is written in *The Zohar* (*VaEra*, Item 89): "Rabbi Elazar started and said, 'Know this day and reply unto your heart that the Lord, He is God.' He asks, 'It should have said, 'Know this day that the Lord, He is God,' and in the end, 'And reply unto your heart,' since knowing that the Lord is God qualifies him to reply so to the heart. And if he has responded to his heart, he certainly has knowledge. Also, it should have said, 'Reply unto *Libcha*' [your heart with one *Bet*] instead of *Levavcha*' ['your heart' with a double *Bet*]."

He replies that Moses said that if you want to insist on this and know that "The Lord, He is God," then "reply unto your heart." Know this: Your heart [with a double *Bet*] means that the good inclination and the evil inclination that dwell in the heart were mingled with one another and they are one, meaning in both your inclinations, turning the bad qualities of the evil inclination into good. At that time, there is no longer a difference between the good inclination and the evil inclination, and then you will find that "the Lord, He is God."

We should understand what is it about knowing this, that if we know that "The Lord, He is God," we come into "Reply unto your heart," which is Rabbi Elazar's question. We should also understand the answer he gives when he says it is impossible to come to know that "The Lord, He is God," before we are rewarded with "Reply unto your heart." What is the connection that one depends on the other, meaning that specifically when he serves the Creator with the evil inclination, too, we can come to know this?

To understand this, we must first present the matter of the purpose of creation and the matter of the correction of creation. It is known that the purpose of creation is to do good to His creations. This means that the Creator wants all creations to receive delight and pleasure. Before they receive this, the perfection in the purpose of creation is not apparent, since there are still discernments in the world that did not attain the delight and pleasure.

For this reason, the perfection of the purpose of creation is apparent specifically when everyone attains the delight and pleasure. This is called, as the ARI says, that "Before the world was created, He and His name were one," as it is written in *The Study of the Ten Sefirot*. This means that the delight and pleasure that He wished to impart upon His creations, there was a *Kli* [vessel] there, called *Malchut de Ein Sof* [*Malchut* of Infinity], which received the light. The light, called "He," and the *Kli*, called "His name," were one, meaning there was no disparity of form. This is the purpose of creation.

Afterward came the matter of the correction of creation, as the ARI says, that "To bring to light the perfection of His deeds, He restricted Himself." He interprets there, in *Ohr Pnimi* [Baal HaSulam's commentary on the ARI], that in order to avoid the shame, since disparity of form causes separation between the receiver and the Giver, and likewise, all things that are not present in the root, cause unpleasantness in the branches, hence, through the *Tzimtzum* [restriction] and concealment that were made, the lower ones were given a place to correct their vessels of reception so they work in order to bestow.

At that time, there will be equivalence of form between the receiver and the Giver, and then all the light that He wished to bestow upon His creations will be revealed among the lower ones, and it will once again be "The Lord is One and His name is One." This means that the delight and pleasure that were revealed in the world of *Ein Sof* in vessels of reception, that light will be revealed in vessels of reception that are corrected into working in order to bestow.

Two things extend from this: 1) The will to receive, which extends from the purpose of creation, since His desire is to do good to His creations. Hence, He created in the creatures a desire and yearning to receive delight and pleasure. The bad, called "evil inclination," whose quality is only to receive for its own sake, derives from this discernment. 2) The desire to bestow, which extends from the *Tzimtzum* and the concealment that were made in order to achieve the correction of creation. It is called the "good inclination," since through the desire to bestow we achieve equivalence of form, which is *Dvekut* [adhesion], by which we receive the delight and pleasure that He wishes to give to His creations, and then the purpose of creation will be achieved in full.

Thus, when a person wants to begin the holy work, to work and toil in order to receive reward, that his reward will be *Dvekut* with the Creator, meaning that all his works will be for the sake of the Creator, at that time the body, which was born—because of the purpose of creation—with a desire to receive for itself, resists with all its might. It yells, "But the purpose of creation is to do good to His creations, and the Creator does not need the lower ones to give Him anything!

"Therefore," he asks, "Why should I exert to make everything for the sake of the Creator without any reward? After all, this is the purpose of creation! If it were true that we must work for the sake of the Creator and not for our own sake, then why did He create within us a desire to receive for ourselves? Instead, He should have created in us a desire to bestow, then all the creatures would work for the sake of the Creator.

"Instead, you are trying to say that since He desires to do good to His creations, He created in us the will to receive, and then He wants us to work for the sake of the Creator. It is great suffering if we want to annul self-reception and revoke our entire selves, leaving nothing within us for our own benefit."

As our sages said (*Sukkah* 45), "Anyone who mingles for the sake of the Creator with another thing is uprooted from the world." This means that if one does everything for the sake of the Creator but mixes into it some for himself, this is called "another thing," and he is uprooted from the world, meaning from the next world. In other words, he cannot be rewarded with the reward one receives for man's work in Torah and *Mitzvot*.

It therefore follows that we cannot understand that His desire to do good to His creations has given us suffering in working for Him. Why does He need us to suffer when we must relinquish our will to receive? Therefore, when we work coercively and exert to overcome the will to receive in us, and we say to our bodies, we do not need to be smart.

Instead, we must believe in the sages who teach us that we must observe the Torah and *Mitzvot* without anything in return, but as they said (*Avot*, Chapter 1:3), "He would say, 'Be not as slaves serving the rav [great teacher] in order to receive reward, but be as slaves serving the rav not in order to receive reward.'"

This means that we must believe that the Creator is not deficient or needs us to work for Him. Rather, we must believe that the fact that we must work for Him is for our sake. That is, by this we will achieve the purpose of creation—that the lower ones will receive delight and pleasure. However, this work is for the purpose of correction of creation.

Yet, since it is against reason, a person does not agree to it, and must constantly overcome, since every overcoming works only for a time, and each time he must overcome anew. This state is called "judgment," meaning that a person is still under the control of the *Tzimtzum* and judgment that took place so as not to reveal the light of His face, so all would feel how the Creator leads the world with a guidance of delight and pleasure.

Instead, each one sees how the quality of judgment is present in the world, since each one feels lacks both in corporeality and in spirituality. At that time, a person says that the world is conducted by the name *Elokim* [God], which is the quality of judgment. And yet, a person must believe that in truth, everything is mercy, but for the time being, he must feel this way, since everything follows the path of correction, where specifically by this it will be possible to achieve the purpose of creation, which is delight and pleasure.

Now we can understand what we asked about the connection between "Reply unto your heart" and the awareness that "The Lord, He is God." Before a person achieves the degree where all his works are for the sake of the Creator, called "in order to bestow," a person cannot see that everything that happens in the world is the Creator behaving with the world as the good who does good.

Instead, he must believe that this is so and say as it is written, "They have eyes and see not." Instead, he sees that the governance of the world is through the quality of judgment, called *Elokim*. But afterward, when he is rewarded with vessels of bestowal, which correct his vessels of reception to work in order to bestow, this means that he can work for the Creator with the evil inclination, too, since the evil inclination is called "the will to receive for one's own sake," from which derives all the evil that we see in the world. This also applies between man and man, as all the wars, thefts, and murders in the world stem from the will to receive for one's own sake.

When he corrects the desire to receive pleasure so as to work in order to bestow, he receives equivalence of form. He receives *Dvekut* with the Creator, and the *Tzimtzum* and concealment that are present in the world depart from him. At that time he sees only good, and that everything he felt prior to being rewarded with *Dvekut* were only corrections, which brought him to equivalence of form. It follows that what he thought, that the governance of the world is with the quality of judgment, called *Elokim*, he sees that it is mercy, called *HaVaYaH* [the Lord].

By this we should interpret the connection of "Reply unto your heart" to "The Lord, He is God." Before we are rewarded

125

with replying to the heart, when it was in disparity of form and remoteness of place, since a receiver for himself is in disparity of form from the Giver, which is called "remoteness," it follows that equivalence of form is regarded as returning the receiver to the Giver. This is called "Reply unto your heart" [in Hebrew, *Hashivota* means both "return" and "reply"].

At that time he sees that everything he thought, that the world was conducted by judgment, which is *Elokim*, now he sees that *HaVaYaH* [the Lord] is *Elokim* [God]. That is, it becomes revealed that to begin with, everything was with the quality of mercy, as it is written, "For the Lord, He is God." However, before one is rewarded with returning the heart, called "equivalence of form," we think that everything is the quality of judgment, called *Elokim*.

Accordingly, we should interpret what they ask, Why if the Creator wanted to bring the people of Israel out of Egypt, He sent Moses to ask and beg him to permit the people of Israel to come out of Egypt? We see that He had made miracles there to our fathers in Egypt, meaning that all the plagues that struck Egypt, the people of Israel suffered none of the plagues. So why did the Creator not bring out the people of Israel against Pharaoh's will?

In the literal, there are many answers, but we will interpret this in the work. It is known that every person is a small world, comprising seventy nations and the people of Israel, namely the quality of Israel in him, which is regarded as *Yashar-El* [straight to the Creator]. This means that everything he does is all for His sake. This quality is in exile among the *Klipot* [shells/peels], which are the seventy nations. *Mitzrayim* [Egypt] means that they *Meitzerim* [afflict/make narrow] the Israel in him, and Pharaoh King of Egypt is the quality that rules and controls the people of Israel. The Creator wants man's body to make a choice, meaning that the evil within man will surrender, that the general will to receive in him will make room to emerge from the governance... (the rest is missing).

126

What Is, "The Righteous Become Apparent through the Wicked," in the Work?

Article No. 15, Tav-Shin-Mem-Tet, 1988/89

It is written in *The Zohar* (*Shemot* [Exodus], Item 370), "'My Beloved is mine and I am His, He pastures among the lilies.' As the lilies have thorns in them, the Creator leads His world with righteous and wicked. As the lilies would not persist without the thorns, the righteous would not be distinguishable without the wicked."

This implies that we need the wicked just so that the righteous will be distinguishable. The question is, Who needs this distinguishing? This cannot be said with regard to the Creator, as He knows all the secrets. With regard to the world, it is written, "Walk humbly with the Lord your God," meaning a person should hide his actions from people. Thus, it means with regard to the person himself.

The question is, Why does one need to recognize the righteous through the wicked? Why do I need this distinction? That is, what does knowing and distinguishing between righteous and wicked do? Is it not enough that he does what the righteous do, but he also needs to know the distinction in the righteous specifically through the wicked, as though otherwise it is impossible to be righteous?

It known that in the work, everything is said within one body. That is, both the wicked and the righteous are within the same body. Therefore, the question is, For what purpose are wicked and righteous required in the same body, as *The Zohar* says, that "the Creator leads His world with righteous and wicked"? Since every person is a small world, it would probably be better if He led His world only through righteous. Why do I need the wicked? The answer is that it is in order for the righteous to be distinguishable. Thus, we need to understand the benefit in distinguishing the righteous through the wicked, meaning what we gain by this distinction.

The thing is that it is known that there is the practice of *Mitzvot* [commandments/good deeds], and the intention of *Mitzvot*, meaning what one wants for one's work when exerting in Torah and *Mitzvot*. We learned that there are two manners of reward in this: 1) *Lo Lishma* [not for Her sake], 2) *Lishma* [for Her sake].

Lo Lishma means that one should be rewarded for his work both in this world and in the next world. As *The Zohar* says, this work is not considered the essence, as *The Zohar* says ("Introduction of The Book of Zohar," Item 190): "Fear that is *Lo Lishma* is not the main fear." (In Item 191) It says, "The main fear is that one should fear one's Master because He is great and ruling, and all is regarded as nothing before Him, and he should place his will in that place, which is called 'fear.'"

From this it follows that there are two kinds of intentions while performing actions, both in learning Torah and in performing *Mitzvot*. The work of the general public is in order to receive reward, and the work of individuals is for the sake of the Creator, and their reward is if they can serve the King. That is, their whole pleasure, which gives them fuel so they can work in order to bestow, is to feel that they are bringing contentment to the King and are praising and thanking the King for giving them the thought and desire to work for Him and not to receive any other reward for their work.

They say that in order to receive reward, "We do not need to feel the greatness of the King. Rather, we need to consider the greatness and importance of the reward we will receive if we observe the Torah and *Mitzvot*." But the Creator can stay for them at the same level of greatness and importance as He was for them at the beginning of their work.

However, if their intention is to bring contentment to the Creator, then if they want to increase the work, they must increase the greatness of the Creator, since to the extent of His greatness, to that extent they can annul before Him and do everything they do only for the sake of the Creator. It is as *The Zohar* says about the verse, "Her husband is known at the gates," each according to "what he assumes in his heart."

Therefore, in order to have fuel to work, those who want to work for the sake of the Creator must try each day to exert to obtain faith in the greatness of the Creator, since the greatness of the Creator is what compels them to work for Him, and this is all the pleasure they derive from their work.

Hence, those people who sometimes think that they can settle for the measure of faith in the Creator that they have, and think that they are already righteous and do not need to increase the faith in the greatness of the Creator, when the Creator behaves with them as righteous, meaning gives them some nearing, and they receive a desire and yearning and taste in the work, they think that they are already complete people who do not lack faith, to believe in the greatness of the Creator. They have no need to advance, except in actions. But the greatness of the Creator that they have is enough for them. This is regarded as the Creator behaving with them as with righteous.

Therefore, in order for a person to progress on the path of the Creator, to be rewarded with all his work being for the sake of the Creator, and now he feels that he is in a state of ascent, what more should he do? For this reason, the Creator leads His world with wicked. That is, at that time the Creator gives him thoughts of wicked—that it is not worthwhile to work for Him, but only for himself. By this, he suffers a descent and thinks that the descent he has received is not because it was given to him so he would advance in the path of the Creator, to be rewarded with knowledge of *Kedusha* [holiness]. Rather, he thinks that he regressed because he cannot work in the manner of individuals, but needs to work like the general public. And since he has departed from the general public, he is left empty handed from here and from there, since he cannot return to the general public.

For this reason, in that state, a person stands between heaven and earth, and feels that his situation is worse than that of the rest of the people. At that time, he can ask the Creator with all his heart, and pray as it is written, "Pardon me, O Lord, for I am wretched. Heal me, O Lord, for my bones are dismayed, and You, O Lord, how long?" That is, how long will I stay in a situation where I feel that my condition is worse than any other person, that I have no grip on spirituality.

For this reason, he has no other choice but to believe what is written, "For You hear the prayer of every mouth." Baal HaSulam explained that a person must believe that the Creator hears the prayer of every mouth, meaning even the worst mouth in the world, of which there cannot be lowlier and worse in the world. Still, the Creator hears him, as our sages said, "He who comes to purify is aided."

He interprets about this in *The Zohar*: "He is given a holy soul." It follows that the Creator gives him the thoughts of the wicked so he will be able to ask the Creator to help him. Otherwise, he will remain in the state he was in at the beginning of his work, and will remain this way for the rest of his life.

By this we can interpret what we asked, What does it mean that were it not for the wicked, the righteous would not be distinguishable? We asked, in whom do the righteous need to be distinguishable, and what is the purpose of this distinction?

The answer is that it is because the Creator leads His world with righteous and wicked. But in this regard, we should also ask why He needs to lead His world with righteous and wicked. Would it not be enough to carry out the purpose of creation, to do good to His creations, if He led the world only with the righteous? It makes sense that if He led His world only with the righteous, it would be easier to carry out the purpose of creation, which is to do good to His creations. Thus, what are the wicked for?

The answer to this is that were it not for the wicked, the righteous would not be distinguishable. This means that the wholeness and greatness of the righteous would not be apparent—the degree that they achieve. Instead, the righteous would remain in the degree of the beginning of their work, and they would not make any progress in the degree of the righteous. For this reason, in order for the merit and greatness of the righteous to be apparent, He had to lead His world with righteous and with wicked. By sending the righteous to a person, the Creator brings one closer to the work of the Creator.

The person, if he did not suffer a descent, would be compelled to remain this way throughout his life, and he would make no progress in the mind of the Torah, where the delight and pleasure contained in the purpose of creation are concealed. The merit of the righteous would not be apparent, since for what purpose would he need a higher level?

Indeed, we must know that the merit of the righteous is as our sages said (at end of *Okatzin*), "The Creator is destined to bequeath each and every righteous 310 worlds, as was said, 'To endow those who love Me with wealth, that I may fill their treasuries.'"

Therefore, in order to have a need to achieve the degree of "righteous," and for their merit to be apparent, He had to lead His world with righteous and with wicked. It follows that in order for the righteous to be evident, wicked are also required, since precisely by leading His world with wicked, too, He gives the thoughts and desires of the wicked to a person, just as He gives the quality of righteous to a person. That is, He gives him the desire for self-love.

But this is done on purpose, so that man would know that the Creator does not want him to remain in the state that he understood the work of the Creator according to his mind at the time, in the beginning of his work in the manner of the individuals, when he assumed to himself what was the degree of the righteous. If the Creator did not behave with him in the manner of the wicked, meaning gave him thoughts and desires that are against the mind and heart, he would think that he is already at the degree of righteous, and the degree of righteous would remain in him in utter lowliness, since he would know that he has nothing to add.

This is regarded as "the Creator leading His world with the righteous," giving man only the degree of a righteous, without feeling any deficiencies, that the Creator should give him a higher level in understanding the meaning of "righteous." This is regarded as the righteous not being distinguishable, as was said, that the merit of the righteous is that he should come to obtain 310 worlds. He would have no need for this.

It is impossible to give a filling if there is no lack, since the person will not be able to keep the Klipot [shells/peels] from taking it into their own authority. Only the Klipot can gain from this, and this will damage the Kedusha, as our sages said, "Tzor [Tyre] was built only out of the ruin of the Jerusalem." Hence, precisely when there is a lack, and he is given a filling for the lack, he knows how to be careful so that no benefit comes from this to the external ones.

It follows that a person must have faith in the sages and how they guide us, to believe in their worlds. He should not say that the fact that he constantly suffers descents comes because he is unworthy of achieving wholeness. Rather, all the descents come to him from above! It is in order for man to have a need to obtain all the NRNHY of his soul. It requires great strengthening to say that the Creator sends him the descents so he would overcome and work coercively. This is called "He is coerced until he," the Creator, "says, 'I want,'" as Baal HaSulam explained.

What Is the Prohibition to Bless on an Empty Table, in the Work?

Article No. 16, Tav-Shin-Mem-Tet, 1988/89

It is written in *The Zohar*, *Yitro* (Item 437): "'You shall not take the name of your God in vain.' Rabbi Shimon started, 'And Elisha said unto her: 'What shall I do for you? Tell me; what do you have in the house?' Elisha said to her, 'Do you have anything on which the blessing of the Creator can be?' We learned that a person must not bless on an empty table. What is the reason? It is because the blessing above is not present on an empty place.'" (In 442) It says, "Hence, we must not mention the holy name in vain, as it is written, 'You shall not take the name of your God in vain.'"

We should understand why there cannot be an upper blessing on an empty table. After all, the blessing is that the Creator wants to give to the created beings delight and pleasure. Thus, why must the receivers first prepare in order to make room for the blessing to be, meaning that they must set up a suitable place to receive the upper blessing?

The thing is that the table is a place on which we eat, meaning the place from which one sustains oneself, and on which various pleasures are set in order to enjoy them. This is called a "table." It must not be empty, but have something from which one enjoys, and only then can one bless the Creator. This means that if one blesses the Creator but there is no pleasure set on the table, it is forbidden, as it is written, "a person must not bless on an empty table."

It is also difficult to understand what Rabbi Shimon brings as evidence, that Elisha asked her, "What do you have in the house?" The question was, Do you have something from which to enjoy? or else, the blessing cannot come. Yet, we see that the cessation of the oil, which is called a "blessing," was because there were no empty *Kelim* [vessels], as it is written, "And he said, 'Go, borrow vessels for yourself, empty vessels, do not get a few.' ...And he said to her, 'There is not one vessel more,' and the oil stopped."

It follows that the cessation of the blessing was not because the table was empty. Rather, the cessation of the blessing of the oil was for lack of empty *Kelim*. This means that there must be empty *Kelim*, as well.

To understand this in the work, we should know about the oppositeness we have in the order of the work. On one hand, we see that a person should establish the praise of the Creator, and then pray. Clearly, while he establishes the praises, he says that the Creator is good and does good to the bad and to the good, and that He is merciful and gracious. At that time, it cannot be said that a person is deficient, meaning that he lacks something whether in spirituality or in corporeality. Otherwise, it means that he is merely saying but his heart is not with him. That is, in his heart, he thinks differently from what he says with his mouth. For this reason, it is impossible to sing and thank the Creator and say His virtues, but a person says about himself that he has abundance and that he lacks nothing. Thus, how can one say so when he finds himself bare and destitute?

Baal HaSulam said about this that a person should depict to himself as though he has already been rewarded with complete faith in the Creator and already feels that the Creator leads the world in a manner of good and doing good. Although when he looks at himself and the world and sees that he and the whole world are deficient, each according to his degree, he should say about this, "They have eyes and see not," meaning above reason. In this way, he can say that he is a complete person and lacks nothing. Naturally, he can establish the praise of the Creator above reason.

He also said that a person should walk on the right line, which is to introspect and say that everything is under guidance and man has no free choice at all. Accordingly, The Baal Shem Tov said that before the fact, a person should say, "If I am not for me, who is for me?" and after the fact, a person should say, "Everything is under Providence." In other words, the Creator gave him a thought and desire to do something in Torah and *Mitzvot* [commandments/ good deeds], and chose him not only from among all the nations to give him a thought and desire to serve Him, meaning to observe Torah and *Mitzvot*, but even within the people of Israel themselves, He chose him from the rest of the people to give him a place to serve Him.

Although it is a small service, meaning that He let him work outside His palace, which is called *Lo Lishma* [not for Her sake], and still did not permit him to enter the palace, meaning He still did not receive permission from the Creator, namely a desire and yearning to work in order to bestow, and everything he does is only for his own sake, regarded as "outside the King's palace," but he considers this, too, a great privilege that He has chosen him from the rest of the people. He feels happy about this, and this can satisfy a person and make him praise and thank the Creator for rewarding him with accepting him into the work.

This is called "right line" in the work. That is, he feels happy when he looks at the rest of the people, who do not have this privilege of serving the King, even if *Lo Lishma*. Still, it is very important, since in terms of the action, he is serving the King, and on actions, we should not add. That is, even if he wants to add to the performance of *Mitzvot*, it is forbidden, as it is written, "You shall not add and you shall not take away." Thus, he considers it a great privilege.

For this reason, when he looks at others, that they have no contact with Torah and *Mitzvot*, and sees their lowliness, in what they are immersed, meaning that all the pleasures they can have are only pleasures clothed in dresses that every animal enjoys, that they were permitted from above to enjoy only these dresses and have no connection whatsoever to Torah and *Mitzvot*, and he believes that everything comes from above, from this a person should derive joy and happiness.

Baal HaSulam said that if a person receives from this joy and happiness, through the joy he is regarded as blessed, and then "The blessed clings to The Blessed." This is called "From *Lo Lishma*, we come to *Lishma* [for Her sake]," since the light in it reforms him, as now he feels that he is blessed and then the upper blessing can be on him, which is regarded as equivalence of form.

But if a person feels cursed, deficient, he has no equivalence with the Creator because the Creator is utterly complete. Consequently, there is no place where the blessing can be due to disparity of form.

That state is called "right line," meaning wholeness, in which there are no deficiencies. And what should one do when he engages in a manner of "right"? He should praise and thank the Creator, and engage in the Torah, for then is the time to receive the light of Torah, since he is in a state of wholeness, regarded as being a person who has blessing and no lacks. Naturally, this is the time for the blessing to be on him, as said above, "The blessed clings to The Blessed."

However, it is impossible to walk on one leg. That is, a person cannot progress on one leg. Since there is a rule, "There is no light without a *Kli*," meaning "No filling without a lack," and since on the right line he is in wholeness, it follows that he has nowhere to progress, no need for the Creator to satisfy his needs, since he has no needs at all.

For this reason, at that time a person must try to see his faults, so as to have room for prayer that the Creator will satisfy his needs. This is regarded as a person having to provide empty *Kelim* that the Creator may fill with upper abundance, which is called "a blessing." If there are no empty *Kelim*, meaning deficiencies, with what can he fill them?

This is regarded as a person walking on the "left line." In spirituality, "left" means something that requires correction. This means that a person should dedicate a small portion of his time to criticize himself and see how much effort he can put into working solely for the sake of the Creator, and not for his own sake, and if he can say that if he does not work in order to bring contentment to his Maker, he does not want to live, and so forth.

At that time he realizes that he cannot do this on his own, but only the Creator can help. It follows that now is the time when he can pray from the bottom of the heart. That is, he sees and feels that he is powerless to change the nature with which he was created, called "will to receive for himself and not to bestow."

But in truth, one must believe that this lack, that he cannot change himself alone, namely his nature, this awareness comes from above. That is, from above, he is notified of this truth that he cannot work in order to bestow.

A person must know that not everyone is shown this. Usually, meaning for people who work like the general public, since they take strength for work like the sacred still, and have no connection to the vegetative, they do not see flaws in themselves. Rather, those who try to walk on the path of individuals, to the extent that they yearn to achieve the degrees of *Dvekut* [adhesion], they receive help from above to see the truth, how far the created beings are from being givers.

It therefore follows that the upper one does not necessarily give them the help to be able to work in order to bestow. Rather, the upper one also gives the *Kli*, meaning the need to get help from above, since they cannot work in order to bestow by themselves. In other words, the upper one also gives the need, meaning the empty

Kelim—that they are unable to overcome the vessels of reception. This, too, the upper one gives.

Yet, help with this lack is given specifically to those who want to walk on the path of individuals. People who work in the manner of the general public are not revealed this knowledge, for the simple reason that they have no desire to work in order to bestow, so what will they reveal to them?

However, there is an issue here, that it is difficult for a beginner to walk on the path of individuals, and he begins to see that bestowing is difficult, and he cannot say that he was given this awareness from above as a gift. Rather, this awareness came to him due to the lowliness of the body itself. He says that all those who walk in the path of the work of bestowal is because "They do not have so much evil in their nature; this is why they can walk on this path. But for me, this is difficult." It is hard for him to believe that this is hard for everyone by nature, and there is no way that a person will have the power to emerge from the control of self-love unless the Creator Himself helps him out of this governance.

This is regarded as the Creator delivering His people from the exile in Egypt, as it is written in the Passover Haggadah [story/narrative], "I and not a messenger, I and not a seraph [type of angel], I the Lord and not another." We should interpret that the Creator said that only He had brought His people out of Egypt, as it is written, "I and not a seraph." This means that the person had the power of the fire of a seraph, which is why he could emerge from self-love. Even if a person has a burning fire, he will still not have the strength to go against nature, but rather the Creator brought them out.

This is the meaning of the words, "I and not a messenger." It means that it will not help a person that he wants to do God's mission, and will thereby have the power to emerge from their control. Rather, nothing will help him. Even if he is the mightiest of the mighty, he will not be able to emerge from this control of the self-benefit, unless the Creator gives the strength to emerge from this exile.

For this reason, a person must say and believe that nothing is difficult for the Creator. Therefore, a person cannot say that this work of bestowal is not for him because it is hard for him. Instead, he must believe that all those descents he has are because with each descent, he gets a need for the Creator's help, since a need is called a *Kli*, and in this *Kli*, the Creator can place light, as it is known that there is no light without a *Kli*.

However, the *Kli* is not made all at once. Rather, each descent gives one a need for His help. For example, one descent creates a one centimeter worth of need, and in the second descent, he gets a need once more, where he must say that only the Creator can help him. It follows that he has received another centimeter, and he has a *Kli* that is only two centimeters deep. When he has a hundred descents, he has a *Kli* that is one hundred centimeters deep. Thus, the *Kli* (grows), meaning the need and the desire that the Creator will help him (and give him) a big *Kli*.

Yet, we should ask, What is the measure of the *Kli?* Baal HaSulam said about this that a person should believe that the Creator knows how much need and desire the size of the *Kli* should have. When the Creator sees that the *Kli* can receive the light, the Creator immediately fills the *Kli* as much as He can. Thus, one should not be impressed by the descents. Instead, he should say, "The salvation of the Lord is as the blink of an eye," and a person must believe that immediately following each descent it may be enough to give him a *Kli*, a desire that the Creator can instantly fill.

However, when he sees that he still did not receive the help from the Creator, he must increase his praying that the Creator will help him and not fall into despair. This order is called "left line," meaning that specifically now he should feel his lowliness, how far he is from the work of bestowal.

However, he must not prolong this work on the left line. He should take only a short time of his work for the Creator to work with the lack. Most of the time, he should engage in work in wholeness, called "right," when he is content with little. That is, whatever taste and feeling in the work he has, he is happy with his lot and feels complete, thanks the Creator for it, and feels that he is the happiest person in the world.

At that time he can bless the Creator because of this good that He has given him—that he has the ability to be a worker of the Creator even at the smallest degree, it does not matter for him. This is so because he sees that he is important to the Creator because he believes that the Creator has chosen him to stand before him and do even the smallest service, while to others, He has not given even this service. For this, he blesses the Creator.

Now we can understand the question we asked, Why is the Creator unable to give His blessing unless there is some food on the table, and it is forbidden to bless on an empty table? The reason is that there must be equivalence of form, as our sages said, "The cursed does not cling to The Blessed." Therefore, when a person blesses the Creator and derives pleasure from the fact that the Creator has given him the meal, meaning a grip on *Kedusha* [holiness], this is regarded as the table not being empty, and the blessing can be in it. This is called "right line," and in this one should be most of the day's work.

We should also interpret what he brings as evidence, that he asked the woman what she has in the house. He learns from this that the table must not be empty. But we see that we do need empty *Kelim*, since the stopping of the oil, called "blessing," was because there were no more empty *Kelim*?

The answer is that in order to advance in the work, we also need the left line, called "deficiencies," which are empty *Kelim*. However, it is one thing to make the *Kelim*, which is when he works on the left line, and the pouring of the abundance into the empty *Kelim*. This is done specifically when a person is in a state where he is blessed and lacks nothing, and "The blessed clings to The Blessed."

What Is the Prohibition to Greet Before Blessing the Creator, in the Work?

Article No. 17, Tav-Shin-Mem-Tet, 1988/89

The *Zohar* writes in *Tetzaveh*, Item 51: "Rabbi Yehuda started, 'Leave off the man whose breath is in his nostrils, for why should he be regarded?' Was the prophet cautioning to avoid the rest of the people, and that the rest of the people should avoid him, so people would never draw near to each other? He replies that the verse speaks of one who comes to the doorstep of one's friend to greet him before he blesses the Creator. It was said about this, 'Leave off.'"

On the face of it, what is the prohibition if a person greets his friend before he blesses the Creator? It is that it seems as though he honors his friend before he honors the Creator. But does the Creator need honor, that we can say that if one does not bless Him before his friend, it is a blemish in His honor?

This is similar to a man walking into a henhouse and seeing that one rooster looks at another and does not pay attention to the man, who is the landlord. Can it be said that the rooster blemished the landlord? It is much more so with regard to the created beings compared to the Creator. His distance from man is far too great for man to be regarded as anything compared to the Creator, that we can say that he has blemished the glory of the Creator.

We should also understand what is written, "The verse speaks of one who comes to the doorstep of one's friend." Why is it specifically the doorstep of one's friend? What does it imply? It is as though if he does not come to the doorstep of his friend, he is permitted to greet his friend? We should interpret this with regard to man's work, for in the work, we speak of everything within one person, meaning that his friend and greeting are also in the same person.

It is known that man's work is to achieve *Dvekut* [adhesion] with the Creator, called "equivalence of form." Since we learn that from the perspective of the Creator, whose desire is to do good to His creations, He created in the creatures a desire to receive that is regarded as yearning to receive delight and pleasure. This is called "the purpose of creation." Yet, in order not to suffer shame, a correction was made, called *Tzimtzum* [restriction] and concealment, so we do not feel the *Kedusha* [holiness] and the delight and pleasure found in *Kedusha*.

Although we say each day, "The whole earth is full of His glory," there is still concealment on it, so we must believe it. Yet, as long as one has not corrected one's actions to work in order to bestow, we do not feel it. Instead, it depends on man's work in obtaining the vessels of bestowal. To that extent, the *Tzimtzum* departs and he begins to feel the existence of the Creator. This is all of our work, to achieve equivalence of form called "*Dvekut* with the Creator."

In order to be rewarded with vessels of bestowal, there is a complete procession of work, as Baal HaSulam interpreted the matter of the three souls within man: 1) *Nefesh* [soul] of *Kedusha*, in which there is nothing to correct, 2) the *Nefesh* of the three impure *Klipot* [shells/peels], in which there is nothing to correct, as this will be corrected only at the end of correction, and 3) the *Nefesh* of *Klipat* Noga [*Klipa* (singular of *Klipot*) of Noga], which is half good and half bad. All of man's work is in this *Nefesh*. If a person performs a *Mitzva* [commandment/good deed], this *Nefesh* connects to *Kedusha*. If he commits a transgression, this *Nefesh* connects to the *Nefesh* of the three impure *Klipot*. Hence, in this *Nefesh* [soul] he can determine between bad and good, and all the work is only in this *Nefesh*.

For this reason, when a person begins to engage in Torah and *Mitzvot* in truth, in order to achieve *Dvekut* [adhesion] with the Creator, he has two ways before him: The reward for the work he does will be for his own benefit and not for the sake of the Creator, regarded as wanting to nurse the *Nefesh* of *Klipa*, that she will receive the reward for his work, or, if he wants to nurse the *Kedusha* through his work, meaning that the reward for his work will be only for the sake of the Creator, then his work feeds the *Nefesh* of *Kedusha*. This is considered that the *Nefesh* of *Klipat* Noga joins the *Nefesh* of *Kedusha*.

However, we should know that achieving the degree where "all your works are for the sake of the Creator" is not done at once. Rather, as our sages said, "Man's inclination overcomes him every day, and were it not for the help of the Creator, he would not overcome it." That is, we see that our sages come to tell us two things: 1) It is impossible to subdue the bad in one time. Rather, each day there is new work, as it is written, "Man's inclination overcomes him every day." 2) A person cannot subdue it without the help of the Creator.

These two discernments are called "light and *Kli*." This means that the deficiency that a person finds—that the evil controls him—is the *Kli*. That is, he feels how far he is from working for the sake of the Creator and the matter of "Love the Lord with all your heart," etc., and not for its own sake. The body cannot understand how can such a thing be, as it is completely against all intellect and reason for such a thing to be in reality.

A person can understand the matter of assuming the burden of the kingdom of heaven only if by this, the Creator will give him all of his heart's wishes. That is, a person can understand that the Creator will serve the man and provide for all his needs. But if it is to the contrary, meaning that man should serve the Creator and always think how he can please the Creator so the Creator will enjoy his work, as it is written, "The Lord will rejoice with His works," meaning that the works of the Creator, who are the creatures, will delight Him, then a person asks, "What will I gain by pleasing the Creator?" since man's body understands only that which pertains to its own benefit.

This lack that a person begins to feel, that he cannot work for the sake of the Creator, is called a *Kli* [vessel], meaning a need for someone to help him have a desire to work for the sake of the Creator. The help he receives from above is regarded as the Creator helping him, is regarded as "light." Those two appear one at a time, and not at once.

This is why it was said, "Man's inclination overcomes him every day." That is, the light and the *Kli* are not completed in one day. Rather, it is as it is written, "Penny by penny join into a great amount," until the *Kli* receives the full measure of the lack that is suitable to receive light in full.

This is as it is written in *The Zohar* ("Introduction of The Book of Zohar," Item 140), "'Day to day expresses utterance, and night to night reveals knowledge,' etc. This is so because prior to the end of correction, before we qualified our vessels of reception to receive only in order to give contentment to our Maker and not for our own sake, *Malchut* is called 'the tree of knowledge of good and evil.' This is so because *Malchut* is the guidance of the world by people's actions. This guidance qualifies us to ultimately correct our vessels of reception in order to bestow and to be rewarded with the delight and pleasure He had contemplated in our favor. ...Often, the guidance of good and evil causes us ascents and descents ... Know that each ascent is regarded as a separate day ... since all those nights are the descents, the suffering, and punishments that stopped the

Dvekut [adhesion] with the Creator until they became many days one after the other. Now, once the night and darkness have also become merits and good deeds ... there are no more stops, and all 6,000 years connect into one great day.

"...This is the meaning of 'Day to day expresses utterance,' since the word that separated between one day and the next has now become a great praise and praises it, for it has become a merit. Thus, they all became one day for the Lord ... since only all of them together, assembled, became worthy of receiving that great knowledge."

It therefore follows that only through the ascents and descents, called "days and nights," when they join into the complete measure to be able to receive the great knowledge, there must be a great *Kli* [vessel], meaning a great need. This happens because of the descents when he sees that each day he becomes more needy of the Creator to help him emerge from self-love. Each day means the ascents, meaning that each time he receives help, called "light and abundance," for the light in it reforms him.

This is considered that the Creator helps him, for specifically through both we obtain a *Kli* that is fit to receive the delight and pleasure that the Creator contemplated in his favor. This is considered that he received the correction and the qualification to receive the purpose of creation, which is to do good to His creations.

However, the most difficult part of the work is that the order of the work is as two writings that deny one another. It is hard to understand how the two can be true.

For example, it is written in the essay about the order of the work by Baal HaSulam that "when attributing the work to the Creator, to believe that the Creator accepts our work regardless of how the work seems." That is, it does not matter if he works with much knowledge and understanding, but if he attributes the work to the Creator, meaning works with the aim to bestow, the Creator accepts his work willingly, even if it is the simplest, without any understanding. However, he must aim to bestow. He said that one way or the other, we must believe that He will hear, even if he does not aim

145

specifically to bestow, but aims that he is speaking to the Creator. Then, a person must believe that the Creator hears his prayer.

On the other hand, it is written in *A Sage's Fruit* (Vol. 1, p 119) that a person must yearn to attain the Creator, meaning adhere to Him with complete recognition, that this is regarded as the Creator. This means that a person must walk on the right line, regarded as wholeness, and pray to the Creator and thank Him, even if he does not find within him anything that desires spirituality. But accordingly, how can he thank the Creator and say that the Creator hears what he says to Him, which is the meaning of attributing the work to the Creator, and He accepts his work regardless of how the work seems?

However, if he relates only to the Creator and says, "I am turning to the Creator and I believe that He can answer my wishes," by this a person becomes happy and feels superior. That is, the rest of the people have no connection to spirituality, and he believes that the Creator has given him [a feeling] that he has no spirituality, in whatever way, but the fact that he has an interest in thinking about spirituality, it makes no difference if he has or hasn't, or that he is now in utter lowliness, meaning that he sees that now he has no desire to ascend in degree and emerge from the lowliness, but he thanks the Creator because at least he is thinking about spirituality, while the rest of the people do not have any thoughts of spirituality.

If he can thank the Creator, it gives him joy, and from *Lo Lishma* [not for Her sake] he comes to *Lishma* [for Her sake]. By this he ascends from his state of wholeness and can thereby come to a state where even if he forgets the state of lowliness he was in prior to making the calculation and thanking the Creator, it appears to him as though he has always been in this state.

This extends from the discernment that "The blessed clings to the Blessed," since the thanks he gives to the Creator makes a person feel whole, and to the extent of the joy he extends, so he can ascend in degree. We must say that this path is true, meaning that man hasn't the power to assess the importance of *Kedusha*, but even touching anything of *Kedusha* is infinitely more important to the Creator than all the corporeal things.

About corporeal things, a person knows that it is worthwhile to thank the Creator for this, since the Creator gave the corporeal pleasures so that the person who receives them will feel joy and elation. Conversely, He gave the *Kedusha* for the purpose of correction, as we learned about the concealment and hiding. However, a person should believe that he can give much gratitude when the importance of a matter is revealed to him, but that which does not appear to him as important, a person does not appreciate. Nonetheless, one who wishes to come into the work of the Creator must believe in the sages and say that a tiny touch on *Kedusha* is regarded as a great thing. He should work on this and appreciate the matter until he can elicit joy from that small thing.

Our sages call this, "Who is rich? He who is content with his lot," who settles for little. That is, even for a small thing he can be grateful as though it were a great thing. For this reason, any contact he has, even a negative one, is still regarded as positive.

In other words, the fact that a person sees and feels that he has no desire and yearning for work, which is truly negative, still, if he can extract from this and see how at least he has a thought to think about spirituality, he thanks and praises the Creator that he has dealings with spirituality, while he sees that there are people to whom the Creator did not even allow to think about the work. He believes that the Creator did choose him to give the knowledge that there is the matter of spirituality, and says that it is only that the Creator has not given him permission to enter and do the holy work. If he can derive joy from that state, it can pull him out of his state of lowliness and admit him into the *Kedusha*.

However, on the other hand, a person must awaken within him the value of the work on the path of truth, meaning what a person must correct. This is as it is written there, that a person must achieve wholeness, be rewarded with 620 times more than he had prior to the descent of the soul into the body. Although this contradicts the quality of the "right," it is still true, meaning the wholeness is precisely to come to correct what he must.

Now we can understand what we asked about the prohibition to greet his friend before he blesses the Creator. We must know that in the work, every person is a whole world. It follows that his friend means the body, in the sense that it has *Nefesh* of *Klipat Orla* [Noga]. To "greet" means to have wholeness before he blesses the Creator. That is, his foundation must be to bless the Creator, meaning that everything he does is for the sake of the Creator and not for his own sake, which is the *Nefesh* of the three impure *Klipot*. For this reason, when he first tries to aim that everything will be for the sake of the Creator, he can then greet his friend, meaning that then he subdues his friend, in that he is subjugated to also work for the sake of the Creator.

It follows that if he blesses the Creator before he greets his friend, it means he wants the glory of the Creator to be revealed, as it is written, "When the Lord favors man's ways, even his enemies will make peace with him." This is how it should be, and not the other way around. This is the meaning of the prohibition to come to the doorstep of one's friend, etc.

What Is, "There Is No Blessing in That Which Is Counted," in the Work?

Article No. 18, Tav-Shin-Mem-Tet, 1988/89

It is written in *The Zohar* (*Ki Tissa*, Item 2): "Come and see: It was established that there is no blessing above on that which is counted. And if you say, 'How were Israel counted?' He took from them ransom for their souls, and they established that they did not calculate until all the ransom was collected and reached the number. It follows that in the beginning, Israel are blessed when receiving the ransom. Afterward, they count the ransom and bless Israel once more. It turns out that Israel were blessed in the beginning and in the end, and there was no plague in them. He asks, 'Why does a plague appear because of the count?' He answers, 'It is because there is no blessing in that which is counted. And since the blessing has departed, the *Sitra Achra* [other side] is on it and can do harm.'"

We should understand the following: 1) If there is no blessing in that which is counted, what is the difference if we count people or the ransom instead of the people, since in the end, we know the number of people? Thus, how does it help if we swap the ransom because finally, we know their number? 2) Why is the ransom specifically a half shekel and not a full or a quarter shekel? What does half mean to us? 3) Why does the verse say, "The rich will not give more and the poor will not give less"? Is there anyone who does not know that if we need to know a certain number and swap, so that instead of counting people, we count something else, it must be the same thing for everyone, or it will not be possible to know the count? What does this come to teach us? 4) How does it benefit us if we are blessed in the beginning and in the end if there is counting in the middle? Do the blessings spoil the counting if there cannot be a blessing in that which is counted?

To understand all this in the work, we must pay attention to the purpose that we must achieve. It is known that every purpose that we want to achieve requires labor. Without labor, nothing can be accomplished. Thus, in the work of the Creator, what is the purpose of that we want to achieve and for which we labor?

The answer is, achieving *Dvekut* [adhesion] with the Creator, which is called "equivalence of form." That is, as the goal of the Creator in creating the world was to do good to His creations, our goal should be to do good to the Creator. In other words, man should do things to please the Creator. This is called "equivalence of form."

This means that when the two forms come as one, the purpose of the Creator dresses in the purpose of the created beings. It follows that His will to do good to His creations, which is the purpose of creation, dresses in the desire to bestow contentment upon his Maker, and this is called "receiving in order to bestow." It follows that we should say that our reward for the labor is the obtainment of the goal, much like corporeal matters, when we exert, and in return achieve the goal that we aspire for, for nothing is given without an effort.

It follows that when a person wants to walk on the path of truth in order to achieve his goal, called "*Dvekut* with the Creator," where all his actions are in order to bestow, he must put in labor, which is called "suffering." This means that a person has to go against his nature, meaning that man was created with Kelim [vessels] to delight himself, and he must walk on the path that will lead to pleasing the Creator and not for his own sake.

However, the body resists it. There are wars over this. Once, the desire to bestow prevails, and once, the will to receive triumphs. Yet, we must know that all the powers we will have so we can go against the will to receive, we must receive from the Torah. It is as our sages said, "I have created the evil inclination; I have created the Torah as a spice."

That is, what is the reward one expects when he engages in Torah and labors in the Torah? It is to aim to be rewarded with the desire to bestow upon the Creator. This is considered that he is learning Torah in order to achieve Lishma [for Her sake], called "in order to bestow." This is regarded as "cling unto His attributes."

Accordingly, there are two manners in labor in the Torah: 1) He labors in the study of Torah in order to thereby obtain self-benefit, such as in order to be called "Rabbi" or for payment of money. 2) He labors in the Torah in order to obtain the power to go against self-benefit. It follows that here there is a different discernment to make in the labor. That is, a person must make great efforts in order to have the strength to labor in the Torah for this intention which is against the body. Moreover, the body resists him as much as it can and does not want to give him energy to exert in the Torah with this intention. But in Lo Lishma [not for Her sake], the body sees that if it gets what it wants to receive in return, the body gives him fuel to work so he can exert in Torah and Mitzvot [commandments/good deeds], since the reward it expects to receive does not go against the body. Hence, the body can give him energy to work.

Therefore, when a person sees that he can obtain self-benefit through labor, he has the power to do things and make great efforts, and there is no weakness in his work. This is how "women, little ones, and uneducated people" are first educated, since it is possible to convince a person to engage in Torah and Mitzvot only through Lo Lishma.

However, when a person should replace the goal, meaning where in the beginning of his work in Torah and Mitzvot, his goal—which he wanted to achieve through the labor—was self-benefit, now he replaces the goal. That is, where he thought, "When will I achieve the goal for my will to receive so I can enjoy?" now he yearns for the goal and says, "When will I be able to delight the Creator and relinquish self-benefit?"

Since this purpose is against nature, he needs more faith in the Creator, since he must always exert to obtain the greatness of the Creator. That is, to the extent that he believes in the greatness of the Creator, to that extent he can work with this intention. For this reason, it is upon a person to pray each day that the Creator will open his eyes so he will recognize the greatness and importance of the Creator, so he has fuel to labor with the aim to bestow.

There are two discernments to make in this: 1) to have a desire to bestow contentment upon his Maker, that this will be his only aspiration, 2) to do things with the aim that the actions will bring him a desire to do things in order to please the Creator. In other words, he must work and toil extensively to obtain light and Kli [vessel]. Light means that he received from the Creator a desire where he craves all day to bring contentment to the Creator. A Kli is a desire, meaning that he wants to bestow upon the Creator. Those two, he should receive from the Creator, meaning both the light and the Kli.

However, a person should demand this, and it is written about this, "Zion, no one requires her." Our sages said, "This means that she ought to be sought," meaning that there must be a demand on the part of the lower ones that the Creator will give them both the light and the Kli.

Accordingly, we should interpret what is written (in the Musaf [supplemental] prayer of Rosh Hashanah): "The far will hear and come, and will give You a crown of kingship." It is known that the order of the work is as it is written, "We will do and we will hear." "Doing" pertains to the created beings. This is called "which God has created to do." That is, the part of doing pertains to us, and by this we will be rewarded with hearing, which is what the Creator lets us hear. But of themselves, the creatures cannot take upon themselves the work for the Creator, which is only for the Creator, without interference of self-benefit.

Yet, the hearing comes from the Creator, as it was at the time of the giving of the Torah, when the people of Israel heard from the Creator "I," and "You shall not have." But preceding this was a preparation to receive the Torah, as our sages said (*Shabbat* 87) that there was the matter of limiting and abstaining, as it is written, "And you shall dedicate today and tomorrow." Subsequently, they were rewarded with hearing the Torah.

By this we should interpret, "The far will hear and come," meaning the fact that they are far, that there is a Torah [law] of life, which is called as it is written, "For with You is a source of life," which is *Dvekut* with the Creator, but man is far from it. This distancing comes also from the Creator, since it is possible to be far from something only when a person clearly knows that there is a reality but he, for some reason, is far from it.

Hence, first a person must have faith in the Creator, and then he can say that he feels far from the Creator. It follows that this feeling that he is far must give him a feeling that the Creator watches over the world, and there is judgment and a judge, except he feels this from afar. Otherwise, who will tell him that he is far from the Creator?

For this reason, when a person feels far from the Creator, the Creator alerts him to this by appearing to a person from afar. This means that when the Creator is hidden from him, a person cannot be in a state of remoteness, for who tells him that he is far? However, by the Creator appearing to him a little bit, the feeling comes to him that he is far.

This is the meaning of "The far will hear," meaning that the Creator sends them hearing so they will feel that they are far and will come near, meaning demand of the Creator to bring them closer so they can achieve equivalence of form, which is vessels of bestowal.

However, a person can obtain these *Kelim* only through help from above. This is called "a light that dresses in a *Kli*," meaning in the desire for this power.

This is as it is written (Psalms 127), "Unless the Lord builds a house, its builders labor in it in vain." The meaning of "Unless the Lord builds a house" is that the heart becomes a building of *Kedusha* [holiness]. "Labor in it in vain" means that the labor is futile. "Its builders" are those who want to build a structure of *Kedusha*. They must know and believe that without His help, for He both gives the *Kli*, the desire and yearning to bestow, as well as the light, which is the power that a person receives so he can work in order to bestow. He gives everything, but a person must first act. That is, before the work, a person must say, "If I am not for me, who is for me." Afterward, he should say, "Unless the Lord builds a house, its builders labor in it in vain."

As it was prior to the giving of the Torah, meaning in order for the people of Israel to be able to hear the Torah that was given on Mt. Sinai, there was preparation on the part of the people of Israel, who were given limitation and abstention. This is considered preparation on the part of the lower one. Afterward, it is possible to receive the Torah from the Creator.

However, during the preparation, before a person is rewarded with a *Kli* called "a need to be able to work so that all his actions are in order to bestow," that need ascends and descends in him. At times he yearns for the Creator to give him the power to be able to do everything for the sake of the Creator and asks the Creator to help him. At times, he later suffers a descent, meaning that he feels no need to bring contentment to the Creator. Rather, he craves only counsels and tactics to satisfy himself with pleasures for the will to receive for himself.

If, during the descent, a thought concerning spirituality comes to him—that he must work in order to bestow—he begins to think about the Creator, why the Creator forbade working for self-benefit and why should the Creator mind if a person does work for his own benefit.

At that time he doubts the Torah and *Mitzvot* altogether, why He wants to afflict us and has given us laws that are hard to observe? If He really is a merciful father, why has He made us observe His *Mitzvot* through many prohibitions? etc. Sometimes, during an ascent, he also thinks about the Creator and why He has given us commandments of interest, such as "Keep your souls."

That is, the fact that man must eat, drink, and so forth, for what purpose did the Creator create these things? Does the existence of these things make a person smarter and more heaven-fearing? Therefore, the person asks, Why are corporeal pleasures needed? since he sees no spiritual benefit from it.

Thus, a person ascends and descends. At times he does not understand why corporeal pleasures were given to us in the first place, since now he understands that man's main purpose is to adhere to the Creator, so why were these corporeal pleasures created?

During the descent, it is the complete opposite. He asks himself, Why were many things prohibited to us? and in general, Why is it forbidden to work for self-benefit and we are as though compelled to work for the sake of the Creator, and if not, then we must suffer in this world and in the next?

This is the order of the work during the preparation period. That is, before a person is rewarded with permanent faith, he is in the catapult, thrown from end to end, and seeing that he has no freedom of choice. Rather, what they want above is what they do with him, while he is like clay in the hands of a potter without any say about himself.

The person should believe that all the states he goes through are for his sake. That is, specifically through the ups and downs he will achieve the desirable completion, as it is written, "A king who puts to death, and brings to life, and brings forth salvation." Through the descents, which are regarded as death in the work, and "brings to life," which is regarded as an ascent in the work, specifically by this He "brings forth salvation," meaning that man achieves wholeness.

Now we can understand what we asked, Why do we need to count Israel in the first place? That is, who needs to know the number when counting is a dangerous matter, as it is written, "There is no blessing in that which is counted." And also, what difference does the correction they were given—of giving ransom—make if in the end, we know the number of Israel? Also, what does it add to us if we bless in the beginning and in the end of the count?

In the work, when speaking of everything within one person, we should know what is the counting of Israel. The work to achieve *Lishma*, meaning to bestow, begins on the right line, called "wholeness." This is regarded as a man on whom there is blessing. From this, a person should be happy and praise and thank the Creator for rewarding him with some grip on *Kedusha*, however much he has, since he knows that this, too, he does not deserve.

This is regarded as being content with little. Thus, he has no reason to count him, to see how many qualities of Israel he has, meaning what percentage of his work can he say is *Yashar-El*, meaning how much effort he is willing to make for the *Kedusha*, called "for the sake of the Creator." This is not interesting at all because he says, "Whatever grip I have in Torah and *Mitzvot* is more important than all the pleasures in the world."

We could ask about this, If this is so important, why does he settle for little? To this he answers himself, "I probably do not deserve to be given by the Creator a bigger share than I have, and I also see that there are people who do not have even this." It follows that he is a person in whom there is blessing since he has something with which to be happy, and he sees that the rest of the people are joyful and happy over nonsense, while the Creator has given him the intellect and understanding to grasp that he should rejoice with the Creator.

This is considered that before he comes to count the *Yashar-El* in him, meaning what he has inside the heart, he first blesses Israel. That is, he says that the Israel in him is blessed, meaning that he has a reason for gladness since he is blessed, and he is content with the little that he has.

Afterward, Israel are counted, meaning he shifts to the quality of the left and begins to introspect how much Torah and fear of heaven he has. At that time, he sees that he is full of faults, and then there can be a plague, meaning that he might come into despair and escape the campaign and say that this work of bestowal is not for him. Yet, he can no longer work in one line because he can no longer fool himself and say that this is real work, since the left keeps telling him what is the work of truth.

This is the meaning of "There is no blessing in that which is counted," since he always has deficiencies, as it is written, "There is not a righteous man on earth who does good and sins not." It follows that according to the rule that where there is a lack, there is a grip to the Klipot [shells/peels], meaning that the Klipa [singular for Klipot] shows him that this is not for him. With these complaints, she kills him, meaning that whatever he had in spirituality, she takes away from him and he remains in the form of "The wicked in their lives are called 'dead.'"

This is the meaning of what is written, that anything that is counted holds no blessing, since it is always deficient and in every lack there is a grip to the Klipot. This is called a "plague," as it is written, "And there will be no plague in them when you count them." That is, through the ransom, there will not be death because of the counting. This means that when working in the left line, meaning although we are walking on the left line and there can be a plague, through the ransom, there will be no plague in them.

For this reason, we were given the advice that the deficiency must be visible to the Klipot: "And they shall each give the ransom for his soul when you count them." That is, they should not regard the deficiencies they find when a person calculates what percentage are included in the quality of Israel.

Rather, they should calculate how many corrections they must do in order to have ransom for their souls to the Creator, meaning that they will not look at the deficiencies, but at the correction of the deficiencies, by which their soul, which was in the Klipot, will emerge from them and cling to the Creator. This is called "And they gave each one the ransom for his soul," counting the corrections they must perform.

Thus, they can only see corrections, as our sages said (*Yevamot* 38), "A bill that is about to be collected is deemed collected." It follows that when looking at the corrections, it is as though he has already performed them and there is no place of deficiency here.

This is the meaning of the verse, "This is what everyone who is numbered shall give." We should interpret that seeing the deficiencies is regarded as "everyone who is numbered." "Half a shekel" means as it is written (*A Sage's Fruit*, Vol. 1, p 95), "A prayer makes half." It is the conduct of one who prays for himself that he has no wholeness but only half, since one who is whole has nothing to pray for. Hence our sages warned us not to work in order to receive reward, but for wholeness.

This means that what a person gives is regarded as half, meaning the *Kli*, which is the will to receive for himself, which has drifted from the Creator and we must pray that this *Kli* will connect to the Creator, who is called "the light." When the light shines in the *Kli*, it is considered wholeness. This is the meaning of "a prayer makes half," where "half" means the *Kli*, for there is no light without a *Kli*.

Therefore, when he prays and feels his lack, there is room to fill the lack. It follows that the words "this they will give," mean the *Kli*, which is half, called "awakening from below," as was said, that the prayer for the deficiency is already considered a correction.

For example, one person gave his coat to the cleaner to remove stains. He tells the owner of the laundromat, "I'm counting the number of corrections you should make so that I will know how much to pay you." He asks the owner of the laundromat to fix and remove the stains. But then, it cannot be said that a person despairs when he sees that he has many stains, since he is not counting the stains so as to see how many deficiencies are in his coat. Rather, he counts how many corrections he must do.

It follows that now he is not thinking of his deficiencies, but about the corrections. Naturally, it cannot be said that there is a plague in them (the stains), meaning that he should escape the campaign and say that the work on the path of truth does not pertain to him.

It follows that it is a great correction that we count the ransom and not the deficiencies in people. This is as our sages said, "A bill that is about to be collected is deemed collected." That is, when we engage in corrections, it is as though it is already corrected because now he is looking at the corrections and not at the deficiencies.

In addition to the abovementioned correction of the ransom, called "ransom for his soul to the Creator," meaning when we speak of corrections, that there will be *Dvekut* with the Creator, we must bless before the count. This means that we must walk on the right line, called "blessing," meaning that he is a person who has no lacks. Afterward, we shift to the left, called "counting," and then again to the right, which is called "blessing." This is the meaning of what is written, that through blessing in the beginning and in the end, the count will come true and there will be no plague in them, but rather by this they will achieve real wholeness.

Why Is Shabbat Called *Shin-Bat* in the Work?

Article No. 19, Tav-Shin-Mem-Tet, 1988/89

It is written in *The Zohar* (*VaYakhel*, Item 180): "What is Shabbat [Sabbath]? Why is it called 'Shabbat'? Is it because that dot ascended and her light shines? At that time, she is crowned in the fathers, who are HGT de ZA, to be one, and everything is called 'Shabbat.' That is, *Malchut* together with the fathers are called 'Shabbat.' Shabbat has the letters *Shin-Bat* [daughter], since the three *Vavs* [3 times *Vav*] in the *Shin* [] imply the three fathers HGT, and she, who is called *Bat* [daughter], crowns in them."

It is also written there (Item 181): "The meaning of the matter is that the dot, wherever it is, is the heart of the eye. That is, it contains *Hochma*, which is called "eyes," and it is called *Bat* [daughter], as he said, 'Keep us like the pupil of the eye.' Because she is the heart of the whole eye [pupil], she is called *Bat*. That is, there are three colors in the eye, which are HGT. The fourth color is a black dot, which is *Malchut*, and only in it is the *Hochma*—called *Ayin* [eye]—revealed. This is why it is the heart of all the colors of the eye." There (Item 177), it says, "All those six days—HGT NHY—unite at a single, holy point, which is *Malchut*, and all the days unite in her."

We should interpret this in the work. Baal HaSulam asked according to the above said, that the six days of work imply ZA, which are HGT NHY of ZA, and Shabbat implies *Malchut*. If this is so, then the six weekdays should have been more important than Shabbat, since ZA is a higher degree than *Malchut*.

He said, "It is true that the six weekdays imply ZA, but the whole world is under the governance of *Malchut*, since *Malchut* is called 'the assembly of Israel,' which means that she contains all the souls of Israel, and anything that is not in *Malchut* is not revealed in this world. However, as long as there is no unification between ZA and *Malchut* and the abundance of ZA does not extend to *Malchut*, it is called 'weekday.'"

Shabbat is regarded as unification, meaning that ZA unites with *Malchut*, which means that all six *Sefirot* of ZA illuminate in *Malchut*. This is why she is called "a Shabbat of holiness," since the *Kedusha* [holiness] of ZA extends to *Malchut*. "Weekday" means that they separated from each other because *Malchut*, who is the *Kli* [vessel] that receives the abundance for the lower ones, "the receiving *Malchut*," is in disparity of form from the Giver, who is ZA. The lower ones must be fit to receive the abundance that *Malchut* wants to bestow upon them, meaning (to be) in equivalence of form, to work in order to bestow.

This is why we were given the six workdays to correct ourselves through work in Torah and *Mitzvot* [commandments/good deeds]. To the extent that we engage in bestowal, to that extent each one corrects the root of his soul above, in *Malchut*, into working in order to bestow. It follows that through the six workdays, *Malchut* is corrected by the lower ones, and then *Malchut* is in equivalence of form with ZA, and the abundance of ZA extends to *Malchut*.

For this reason, Shabbat is regarded as *Malchut* and is more important than the six weekdays, although the six days imply ZA, which is a higher degree than *Malchut*. However, all the degrees are measured by the extent to which they bestow upon the lower ones. Since on the six workdays they are in the midst of the work of correcting *Malchut* into working in order to bestow, ZA still cannot bestow. Only on Shabbat, when the work of bestowal of *Malchut* is completed, Shabbat is considered more important because then the degree of ZA shines to the lower ones through the correction of *Malchut*. This is why Shabbat is called "the secret of the One," which is the unification of ZA and *Malchut* through equivalence of form. This is why she is called "Shabbat of peace," meaning that it is considered that on Shabbat there is already peace between ZA, regarded as the giver, and *Malchut*, regarded as the receiver.

On Shabbat, *Malchut* is already corrected into working in order to bestow and there is no separation between them whatsoever. For this reason, it is called "a blessed Shabbat of peace," for then the blessings extend to *Malchut* and to the lower ones. For this reason, Shabbat is more important than the six workdays.

Our sages said (*Avoda Zara* 3), "The Creator said to them: 'Fools, he who toiled on the eve of Shabbat will eat on Shabbat. He who did not toil on the eve of Shabbat, from where will he eat on Shabbat?'" This means that the Shabbat meal is regarded as a reward for the work. If a person did not work, from where will he be rewarded? Without work, it is possible to receive almsgiving or a gift, but not a reward [*Sachar* means both "reward" and "salary"], as there is reward specifically in return for work. This is why the Creator said to them, "He who did not toil on the eve of Shabbat, from where will he eat on Shabbat?"

Yet, this is truly perplexing. Why did the Creator say, "He who did not toil on the eve of Shabbat, from where will he eat on Shabbat"? After all, the Creator can give them as almsgiving or as a gift.

The answer is that without work it is impossible to enjoy the meal due to the known reason that in order not to have the bread of shame upon the reception of the pleasure, a correction was made, called "*Tzimtzum* [restriction] and concealment on the upper light," and the delight and pleasure that the Creator wishes to impart upon the creatures is not revealed.

Instead, through labor in the *Segula* [remedy/virtue] of Torah and Mitzvot, we obtain the vessels of bestowal, and to that extent the concealment is removed and it is possible to receive the delight and pleasure. But before we obtain the vessels of bestowal, it is impossible to enjoy the purpose of creation, which is the delight and pleasure. This is why there is no point saying that the Creator should give him as a gift or as almsgiving, since there will certainly be shame there, and this shame spoils the taste of the pleasure.

As we see in corporeality, a person is ashamed to eat the bread of shame [receive handout], but specifically through labor. Here, the labor is to turn the vessels of reception, with which man was born, and to provide for himself vessels of bestowal, which are against nature, and anything that is against nature is hard to do and requires great efforts to obtain the vessels of bestowal. It was said about this, "He who comes to purify is aided." That is, without His help, a person has no chance of being able to obtain them.

Now we can understand that the six workdays constitute the matter of making the vessels of bestowal, which pertains to ZA, for the degree of ZA is to bestow upon *Malchut*. In order for *Malchut*, who receives the abundance from ZA, (to be able to) give to the lower ones, we must correct *Malchut* into being a giver like ZA. This is called "unification," meaning equivalence of form.

For this reason, the six workdays are called "days without holiness," due to this work of emerging from the will to receive for oneself and admitting it into *Kedusha*, meaning that it will serve the *Kedusha*. That is, the work is to make the secular holy. Although a person corrects one quality each day, where the first day [Sunday] corresponds to the quality of *Hesed*, the second day [Monday] to the quality of *Gevura*, etc., each correction does not become apparent right away.

Instead, when all six days have been corrected, the Shabbat becomes apparent. In other words, as long as the procession of the work of seven days has not been completed, the state of Shabbat does not become apparent in a person. This causes man not to be able to see or feel if he is advancing in the work or standing still in the same state as when he began the work.

Sometimes, a person sees the opposite—that he has regressed. That is, before he began the work of bestowal, he had more passion for Torah and work, and now he sees that his motivation for the work has weakened. This is so because each week is considered one degree. In the middle of the degree, it is impossible to see the situation as it truly is, for it is like a turning wheel, where that which was below before, ascends upward, and that which was above, descends, and as a result of all this, the machine moves forward.

Only at the end of the work, when Shabbat arrives, it means he has completed the six workdays that pertain to this Shabbat. Then it is considered that ZA, which are vessels of bestowal, have entered *Malchut*. This is called Shabbat.

For this reason, although the six workdays belong to ZA, they still do not shine in *Malchut* because the heart of our work is in *Malchut*, as it is written, "to correct the world in the kingdom [*Malchut*] of *Shadai* [the Lord]."

It follows that the work of the *Kelim* is to eject the will to receive for oneself and install instead the desire to bestow. This is called the work of the weekdays, which is the correction of the *Kelim*. This work is forbidden on Shabbat because Shabbat is called "the time of dining," when the light can shine inside the *Kelim*. This is why it is written, "He who did not toil on the eve of Shabbat," meaning did not prepare the vessels of bestowal, "from where will he eat on Shabbat?" since he has no *Kelim* where the meal, which is the delight and pleasure, can clothe.

By this we will understand what we asked, Why can He not give them the meal as a gift or almsgiving? since with a gift or almsgiving, there are no vessels of bestowal there, where the delight and pleasure can enter, due to the *Tzimtzum*.

Yet, we find that Shabbat is called "a gift," as our sages said (*Beitza* 16), "'To know that I the Lord sanctify you.' The Creator said to Moses: 'Moses, I have a good gift in My treasury, whose name is Shabbat, and I wish to give it to Israel, go and let them know.'"

This is perplexing. Why did He say, "He who did not toil on the eve of Shabbat, from where will he eat on Shabbat"? In the work, we should also ask, But He could have given them the Shabbat meal as a gift, since Shabbat is called "a gift," which means that it is possible to give the Shabbat even without work?

However, we should ask about what our sages said, that the Creator said to Moses, "Go and let them know." We should ask, For what purpose did He have to give them a fore notice about the gift? We understand that if we want something in return for the gift, then they should be notified so they will meet the conditions required for the giving of the gift. Therefore, it means that here, too, when He said, "Go and let them know," He must be demanding something in return for the gift.

Yet, we must understand how one can ask something in return for a gift, since if the receiver of the gift gives something, it is no longer considered a gift? We should interpret that when He said, "Go and let them know," He gave them awareness that since He wants to give them a gift, there was fear that it would be stolen from them. Therefore, the Giver of the gift required that they would make a safe place for the gift where no one would be able to take this important gift away from them. Otherwise, the Giver of the gift would not even be able to notify them of the importance of the gift, since those who should not hear would probably hear that it is important and would be able to take the gift away from them.

Therefore, in order for Him to give them the gift, He first needed to let them know that He wants to give them a gift, as it is written, "Go and let them know," "and I will notify them of the importance of the gift so they will be able to enjoy the gift." Then he let them know that they should do much preparation for the gift, so it is kept from the external ones, to prepare a place for the gift. It follows that the condition He had set in order to give them the gift was that they would prepare a safe place for the gift. This is not regarded as giving a present in return for the preparation.

What is the keeping from the external ones? It is that if they prepare vessels of bestowal, in these vessels they will receive the Shabbat, which is called "a gift." This is called "keeping from the external ones," whose whole grip is on the vessels of reception. This is not so with vessels of bestowal; from these they run away. This work of preparing the *Kelim* is called "weekdays," where on each day we must admit the implied *Kelim* into the *Sefirot* of ZA, which are called *HGT NHY*.

When the work of bestowal is through, the light of Shabbat arrives, which is called "a meal," and dresses in the *Kelim* that were acquired during the six workdays. It follows that the whole of the revealing of the work is apparent on Shabbat, which is called "the meaning of the One," when *Malchut*, called "vessels of reception," has been turned into bestowal during the work of the six workdays.

That is, the work of the vessels of bestowal that they acquired during the weekdays enter the Shabbat. This means that the fact that Shabbat is called "*Malchut* that shines in *Gadlut* [greatness/ adulthood]" is due to the preparatory work prior to the reception of the gift. At that time the light of Shabbat, which is called "a gift," can clothe in these vessels of bestowal. Then, the external ones have no control because the vessels of reception, to which the external ones grip, are absent. Hence, Shabbat is called "And all the judgments pass away from her."

This is why a gift is called Shabbat, since the Creator did not give the Shabbat in return for labor, but gave the Shabbat as a gift. And the reason why we need to work during the six workdays is in order to make a place for her, meaning a safe place where the external ones cannot hold her, since on Shabbat, the vessels of bestowal have already been corrected and they flee from a place where they see that the vessels of bestowal govern.

For this reason, Shabbat is called "holy," for the external ones run from the *Kedusha* of the Shabbat, when everything shines in vessels of bestowal because of the preparation during the six workdays.

According to the above, we should interpret what is written, "Moses will rejoice with the gift of his share." We should understand why it is written, "He who hates gifts shall live" (Proverbs 15:27). If so, then what is the meaning of "Moses will rejoice with the gift of his share," if "He who hates gifts shall live"?

The answer is, "For You have called him a faithful servant." What is "a faithful servant"? It is as our sages said, "Be as slaves serving the rav [great teacher] not in order to receive reward," meaning that all of one's work is only to bestow and not to receive anything.

It follows that the fact that he does receive is because the Creator wants to give him. Thus, his reception is called "receiving in order to bestow." It follows that the gift he is receiving is not because he wants to receive for himself, but because he wants to bestow. Since it is the will of the Creator to do good, he therefore accepts the delight and pleasure, to satisfy His wish, since he wants to delight the Creator.

But what does the Creator need? Certainly, it is for the purpose of creation to be carried out in full. Therefore, he accepts the King's gift in order to please the King. This is the meaning of the words, "For you have called him a faithful servant."

Now we can interpret the words of *The Zohar*, which asks, "What is the Shabbat?" and replies, "*Shin-Bat*, since the three *Vavs* in the *Shin* imply the three fathers, *HGT*, and *Malchut*, called *Bat* [daughter], crowns in them," since in her is the majority of the *Hochma*, as it is written, "Keep us like the pupil of the eye," which is the heart of the eye. There are three colors in the eye, which are *HGT*, and the fourth color is a black dot, which is *Malchut*.

In the three *Vavs*, each *Vav* implies the six workdays, which is the time of work, when a person must provide for himself vessels of bestowal. Indeed, each and every day, a person must walk on three lines, implied by the three *Vavs* in the *Shin*.

In other words, by walking on the right and left each day, we come to the middle line, which consists of both. In other words, we begin to walk on the right, called "the state of wholeness," and then shift to counting, when he begins to count the profit he has gained through the labor. Afterward, he returns to the right.

Through this turn of left and right, we arrive at the middle line, born out of the two lines. Then, through the work of the three *Vavs*, we come to the state of Shabbat, where Shabbat is called "the dot of *Malchut*," which is black, and is called "a black dot [or point]," since the *Tzimtzum* was on *Malchut*, which is called "the receiving *Kli*." For this reason, the light does not shine on her own self. However, through the correction of the three *Vavs*, which is the work on the six workdays in their three lines, she can receive the light that belongs to her essence, which is the light of *Hochma*. She is called *Bat-Ayin* ["pupil" but also "daughter of the eye"], where *Ayin* [eye] is called *Hochma*, and in the black dot, the light of *Hochma* is revealed. This is the Shabbat, where through the workdays, the Shabbat appears.

What Does It Mean that the Evil Inclination Ascends and Slanders, in the Work?

Article No. 20, Tav-Shin-Mem-Tet, 1988/89

I t is written in *The Zohar, Tzav* (Item 20), "'This is the law' is the assembly of Israel. *Malchut* that ascends is an evil thought that comes up in one's mind to divert him from the way of truth. It is the burnt-offering that ascends and slanders a person, and must be burned in fire so as not to allow it to slander. For this reason, On its firewood upon the altar all night.' Who is the 'Night'? It is the assembly of Israel, *Malchut*, which is the one who comes to purify the man from that desire. For this reason, it must never be quenched, but an everlasting fire shall burn in it.'"

We should understand the meaning of a bad thought that ascends and slanders a person. We should also understand what it means that "night" is called *Malchut*, and what it means that with

169

the fire, we burn the bad thought so it does not slander above, and what it means that this fire will not be quenched. What is this fire?

It is known that our basis is faith. That is, although we do not feel or understand everything our sages told us, we must believe. Without faith there is nothing to talk about. That is, we must believe what they told us, "I labored but did not find, do not believe." Rather, once a person has put in the necessary effort, we will achieve what our sages told us.

That is, first we must believe that the purpose of creation is "to do good to His creations." But the creatures do not attain the delight and pleasure right away, meaning that each one can say, "Blessed is He who said, 'Let there be the world,'" meaning that each one will rejoice in being created and in being able to enjoy a world that is full of abundance. However, we see that all creations suffer, whether less or more. They all ask, "Where is that delight and pleasure that the Creator wants to give us?" The answer is that there was a correction in order to bring to light the perfection of His deeds. That is, so that the creatures will not feel shame when receiving the delight and pleasure. For this purpose, there was a Tzimtzum [restriction] and concealment, where the delight and pleasure are concealed from us until we obtain the Kelim [vessels] that are fit to receive the good, and that they feel no deficiency in it, called "bread of shame."

For this reason, we must believe that although we still do not see the good, if we qualify ourselves to obtain the Kelim that are suitable for this, we will receive the abundance, as our sages said, "I labored but did not find, do not believe." Rather, anyone who exerts to obtain the vessels of bestowal will receive the delight and pleasure. Therefore, a person must not decide that if some time has passed in his engagement in the work of bestowal and he has labored for it, he must believe that he must have not given the required effort, and this is why he has not been awarded these Kelim.

However, in order to receive these (Kelim), meaning vessels of bestowal, there is the opposite work here. That is, normally, when a person learns a trade, each day he makes some progress, some more, some less. All those who quit the profession do not leave because they see no progress. Instead, they are advancing, but very slowly, and see that at the very least, they will need to learn this profession many years since they are advancing very slowly. Therefore, they drop out.

However, in learning the work of bestowal, the order is to the contrary: Not only do they see no progress in the work, they even see that they are going backward. Indeed, the question is, Why do they need to regress, meaning see that instead of what he should have seen, that the will to receive for himself separates him from Kedusha [holiness], and each time he must loathe the bad, meaning not want to work for self-reception, but always crave to work for the Creator, now he sees that he has received a greater yearning for self-love and cannot do anything in order to bestow?

Baal HaSulam said about this that in fact, a person does advance, meaning that each time he advances toward seeing his true state—that he is so immersed in self-love. This is so because there is a correction from above not to see one's true state before he can correct it. Therefore, to the extent that it is seen above that he exerts to emerge from self-love, to that extent the evil in him is revealed to him, so he will know that he is the worst person in the world. That is, in other people, the evil is not as exposed as it is in him. For this reason, he sees what he is lacking, and then he can ask the Creator to save him and bring him out of the bad within him.

By this we should interpret what is written, "The Lord is near to all who call upon Him, to all who call upon Him in truth." That is, in truth, they see their lowliness, that they are lower than the rest of the people and are unable to emerge from the control of the evil in them by themselves. For this reason, this is called "who call upon Him in truth," since they see that it is utterly impossible to emerge from the control of the self-love.

For this reason, they have a complete thing, meaning a complete desire for His help. It is as Baal HaSulam said, "A prayer makes half." That is, when a person gives an awakening from below, called "a prayer makes half," meaning the Kli [vessel], called (desire) for the thing he wants the Creator to satisfy. When the half of the *Kli* is completed, the filling comes. Here, "half" means that he sees that he has a deficiency but no vessels of bestowal.

It turns out that when he knows about himself that he is utterly unable to correct his lack, meaning that he has already done all that he could to be able to obtain the desire to bestow, he can say that he knows one hundred percent that if the Creator does not help him, he will remain in self-love. This is called "having a complete *Kli*," meaning a lack. At that time, the satisfaction of the lack comes, as the Creator gives him the desire and yearning to bestow.

The order is as our sages said, "There are three partners in a person: the Creator, his father, and his mother. His father gives the white," as it is said (*Nida* 31), "Our sages said, 'There are three partners in man: the Creator, his father, and his mother. His father sows the white, his mother sows the red, and the Creator places in him a spirit and a soul.'"

"Right" is named after his father, meaning the light of *Hochma*, which is the light of the purpose of creation. The light of *Hochma* is the light of "doing good to His creations," and this light comes specifically to the vessels of reception. There were *Tzimtzum* and concealment on that light, so it will not illuminate to the vessels of reception before they are corrected and can aim to bestow.

Therefore, when this light shines, we see that along with it shines the fact that there is also a *Tzimtzum*, meaning that through this light, we feel that we might come to separation. At that time a person becomes worse than he was. That is, he wants to receive spiritual light and pass it on to the *Klipot* [shells/peels], which want to receive abundance in order to receive. For this reason, a person takes upon himself not to use the vessels of reception any longer. This is regarded as his father, called *Hochma*, gives the white, meaning that he "whitens" a person not to use the will to receive for himself, since the light made him see how engaging with the will to receive for oneself removes one from the Creator. Hence, he decides not to use the will to receive any more, and this is called "white."

Yet, without a desire, it is impossible to do anything, and for himself, he no longer wants to receive. For this reason, "His mother gives the red." "His mother" is called *Bina*, whose quality is the desire to bestow. It is known that *Malchut* is called "black," meaning the will to receive, who is called *Malchut*, on whom there was a *Tzimtzum*, meaning that the light will not shine into her. This is why she is called "darkness." When *Malchut* is included in *Bina*, *Bina* is called "red." This is the meaning of his mother, meaning *Bina*, giving to a person the desire to bestow, and then a person can perform acts of bestowal. This is regarded as the Creator "giving a spirit and a soul," meaning upper abundance that comes into the vessels of bestowal. This is called "the birth of the *Partzuf*," meaning that a new degree is born.

It follows that everything comes from above. That is, the power to throw away the will to receive is not in one's own hands to do on his own. Rather, this is called "His father gives the white." Also, it is not within one's power to be able to do everything in order to bestow. Rather, this forces of wanting to perform only acts of bestowal comes to us from above. This is called "His mother sows the red."

According to the above, we can interpret what we asked, What is the meaning of saying, "She ascends and slanders a person"? It is written, "This is the Torah," meaning the order of the work, which gives one forces from above. He says that the Torah is called the "Assembly of Israel," *Malchut*, and a person should take upon himself the kingdom of heaven. Then comes the order that first a person begins to feel the bad in him, since before he began the work of bestowal, it appeared to him that he was already righteous, since he was sitting and learning Torah and observing *Mitzvot*, and what else should he do?

Certainly, there are greater righteous, who learn more and are more meticulous about the *Mitzvot* [commandments/good deeds], but nonetheless, he is also righteous, though he believes that there are greater righteous. Because of (this), he feels his lowliness, that he is not as righteous as they are, and he takes his lowliness only from this.

However, when a person begins to come into the work on the path of truth, which is the work of bestowal, a person begins to see each time that he is immersed in self-love, and cannot do anything in order to bestow. Rather, each time he sees that by observing Torah and *Mitzvot*, the will to receive for himself will enjoy it, he is able to work. Otherwise, he is completely powerless.

This is called "This is the Torah [law] of the burnt offering." *The Zohar* says, "It is a bad thought that comes up in a person's mind to divert him from the path of truth." That is, who is the one giving him the bad thought that will come up in his mind? After all, before he began the work, he was righteous, and now, why does he get a bad thought?

Reasonably thinking, it should have been the opposite, that now that he wants to work on the path of truth, he should have had good thoughts and not bad ones. The answer is that "This is the Torah of the burnt offering," meaning the Assembly of Israel, who is *Malchut*, sends him these bad thoughts. Otherwise, if she does not notify him of the thoughts of wickedness, he would never be able to correct.

It turns out that the Torah sends him the bad thoughts, but then he falls into despair. He comes to such lowliness that he cannot believe that the Creator can help him, judging by the lowliness he sees, that he is so immersed in self-love. This is the meaning of what is written, "She ascends and slanders a person." This bad thought comes up in one's mind and makes him see that he is not worthy of the Creator's help. Rather, the Creator helps only people who are more important than you. This is the meaning of "ascending and slandering" in the work. We must burn with the fire of the Torah, as it is written, "Such is my word, like fire." However, the Creator helps every person.

What Is, "A Drunken Man Must Not Pray, in the Work?

Article No. 21, Tav-Shin-Mem-Tet, 1988/89

Our sages said (*Iruvin* 64), "A drunken man must not pray. And if he prays, his prayer is an abomination." This means that it is better if he does not pray because his prayer is an abomination. But what does "abomination" mean?

We find the word "abomination" in relation to incest, too. In general, "abomination" means something loathsome, as it was said, "You shall not eat any abomination," "Come and see the evil abominations they are committing here," etc. We should understand this in the work. Why is it better if he does not pray if he is drunk, since this is loathsome?

The *Zohar* asks (*Shmini*, Item 61) about the verse, "Do not drink wine or ale": "Rabbi Hiya opened, 'and wine makes man's heart glad.' He asks, If the priest should be happy and in illumination of the face more than everyone, why is he forbidden to drink wine? since there is joy and illumination of the face in it. However, in the beginning, wine is gladness and its end is sadness. And the priest should always be happy. Moreover, wine comes from the side of the Levites, since the Torah and the wine of Torah are from the side of *Gevura*, while the side of the priests is *Hesed*."

It is also written there (Item 66), "For this reason, when a priest enters the Temple in order to work, he is forbidden to drink wine, since his actions are secretive and wine reveals secrets. This is why it is to raise the voice," and this raising of the voice pertains to the Levites.

We should understand what is a priest in the work, what "The priest's work is secretive" means in the work, and what is a Levite. Also, why do the Levites need to raise their voices, the opposite of the priests, and why wine is gladness in the beginning and sadness in the end, meaning what is regarded as "beginning" and what is regarded as "end"?

First, we need to know what is work. It is known that there are two manners in the work of the Creator: 1) *Lo Lishma* [not for Her sake], 2) not in order to receive reward. This means that he believes in the Creator, that He is the King of the world, and to the extent of his faith in the greatness of the Creator, so he feels that it is a great privilege to serve the King.

But with what can he serve the King that the King will enjoy? The answer is that we must believe that the Creator has commanded us through Moses how we can serve Him: He has given us Torah and *Mitzvot* [commandments/good deeds], as well as faith in the sages, to observe everything that our sages added to us, which is called *Mitzvot de Rabanan* [commandments of our great sages]. Also, He has given us customs to follow, which they have given us to observe. By observing all these, it is in order to bring Him contentment by observing the Torah and *Mitzvot*, and all of our pleasure is in having this great privilege, and from this we derive our entire life.

That is, since it is impossible to live without delight and pleasure, which extends from the fact that the purpose of creation was to do good to His creations, a desire and yearning to receive pleasure was therefore imprinted in the creatures, or else a person cannot exist in the world. For this reason, all the creatures, as soon as they are born, must receive pleasure.

The only difference between small and great is in the clothing. That is, the pleasure must be dressed in something. Hence, according to one's maturing, the dresses for a person change accordingly. For example, a child enjoys games, and when he matures, he changes the dresses.

Likewise, a person begins to do the holy work in order to derive pleasure in observing Torah and *Mitzvot*. We must promise him a reward in return for his work, just as in corporeal work. Although a person derives great pleasure from rest, he relinquishes it and goes to work because the work will give him a reward, meaning things he will enjoy.

This pleasure, which he receives from the work, comes in two ways: 1) Payment, called "salary." Through the salary, he will be able to buy things that will give him pleasure. 2) Some people work not in order to receive a salary for their work, but for respect. This is what they enjoy and what gives them fuel for work.

It is the same in the holy work. Some work in order to receive reward or respect for their work. In this, too, there are two manners: 1) The created beings will give them money or respect. 2) They want the Creator to give them money and respect, etc., in return for their work. As *The Zohar* writes, they want the Creator to give them the next world in return for their work. All this is called "in order to receive reward."

However, those who want to work only in order to bestow, whose motivation is that they are serving the King, as *The Zohar* says ("Introduction of the Book of Zohar," Item 191), "Fear, which is the most important, is when one fears one's Master because He is great and ruling, the essence and the root of all the worlds, and everything is considered nothing compared to Him... And he will place his will in that place, which is called 'fear.'"

Here, in this work, begins the main heaviness, since a person must muster motivation not from what is generally accepted, which the general public can understand, that he receives reward in return for work. That is, the work is in Torah and *Mitzvot*, but he receives the reward from something else, and only this, that he hopes to receive the reward, obligates him to work. That is, according to the reward he hopes to receive, he measures himself in the work, meaning how much effort to exert in the work, according to the reward he will receive.

But those who want to work for no reward at all, but in order to bring contentment to their Maker, their measurement is the greatness of the Creator. That is, to the extent that a person assumes the greatness of the King, to that extent he has the energy to work. It is written ("Introduction to The Study of the Ten Sefirot," Item 14), that there is partial faith, where each one has a certain measure of faith that determines how much effort he should put into the work of the Creator.

This is as he says in *The Zohar* about the verse, "Her husband is known at the gates, each according to what he assumes in his heart." This means that each person has a measure of greatness of the Creator, and the greatness of the Creator in a person is according to what he assumes in his heart. That is, there is no measure to the greatness of the Creator so that one can have the real measure of the greatness of the Creator, as it is written, "His greatness is unsearchable. One generation shall praise Your works to another." We learn that the matter of "one generation to another" in the work is in the same person, meaning each state is called a "generation."

Thus, during an ascent, a person has a certain measure of greatness of the Creator. During a descent, a person has a different measure of greatness of the Creator. This is called "One generation to another." This means that through these generations, meaning through the ascents and descents, when a person calculates how much he appreciates His greatness in those two states, and he strengthens himself in the work, by this he is later rewarded with "will praise Your works." That is, he sees that even the states of descent were for better and not for worse.

This is so because a person can evaluate something only from its opposite, as was said, "As the advantage of the light from within the darkness," as Baal HaSulam explains (Shamati, Essay No. 34, "As the Advantage of the Light from within the Darkness" ["The Profit of a Land"]). It follows that "One generation to another" means that from both together we come to the state, "will praise Your works." Through these states, which are repeated every time, and there can be several states, called "generations," each day, from all those "many generations" we achieve wholeness. However, it is provided we do not escape the campaign in the middle of the work.

Accordingly, we see that in order to have fuel to work in order to bestow and not receive any reward, but the work itself will be the reward, we must believe in Him, meaning believe in His greatness. We must make great efforts to obtain faith in the greatness of the Creator. Without faith in the greatness of the Creator, there is no power to work in order to bestow. That is, precisely when we feel the greatness of the Creator, a person is ready to work without any reward.

Instead, the work itself is the reward, since serving a great King is more valuable to him than any fortune in the world, compared to this service, that the Creator permits him to come in and serve Him. Hence, we must focus all our thoughts on how to come to feel the greatness of the Creator, and then everything follows that point.

It is known that when we begin the work, we must begin on the right line, called "wholeness." That is, a person should try to believe above reason as much as possible, and say that although he can only do a small service in Kedusha [holiness], he should believe that it is very important and he does not have the brains to appreciate the importance of the matter.

This is as our sages said, "Walks and does not do, the reward for walking is in his hand." This means that one should appreciate even a tiny contact with spirituality, in whatever manner. The Creator accepts everything and registers it under that person's account, and penny by penny join into a great amount.

This is as it is written in Baal HaSulam's essay, "The Order of the Work," that we should address the work to the Creator and believe that He accepts our work, and it makes no difference how this works seems. That is, the Creator takes everyone into consideration if he does something in the work, and it makes no difference what aim a person has at the time, but the Creator takes everything into the account. For this reason, the person, too, should certainly think about everything that is something in the work of the Creator, and a person should derive delight and joy from everything, in that he has the privilege of having any contact with spirituality.

A person must give many thanks to the Creator for rewarding him with anything in spirituality, as was said, that even if he walks but does not do, the reward for walking is in his hand. Thus, one must thank the Creator for at least rewarding him with going to the synagogue. When a person thanks the Creator for this, and not merely thanks, but he should be happy with it, this is called "right," wholeness, and this is the quality of *Hesed* [mercy], the right line.

In other words, he says that the Creator has dealt mercy with him by permitting him to do something in spirituality. This quality is called "priest," meaning that he is regarded as doing the holy work.

When a person walks on the right line, he can always be happy, called "desiring mercy." That is, he is content with his lot, with what he has, and does not slander the Creator. In other words, when a person is happy, there is no room for slander since when he is happy, he has no complaints to the Creator that He does not treat him as The Good Who Does Good. In that state, a person is regarded as "blessed."

It is written in the essay, "Faith in His Rav [Teacher]," this is when a person can be awarded a high degree because "the blessed cling to the blessed." But when a person slanders, even if he wants the Creator to give him spirituality and not corporeality, there is still no difference between them. Rather, when he has complaints and discontent with his situation, and he cannot say that the Creator treats him as The Good Who Does Good, this is considered slander, and the prohibition on slander is known to all.

Therefore, when a person walks on the right line and slanderous thoughts come to him, he should reject them and say that it is forbidden to listen to slander. He should do all that he can to repel and expel from himself all the bad thoughts that slander, although when these thoughts come to a person, they say, "We are not foreign thoughts. On the contrary, we want you not to deceive yourself, but to see that the state of your work is incorrect and fix it. Thus, we bring good thoughts about the person."

At that time, he should say, "If you are saying this for my sake, why don't you come to me when I am on the left line?" meaning when a person concludes that he should be walking and not standing in one state. "Right" means that he is content with little. But it is known that two are required, and to tell me where I am wrong.

"Instead, precisely when I want to walk on the right line, you come to me. Hence, I do not want to listen to you." This is called "the wholeness of the right." This quality is always in wholeness, since he is content with his lot, and is not interested in anything but to give many thanks to the Creator. This quality is considered a "priest," and it is perpetual happiness.

However, this work is regarded as concealed, meaning it does not reveal its wholeness outward. This is called "covered *Hassadim* [mercies]," meaning that he cannot show its importance outward because he has nothing to show to the external ones, for they will immediately ask him, "What are you looking at? We see that you are happy and content with your lot, so do show us what you have, what possessions have you acquired in spirituality, for which you are happy."

He answers them, "I am content with my share." But they tell him, "We see that you have nothing real in spirituality, yet you are still happy. Thus, you are fooling yourself." And what is the truth? He says, "I am going above reason, so I have no need to answer the questions you are asking me within reason."

However, we must know that "external ones" does not mean other bodies. Rather, the person himself consists of many thoughts, as it is written in *The Zohar*, "Man is a small world and consists of all the nations of the world."

Now we will explain what is a Levite, why he raises his voice, contrary to a priest, whose work is secretive, meaning above reason. Since there is wholeness there, he can always be in gladness. The Levites are "left," which is illumination of *Hochma*, and *Hochma* comes in vessels of reception. Conversely, *Hassadim*, which are regarded as a priest, come in vessels of bestowal.

Vessels of reception require constant guarding so they will not be taken after the *Kelim* [vessels] that engage in reception. Their guarding is that they also draw *Hassadim*, and these *Hassadim* look after the intention to keep it in order to bestow. This is called "receiving in order to bestow." As soon as he is taken after the act, which is reception, he falls from his degree, since he becomes separated from *Kedusha*.

Hence, the work of the Levites is with a raised voice, meaning that illumination of *Hochma* shines there, called "revealing the *Hassadim*." Revealing is called "raising the voice," since it is revealed outward, in vessels of reception. This is why he says that in the beginning it brings joy, and its end is sadness.

We asked, What are the "beginning" and "end"? "Beginning" means when he is mingled with *Hassadim*. At that time he can use the *Hochma*, too. But in the end, when his *Hassadim* ends, as much as he was mingled with *Hassadim*, he remains with the core, meaning only with *Hochma*. At that time, it is impossible to use *Hochma* without *Hassadim*, and this brings him sadness because he always needs the clothing of *Hassadim*, but he does not have it.

Conversely, a "priest," who must always be content, should walk only on the right line, which is *Hesed*, for "he desires *Hesed* [mercy]," and he is happy with his share and has no need for *Gadlut* [greatness, adulthood]. Naturally, he can always be in gladness.

This is similar to what was written (*The Study of the Ten Sefirot*, Part 14). It is written there that there are two discernments: 1) blessing, 2) freedom, which is carved. He interprets there in *Ohr*

Pnimi [Inner Light] that "covered *Hassadim* are called 'free,'" when he lacks nothing because he needs nothing. For this reason, he feels himself free, that he has no enslavement by something he needs to receive. It follows that he is enslaved to nothing.

This is so precisely when he is content with his share, and this is called a "priest," whose work is secretive and he does not reveal what he has outwardly. That is, he does not need the possessions to be revealed outwardly, but believes above reason that everything he has is enough.

However, the Levites belong to the left, meaning *Hochma*, which is "the wine of Torah." The Torah should actually be revealed because the Torah should be with knowledge, for *Daat* [knowledge] is called the "middle line," which decides between right and left, meaning that he will not take more *Hochma* than he has *Hassadim*. If he wants to receive more *Hochma* than *Hassadim*, it is considered "drinking more wine than he can." At that time he becomes "drunk" and loses his *Daat*, called the middle line, which weighs to see that he does not have more *Hochma* than *Hassadim*.

By this we should interpret what our sages said, "A drunken man must not pray. And if he prays, his prayer is an abomination." That is, when he loses the *Daat*, which is the middle line, and he prays to be given more *Hochma* than *Hassadim*, this is called "abomination," for it is loathsome because he prays to the Creator to give him *Hochma* without *Hassadim*, which will go to the external ones and not to *Kedusha*.

Accordingly, we should interpret what our sages said (*VaYikra Rabbah* 1:15), "Any wise disciple in whom there is no *Daat*, a carcass is better than him." That is, he receives more *Hochma* than *Hassadim*. It follows that there is no middle line in him, called *Daat*, which decides between "right" and "left." As was said, "a carcass is better than him," meaning he is loathsome since there is no *Daat* in him, and he is considered a "drunk" who "drank more wine than he should," meaning more than *Hassadim*. When he prays in this way to be given Torah, called "wine of Torah," his prayer is an abomination, meaning that he is regarded as loathsome.

We can understand this as our sages said (*Avot*, Chapter 3), "Anyone whose wisdom is more than his actions, what is he like? a tree whose branches are many and roots are few, and the wind comes and uproots it." That is, action is called "right," *Hesed*, and he need not understand with his knowledge and intellect that it is worthwhile to do the holy work in order to bestow. Instead, he can go above reason, although the reason comes to him with Pharaoh's questions, who asks, "Who is the Lord that I should obey His voice," or the wicked man's question, who asks, "What is this work for you?" To this he replies to them that he is going above reason. This is called "an act," since he does not answer them with wisdom and intellect. Rather, he answers them that he is working in practice, and not in theory, and this is all of his joy, that he maintains faith above reason.

Afterward, when he is rewarded with *Hochma*, he does not want to use the *Hochma* as support, and say, "Now I no longer need faith because I have the intellect as a basis." This is called "His knowledge is more than his actions." However, he receives the *Hochma* because the Creator wants him to receive. He receives, but not for his own sake.

If he wants to receive *Hochma* more than his actions, this is called "drunk" and his prayer is an abomination. Thus, everything should be with reason, which is the middle line, so there is no more left than right.

Why Are Four Questions Asked Specifically on Passover Night?

Article No. 22, Tav-Shin-Mem-Tet, 1988/89

As we see, when does one ask questions? When he is lacking. He is asking, "Why do I need to suffer from not having what I think I need?" He comes to the Creator with complaints and demands and asks, "Why do I need to suffer?" But when a person has abundance, what questions are there to ask when he feels that he is free, that he is not enslaved by anything, or feels that what he does not have pains him, giving him room to ask, "Why"?

Therefore, we should understand why we ask questions specifically on Passover night, which is the festival of freedom. Also, they are called "four questions," meaning four times "Why," precisely when he is not lacking anything.

According to what the ARI says, Passover night is more complete than the eve of Shabbat [Sabbath]. He says that on the eve of Shabbat there is an ascent of *Malchut* to *Mochin de Neshama*, but on Passover night, there is an ascent of *Malchut* to *Mochin de Haya*, such as on the day of Shabbat (see *Shaar HaKavanot*). Thus, we should understand why we ask questions specifically at a time of wholeness. Certainly, there are many answers to this, and we will interpret this in the work.

It is known that the work we were given in Torah and *Mitzvot* [commandments] is so that through them we will correct ourselves to be worthy of receiving delight and pleasure, since for this man was created, as it is known that the purpose of creation is to do good to His creations. However, to avoid the shame upon reception of the pleasures, since every branch wishes to resemble its root, and since the root bestows upon the creatures, there is disparity of form between the giver and the receiver, which causes us shame.

Therefore, to correct it, a *Tzimtzum* [restriction] and concealment were placed on the upper Providence. Thus, through the *Tzimtzum* and concealment, a place was made in which we are so far from the Creator that it causes us to have very little understanding of His guidance over His creations. It is written about it in the "Introduction to The Study of the Ten Sefirot" (Items 42-43), where he says that if Providence were revealed, and for instance, one who ate something forbidden instantly choked, and one who performed a *Mitzva* [commandment/good deed] immediately discovered a wonderful delight in it, similar to the greatest pleasures in our corporeal world, what fool would even contemplate tasting something forbidden when he knew he would immediately lose his life for it, or wait to receive a great corporeal pleasure when it came into his hand? Thus, the *Tzimtzum* and concealment, which were made to correct the shame, cause us all the labor and remoteness from the Creator.

It follows that the *Tzimtzum* and concealment were made to benefit the lower one. Thus, there is no point in asking about Providence, "Why is the Creator treating us as it seems to us, for we do not see the good and we suffer in exile, poverty, and so on?" In other words, everyone complains about why the Creator behaves with undisclosed guidance toward us, that it is only good.

For this reason, it is forbidden to slander His guidance—the way He behaves with the creatures. Instead, we must believe with faith above reason that it should be precisely as we see it. And concerning what we feel, we should walk in the ways of Torah, as the sages have instructed us how to behave with all these feelings that we feel, and to say about them with faith above reason, "They have eyes and see not," as is written in the article from 1943.

It is known that there is a prohibition on slander. However, it is commonly thought that slander, which is so bad, is between man and man. But in truth, slander is primarily between man and the Creator, as it is written (*Shemot Rabbah*, Chapter 3, 12), "Moses caught the act of the serpent, who slandered his Creator, as it is said, 'For God knows that in the day you eat from it, your eyes will be opened and you will be as God, knowing good and evil.'"

With the above-said, we can see why slander is worse than other things. It is because slander is primarily from the serpent, who slandered the Creator and told him, "The Creator commanded you not to eat from the tree of knowledge, but to keep it in concealment and in hiding." The serpent told him about that, "You shouldn't obey what He told you, that the tree of knowledge should remain hidden from the lower ones." Instead, his argument was that everything should be open.

That was the serpent's slander. It follows that he spoke about Providence, that the Creator's conduct with the creatures of undisclosed guidance was wrong. But in truth, the concealment is only so that the creatures will be able to receive the delight and pleasure without shame. This can only be when the creatures receive everything for the sake of the Creator, meaning that all the reception will be only in order to bestow.

It follows that the serpent's slander is not a part. Rather, he spoke about the entire correction that was executed on *Malchut* so that the lower ones, who extend from her, would be able to achieve *Dvekut* [adhesion], called "equivalence of form," by which there would be the correction that enables them to receive the delight and pleasure without any unpleasantness, called "shame."

Because of this correction, we were given the Torah and *Mitzvot* by which to be able to emerge from self-love, which is separation from the Creator, and achieve equivalence of form, as our sages said, "I have created the evil inclination; I have created the spice of Torah." According to the serpent's slander, there will be open Providence, meaning everything will be disclosed, even though the Creator explicitly told Adam, "But of the tree of knowledge you shall not eat." Instead, this discernment must be covered and only at the end of correction will it be possible to illuminate this discernment.

About that, too, the serpent told him not to obey the Creator. In other words, the Creator did not do this in Adam's favor, that the Creator's guidance over the creatures—the Good who does good—will be undisclosed, but for other reasons. It turns out that the serpent's slander was a general thing, meaning he said that all the corrections we should do by the power of Torah and *Mitzvot* are not for the man's purpose.

This is the reason why slander is the most severe of all prohibitions, since it encompasses the whole of the Torah. In other words, with this slander, all the corrections that were made should not be made. Thus, since it is so grave between man and the Creator, the prohibition between man and man is a grave matter, too, as we said about "love your friend as yourself," which Rabbi Akiva said was the great rule of the Torah.

It follows that one who slanders acts the opposite of the rule, "Love your friend as yourself." Hence, slander between man and man is also a rule. This is why it is such a grave prohibition.

With the above, we can interpret what our sages said (*Sanhedrin* 38), "Rav Yehuda said, 'Rav said, 'Adam HaRishon was heretical.' And RASHI explains, "Was heretical' means that he leaned toward idolatry.'"

This is very difficult to understand. Adam HaRishon spoke to the Creator. How can one who speaks to the Creator be heretical—that his heart will lean toward idolatry? After all, the Creator spoke to him, so how can he be mistaken to the point that his heart leaned toward idol worship?

As we said above, the Creator told him that the tree of knowledge should be in concealment and must not be disclosed before the end of correction. When the serpent came to him and told him not to obey the Creator, that this great pleasure was found in the tree of knowledge, which the Creator hid from him, he took to heart the serpent's slander. This is called that he "was heretical."

RASHI interpreted that his heart leaned toward idolatry, meaning that his heart leaned toward what the serpent told him—that it would be better if there were open Providence in the world, as the serpent advised him. This is called "heretic," one who does not like His governance. This means that he thought, according to the serpent's advice, that if the tree of knowledge were revealed and there were open Providence, many would engage in the holy work, for the above reason that everyone would observe Torah and Mitzvot because it would all be clothed in the intellect, within reason, and not that everything must be above reason.

In other words, the tree of knowledge means that everything is revealed within reason, and on that was the commandment to refrain from eating. That is, our work toward the Creator should be above reason and not within reason, although it is reasonable to think that if everything were clothed within reason, the servants of the Creator would proliferate.

This is the meaning of the serpent's slander, who spoke badly about Providence. Since the Creator made the work of the Creator above reason, it does not mean that the Creator could make everything within reason. Instead, we must believe, although we do not understand, that this guidance is the best.

And so did Baal HaSulam say—that the Creator chose the way of faith above reason because the Creator knows it is the most successful way for the lower ones to reach the goal called "Dvekut with the Creator," which is equivalence of form, called "receiving in order to bestow."

Although the sin of the tree of knowledge relates to high degrees—the light of the end of correction—as explained in the "Introduction to the Book, Panim Meirot uMasbirot," with regard to our work—we should interpret that one who slanders Providence, saying that he does not want to believe that His guidance over the creatures is benevolent, and that it is so to believe above reason.

However, a person says, "If there were open Providence, if I could see with my mind that the Creator bestows benevolently upon all creations, and if it were within reason, only in this way would I be able to observe Torah and *Mitzvot*." This comes because of the sin of the tree of knowledge—that a man wants to go specifically within reason and not believe above reason. Hence, when he does not believe that He is good and does good, he is slandering the Creator. This is rooted in the time when the serpent slandered the Creator to Adam HaRishon.

A person wanting to go within reason is called "the sin of the tree of knowledge." This sin appears in two ways, in two questions that extend from it: 1) Pharaoh's question, who asked, "Who is the Lord that I should obey His voice?" meaning it is hard for him to believe anything that contradicts reason. And another thing extends from it, a second question, "Why should one work to benefit the Creator and not himself?" In other words, he is asking, "What will I gain by working for the sake of the Creator and not for my own sake?"

With the above-said, we can understand what we see, that even after one has overcome and said that he is taking upon himself to walk on the path of truth, and begins to believe in faith in the sages, reason dictates that each day he should advance and move forward. Yet, he sees that it is actually the complete opposite—each day he is regressing. Thus, reason makes him say, "This work of going in bestowal is not for me. Rather, it is work for a chosen few." He understands that he would be better off escaping the campaign.

And what is he told? That he should once again go with faith above reason and disregard what reason compels him to do. As it is written in the essay "Faith in His Rav" (1943), one cannot see his true state.

Instead, he should go above reason, and only in this way can we reach the goal and be rewarded with *Dvekut* [adhesion] with the Creator.

However, we should understand what it gives us to feel within reason that we are regressing instead of progressing. In other words, for what purpose does one need to feel that he is in decline? What is the benefit in that? We see that in a state of ascent, when one has a desire for spirituality and regards mundane pleasures—which the whole world chases so as to obtain these pleasures—as though they were created needlessly, meaning that it would be better if the Creator created all creations enjoying spiritual things.

Thus, regarding thoughts of declines, what does one gain by the fact that after each ascent he comes to a descent? As a result, a person always asks, "How many are the ascents and descents and why are they needed anyway? It would be better if I could stay in the state of ascent."

But the answer is that it is impossible to appreciate anything without knowing its importance. In other words, there is a rule that the joy that a person takes in something depends on the importance of the matter. Sometimes a person is given something important, and if he could appreciate it, he could receive great pleasure from it. But since he does not know the value of the thing, that person cannot enjoy it, except to the extent that he understands its importance.

For example, a person buys an object, a book, which is not so beautiful on the outside, and later that book is reprinted and costs more, but since he did not have much money, he bought this book. The seller, too, was not aware of the importance of the book and sold it to him for a low price. But sometime later, a man comes to his house, sees the book, and says, "Since this book was printed 300 years ago, this book is worth a fortune, as there are only three such books in the world." Now that he hears about the great value of the book, he begins to take pleasure in the book.

The lesson is that we do not know how to appreciate the ascent. That is, we do not understand the value of a single moment of having the power to believe in the Creator, and to have some sensation of the greatness of the Creator. In a state of ascent, we desire to annul before Him without any rhyme and reason, like a candle before a torch. Naturally, we cannot enjoy the fact that the Creator has brought us closer and has given us some nearness, from which we should derive the joy and elation that it should bring us. But since we haven't the importance to appreciate it, we can only enjoy according to the importance, as explained in the allegory.

This is why we were given descents: to be able to learn the importance of the ascents, as it is written, "as the advantage of the light from the darkness." Specifically through descents, one can come to know and appreciate ascents, and then he can enjoy the ascents and come to feel that "They are our lives and the length of our days." But when one does not know the need for faith because he thinks that engaging in Torah and observing Mitzvot is enough for him to be considered a servant of the Creator, he is not given descents from above so as to appreciate the ascents.

Their work is on the outside. They have no intention of entering the inside. That is, they have no intention to completely annul before the Kedusha [holiness/sanctity]—and holy means "retired and separated from himself," as it is written, "You will be holy for I am holy,"—at which time there is only the authority of the Creator because the lower one wishes to annul before the root, and all he sees is that it is worthwhile to live only to benefit the Creator.

For a person to be in a state where he wants to live only in order to give contentment to the Creator, he must provide himself with great faith in the greatness of the Creator, to make it worthwhile to annul himself for the sake of the Creator. The faith he has acquired during his upbringing is not enough for him. With the faith that he has acquired during the upbringing, he can already work and observe the Torah and Mitzvot in all its details and precisions. This is because he does not have to annul himself before the Creator. Instead, he asks of the Creator that in return for his observing the Torah and Mitzvot that the Creator commanded us through Moses, the Creator will grant all his wishes.

He believes in reward and punishment, and certainly, as our sages said (Avot, Chapter 2, 21), "If you studied much Torah, trust your landlord to pay the reward for your work." Hence, since the basis obligating him to observe Torah and Mitzvot depends on the reward, not on the giver of the reward, he does not have to engage in the greatness of the faith in the Creator, but in the greatness or smallness of the reward. Hence, there is no question of ascents and descents, believing in the greatness and importance of the Creator. Rather, the only thing that is pertinent there is that he engages in Torah and Mitzvot or that he grows weaker in observance because he does not always believe in the reward.

This causes those who engage in Torah and Mitzvot in order to receive reward—who are sometimes among people who do not believe in reward and punishment—to be able to influence a person with their thoughts. This might cause him even to stray completely from Judaism. Hence, they must not come in contact with people who are free in their views, since they bring them foreign thoughts about faith in reward and punishment. But on the whole, those who engage Lo Lishma [not for Her sake] do not experience ups and downs, meaning there is no need for the presence of descents.

But those who wish to work because of the importance of the Creator, who always need to increase the faith in the importance and the greatness of the Creator, that only the importance and the greatness of the Creator obligates them to observe Torah and Mitzvot in order to achieve Dvekut with the Creator, those people must always assume and value the greatness of the Creator. They must always assess that if they have some grip on spirituality, it is because the Creator is bringing them closer, while they themselves are completely powerless unless they see that they will derive from it some benefit for themselves. It follows that the main work is to annul himself. Yet, this is against nature; only by His salvation can they achieve it.

Thus, during the ascent, a person thinks that it is natural and that he does not need the Creator's help at all. Hence, a correction was made, called "descents," where one is always shown the measure of his strength—what he can do by himself and how he sees it. But when he is tossed off from his state, where he thought he was already human and not like the beasts that work for themselves, suddenly he cannot even feel that they wish to throw him down into this baseness, in which he discovers himself afterwards.

And yet, during the descent, he does not see that he is beginning to decline. Rather, when he descends, he remains unconscious. After being down for some time, he also gets help from above and he is told, "Know that now you are in decline." Before he is told that he is unconscious, he does not know a thing. However, one should believe that this, too, is so, since knowing does not come by itself. Instead, one should know that these descents were given to him to learn how it is possible to appreciate the state of ascent. But during the descent, one cannot learn anything from it.

However, during the ascent he can make a true judgment and say, "Now I am in a state of faith, and this came to me from the Creator. Otherwise, I would immediately fall into a state of self-love." If he does not make this calculation and thank the Creator for bringing him closer, he is immediately thrown. It turns out that it is impossible to obtain real pleasure from nearing the Creator unless he can appreciate it, as said above, "As the advantage of the light from the darkness."

It follows that for the creatures to receive the delight and pleasure and feel it, those descents were all necessary. They are called "exile," and this is called "Shechina [Divinity] in exile" or "Shechina in the dust." Only by this will one have the Kelim [vessels] to feel the delight and pleasure.

With the above-said, we can understand why specifically at the time of freedom, which is Passover night, the complete wholeness, as the ARI says, that Malchut has the same Gadlut, since Malchut has Mochin de Haya, and so it is on Passover night.

The answer is that precisely during an ascent, when one thinks of descents they had the power to elicit the importance of ascents. Otherwise, it is akin to one who is given something that is worth a fortune and he uses and enjoys it as though its worth was a few pennies.

Thus, specifically at the time of freedom, it is possible to ask the questions. That is, it is not about the questions, but we need the questions in order to understand the answers, as Baal HaSulam said about what is written, "Speak now in the ears of the people, and let them borrow every man of his neighbor." RASHI interprets that he warned them that that righteous will say, "He kept, 'And they shall serve them and they shall afflict them,' and He did not keep, 'Afterward they will come out with great possessions.'" There is a question: "If the Creator wished to give great possessions to the people of Israel, could the Creator not give them? Did he have to tell the people of Israel to be fraudulent and borrow vessels of silver and vessels of gold from the Egyptians?"

The answer is that when the Creator told Abraham, "To give this land unto you to inherit it," Abraham asked, "By what will I know that I shall inherit it?" "And he said unto Abram, 'Know for certain that your seed will be a stranger in a land that is not theirs ... and afterwards they will come out with great possessions.'" He asked, "What do we see in the Creator's reply to Abram's question, 'By what will I know...,' that by being in a land that is not theirs, meaning in exile, Abram could be certain that they would inherit the land?"

He said that since there is no light without a Kli [vessel]—meaning no filling without a lack, and Abram said to the Creator that he did not see that they would need such great lights, called "the land of Israel"—the Creator told him that by being in exile and by asking the Creator to deliver them from exile, how will He deliver them? Only with great lights, since "The light in it reforms him." Thus, then they will have the need for the great lights.

He explained about this that this is why the Creator said to borrow Kelim [vessels] from the Egyptians—meaning take the hardness of the Egyptians, but as a loan—to receive the lights, and then return the Kelim to them. In other words, they took the questions in order to understand the answers. It is as was said above, it is impossible to understand the light if not from within the darkness. This is why all the questions come specifically at the time of freedom.

What Is, If He Swallows the Bitter Herb, He Will Not Come Out, in the Work?

Article No. 23, Tav-Shin-Mem-Tet, 1988/89

It is written in *Shaar Hakavanot* [*Gate of Intentions*], "This is the meaning of the *Maror* [bitter herb], which is 'death,' in *Gematria*. They are the judgments in her, in which the *Klipot* [shells/peels], which are called 'death,' grip, and to sweeten her by drawing of life. This is also why he must taste bitterness, and if he swallows it, he does not do his duty, since the grinding of the teeth sweetens through the thirty-two teeth." We should understand what is the bitter herb, which is called "death," in the work, and what it means that through the chewing of the teeth, which are thirty-two, the bitter becomes sweetened, and if he swallows it, he no longer tastes bitterness. How is all this clarified in the work?

To understand this, we first need to know why we need work in the first place. We see that even in corporeality a person does not achieve anything without effort. The answer to this is known, that since every branch wants to resemble its root, and since our root, which created us with the aim to do good to His creations, meaning to bestow, therefore, when the created being receives, it feels unpleasantness when receiving the abundance from another. This is why we were given work.

When a person receives reward for his work, there is no shame. We say that a person is not willing to eat the bread of shame because in return for the bread, he gives work. This seems like a tradeoff, where they swap with one another, where one gives work and the other gives bread, or money, and so forth.

In corporeality, among people, this is very clear. But between man and the Creator, how can we say that the person works in Torah and Mitzvot [commandments/good deeds], and in return, He rewards him? After all, our sages said that we should work not in order to receive reward. Thus, what is the benefit from the work in Torah and Mitzvot? We can understand that in corporeality, we need to work because reward without work causes shame. Therefore, when he wants to receive reward, there is a correction on the reward that a person works for the reward so it will not be as bread of shame upon the reception of the reward.

For this reason, we understand that the work is a correction on the reward. But in working not in order to receive reward, why do we need the work? What purpose does the work serve if there is nothing to correct, since he is not receiving any reward, so why the work? Concerning the work, we should also understand that in corporeality, when a person needs to work, it is because the work that one does for another, the other needs that work. For example, a bakery owner needs employees, or he will not be able to produce the amount of bread he needs. This is not so with regard to the Creator. Is He deficient and needs the creatures to complement what He is lacking by their work for Him?

It follows that the question has two aspects: 1) We were given work in order to be able to receive reward in return for the work.

By this, the shame will be corrected so it is not as though he eats the bread of shame. This cannot be said regarding the work of the Creator because we work not in order to receive reward. 2) This can be said between man and man because his friend needs his work. But between man and God, how can we say that the Creator needs man's work?

The answer is that in truth, we should ask why our sages said that we should work not in order to receive reward, since the whole matter of the work was established so there would not be the bread of shame? Therefore, we see that in corporeality, too, between man and man, this rule of not eating the bread of shame applies, as well, because of the shame. Thus, why do we need to work without reward with respect to the Creator, if the work corrects the delight and pleasure so there will not be shame in it upon reception, for then it is no longer considered a gift or charity? Rather, now the delight and pleasure acquire a new name: "reward." Accordingly, why do we need to work not in order to receive reward?

The answer to this is brought in *The Study of the Ten Sefirot* (Part 1, *Histaklut Pnimit*, Item 7), where he asks about what our sages said, that in order to correct the bread of shame there was a correction that He created this world. Here, there is a reality of work, "for they take their reward from the Whole One in return for their work, and by this they are saved from the blemish of shame." He asks there about this: "But their answer is odd indeed. What is this like? It is like a person who says to his friend, 'Work with me for just a minute, and in return, I will give you every pleasure and treasure in the world for the rest of your life.' There is indeed no greater free gift than this, since the reward is utterly incomparable with the work, since the work is in this world, a transient, worthless world compared to the reward and the pleasure in the eternal world." And there (in Item 20), he replies, "Since there is disparity of form between the Creator and the created beings, which causes the shame, through engagement in Torah and *Mitzvot* in order to bring contentment to his Maker, they invert the vessels of reception of the soul into vessels of bestowal. That is, for herself, she has no desire for the momentous abundance, but she receives the abundance in order to bestow contentment upon her Maker, who wants the souls to enjoy His abundance."

Now we can understand what we asked, that we can understand that between man and man, the work that a person does for a reward is in order for him not to eat the bread of shame, as it is known that this causes shame, and through the work, the blemish of shame is corrected because he receives reward for the work. But with respect to the Creator, what is the correction of the work, if we must work not in order to receive reward?

Also, we said that we can understand that between man and man, a person needs his friend's work, but as for the Creator, why does He need man's work? Is He deficient and needs man's work?

Indeed, between man and God, it cannot be said that the work corrects the reception of delight and pleasure so the flaw of shame will not be felt. This is so only between man and man, since the giver of the work pays him according to his work. It follows that work for a reward is a kind of tradeoff where they swap with one another, and there is no shame here anymore, since both receive—one receives work and the other receives reward. But with respect to the Creator, there is no equality that we can say that one receives work and the other receives reward.

This is so for two reasons: 1) It cannot be said that the Creator receives work from man, since the Creator is not deficient or needs man's work. 2) As he says there in *The Study of the Ten Sefirot*, the reward that a worker of the Creator receives is not equal to the work, since the work, compared to the reward, is like a person working for his friend for one minute, and in return receives provision for the rest of his life, for the worker of the Creator works only in this world, and in return receives reward in eternity. But between man and man, this is not so.

Therefore, as it is written there, man's work in Torah and *Mitzvot* is not for the purpose of tradeoff, as between man and man. Rather, the work is that through work in Torah and *Mitzvot*, a person will receive something new, a second nature. That is, instead of the nature of wanting to receive for himself with which he was born, by engaging in Torah and *Mitzvot* in order to bestow and not receive reward at all, he will receive reward in return for his work.

Yet, what is the reward he expects to receive for his work in Torah and *Mitzvot*? It is that the Creator will give him a second nature: vessels of bestowal. Until now he had vessels of the will to receive in order to receive. Now he will obtain new *Kelim* [vessels] called "vessels of bestowal." Hence, during the work in Torah and *Mitzvot*, he should aim to engage in order to bestow. That is, all the time during the work, he must aim which reward he hopes that the Creator will give him in return for his work in Torah and *Mitzvot*.

There are two things in this intention that he aims in order to bestow: 1) to know which reward he hopes for, 2) to feel a good taste in the reward, meaning to enjoy this reward. That is, the measure of the reward depends on the yearning for it. In corporeality, there is a great reward and a small reward, which is measured by the importance of the matter, since normally, something that is rare, that not many people have and is difficult to obtain, is regarded as important in corporeality.

Likewise, everyone thinks that he can come to do everything for the sake of the Creator since it is only an intention, to aim during the work that he wants the work to be for the sake of the Creator. The person thinks that only actions are hard to do, but intentions are very easy, and depend only on his will, and if he wants to, then he can.

But those who begin to walk on this path, who want their actions to be for the sake of the Creator, the more those people increase their efforts in actions and intentions to bestow, the more they discover the truth that they are far from it. That is, there is a *Segula* [power/ remedy/quality] in this work—the truth is revealed to him from above, that he has no connection to acts of bestowal. But before a person begins the work of bestowal, there is a correction that we cannot see the truth that a person is far from this path, as it is against nature.

Man is born to do everything for his own sake. In order not to feel shame, he must do everything for the sake of the Creator and annul his entire being. How can the body agree to this? As *The Zohar* says about the verse "Or make his sin known to him," the Creator makes this known to him, meaning that from above, when they see that a person wants to correct the will to receive for himself, they alert him to the truth that he is far from it. Then he begins to see that not anyone can achieve this reward, and he begins to see the importance of the matter.

It follows that only then does he begin to see how this reward, called "vessels of bestowal," is hard to merit, and only the Creator can give him these *Kelim*. As a result, his reward becomes important in his eyes since it is a precious thing that not just anyone can achieve.

Accordingly, we see the importance of this reward—to be rewarded with vessels of bestowal. It is impossible to understand the importance of the matter before one sees how difficult it is to obtain. When he obtains vessels of bestowal, he sees that he has been rewarded with a great reward, which is such a precious thing since he cannot obtain this great thing by himself, and only the Creator Himself can give him these *Kelim* as a gift.

Thus, their saying that it is forbidden to work in order to receive reward is because if he wants reward for the work then he escapes from the real reward. By this we will understand why we need to work, since the Creator does not need our work, to help Him in any way. The answer is that this work is only for us. That is, through the work, we obtain the importance of the reward. And it is not merely importance, but through the work, we attain that the importance is because it is our entire life, for without *Dvekut* [adhesion] with the Creator, we are far from Him, and all the delight and pleasure that the Creator created in order to do good to His creations depends on having equivalence with the light.

As the ARI says, the reason for the breaking of the vessels was because the *Kelim* could not tolerate the light. Hence, the lights departed and the *Kelim* broke. This means that there is an inverse relation between the light, which is the giver, and the *Kli* [vessel], which is the receiver. In order to have equivalence, there was a correction that the receiver does not receive because of his own benefit, but because he wants to do the Creator's will, who wants to do good to His creations, and only for this reason does he receive the delight. This is called "equivalence," since now both are equal for they are both considered givers. That is, as the light gives by giving to the *Kli*, the *Kli* receives only because it wants to bestow upon the Giver.

Now we can understand what Baal HaSulam said about the words that Moses asked of the Creator (Exodus 33:18-21): "And he said, 'Show me please Your glory.' And the Lord said, 'Here is a place with Me.'"

He said, "What is the meaning of 'Here is a place with Me'?" He said, "*Iti* [with me] is an acronym [in Hebrew] for faith, prayer, and labor. That is, this is the place by which we can be rewarded with the glory of the Creator. We can interpret the glory of the Creator the way we pray (in the Eighteen Prayer of *Rosh Hashanah*) "Give glory to Your people," which means that the glory of the Creator will be revealed within the people of Israel, so each and every one will feel the greatness of the Creator to an extent that people's only worry will be to do something, to bring some contentment to the Creator, and nothing else will interest them.

Conversely, when it is the opposite, when the *Shechina* [Divinity] is in the dust, the greatness of the Creator is concealed and we neither see nor feel the importance of the Commander, who commanded us to observe Torah and *Mitzvot*, it is not because He needs our work. Rather, He wants to reward us. We were given Torah and *Mitzvot* because as our sages said, "The Creator wanted to cleanse Israel, hence, He gave them plentiful Torah and *Mitzvot*," as it is written in the beginning of the essay, "Preface to the Wisdom of Kabbalah." Therefore, to achieve the glory of the Creator, we can interpret that this is why he said, "Show me Your glory." Although there are many interpretations to this, in the work, this is how we should interpret the verse—"Show me Your glory" means that the glory of the Creator will be revealed.

We should interpret that the order of "a place *Iti* [with Me]" is that one should take upon oneself faith, to believe that each and every one can be rewarded with the glory of the Creator. When he believes this, he must know why the glory of the Creator is not revealed even before he begins the work, and only the concealment is revealed. He must believe the words of our sages that this is a correction so that man will be able to acquire equivalence of form, regarded as "giving to the Creator and not for himself."

For this reason, concerning the faith that one should take upon himself, he should also believe that it is impossible to be rewarded with the glory of the Creator, meaning that the hiding and concealment would be removed from him, if he has not been rewarded with "fear of heaven." Fear means as it is written ("Introduction of The Book of Zohar"), "He cannot have faith before he has equivalence of form." In order to have equivalence of form, he must try to have fear in everything he does, as it is written (there), "Fear means that he is afraid lest he will diminish in bringing contentment to his Maker."

It follows that when one begins the work, he begins with faith, but the body resists this work, and then comes a state of labor, when he must overcome the body and seek all kinds of counsels, as our sages said, "In trickery shall you conduct war," since the body does not want to relinquish self-benefit. To the extent that he exerts, to that extent he begins to feel that he is incapable of doing anything since in his view, he has done everything he could. After the labor, he comes to know that only the Creator can help, and it is out of his hands. Then comes the third state—a prayer—and then the prayer is from the bottom of the heart, since it is utterly clear to him that no one can help him but the Creator.

However, even when he comes to know that the Creator can help him, and he understands that the real advice is only prayer, the body comes and makes him see that "You see how many prayers you have already prayed but you received no answer from above. Therefore, why bother praying that the Creator will help you? You see that you are not getting any help from above." At that time, he cannot pray. Then we need to overcome once more through faith, and believe that the Creator does hear the prayer of every mouth, and it does not matter if the person is adept and has good qualities, or to the contrary. Rather, he must overcome and believe above reason, although his reason dictates that since he has prayed many times but still received no answer from above, how can he come and pray once more? This, too, requires overcoming, meaning to exert above reason and pray that the Creator will help him overcome his view and pray.

It follows that although faith, prayer, and labor are three successive things, in truth, they are indeed three things, yet these three things are intermingled. That is, in every state, he works with all three together. In other words, although we begin with faith, all other discernments are included in faith, since when he begins to overcome, he must believe in the sages, who said, "Man must say, 'If I am not for me, who is for me?'" In other words, a person must toil and achieve the goal by himself. When he sees that he cannot overcome and exert, he must believe that a prayer helps, as it is written, "For You hear the prayer of every mouth," although he sees no change when he prays for the Creator to help him. Thus, here, too, there is the matter of above reason. However, the general order is to begin with faith, then labor, and then prayer.

It follows that the most important is faith, since with it we must work in everything we do. That is, the basis of all the Kelim with which one works is faith. This is why the light that is revealed is called "light of faith," after the Kli. This Kli is built on the basis of faith in the sages and faith in the Creator, as it is written, "And they believed in the Lord and in His servant, Moses."

Now we can understand what our sages said, "If he swallows the bitter herb, he will not come out." The ARI said that Maror [bitter herb] is death in Gematria. We should understand what this implies to us that Maror is death in Gematria, that it is the judgments in her, to which the Klipot grip. We should interpret that it is as we say (in the Passover Haggadah [story]), "This Maror that we eat, what for? For the hard work with which the Egyptians made their lives bitter."

The hard work was that the people of Israel wanted to emerge from the control of the Egyptians, called "self-love," that when they overcame to do something in order to bestow, thoughts of the Egyptians immediately came to them, asking the wicked man's question: "What is this work for you?" To work for the sake of the Creator. Every time they prevailed, the questions of the Egyptians immediately came. This is called "hard labor," that it was difficult for them to emerge from their control because the Egyptians made their lives bitter.

The ARI says about this, that *Maror* in *Gematria* is death, meaning that the Egyptians did not want to let them out of their control, but to remain as they wanted, as the wicked man's question. This is the meaning of staying in the form of "The wicked in their lives are called 'dead.'" It follows that this is not just bitter, but it is actual death. Thus, "made their lives bitter" means that they wanted the people of Israel to remain dead.

It therefore follows that hard labor, when they tasted bitterness, means that they tasted the taste of death by working for their own sake. This is the meaning of what he says, that *Maror* is regarded as death, and judgments to which the *Klipot* grip, where judgment means that they were under judgment, meaning forbidden to use the vessels of reception, and all the nursing of the *Klipot* comes from the vessels of reception, which want to receive in order to receive. Then, when a person is in a state of reception, the person is in a state of concealment and hiding from spirituality.

Its correction is as it is written, "This is the reason why he should taste bitterness, and if he swallows it, he does not do his duty, since the grinding of the teeth sweetens through the thirty-two teeth." We should interpret that it is known that the thirty-two teeth imply the thirty-two paths of wisdom, meaning that specifically by a person achieving a state of ascent, regarded as being in a state of life and wisdom, then he should chew the bitter herb, so as to taste bitterness, for only during an ascent can we feel what is *Maror*, meaning what descent tastes like, as in, "the advantage of the light from within the darkness."

That is, it is impossible to taste a real taste in life and light unless he has the taste of darkness and death. Thus, the *Maror* is sweetened through the ascent, for only through the darkness, which is a descent, does he feel a taste in the light. It follows that the darkness has now been corrected. This is the meaning of the words, "And to sweeten her by extending life."

What Is "Do Not Slight the Blessing of a Layperson" in the Work?

Article No. 24, Tav-Shin-Mem-Tet, 1988/89

The Zohar (Nasso, Item 10) says, "Do not slight the blessing of a layperson." This is, 'In the daytime, the Lord will command His mercy.'" In the Megillah (p 15) he says, "Never slight the blessing of a layperson."

We should understand what this comes to teach us in the work of the Creator, meaning when we learn within one person, what is the meaning of "layperson." First, we need to understand the meaning of a "layperson" altogether.

In Masechet Megillah (p 12b), Rav Kahana said, "It follows that a layperson jumps first." This means that the meaning of "layperson" is said in his condemnation, that he is a simple person, who nonetheless likes to show himself and appear as wise. Thus, how should we interpret "the blessing of a layperson" in the work? Also, we need to understand what The Zohar says, "Do not slight the blessing of a layperson." This is, 'In the daytime, the Lord will command His mercy.'" What is the connection between the blessing of a layperson and His mercy?

It is known that man's work is in two lines, called "two writings that deny one another until the third writing comes and decides between them." It is as our sages said (*Sotah* 47), "The left always pushes away, and the right pulls near."

In the work, we should interpret "the right pulls near." When a person is advancing in the work and wants to be in a state nearing the Creator, and does not want to see any deficiency in himself because now he wants to engage in songs and praises for the Creator, and if he sees some deficiency in himself he will not be able to thank the Creator with all his heart because he has deficiencies and he wants the Creator to fill his deficiencies. It follows that now he is praying for the Creator to fill the lacks. Thus, his gratitude is already deficient. That is, in the midst of saying thanks, he claims that the Creator has not given him everything he needs. Therefore, when he wants to engage in wholeness so that the thanks he gives to the Creator will be from the bottom of the heart, he must not see any lack in himself.

However, we must understand how a person can say that he has no lacks, and instead, he thanks and praises the Creator that he is working for the Creator, when he sees that his work is full of flaws. How can he lie when he sees his own incompleteness in the Torah and work? The answer is that when one introspects and sees his lowliness, that he is worse than the rest of the people in skills and qualities, and yet the Creator has given him a thought and desire to do something in Torah and *Mitzvot* [commandments/good deeds], and he knows that this service is worthless and sees that there are many people more important than him, yet the Creator did not give them a thought or desire to do something in matters of *Kedusha* [holiness], and He did give him a thought and desire. For this he thanks the Creator as though he has obtained a fortune in corporeality. What spirit would the corporeal things yield in them? From this depiction, he receives joy and happiness and it gives him satisfaction.

This causes him to later have ears to hear things toward which previously his ears were deaf. Now, through the joy, all his organs have become alert and understand and contemplate everything, since the joy that came to him through the joy of Mitzva [singular of Mitzvot] causes him that in corporeality, too, he will be a completely different person now. All this came to him because he appreciated matters in Kedusha.

However, one must believe that even though he appreciates the importance of Kedusha with all his might, he still has not come to give the measure of importance where there is the real importance, because no person can evaluate the measure of importance of the Kedusha, and only those who have ascended know how to appreciate a spiritual matter.

Our sages knew what importance to attribute to spirituality, as our sages said (Berachot 7), "Rabbi Zira said, 'The reward of learning is in running.'" RASHI interpreted that the reward of people who run to hear a lesson from a sage is mainly the reward for running, since most of them do not understand. The MAHARSHA interprets that "The wise do not need the learning, for they already know the laws, as was said, that in any case, their reward is the running," meaning the reward for running.

"Abaye said, 'The reward of the Kallah [Shabbat before a pilgrim festival] is in the squeezing.'" RASHI interpreted, "On a Shabbat before the pilgrimage, everyone gathers to hear the laws of the pilgrimage." The meaning is that although there are people who do not understand the laws, they still have reward for standing pressed together. The MAHARSHA says about this, too, "If the listener is a wise disciple and has no need for this, he has the reward for squeezing."

Accordingly, we can see how our sages appreciated the importance of spirituality, for they said, "Even if people do not understand what the sage is saying, they still have reward in that they run to hear the sage's words." Moreover, we see that the MAHARSHA says, that even those who are themselves wise disciples and know the laws on their own, still, if they come to listen to the sage's words, they have reward. And certainly, reward is given only for work.

It follows that a person should be happy that he has been rewarded with the work of the Creator. Even if he comes to the seminary or the synagogue and does not learn, he has the reward for walking, meaning that it is defined as work of the Creator. The evidence of this is that there is reward for this work.

It follows that when a person walks on the right line and wants to engage in work of singing and praising the Creator, he must see that he has wholeness. That is, he must appreciate his lowliness and how the Creator has given him a desire and yearning at least to walk to the seminary, although he understands nothing, and to say, "I cannot appreciate the importance of my fortune that the Creator has chosen me for at least some service." He should be happy as though he has struck a fortune in corporeality, how he would be happy. That joy gives him the strength to believe in the Creator, that He is good and does good.

But when a person begins to calculate how much he earned in spirituality through the labor he has already given, and begins to see that he did not advance, although what he sees is true according to his attainment, in that state, he is separated from the *Kedusha* [holiness] because in that state, he is slandering His Providence and cannot say that the guidance of the Creator is in the form of good and doing good.

It follows that by this he becomes more remote from the *Kedusha*. That is, to the extent that he sees that he is deficient, and sees all that he is lacking, and that he has prayed to the Creator several times but the Creator did not give him anything for his plea, he immediately blemishes the belief that "You hear the prayer of every mouth."

It follows that in this state, he says that now he is walking on the path of truth and does not want to deceive himself that he is a person who has wholeness, and he is certain that the road he is marching is true. However, a person cannot make ways for himself, but must accept the path that our sages have arranged for us.

About such matters, Baal HaSulam asked about what we say (in "You Have Chosen Us"), "And lifted us from among all the tongues." Yet, there is only one tongue in the world, that of the evil inclination. Thus, it should have said, "And lifted us from all the tongue." What is the meaning of "all the tongues," in plural form? He said that there are holy angels and there are impure angels. That is, sometimes, the evil inclination prevents us from doing something good through a power that incites us and says that we have no need to engage in Torah and Mitzvot, since we will not gain anything from this. Sometimes it comes to us and tells us, "You should not do this; it will only interfere with your engagement in Torah and Mitzvot." It follows that it says to us the opposite, that he wants us to engage in Torah and Mitzvot, which is why he advises us not to do what we want to do, or learn, or think, etc.

It follows that when a person should walk on the "right line," the holy angel comes to him and tells him, "Look at your baseness, see how you are devoid of Torah and devoid of faith, and you are also lacking in observing Mitzvot." He lowers him to the netherworld and speaks to him like a holy angel.

And what happens? In the end, the person falls into a descent and cannot think of doing anything in Kedusha. For this reason, when he must walk on the right line, he must fight against all those who object to the wholeness of the right, and believe above reason that the Sitra Achra [other side] speaks to him dressed as a holy angel.

However, afterward a person must shift to the other side, called "left line," where great care is required. He must be ready, when he sees his past, that he is full of flaws, to have the ability to pray for the flaws. Otherwise, it is forbidden to begin the work on the left, as it is written in The Zohar, that it is "forbidden to raise the hands without prayer and plea." "Raising the hands" means that he looks in his hands, meaning what spirituality he already has in his hands, if he has advanced a bit or not.

It is forbidden to look, except in a way that he is willing to make an honest prayer and plea right away. Otherwise, he will fall into despair and sadness and melancholy, and will have to escape the campaign. It follows that where he should have received from the left line a place for prayer, that this is the only reason he should move to the left line, hence, if he cannot be certain that he can make an instantaneous prayer, he should remain on the right line until he is certain that by this he will have the strength to pray that the Creator will help him, and he will believe that "The Lord hears the prayer of every mouth."

Otherwise, it is forbidden because in that state, he cannot give thanks and also cannot pray to the Creator to deliver him from that state. When a person is in a state where he begins to slander Providence, he immediately loses the power of prayer because the body does not believe that the Creator "hears the prayer of every mouth." It follows that he remains empty handed both ways. For this reason, he must stay on the right line and not enter the left line.

This is the meaning of what our sages said (*Yoma* 16), "Any turn you take should be only through the right." The meaning of "any" is "generally." That is, generally, a person should walk on the right line. It is permitted to walk on the left line only when he is certain he will be able to pray for his deficiencies. Otherwise, he must remain on the right until he feels that he is ready for it.

Therefore, if thoughts that he is at fault have awakened in him against his will, and how can he speak words of Torah and prayer to the Creator when his thoughts tell him, "You are filthy! How are you not ashamed to engage in matters of *Kedusha*?!" About this, a person (must) say that it is written, "I am the Lord, who dwells with them in the midst of their *Tuma'a* [impurity]." That is, even though I am in the lowest possible baseness, I still believe what is written, that the Creator dwells even in the worst lowliness.

However, He is not among the proud, as our sages said, "Anyone who is proud, the Creator says, 'I and he cannot dwell in the same abode.'" For this reason, when a person feels whole, according to the right line, when he appreciates his lowliness and says that nonetheless, the Creator has given him some grip on *Kedusha*, and that "some," compared to the *Kedusha* that a person should attain, that "some" is called "layperson."

But if he says according to his lowliness, "I thank and praise the Creator for this," it can be said about this what is written, "I am the Lord, who dwells with them in the midst of their *Tuma'a*." When he is happy about this, he can be rewarded with, "The *Shechina* [Divinity] is present only out of joy."

It follows that through this lowliness, that because the Creator has given him some grip on *Kedusha*, he can climb the rungs of holiness if he only takes from this the joy and appreciates it. Then, a person can say, "Raise the poor from the dust," "He will raise the destitute from the litter." That is, when a person feels his lowliness, that he is meager, meaning poor, as our sages said (*Nedarim* 41), "Abaye said, 'In our tradition, there is no poor but in knowledge.'" That is, it has been handed down from our father, a custom from our forefathers that "there is no poor but in knowledge."

This is why he says that he is meager, meaning poor, for he has no knowledge of *Kedusha*–he is called "poor and meager." Then, if there is any grip on *Kedusha*, even though he is poor, he says, "Raises the poor from the dust." That is, he says a prayer, for even though he is poor, the Creator still raised him. "He raises the destitute from the litter." Although he feels that he is destitute, the Creator still lifted him, and for this, he praises the Creator. If there is any grip on *Kedusha*, we can already praise and thank the Creator.

We can interpret what is written (Psalms 97), "Be glad in the Lord, you righteous ones, and give thanks to the memory of His holy name." We should interpret that "righteous" is one who says that the Creator is righteous, since any grip that he has on *Kedusha*, he immediately says, "The Lord is righteous" in that He gives one who is as poor and destitute as him some grip on spirituality. These are called "righteous," as it is written, "Who is righteous? He who justifies his Maker."

The measure of grip on spirituality is that he can say about it, "I am happy with it." The verse says, "And give thanks to the memory of His holy name," meaning they thank "the memory of His holy name," the fact that they remember His holiness—for this they thank and praise. This is the meaning of the words, "Give thanks to the memory of His holy name." That is, if they merely remember the Holy name, for this alone they already thank the Creator, meaning on the mere remembering, they are immediately awakened to thank the Creator.

But one who has some pride and says that "The rest of the people, who have no brains, can come to be servants of the Creator without any intellect and reason, but a man like me, who has brains and is not as stupid as other people," he says, "If the Creator wants me to work for Him, He must be considerate with me and give me the taste of Torah and prayer. Otherwise, I will serve the way I understand it and not the way You require."

It is written about this, "The Lord is King, He dresses in pride." That is, the Creator behaves toward such people a garment of pride and is not impressed with them, and they remain with nothing but their pride. This is why it is written, "The Lord is high and the low will see." With his lowliness, a man can see. But one who is high, who considers himself higher than others, is called "And the high from afar," meaning he moves afar from *Kedusha*.

Now we can understand what we asked, What is "Do not slight the blessing of a layperson"? It means that when a person feels that he is a layperson, that he has only a slight contact with *Kedusha*, which is considered "layperson" compared to the wholeness that one should achieve, still, when he blesses and thanks the Creator, "Do not slight it." Rather, a person must appreciate it as though he has obtained a fortune and thank and bless the Creator as though he has attained true wholeness.

What Is "He Who Has a Flaw Shall Not Offer [Sacrifice]" in the Work?

Article No. 25, Tav-Shin-Mem-Tet, 1988/89

It is written in *The Zohar* (*Emor*, Item 41): "'Whosoever he be of your seed throughout their generations who has a blemish.' Rabbi Yitzhak said, 'The reason is that he is flawed, and one who is flawed is unfit for serving in the holy.' We established that one who is flawed has no faith in him and that flaw testifies of him. It is all the more so with a priest, who must be more complete and full of faith than anyone."

We should understand this: According to this, if a person is born with some defect, does he have a choice to achieve faith in the Creator or does he have no choice and must remain without faith? What should that person do if he is told, "First you must go to the doctors to see if they can heal you from your flaw, and then you can come to learn about faith." Can this be?

The thing is that we learn everything from the perspective of branch and root. This is the revealed part in the Torah, that all the work of *Mitzvot* [commandments/good deeds] were given to us by way of branch and root. But when speaking of the hidden, meaning the intention and not the action, we interpret everything with regard to the work. Thus, that which is called "flaws or defects" does not pertain to the act, but to the aim.

We should know from where the flaws and defects in spirituality extend. They come to us because of the shattering that took place, when sparks of *Kedusha* [holiness] fell into the *Klipot* [shells/peels]. Through these sparks, the *Klipot* gained the power to remove a person from the work of the Creator, by giving him pleasures when he engages in order to receive pleasure, and a person cannot relinquish the pleasure he receives in *Kelim* [vessels] of self-benefit and work for the sake of the Creator.

When he engages in matters of bestowal, a person feels in all those actions that they have no flavor or fragrance. When he overcomes and does perform acts of bestowal, this work is not with all the organs. That is, not all the organs agree to this work. It follows that he is flawed. That is, when he works with the aim to bestow and wants to work only for the sake of the Creator and not for his own sake, even after all the overcoming, there are still some organs that disagree with this work. It follows that he is missing organs, which is called "flawed" in the holy work.

All this, meaning that the organs do not agree with his work, is because they feel that there is a flaw in the work of bestowal. Thus, they themselves, meaning the workers themselves, say that there is no wholeness in this work, but that it is completely flawed. In such a state, how can it be said that there is wholeness in the work, when they themselves say that there is a blemish in the work? And how can work with flaws be given to the Creator?

In corporeality, this is like a person who gives a gift to a king and wants to show him that he is a loyal subject. Yet, his heart is not with him. That is, he has organs that ask him, "What will you get out of working for the king? Do you think that the king will pay you for working for him devotedly?" It follows that the person himself says that this work is flawed. It is as it is written (*Midrash Rabbah, Nasso* 13), "Woe unto that dough whose baker testifies that it is bad."

However, we should ask, Why does the person himself say that he is flawed? The answer is that he lacks faith. If the person truly had faith in the Creator, that He leads the world as The Good Who Does Good, and believed in the greatness of the Creator and His importance, it would not be possible that that man would have any resistance in him. This is so because we see in our nature that the small one annuls before the great one like a candle before a torch; it has no freedom of choice. As long as it has not been established in his heart that He is great, there is choice, meaning to choose and say that He is great—either by himself, since he attains that He is great, or by others, who tell him He is great and he follows their view. Afterward, he has no freedom of choice not to annul, but he is drawn like a candle before a torch. Then he considers it a great joy if he can serve the great one and he has no greater pleasure than this.

It therefore follows that anyone who has a flaw in the work, his work is flawed. Why is it flawed? It is because he has no faith in the Creator—that He is the King of the world and leads the world as The Good Who Does Good. Otherwise, he would not have a flaw at all, since all the organs would agree to serve the great King. But since he has no faith in the greatness of the King, his work for the sake of the King is flawed.

That is, since his work is tasteless, a person cannot do it with all the organs. It follows that there are several flaws in his work. Either an organ is missing, or it functions not as it functions with something that is tasteful.

Thus, what can one do when he sees that he is flawed? His only work is to ask the Creator to give him the power of faith, to have the strength to believe in the greatness of the Creator, meaning that in everything he does in Torah and *Mitzvot*, he should aim that through his actions that he does as an "awakening from below," the Creator will give him the power from above to believe in His

217

greatness with all his heart. At that time there will be wholeness in the things he does.

That is, there will be thought, speech, and action in his work, since in anything that is complete there are three discernments: 1) the act, 2) the thought, where through the act the Creator will give him the power of faith in the greatness of the Creator, 3) speech, meaning prayer, since the thought causes him to pray to the Creator, which is called "speech and prayer." To the extent of attainment of the lack of faith, so the prayer is measured, since the lack that a person feels and wants the Creator to satisfy his lack, this is called a "prayer." However, when a person sees with his mind that he has already prayed to the Creator but the Creator still did not help him, he loses the power of prayer.

But a person should also pray for the ability to pray. He must believe in the sages and say, "What I see and what the mind obligates me is called "within reason." Yet, I must believe above reason in what the sages said (*Berachot* 32), "Rabbi Hama Bar Hanina said, 'If a person sees that he has prayed but was not answered, he must pray again, as it was said, 'Hope for the Lord, be strong, brace your heart, and hope for the Lord.'"" It follows that without faith in the sages, a person cannot do anything on the path of correction, as it is known that "The view of landlords is opposite from the view of Torah." Hence, a person cannot make ways in the way of the Creator, except that which is accepted among the servants of the Creator.

The main lack is that when a person engages in Torah and *Mitzvot* and the body does not resist him, meaning does not bring him foreign thoughts, in that state, a person does not think that faith is what he lacks in order to enjoy what he does as though he has obtained a great fortune in corporeality, for then he would certainly be very inspired and elated from obtaining something important that the whole world appreciates. What pleasure he would have then?!

If a person believes that he is serving a great King, why is he not elated now and full of joy over the matter of *Kedusha* in which he is engaging? The reason is that he lacks faith. For this reason, a person should not be content with little, since he is lacking what is essential, not a supplement. If a person does not pay attention to this, then he must remain in the state of "general public," who work only in action. However, we must not forget that "An act without an aim is as a body without a soul." Hence, a person must overcome and be unlike the rest of the workers, but rather join the servants of the Creator, who aim for the sake of the Creator.

Although we learn that a person should walk on the right line and say that he is not deficient, and he is happy with what he has, but on the right line, too, there should be great inspiration and elation because he is working for and serving a great King. Although he cannot value the magnitude of the importance of the Creator, he should still work on it, on being happy with settling for little as though it were a great thing. And the fact that he does not feel the great importance, for this, too, he thanks the Creator, for seeing that he has some grip on spirituality. For this, he gives great praise to the Creator.

Yet, in truth, the order is that he must shift from the right line, which is wholeness and settling for little, to the left, meaning to reflect on why he has no grip and why the Creator does not want to give him more grip on spirituality. There must be something missing here that should be corrected through good deeds, and not remain "poor in knowledge," but make all kinds of efforts that the Creator will help him as He helps others who want to be considered servants of the Creator.

However, a person should be careful not to mix the lines with one another, or else he will not be able to see the actual reality of each line. Rather, once he sees the distances, he can go forward because now he can work on two legs. It is known that a person cannot walk on one leg, meaning that one leg is considered giving praise and gratitude to the Creator, which is the beginning. And the praise is in that he can believe, to some extent, that he is speaking to the Creator.

It follows that to the extent that he has some faith, he thanks the Creator. For everything he does, he thanks the Creator for rewarding him and giving him the thought and desire to observe

His commandments. For this, he is able to bless the Creator and thank Him for this.

As we should bless for each Mitzva [commandment/good deed], we should also bless the Torah. We should know that "blessing" means that we bless Him for this boon. One who does not bless Him for this, it is because he does not feel the Mitzvot as something important, worth blessing Him for it. That is, the gratitude He gives us is like the gift, as it is customary that to the extent of the gift, so is the extent of the thanks we give.

It therefore follows that before a person comes to perform a Mitzva and bless on it, he must first take upon himself faith above reason. That is, although he still does not feel the importance of Torah and Mitzvot, he should believe above his intellect that they are very important things. Because a person is still unfit to feel the greatness of Torah and Mitzvot, since there is a correction regarded as "avoiding the bread of shame," for which there is a concealment on the Torah and Mitzvot, for this reason we must begin with work above reason and disregard our feelings. Rather, we must say, "They have eyes and see not." To the extent that we overcome through faith in the importance of Torah and Mitzvot, to that extent we can give thanks. That is, the blessing that a person gives to the Creator depends on the measure of importance of Torah and Mitzvot.

According to the above, we should interpret what our sages said (Nedarim 81), "Why do wise disciples not yield wise disciples from their sons? Rabina said, 'Because they do not bless in the Torah first.'"

We should understand how can it be said about wise disciples that they did not bless in the Torah first. After all, we see that when ordinary people come up to read the Torah [during service], before the leader of the prayer reads in the Torah, they say a blessing. But concerning wise disciples, our sages said that there are wise disciples who did not bless in the Torah first, and therefore their sons are not wise disciples.

The literal explanation has many answers. But in the work, where we learn within one body, what are wise disciples and the sons of wise disciples in the same body? We should interpret that the blessing we must give first pertains to the intention. That is, they do not set their hearts on appreciating the Torah in order to bless the Creator for giving us a great gift. Naturally, the blessing they do—namely the thanks they give to the Creator for the gift—is not as it should be. It follows that they lack the importance of the Giver of the Torah.

This is the meaning in what was said, that they did not bless in the Torah first. "First" means that before they said the blessing, they did not think about the importance, and from this extends that their sons, meaning their understanding, is not that of wise disciples. That is, it is those who learn Torah and see that they have still not achieved the view of Torah, meaning understood that the view of Torah is annulment of the authority, meaning that they must understand that working for self-benefit is what they must annul, and they see that although they are learning Torah, they still do not understand that the body should annul its entire being and work only for the sake of the Creator.

This is as our sages said about the verse, "If a man dies in a tent." They said, "The Torah exists only in he who puts himself to death over it." The person asks, "What should I correct so as to come to this understanding?" They said that the reason is that "they did not bless in the Torah first." That is, the blessing on the Torah that they gave to the Creator was not with all their hearts, since they did not grasp the importance of the Torah, meaning what the Torah should give us and for what purpose a person needs the Torah and *Mitzvot*.

When a person reflects on the benefit and the degree that the Torah and *Mitzvot* should bring him, then, according to the importance of the matter, he will bless the Creator. But a person who does not make the real calculation, although he blesses the Creator, "his heart is not with him," since he cannot appreciate its importance.

Therefore, when he hasn't the preparation, meaning he does not have the intention before him, to aim why he needs the Torah and *Mitzvot*, a person cannot achieve an understanding of a wise disciple. This is as Baal HaSulam said when he asked Why did they say, "wise disciple," and not simply "wise"? It is because "wise" means the Creator, and one who learns from Him the quality of the Creator is called a "wise disciple."

This is as our sages said, "Cling unto His attributes: As He is merciful, so you are merciful." It follows that the question, "Why do wise disciples not yield wise disciples from their sons?" means that they should understand that the most important is that they will take upon themselves the work of bestowal and not for their own sake. This is called "a wise disciple." This is why they said that the advice to a person who wants to yield sons who are wise disciples is to understand that we must work for the sake of the Creator. Prior to the blessing, he must aim for what he is blessing, meaning why he thanks the Creator. This is called "Because they did not bless in the Torah first." That is, before they made the blessing, they did not pay attention to what the Torah and *Mitzvot* should bring him.

However, when he aims that the Torah and *Mitzvot* were given in order to cleanse people, as Rabbi Hanina Ben Akashia said, it follows that all the gain from Torah and *Mitzvot* is the cleansing. What comes after the cleansing, meaning what will they gain by receiving the cleansing? The answer is that we must believe in the purpose of creation, which is to do good to His creations, to the extent of His ability. Then, they will be rewarded with the delight and pleasure that a person cannot appreciate. As our sages said, this is regarded as "The eye has not seen a God besides You, will do for those who await Him."

Now we can understand what we asked, What is the meaning of what *The Zohar* said, "A man in whom there is a flaw must not offer [sacrifice]." This is so because he is flawed, and a person who is flawed has no faith in him, and that flaw testifies to him. This is true for every person, but even more so for a priest. We asked about this, What can one do if he sees he has a flaw? Can he no longer have faith? Can it be said that there is a person in the world without freedom of choice although he did not commit any sin? Why is it his fault if he is flawed?

The answer is that when speaking of the holy work, meaning that his work will be in holiness, it is as it is written, "You will be holy for I am holy." That is, everything they do will be for the sake of the Creator, is in order to bestow. This work begins in *Lo Lishma* [not for Her sake], as our sages said, "From *Lo Lishma* we come to *Lishma* [for Her sake]."

The reason why we must begin in *Lo Lishma* is as he writes in the book *A Sage's Fruit*: "Since man is born with a *Kli* called 'will to receive for his own sake,' it follows that it is impossible to begin in order to bestow. Rather, we begin in *Lo Lishma* and "the light in it reforms him." In order for a person to know that he does not need to stay in the state of *Lo Lishma*, there are flaws in his work when he wants to work for the sake of the Creator. At that time, not all the organs agree to this work. Therefore, we were given two lines to walk in, called "two legs." Prior to this, he has flaws and defects, and all because he lacks faith. For this reason, one must ask of the Creator to give him the power of faith.

What Is "He Who Defiles Himself Is Defiled from Above" in the Work?

Article No. 26, Tav-Shin-Mem-Tet, 1988/89

It is written in *The Zohar* (*BeHaalotcha*, Item 67), "What is 'Or on a far off road'? It is because a person who defiles himself is defiled from above. Thus, he is on a far off road from that place and road to which the seed of Israel adhere, for he has clung to a far off road, has moved away from approaching you, Israel, referring to the *Sitra Achra* [other side], which is far from *Kedusha* [holiness]. Rabbi Yitzhak said, 'It is written, 'If he is defiled for a soul or on a far off road.' This means that they are two things.' Rabbi Yosi said, 'Here, when it says 'defiled for a soul,' it means before he has been defiled from above. And here, when it says, 'on far off road,' it means that it is after one has been defiled above and fell to a far off road, which is the *Sitra Achra*.' This means that on both, the *Kedusha* of above will not be on them and they will not do the Passover when Israel do it."

Also in *The Zohar* (*BaHar*, Item 46), it says, "'His kingship rules over all.' For this reason, the *Shechina* [Divinity] is called 'an offering to the Lord,' 'a burnt offering to the Lord.' Everything should be sacrificed to the Lord and to His *Shechina*. Afterward, the *Shechina* imparts to all, as it is written, 'And gives prey to her household.' Even food for animals, and even for dogs, she imparts everything, in order to fulfill, 'And His kingship rules over all.'"

We should understand why one who defiles himself is defiled from above. Why is it man's fault that he is defiled from above? Why is he punished with not being able to do the Passover, which *The Zohar* says is the meaning of the words, "If he is defiled for a soul or on a far off road"? He is "defiled for a soul" before he is defiled from above, and "on a far off road" after he has been defiled from above, and neither will do the Passover when Israel do it.

We should understand this. If he has defiled himself, he can no longer do the Passover offering, so for what purpose is he defiled from above? Also, why is he defiled from above if *Tuma'a* [impurity] that is done from above is not his fault?

Therefore, we should understand the following: 1) For what purpose is he defiled from above if he cannot make the Passover offering because he is impure? 2) Why is he defiled, since choice is something that a person makes, and when he is defiled from above, this *Tuma'a* does not come to him by choice? 3) We should also understand what *The Zohar* writes about the verse, "His kingship rules over all," that the *Shechina* [Divinity] imparts nourishments to all—to animals and beasts, and even to dogs and donkeys, which are the *Klipot* [shells/peels]. Why must the *Shechina* provide them with nourishments, as they are her adversaries and enemies of the *Kedusha*?

To understand the above, we must first know what are *Kedusha* and *Tuma'a* in the work. In actions, *Tuma'a* and *Tahara* [purity] are clear, as it is written in the Torah or what our sages added concerning *Tuma'a*, *Kedusha*, and *Tahara*. But in the work, what is the meaning of *Tuma'a*, *Tahara*, and *Kedusha*?

225

First, we must always remember our two tenets, that all the conducts in the world follow, and from which we have conducts in the work of the Creator, which often seem to be conflicting.

1) The purpose of creation, which is His will to do good to His creations, and for which He created in the creatures a desire and yearning to crave pleasures. This is called "will to receive for himself." All creations, which are called "existence from absence," emerged with this nature, meaning with this desire that was created, which is considered a lack that the creatures yearn to satisfy. This *Kli* [vessel] comes to a person without work, since we attribute this *Kli* to the Creator, and we have no work expanding the *Kli*, but wherever this desire (sees or feels) that it has some pleasure to receive, it promptly runs there with all its energy. It seems as though it is going to satisfy the Creator's will, meaning what the Creator wants—that the creatures will enjoy the pleasure He wants to give them.

2) The correction of creation, so as not to feel shame upon the reception of the pleasures. It is known that this happens because every branch wants to resemble its root. Hence, a correction was made that from the perspective of his will to receive, a person wants to decline and not receive any pleasure. Instead, he comes to receive the pleasures because the Creator wants the creatures to receive delight and pleasure, as this was the purpose of creation. Then he will not feel shame because now there is equivalence of form, meaning that as the Creator wants to bestow, so the creatures want to bestow upon Him, so He will enjoy that "He said, and His will was done," and only because of this they want to receive delight and pleasure.

However, this *Kli*, called "receiving in order to bestow," is the complete opposite of the *Kli* called "will to receive for oneself," which we attribute to the Creator, who created it existence from absence. Hence, if we want to work only for the sake of the Creator and not for our own sake, it is hard work, since we must fight against the *Kli* that the Creator created.

From this work come all the lacks we learn about, such as the departure of the lights, the breaking of the vessels, *Kedusha, Tuma'a,*

Sitra Achra [other side], and Klipot. Also, all the names we see explained in The Zohar and in books of Kabbalah extend only from the correction of creation.

This is so because we attribute the Kelim of the correction of creation to the creatures, as it is written in the beginning of Tree of Life, and as he explains in The Study of the Ten Sefirot, that the first will to receive, called Malchut de Ein Sof, said that she does not want to receive in order to receive, but in order to bestow.

Naturally, if we want to go against the nature that the Creator created, which is the opposite, it comes to us by hard work. In the upper worlds, this caused the departure of the lights and the breaking of the vessels, and then the Klipot emerged and the distance between Kedusha and Tuma'a was made.

Kedusha is called "equivalence of form." This is the meaning of Dvekut [adhesion], as it is written, "You will be holy for I am holy." This means that as the Creator wants only to do good to His creations, the creatures should also want to be on a degree of doing good to the Creator and not to themselves.

It follows that before we achieve the correction of creation and while still immersed in self-love, a person cannot receive the delight and pleasure, and the Tzimtzum [restriction] and concealment that occurred are on him. That is, we must say that all the concealments we suffer are because such is the order of corrections, that by this, all the creatures will arrive at the end of correction, meaning that all the Kelim that emerged with the quality of receiving for themselves will be corrected into working in order to bestow. Naturally, they will be able to receive the delight and pleasure. It follows that then, at the end of correction, there will no longer be a need for the Tzimtzum and the concealment. This is the meaning of the words, "And your Teacher will no longer hide Himself."

It follows that remoteness and closeness are that if a person does everything in order to bestow, he is close to Kedusha, as was said, "You will be holy." If he does everything for his own sake, he is far from Kedusha.

Accordingly, we should ask, If the delight and pleasure cannot shine in vessels of reception because of the *Tzimtzum* that took place, how will the created beings exist in the world before their vessels of bestowal are corrected? From where can the creatures derive pleasure? for without pleasure, it is impossible to live, since such was the order of creation.

Therefore, we learn that promptly after the *Tzimtzum*, when there was the departure of the light, *Reshimot* [recollections] remained in order to sustain the *Kelim*. The first *Kelim* from which the light departed are called *Kelim de Igulim* [vessels of circles], and the *Reshimo* [singular of *Reshimot*] that remained of the light sustains the *Kelim*. Yet, this can be said only about the *Kelim* of *Kedusha*, as was explained that in the *Partzufim* of Adam Kadmon the *Reshimot* remained in the *Kelim* after the departure of the lights.

Conversely, in the world of *Nekudim*, where the *Kelim* fell to the *Klipot* after the departure of the lights, we learn that the *Reshimot* remained in the place of *Atzilut*, since the *Reshimot*, which are parts of the light, cannot enter the *Klipot*. Rather, only sparks fell into the *Kelim* to sustain them. That is, the *Kelim* that fell into the *Klipot*, and all of their vitality, is only because sparks of *Kedusha* fell into them. From this comes all the vitality of the *Klipot*, as the ARI interprets, only a "slim light," called "very thin light" compared to what is found in the *Kedusha*, is all the vitality that fell into the corporeal world.

In other words, all the life and the corporeal pleasures that the entire world chases in order to obtain, since they feel that this is their entire life, are but a very thin light compared to the spiritual pleasures, and on the spiritual pleasures was the intention to do good to His creations, called "the purpose of creation."

By this we will understand why the *Kedusha* must give nourishments to the *Klipot*, for otherwise they will not be able to exist, since the desire to do good to His creations causes that if the creatures have no delight and pleasure at all, they cannot exist and must die. Since man is born with an inherent nature to receive only for his own sake, he is under the control of the *Klipot*. At that time, it is impossible to receive vitality from the *Kedusha*. Hence, even when he begins to engage in Torah and *Mitzvot*, he must begin in *Lo Lishma* [not for Her sake], or else from where will he have life? Therefore, the *Kedusha* gives nourishments to the *Klipot* so the *Klipot* will have life and nourishments, which sustain the creatures while they are under their control.

Only through the reforming light in Torah and *Mitzvot*, when they achieve *Lishma* [for Her sake], meaning when they can work in order to bestow, then the concealment and hiding called *Tzimtzum* depart from them. Then, they can receive their vitality from the *Kedusha*, where the real pleasures are revealed, and not as they received, only a "slim light" of *Kedusha*, but real light of *Kedusha*.

By this we will understand what we asked about what *The Zohar* says, "And His kingship rules over all," that the *Shechina* imparts nourishments to all, to animals, beasts, and even to dogs and donkeys, which are the *Klipot*. We should understand for what purpose the *Shechina* should sustain them.

Since it is impossible to exist without light and pleasure, and there is no other power in the world that can sustain them, as it is written, "There is none else besides Him," hence, the *Shechina* sustains them and gives them nourishments so as to sustain them. The *Shechina* imparts the nourishments to each one according to his degree, as he says, "Although all the offerings are to the Lord, of them he gives to the dogs, which are the disqualified offerings, which he gives to *Samel*, who is called a dog, and some of them are as "ministering angels" and some of them are as "humans."

This means that the *Shechina* imparts nourishments to each one according to his quality. There are people who are as "humans," there are those who are as "pure beasts," and there are those who are as "dogs." The *Shechina* imparts nourishments to all. However, according to one's efforts to ascend on the rungs of *Kedusha*, so is the abundance he receives. That is, if a person comes to a degree where his only pleasure is in serving the King, he receives abundance suitable for *Kedusha*. If the person can work only in order to receive for himself, he receives according to his merit.

For this reason, those who wish to walk on the path of truth but cannot overcome the will to receive for oneself, but want nourishments so they can overcome it, they receive from *Kedusha*, which is called "the light in it reforms him." They receive nourishments according to their preparation. That is, they receive vitality in being able to perform acts of bestowal.

Conversely, those who are still as "dogs"—as it is written in *The Zohar*, that they howl as dogs *Hav-Hav* [Give, Give]—must receive vitality within the vessels of self-benefit.

This is not so with people who want to exit self-love. Sometimes they receive nourishments, meaning vitality, from wanting to work in order to bestow, but when they do not appreciate the nourishments they received with the vessels of bestowal, they are given some lust that they crave and they begin to think about the pleasure of the lust. At that time they completely forget about the spiritual work and suffer an immediate descent until they no longer feel the situation they are in. In truth they are in a state of unconsciousness, meaning that they do not recognize that there is the matter of spirituality, in which they previously engaged with all their hearts, but suddenly they have completely forgotten about it.

Finally, they recover and begin to feel that they are in descent. However, it is as though they were in a car accident and were left unconscious. When they recover, they see that they are in a hospital.

Likewise, a person who was walking on the path toward achieving the aim to bestow was suddenly hit by some passion, which entered his heart and he became unconscious. That is, he fell into the corporeal world. After some time, he recovers, meaning that he heard a clarion from above that he is not all right.

The matter of the passion is not the same for everyone. Sometimes, a person is encountered by a thought that it would be better for him to work for his own sake and not for the sake of the Creator. When this thought hits him, it is called a "road accident," if he did not see the danger in advance, while he still had time to overcome the thought so it would not penetrate his heart. However, the form of the passion is not the same for everyone. In each person, the passion dresses in a different form. Even within the same person, not all times are the same, and each time, the passion dresses in a person in a different way, all according to the time.

The passion is like a bait. When we want to catch fish, we take the rod and hang on it some animal or a piece of meat. When the fish sees the meat, it sees the pleasure it can receive from it. And when it sees the pleasure, it has no other thoughts, and then it cannot conceive that by this, meaning if it bites into the bait, it will die, since the man will pull it out of the water so it will die. At that time, it has no interest in thinking about this.

Likewise, when a person sees some lust, it is a bait that lures him into receiving this passion, and then he has no time to think that by this he will die in the spiritual sense, that all the work he thought had to be done for the sake of the Creator, when he looks at the lust, it is a bait that pulls him out of the spiritual water where he lived. And as soon as he is pulled out of the spiritual water, he dies in spirituality and remains unconscious. In other words, he is unaware that he has already died in spirituality because he does not even remember that there is spirituality in the world, and he forgets about everything.

However, afterward, recovery comes to him from above, and he sees that now he is in a state of descent. That is, during the ascent, he looked at all the lusts as something separate from him, meaning that he was not attracted to them. He felt he had within the heart a rejecting force that he did not even want to think about them. But suddenly, he receives a direct relation to them, meaning that they become close to his mind and feeling, to the point that when he recovers, he does not understand how the relationship between them was created.

However, there is a rule: "When the upper one descends to the place of the lower one, He becomes like him." That is, they become seemingly together, without any distance between them, as there were while the upper one was in His place above. Likewise, when the lower one ascends to the place of the upper one, he receives a common relation, as though he has always been in the place of the upper one. He receives distance from the state of the lower one (according to the rule: "When the lower one ascends to the place of the upper one, he becomes like Him").

It follows that this bait is akin to "vision." "Vision" is not necessarily with the eyes. Rather, "vision" is also thought, meaning the vision of the mind. In other words, if some sinful thought comes along, whether in the mind or in the heart, and there is a rule that "the eye sees and the heart covets," so by seeing he will certainly come to covet. And although a person cannot be held accountable for seeing, meaning when some thought comes to a person, why is it his fault, or when he suddenly see with his eyes, what can he do?

Baal HaSulam explained about it, asking about what our sages said, "A person does not sin unless a spirit of folly has entered him" (Sotah 3). He asked, Why is a spirit of folly permitted to enter him so he would sin? Had the spirit of folly not entered him, he would not have sinned. Thus, why is it man's fault that a spirit of folly has entered him? He replied that there is a rule that "the eye sees and the heart covets." It follows that although seeing is not man's fault, but if he does not repent the seeing, although he is as though misled in this, he must come to covet, and coveting is already a sin.

It follows that the fact that a spirit of folly entered him is a great correction for a person, so he will not blemish the Kedusha so much, since during the sin, he no longer feels the importance of Kedusha because the spirit of folly is already in him, and naturally, the Kedusha escapes from him. That is, had he repented the mistake right away, he would not have come to an actual sin, which is the coveting. And if he does not repent, the spirit of folly comes.

Now we can understand what we asked, Why is it that when a person defiles himself, he is defiled from above, as The Zohar says about the verse, "If he is defiled for a soul or on a far off road"?

The answer is that it is because he defiled himself in the work. We should interpret—in vision. If he defiled himself and did not repent, he must be defiled from above, meaning that they let a spirit of folly enter him.

This is for man's best, for when one works without reason, it is as though he works without an intention to sin, since he has no reason that we can say that he acted deliberately. Hence, being defiled from above is a correction, and naturally, there is no question why he is defiled, since by this they do him a favor. Naturally, whether he is defiled only by seeing, which is certainly considered a mistake, and all the more so afterward, when he is defiled by coveting, they already show that they are not close to *Kedusha*.

Although seeing was by mistake, still, there was no spirit of folly in him. But at the time of coveting, he already had the spirit of folly. Although we could ask, but when he is defiled from above, there are two things in him, meaning seeing and coveting. Perhaps he wants to say that even when he had the possibility to be one thing, he was already unworthy of nearing.

233

What Is the Meaning of Suffering in the Work?

Article No. 27, Tav-Shin-Mem-Tet, 1988/89

On *Yom Kippur* [Day of Atonement], in the "Eighteen Prayer" ("My God, Until I Was Created"), we say, "That which I sinned before You, erase with Your many mercies, but not through suffering." We should understand how is it that when we pray that we want Him to erase our sins, we stipulate conditions before Him, or else we do not want Him to erase our sins. Thus, what is the condition, "but not through suffering"?

The Zohar (*BeHukotai*, Item 42) writes, "Rabbi Yosi started, 'My son, do not reject the discipline of the Lord or loathe His admonition.' How beloved are Israel, that the Creator wishes to admonish them and lead them on the straight path. And out of His love for him His cane is always in His hand, to lead him on the straight path and so he will not stray right or left. One whom the Creator does not love but loathes, He removes His admonition from him. 'But Esau I hated,' which is why I removed from him the cane, removed from him the admonition so I would not give him a part in Me, for My soul loathes him. But you I love indeed, and do not loathe His admonition.' What is, 'Do not loathe'? It is, do not loathe it, as one who runs from thorns, for those kings who enslave Israel are as thorns in one's body."

We should understand this. Common sense mandates that the Creator should hold the cane for the gentiles, who act against the Creator. But to the people of Israel, whom He loves, it should be as it is written, "Love will cover all crimes." So why does He afflict specifically Israel—whom He loves—with a cane?

We should also understand what it interprets, "Do not loathe His admonition," that the kings' enslavement of Israel is like thorns in a person's body. Yet, it says, "Do not loathe," meaning do not run away from the thorns, meaning from the enslavement of the kings. Can be it be that He tells them not to run from the kings' thorns only because He loves them?

We should also understand the words "But Esau I hated," which is why He removed from him the admonition, "so I would not give him a part in Me." It seems as though if He did admonish him, he would have a part in the Creator. How are they connected? It is as though the suffering causes them to have a part in the Creator.

We should know that when speaking in matters of work, both Israel and Esau speak of people who observe Torah and Mitzvot [commandments/good deeds], and not of the nations of the world or secular people. Rather, it is only about people who have faith and observe Torah and Mitzvot. Thus, what is the difference between the quality of "Israel" in a person and the quality of "Esau" in a person?

According to the rule in observing Torah and Mitzvot, we should also discern the intention—if the observance of Torah and Mitzvot is in order to receive reward in this world or in the next world, or is his intention to bestow and not receive anything. In the quality of "Israel," the aim is Yashar-El [straight to the Creator], when he does not want to receive anything in return but that everything will go straight to the Creator. This is regarded as the "quality of Israel" in a person in the work.

But if he does want reward in return for observing Torah and Mitzvot, it is regarded as "Esau." Esau means Asu [did], meaning that he made a domain for himself and wants the Creator to fill his domain. He does not want to revoke his own domain, which is called Yashar-El, meaning cancel his domain and annul before Him, which is called "straight to the Creator," and this is his only aim. This, he does not want. For this reason, we discern two qualities in man's work: "in order to receive reward" or "not in order to receive reward."

We should remember that man's work in order to bestow, when he wants Dvekut [adhesion] with the Creator, is where one begins a procession of ascents and descents. That is, when a person focuses everything he does in the work on receiving reward in return for this, then, when he believes in reward and punishment, his inherent will to receive does not object to receiving greater pleasures.

However, when a person wants to walk on the path of not receiving reward, since it is against nature, the real war with the evil inclination begins, since a person wants to remove the evil inclination from the world, for only here is its existence. And concerning the name of the will to receive, "evil inclination," it is because it depicts to us the path that the people of Israel want to march as bad. That is, it argues that a person's desire to annul his own authority and annul before the Creator is suicide. Instead, what would be called "good"? That would be if a person demanded of the Creator to expand man's domain and satisfy all his lacks, and not that man would work for the Creator.

In other words, the evil inclination asks a person, "Where is your brain, that you are working so hard in Torah and Mitzvot, and for what reward?" It is as our sages said, "The light in it reforms him." This means that since the evil does not want to annul before the Creator, but rather the evil in a person wants man to exist, man is advised that if he engages in Torah and Mitzvot he will thereby be rewarded. That is, without Torah and Mitzvot, it is impossible to receive such as great reward, and only by the power of Torah and Mitzvot can we achieve such a great reward that a person will annul before the Creator and man's authority will not be apparent, and the Creator will take everything.

About such a reward, the evil inclination cries out, "But you are losing your very being! You are performing actions that will cause you to cease to exist! Should one work and toil for this?!" It follows that the evil inclination depicts to him bad pictures concerning the order of his work.

This is called "suffering." That is, when a person wants to walk on the path of truth and achieve *Dvekut* with the Creator, called "equivalence of form," these questions come to him and he suffers a descent, meaning he cannot overcome its arguments. This manifests immediately, in mind and in heart. When that person recovers from the descent and begins to contemplate the situation he is in, he suffers from being far from the Creator.

Once he has been rewarded with an ascent in spirituality, he begins to think that from now on he will be strong and immune to the words of the kings of the nations of the world who slander the Creator. That is, they do not necessarily say that it is not worthwhile to engage in Torah and *Mitzvot*. Rather, they say that it is not worthwhile to engage for this reward of losing himself, and also that he wants all the labor to be for the sake of the Creator and not at all for himself.

This inflicts upon a person great sufferings, which are as thorns in one's body, and he wants to escape the situation he is in. He says, "I am probably unworthy of this work, or I would not suffer descents." It follows that these sufferings are that he hears from them that it is not worthwhile to work for Him with this intention.

Thus, there are two things here: 1) The kings' arguments, who enslave Israel with their words. That is, a person falls under the control of the kings, who enslave a person so he can work only for his own sake because of the suffering of the bad depictions that the evil inclination depicts to him.

Generally, all the kings of the nations of the world are called "evil inclination." Each king has his own view, and he says to a person, "Walk in my way; I will give you pleasure in the work." In other words, all the kings say the same thing: It is better for you to work for yourself rather than for the Creator."

It follows that the suffering that one sees—that he cannot work for the sake of the Creator—causes him to want to escape the campaign. These sufferings make him see that this work is not for him, for this path requires chosen people, a select few, and mere ordinary people cannot approach this work, called "working with the aim to bestow."

Worse yet, the evil inclination comes to him dressed as a holy angel and says to him, "But you see that I am right. Look back at how vigorously you engaged in Torah and *Mitzvot* and how enthusiastically you used to pray. If you ask, Why was it like this before? It is as I am saying, since you worked for your own benefit, to receive reward. This is why you had the strength to work. Thus, what is the point in overcoming each time if you see that you keep descending, which is called 'The shattered is greater than the whole,' meaning that there are many more descents than ascents."

The evil inclination also tells him, when it dresses in the clothes of a holy angel, "Previously, you advanced in the work and each day you acquired a possession of *Kedusha* [holiness] in Torah and *Mitzvot*. But you denigrate this and say that you want to work only for the sake of the Creator. But you see that you are going backward in this work, that you have descents, meaning that your bad is becoming increasingly evil. While you were observing Torah and *Mitzvot* in practice in the work, you were more successful. You saw for yourself how you progressed. But now, where are your energy and excitement in the work? Thus," it says to him, "turn away from this path."

It follows that through the words of the evil inclination, which is all the kings of the nations of the world, they enslave Israel and sting the bodies of those workers who want to work in order to bestow. This brings up the question, Why do these people, who want to walk on the path of truth, achieve *Dvekut* with the Creator and annul before Him, deserve such suffering, such descents that they cannot tolerate the suffering and want to escape the campaign?

And conversely, those who work in order to receive reward do not have the suffering of feeling that they are far from the work of the Creator. Instead, they feel that they are advancing every day. Certainly, when they see the progress, there is energy to work. They do not feel that they have any descents, but only that sometimes they advance more and sometimes they advance less, but they do not regress.

The answer is that when a person does not feel a lack and corruption in the work, he has nothing to correct. Therefore, these are people who can work only in practice, and on practical Mitzvot, there is nothing to add or subtract, as it is written, "Do not add, and do not take away."

And since they still have no need for the intention, and intention means achieving equivalence of form, called "in order to bestow," naturally, they do not want to adhere to Him. That is, they have no understanding about working not in order to receive reward. For this reason, the Creator does not give them suffering, namely the sensation of remoteness from the Creator, so they will ask the Creator to bring them closer.

This is as Maimonides writes, that "women, little ones, and uneducated people are taught to work in order to receive reward," for they will not understand otherwise. When "they gain knowledge and acquire much wisdom, they are taught that secret," that we should work Lishma [for Her sake], which is in order to bestow.

Now we can understand what we asked, Why does the Creator afflict Israel, who are the Creator's beloved ones? Moreover, He tells them, "Since I love you, I want you not to loathe the thorns," since those kings who enslave Israel are as thorns in their bodies.

It is written, "Do not loathe His admonition," meaning do not escape the campaign and say that this work on the aim to bestow is not for you. This means that those whom the Creator loves, referring to the quality of Israel, who want to annul Yashar-El [straight to the

Creator], and the will to receive that exists in a person, this they want the Creator to give them the power to subdue it so he will annul before the Creator.

However, a person cannot overcome the will to receive, since the will to receive makes him see that the main reason why a person should labor and toil is to be able to satisfy his self-love. But that person wants the opposite—to revoke his self-love and be able to work only on what pertains to love of the Creator. That is, he does not want to work for his own sake, but for the sake of the Creator, meaning for what pleases the Creator.

That person says that he derives no satisfaction from having the strength not to work for himself, as there are many smart-alecks who say that man achieves wholeness if he does not work for himself. He, however, says that this is not why the Creator created the creatures, so they will not enjoy. Rather, the purpose of creation was to do good to His creations. Therefore, the creatures, too, should work in equivalence of form, meaning so all their yearning will be to do good to the Creator.

It follows that one who says that man's purpose to achieve wholeness is only so as not to work for himself, that only this is man's purpose and why he was created, this is not the truth. Instead, one should always examine oneself to see if he is working for the sake of the Creator, meaning that the Creator will enjoy. That is, he wants to replace self-love and achieve love of the Creator, for only in this way will the creatures achieve the goal for which they were created, called "to do good to His creations."

Therefore, those who want to achieve love of the Creator, although this degree is still far from them, yet they nonetheless want to achieve it, these are called "those who love the Creator." It is as Baal HaSulam said about the verse, "will give wisdom to the wise." He asked, "It should have said, 'will give wisdom to the fools?!'" Since they are already wise, what does wisdom give them? Also, from where would they have wisdom before the Creator gives them? Only afterward, when they already have wisdom.

He said that the meaning of "wise" is those who want to be wise. Although he still does not have wisdom, but he desires wisdom, he is already called "wise," after his purpose. Hence, one who wants to be wise should believe that the Creator will give him wisdom.

In this way, we should interpret that one who wants to love the Creator is already regarded as one who loves the Creator. For this reason, the Creator wants to give them love, meaning annulment of self-love and to be rewarded with love of the Creator. *The Zohar* says to them that the Creator holds in His hand a cane to lead them on the straight path. That is, they should believe that the sufferings they suffer from the descents they undergo come from the Creator. That is, these foreign thoughts they are receiving, which are as thorns in their bodies, the Creator is the one who sends them.

Although a person understands it would be better if the Creator sent more ascents, and why do I need these descents, meaning what is their purpose, the answer to this is that this is called "the cane in the Creator's hand to lead him on the straight path." Otherwise, if a person remains in a state of ascent, he will think that he has achieved completeness and will remain in his state of lowliness because he will not feel any lack that he must correct.

For this reason, the Creator shows him his lowliness and shows him that as much as he already thought that he was superior, that he did not have such lowly thoughts that other people have, suddenly he sees that he has worse thoughts than people who work like the general public, who are regarded as working in order to receive reward.

He says that he wants to work only for the sake of the Creator and not for his own sake, and he is certainly at a higher degree than they are. But suddenly, he sees that he is lower than they are. It follows that the suffering he feels causes him to need to ask the Creator to truly bring him closer. This is why this pertains specifically to people who are regarded as Israel, who want to be "Israel." In order not to fail in the work, He sends them these descents. This is considered that He is "holding the cane in His hand, to lead them on the straight path." The "straight path" is the path that leads straight to the King's palace.

This is not so with those who are regarded only as Esau. This is only action, without the intention that the actions will lead to annulment of self-benefit, and they do not want to do things for the sake of the Creator, but settle for the action, without the aim that they will lead to *Dvekut* with the Creator and do not think of the matter of *Dvekut* with the Creator, as it is written, "And to cling unto Him." For them, the Creator does not hold the cane in His hand to admonish them.

He says, "But Esau I hated, which is why I removed the cane from him, removed the admonition from him so I would not give him a part in Me." That is, "I do not want him to have *Dvekut* with Me." This is why He says, "My soul loathes him," meaning that because their whole work is only for their own sake, "My soul loathes him," and I will not give him a part in Me. That is, I will not give him suffering by which to cling to Me. Since they have no desire for Me, I have no desire for those who are in the quality of Esau, who feel themselves as whole. "Esau" means that he has already *Asah* [did] his bit and regards himself as whole.

Yet, what can one do in order not to undergo a descent, called "suffering" from feeling remote from the Creator? since all the suffering is in order for a person not to remain on a low degree because he is content with little, since he already thinks that he has already been rewarded with a spiritual degree. Therefore, it is necessary to lower the person in importance, meaning that he will see for himself how deficient he is. Then he will come to ask the Creator to deliver him from his lowliness.

Thus, how can he not fall into a state of lowliness? The advice for this is that if a person calculates and sees, through thought and desire, that he is still far from *Dvekut* with the Creator, meaning that even during an ascent he still considers himself, and begins to feel his faults, then he does not need to fall from his state, meaning to be given lowly thoughts until he feels that he is in a state of deficiencies.

Rather, even during an ascent he begins to seek advice how to ascend in degree. In that case, he does not need to be given descents from above, since he himself begins to seek advice even before he has fallen into lowliness. Now it seems that in the situation he is in, he is full of faults. By this he can rid himself of the need to be given descents from above.

However, normally, the order is that during an ascent, a person does not want to search for faults in himself. Therefore, he must be given descents from above.

By this we can interpret what our sages said (*Shabbat* 152), "What I did not lose, I seek." That is, an old man walking bent, always looking at the ground as though searching for something. He says, "I have lost nothing, yet I search." We should interpret "Old is he who has acquired wisdom." That is, he is "Wise, who sees the future." Since he can come to a descent in order acquire empty *Kelim*, so the Creator may fill them or he will remain in a state of lowliness because he will not feel deficient. Then, when he loses the state of ascent, he begins to seek advice how to ascend in spirituality once again.

Therefore, one who is old, meaning wise and sees the future, begins to search how to ascend in spirituality even before he loses the state of ascent. He begins to follow all the counsels about the ways to ascend on the spiritual degrees, and this is done by seeking deficiencies in the state he is in. In that case, there is no need to throw him down in importance so he will find and see deficiencies in himself, since he himself will be looking for deficiencies so as to have empty *Kelim* that the Creator may fill.

The best advice in a state of ascent is that when a person feels that now there is a state of spirituality, and he wants to find deficiencies, in that state he should delve in the Torah and find the connection between the Torah and man. From this he will be able to take knowledge about how to serve the Creator, as it is written, "a soul without knowledge is also not good," and as it is written, "grant us wisdom, understanding, and knowledge from You." In that state, he will see the lack in him and will have empty *Kelim*. By this, he will be saved from coming into a real descent.

Now we will explain the question, Why, when we pray to the Creator to erase our sins, do we stipulate before Him conditions and say, "but not through suffering," meaning "not through descents"? During a descent, we are separated from Him, since during a descent, everything is in lowliness. This is called "*Shechina* [Divinity] in the dust." Because we must feel our lowliness, we cause the *Shechina* to be in exile, too, just as we have drifted from the holy land. That is, we do not have the desire of *Kedusha* [holiness]. Instead, during a descent, we receive the desire of "the land of the nations," and by this we degrade the *Kedusha*.

For this reason, we ask Him to help us erase our sins so we may enter *Kedusha*. However, that it will not come by suffering, called "descents," for these descents cause the degrading of *Kedusha*, which is called "*Shechina* in the dust" or "*Shechina* in exile." We pray that this suffering will not come, since we are causing the degradation of *Kedusha*.

Our sages say (*Berachot* p 5), "Rabbi Yohanan was weak. He went to Rabbi Haninah. He said to him, 'Are you fond of suffering?' He replied, 'Neither they nor their reward.'" Everyone asks about this. After all, many righteous took upon themselves suffering, so why did Rabbi Yohanan say "Neither they nor their reward"?

Baal HaSulam interpreted this and said that they were arguing over the exile of the *Shechina*, which is delayed because not all the sparks of *Kedusha* that have descended into the *Klipot* [shells/peels] have been corrected. For this reason, although there is reward, namely that everything that descended to be among the *Klipot* will return to the *Kedusha*, which is a very big reward—that everything will be corrected—but in the meantime, until everything is corrected, the *Shechina* is in exile, everyone degrades her and exalt the maidservant, namely the *Klipa* [singular of *Klipot*]. This is the sorrow of the *Shechina* that he cannot tolerate. It is about this that he said "Neither they nor their reward."

We see what is suffering in the work. It is that they suffer that the *Shechina* must be in lowliness because of them. To understand this, we should examine the essay "Divinity in Exile" (*Shamati*, Essay No. 1), where it says that when a person regrets being far from the Creator, that he is inside the will to receive only for his own benefit, like animals, which is unbecoming of the "human" quality, he should direct the suffering so it is not because he wants to be a man, and this is why he suffers, but rather that it is because of the sorrow of the *Shechina*.

He says an allegory about this, that a person who has a pain in a certain organ, feels the pain primarily in the heart and in the mind, which is the whole of man. Likewise, man is a specific part of the *Shechina*, called "the assembly of Israel." She feels the majority of the pain, and this is what he should regret. This is called "suffering" in the work.

Who Needs to Know that a Person Withstood the Test?

Article No. 28, Tav-Shin-Mem-Tet, 1988/89

*T*he *Zohar* says (*BaMidbar*, Item 7), "When the Torah and the tabernacle were erected, the Creator wished to count the armies of the Torah, how many armies are in the Torah, in ZA, and how many armies are in the tabernacle. ...For this reason, Israel, who are the armies of ZA and *Malchut*, are counted, so they are known by them."

We should understand this matter, to know that the Creator wanted to count Israel in order to know how many armies there are. Who needs to know? Is it the Creator? But everything is revealed and known to Him. Does He need to actually count them below in order to know the number? Thus, for whose need can we say that the Creator said to count Israel in order to know the number of the armies of ZA and *Malchut*, as it is written, "the Creator wished to count the armies of the Torah, how many armies are in the Torah"?

Baal HaSulam asked a similar question concerning what it says in regard to Abraham: "And He said, 'Do not stretch out your hand against the lad, and do nothing to him, for now I know that you fear

God.'" He asked, Did the Creator not know that Abraham feared God before the test? Thus, what does "for now I know" mean? He said that "for now I know" means that you know that you fear God, since you withstood the test.

Still, we should understand for what purpose a person should know that he fears God. This can give him satisfaction in the work, since what else is there to do in the world, as our sages said (Berachot 33), "Rabbi Hanina said, 'Everything is in the hands of God except for the fear of God.'" This means that the Creator does everything, and all that man needs to do is fear God, as was said, "And now, Israel, what does the Lord your God ask of you but fear?" Thus, why does one need to undergo a test in order to know that he fears God? It would be better if he did not know whether he fears God, and this would make him need to increase the holy work so as to come to be God fearing.

We see that our sages said (Berachot 61b), "Raba said, 'One should know in one's soul if he is a complete righteous or not.'" Here, too, there is the same question: Why does one need to know one's state, since knowing this will give him satisfaction, so what is the benefit in the work from knowing this?

To understand all this, we must remember the two tenets we have in the holy work: 1) The purpose of creation is to do good to His creations, namely for the created beings to receive delight and pleasure. Before we achieve this state, of receiving delight and pleasure, we have not achieved completion, meaning the purpose of creation. 2) The correction of creation. It is known that in order not to have the bread of shame, meaning for the creatures to feel unpleasantness upon reception of the delight and pleasure, the Tzimtzum [restriction] and concealment were made, so they would not feel the delight and pleasure in the purpose of creation, and would be able to work for the sake of the Creator and not for their own sake. This would remove the shame from man because everything he enjoys in the world would not be for his own sake, but because the Creator wants the creatures to enjoy in the world, and this is the only reason they enjoy. For themselves, meaning

247

to enjoy because they want to enjoy, they do not want this and relinquish all the pleasures in the world.

That is, he does not want to receive anything for his own sake, but in everything, he thinks that if receiving the pleasure and enjoying will bring contentment above, only then does he receive the delight and pleasure. Otherwise, he relinquishes it. This is called the "correction of creation," meaning that the purpose of creation is received in a clothing, and this clothing does not let the shame come in when the pleasure is received. That clothing is called "desire to bestow."

Now we can understand what is fear in the work. It was said about fear, "Everything is in the hands of God but fear of God." But why is it not in the hands of God? As we learn, we attribute everything to the Creator, that the Creator gives everything to the created beings. Not giving does not belong to the Creator, since His will is to do good to His creations.

Since the meaning of fear is as it is written in the "Introduction of The Book of Zohar" (Item 203), "Fear means that he is afraid that he will decline in bringing contentment to his Maker." For this reason, he avoids asking the Creator to impart upon him delight and pleasure, as it might not be for the Creator's sake, but for his own, which is regarded as the abundance going to the *Klipot* [shells/peels]. It follows that fear not to receive pertains to man, meaning that man does not want to receive, for fear that it will not be for the sake of the Creator. This work pertains to man. That is, we attribute not receiving in order to receive to the lower ones, since from the perspective of the Creator, He only bestows.

This is called the name *HaVaYaH*, where there are no differences, as it is written, "I the Lord [*HaVaYaH*] do not change." Rather, He always wants to give. For this reason, fear, where he is afraid to receive, belongs to the creatures, and this is all of their work. All the corrections in the world concern this point—correcting ourselves in order to come to a degree where we do not receive anything for our own sake, but as our sages said, "All your works will be for the sake of heaven."

248

Now we can interpret this awareness—that he has fear of God. A person should know this in order to want to go and ask the Creator to give him the light of Torah, where there is the real pleasure, called "His will to do good to His creations." He sees for himself that he has already been through several trials and have endured them because he already has fear of heaven, meaning that he is already certain of himself, that anything he receives will be in order to bestow. Otherwise, he would not have withstood his tests because the only reason a person cannot withstand a test is because he is immersed in his will to receive for himself. But a person who has already departed from receiving pleasures for his own sake, and in every pleasure, he first examines what contentment this will bring to the Creator, then he receives the pleasure.

This is called "for now I know that you fear God," meaning a person already has this awareness. At that time, that state is called "bestowing in order to bestow." Afterward, when he has acquired this degree of fearing God, which is called "man's work," a person should go forward and ask the Creator to give him the delight and pleasure that He wishes to give to the created beings, since he wants to impart pleasure upon the Creator, and his pleasure is in carrying out His thought—that the creatures receive from Him delight and pleasure. This is all of his delight. For this reason, a person needs the awareness.

Now we can interpret what we asked about what *The Zohar* says, "When the Torah and the tabernacle were erected, the Creator wished to count the armies of the Torah, how many armies are in the tabernacle." We asked, Who needs to know this? Does the Creator not know even without actually counting? The answer is the same as with Abraham, "for now I know," meaning that the Creator knows that now Abraham, too, knows that he fears God.

Likewise, we should interpret similarly, meaning that the people of Israel needed this awareness so as to know to which degree they now belong, whether to the quality of the Torah or to the quality of the tabernacle. He says there that Torah and tabernacle pertain to ZA and *Malchut*, meaning the "unification of the Creator with

His *Shechina* [Divinity]." This is why *The Zohar* says, "how many armies are in the Torah," meaning to know to which degree they belong, "how many armies are in the tabernacle," meaning how many of them belong to the *Shechina*. It follows that the whole point of counting is only for man to know. But as for the Creator, He certainly knows everything without actually counting.

It follows that the most important is for man to know to which state he belongs. It is as Rabba said, "One should know in one's soul if he is a complete righteous or not." It is all in order for man to know whether he is on the right track, meaning knows what he must do in order to achieve the goal for which he was created, as was said, "so we will not toil in vain."

In order to understand how an ordinary person can be taken after the general public, and in order for one to have the strength to emerge from what is accepted by the general public and become an individual worker, meaning to understand what he must do individually, and how to be extremely careful, how to be saved from having to work only for his own benefit, I will present here a story by The Seer of Lublin, presented in the book *Talks of Life* (p 34).

"The Rabbi of Mogalitza once said that when the Rabbi of Lublin was confined in his room on the eve of Shabbat [Sabbath] before the *Kiddush* [the beginning of the Sabbath], the rabbi suddenly opened the door and the house was full of great rabbis and sages from his greatest disciples. The rabbi turned to them and said, 'It is written, 'and repays those who hate Him to their faces, to destroy them.' The translation is, He pays His enemies with good deeds that they do in this world in order to lose them from the next world (explanation: The Creator pays His enemies for good deeds that they did in this world in order to lose them, so they will not have the next world). Therefore, I ask you, I can understand that if a wicked man is taken after money, fine, he is paid much money. And if the wicked man takes after respect, he is given great respect. But if the wicked man wants neither respect nor money, but rather loves degrees or wants to be a rabbi or a teacher, how is he paid? The good deeds he did in this world—to remove him from the next world (explanation: How are those people who did good in this world paid so they will not have the next world?). Indeed, one who wants to be a rabbi or a teacher is given this from above, and one who loves degrees is given degrees so he will lose the next world.' Promptly, he shut the door." Thus far the story.

This story shows that there are people who think that they are complete because they relinquish lusts and respect. They look at people who are immersed in lusts or pursuit of honor as unworthy of looking at, much less speaking with them. That is, they see people observing Torah and Mitzvot [commandments/good deeds] in order to satisfy their will to receive, though certainly it is permitted lusts, or they would not be regarded as doing good deeds, and also those who observe Torah and Mitzvot in order to receive respect, while they, meaning those who want high degrees or to be a rabbi or a teacher, probably think that they want this for the sake of the general public.

The Seer of Lublin said about them that they are those who hate the Creator. However, since they do engage in Torah and Mitzvot, the Creator rewards them according to what they want, meaning according to what they pray to the Creator to give them. It follows that the Creator fulfills their wishes. However, they must know that what they are receiving is because the Creator is fulfilling their wish, but they must know that by wanting the Creator to grant their wishes, they lose the next world since by this they become haters of the Creator, as it is written, "and repays those who hate Him to their faces, to destroy them." Thus, they must know that by receiving what they want, meaning by His fulfilling their wish, they will thereby lose the next world.

There are two things to understand here: 1) Why if they are rewarded in this world, they must lose the next world? After all, our sages said (Berachot 8a), "Great is he who enjoys his labor more than he who fears God." And concerning one who fears God, it is written, "Happy is the man who fears the Lord." Concerning one who enjoys his labor, it is written, "If you eat through your own labor, happy are you in this world and happy are you in the next world." We therefore see that one who is rewarded in this world does not have to lose the next world. Thus, why, concerning those who hate the Creator, if he receives reward in this world, we say that he is losing?

2) We should understand, if he observes Torah and Mitzvot, which is called "good deeds," why is he regarded as hating the Creator?

We see that the evil inclination is called "enemy" [hating], as it is written, "If your enemy is hungry, feed him bread." We should understand why the evil inclination is man's enemy. On the contrary, he advises man to commit transgression not in order for man to torment himself, but in order for him to enjoy himself. It follows that one who brings joy to a person should certainly be called "loving," so why is it called "hating"?

We must believe in our sages, who said that all of our work in this world is to be rewarded with Dvekut [adhesion] with the Creator. That is, He wishes to give delight and pleasure to the creatures, which is called "the purpose of creation." Yet, this is impossible to give us before we correct our will to receive to work in order to bestow, or we will feel shame.

Therefore, we need Dvekut, called "equivalence of form," meaning that all the delight and pleasure we want to receive from the Creator is not for our own sake, since we want to annul our authority and to have (only) one authority: the authority of the Creator. Then we will have the real pleasure, in that "He said, and His will was done," meaning that the will of the Creator was fulfilled completely, meaning that the creatures can receive what the Creator wants to give them, namely the delight and pleasure.

It follows that the evil inclination incites a person not to work for the sake of the Creator but for one's own sake, and thereby harms a person. This is why it is called "evil inclination."

Now we can understand the question, Why is it that when one observes Torah and Mitzvot and does good deeds—and the evidence that they are good deeds is that the Creator rewards him for the good deeds—yet he is called an "enemy of the Creator," as it is written, "and repays those who hate Him to their faces, to destroy them"? This is so because although he does good deeds, it is not because he loves the Creator, but because he believes that the Creator will reward him for this. He does not work and observe Torah and *Mitzvot* because he loves the Creator, but because of his own benefit.

However, we must understand, 1) Does one who works for another and aims for the reward and does not work for him or does and observes his commandments out of his love for him, should he therefore be regarded as his enemy? We can only say that he does not work for him for love, but because that person loves himself. But why is he regarded as an enemy of the Creator? What makes him the Creator's enemy if he is working for his own sake?

2) What is the meaning of the commandment to love the Creator? Does He want us to love Him? Does He need our love? Is He deficient and this is why He has commanded us to love Him, as it is written, "And you shall love the Lord your God"? The answer is that He has commanded us to love Him for our sake. That is, loving Him will make us observe Torah and *Mitzvot*. In other words, we observe Torah and *Mitzvot* because we want to please Him, to give Him contentment, for it is the nature of those who love that the love obligates them to want to bring them contentment.

It is like parents' love for their children. They want their children to enjoy and try to give to the children because they love them, so they will enjoy life. The lesson is that they observe Torah and *Mitzvot* because of their love for the Creator. Naturally, they want nothing in return. Thus, they will not receive all the delight and pleasure that the Creator wants to give them in the vessels of reception, but in the vessels of bestowal. That is, they receive the delight and pleasure because they know that the Creator enjoys it, that the purpose of creation, to do good to His creations, is carried out, as He wants it. In other words, there is wholeness in their receiving the delight and pleasure and there is no shame in them.

It follows that one who observes Torah and *Mitzvot* for a reward, meaning that he wants a reward, is considered the Creator's enemy because he obstructs the Creator, delaying what the Creator wants—to give to the created beings, as this is the pleasure of the Creator, and that person delays carrying it out because the *Kli* [vessel] and clothing are missing there, which remove the shame upon reception of the abundance. This is why he is considered an enemy of the Creator.

A person should believe the words of our sages, who said, "He who comes to purify is aided." This means that once a person has come to purify, meaning feels that he is in *Tuma'a* [impurity] and is still far from *Kedusha* [holiness], he should say that this awareness comes from above. That is, the fact that he came to purify is because he received help from above and was notified that he is far from *Kedusha*.

This means that he should appreciate this awareness and say that this is called "revelation from above," when he was notified that he should feel about himself unpleasantness in that he is far from *Kedusha*. Normally, a person has no concern for lack of *Dvekut* with the Creator. A person might feel a lack about anything, and hurt because he does not have it. But to feel pain at being far from the Creator, although a person is remote, he does not notice it because he has more important worries whose absence he feels.

Only sometimes does he feel that he is beginning to feel shame that he is in such a lowly state. Before this, although he was previously in that state, too, he did not notice it. At that time, a person should believe that this came to him from above, as in "He who comes to purify is aided." In other words, why has he now come to purify and cannot tolerate his state of lowliness? He should say that this came to him from above.

However, a person must not say, "I'll wait until this awareness comes to me from above, and then I'll think that I should purify myself." Baal HaSulam said about this, that before the fact, a person should say, "If I am not for me, who is for me?" meaning that only I can help myself, if I brace myself and do things that lead to *Dvekut*. Afterward, meaning after the fact, a person should say that everything comes from above and he must not say, "My power and the might of my hand have gotten me this wealth."

We therefore see that on one hand, a person should say that from all the tests that the person has withstood, he should know that on the one hand, he is a mighty man, as was said, "for now I know that you fear God," meaning that the person is the mighty one. On the other hand, he must say, "The Creator helped me." But from whichever side, he sees that he has withstood the test. Knowing this gives one confidence that now he can demand of the Creator to let him go and achieve the goal.

What Is the Preparation to Receive the Torah in the Work?

Article No. 29, Tav-Shin-Mem-Tet, 1988/89

Our sages said (Shabbat, p 87), In the matter of preparation, which was there, at the time of the giving of the Torah, that there was the matter of the kingdom of priests, and the Mitzva [commandment/good deed] of limiting, and the matter of abstention. This was for the general public.

There are people who observe Torah and Mitzvot [plural of Mitzva] in general, meaning only in practice. That is, they mean that the Creator commanded us to observe Torah and Mitzvot, and in return for obeying Him, He will reward us for the labor or relinquishing many things that the body craves. This is a great effort for us not to obey what the body demands, yet we try to observe the voice of the Creator, meaning what the Creator wants. That is, we annul our will before the will of the Creator. In return for this, He will reward us in this world and in the next world, as was said,

"Happy are you in this world, and happy are you in the next world." This is the work of the general public.

And then there is the work of individuals. They want to observe Torah and Mitzvot individually. That is, they do not care what the general public does; they want to know why the Creator commanded us to observe Torah and Mitzvot. Is He deficient, needing someone to do Him a favor and observe his Torah and Mitzvot? Rather, it must be that the Torah and Mitzvot He has given us is for our sake. Then, they begin to think and pay attention, what benefit will come out of this to the created beings if they observe the Torah and Mitzvot. That is, what they lose by not observing, and what they gain by observing what the Creator has commanded us.

This is as our sages said (Avot, Chapter 2), "Be careful with a light Mitzva as with a grave one, for you do not know the reward for the Mitzvot, and consider the cost of a Mitzva compared to its reward, and the reward for a transgression (the joy you experience in the transgression) compared to its cost." Therefore, when they begin to think about the benefit of observing Torah and Mitzvot, meaning who gains from this, they see what our sages said (Avot, Chapter 1), "Be as slaves serving the rav [great one] not in order to receive reward, and the fear of heaven will be upon you."

This means that the fact that we must work not in order to receive reward means that it is because observing Torah and Mitzvot is not for the Creator, that He needs to be served. If this were true and He needed our work, He would certainly have to pay, just as we work for someone in this world. If a person needs the work of an employee, he certainly pays, as this is how the world works. Since our sages said to work not in order to receive reward, the reason must be that this work is for us, meaning for our sake.

Thus, how can we say that one who does some work for his own sake, meaning that he needs the work, but someone only gave us the work-plan so we would know how to work so it results in a complete product that we will enjoy, can we say that the person who he gave him the work-plan should also pay him for his work? In our world, we see the opposite: A person has to pay for the work-plan he has given us, and the one who gave the work-plan does not pay the person for working according to the work-plan he has received.

This is similar to one who wants to build a house. He goes to an engineer to make a work-plan for him. Then, who has to pay? Is it the engineer to the person who received the work-plan or does the person pay the engineer for giving him a work-plan by which he can build himself a house? Clearly, the person pays the engineer.

According to the above, it is clear that the Creator has given us the Torah and Mitzvot in order to correct ourselves, so we will have a structure of Kedusha [holiness]. Thus, who needs to pay for the plan? It is certainly we, since without Torah and Mitzvot, which is our plan for a structure of Kedusha, it would be utterly impossible to build us a structure of Kedusha. This is as our sages said, "If not for My covenant day and night, I would not put the ordinances of heaven and earth." That is, without Torah and Mitzvot, namely the ordinances of heaven and earth, which is the structure of the world, it would not be able to exist. Rather, specifically if we build the world according to the Torah, the world can exist.

From this we understand that although we have nothing with which to pay the Creator for giving us the plan of Torah and Mitzvot, and we can only thank and praise for it, we should not ask for a reward in return for observing Torah and Mitzvot, that He should pay for our observing Torah and Mitzvot, meaning for using His plan to build for ourselves the house.

People who understand this are regarded as "walking in the work of the Creator on the path of individuals." They have a different perspective on the issue of observing Torah and Mitzvot compared to the way that the general public understands the observance of Torah and Mitzvot—that the Creator should pay them for following the laws of the Torah, which is the Creator's work-plan. They understand that the Creator wants them to follow the plan He has given them, and that it is for the sake of the Creator. Therefore, He should pay for this work of following His plan.

This is as our sages said (*Midrash Rabbah*, Portion 1:1), "Another interpretation: *Amon* is a craftsman [*Uman*]. The Torah says, 'I was the working tool of the Creator.' When a flesh and blood king builds a palace, he builds it not with his own skill but with the skill of an architect. And the architect does not build it out of his head, but employs plans and diagrams (which are books containing various diagrams of buildings by which the craftsman makes a plan how to build the palace). So God looked into the Torah and created the world."

We should understand what this comes to teach us about the way of the work, how there was the creation of the world, that the Creator looked into the Torah, meaning that the Torah is the plan by which He created the world.

It is known that the purpose of creation was to do good to His creations. This was the reason for the creation of the world. For this reason, the Creator created in the creatures a desire and yearning to receive pleasures, and without pleasure, it is impossible to exist.

As we see, one who commits suicide, it is because he cannot see that he will get pleasure anywhere now, which is called "the present," and he also does not see that in the future, he will be able to receive pleasure. Instead, he sees that the world has grown dark on him and does not shine for him. Then he has no other option but to commits suicide because he thinks that by this he will escape the torments.

For this reason, the fact that a person always wants to receive pleasures is the nature that the Creator created, that each created being aspires only to receive pleasures. We must know that everything we call the "evil inclination" is only this quality called "desire to receive pleasure in order to satisfy the yearning."

The reason why the will to receive for oneself is called "evil inclination" is explained with respect to the correction of creation that was done. That is, when the creature receives from the Creator, there is disparity of form in this, which results in a person being ashamed to receive for himself from his friend. For this reason, a person is ashamed to eat the bread of shame. It follows that if a person would receive the delight and pleasure in vessels of reception, he would feel unpleasantness while receiving the abundance. Hence, there as a correction that as long as one does not revoke the *Kelim* [vessels] of the desire to receive for himself, he cannot receive delight and pleasure. It follows that the only obstructor on receiving the delight and pleasure is the will to receive for oneself. This is why this will to receive is the evil inclination.

However, how can it be revoked, as it is written, "Annul your will before His will"? He is the Torah, as our sages said, "The Creator said, 'I have created the evil inclination; I have created the Torah as a spice.'" This means that the Creator says, "The fact that I created the will to receive pleasure, and that this is the nature of creation, as was said, that creation is called 'existence from absence,' means that a new thing was created here." This was said about this will to receive. The Creator said, "I created the Torah as a spice." That is, through "the light in it reforms him."

It therefore follows that if there were no Torah, there would not be existence to the world, for because of the concealment and hiding that was because of the correction of the world, the creatures would have had to remain in the dark, without light. Naturally, there would be no existence to the world. This is the meaning of the Creator looking in the Torah, meaning that the Torah is the work-plan. That is, according to this plan, the world will be built through the Torah and there will be existence to the world. This is called "I have created the evil inclination; I have created the Torah as a spice."

Concerning the study of Torah, our sages said (*Hagigah* 13), "A word of Torah is not to be given to an idol-worshipper, as was said, 'He did not do so for any nation, and let them not know the ordinances.'" We should understand the meaning of idol-worshippers in the work. In the work, we learn everything in one body, as it is written in *The Zohar*, that man is a small world. Thus, what are idol-worshippers in the work, and what is Israel in the work?

We already said that Israel means that he wants all his actions to be for the sake of the Creator and not for his own sake. This is called *Yashar-El* [straight to the Creator], meaning that all his actions are directly to the Creator. The idol-worshipper is the complete opposite: All his actions are for his own sake. That is, he wants two authorities. This means that he wants to extract delight and pleasure from the authority of the Creator into his own authority.

In other words, he wants there to remain two authorities in the world—the authority of the Creator and his own authority. This is called "idol-worshipping," which is work that is foreign to us. "Israel" means that he is working for the sake of the Creator, meaning that he is considered a "worker of the Creator," whose actions are all for the sake of the Creator. But if a person works for his own sake and not for the sake of the Creator, this is regarded as his work being idol-worship and not work for the Creator.

It follows that the whole difference between idol-worshippers and Israel in the work is that "Israel" means that he wants to work for the sake of the Creator, and although he is still enslaved to the evil inclination and cannot subdue it, because he is walking on the path that leads to working for the sake of the Creator, he is already regarded as "Israel," since he wants to achieve this degree.

But when a person wants to work in a state of "Israel," which we said is regarded as working in the state of "individuals," then all the bad in a person stands against him. That is, before he decided to go as "Israel" and his work was in the manner of the general public, he looked at the things he was doing and believed that for every single action he would receive a reward—a reward of this world and a reward of the next world. It was easy for him to do good deeds because this was not against the evil inclination, called "will to receive for himself."

But now that he wants to work in order to annul his own authority and leave only one authority in the world—the authority of the Creator—the will to receive for himself objects to this. Then comes the wicked's question, who asks, "What is the work for you? The fact that you want to work not for your own sake, what will you get out of it?" There is no answer to this, but as it is written, "Blunt its teeth."

It follows that then a person needs help in order to be able to emerge from the control of the evil inclination. At that time, his only choice is what the Creator said, "I have created the evil inclination; I have created the Torah as a spice." It follows that now is the real time when a person needs the help of the Torah to pull him out of the control of the evil inclination.

According to the above, what should one prepare in himself in order to receive the Torah? It is the need for the Torah, and a need is called a *Kli* [vessel]. There cannot be filling without a lack. This is similar to a person asking his friend when he invites him to come in the evening for a meal that he has prepared for him, "How should I prepare myself for eating at your place?" He will probably tell him, "Be careful not to eat at home before you come to me because then you will not be able to eat at my place."

Likewise, in order to receive the Torah, a person must prepare himself—to have a need called a *Kli*, that the Torah can fill. This applies specifically when he wants to work for the sake of the Creator, for then he encounters the resistance of the body, which yells, "What is this work for you?" But a person believes in the sages, who said that only the Torah can deliver a person from the control of the evil inclination. This can be said only of those who want to be "Israel," meaning *Yashar-El* [straight to the Creator]. They see that the evil inclination does not let them emerge from their control, and then they have a need to receive the Torah so the light of the Torah will reform them.

Now we can understand what our sages said, "A word of Torah is not to be given to an idol-worshipper, as was said, 'He did not do so for any nation, and let them not know the ordinances,'" since they have no need for the Torah. One who does work that is foreign to us, meaning for his own sake, can live without the Torah, for he does not need the help of the Torah. Only Israel—those who want to work for the sake of the Creator—need the light of Torah, for "the light in it reforms him." That is, it is impossible to defeat the evil within him without the Torah.

By this we can interpret what our sages said, "The Torah exists only in one who puts himself to death over it." We should understand the word "exists." What does it tell us? We should interpret this according to what our sages said, "The Creator said, 'I have created the evil inclination; I have created the Torah as a spice.'" That is, the Torah should be a spice. In whom is this so, since "There is no light without a *Kli*, no filling without a lack"?

For this reason, they said that those who want to put their selves to death, meaning want to put to death the will to receive for their own sake, and want to do everything for the sake of the Creator, see that they cannot do this on their own. To them the Creator said, "I have created the evil inclination; I have created the Torah as a spice."

But in those who do not want to annul themselves and want there to be two authorities—meaning that man's authority will remain and the Creator will give them and they will extract the delight and pleasure at His disposal and hand it over to the receivers—the Torah does not exist. That is, the Torah does not become a spice for them, since they do not want it to be a spice, and if there is no desire and need, which are the *Kli*, there is no light.

Now we can understand why it is forbidden to teach Torah to idol-worshippers in the work. It means that one who is practicing work that is foreign to us, meaning works for himself, since the Torah is for the evil inclination, so that one who wants to revoke it but cannot, it was said about him, "I have created the evil inclination; I have created the Torah as a spice."

But one who wants to work for his own sake—which is idol-worship—has no need for the Torah. Therefore, if he learns Torah, the Torah will not exist in him in terms of what the Torah is meant to give. Thus, what is the preparation for the reception of the Torah? The need for the help of the Torah. And this is done by wanting to aim everything for the sake of the Creator. Then we need the Torah to give the help.

What Is the Meaning of Lighting the Menorah in the Work?

Article No. 30, Tav-Shin-Mem-Tet, 1988/89

Concerning the verse "When you raise the candles," RASHI interprets—after the rising of the heart. It is written, "when they are lit up," implying ascent, that they must be lit until the flame rises by itself.

"The seven candles will shine before the front of the menorah [lampstand]." There are many interpretations to "the front of the menorah." Literally, it means that all seven candles will shine before the front of the lamp. Thus, who is the front of the menorah? We should understand the whole matter of the menorah in the work.

It is written, "A candle is a Mitzva [commandment/good deed] and the Torah [law/teaching] is light." This means that through the Torah, we light the candle. Also, "The Lord's candle is man's soul." We see that in corporeality, we need to light a light so it will shine only in a place of darkness, as it is written, "as the advantage of the light from within the darkness." This means that "there is no light without a *Kli* [vessel]," and a *Kli* is a lack and a need. This means that a *Kli* is not something that is empty without anything in there. This is not regarded as a lack. Rather, a *Kli* that is fit to receive filling must have a lack for the filling. That is, anything that a person wants to receive is in order to enjoy receiving it.

Otherwise, although he may receive something without a lack, enjoying it depends on the measure of the yearning for what he lacks. Thus, the yearning determines the measure of the pleasure. Therefore, in order to enjoy the light so it will shine, a person must provide for it a lack and yearning for the light. This cannot be achieved without a need. In order to provide a need, the only way is to think about the purpose of creation, meaning why the Creator created creatures, and what should the creatures do in order to satisfy the Creator's will.

In other words, once a person believes in the purpose of creation, that it is to do good to His creations, when a person calculates and wants to see how much delight and pleasure he feels all day, for which he should thank the Creator for receiving from Him only delight and pleasure so he can say, "Blessed is He who said, 'Let there be the world,'" since he enjoys the world so much, at that time he begins to see that all his days are few and bad. Sometimes, his life is meaningless, and instead of saying, "Blessed is He who said, 'Let there be the world,'" a person says, "Better not created than created."

When a person believes in the purpose of creation, which is to do good, he begins to contemplate the reason that he does not see the delight and pleasure revealed to all. When he wants to know the reason for the concealment hiding on the delight and pleasure, he must also believe in the sages who said that there was a correction on the purpose of creation.

That is, in order for the purpose of creation to be complete, without shame, it is known that by nature, every branch wants to resemble its root. Hence, as the Creator gives, likewise, when a person must receive for himself, he feels unpleasantness. To correct this, there was the *Tzimtzum* [restriction], concealment, and hiding, so as to give room for choice. That is, through the concealment and hiding there is room for work, if a person wants to work in order to bestow. In other words, there is room for work so that after his work he will be able to receive in order to bestow, which is called "equivalence of form."

Conversely, if the delight and pleasure clothed in Torah and Mitzvot [plural of Mitzva] were revealed, as it is written in The Zohar that there are 613 counsels during the period of concealment and hiding, where by observing the Torah and Mitzvot as counsels we are then rewarded with 613 deposits. It is written in the Sulam [commentary on The Zohar] that it means that afterward, after the completion of the process of 613 counsels, we are rewarded with 613 deposits, which are 613 lights deposited in the 613 Mitzvot. Only then does what exists within the Torah and Mitzvot become revealed. These are called "holy names," which are details that reveal the general name of the Creator, who is called The Good Who Does Good. In the words of The Zohar, this is called "The Torah and the Creator and Israel are one."

Accordingly, we can understand man's work, meaning what man must do in order to carry out the Creator's purpose of creation for the creatures to receive delight and pleasure and for the Tzimtzum and concealment to depart. There is only one thing, and it is called Dvekut [adhesion], "equivalence of form." This is all the correction that the created beings should do, since all the bad in us disrupts us from receiving the delight and pleasure because of the disparity of form, called "separation." This is what we must correct, and then everything will fall into place.

However, since the nature we are born with is a desire to receive for ourselves, and not to bestow, when a person wants to walk on the path of the work to achieve the truth, meaning that a person wants to acquire a desire to bestow contentment upon the Creator and not for his own sake, the body begins to resist with all its might.

A person says to his body, "Know that by wanting to exist in the world for your own sake, without caring for anything else in the world, where your only concern in everything you do is how much the will to receive will gain from performing acts of bestowal, and without even wanting to think about the benefit of the Creator, by this you obstruct the purpose of creation, which is that the Creator wants to give to the created beings delight and pleasure. You are the obstruction, and I cannot revoke your reason, but I believe in the words of our sages, who said that the Creator said, 'I have created the evil inclination; I have created the Torah as a spice.' Therefore, I want to observe Torah and Mitzvot, by which I will be able to completely revoke you. I want to observe what our sages said, 'The Torah exists only in one who puts himself to death over it.' Therefore, I want to put you to death with the Segula [remedy/virtue] called Torah."

Thus, he tells the body, "Leave me alone with your views, since I want to learn Torah so I can put you to death." Naturally, at that time the body resists with all its might and follows the verse, "He who comes to kill you, kill him first." For this reason, the evil inclination exerts with all its might to obstruct him from observing Torah and Mitzvot with this aim. Either it interferes with his actions, or disrupts him through foreign questions and thoughts that it brings him every time in order to disrupt his holy work.

As a result, those who want to walk on the path of truth and revoke the will to receive for themselves and do everything for the sake of the Creator go through ups and downs. This is not so with people who observe Torah and Mitzvot in order to receive reward. They do not have such descents because they are not going against nature, namely against the evil inclination. However, since "From Lo Lishma [not for Her sake], we come to Lishma [for Her sake]," at times, these people, too, experience descents.

But for people who want to revoke the evil inclination and this is why they engage in Torah and Mitzvot, this is a daily battle. That is, sometimes a person receives help from above, as it is written, "He who comes to purify is aided," and thinks that now he is on top of it, meaning that now he will advance and climb the rungs of Kedusha [holiness]. But suddenly, he falls back down. Such is the procession of the war against the evil inclination, until he comes to a state where he is rewarded with permanent faith, which is called "rewarded with opening his eyes in the Torah."

It is written about it (in the "Introduction to The Study of the Ten Sefirot," Item 98), "Every person can labor in the Torah until he finds the attainment of His open Providence. When one attains open Providence, the love extends to him by itself through the natural channels. And one who does not believe that he can attain this through his efforts, this must be because of disbelief in the words of our sages, 'I labored and found.' Instead, he imagines that the labor is not sufficient for every person."

Accordingly, we should interpret the meaning of the menorah in the work, which RASHI interpreted that it is written "when you raise" after the rising of the flame. It is written, "When they are lit up," as in ascent, that they must be lit until the flame rises by itself.

We should interpret that the purpose of creation, which is to do good to His creations, is the light, and the created beings are the *Kelim* [vessels] receiving the light. However, the *Kelim* must be made suitable. They must be clean so as not to spoil the light extended into them. Since, as we learned, the essence of the creature is the will to receive for oneself, as it emerged from *Ein Sof* [infinity/no end], that *Kli*, as it is, lacks correction.

In other words, although the Creator created the will to receive to desire and yearn to receive the delight and pleasure that He wants to give, the completeness of His works was still missing, namely, there was shame that the lower ones feel upon reception of the abundance. This is called "the correction of the *Kelim*." That is, the bad, which is called "separation," due to the disparity of form between the receiver and the giver, this bad, called "will to receive for oneself," must be cleansed. When the *Kli* is cleansed from the will to receive for oneself, it will be fit to receive the abundance, called "delight and pleasure." As in corporeality, a person will not pour wine into a vessel filthy with waste, since the waste spoils wine. Therefore, the vessel must first be cleaned, and then it can receive the drink, and not before.

This is what took place with the menorah. The amelioration of the candles, when the menorah would be cleaned from residue of oil and coal, and afterward the oil would be placed in them, implies to us that in the work, our bodies must be cleansed of the waste in them, which is the will to receive for oneself. Subsequently, the body can receive the light of Torah. But before the body is clean, it cannot contain the light of Torah.

However, it is very difficult to cleanse the body from the will to receive for oneself, so all his works will be only for the sake of the Creator, since it is against the body's inherent nature. We were given Torah and Mitzvot, by which to cleanse the evil in it, so that the light of the Creator can be in it, as our sages said, "I have created the evil inclination; I have created the Torah as a spice." But at the same time, in itself, observing Torah and Mitzvot is not enough to be able to cleanse the will to receive; it requires prayer, as well.

Prayer means that he should know that the Torah and Mitzvot he is observing are not for the sake of the Creator but for the sake of the created being. This means that since he wants to purify his heart, as it is written, "Purify our hearts to serve You in truth," it follows that through prayer, when a person prays for the purification of the heart, he will remember that the Torah and Mitzvot that a person observes is for man's sake. At that time, he sees how the evil controls a person and he cannot emerge from its governance. In other words, by observing Torah and Mitzvot and praying, these bring him the purity of the heart.

But before a person begins to think about the purity of the heart, he thinks that everything is up to him. That is, he thinks that if he wants to do things only for the sake of the Creator and not for his own sake, since he does not wish to use these desires, it is up to him. This is so because a person cannot appreciate the evil in man's body. This becomes revealed gradually, according to man's work. When he wants to revoke the evil in him, to that extent the evil within him is revealed until he comes to feel that unless the Creator helps him, he is doomed.

At that time, a person begins to ask, "Why did the Creator do this? That is, on one hand, He tells us we must make a choice, meaning loathe the evil, which is the will to receive for ourselves, and choose the good, namely the desire to bestow upon the Creator. But at the same time, I see that I cannot emerge from the governance of the will to receive for myself and work in order to bestow."

The answer is that only when a person comes to a state where he says, "Salvation by man is in vain," meaning that one cannot help himself and choose the good. In other words, when a person sees that this matter is difficult from every angle, then the help from above comes to him and the verse, "He who comes to purify is aided" comes true. That is, when a person comes to purify and begins to walk on the path of achieving bestowal and uprooting the evil from within him, he sees that it is out of his hands. At that time, the *Kli* is completed from man's perspective, meaning the lack, when he becomes needy of the Creator to help him emerge from the control of the evil.

Prior to this, he thought that he could defeat the evil in him by himself. In that case, he would not need the Creator and would receive the purification of the body from the will to receive by his own strength. In that state, he had no importance for *Dvekut* with the Creator as it should be, and this was considered a flaw.

This is similar to a person who is given a vessel of gold and he considers it a vessel of copper. He thanks the person for it as one would thank a person for a vessel of copper. What sorrow that person would inflict upon the giver of the gift, although the giver does not need the gratitude that he would give in return for the gift. Rather, the giver's sorrow is because the giver wants the receiver to have great pleasure. When the receiver feels great pleasure, this is the giver's joy. It follows that when the receiver cannot appreciate the importance of the gift, the receiver is not delighted as the giver intended. Thus, the giver of the gift feels sorrow.

The lesson is that when the Creator gives something to a person, it is in order to enjoy it. Yet, a person cannot appreciate anything according to its importance, but according to how the receiver appreciates it. It is written about it, "As the advantage of the light from within the darkness," meaning that the darkness is how a person feels the lack in him. According to the sensation of the lack, he will later be able to enjoy the light.

I once said that we can see about ourselves that thank God, we are walking on our legs. Certainly, we enjoy the fact that we can use our hands and legs. But where is our joy? We should be delighted that we have such important things that we can use, like hands and legs.

For example, if we were to walk into a hospital where there are paraplegics, one in the leg, one in the hand, or in both, and we would tell them that we have a cure that as soon as you take it you will be able to tend to yourselves, meaning you will be able to walk on your legs and use your hands. Can we imagine the joy that they would feel? We cannot even appreciate the true elation that they would feel.

It follows that all we need in order to be as happy as they are is darkness. That is, if we felt the darkness that they feel, we would be as happy as they are.

Now the question is, Should we really be happy that we can use our hands and legs, meaning that it is an important thing and we should thank the Creator for it and be happy about it?

Or, in fact, this is a small thing, not worthy of rejoicing over and saying, as we do, this is how it should be. That is, we are not obligated to be happy about it because we do not feel the importance of the matter. Or, perhaps, we should in fact thank the Creator for not being paraplegic, and rejoice over this?

However, we see that even if we introspect and thank the Creator, we cannot receive joy from this because as said above, the advantage of the light is from within the darkness. By this we can see why the matter of choice, choosing the good, namely the desire to bestow, and loathing the bad, is so difficult. It is because we must taste the taste of darkness.

However, we must not be shown the darkness as it truly is. If we saw the measure of bad within us, we would immediately escape from the work. Then we would not feel darkness because he does not mind that the will to receive for himself is the ruler as he does not feel this as darkness. Only one who labors and works as much as he can, and goes through ups and downs, can say that he tastes the taste of darkness because he cannot overcome his will to receive for himself.

Thus, the descents that a person receives when he wants to walk on the path of truth are instruments for the sensation of the help he will receive. We must believe the words of our sages who said, "He who comes to purify is aided." A person must not escape the campaign when he sees that he is not making progress. Sometimes he gets thoughts of the spies, who said that this work is not for us and requires special people who can walk on the path of overcoming.

All this comes to him because he understands that each time, he must see how he is making progress. However, it does not occur to him that he must advance in obtaining darkness, that this is the only Kli he needs to acquire. A Kli is a need for a filling. That is, if he has no filling for the lack, he feels that he is in the dark. For this reason, a person must not say that he is not advancing in the work.

Hence, he wants to escape the campaign, for it is not the truth, since he sees each time how far he is from obtaining the light, meaning for the Creator to give him the Kli called "desire to bestow." He cannot obtain the desire to bestow by himself, and then he comes to feel that the world has grown dark on him. At that time, the light comes, meaning help from above, as it is written, "He who comes to purify is aided."

Accordingly, in the work, the menorah implies the body, that the body must be lit so as to shine, as it is written, "The Lord's candle is man's soul," meaning that the body must obtain the soul. At that time, the name of the Creator is named after the person, as was said, "The Lord's candle."

When is the body regarded as the Lord's candle? It is when we must light it so it will shine, which is when a person obtains the soul, meaning acquires the desire to bestow. This is regarded as a soul, as *The Zohar* says, "He who comes to purify is aided." *The Zohar* asks, "How is he aided?" and it replies, "with a holy soul," meaning that he is given from above a soul. At that time, the body is called "The Lord's candle," since the soul of the Creator is clothed in the body. That is, preceding the arrival of the assistance from above, the will to receive for himself was clothed in a body. Now the desire to bestow is clothed in the body.

However, until one obtains help from above, a person is in the dark. Each time he overcomes and lights up the menorah, meaning the body, so as to be in the form of "All your works will be for the sake of the Creator," he experiences ups and downs. For this reason, the verse calls the lighting of the menorah, "When you raise the candles," since the flame does not go up as soon as it is lit. That is, during the overcoming, he lights up the body and begins to do the holy work, but afterward he descends from this degree.

It follows that when a person lights the menorah, so the body will work in order to bring contentment to his Maker and have love of the Creator, "as cinders of fire is the Lord's flame," it stands to reason that when he overcomes and begins to walk on the path of doing everything in order to bestow, the fact that he received a descent in the middle of the work and fell once more into the vessels of reception, although afterward, he receives a desire and yearning to work in order to bestow once more, but again he falls from his degree.

This repeats itself until he sees that this is endless. Therefore, he says, "I see that there should have been progress in the work," that this would be a sign that the work he is doing is for Him, meaning he will accomplish what he wants, meaning come to do everything for the sake of the Creator. Yet, he sees the opposite. Therefore, a person wants to say, "This thing, that I want to light the menorah, meaning the body, is not for me. Otherwise, I would not have such descents in the work."

For this reason, the text tells us, "When you raise," and not "when they are lit," to tell us that everything that appears to our eyes when we engage in lighting the menorah, everything—all the states—are ascents. In other words, even the worst descents that we receive during the work belong to ascents, since the advantage of the light is from within the darkness.

This means that a person cannot say that this work to bestow is not for him, as he sees by his descents. The verse says about this, "When you raise the candles," in order to tell us that everything is regarded as an ascent. Hence, one should not say that this is not for him but for more gifted people. In order to know more, that this is the order of the work of bestowal, the verse comes and says, "This was the workmanship of the menorah, hammered work."

It is written in the *Midrash* [*Beha'alotcha* (When You Raise)]: "The workmanship of the menorah, how was it? When Moses went up, the Creator showed him on the mountain how He would make the tabernacle. When the Creator showed him the workmanship of the menorah, Moses was perplexed. The Creator said to him: 'Behold, I do in front of you.' Still, Moses was perplexed about it. He said, 'The menorah will be made of hammered work,' meaning it is very difficult to do. The Creator said to him, 'Throw the gold into the fire and the menorah will be made by itself, as was said, 'the workmanship of the menorah was hammered work.'"

RASHI interprets the verse, "This was the making of the menorah": "It was done by itself by the Creator." We should understand what it implies to us in the work that it was difficult to make the menorah. The menorah indicates the body, that the body must be lit so as to do the holy work, such as a menorah is lit up so it will work in corporeality.

However, this is very difficult because in order to work for the sake of the Creator and not for one's own sake, it is against nature. Hence, Moses found it difficult. That is, how could he say to all of Israel that they should do the work of the menorah, that it must be lit before the front of the menorah, where "before the front of the menorah" is the Creator?

In other words, the Creator is the one standing before a person, as it is written, "The Lord is ever before me." When the body is lit up, it must shine not for its own sake. Rather, the body must shine for the sake of the Creator. This is called "The seven candles will shine before the front of the menorah," where the seven candles are the six days of work and the Sabbath. This means that the body must shine from the light of the soul, as in "The Lord's candle is man's soul," where everything must be "before the front of the menorah," meaning it should all be not for his own sake, but for the sake of the Creator.

By this we should interpret, truly perplexing, why the Creator said, "This was the workmanship of the menorah, a hammered work of gold." That is, why did the Creator say "hammered work," which means that making the menorah should be difficult? We should interpret that this is the meaning of what our sages said, "When the Creator showed him the workmanship of the menorah, Moses was perplexed." That is, he asked, "Why did the Creator make it so it would be difficult?" We should answer this with what was said above, "As the advantage of the light from within the darkness." This is why He made the menorah deliberately difficult, so they would taste the taste of darkness and will know the importance of nearing the Creator by His giving them vessels of bestowal.

However, Moses asked, "It is true that there should be darkness so as to distinguish between light and darkness. However, since they are unable to emerge from the control of the will to receive, what is the benefit in it being difficult? True, they will taste the darkness, but they will never be able to come to the light. Thus, they will never be rewarded with the advantage of the light from within the darkness. In other words, they will receive darkness but how will they ever be rewarded with the light, meaning with vessels of bestowal?"

We should interpret that it is about this that the Creator's reply came. "The Creator said to him, 'Throw the gold into the fire and the menorah will be made by itself.'" This means that it is true that the Creator agreed with Moses that man cannot obtain vessels of bestowal by himself. And your question, "How then will they obtain vessels of bestowal?" Tell them, "Throw the gold," meaning the will to receive, which is called *Ze-Hav* [Hebrew: "give this," but also *Zahav* (gold)]. In other words, only if they want to throw away the will to receive for themselves, the menorah, meaning the body, so it will shine "before the front of the menorah," and before the menorah is the Creator, this means that the menorah will be done by itself.

Naturally, the Creator can certainly give a person vessels of bestowal, as He has given man vessels of reception. This is the meaning of what RASHI interpreted about the verse, "This was the workmanship of the menorah." The question is, Who made the menorah? Through the Creator, it was made by itself. It follows that one should not look at the descents he has, for everything is regarded as ascents, as it is written, "When you raise."

What Is the Prohibition of Teaching Torah to Idol-Worshippers in the Work?

Article No. 31, Tav-Shin-Mem-Tet, 1988/89

It is written in *The Zohar* (*Hukat*, Item 2): "It is written there, 'But *Zot* [This] without the addition of the *Vav*, is the statute of the Torah,' which is *Malchut*, called 'Statute,' and comes from ZA, who is called 'Torah.' Yet, not the Torah itself, which is ZA, but only the judgment of the Torah, the decree of the Torah, which is *Malchut*. Conversely, 'This is the Torah' is to show that all is in one unification, to include the Assembly of Israel, which is *Malchut*, in the Creator, so all will be one."

We should understand why *The Zohar* calls *Malchut* by the name "statute." That is, why must *Malchut* be only a law, without intellect, as RASHI interpreted, "'This is the statute of the Torah,' since Satan and the nations of the world count Israel to say, 'What is this *Mitzva* [commandment/good deed] and what point is there to it?'

277

Hence, it is written about it, 'It is a statue, a decree before Me; you have no permission to doubt it.'"

Thus, when is it considered a law? Only when the nations of the world ask, "What is this *Mitzva*"? and we must answer them. What is the answer? A law, a decree." This implies that man upholds the law precisely when they ask "Why?" Then it can be said that he is observing the *Mitzva* because of a law. Otherwise, there is nothing that shows that he is observing this *Mitzva* because it is a law.

We should also understand this: Would it not be better had this *Mitzva* been clothed in intellect? That is, it would be easier to observe the *Mitzva*. Why does the Creator want it to be as a law, which is harder to observe the *Mitzva*? After all, there is a rule, "The Creator does not complain (comes with libel) against His creations" (*Avoda Zarah* 3).

We should understand why He wants this *Mitzva* as a law. When speaking of the work, we must discern two things: 1) the practice, 2) the intention.

In the corporeal world, we see that a person looks mainly at the reward. That is, if a person works for an employer who gives him the work and tells him, "I want you to work for me, but you haven't the brains to understand why I need this work. You may think that it would be better for me if I did not need to command you to do the things that I am commanding you, but I cannot explain to you why I need you to do these things for me. In return, tell me how much you earn working for other people, with whom you do understand why you are working, and since I want this job, I will pay you ten times more than you would earn with others."

Certainly, many people would jump on such a job, since they are all looking at the reward and the salary, since he is paying ten times more. For example, the usual pay is $1,000 a month, and he will pay $10,000. Certainly, with such a job, he will not say that they are working above reason, that their job is called "a law," since it is within reason that it is worthwhile to do this job, as it is common sense that the main reason that a person works is for the pay. Hence, one who pays more, there you need to work. This is called "within reason."

What do the created beings call "above reason"? When one must work without any pay or reward, this is called "above reason." This is so because of the purpose of creation, which is to do good to His creations, meaning for the creatures to receive delight and pleasure, which is called "desire to receive for oneself." That is, everything he does will be for the sake of the creature, for so was His wish. For this reason, when a person is told that he must work without reward, it is called "above reason," which is against the intellect, meaning against the purpose of creation.

Then, when a person is told that he must work in order to bestow, there immediately comes the question of the wicked: What is this work for you, that you are not caring for your own benefit but for the benefit of the Creator? Clearly, we must provide a reasonable answer, since he is making a straightforward argument, saying "You want to go against nature!" But what did our sages say about what to answer? "Blunt his teeth," meaning there is no answer to this, only a law.

When we want to overcome him and say that it is worthwhile to work for the King, he becomes smarter and begins to ask the question of wicked Pharaoh, who says, "Who is the Lord that I should obey His voice?" It follows that there are two just arguments here. And according to what Baal HaSulam said, it is only one argument, except he wants to remain in self-love, and therefore argues like a wise one. That is, "In truth, I am a mighty man, not one of the ordinary folk, who cannot overcome. However, I don't know the Creator. If the Creator were revealed to me and I would not have to believe in Him, I would immediately work for the sake of the Creator."

It turns out that he is in pride. That is, he wants to remain in self-love, and therefore makes the argument of the wise one, that he is not like other people who cannot overcome, who are like little children who want what they see and have no power to overcome and see if this is good for them or not. "I, on the other hand, am what is called 'a man,' and I can control myself. But if the Creator wants me to work for Him, He shouldn't hide Himself so we can't perceive Him and must only believe in His Providence. This doesn't make sense."

It turns out that he is clothing the self-love in a garment of pride. That is, his will to receive for himself causes him to be proud. In other words, everything that a person says, that he does not want to believe, is really that he does not want to annul his will to receive for himself.

Baal HaSulam said about this that we must believe that this path of faith above reason, and also the fact that we must work for Him and not for our own sake, is not because the Creator wants all those things for His own sake. Rather, it is all for man's sake. In other words, the Creator's desire to give to the created beings delight and pleasure, and to have in this complete delight, meaning that they will not to feel any shame while receiving the delight, He has given us an advice: to work for Him. By this we will be able to receive delight and pleasure and will not feel any unpleasantness while receiving the delight.

For this reason, in order not to feel shame, we were given another thing, called "faith above reason." "If Providence were revealed," as he says in the introduction, "it would be utterly impossible to do anything for the sake of the Creator. Rather, everything would have to be for one's own sake," if the pleasure in Mitzvot [plural of Mitzva] were revealed more than in corporeal pleasures. We see how difficult it is to relinquish corporeal pleasures and to say, "I will receive the pleasure only when I can aim for the sake of the Creator. Otherwise, I do not want to receive the pleasure."

With the flavors of Torah and Mitzvot, we must believe what the ARI says, that because of the breaking, holy sparks fell into the Klipot [shells/peels]. The Zohar calls it "slim light," meaning a small illumination from the Kedusha [holiness]. From this come all the pleasures in the corporeal world.

By this we can calculate that if it is difficult to make a choice over small pleasures and say that he is careful not to receive the corporeal pleasures only for the sake of the Creator, meaning he is willing to relinquish every single pleasure he receives if he cannot aim for the sake of the Creator, how difficult it is, it is much more so if the delight and pleasure clothed in Torah and Mitzvot were revealed. Then the creatures would not be able to choose to do everything for the sake of the Creator, but would receive the delight and pleasure for their own sake.

Therefore, in order for the creatures to be able to correct themselves, in order to have Dvekut [adhesion] and equivalence of form while receiving the delight and pleasure, there was the Tzimtzum [restriction] and concealment. Then, if the delight in Torah and Mitzvot is not revealed and a person observes Torah and Mitzvot because of faith, meaning that he chose Torah and Mitzvot not because he derives pleasure from Torah and Mitzvot, since the delight and pleasure is still not revealed, since before a person corrects his vessels of reception, so everything he does will be for the sake of the Creator and not for his own sake—on that person there are still concealment and hiding. At that time, there is room for choice, meaning to choose and see if he is working for his own sake or for the sake of the Creator.

Conversely, if the reward and pleasure were revealed, the created beings would be compelled to remain in a state of receiving for themselves, since they would not be able to retire from Torah and Mitzvot because of the open Providence. It is as he says (in the "Introduction to The Study of the Ten Sefirot," Item 43), "If, for example, the Creator were to establish open Providence with His creations in that, for instance, anyone who eats a forbidden thing would suffocate on the spot, and anyone who performs a Mitzva would discover such wonderful pleasures in it, like the finest delights in this world. Then, what fool would even contemplate tasting a forbidden thing, knowing that he would immediately lose his life because of it, just as one does not consider jumping into a fire? Also, what fool would leave any Mitzva without performing it as quickly as possible?" It follows that this matter of faith, and this matter of work in order to bestow and not for one's own benefit are all for man's sake.

According to the above, we can understand the question we asked, Why were we given the order of the work by way of faith above reason? It makes sense that if the Creator were to give us the work in Torah and *Mitzvot* within the reason and the intellect, it would be easier to do the holy work, and the Creator does not complain against His creations, so why did He do this?

The answer is that only by way of concealment and hiding is it possible for the created beings to achieve wholeness, meaning to receive the delight and pleasure in wholeness, meaning not to feel unpleasantness while receiving the pleasures. Therefore, it turns out that precisely when we can go with our hearts and minds toward the Creator, precisely this way is the most successful, and not as everyone thinks, that if the Creator gives us the work in the intellect, meaning to have open Providence, from this the created beings will achieve wholeness. We can say about this, as it is written, "For My thoughts are not your thoughts."

According to the above, we can interpret what we asked, Why is *Malchut* called a "statute," as it is called "the statute of the Torah"? *The Zohar* says there that *Malchut* is called "the statute of the Torah," and not the Torah itself, the decree of the Torah, which is *Malchut*, but we must include *Malchut* and the Torah in one unification.

We asked, Why is *Malchut* called "statute"? The answer that *Malchut* is called the "kingdom of heaven," which is faith, to believe in the Creator, that He watches over the world with a guidance of good and doing good.

When a person begins to introspect, he sees that he is full of faults. Thus, how can the body understand that these are all bestowals? Although we are given the prayer for the bad states that we feel, whether in corporeality or in spirituality, but afterward, meaning after the prayer, when a person prayed but his prayer was not answered, if he sees that he is in utter lowliness, whether in corporeality or in spirituality, at that time he needs to overcome and say that the name of the Creator is The Good Who Does Good.

This is a lot of work, since he has no rational answers to the questions that the body asks. Instead, he must say, "I take upon myself the burden of the kingdom of heaven above reason and say that such is the decree of the Creator." Our sages said about this, "Since the nations of the world count Israel to say, 'What is this Mitzva and what is its taste?' What should we reply? 'I have set a law, a decree before Me, and it is forbidden to doubt it.'"

This is why the kingdom of heaven is called a "statute." However, it is the law of the Torah and not the Torah itself. That is, in order to be rewarded with the Torah, we must take upon ourselves the rules that the Torah has given us. Otherwise, it is impossible to receive the Torah. When a person takes upon himself the kingdom of heaven, he is called "Israel," since through the kingdom of heaven that a person takes upon himself above reason, he exits self-love, and then he is able to receive the Torah herself.

Otherwise, if he was still not rewarded with vessels of bestowal, all the Torah that he takes will go to the Sitra Achra [other side] and not to Kedusha. That is, that light of Torah, which is the delight and pleasure that the creatures must receive, will go to the Klipot. This is why there was the Tzimtzum and the concealment, so that everything would enter the Kedusha. Hence, precisely when a person is rewarded with being Israel, when he has already been rewarded with the kingdom of heaven, namely that in everything he does, he has no other thought but to bestow contentment upon his Maker, then he can be given the Torah.

It therefore follows that in the work, the prohibition on teaching Torah to idol-worshippers means that it is impossible to learn Torah as long as one is in a state of idol-worshipping, when he is still immersed in self-love. That is, faith above reason, called "kingdom of heaven," which is a statute, is a way to emerge from self-love and thereby be rewarded according to the order of the work that is given when a person wants to take upon himself the kingdom of heaven in mind and heart. At that time a person is rewarded with the quality of "Israel," meaning that all his actions are only for the sake of the Creator. Then is the time when he can receive the Torah, and the *Klipot* cannot suck from the *Kedusha*.

By this we can interpret what our sages said (*Hulim* 89), "The world exists only for one who restrains himself during a feud." We should understand why if a person does not restrain himself but replies to the other during a feud, because of this the world cannot exist. In the work, this means that the "world" is the person himself, as it is written in *The Zohar*, "Every person is a small world in and of itself." Therefore, this means that when a person begins to quarrel with the body and wants to obey what our sages said, "One should always vex the good inclination over the evil inclination," and RASHI interpreted that he should make war with it, called "the war of the inclination," meaning when a person demands of the body to do everything for the sake of the Creator, this infuriates the evil inclination as he wants to annul its authority altogether, and everything a person does, he wants it all to be for the sake of the Creator, at that time, the body comes to him with just arguments that the body is making rational arguments.

But if a person wants to live, meaning he wants to achieve the complete wholeness and observe the will of the Creator, whose desire is to do good to His creations, meaning to be rewarded with the light of Torah, which is the delight and pleasure in the thought of creation, at that time it is forbidden to answer the body with rational arguments, meaning to say that he is going within reason, since within reason must be in order to receive. Instead, he restrains himself during the feud and tells it, "From the perspective of the intellect, you are correct, but I am going above reason."

What Does It Mean that Oil Is Called "Good Deeds" in the Work?

Article No. 32, Tav-Shin-Mem-Tet, 1988/89

It is written in *The Zohar* (Balak, Item 43): "'The wise, his eyes are in his head.' He asks, 'Where else would man's eyes be? Perhaps in his body or on his arm, as the wisest in the whole world told us?' We learn that 'One must not walk four steps bare-headed.' What is the reason? It is because the *Shechina* [Divinity] is on his head, and any wise man, his eyes and his words are in his head. That is, on the same line. It stands on his head, which is the *Shechina*, and when his eyes are there, in his head, which is the *Shechina*, he should know that that light which burns on his head needs oil, since man's body is the wick, and the light burns above the wick. King Solomon shrieked and said, 'Let not oil be lacking on your head,' since the light in his head needs oil, which is the good deeds. It is about this that he says, 'The wise, his eyes are in his head,' and not elsewhere."

We should understand why if the Creator wants to give the light of the Creator to a person, the person needs good deeds, like the oil. That is, according to the amount of oil in the wick, to that extent the candle burns. In other words, in corporeality, we see that the wick can burn only according to the amount of oil in it. Yet, how does this relate to spirituality? Why is it that when there is a lack of good deeds, the Creator cannot give to a person, so the light will not stop from him? After all, the fact that the Creator gives light to a person is because of the purpose of creation, which is to do good to His creations. Thus, why does the Creator need the lower one to give Him good deeds?

To understand what we asked, If He wishes to give delight and pleasure to the created beings, why does He need them to give Him oil? The answer is that in order to achieve the completion of His works, there was the matter of concealment and hiding, so that His guidance will not be in open Providence. Only once the created beings correct their *Kelim* [vessels] from the will to receive for themselves and achieve equivalence of form, called "desire to bestow," by this the matter of shame—which derives from the oppositeness of form from the Giver—will be corrected.

It therefore follows that although from the perspective of the Giver there is no cessation of abundance, but as it is written, "I the Lord do not change," from the perspective of correction that was carried out in the first receiver, called *Malchut de Ein Sof*, this correction is derived, where as long as the lower one cannot receive everything in order to bestow, the light stops shining to the lower one. Therefore, in order for the light to shine on one's head, he must do good deeds, meaning acts of bestowal. This will lead him to do everything in order to bestow, and then there will be a place where the light can be present permanently.

Now we can interpret what is written, "The wise, his eyes are in his head." Baal HaSulam said that "wise" means that one who wants to be wise is already called "wise." Accordingly, this means that one who wants to be wise should look in his own head, meaning believe that the *Shechina* is on his head, which is the reason why our sages said, "One must not walk four steps bare-headed." We explained that man's head means man's mind, and the mind must not be revealed, meaning he should cover his mind and reason as though he has no reason and go above reason, for precisely above reason can he receive everything in order to bestow. In this way, a person can be rewarded with feeling that the *Shechina* is over his head, meaning above reason, by which he will come to feel.

This is as Baal HaSulam says, that when a person comes to feel that now he is in ascent, he should not say, "Now I do not need to believe that His guidance is in the form of good and doing good because now I feel that this is so." By this he goes back within reason and promptly loses his degree, since he has flawed the faith above reason by saying that now he no longer needs to go above reason.

This is called falling once more into self-love, on which there was a *Tzimtzum* [restriction] and concealment, for which the light departed from him and he remained in the dark. When it says, "His eyes are in his head," it means he is looking at the *Malchut* [kingdom] of heaven in his head, which is precisely when his head is not revealed but covered, and he goes above reason. This is called "good deeds." And what is the good deed? It is that he covers his head by going above reason.

It follows that man's body is the wick that needs the light in his head, and the light shines as long as he has oil. When he has no oil, the light departs from the wick.

As was said above, "oil" means good deeds. As long as he adds oil, the candle burns, meaning that as long as he "covers his head," meaning his feeling, that is, he is not taking this ascent—meaning that now he feels the light within reason—as support.

This means that now he has something on which to base his kingdom of heaven. It follows that now he no longer has oil, meaning good deeds, called "above reason." Hence, the wick is quenched for lack of oil. This is the meaning of what we asked, "What does it mean that oil is called "good deeds"?

The answer is that good deeds are like the oil in the wick. When the oil runs out, the light stops. Likewise, when the good deeds stop, the light departs and descends once more to the place of lowliness.

Baal HaSulam said that when he comes into a state of ascent, meaning that he feels that it is worthwhile to work in order to do everything in order to bring contentment to his Maker, he should not say, "Now I have a basis on which to build the kingdom of heaven, since now I no longer need to go above reason." Rather, he should say, "Now I see that I must go specifically above reason, and the evidence of this is that specifically by going above reason, the Creator brings me closer and loves me."

How does he know that the Creator loves him? Baal HaSulam said a rule about this: If a person has love for the Creator, he should know that it is because the Creator loves him, as it is written, "The Lord is your shade." "Therefore, from here on I take upon myself to go only above reason, for in this way I see that the Creator brings me closer." Thus, he does not relate to the ascent as a basis, that because now he feels, he wants to be a worker of the Creator. Rather, he takes this ascent as proof that the way of the Creator is specifically above reason, and henceforth, he will try to go only above reason.

Accordingly, we can understand what *The Zohar* says (Balak, Item 71), "'And it shall come to pass that when you eat from the bread of the earth you will raise a contribution to the Lord' was said about the sheaf of the "wave offering." Why "wave"? Is it a wave because the priest would wave it up? How does it concern us if he waved up or lowered down? We said that *Tnufa* [waving] means *Tnu-Peh* [give-mouth], which are the letters of *Tnufa* [in Hebrew]. It means, "Give glory to the Lord your God, since *Peh* is glory, meaning *Malchut*, which is called "glory," which should be given to the Creator. For this reason, we must raise her, since there is glory to the upper one, ZA, only when Israel establish this glory, which is *Malchut*, and give it to the King of Glory. This is the meaning of *Tnu-Peh*, "give glory." This is certainly elevating, meaning raising *Malchut* to ZA.

Waving implies work. That is, although the literal meaning is that we must raise the sheaf, as it is written, "the sheaf of the wave offering," but *The Zohar* asks what this comes to teach us in the work. It explains about this that we must raise the kingship to the Creator, for *Peh* [mouth] is called kingship and *Peh* is also called "glory," as it is written, "Give glory to the Lord your God." Thus, we must give the *Peh*, which is the kingship [*Malchut*], to the Creator.

We should understand what it means that we must give the kingship to the Creator, and what it means that they should give the *Peh*, meaning glory, to the Creator. When we speak about observing Torah and *Mitzvot* individually, meaning in order to thereby achieve *Dvekut* with the Creator, which is equivalence of form, namely relinquish self-benefit and do only that which benefits the Creator, this work is called "*Shechina* [Divinity] in the dust," or "*Shechina* in exile."

In other words, when a person works for his own benefit, meaning to receive reward for his work, he has fuel to work because he considers the reward. But when a person wants to work not in order to receive reward, the body asks, "What is this work for you?" Therefore, at that time, this work tastes like dust to him. Although he overcomes and observes the Torah and *Mitzvot* [commandments/good deeds], he works with great efforts since the body does not enjoy it.

Conversely, if a person says to the body, "If you ask me why I observe Torah and *Mitzvot*," the person should say, "Until now, I worked for you. Now I have come to realize that we must work for the sake of the Creator. Since I cannot fight, as you are stronger than I, as it is written, 'And redeemed him from the hand of he who was stronger than him,' therefore, I want to observe Torah and *Mitzvot* and I believe in our sages who said, 'The light in it reforms him,' that by observing Torah and *Mitzvot*, I will be able to overcome you. Therefore, I ask that you will not disturb me, or I will not be able to annul you."

Clearly, what does the body answer? There is the known rule, "He who comes to kill you, kill him first." Naturally, the body does what it can. It brings him many bad thoughts, to the point that he cannot overcome it.

What should one do when he sees that he cannot overcome it by himself? His only choice is to believe in our sages, who said, "He who comes to purify is aided." That is, at that time he must pray to the Creator to help him from above so he will have the strength to defeat his body.

For what should one ask for the Creator's help? He cannot defeat the evil in him, called "will to receive for his own sake," because the *Shechina* is in the dust. In other words, since there is a natural law that the small annuls before the great as a candle before a torch, a person cannot work for the sake of the Creator because the King is not important in his eyes. This is called "*Shechina* in the dust."

It follows that he asks of the Creator to raise the *Shechina* from the dust. In other words, the *Shechina* is called "kingdom of heaven," and its value is the same as that of dust. It is as we say in the blessing for the food, "The Merciful One will raise for us the fallen hut of David," where the "hut of David" means the kingdom of heaven, which is lying in the dust. We ask the Creator to raise the kingdom so that we can see its importance, and not as it appears to us, that it is lying in the dust, which is why we cannot annul the evil in us.

Conversely, if the glory of heaven were revealed, the body would annul like a candle before a torch. This is the meaning of what we say in the *Musaf* [supplemental] Prayer: "For our sins, we have been exiled from our land and drew far off from our land." That is, because of the sins, called "vessels of reception," we have become "far off from our land." *Adama* [land] comes from the words, "*Adameh* [I will be similar] to the Upper One." Similar to the upper one means that the lower one, too, wants to be as a desire to bestow, like the upper one. He drew far off from it because he wants only to receive for himself.

For this reason, we ask of the Creator and say, "Our Father, our King, reveal the glory of Your kingship upon us soon." That is, by the Creator revealing His glory to us, meaning raising the *Shechina* from the dust and glorifying *Malchut* [the kingship/kingdom], we will be able to annul our will to receive through the rule, "the small annuls before the great."

Yet, the question is, Why must we ask the Creator to raise *Malchut* from the dust? Why does He not show the importance of *Malchut* on His own, but made it so that in our eyes, she is lying in the dust?

The answer is that if the glory of *Malchut* were revealed, we would not be able to make a choice, and everything would go into the vessels of reception. It would be utterly impossible to emerge from the control of the will to receive for oneself. But while there is concealment on the kingdom of heaven and we must accept the burden of the kingdom of heaven above reason, it is rooted in a person that there is a prohibition to receive abundance in vessels of reception. For this reason, a person begins to work not in order to receive reward, but because of the glory of the King. Hence, he asks the Creator not to hide Himself from the lower ones, but to "Reveal the glory of Your kingship over us" so we will have the strength to annul ourselves and work only because of the glory of the King.

Now we can understand the meaning of *Tnufa*, which he says means *Tnu-Peh* [give-mouth]. We should interpret what it means that the created beings must give a mouth to the Creator, which is *Malchut*. It means that the lower ones should take upon themselves the kingdom of heaven, meaning that they must elevate *Malchut*, which is lying in the dust, and say that she is not lowered and lying in the dust, but that her place is in heaven. This is called "the kingdom of heaven," meaning that she is raised from the dust and placed back in her place, which is her important place—in heaven. Then, *Malchut* is called *Peh*.

It says, "Give glory to the Lord your God," since *Peh* is glory, for there is no merit to the high King unless when Israel establish this glory, which is the kingship, and give it to the King of Glory.

That is, all our work is to aim all of our actions to raise the *Shechina* from the dust, meaning to raise *Malchut*. This means that we take upon ourselves the kingdom of heaven to make her respectable, to understand her merit, and that it is worthy to work for the sake of the Creator and not for our own sake.

Yet, this work is difficult because it is against nature. Hence, this work causes us many ascents and descents, until sometimes a person despairs and says, "This work is not for me," and wants to escape the campaign since he sees no progress in the work. Moreover, he sees that he has regressed and not progressed, namely that now he is more immersed in self-love, and that before he began the work of bestowal, he was not so worldly.

It follows that now he sees that he has more evil. But the question is, What is the truth? Was all the effort he had put into achieving love of the Creator pointless and useless? According to the rule that our sages said, "One should always see oneself as half guilty, half innocent. If he commits one Mitzva [singular of Mitzvot], happy is he, for he has sentenced himself to the side of merit." Thus, the question is, Once he has sentenced himself to the side of merit, how can he be half guilty, half innocent, since now he is mostly worthy?

We should answer according to what our sages said (Sukkah 52), "Anyone who is greater than his friend, his inclination is greater than him." But why is he given a greater evil inclination? The answer is that each time a person subdues some evil and the evil enters the Kedusha [holiness], he is given a bigger portion of evil to correct. It follows that now that he has subdued the previous evil, he is given evil once again, and more of it. That is, according to the measure of the good, so he is given a measure of the bad.

Thus, according to the rule, "Anyone who is greater than his friend, his inclination is greater than him," it means that the good and the bad are always of equal weight. It therefore follows that the evil is recognized only according to the extent of good that a person has obtained, and to that extent, the evil in him appears.

Accordingly, one who has only a little bit of good will have only a little bit of bad, for otherwise he will not be balanced and will not be able to make a choice, for the bad will be more than the good. For this reason, a person is shown the evil in him only to the extent of the good in him, meaning that a person is always in a state of half good and half bad.

It turns out that through descents and ascents, the evil is gradually corrected, and a person must always remember and believe what our sages said, "He who comes to purify is aided." However, a person must give an awakening from below, and then he is rewarded with a *Peh* of *Kedusha*, as was said, "Give a mouth, give glory to the Lord your God."

What Are Spies in the Work?

Article No. 33, Tav-Shin-Mem-Tet, 1988/89

It is written in *The Zohar* (*Shlach*, Item 18): "I looked in this verse, since Solomon said, 'For the fate of the sons of men and the fate of beasts is the same. As one dies so dies the other, and there is one spirit to all,' for here there is an opening for the faithless. He replies, 'He repeats those words that the fools of the world say—that this world is runs on chance and the Creator does not oversee them. Rather, the fate of man and the fate of beast is the same.' What did Solomon (tell) them? He said, 'Who knows the spirit of the sons of men, if it ascends upward? And the spirit of the beast, if it descends down to the earth?' Does it go up to the high place, and the spirit of the beast, does it descend down to the earth, as it is written about it, 'He has made man in the image of God,' and it is written, 'Man's soul, the Lord's candle.'"

It follows that there is a question: Since Solomon said, "For the fate of the sons of men and the fate of beasts is the same. As one dies so dies the other, and there is one spirit to all," *The Zohar* asks, Does this mean that Solomon opens a door to those who are faithless? It replies that Solomon said this in the eyes of the fools. When Solomon looked at the fools, he called them "beast," as it

294

is written, "I said to myself concerning the sons of men: 'God has sorted them to see that they are but beasts.'" "Sorted" means that God sorts them out so they remain alone and do not connect to people and bring this view to people.

What did Solomon reply to them? "Who knows the spirit of the sons of men, if it ascends upward?" meaning to a high place, a holy place, to feed on the upper light, while the spirit of the beast, which descends down to the earth, and not to that place that is for all the sons of men?

We should understand this in the work. That is, how we learn this in one person, who consists of all those states, meaning has all the questions. The thing is that when a person wants to begin to observe Torah and *Mitzvot* [commandments/good deeds], the person sends spies to spy on the work of the Creator to see if it is worthwhile. At that time the evil inclination shows him images of those who engage in Torah and *Mitzvot*, that they are concerned only with their own benefit. They say that they are servants of the Creator, but he sees that they are working for themselves. The only difference is that they say that they want the Creator to pay for their work, and secular people say that they settle for payment from a person like himself. Yet, they all work for their own benefit.

But we heard that you say that our sages said, "The wicked in their lives are called 'dead,'" for because the Creator is the giver, those who work for their own benefit are separated from the Life of Lives and are therefore called "dead." They even present evidence to their words in what our sages said (*Berachot* 17), "Anyone who engages in Torah *Lo Lishma* [not for Her sake] is better off not being born."

Therefore, *The Zohar* says about the spies within man that Solomon said about them, meaning repeated those words that the fools of the world say—that this world runs on chance and the Creator does not watch over them, but rather the fate of man and the fate of beast are the same; as one dies, so dies the other, and all have the same spirit. That is, both are called "dead"; whether religious or secular, all work for their own sake.

Solomon said, "Who knows the spirit of the sons of men, if it ascends upward? And the spirit of the beast, if it descends down to the earth?" That is, we must believe the words of our sages, who said (*Pesachim* 50), "One should always engage in Torah and *Mitzvot*, even if *Lo Lishma*, since from *Lo Lishma* he comes to *Lishma* [for Her sake]."

Therefore, although when he begins the work, he begins *Lo Lishma*, meaning for his own sake, like the people who are as beasts, meaning engage only in beastly lusts, but those who engage in beastly lusts, what degree will they ultimately achieve? Solomon said about this that they will achieve the degree, "the spirit of the beast," which "descends down to the earth." That is, they will remain in earthliness, in vessels of reception for their own sake, which is the lowest thing, called "earth."

But those who engage in Torah and *Mitzvot*, although it is *Lo Lishma*, meaning for their own sake, still, from *Lo Lishma* he comes to *Lishma*. For this reason, they will emerge from self-love and achieve equivalence of form called "*Dvekut* [adhesion] with the Creator," and will be rewarded with life, as it is written, "And you who cling to the Lord your God are alive every one of you this day."

This is why Solomon says, "Who knows the spirit of the sons of men, if it ascends upward," to a high place? "Who knows" means we must believe in the words of our sages, who said, "And from *Lo Lishma*, he comes to *Lishma*," and "He who comes to purify is aided." Thus, he who knows how to appreciate this and believe in the words of our sages will therefore achieve *Dvekut* with the Creator, which is regarded as "the spirit of man." That is, it is those who engage in the quality of "man," although they are still in the quality of "beast," meaning still engaging only for their own benefit.

Baal HaSulam interpreted the verse, "will give wisdom to the wise." A common question is, It should have said, "will give wisdom to the fools." He answered in regard to this, that he who wants to be wise is already called "wise." But one who has no desire for wisdom is called a "fool," as it is written, "The fool has no desire for understanding."

Therefore, those who want to be "men," as our sages said, "You are called 'men,' and the nations of the world are not called 'men,' where "nations of the world" means the self-love within a person; this is called "the nations of the world." But "Israel" means *Yashar-El* [straight to the Creator], meaning that within "Israel," everything he has is straight to the Creator.

For this reason, one who wants to walk on the path toward achieving the quality of "man," the verse says about him, "the spirit of the sons of men, if it ascends upward," to the high place, meaning to the Creator, as it is written about it, "He has made man in the image of God," and as it is written, "Man's soul, the Lord's candle."

This means that "in the image of God" means that as the Creator is the giver, so man should achieve this degree of being a giver. Yet, since man begins the work in *Lo Lishma*, how can he achieve the degree of a giver? The answer is as our sages said, "He who comes to purify is aided." *The Zohar* asks, "With what?" and it replies, "with a holy soul." That is, the Creator gives him a soul by which he receives the assistance. This is the meaning of "Man's soul, God's candle."

This is the meaning of the verse, "I said to myself concerning the sons of men: 'God has sorted them.'" *The Zohar* interprets that "sorted" means that God sorted them out so they remain alone and do not connect to the sons of men, so they will not express this view to people. In the work, this means that a person should be careful from the argument of his spies, who want to bring him the view of the beast and say that he should not mind the view of man, meaning that the body can achieve the quality of man, and their beastly view does not let them consider the view of man. For this reason, Solomon warns them that they need extra care not to be lured after their view.

This is why he says, "sorted," meaning he sorted them so they remain alone. This means that the spies come with complaints that they have the same fate, meaning that both remain as "dead," meaning separated, since they both work for their own sake, and both are called "the wicked in their lives are called 'dead.'" Yet, we must brace ourselves and not listen to the spies or look at their view when they say it is a waste of work since in any case, you will remain as "the wicked in their lives are called 'dead,'" so why work for nothing if you know you will not gain anything? By this, these fools, who are as beasts, govern man's body.

But the main argument of the spies is that it is true that it would be worthwhile to work for the sake of the Creator if the taste of Torah and Mitzvot were revealed, at least to the extent that the pleasure in beastly lusts is revealed. But we see that in Torah and Mitzvot, of which we say that "They are our lives and the length of our days," we have no taste of feeling, while in beastly lusts we do feel the taste. So, why did the Creator place such a concealment before us? It would be better if the Creator revealed Himself to the lower ones. Why do we need to do everything in faith, since the path of faith pushes people away from walking in the path of the Creator? Therefore, the spies say, this way is completely unacceptable.

Baal HaSulam said about this, that if the taste of Torah and Mitzvot were revealed, it would be impossible to have free choice, meaning to do something for the sake of the Creator. In corporeal pleasures, we see that there, the ARI said that all the flavors we have in corporeality are but a tiny light compared to what is found in spirituality, and how difficult it is to direct them in order to bestow. Certainly, with great pleasures, it will be utterly impossible to observe them in order to bestow.

We could ask, If His Providence were revealed in the form of The Good Who Does Good, all creations would annul before Him "as a candle before a torch." The answer is that when the delight and pleasure are felt, the will to receive cannot look at the shame. Instead, it wants to receive despite the shame, just as in corporeal lusts, a person does not look at any shame, and the passion drives him to receive. Only afterward he regrets, meaning after the passion has left him, he begins to be ashamed of how he behaved like a beast, without any shame. This is the meaning of what our sages said, "The wicked are full of remorse," for in the work, "wicked" means that the person himself comes to feel that he is wicked. Then he begins to be ashamed of what he had done.

It is likewise in spirituality. If the delight and pleasure were revealed, the person would receive it in order to receive. Only afterward, once he has satisfied his wish, he would be ashamed. But he would have no way to correct himself. But while there is concealment, and a person begins to work with faith above reason, the person begins to exercise prohibiting self-reception. For this reason, once he has exerted in the work of bestowal, although the person cannot achieve this degree without help from above, when he asks for help, he asks to be given help to have the strength to receive in order to bestow. For this reason, it cannot be said that the person would see the greatness of the Creator and would annul before Him. Rather, he would receive a pleasure of the will to receive for himself.

But when a person first works in order to bestow during the period of concealment, he says to the Creator, "I want to serve You unconditionally, even if I do not feel Your greatness. I want to believe that You are great and worth serving." It follows that he agrees to serve the Creator unconditionally. Although he cannot, he asks the Creator to give him this power to serve even without any feeling, but only for the sake of the Creator.

When a person achieves this degree, where he is willing to work without any reward, our sages call this learning "Torah *Lishma*," without any reward. At that time, he is rewarded with the revelation of the secrets of Torah.

At that time begins the work of the *Masachim* [screens], when he can already see the meal. However, at that time he must calculate how much of the meal he can receive in order to bestow. That much he should take, and not more.

It follows that we should discern here, for example, that he sees that he was given, for example, five dishes of food. Yet, he only sees them. He does not know how they taste because he has not tasted any of them. But since he is a faithful person, meaning he is certain that he will not receive in order to receive, he can already see the meal, since he has achieved the degree of not receiving in order to receive.

For this reason, although he sees the meal, he still did not taste, prior to making a *Zivug de Hakaa* [lit. coupling by striking] called the "intention," how much of the meal he can receive in order to bestow. Once he has made the *Zivug de Hakaa*, he tastes from the meal. But if he still cannot receive in order to bestow, the *Tzimtzum* [restriction] and concealment are still on him and he cannot see a thing. Hence, precisely when a person can work without any reason or intellect, but only above reason, which is called *Lishma*, then he is rewarded with the secrets of Torah.

It follows that the primary sin of the spies is that although they do not lie, but tell the truth, for they speak according to their intellect and reason, therefore, the whole sin is that they do not believe that the Creator helps everyone, that we must believe that "The Lord supports all the fallen." If a person says that he is so lowly that the Creator cannot help him, he is blemishing the faith, for he does not believe that the Creator is almighty. In such states, when such thoughts come to a person, it is very difficult for him.

And the hardest is that a person thinks he sees the truth. He does not blame anyone for his escaping from the campaign, but says, "It's true that the Creator is righteous, but what can I do if I haven't the power to overcome my will to receive, since my bad qualities are not like those of others? Therefore, I must leave the work and I have nothing more to hope for."

But sometimes he says otherwise: "I am not saying that my friends are better. Rather, it is that they do not really see the truth and think that they are doing something in spirituality. For this reason, they do not feel the situation in the current state—that they are not moving one step forward. This is why they can continue the work and no lack is apparent in their work. This is why they are always content."

It does not matter what is the reason for which a person escapes the campaign. What matters is that at that time, it is difficult for a person to believe that the Creator can help everyone, that with respect to Him, it cannot be said that He can help only the great ones, but not the small ones. It follows that by this he blemishes the faith in the Creator. Instead, a person must believe what is said, that "The Lord supports all the fallen."

It therefore follows that the matter of spies is for lack of faith. That is, all the faults they mention to a person: 1) That it is difficult because it contradicts the body's nature, since the body wants to exist, and here it is told that it must serve the Creator "with all your heart and with all your soul." This is from the perspective of the heart. 2) We must believe that all the work is based on a foundation that is above reason. Thus, how is it possible to walk on this path?

We therefore see that these spies are not lying. So what is the sin in the words of the spies, who slandered the land of Israel, as *The Zohar* says, that the land of Israel means the kingdom of heaven, called "the land of Israel," and this pertains only to the quality of "Israel"? But they said, "We do not see that it is possible to be rewarded with it for the two above reasons." Thus, the sin is that they did not believe in the greatness of the Creator, that He is almighty, and had no faith in the sages, who said, "He who comes to purify is aided."

Hence, the correction is to pray to the Creator, that only He can help with this, and believe that "You hear the prayer of every mouth," as Baal HaSulam explained that "every mouth" means even the lowest possible mouth.

What Is Peace
in the Work?

Article No. 34, Tav-Shin-Mem-Tet, 1988/89

The verse says, "Therefore say, 'Behold, I give him My covenant of peace ... because he was jealous for his God and made atonement for the children of Israel.'"

We should understand this in the work. 1) What is, "because he was jealous for his God"? 2) What is, "and made atonement for the children of Israel"? 3) What is "My covenant of peace"?

It is known that the order of the work is that a person must achieve the completion of the goal, which is that he will receive the delight and pleasure that was in His desire to do good to His creations. However, in order for man to merit receiving it, he must fight with the *Sitra Achra* [other side], which is the quality of the "nations of the world," which opposes the quality of "Israel."

"Israel" means that all their actions are *Yashar-El* [straight to the Creator], while the "nations of the world" are the opposite of *Kedusha* [holiness], and want everything for their own sake, for which they are separated from the Life of Lives. Because of this, they are called "dead," as it is written, "The mercy of the nations is a sin," and *The Zohar* interprets, "All the good that they do, they do for themselves." This means that they only work for their own benefit, since man is born with a desire to receive for himself, which is a *Klipa* [shell/peel].

It is written in the "Introduction to The Book of Zohar" (Item 11), "And he remains under the authority of that system for the first thirteen years, which is the time of corruption. And by engaging in *Mitzvot* [commandments/good deeds] from thirteen years of age onward, in order to bestow contentment upon his Maker, he begins to purify the will to receive for himself, imprinted in him, and slowly turns it to be in order to bestow. By this he extends a holy soul from its root in the thought of creation. And it passes through the system of the worlds of *Kedusha* and dresses in the body. This is the time of correction. And so he accumulates degrees of *Kedusha* from the thought of creation in *Ein Sof* [Infinity], until they aid him in turning the will to receive for himself in him, to work entirely in order to bestow contentment upon his Maker, and not at all for his own benefit. By this one acquires equivalence of form with his Maker."

It therefore follows that a person should qualify himself to have equivalence of form, for precisely through vessels of bestowal he can receive the completeness of delight and pleasure. However, in order to be rewarded with vessels of bestowal, which are vessels that work for the sake of the Creator, and which are against the nature with which man is born, since man is born the opposite—with a desire to receive only for himself—therefore, as long as he works for reward and punishment, called *Lo Lishma* [not for Her sake], the body does not resist the work so much.

But when a person wants to engage in the holy work, to make it a means by which to obtain vessels of bestowal—which is completely against nature—the body comes with "who" and "what" questions, meaning questions corresponding to the mind and to the heart, which is called "spies." Although the person overcomes each time, the order is that then the entire order of the work is in ascents and descents, and a person comes to a state where he wants to give up on ever achieving equivalence of form.

Also, many times he wants to escape the campaign because he sees that his work is in vain and he has no reason to hope that it will ever be good, as he sees from the past. For this reason, many people who begin the work of bestowal, see that it is too difficult and therefore leave this work and say that this work is only for great people, and not for ones like him.

This is the time when a person has complaints and demands to the Creator, and he is in dispute with the Creator and argues, 1) Why did the Creator create him with a nature of wanting to receive? 2) Why does the Creator want him to cancel his vessels of reception? After all, the Creator is good and does good, so why is He not behaving toward us as we understand? We understand the ascents and descents in such a way that sometimes, during the ascent, we are at peace with the Creator and say about Him that He leads the world as the good who does good. But during the descent, we haven't the strength to say that He behaves with a guidance of the good who does good. Hence, we are always in dispute.

Indeed, why is the order of the work so difficult that it requires ascents and descents? The known answer to this is what is written, "As the advantage of the light from within the darkness." In other words, it is impossible to receive light if he has no lack and need for the light.

For this reason, when a person sees that the nations of the world in him object to the Creator, and he cannot tolerate the enemy of Israel within him, he becomes jealous for his God and does not look at any descents he has, and does what he can and cries out to the Creator to help him be able to defeat the wicked ones within him.

By this he overcomes and does not escape the campaign. At that time, the Creator gives him the covenant. That is, he makes a covenant with Him that there will be peace between him and the Creator, by receiving a gift from the Creator, which is the vessels of bestowal. This is regarded as making the covenant, which is the Klipa [shell/peel], called "will to receive for himself," and instead of the foreskin, the Creator gives him vessels of bestowal, and by this they make a covenant, meaning peace.

It follows that through one's jealousy for one's God, when he sees that all the nations of the world in his body slander the work when a person wants to work for the sake of the Creator, even though a person often overcomes their views and says, "I am certain that the Creator will help me, as it is written, "He who comes to purify is aided," they laugh at him and tell him, "But you see for yourself how many times you said that the Creator would help you, yet you are standing in the same situation as when you started to work. Therefore, leave this path."

Here, a person needs great strengthening, called "because he was jealous for his God." At that time a person prays to the Creator and says, "Not to us, O Lord, not to us, but to Your name give glory. Why should the nations say, 'Where is their God?'"

It turns out that at that time, a person cries out for the glory of the Creator, how the nations within him mock him when he says, "I trust the Creator to help me." At that time, they say, "Where is their God, for you, Israel, say that the Creator will help you?" And when a person is jealous for the Creator, when he is concerned with the glory of the Shechina [Divinity], meaning regrets that the Shechina is in the dust, and cannot stand how they despise the work in order to bestow, this is called what is written about Pinhas, "Therefore say, 'Behold, I give him My covenant of peace, because he was jealous for his God.'"

This is as it is written in the book Shamati [I Heard] (Essay No. 1), that when a person regrets the Creator not bringing him closer, he should be careful that it will not be for his own sake, meaning because he is far from the Creator, since by this he becomes a receiver for his own benefit, and a receiver is in separation. Instead, he should regret the exile of the Shechina, meaning that he is causing the sorrow of the Shechina. A person should depict to himself that it is like a person feeling pain in some small organ. Nonetheless, the pain is felt primarily in the mind and in the heart, for the mind and the heart are the whole of man. Likewise, the pain that a person feels when he is far from the Creator, since man is but a particular part of the holy *Shechina*, and the *Shechina* is the whole of the soul of Israel, for this reason, the personal pain is incomparable with the general pain. This is called the "sorrow of the *Shechina*."

When a person regrets this, it is called "because he was jealous for his God." To such a person, the Creator says, "I give him My covenant of peace." "Peace" means as it is written (Psalms 85), "I will hear what God the Lord will say, for He will speak peace unto His people and unto His followers, and let them not turn back to folly." In other words, at that time the Creator tells them "Peace," meaning that then, peace is made because the Creator gives him as a present, the vessels of bestowal, and naturally, he no longer has anyone who objects to working for the sake of the Creator.

But before he receives the covenant of peace, all the vessels of reception, which belong to the nations of the world, object to a person working for the sake of the Creator, as it is written, "I will hear what God the Lord will say, for He will speak peace, and let them not turn back to folly."

This means that they will no longer have descents, where they want to work for their own benefit, since a "fool" is one who does not walk on the path of *Kedusha*. But one who wants to walk on the path of *Kedusha*, that all his actions will be in order to bestow, is called "wise." It is as Baal HaSulam said, "Who is a wise disciple? He who learns from the Creator, who is called 'Wise.'" In other words, he learns from Him the quality, "as He is merciful, so you are merciful." This means that when a person learns to be a giver just as the Creator is the giver, he is called "wise." It follows that the opposite is called a "fool."

Thus, the fact that a person has been rewarded with the covenant of peace is "because he was jealous for his God," meaning that he saw that the nations of the world in him despise the holy work, which is to work for the sake of the Creator.

This is the meaning of what is written, "and made atonement for the children of Israel." That is, he was jealous for his God in that he wants that by this there will be atonement for the children of Israel, so they will have the strength to work for the sake of the Creator, which is called *Yashar-El*, meaning that they will be able to work for the sake of the Creator. By this they are rewarded with His covenant, so he will not turn back to folly.

However, there is a difficult question here: What can one do if he hasn't the power of jealousy, and when he hears the argument of the spies and wants to run away from them so as not to hear the slander they speak, but as much as he moves away from them, they awaken in him a desire and yearning to nonetheless listen to what they say, and at that moment he descends from his degree and falls into their net?

The only advice for this is prayer. That is, he should ask the Creator not to be taken after the view of the spies. But only when the thoughts of the spies chase him, this is the heart of the work not to be taken after the spies. But why indeed is there room for the argument of the spies? The answer is that it is impossible to feel a good taste in the light unless from within the darkness, as it is written, "As the advantage of the light from within the darkness."

It is written in *Midrash Rabbah* (96): "Her ways are ways of pleasantness and all her paths are peace. All that is written in the Torah, was written for the purpose of peace. And even though wars are written in the Torah, even the wars were written for the purpose of peace."

We should understand what it means that the wars were written for the purpose of peace, and that because of it, the Torah is called "and all her paths are peace." There must be explanations to this in the literal, but in the work, we should interpret that we asked, Why do we need the argument of the spies and all those descents?

We explained that the reason is that it is impossible to understand anything except according to the need for the matter. Since "There is no filling without a lack," it follows that all the wars that were written in the Torah, when pertaining to the work, it follows that all the wars are in relation to work. And since it is impossible to feel a good taste in peace if there is no war, meaning that only when there is the war of the inclination, which wants to work only for itself, and a person wants to work for the sake of the Creator, then there is the matter of darkness, meaning ascents and descents. Then, a need is born within man that the Creator will help him, since he sees that by himself, he does not see how he will be able to emerge from the control of self-love.

At that time, he truly needs the Creator to help him. Then the Creator gives him "My covenant of peace." That is, the Creator gives him a gift: vessels of bestowal, by which he is rewarded with *Dvekut* [adhesion] with the Creator. And then the verse, "And you shall love the Lord your God with all your heart" comes true, as our sages said, "with both your inclinations, the good inclination and the evil inclination." This is called "My covenant of peace."

What Is, "He Who Is Without Sons," in the Work?

Article No. 35, Tav-Shin-Mem-Tet, 1988/89

Our sages said (*Masechet Nedarim* 64), "Any person without sons as regarded as dead." *The Zohar* (Pinhas, Item 92) writes, "A man without sons is called 'barren,' and his wife is called 'barren.' Likewise, Torah without *Mitzvot* [commandments/good deeds] is called 'barren.' For this reason, we learn that it is not the learning that is most important, but the act." Also in *The Zohar* (Item 91), it says, "The Torah is called 'a tree,' as it is written, 'It is a tree of life for they who hold it.' Also, man is a tree, as it is written, 'For man is the tree of the field,' and the *Mitzvot* in the Torah are as fruits." In other words, since the Torah and man are called "tree," therefore, as a tree that does not bear fruit is akin to a barren person, who begets nothing, so man and the Torah are called "barren" if they have no sons.

We should understand this. We can understand that a man and a tree who do not bear are called "barren." But if a person learns Torah but does not observe the *Mitzvot* of the Torah, why is the Torah called "barren"? Why is it the fault of the Torah if a person does not want to observe the *Mitzvot* in the Torah? In this regard, he references what our sages said, "Great is the learning that leads to action." This means that the Torah should lead to action, and if it does not, it is as though the Torah is to blame for not leading to action. Thus, it is as though the fault does not lie with the person, but with the Torah. Can this be?

To understand the above said, we should first understand the whole issue of Torah and *Mitzvot* that the Creator gave us, and for which we bless Him for this gift, as we say, "Who has chosen us from among all the nations and has given us His law [in Hebrew: Torah]." We understand the matter of Torah in two ways, as it is written in *The Zohar* ("Introduction of The Book of Zohar," "General Explanation for All Fourteen Commandments and How They Divide into the Seven Days of Creation"): "The *Mitzvot* in the Torah are called *Pekudin* [commands/deposits], as well as 613 *Etzot* [counsels/tips]. The difference between them is that in all things there is *Panim* [anterior/face] and *Achor* [posterior/back]. The preparation for something is called *Achor*, and the attainment of the matter is called *Panim*. Similarly, in Torah and *Mitzvot* there are 'We shall do' and 'We shall hear.' When observing Torah and *Mitzvot* as 'doers of His word,' prior to being rewarded with hearing, the *Mitzvot* are called '613 *Etzot*,' and are regarded as *Achor*. When rewarded with 'hearing the voice of His word,' the 613 *Mitzvot* become *Pekudin*, from the word *Pikadon* [deposit]. This is so because there are 613 *Mitzvot*, and in each *Mitzva* [singular of *Mitzvot*], the light of a unique degree is deposited, and this is the *Panim* of the *Mitzvot*."

Yet, we should know and understand the matter of Torah and *Mitzvot* in general, how "doing" pertains there, and what is the meaning of "hearing." That is, if hearing is the most important, for what purpose does one need to begin the order of the work as "doers of His word," which is called *Achor*? Why do we not begin with *Panim*, called *Pekudin*, right away? It seems as though this work is pointless.

It is known that there are two matters before us: the purpose of creation and the correction of creation. The purpose of creation is that His desire is to do good to His creations, meaning that the created beings will receive from Him delight and pleasure. For this reason, He created in the creatures a desire to receive pleasure. In order to calm the yearning that exists in the created beings, this *Kli* [vessel], namely the desire to receive delight and pleasure, comes from the Creator because He created it for His purpose, for without yearning for something, it is impossible to enjoy it. It is known that the whole pleasure from something can be received only according to the yearning for it. This is the measure of the pleasure, and it does not matter what a person wants, but the yearning for something makes it important.

Therefore, this *Kli* that comes from the Creator has completeness. That is, wherever a person sees that he can elicit pleasure from something, he promptly does all that he can to obtain the pleasure. But the *Kli* that the creatures must make is in oppositeness of form from the *Kli* of the Creator, and this is very difficult to do because it contradicts the quality of the *Kli* that the Creator created. A person cannot create this *Kli*, as our sages said, "Man's inclination overcomes him every day, and were it not for the help of the Creator, he would not overcome it."

The question is, If a person cannot overcome it, what must he do if only the Creator can give the overcoming over the evil inclination? The answer is that a person must begin the overcoming, meaning he must see that he has a desire to defeat the evil inclination. If a person has no desire to defeat it, how can he be given help? Help means that a person wants something that is difficult to obtain. Then it can be said that he is given help to obtain what he wants. But when a person has no desire, how can we say that we are helping him get something that makes him suffer? "Help" means that a person is given help so he will enjoy, not that he is given help so he will suffer.

For this reason, if a person truly wants to do the work of the Creator in *Lishma* [for Her sake], which is in order to bestow, he must want to do everything for the sake of the Creator. When a person truly wants to work for the sake of the Creator, the body begins to show its might, that it wants a person to do everything specifically for one's own sake, and resists this work with all its might, presenting him with all the arguments of the spies that it is right. Then, if someone comes and helps him, that person will be happy with this help and will be very grateful for the help. Then it can be said that he is receiving help from above, as our sages said, "He who comes to purify is aided."

Yet, if a person did not begin this work, two things are missing: 1) He thinks that he does not need help, that he can do this if he wants to, that he is a man. Therefore, he has no need for help. It follows that he has no *Kli* for the light. 2) If he did not exert in order to achieve the state of "All your works will be for the sake of heaven," then he does not even want to be given the strength not to work for his own sake but for the sake of the Creator. Instead, he wants to work for his own sake. If he hears that by observing Torah and *Mitzvot* he will have nothing for his own sake, he regards it as a curse, not as a blessing.

For this reason, he must begin this work on his own. Then, he gradually acquires a desire that it is worthwhile to work for the sake of the Creator, and the procession of ascents and descents begins for him. That is, once he sees that it is worthwhile to work for the sake of the Creator, and once he surrenders to the argument of the body, which asks, "What is this work for you?" Working for the sake of the Creator. Through the ascents and descents, he begins to understand the benefit in working in order to bestow, and what he loses if he cannot emerge from self-love.

When a person overcomes and does not escape the campaign, but overcomes and increases his prayer that the Creator will help him and give him the help required to be able to emerge from receiving for himself, then he needs great overcoming to believe that the Creator will help him. That is, he must believe that everything he sees, that it is harder to emerge from the control of the receiver, and sees that each time, he begins to see that his evil is worse than that of others, at that time he must say that now the Creator will certainly help him because "Now I have come to know the truth, that without the Creator's help, it is impossible."

All the actions he contemplated doing so as to help him emerge from the control of the receiver did not help him. On the contrary, the receiver grew stronger and shows greater resistance to the work in order to bestow. At that time, a person must overcome and not yield to the counsel of the spies, but overcome above reason that the Creator will help, as our sages promised us, "He who comes to purify is aided."

However, from where can one receive the strength to overcome so he can have faith in the sages? This is only by the power of the Torah. It is as our sages said, "The Creator said, 'I have created the evil inclination; I have created the Torah as a spice.'" That is, through the Torah, he receives the power to overcome during the war, when he must acquire Kelim [vessels] of darkness so that afterwards he will have the discernment, "As the advantage of the light from within the darkness." It follows that the Torah sustains him during the work until the Creator knows he has Kelim that are suitable to receive the light, and then he is rewarded with 613 Pekudin.

However, during the work, while he still has spies, the Torah and Mitzvot are called 613 Etzot, meaning 613 counsels how to be saved from the spies. Hence, when a person engages in Torah and Mitzvot, he should aim that the reward he wants for his work will be the strength to fight against the spies.

It follows that he wants the Torah to give him this reward. If he does not receive this strength, then the Torah is like a tree that does not bear fruit, or a person who has no sons. In other words, the Torah did not beget for him the sons, which are the powers to fight against the spies. When the Torah does give him this strength, it is called "a tree that bears fruit," and it is like a person who has sons.

By this we will understand what we asked, Why is man like a tree? It means that both must yield fruit. And as the tree must be given what it needs in order for it to bear fruit, which is called "tilling the land," so man must give himself the nourishments he needs in order to be able to achieve the goal, called 613 Pekudin [deposits], meaning to observe Torah and *Mitzvot* with the aim that the light in it will reform him.

Thus, we need action, which is to turn the will to receive for oneself, which is man's tool of action, into vessels of bestowal. This is called "turning the vessels of reception into vessels of bestowal."

This is called "action." That is, since man is unable to do this action, then as the Creator gave us vessels of reception, He should give us vessels of bestowal. However, "there is no light without a *Kli*," as said above, "there is no filling without a lack." For this reason, a person must work and execute all the tactics at his disposal in order to satisfy that need. To the extent of his work, he receives a need for the Creator to help him in this. At that time the Creator gives these tools of action called "vessels of bestowal." This is done through the Torah and *Mitzvot*, since "the light in it reforms him."

This is the meaning of what is written, "Which God has created to do." As Baal HaSulam said, "created" means something new, existence from absence. This refers to the will to receive, which is something new because before He created it, there was no concept of reception in reality. It follows that the Creator created the will to receive, and the creatures must turn it into a desire to bestow. This is the meaning of "do," to make of it a desire to bestow.

Yet, we cannot change the work of creation, and if the Creator created it in such a way that the will to receive is what operates, how can it be changed? The answer is that man must seek advice how to come to the desire for it. This is called "doing." Although we said that a person cannot do this, but the Creator Himself must do this, since we cannot change the work of creation, it is still named after the person.

We can understand this through what Baal HaSulam said about the verse, "will give wisdom to the wise." He asked, "It should have said, 'will give wisdom to the fools.'" He replied that "wise" is he who seeks wisdom although he still does not have it, for a fool does not seek wisdom, as was said, "The fool will not desire wisdom." For this reason, when a person seeks advice and tactics how to obtain vessels of bestowal, this is called "doing," as was said, "to do."

By this we can interpret what is written, "It is not the learning that matters most, but the work." *The Zohar* brings evidence that if he has no Mitzvot but only Torah, he is called "barren" and the Torah is called "barren," since the Torah has no fruits, which are Mitzvot, and man has no sons. This implies what our sages said, "Any person without sons is regarded as dead." When we speak of work, this will mean that one who has no Mitzvot is considered "barren," as *The Zohar* likens him to the Torah, when it says "tree of life." Also, "Man is a tree of the field" means that the Torah being called "barren" if he has no Mitzvot was said about the person. That is, a person must know that for him, the Torah is barren if the Torah he is learning does not lead him to Mitzvot. *The Zohar* says about this, "For this reason, we learn that it is not the learning that is most important, but the act." Hence, if the Torah does not have the Mitzvot of the Torah, the Torah is considered barren.

By this we can interpret what we asked, Why is the Torah called "barren" is a person has no Mitzvot? The Torah is called "barren" with respect to him because "it is not the learning that is most important, but the act." That is, since the Creator said, "I have created the evil inclination; I have created the Torah as a spice," it means that for a person to be able to defeat the evil in him, it takes the light of Torah. Thus, one who learns Torah but does not intend for the Torah to bring him the light, so he can do his actions for the sake of the Creator, which is against the evil inclination, for the evil in man wants to work specifically for one's own sake, and resists with all its might to aim for the sake of the Creator, and it cannot be defeated. For this reason, the Creator has given us the counsel of the power of the Torah, meaning that the Torah should give us the strength, through the light in it, which reforms him.

This means that the Torah turns the bad in a person into good, meaning that through the Torah, he can obtain the vessels of bestowal. This is called "action," as was said, "Which God has created to do."

It therefore follows that if the Torah does not give the assistance it is meant to give, it is regarded that the Torah is barren in that person. And a person who receives the Torah without the assistance it is meant to give, both the person and the Torah are called "barren," meaning they engender nothing.

Now we can interpret what our sages said (*Nedarim* 81), "Why do wise disciples not yield wise disciples from their sons? Because they do not bless in the Torah first." The reason for this is very difficult to understand. We see that even simple landlords say the blessing of the Torah when they are invited for the reading of the Torah [on the Sabbath service]. They, too, say the blessing. So how can it be that wise disciples do not bless in the Torah first? According to the above-said, we should interpret learning Torah and not aiming why are they learning prior to the learning of Torah, meaning what they want to achieve in return for engaging in Torah, since nothing is done unless to bring them some benefit.

The answer is that they did not bless in the Torah first. That is, they did not have the initial intent that the Torah will bring them blessing, and blessing means bestowal. In other words, they did not intend for the Torah to give them *Kelim* of blessing, meaning vessels of bestowal. This is why their Torah cannot deliver sons that will be recognizable as wise disciples. Instead, the Torah they learn does not yield for them *Mitzvot*, which are acts of bestowal; they remain barren, and their Torah is barren.

In other words, these wise disciples who are learning Torah do not beget their sons, meaning the acts called *Mitzvot*, that it will be evident that they come from wise disciples, meaning that they are good deeds, called "acts of bestowal" that the light of Torah engendered. This is called "Wise disciples do not yield wise disciples from their sons," meaning it is not evident by their actions that they had to be born by the light of Torah, which is called "wise disciple." That is, they learn Torah and the light of Torah should yield actions, meaning that all his actions will be for the sake of the Creator and to be rewarded with *Dvekut* with the Creator, to adhere to the Life of Lives. Why do they not have it? It is because "they did not bless in the Torah first." That is, prior to learning Torah, they did not aim their minds that they are going to learn in order to the light of Torah to bring them the *Segula* [remedy/power/quality] that it will reform them.

Accordingly, we can understand what our sages said, "Any person without sons as regarded as dead," since sons are *Mitzvot*, meaning that all the *Mitzvot* he does are in order to bestow. This is called *Dvekut* with the Life of Lives. Naturally, if he has no vessels of bestowal, he is separated from the Life of Lives, and is therefore regarded as dead, as our sages said, "The wicked in their lives are called 'dead.'"

Now we can understand what our sages said about the verse, "Zion, no one demands her, meaning that a demand is required." This means that Zion is called *Malchut* [kingdom/kingship], meaning the kingdom of heaven. This means that all of one's actions should be for the sake of the Creator and not for his own sake, as it is written, "I remember God and I moan when I see every city built on its ruins, and the city of God lowered to the bottom of the netherworld."

That is, that which concerns his own benefit is fine, and everyone tries that this will be in utter completeness. But the "city of God," which is the holy work, to work for the sake of the Creator, this work is one of lowliness.

This requires the light of Torah. That is, one who learns Torah, before he learns, he must demand of the Torah to give him this light so he can work for the sake of the Creator.

What Is "For It Is Your Wisdom and Understanding in the Eyes of the Nations," in the Work?

Article No. 36, Tav-Shin-Mem-Tet, 1988/89

It is written (Deuteronomy 4:6), "So keep and do them, for it is your wisdom and your understanding in the eyes of the nations, who will hear all these statutes and say, 'Surely this great nation is a wise and understanding nation.'"

We should understand this, since we do not see that the nations of the world are saying that Israel is a "wise and understanding nation."

Also, it appears from the text that specifically by "keep and do them," the nations will see the wisdom and understanding in the people of Israel. Even within the people of Israel we see that the secular despise the religious for observing the Torah and Mitzvot [commandments/good deeds], so how can we say that the nations of the world will respect the people of Israel for keeping them and doing them?

We should interpret this in the work. It is known that in the work, the person himself is a small world consisting of all the nations in the world. Since each nation has its own specific lust, as it is known that there are seven qualities of *Kedusha* [holiness], and opposite them seven qualities of *Tuma'a* [impurity], and each quality consists of ten, thus, in general, there are seventy nations. Then there is Israel.

The seventy nations want to control the quality of Israel, since Israel want all their actions to be for the sake of the Creator, for *Yashar-El* [straight to the Creator] indicates that all his actions will be for the Creator. But the nations of the world in a person want specifically that everything they do will be only for their own sake. We call the evil inclination, "nations of the world," and we call the good inclination, "Israel."

The order of the work is that when a person wants to work only for the sake of the Creator, the evil inclination, which is the nations of the world, come and resist with all their might. Each one makes a person think that he should go its way, according to the root of the lust in each and every nation. They make a person think that they are correct through intellectual and reasonable arguments.

Each time they see that the person does not want to listen to them, they come with stronger arguments and clearer evidence that they are right. They are certain that according to the reasoning and arguments that they make a person understand, he will have nothing to reply to them. Hence, they are certain that they are the smartest in the world, since they see, according to their intellect and reason, that man's mind, can only give them silly answers, and the answers will be dismissed before their intellect and reason. Then, naturally, the person will have to follow the path of the nations of the world and idol-worship, meaning do work that is foreign to us, to the *Kedusha*, since *Kedusha* means working for the sake of the

Creator, while they want to work for their own sake. Their entire certainty lies in their intellect, that they are making sense.

Indeed, how can a person defeat his evil, even though his evil speaks with reason, wisdom, and knowledge, and know that they are the smartest in the world? They are so sure of their arguments and that man will stay with them, under their control, forever.

We must know that the power of *Kedusha* is faith above reason. That is, when they come with their arguments and show how correct they are, one should not tell them that their arguments are wrong. Instead, he should tell the nations of the world within him, "Know that everything you say is true. Reasonably speaking, you are correct, and I have nothing to reply to you. However, we were given the work above reason—that we must believe above reason that you are incorrect. And since the work on faith must be above reason, I thank you very much for your correct arguments that you have brought me, since it cannot be said that a person goes above reason unless he has reason and intellect. Then, it can be said that he is going above the intellect.

But when there is no reason, it cannot be said that he is going above reason. That is, "above reason" means that this path is more important than the path within reason. However, when there is no other way to tell him, "Walk in this path!" it cannot be said that he chooses the path of faith above reason. For this reason, precisely through the power of faith above reason is it possible to defeat the views of the nations of the world within man.

Now we can understand what we asked, What is the meaning of, "for it is your wisdom and your understanding in the eyes of the nations"? The writings says, "keep and do them." We asked, What does "keep and do them" imply?

According to the above said, that all the power we have against the arguments of the nations, who come with sensible arguments that their way—within reason—is the path of truth, all we can reply to them is by way of faith above reason. Above reason means "doing," since they are not given an answer within reason. When we answer not with reason, this is called "doers of His word."

This is the meaning of "Man and beast You save, O Lord." Our sages said, "Those who are as cunning in reason as men, and pretend to be as beasts." That is, they go above reason as though they have no reason, and by this they defeat the nations of the world within them.

It is as it says (*Midrash Rabbah*, Ecclesiastes, p 12) about the verse, "I said to myself concerning the sons of men." These are its words: "'Concerning the sons of men,' concerning words that the righteous say. And why did God create them? To clarify to them the measure of their righteousness, so they will see that they are beasts, to see and to show the nations of the world how Israel follow Him like a beast."

We should understand why we need to show the nations of the world how Israel follow Him like a beast. According to the above, the nations of the world means the nations of the world within man's heart. They must be shown that the fact that we want to work for the sake of the Creator and not for our own sake, we do not do this within reason, as you want to argue with us who is right. Rather, we do everything with faith above reason. We do this like beasts, without any rhyme or reason. Therefore, do not think that we will ever listen to your views because for us, everything is above reason.

We ask the Creator about this, that He will help us from above to overcome all the answers you require. Your questions are included in two questions, called "Who" and "What." We believe with faith in the sages that we must seek the Creator's help, and He will certainly help us, as our sages said, "He who comes to purify is aided." That is, He will help us follow Him above reason, to show the nations of the world how Israel follow Him like a beast. This is the meaning of the works, "So keep and do them, for it is your wisdom and your understanding in the eyes of the nations."

That is, your observing the action, which is the above reason, and by not veering off from this path, you will certainly succeed in emerging from the control of the nations of the world, and the nations of the world within you will annul before the *Kedusha*, as it is written, "And you will love the Lord your God with all your heart." Our sages said, "With both your inclinations," meaning that the evil inclination will also turn to good. It follows that his "nations of the world," called "evil inclination," will also be servants of the Creator.

Then, the nations of the world in man will see that once they, too, have been rewarded with the good, since all the wisdom—by which they could defeat the nations of the world and admit them into *Kedusha*—was faith above reason, called "do them." That is, all the wisdom in the quality of Israel is specifically in acting like a beast, and this was their entire wisdom.

This is the meaning of the words, "who will hear all these statutes and say, 'Surely this great nation is a wise and understanding nation.'" That is, the nations of the world, too, once they have also been admitted into *Kedusha*, as in "with all your heart, with both your inclinations," when the evil inclination, which are the nations of the world, also enters the *Kedusha*, then they see that all the wisdom that Israel had was that they heard the statutes, which is an act.

Then they are a wise and understanding nation, for all their wisdom was not as we think, that we will obtain wisdom only with inquiries and intellect. On the contrary, they were rewarded with wisdom precisely by following Him like a beast, meaning that precisely by "doing," which is called "working above reason," they were rewarded with wisdom. It follows that they are called a "wise and understanding nation" because they followed Him like a beast, and not with wisdom. This is all of the wisdom of the people of Israel.

Concerning doing, which is called "above reason," we should interpret what it says (*Midrash Tanchuma*), "'And it shall come to pass that because,' as the verse says, 'Why should I fear in the days of evil, the iniquity of my heels shall surround me (encircle me).' Because there are light *Mitzvot* among them, which people do not notice, but throw them under their heels, meaning that they are light, for this reason, David feared the day of judgment. He would say, 'Lord of the world, I do not fear the grave Mitzvot; what I fear is the light Mitzvot.'"

We should understand the meaning of light and grave Mitzvot in the work. "Light" means that it is unimportant. The fact that a person should work above reason, a person finds no importance in the matter, and this work tastes like dust to him. It is called "Shechina [Divinity] in the dust." That is, the fact that a person must take upon himself the burden of the kingdom of heaven above reason, this work is "in the dust."

Yet, we must observe Mitzvot and do good deeds and learn Torah so the Creator will raise this work from the dust, meaning from its lowliness, as we pray—that the Lord will raise the Shechina from the dust, as it is written, "The Merciful One, He will raise for us David's fallen hut." The reason why she is in lowliness is the concealment that the Creator has made, so there would be room for choice, meaning so we will be able to work in order to bestow, called "Dvekut [adhesion] with the Creator." This is why we were given this work in the form of concealment of the face.

Hence, the heart of our work is to make for ourselves vessels of bestowal through the preparation we make during the work at the time of concealment. We have vessels of reception from the Creator, and on these Kelim [vessels], there was a correction not to use them because they cause separation as they are in oppositeness of form from the Creator. Hence, we were given Torah and Mitzvot by which we will be able to obtain the vessels of bestowal.

For this reason, all the slanderers and accusers appear over this work and say, "We agree to serve the Creator, but the goal you want to achieve through observing Torah and Mitzvot, to this we do not agree. They bring a person many arguments, meaning thoughts that make him think that this whole purpose is not worth working for. Hence, if a person does not agree to change the goal of obtaining vessels of bestowal, they do not let a person observe Torah and

Mitzvot for this purpose, and anything a person does comes to him with great efforts.

As soon as a person forgets the goal and begins to work like the general public, meaning to receive reward for the work, he once again has the strength to respect it and to work with energy, since the purpose of the work is not against man's will. But when a person begins to work and forgets the goal, and finally awakens once again and wants to work in Torah and Mitzvot in order to obtain vessels of bestowal, the arguments of the spies rise against him once again and make him feel the taste of dust in this work. Then it is difficult for him once more to move ahead. This is called "light Mitzvot," meaning working with the aim of obtaining vessels of bestowal, namely for the sake of the Creator and not for one's own sake. There is reason to fear in this work because he has many dissidents.

This is not so with "grave Mitzvot," meaning that which is important to a person. That is, if a person works in order to receive reward, he regards it as a grave matter, since his self-benefit would lose if he did not observe the Torah and Mitzvot. But if the reward and the loss are for the sake of the Creator, this is not so important to a person.

For this reason, here a person slights because he introspects and says, "Since in any case, I will not lose a thing," since he says that he will not receive anything for himself, for he says that the Torah and Mitzvot should be done primarily for the Creator and not for his own benefit, then who can benefit from his work? Only the Creator. By this, a person slights and belittles in this work. Hence, a person often tells himself, "I should not even bother exerting in the work. If it comes easy, I can work. But if I have a small disturbance, I have no power to overcome."

The reason is that working Lo Lishma [not for Her sake] is not important, so it is not worth exerting over it. At the same time, what will he get out of working Lishma [for Her sake]? Therefore, usually, a person says that it is best to go to sleep and get some rest from all these things, as they bring him nothing but despondency and discontentment. This is called "light Mitzvot," "which people do not notice, but throw them under their heels."

David said about this, "Why should I fear in the days of evil, the iniquity of my heels," the light Mitzvot that a person slights? That is, when we want to go in the work of bestowal, I fear this —perhaps I will not be able to observe them. In this regard, meaning regarding obtaining the vessels of bestowal, only the Creator can help. That is, as the Creator gave man the vessels of reception, we must ask Him to give the vessels of bestowal instead of the vessels of reception.

That is, just as a person enjoys working for his own benefit, so he will receive great importance and pleasure from working for the sake of the Creator. That is, he will feel that it is a great privilege for him to serve the King, and we obtain this by "keep and do them, for it is your wisdom and your understanding in the eyes of the nations."

What Is "A Road Whose Beginning Is Thorns and Its End Is a Plain" in the Work?

Article No. 37, Tav-Shin-Mem-Tet, 1988/89

It is written in *Midrash Tanchuma* (p 318b): "Behold, I place before you. It is written, 'From the mouth of the upper one, the bad and the good will not emerge.' Moses, too, set before them two ways—the good and the bad, the path of life and the path of death, a blessing and a curse. There is an allegory about an old man who sat by the roadside before two roads: One, whose beginning is thorns and its end is a plain, and one whose beginning is a plain and its end is thorns. He sat at the beginning of the two and warned passersby, telling them, 'Although you see that this one begins with thorns, take it, for its end is a plain.' Anyone who was wise, listened to him and took it. He exerts some, but he goes in peace and comes in peace. But those who did not listen to him went and failed in the end. Therefore choose life; you and your descendants."

To understand this in the work, meaning in the work of observing Torah and *Mitzvot* [commandments/good deeds], we should discern two ways: 1) *Lo Lishma* [not for Her sake], 2) *Lishma* [for Her sake].

It is known that in the work, we should discern between the purpose of creation and the correction of creation. The purpose of creation is for man to achieve wholeness, meaning to be rewarded with the delight and pleasure that the Creator wishes to give to the created beings. This is called "His desire to do good to his creations." Because of this, all created beings yearn only to receive delight and pleasure.

Therefore, each and every day, a person yearns anew to receive delight and pleasure, and does not settle for what he had in the past. Rather, each day a person begins to receive delight and pleasure. This means that each day, a person must receive delight and pleasure. Some people receive pleasure now from what gave them delight and pleasure in the past. However, if they cannot receive pleasure from the past now, it is not regarded as enjoying the past now. That is, a person must feel pleasure every day. A person can feel pleasure even from what he gained yesterday, or he can feel pleasure today because yesterday he received respect, and so forth.

It follows that "His desire to do good to His creations" must mean that a person will feel each day anew that he receives pleasure. However, he can enjoy only from the pleasure he receives in the present from both the past and from the future. In feeling pleasure, if he enjoys in the present, this is regarded as having pleasure.

For this reason, in both corporeality and spirituality, a person must feel that he enjoys life now, regardless of the past or the future. Even with the greatest delight and pleasure, if he does not feel the delight and pleasure in the present, he could die because of the torments he is feeling now because he has nothing to enjoy.

But this depends on the level of suffering he is feeling now, and in this, meaning in the measure of the suffering, no two people are the same. Yet, all people must feel pleasure in the present. But as in corporeality, such as in eating, drinking, and sleeping, some people need to eat a lot, drink a lot, and sleep a lot, etc.

Likewise, in feeling pleasure, there are differences between people in the amount of need to feel pleasure. Some people need to feel a lot of it, and some can do with little. But they are equal in that they all need to feel pleasure in the present. If they cannot provide for themselves pleasure in the present from what they had in the past, and cannot depict for themselves some future pleasure that will shine in the present, they cannot exist in the world. This extends from the fact that the Creator's will in the purpose of creation was His will to do good to His creations.

For this reason, each day we are given one hundred blessings to bless, as our sages said (*Minchot* 43), "One must bless one hundred blessings every day. Also, each day, one must say four *Shema* readings [text that is read four times a day]: '*Shema* of offerings,' '*Shema* of Maker of Light,' 'Evening *Shema*,' and '*Shema* by the Bedside,' as well as to pray three times a day."

This shows that in spirituality we must draw a unique light each time, which pertains to the work that one is doing. The reason is that the creatures are incapable of receiving the delight and pleasure that the Creator contemplated giving to the creatures all at once, due to the correction that took place, which is called *Tzimtzum* [restriction]. For the creatures to receive the delight and pleasure in vessels of bestowal and not in vessels reception in order to receive, according to the work of the creatures, the abundance extends down to them.

It therefore follows that when a person begins the work, since by nature he does not understand that it is worthwhile to do any movement unless it is for his own sake, Maimonides says that we must begin with observing Torah and *Mitzvot* in order to receive reward, since a person cannot understand otherwise. But afterward, a person is shown that he must do all his deeds in order to bestow.

Since the body cannot agree to this path, the person begins to ask, "Why can't I work like the rest of the world, whose labor is all about the acts, and who have no work on the aim to bestow? But when I am told that I must walk on the path of bestowal, my work is twofold. That is, I have work observing Torah and *Mitzvot* in practice, as well as work on the aim to bestow. It follows that I have twice the work as the rest of the world. So," his body yells, "What do you want from my life?!"

This means that the body asks, "Why do I deserve such a punishment, more than other people, in that I have extra work that the general public does not do? For this reason," says the body, "I will not let you work even in action. Even though you cannot aim to bestow, I have no interest in them whatsoever. Therefore, I will object to your actions because you do not want to work for yourself."

It follows that if a person wants to walk on the path of truth, he should make three discernments in his work: 1) Work to observe Torah and Mitzvot in practice, 2) Work on the intention. That is, he does not want any reward for observing Torah and Mitzvot, but works not in order to receive reward. 3) When a person wants to work, meaning observe Torah and Mitzvot without any reward, his work is twofold: on the action, meaning that he has great resistance to observing Torah and Mitzvot, even on the act itself, since the body objects to observing Torah and Mitzvot without any reward. It follows that although he still cannot aim to bestow during the work, since the body objects to these intentions, there is also resistance to the act itself, even without the aim. The body asks, "What are you doing?! You say that you do not want any payment for your work in observing Torah and Mitzvot." It follows that he not only has work on the aim, which does not happen in the work of the general public, but he has twofold work in the act, as well, as it is more difficult to observe Torah and Mitzvot in practice.

Conversely, the bodies of those who work in the manner of the general public do not resist the work in practice all that much, since there, the body cannot ask, "What is this work for you?" because it gets immediate answers when he says to it that he believes in reward and punishment so he is not working for nothing, but he will be rewarded for his labor.

But with those who want to work on the path of truth, meaning in order to bestow, although reward and punishment apply to them, as well, meaning that they, too, believe in reward and punishment like people who work like the general public, yet, their reward and punishment are not similar to one another. The reward and punishment of the general public is in self-benefit. That is, they believe that if they observe Torah and *Mitzvot* they will receive reward for their own sake. And if they do not, they will be punished and will also lose the reward for their work.

But those who work in the way of the individuals, their reward is that the Creator gives them the privilege of working only for the sake of the Creator and not for their own sake. All of their pleasure is in being able to bring contentment to the Creator, and the punishment is if they stay under the governance of the will to receive for oneself. This is their whole punishment.

They believe in what our sages said, that the Creator said, "I have created the evil inclination; I have created the Torah as a spice." That is, they learn in order to receive reward, which is that they will emerge from the control of the evil inclination, which is the will to receive only for themselves, and will be able to work solely for the sake of the Creator. Certainly, on such an aim, the body, which is the desire to receive for one's own sake, must resist giving one the powers to be able to uproot it from the world.

It is as our sages said with regard to King David about the verse, "And my heart is slain within me." Our sages said that David killed the evil inclination by fasting. Naturally, even to the act—when a person still cannot aim in order to bestow—the body immediately resists and does not let him make a single move, since the body knows he wants to use those actions in order to kill it, as said about King David.

It follows that even when actions are without the aim, the body already shows great resistance. The only way is that in everything he wants to do, he must have the Creator's help. That is, for every little thing a person wants to do on the path of individuals, he must ask the Creator to help him do them. Yet, we must know that the fact that the person must ask the Creator for every single thing he wants to do because it is difficult for him, this is a great correction by which one gains the need to always pray to the Creator.

In other words, a person has what to pray for. Otherwise, it might happen that a person will not need the Creator's help. Therefore, a person gains in that he is always connected to the Creator in that he needs Him. Otherwise, a person might do the best deeds, but the deeds will not obligate him to remember the Creator while performing the act, although he goes to do good deeds. This can be because he has been brought up this way, and it can also be without remembering who commanded him to do so, but simply out of habit.

Conversely, when it is hard for him to do those deeds, he must ask the Creator to help him. It follows that during the act, he remembers the Creator because he is asking Him for help to do the act. This is a great benefit that a person should pay attention to the fact that he has something that reminds him that there is a Creator in the world and we must serve Him.

According to the above, we can understand what we asked, What is a road whose beginning is thorns and whose end is a plain, in the work? The thing is that there are two ways in the work of the Creator: 1) for one's own benefit, 2) for the Creator's benefit.

The way of self-benefit is called "whose beginning is a plain," since the body does not resist it so. Because the body believes in reward and punishment, it agrees to work although it exerts itself in this work. But when it looks at the reward, this work is regarded as "whose beginning is a plain," meaning that the body understands that this way is acceptable because it is for one's own sake.

But "its end is thorns." That is, in the end, he sees that he cannot feel His Providence as The Good Who Does Good, as it is written ("Introduction of The Book of Zohar," Item 138), "As long as the receivers have not been completed so they can receive His complete benevolence, which He had contemplated in our favor in the thought of creation, the guidance must be in the form of good and bad, reward and punishment. It is so because our vessels of reception are still tainted with self-reception. When we use the vessels of reception contrary to how they were created, we necessarily sense evil in the operations of Providence in relation to us."

Thus, "its end is thorns." "Thorns" means that this way inflicts pain, meaning that after all the work that one has exerted in Torah and *Mitzvot*, he still does not feel His Providence as good and doing good.

This causes him the matter of reward and punishment in his work. That is, the fact that His guidance is in the form of good and evil, from this extends reward and punishment, as it is written there in the *Sulam* [Baal HaSulam's commentary on *The Zohar*], "Hence, when one feels bad, denial of the Creator's guidance lies upon him and the superior Operator is concealed from him to that same extent. This is the greatest punishment in the world.

"Thus, the sensation of good and evil in relation to His guidance brings with it the sensation of reward and punishment, for one who exerts not to part from faith in the Creator is rewarded even when he tastes a bad taste in Providence. And if he does not exert, he will be punished because he is separated from faith in the Creator."

According to the above, we can understand what we asked, What is a way whose beginning is a plain and whose end is thorns in the work? It means that the way that the general public works, in order to receive reward, "its beginning is a plain." That is, the body does not resist this way because it is told, "You must believe in reward and punishment for your own benefit."

That is, if it observes Torah and *Mitzvot*, the self-benefit will gain. And if it does not observe, the self-benefit will lose. A person can understand this because this is man's inherent *Kli* [vessel], called "will to receive for oneself."

But "its end is thorns." That is, in the end, he does not achieve wholeness, the reward of seeing that His Providence is in the form of good and doing good. Instead, he is placed under the governance of good and evil. It follows that although "He alone does and will do all the deeds," this is nonetheless hidden from those who feel good and evil, since at the time of "bad," the *Sitra Achra* [other side] is given the power to conceal His guidance and the faith in Him, as written in the *Sulam*. Thus, they will "die without wisdom." This is called "its end is thorns."

Conversely, the way "whose beginning is thorns and its end is a plain" means that those who want to walk on the path of truth and achieve the degree of bestowing contentment to the Maker, its beginning is thorns, since when a person wants to work only for the sake of the Creator and not for himself, the body objects to every single thing he does, and each time, he must overcome anew, and every time he overcomes and the body resists, it stings him and afflicts him like thorns.

It follows that the way he is walking is as though walking on thorns, and each time, he wants to escape from the campaign. But "Anyone who is wise, listens to him." That is, one who has faith in the sages listens to him. "He takes it. He exerts some, but he goes in peace and comes in peace," as it is written, "For her ways are ways of pleasantness and all her paths are peace," since afterward, when he is rewarded with vessels of bestowal, he walks in a way that is on a plain.

This is as it is written, "When the Lord favors man's ways, even his enemies will make peace with him," since then he is rewarded with the delight and pleasure found in the thought of creation, which is to do good to His creations. When they are rewarded with vessels of bestowal, it is written there in the *Sulam*, "At that time, His private Providence will be revealed throughout the world, since now, once the evil and the punishments have become benefits and merits, it will be possible to attain their Doer, for they have now become fitting for the work of His hands. Now they will praise and bless Him," as it is written, "Therefore choose life; you and your descendants."

What Are Judges and Officers in the Work?

Article No. 38, Tav-Shin-Mem-Tet, 1988/89

It is written, "You shall appoint for yourself judges and officers in all your gates." We should understand what are "judges" and what are "officers" in the work. We should also understand what is "in all your gates" in the work. And we should also understand what is written, "You shall not plant for yourself an Asherah [tree for idol-worship], any tree beside the altar." Our sages said, "Anyone who appoints an unworthy judge, it is as though he plants an Asherah in Israel." We should also understand what is an unworthy judge in the work, and why is the prohibition so severe, as though he "plants an Asherah."

In corporeality, we see that there is a courthouse, and the order there is that each one claims that justice is on his side, and the judges give the verdict and decide who is right. But even when the judges have already decided who is right, it is only in potential. We see the justice, but the one who was found guilty does not want to obey the justice of the judges, so the verdict is given to the police and the officers execute the verdict. That is, the officers overcome the guilty party and execute the verdict against his will. But as long as there is no court order to execute the verdict, the person says that the judges are fine, but he cannot obey the verdict although he does not dispute it.

The order is that when the officers come to execute the verdict, it is impossible to argue with the officers because they are only messengers of the courthouse. Therefore, there is no place to argue with the officers, since only in court is it possible to argue and say everything that is on one's mind. When someone does want to argue, the officers laugh at him and say, "You are wasting your words; we must follow what the judges said."

The same applies in the work. When a person wants to walk on the path of truth, a war begins between the good inclination and the evil inclination, where each one claims, "It is all mine." That is, the evil inclination claims that the whole body belongs to it, meaning that the body should work only for one's own sake. The good inclination argues that the whole body should work only for the sake of the Creator. And what should be done when two parties quarrel with one another? We go to a judge to give his verdict. The judge will say to whom the body belongs, meaning for whom the body should work.

Hence this judge in one's heart—and a person wants to obey it, as he must say to whom the body belongs—this judge must be worthy. But how do we know if this judge is worthy? This depends only on the greatness of the judge. In other words, we must see to what extent the judge understands the greatness and importance of the work, meaning whether we serve a great or a small king.

"A worthy judge" means if he understands that he assumes in his heart that the King for whom we must work is a great and important King, worth relinquishing any pleasure that one can have in beastly lusts. He understands that the pleasure of serving the King is so important, more than all the pleasures of this world. This matter, that it is worthwhile to relinquish, can be only if the judge knows and has attained the greatness of the Creator.

Or, it can be otherwise: If he believes in the sages, who told us that we must believe in the greatness of the Creator above reason. That is, although he has not been rewarded with seeing the greatness of the Creator within reason, but on the contrary, each time a person wants to take upon himself the burden of the kingdom of heaven above reason, it resists. And then, what can one do if the body, meaning the judge in his heart, is not impressed with everything the person tells it? Although he listens and does not say to the person that he is not making sense, but it is similar to what is written, "Like a deaf viper that does not hear the sound of the whisperers."

First, he must say that the fact that he has come to a resolution that the body does not want to obey the arbiter and the judge that it is worthwhile to work for the sake of the Creator, this is natural, since by nature, man is born with a will to receive for himself. Therefore, although the judge said that we should work for the sake of the Creator, he simply does not understand it, meaning how is it possible to do something that a person does not enjoy. But the judge told him that he should achieve a degree where all his concerns are the joy of the Creator. Although the judge brings him evidence from the Torah, which says, "Blessed is our God, who has created us for His glory," and "All the works of the Lord are for His sake," the body insists and says, "I see that I must do something against my mind and reason."

Therefore, there are two manners to this state: 1) "I do not want to obey you, even though you are correct. Hence," the body says, "I will not obey your order." 2) It says, "Sometimes I do want to obey you, but I can't because whenever I do something that is not according to nature, I suffer torments and I cannot tolerate such torments, meaning to work for the sake of the Creator. This is actual death, and how can I put myself to death?"

Therefore, a person must act coercively. That is, he must believe what our sages said, "He who comes to purify is aided." This means that a person must tell his body, "What you say—that you cannot do things that contradict nature—is true. However, we must know that the actions are mainly in the intention, meaning that the intention should be that the act he does will be for the sake of the Creator."

Although the body cannot understand this, because it is against nature, meaning against the reason and the intellect, it does this only out of faith and not through its own intellect. This is why it is called "an act." And when a person wants to observe Torah and Mitzvot [commandments/good deeds] in action and not in the reason, if a person wants to achieve the truth, he must say—when he wants to execute what the judges said—that we must work for the sake of the Creator. This is called "officers," and with officers, we see that there is no point arguing with them, that there is no arguing with the officers, meaning that they do not hear what is being said to them.

It is likewise in spirituality. A person must not argue with the body when he goes above reason. He should say to the body, "It does not matter to us if you are right or wrong." Perhaps the body is one hundred percent correct, but the officers follow the judge's order, and a person should pray to the Creator to give strength to the officers so they can overcome the guilty one. In spirituality, this means that a person should pray to the Creator to give the power and might to his overcoming, so he can prevail over the body and execute what the judges said.

By this we will understand what we asked, What are "judges and officers" in the work? It is that we must appoint judges who will determine whose is the body. That is, when this body works, who profits from its work? Does the profit go to one's own benefit or to the benefit of the Creator? Afterward, one needs the power to overcome, to execute the judges' verdict, and the power to overcome is called "officers." This should be "in all your gates."

We asked, What is "in all your gates"? Literally, it seems to mean that in each gate there must be judges and officers. We should interpret "your gates." It is as *The Zohar* says about the verse, "Her husband is known at the gates." It interprets that "in the gates" means "Each one according to what he assumes in his heart." That is, in each measure that a person assumes in his heart the greatness and exaltedness of the Creator, a person should appoint there "judges and officers" in order to be able to carry out everything.

Now we can understand what we asked, What does "You shall not plant for yourself an Asherah, any tree beside the altar," mean? Our sages said, "Anyone who appoints an unworthy judge, it is as though he plants an Asherah in Israel." We asked, Why is the prohibition so severe that it is as though he plants idol-worship in Israel?

According to the above, since in the work, every person is a small world, it follows that when there is a feud between the evil inclination and the good inclination, each one claims, "It is all mine," meaning "the body belongs to me." The evil inclination claims that the body should work not for the sake of the Creator, but for one's own sake, that working for the sake of the Creator is foreign work to us. And since we must obey the good inclination, which says that the body must work for the sake of the Creator, as a result, when a person appoints an unworthy judge, meaning who does not know to say that we must work for the sake of the Creator, but says that we must work for the sake of the body, it follows that he plants idol-worship in Israel, since the judge does not understand that we must work for the sake of the Creator but says that we must work for the sake of the body, which is foreign work to us.

This is why the prohibition on an "unworthy judge" is so severe, since the judge tells him to do idol-worship, called Asherah. Hence, if a person wants to know what to do and wants to trust the judge within a person, he must first see if this judge can give a judgment that is the whole truth, meaning to tell him to walk on the path of truth, meaning to work for the sake of the Creator.

According to the above, we should interpret what our sages said (Tanhuma 8), "Anyone who makes a judgment that is the whole truth is rewarded with the life of the next world." This implies that one who wants to be rewarded with the life of the next world, there is a very easy way that does not require so much labor in Torah and work. Instead, if one tries to give a judgment that is the whole truth, he will be rewarded with the next world. According to the above, a "judge" in the order of the work is one who gives the verdict—to whom the body belongs, meaning whether the body should work for the sake of the Creator or for one's own sake.

It follows that this judge, which a person establishes within one's heart so as to give the verdict, to whom the body belongs, meaning for whose sake it should work, for the sake of the Creator or for one's own sake and not for the sake of the Creator, if he is not a worthy judge and does not know to appreciate the greatness of the Creator, and he is still biased by the will to receive for himself, and the person says, "I will listen to what the judge decides and says about whom one should work for," it follows that that judge seemingly plants an Asherah, meaning idol-worship.

That is, this judge, which a person wants to obey, tells him it is not worthwhile to work for the Creator. It follows that if he listens to this judge, he will have to commit idol-worship and not work for the sake of the Creator.

This is why our sages said, "Anyone who appoints an unworthy judge, it is as though he plants an Asherah." We asked, What is the severity in the matter, that if the judge is not worthy, it is as though he commits idol-worship? The intimation is that in the work, it is truly idol-worship because he tells him that we need not work for the Creator. It says, "It is as though he plants an Asherah in Israel," since every person should have the quality of "Israel," meaning Yashar-El [straight to the Creator], namely that "all your works will be for the sake of the Creator." Yet, the unworthy judge says that it is better to work for oneself. This is called "idol-worship."

By this you will understand what we asked about what our sages said, "Anyone who makes a judgment that is the whole truth is rewarded with the life of the next world." Thus, why should we work and toil so much in order to be rewarded with the life of the next world? After all, there is an easier way—to try to make a judgment that is the whole truth and thereby be rewarded with the life of the next world.

In the work, this means that there is the "truth," and there is the "whole truth." "Truth" means that the judge within his heart tells him he must observe Torah and *Mitzvot*, but in order to receive reward. That is, the Torah and *Mitzvot* that he performs should be with a reward and punishment of self-benefit. It follows that on one hand, this is called the "truth." It is as Maimonides says, "Therefore, when teaching little ones, women, and uneducated people, they are taught to work only out of fear and in order to receive reward. Until they gain much wisdom, they are shown that secret bit by bit" (*Hilchot Teshuva*, Chapter 10).

This means that the judge gives a judgment of truth.

Conversely, the "whole truth" means that the judge tells him we must work for the sake of the Creator and not for our own sake. This is called the "whole truth," meaning that the act is true and the intention is also true. This is called the "whole truth."

However, we should interpret what is the meaning of the "whole truth." It means that the truth is that it is true, that everyone admits that it is true, and not simply that he says that it is the truth. We can understand this according to what is written in *The Study of the Ten Sefirot* (Part 13), where he interprets the seventh correction of the thirteen qualities, which are 1) *El* [pronounced *Kel*], 2) Merciful, 3) Gracious, 4) *Erech* [long], 5) *Apaim* [face. *Erech Apaim* means "long face" or "patient"], 6) Great in Mercy, 7) And True.

He interprets what is "And True." In his words, "Therefore, he calls this correction by the name, 'And True,' since by the revealing of the two Holy Apples below, the truth of His Providence over the lower ones is revealed. Therefore, the revelation of His Providence is called 'And True,' for it is the truth of His will, and all the concealments in the worlds come only to reveal this truth about His

Providence, which is to do good to His creations. For this reason, this correction in ZA is called 'And True.'"

According to the above, we can understand the meaning of "Anyone who makes a judgment that is the whole truth is rewarded with the life of the next world." It means that then, all the nations of the world in his body see the truth—that they are rewarded with the delight and pleasure found in the will of the Creator, which is His will to do good to His creations. And this is called the "whole truth."

What Is, "The Torah Speaks Only Against the Evil Inclination," in the Work?

Article No. 39, Tav-Shin-Mem-Tet, 1988/89

It is written, "If you go out to war against your enemies, and the Lord your God delivers them into your hands, and you see among the captives a beautiful woman, and you take her for yourself as a wife." RASHI interprets, "The Torah speaks only against the evil inclination, that if the Creator does not permit her, he will marry her under prohibition."

We should understand this. Would it not be better if the Creator had not empowered the evil inclination to incite him into transgression? Then, it would not be needed to permit her because he would not marry her under prohibition. We should also understand what RASHI's interpretation means in the work, concerning the verse "If you go out to war," that it speaks of "optional war." What is "optional war" in the work?

Also, we should understand what our sages said (*Kidushin* 30), "I have created the evil inclination; I have created for it the Torah

342

as a spice." It seems as though I have created the Torah for the evil inclination. That is, were it not for the evil inclination, there would be no need for the Torah. Here, too, we should ask, But He had another way, namely not to create the evil inclination, and then there would be no need for the Torah.

It is known that only thanks to the Torah, the world exists, as our sages said, "Were it not for My covenant day and night, I would not establish the ordinances of heaven and earth." But here it implies that He created the Torah because of the evil inclination. We should understand this in the work.

We must know who is the evil inclination, for whom the Torah had to be created, as it is written, "I have created the evil inclination; I have created for it the Torah as a spice." We should also understand why the Torah is called a "spice." We see that when we cook some dish for a meal, in order for the dish to be tasty, we put a spice in the dish. This means that the main thing is the dish, and the spice is only an addition that gives flavor. But according to what is said, the Torah is only a spice. It follows that the main thing is the evil inclination, and the Torah only gives flavor to the evil inclination. How can we understand this, since the Torah is the main thing, as it is written, "For they are our lives and the length of our days"?

According to what is explained in the "Introduction to The Study of the Ten Sefirot," we understand that the evil inclination is the will to receive delight and pleasure, which is called "evil inclination." This is the "heart of creation." That is, the thing of which we can say that a new thing was made in the world, which did not exist before He created it, is only the desire to receive pleasure. This desire, the yearning to receive delight and pleasure, did not exist prior to the creation of the world, since in the Creator, there are no lacks or desires that He needs to receive.

He says there, Why did He create this desire? It is for the purpose of creation, since the creation of the world was because He desires to do good, and we see in our nature that the Creator created that there are delight and pleasure only from things the body craves.

Moreover, the measure of delight and pleasure depends on the yearning. For this reason, He created in us a desire to receive delight and pleasure, and this is the heart of creation. In other words, if this will to receive did not exist in the world, there would be no one to receive the delight and pleasure that He wishes to give to the creatures.

It follows that the heart of creation is the will to receive delight and pleasure, and without it, it is impossible to speak of creation. However, we should understand why the will to receive is called "evil inclination," and if it is truly evil, why did He create it?

The thing is that since the Creator wanted them not to feel unpleasantness when they receive the delight and pleasure, and it is also in the nature that the Creator created, that every branch wants to resemble its root, and since our root, meaning the Creator, is the Giver, and the created beings, who must receive from Him, are opposite from the Creator, they feel shame about this. For this reason, a *Tzimtzum* [restriction] and concealment were placed, where the delight and pleasure do not shine for the *Kelim* [vessels] of the will to receive for oneself, but only where they want to receive the delight and pleasure because the Creator wants to give, as this was the purpose of creation, for His desire is to do good to His creations, and the creature wants to obey the King's commandment and therefore receives.

This is a correction called "receiving in order to bestow." For this reason, two systems were made: systems of *Kedusha* [holiness], and systems of *Tuma'a* [impurity] and *Klipot* [shells/peels]. It is as it is written in the "Introduction to The Study of the Ten Sefirot" (Item 10), "He imprinted the desire to bestow in the system of *ABYA* of *Kedusha*, removed the will to receive for themselves from them, and placed it in the system of the worlds *ABYA* of *Tuma'a*. Because of this, they have become separated from the Creator and from all the worlds of *Kedusha*."

It follows that this will to receive is called the "evil inclination" because it causes all the evil in the world. Because of it, the creatures cannot receive delight and pleasure, and because of it they remain without vitality of *Kedusha*, since the light and abundance cannot shine in a place where using it was prohibited. This happened to us because of the cascading of the worlds, where from this will to receive emerged the *Klipot* into the world, and govern man, and he is utterly incapable of emerging from their governance, unless by the power of Torah and *Mitzvot* [commandments/good deeds], where there is the light of Torah, and "the light in it reforms him," meaning sets him free from the governance of the will to receive for himself.

Now we can understand what we asked, why RASHI interpreted the verse, "and you take her for yourself as a wife," by bringing the explanation of our sages (*Kidushin* 21), "The Torah speaks only against the evil inclination. Let him eat the flesh of slaughtered carcasses, but not the flesh of carcasses that were not slaughtered." Some ask, Why did the Creator give the evil inclination the power to incite him into transgression? Would it not be better if the Creator had not empowered the inciter and there would be no need to permit him the forbidden? Our sages said about this, "The Torah speaks only against the evil inclination."The answer is that in the work, the evil inclination is called "the will to receive for oneself." Without the will to receive, there would not be creation whatsoever. Wherever the will to receive sees some pleasure, it wants to satisfy its want, and by wanting to satisfy its want, it is possible to enjoy the thing for which it yearns. Since the Creator created this nature, it does not suffer changes. However, there is a place for corrections, which is not to cancel them but to add to them something by which this thing is corrected. However, this does not change nature, since the Creator created nature and the will to receive is something that the Creator created. Hence, man is powerless to cancel it.

The general correction is the intention to bestow. This is called "mitigation of the judgments." That is, the judgment that was done, where it is forbidden to use the will to receive and enjoy for one's own benefit, is because by this we come into disparity of form from the Creator. However, when receiving because the Creator wants us to receive, and for ourselves, we would rather not receive, by this the judgment of prohibition on reception is mitigated.

However, we must know that this quality of receiving in order to bestow is a real correction. That is, the purpose of creation, which is to do good to His creations, cannot come true unless in this manner, when he does use the desire to receive pleasure, yet remains in *Dvekut* [adhesion], which is equivalence of form. That is, if he receives but does not enjoy, this reception is not regarded as "doing good," since we do not speak of what he receives, but of what he enjoys. In other words, the upper one wants the lower one to enjoy, and if a person does not enjoy, then he has received nothing from the upper one. This is called "mitigation of the judgments."

This is the heart of the wholeness. However, there are things that can be sorted from the perspective of the upper roots, so they work in order to bestow, and there are things that are forbidden to use, even in order to bestow. In other words, a person cannot say that he wants to do something that is forbidden, yet aim to bestow. If the thing is forbidden, it is because with respect to branch and root, there are things that the Torah prohibited and there are things that the Torah permitted.

In general, we should make three discernments in the Torah: 1) *Mitzva* [commandment/good deed], 2) permission, 3) prohibition.

We must be careful with *Mitzva* and with transgression, even with an act without an aim, for there is a matter of *Mitzva* in practice even when he has no intention. Likewise, with prohibition, there is a transgression in the action, even without any intention. But the main work on the intention is in what is permitted, when there is no *Mitzva* in doing it, yet no transgression if he does not do it. Then, when he does what is permitted, meaning when he aims for the sake of the Creator while performing the permitted thing, that permitted thing enters the *Kedusha*.

Then it is called a *Mitzva*. In other words, it emerges from being "permission" and enters the realm of *Mitzva*. And precisely here is the heart of the war against the inclination, since the body tells him that there is no prohibition, so why deny yourself from doing it? But when a person must answer it, he can tell it, "I must perform a Mitzva. Therefore, when I perform a Mitzva, I have done something. When I do not commit a transgression, I also have a Mitzva, as our sages said, 'If he sat and did not commit a transgression, it is as though he performed a Mitzva.'

"However, when you tell me to do something that is permitted, even though I cannot aim for the sake of the Creator, this is not a Mitzva. Therefore, I have done nothing. And I do not want to be an idle worker, meaning to do things that are a waste." It follows that with the work of Mitzvot and transgressions, the work is mandatory. But with what is permitted, where there are no imperatives pertaining to this act, specifically then the intention makes it a reality, admitting it into Kedusha.

According to the above, we should interpret what RASHI interpreted about the verse "If you go out to war," that it speaks of "optional war." In the work, we should interpret "permission" as having to aim in order to bestow. There is the main work on the inclination. Since there is no prohibition on the act, the inclination sees that the person wants to uproot it from the world. That is, with regard to Mitzvot and transgressions that a person does in action, the inclination does not show much resistance, since the person does not say that he wants to work only for the sake of the Creator. But when he begins to work on the aim to bestow and not for the sake of the body, the real work with the evil inclination begins.

Since the Torah and Mitzvot were given in order to cleanse Israel, as it is written (in the essay, Matan Torah ["The Giving of the Torah"]), "These are the words of our sages when they asked, 'Why should the Creator mind if one slaughters at the throat or at the back of the neck? After all, the Mitzvot were only given to cleanse people,' and that cleansing means the cleansing of the turbid body, which is the purpose that emerges from the observation of all the Torah and Mitzvot."

It follows that only when speaking with the body concerning the intention for the sake of the Creator, when we want to annul self-benefit, then is the real dispute with the body. This is evident precisely when there is a war against the inclination on permitted matters. At that time, the war is not over the act, since there is no prohibition on the action. The war can be only on the aim, where a person wants it to be only for the sake of the Creator and not for the sake of the body. Rather, he wants to kill the body, as our sages said, "The Torah exists only in one who puts himself to death over it."

Now we can interpret what we asked, Why did the Torah permit the beautiful woman, since the Torah speaks only against the evil inclination? After all, the Creator had an easier way, where He would not need to permit a beautiful woman, meaning He would not give the evil inclination the power to incite him and He would not need to change and permit something forbidden.

What is the answer? "The Torah speaks only against the evil inclination." Literally, it is very difficult to understand the matter of the prohibition of a beautiful woman. It is just as there are those who ask, Why did the Torah not permit other prohibitions when he has a great lust for the prohibited thing? Indeed, we should answer about this that we have no idea about Torah and *Mitzvot*, that it is inconceivable to the human intellect. Instead, this is a spiritual matter that the Creator sentenced, as our sages said (*Safra*, RASHI, *Kedoshim*), "One should not say, 'Pork flesh is impossible,' but rather, 'It is possible, but what can I do if my Father in heaven so decreed upon me?'" In other words, the whole of the Torah and *Mitzvot* are decrees of the Creator, and man's intellect does not reach there. Naturally, we cannot ask, Why the Torah permitted a beautiful woman? (See in *Ohr Chaim*, *Ki Tetze*).

We should interpret what we asked, What is the meaning of "I have created the evil inclination; I have created for it the Torah as a spice"? This implies that the evil inclination is the heart of the matter, and the Torah is not the main item, but is like an addition to the dish. According to what is explained in the "Introduction to The Study of the Ten Sefirot," the heart of creation is the will to receive delight and pleasure. The reason why the Creator created the will to receive is that He wishes to do good to His creations. But due to disparity of form between the Giver and the receiver, it was given to us to correct it into working in order to bestow, by which the disparity of form in the will to receive will be corrected.

It therefore follows that what receives delight is mainly the will to receive. However, if it receives for its own sake, it is called "evil inclination" because the disparity of form in it causes it to separate from the Creator, and the delight and pleasure do not reach the separated *Kelim* because of the correction of the *Tzimtzum*. Hence, in order for the will to receive to be able to receive the delight and pleasure, the evil inclination must be given a spice, by which there will be a flavor in the will to receive, meaning that there will be delight and pleasure in the will to receive.

If it is not given the spice, which is the desire to bestow, there will be no flavor in the will to receive because it will have nothing, since the delight and pleasure does not reach there.

However, there are four discernments to make here: 1) The *Kli*, which receives the pleasure. 2) The pleasure that the *Kli* receives must have a pleasant taste. That is, it must not have shame in it, but they must feel a good taste. 3) The good taste is the will to bestow. This is called that the desire to bestow spices up the dish so it is tasty. 4) It is possible to receive this flavor, called "desire to bestow," specifically through the Torah, as it is written, "I have created the evil inclination; I have created for it the Torah as a spice." This means that the Torah, meaning the light in it, gives the desire to bestow, and the desire to bestow gives a flavor that removes the shame from the dish, for the shame spoils all the flavor that can be found in the dish, and why the Giver cannot give any of the real pleasures, since when it reaches the *Kelim* of the lower ones, everything will be spoiled. This is all of our work—to obtain *Kelim* that are suitable for the abundance.

Now we can interpret, "The Torah speaks only against the evil inclination." Everything that is forbidden or permitted is according to what the Creator decreed. That is, there are things that can be corrected and admitted into *Kedusha* even before the end of correction, and this is why we were given 613 *Mitzvot*. This is the reason why the Torah permitted the beautiful woman through the corrections presented in the Torah. This is above our intellect to attain what the Creator permits and what the Creator prohibits. Hence, we have no clue that we can ask, Why did the Torah permit? since the whole matter of Torah and *Mitzvot* is "to cleanse Israel with them." Hence, the permission that the Torah permitted a beautiful woman through the corrections is also with the intention to cleanse people.

What Is, "Every Day They Will Be as New in Your Eyes," in the Work?

Article No. 40, Tav-Shin-Mem-Tet, 1988/89

Our sages (RASHI, *Tavo* 3 (Deuteronomy 26:16), in *Yitro* 13:10) said about the verse, "This day the Lord your God commands you to do these statutes and ordinances. You shall be careful to do them with all your heart and with all your soul," "Each day, they will be as new in your eyes, as though you received them today from Mt. Sinai, as though on this day you were commanded them."

We should understand what "as though on this day you were commanded" adds to us. Why is simply, "as you received the Torah then, on Mt. Sinai," not enough, and we need to take them upon ourselves "as though today you were commanded them"? What does this add to us in the work?

He says in *Shaar HaKavanot* [*Gate of Intentions*] (Part 2) that "The *Shema* reading [section in every prayer] and the prayer we pray every day always three times, evening, morning, and noon, on weekdays and on Shabbat [Sabbath] and good days, know that there is a big difference between the prayers on weekdays to those on Shabbat and beginnings of months, and the prayer on a good day or the weekdays of the festival. Moreover, even among the good days themselves, the prayer on Passover is not the same as the prayer on *Shavuot* [Feast of Weeks]. Also, during the weekdays, there is a big difference between the prayer on one day and the prayer of the next. There is not a single prayer since the world was created until the end of the world that is like another, and there is not a person who is like another, and one corrects what the other does not correct, since the purpose of the commandment of the prayer is to make the sorting of the seven kings of Edom who died. Each day, each and every prayer sorts out new sparks."

In order to understand the matter of the shattering of the seven kings of Edom—which we must sort through the Torah, *Mitzvot* [commandments/good deeds], and prayer—we must remember the two known things: 1) the purpose of creation, 2) the correction of creation. The purpose of creation is to do good to His creations, meaning for the created beings to receive delight and pleasure. The correction of creation is that when they receive the delight and pleasure, they will not feel the shame due to the disparity of form between the receiver and the Giver. The way is that there was a correction that the light no longer shines on receiving in order to receive for oneself. Therefore, when a person is immersed in vessels of self-reception, concealment and hiding are on him and he cannot feel the importance of *Kedusha* [holiness], since there is *Kedusha* precisely where one wants to bestow contentment upon one's Maker.

Prior to this, as long as one has not been rewarded with vessels of bestowal—for the upper light is present only in those *Kelim* [vessels]—a person must accept everything on faith, to believe that the Creator leads the world by way of good and doing good, and believe in the greatness of the Creator "because He is great and ruling." He should believe that it is a great privilege to serve a great King.

But saying that it is a great privilege does not mean verbally. Rather, a person must feel great delight in serving a great King. That is, when can one say that he is serving a great King? It is when he feels great delight. If he is still not delighted when serving the King, it is a sign that he has not achieved a degree where he believes that he is serving a great King.

We must believe what is written, "His kingship rules over all." Baal HaSulam said that there is no other force in the world, but that He alone does and will do all the deeds. Also, the *Kedusha* sustains the *Klipot* [shells/peels], and the *Klipot* have no vitality but that which the *Kedusha* gives them. This is the meaning of the words, "You sustain them all." The meaning of "His kingship rules over all" is that *Malchut de Atzilut* gives them life, or they would not be able to exist.

It therefore follows that what we learn, that the Creator created the will to receive in order to receive pleasure, it must receive pleasure and delight or it cannot exist in the world. That is, although a *Tzimtzum* [restriction] and concealment were placed on the will to receive for oneself, so delight and pleasure do not reach there, in order for this desire to exist—for if it were revoked, there would be nothing to correct—hence, in order for it to exist, it receives minute vitality so it will not be revoked. This vitality that they receive comes from the breaking of the vessels, when holy sparks fell into the *Klipot* so they would receive vitality and would not be canceled.

It follows that without pleasure, we cannot live. However, as long as one has not taken upon himself the burden of the kingdom of heaven, that person receives vitality only from the Creator. But the person does not have faith in the Creator, to say that the Creator gives him his life. For this reason, he says that his life comes from nature.

But we must say that in truth, the Creator hides himself in those dresses from the secular ones. Yet, they do not believe this, meaning that the Creator hides Himself from this person, for that he will not be able to believe that the Creator is the bestower. The Creator hides Himself in a clothing of separation, so the pleasure of the Creator comes to a person clothed in dresses, and the pleasure is clothed in these dresses.

Similarly, we see that there is food for man, who sits and eats a meal of meat, fish, and so forth. From this a man enjoys. The leftovers that remain from the food, he throws in the trash for the cats to eat this waste. But the cats enjoy the waste. We see that they are completely satisfied with the food they find in the trash. Therefore, we see that dogs, chickens, and so forth, all enjoy the food, but there is a difference in that man's pleasure is not from the waste, whereas for them, the leftover waste is satisfactory.

It is likewise with the work of the Creator. Some people enjoy the waste, meaning the *Klipot*—the slim light that the *Kedusha* gives them—and derive complete satisfaction from this. Then there are people whose pleasure is what they receive like the rest of the people. These are regarded as "waste of *Kedusha*." However, that food does not satisfy them because they have an inner drive where they feel that it is not worthwhile to be born to derive pleasure from waste.

In other words, they feel that it cannot be that the same food given to animals, meaning to beasts, animals, and poultry and so forth, will be food for man, who is regarded as "speaking," that he will be similar to animals, meaning that the same thing that sustains animals will sustain the speaking. That sensation does not let them rest and they begin to search for another source of sustenance that they will be able to say that it is worth being born for and enjoying life.

This causes them to search for spirituality, and causes them to take upon themselves the burden of the kingdom of heaven and the burden of Torah and *Mitzvot*. But here, too, once they have taken upon themselves the burden of Torah and *Mitzvot*, some of them derive satisfaction from *Lo Lishma* [not for Her sake]. It is as Maimonides says, that first they are taught to engage in Torah and *Mitzvot* in order to receive reward. And so it should be, so they will not change the order of their work. However, "Until they gain knowledge and acquire much wisdom, they are taught that secret bit by bit."

The question is, How do we know that they are in the form of "until they gain knowledge"? The answer is that he receives an inner drive and feels that it cannot be said that this is the meaning of what is written, "For He is your wisdom and understanding in the eyes of the nations." At that time it is evident that his knowledge has increased, and it is for him as Maimonides says, they "acquire much wisdom." In other words, he has become wise and begins to feel that there is also internality in the Torah and Mitzvot.

Then "they are taught that secret," that we must work on the intention, too, meaning that one should try to do all his works in order to bestow. At that time a person achieves Dvekut [adhesion] with the Creator and is rewarded with the delight and pleasure of the purpose of creation. Then, the person feeds on the food suitable for man, and not on waste that the Kedusha throws to the Klipot so as to sustain them.

However, this is only a slim light, enough to sustain them so they will not be canceled from the world. If the will to receive is canceled in the world, there will be no one to correct. But as we learn, the heart of creation is the will to receive; it is all the substance of creation, except there is the matter of the correction of creation, meaning that creation is called "will to receive," and this quality was created because of the purpose of creation. In other words, the desire to do good to His creations created the will to receive existence from absence.

The correction of creation is that the intention to bestow is placed on it, and then a person is fit to receive the delight and pleasure. At that time, by being rewarded with Dvekut, which is equivalence of form, we achieve the degree, "For He is your wisdom and understanding in the eyes of the nations." That is, only when we emerge from the governance of the nations, called "multiple authorities," and achieve the single authority, when a person has only the authority of the Creator, then we are rewarded with the light of Hochma [wisdom] and Bina [understanding].

However, although a person has already received an inner drive and wants to work in order to bestow, and not merely in an act in order to receive reward, the mind asserts that man must go forward and each day he should grow stronger than the day before. In fact, a new order begins here, which is completely irrational. That is, a procession of ascents and descents begins here, where sometimes a person says, "The first days were better than these."

There can be several ascents and descents in one day or several ascents and descents in a single week, to the extent that a person often falls into despair and says that he does not see that he will ever be able to emerge from the control of the bad, and he must surrender under the will to receive.

But since he has already realized that the majority of the work in Torah and *Mitzvot* is not so important because the primary importance in observing Torah and *Mitzvot* should be in observing it for the sake of the Creator, this means that he realizes that the most important is to work for the sake of the Creator. This awareness causes him to feel lack of importance, meaning that it is not important to work in action without an aim.

Although he knows what our sages said, "One should always learn *Lo Lishma*, and from *Lo Lishma* he will come to *Lishma* [for Her sake]," at that time the evil in a person makes him think that it is true that it is important since from *Lo Lishma* we come to *Lishma*, but–says the evil in a person– you see that you cannot achieve *Lishma*. You can see this for yourself.

That is, first the evil in him makes him think that he must give up on achieving a degree where he can work for the sake of the Creator. After it has given him thoughts of despair, it tells him, "You, who have already come to know that the main point is for the Creator, you understand that not for the sake of the Creator is worthless." Therefore, it makes him think that he does not need to make such efforts in order to sustain all the actions, since you already know from experience that the *Lo Lishma* is not so important. Hence, you can make allowances in the Torah and the prayer and so forth.

It follows that during the descent, a person declines and follows what his mind makes him think. When the person is in a state of descent with all his lowliness, he prides himself and says he sees those people who observe the Torah and *Mitzvot* with all the details, but although he sees that they are not working for the sake of the Creator, he cannot be like them.

He excuses himself with an excuse of pride. That is, they have not yet come to this important knowledge that what matters is to do everything for the sake of the Creator, whereas I am at a higher degree than they are, and I do know that for the sake of the Creator is what matters. For this reason, I do not see in observing only in action, without the aim for the Creator, much use, that it is worth exerting to observe with all the details.

This is called "transgression induces a transgression." That is, the transgression of despair causes him to degrade the work *Lo Lishma*. Once he has degraded the work *Lo Lishma*, it causes him to come to the degree of pride, meaning to consider himself superior to others, that he knows better than the rest of the people, who do not understand the truth as he does.

If a person nonetheless does not escape the campaign, meaning he does not disclose his sins in public, after some time, he is pitied from above and is given another awakening, and he receives an ascent once more. Then, the evil comes to him once more to argue with him and the same sequence repeats itself. The advice is not to run from actions he was accustomed to do, but on the contrary, do more actions.

Yet, he can do this only above reason. A person must believe that this work he does during the descent, when he adds actions in externality on the basis of above reason, by this he takes big strides toward the goal, called "*Dvekut* with the Creator." Baal HaSulam said about this issue, that this is the meaning of what is written, "For the ways of the Lord are straight; the righteous walk in it, and the transgressors fail in them."

If he can add actions on the basis of going above reason in that state of descent, since his reason shows him a procession of "transgression induces a transgression," and he grows stronger above the intellect, he brings the time of his work closer and can achieve the goal sooner.

Therefore, during the ascent, a person must put in order the actions and the intentions. That is, when he feels that the aim is what counts, he must think that the act is also very important, since he is observing the King's commandments and we cannot grasp how important is the act to Him. As Baal HaSulam said, as much as we can appreciate the importance of *Lishma*, to the Creator, the *Lo Lishma* is far more important, and we cannot even fathom the importance of *Lishma*. Hence, during the ascent, a person must remember not to belittle the action he is doing.

But at the same time, a person must try to do his work only for the sake of the Creator. There is a rule: Anything to which a person is accustomed becomes to him like a conduct, meaning something he does not need to know why he is doing it. This is called "by rote," meaning he is used to them.

But since the Torah and *Mitzvot* were given in order to cleanse people, it follows that while performing the *Mitzvot*, he must aim that this work will yield for him a state of *Dvekut* with the Creator. It follows that the person must know what he wants from this work.

Therefore, if a person works out of habit, he does not need any reward. Thus, on one hand, observing Torah and *Mitzvot* out of habit is also a sublime thing, as our sages said, "The Creator adds a good thought to an action." That is, when a person is rewarded with a good thought, meaning he is rewarded with being able to aim his actions in order to bestow, then all the things he did, which were still not with the intention for the sake of the Creator, the Creator adds to all the actions that were done before and all of them enter *Kedusha*. It follows that the more actions he has, the more the thought for the sake of the Creator is on them later.

Now we will understand what our sages said, "Each day, they will be as new in your eyes, as though today you received them from Mt. Sinai, as though on this day you were commanded them."

There are two meanings here: 1) As then they had preparation to receive the Torah, likewise, each day, a person must prepare to receive the Torah and *Mitzvot*. Through the preparation, we can attain it.

But if a person works without preparation, but out of habit, by this, a person is not rewarded with the purpose of creation. Although this is a big thing, too, in a place where he can thereby achieve the degree, "know the God of your father," which is certainly directly to the goal, for this reason, they said, "they will be as new in your eyes," for by this they will achieve *Dvekut* with the Creator.

2) If they are not "as new in your eyes," it will be to him as going "by rote," meaning out of habit. At that time, he will not be able to observe the Torah and *Mitzvot* above reason because by working above reason, he later merits being rewarded with the knowledge of *Kedusha*. It follows that when he works out of habit, meaning feels that he should observe Torah and *Mitzvot* as a custom that is fixed into his schedule, he cannot advance. This is why they said, "Each day, they will be as new in your eyes," for by this, the person will be rewarded with the purpose of creation, which is for the creatures to be rewarded with receiving the delight and pleasure.

According to what is written in the book *Shaar Hakavanot* [*Gate of Intentions*], "the meaning of "Each day, they will be as new in your eyes" is that because this is the truth. That is, each day a person corrects new discernments from those that have fallen during the breaking of the vessels, as explained there in the book. It follows that a person does not repeat the Torah he had received on Mt. Sinai, he does not repeat the same things. Rather, with the Torah that was given on Mt. Sinai he must correct new discernments each day. It follows that it is "as though on this day you were commanded," meaning that each day there are other discernments to correct with the Torah.

From this we learn why a person needs to eat each day, and it is not enough to eat once a year so it suffices for the rest of the year. According to the words of the ARI, in each eating, new discernments from the shattering are sorted, although not each one feels it. However, this is given to the whole of Israel, and all the individuals in the collective should come to this degree, as it is written, "For they shall all know Me, from the least of them unto the greatest of them."

The Daily Schedule

Article No. 41, Tav-Shin-Mem-Tet, 1988/89

1) Midnight Correction: to mourn over the exile of the *Shechina* [Divinity].

2) Establish the faith in quantity and quality.

3) Concerning the bad: Depict the suffering and pain that the bad causes in the worlds above and below, in this world, that it inflicts death upon the created beings, and causes suffering to all of creation. For this reason, the bad of the individual causes the general, since the general and the individual are equal and there is no difference between them.

4) Also, to hate the evil because "You who love the Lord, hate evil, who preserves the souls of His followers; He delivers them from the hand of the wicked," and his aim will be to separate the bad completely.

5) Depict the state of the souls that are robbed, and ask for mercy for them.

6) Depict the exaltedness of the Creator.

7) Depict the love in manners of revealing love.

8) The order of the learning should be *Lishma* [for Her sake]. This means that he wants the learning to bring him the light of Torah so the light will reform him, as our sages said, "The light in it reforms him." Without help from above, a person cannot work in true faith and bestowal, without fooling himself saying that he has faith in the Creator, and he is ready to work in order to bestow without the Creator's help, for only "the light in it reforms him."

For this reason, it is good to dedicate a fixed time for learning only matters that speak of faith and bestowal, since when he learns these matters, he clings to such thoughts and then it is easier to accept to cling to the light of Torah.

However, we obtain this only to the extent that we work on hating evil. Hating evil is called "doers of His word," and the light of Torah is called "to hear the voice of His word." Both together are wholeness, for everything must [consist of] two things: right and left, meaning the hatred of evil and the love of the good, which is like light and *Kli* [vessel].

Tav-Shin-Nun
(1989 - 1990)

What Does "May We Be the Head and Not the Tail" Mean in the Work?

Article No. 1, Tav-Shin-Nun, 1989/90

Our sages said, "Be a tail to the lions and do not be a head to the foxes" (*Avot*, Chapter 4). Therefore, what does it mean when they say, "May we be the head and not the tail"?

The order of the work is that when wanting to walk in the path of correction, called "in order to bestow," the basis of the work should be faith above reason. That is, when the body sees that a person wants to work for the sake of the Creator and not for oneself, the body comes with the question of wicked Pharaoh, who asked the "Who" question, and the question of the wicked one, "What is this work for you?" Reasonably thinking, we should answer these questions with the mind, which is the intellect, and not answer as though we have no head. In other words, we should delve and scrutinize with our minds what to answer to these questions.

It was said about this that we should say to the body, "In terms of the intellect, you are correct and I have no reply to you. However, the path of Torah is that we must go above the reason and the intellect."

Accordingly, we should interpret "Be a tail to the lions and do not be a head to the foxes." That is, when the body comes with the "Who" and "What" questions, do not answer it with the head, meaning with the intellect and within reason. Rather, "Be a tail to the lions." A "lion" is the quality of *Hesed* [mercy], since in the upper *Merkava* [structure/chariot] there are a lion and an ox, which are *Hesed* and *Gevura*, and a vulture, which is the quality of *Tifferet*. He says "to the foxes" because the questions they ask are in the intellect and a fox is considered clever; this is why they are called "foxes."

A person should reply, "I do not reply to you with the intellect, meaning with the mind. Rather, I am following the lions as a tail follows the head. As for me, I have no head, but I am following the quality of *Hesed*, which is covered *Hassadim* [mercies]." That is, even though he does not see that they are *Hassadim*, meaning that it is covered from him, he still believes above reason that they are *Hassadim*.

This is called "Be a tail to the lions." This means that he says, "I am following the quality of *Hesed*, which is only to bestow. A person should say that since he believes above reason that the Creator watches over the world with the quality of good and doing good, he therefore believes that although he sees concealment on Providence, since according to a person's eyes it should have been otherwise, he still believes that the Creator wants that this way it will be better for man if he can accept everything with faith above reason, for by this he will be able to emerge from self-love and work for the sake of the Creator.

This means that if Providence were revealed to all, even before a person has obtained vessels of bestowal, it would be utterly impossible for man to be able to receive the good in order to bestow. Rather, once a person has made every effort to obtain the vessels of bestowal, he can receive the delight and pleasure in order to bestow, as the correction should be.

It is known that our sages said, "Everything is in the hands of heaven except for fear of heaven." This means that the Creator gives everything but the fear of heaven. This, the Creator does not give.

Indeed, we should ask, Why does He not give it? But first we should know the meaning of fear of heaven. As it is explained in the "Introduction of The Book of Zohar" (Item 203), fear is that he is afraid that he will "decline in bringing contentment to his Maker." Therefore, he is afraid to receive the abundance. This is as it is written, "And Moses hid his face for he was afraid to look." Our sages explained that "In return for 'Moses hid his face,' he was rewarded with 'The image of the Lord he beheld.'" It follows that we attribute to the Creator only giving, and not giving does not pertain to the Creator. This is why we say that fear of heaven pertains to the created beings, who detain themselves from receiving as long as they are uncertain that it will be only for the sake of the Creator.

This is all the work of the created beings, that they must work above reason. It is impossible to do anything without faith in the sages, who arranged for us the order of the work. Once a person has accepted his work as "a tail to the lions," he follows the sages, to walk only as they had arranged for us.

This is as our sages said (Avot, Chapter 1:4), "Be dusted by the dust of their feet (of the sages)." The Bartenura interprets that you should follow them, for one who walks kicks up dust with his feet, and one who follows him fills up with the dust that they raise with their feet.

We should understand what our sages imply to us with this allegory. We should interpret that one who goes after faith in the sages looks at their way, and they say that we must go above reason. Then, a person begins to be as spies, to see if it is truly worthwhile to follow their path. This is regarded as the feet of the sages kicking up dust, which goes into the eyes of their followers. That is, when a person wants to understand the path of the sages, they tell us that we must follow them with our eyes shut, or dust will enter. Something unimportant is called "dust," meaning that there cannot be greater lowliness than this.

Since man was given the reason and intellect in order to understand everything according to the intellect, and here we are told to walk by accepting faith in the sages, and a person wants to understand this path, and since as long as one is placed under the governance of the will to receive for himself, he cannot know what is good and what is bad, but must accept everything the way the sages determined for us, or dust and dirt will enter his eyes and he will not be able to move forward, but when we do not criticize the words of the sages and do not want to accept their words within reason, specifically by this we are rewarded with knowledge [reason] of *Kedusha* [holiness].

This is so because the whole reason why we need to go above reason is that we are immersed in self-love. Hence, through faith above reason, we are rewarded with vessels of bestowal, and then the delight and pleasure in vessels of bestowal is revealed. In the words of *The Zohar*, this is called "Reason spreads and fills rooms and corridors." That is, when the *Kelim* [vessels] are proper, reason spreads both in the inner *Kelim* and in the outer *Kelim*.

By this we should interpret what we say, "May we be the head and not the tail." It is known that there is the order of the purpose of creation and the order of the correction of creation. Therefore, in the order of the correction of creation, we must obtain vessels of bestowal, or it is impossible to receive the delight and pleasure. Therefore, the conduct is "be a tail to the lions," and then the conduct is everything above reason.

Later, when he is rewarded with the vessels of bestowal through it, he is rewarded with a mind of *Kedusha*, called "reason of *Kedusha*," as it is written in *The Zohar*, that the reason fills rooms and corridors. In other words, the reason of *Kedusha* in a person who is rewarded is called the "head." Therefore, when we ask of the Creator and say, "May it be," we ask to achieve the purpose of creation, which is "reason" and "head."

This is the meaning of "May we be the head and not the tail," meaning that we will not remain a tail of the *Sitra Achra* [other side], who has no reason, as it is written, "Another God is sterile and does not bear fruit." Rather, we will be rewarded with "reason," which is the fruits one obtains following the work of obtaining vessels of bestowal, which are *Kelim* that are fit to receive the delight and pleasure that He wishes to bestow upon His creations.

For this reason, if a person sees that he has still not been rewarded with "reason of *Kedusha*," called "head," it is a sign that he has still not been purified from vessels of self-love. This is why he still has no "reason." In other words, it is because he did not initially walk in the manner of accepting faith above reason, by which one is rewarded with vessels of bestowal, which are *Kelim* where the *Kedusha* can clothe. This is why he has no reason of *Kedusha*.

This is similar to what the Sayer of Duvna said about the verse, "You did not call upon Me, Jacob, for you labored, Israel." If a person still feels labor in the work of the Creator, it is a sign that he is still not working for the sake of the Creator, but is rather working for his own sake. This is why he has exertion in his work. Conversely, when he has corrected his *Kelim* so as to work in order to bestow contentment upon his Maker, he enjoys the work because he feels that he is serving a great King, and this is worth a great fortune to him. It follows that a person should come to a state of head, intellect, and reason of *Kedusha*, since this is the purpose of creation.

According to the above, we should interpret what *The Zohar* says (Pinhas, Item 143), "Rabbi Aba said, 'I remember something I had heard from Rabbi Shimon, who had heard from Rabbi Eliezer. One day, a sage from the nations came to Rabbi Eliezer and said to him, 'Three questions I would like to ask you: 1) You say that another Temple will be built for you, but there can only be building twice ... for the writing called them 'The two houses of Israel.' Also, it is written about the Second Temple, 'The glory of that last house will be greater than the first.' 2) You say that you are closer to the High King more than all other nations. One who is close to the King is always happy, without sorrow ... but you are always afflicted, in trouble, and in more grief than all the people. 3) You do not eat carcass or nonkosher food so that you will be healthy, etc. We eat whatever we want and we are robust in strength, etc. Old man, old man, tell me nothing for I will not hear you.' Rabbi Eliezer raised his eyes, looked at him, and turned him into a pile of bones. When his anger subsided, he turned his head and wept. ...These words that the wicked man asked him, I asked Elijah one day, and he said that in the seminary of the firmament, the words were laid out before the Creator, and so they are.'"

We should understand why when the gentile asked him the three questions, Rabbi Eliezer turned him into a pile of bones, while he was rewarded with the revelation of Elijah and asked him the same three questions. Why was Rabbi Eliezer permitted to ask those questions?

According to the above, meaning that we must go above reason, there is no room for questions. That is, it is forbidden to be a head to the foxes, meaning answer the questions with the head, meaning with reason and intellect, namely the questions of "Who" and "What." Rather, "Be a tail to the lions," meaning we must say that common sense is as the body says, but we are going above reason. By this we are later rewarded with "reason of Kedusha," which is being the head and not the tail. In other words, we are rewarded with the head of Kedusha.

By this we should interpret what is this act, that he tells us the argument that Rabbi Eliezer had with the gentile. What does it give us in the work? In the work, we should interpret this in one person. That is, when the body asks questions and wants to understand everything within reason, we must tell the body, "Your questions do not interest me, since I am going above reason." This is the meaning of the saying that he "looked at him and turned him into a pile of bones." That is, turning him into a pile of bones refers to his questions, since when one goes above reason, there are no questions and everything is canceled. Afterward, "when his anger subsided" over the questions that the wicked man asked him, he was rewarded with the revelation of Elijah, and Elijah gave him the reason of Kedusha on all the questions, according to what is learned above.

What Is the Meaning of Failure in the Work?

Article No. 2, Tav-Shin-Nun, 1989/90

It is written (Hosea 14), "Return, O Israel unto the Lord your God, for you have failed in your iniquity." The RADAK interprets "You have failed in your iniquity," that you see that you failed in your iniquity because nothing raises you from your fall but your repentance [return] to Him. It says "unto" as in "to." Our sages said, "Great is repentance, for it reaches unto the throne, as was said, 'unto the Lord your God.'"

We should understand what is "for you have failed in your iniquity." It seems as though he did something and there was a failure, some blunder that he did not see in advance. But if a person commits iniquities, what failure is there here? From the start, he intended to do something inappropriate, for he committed something that is forbidden to do.

A failure means that it is not really the person's fault, but that he failed in it. And we should also understand the meaning of the words "unto the Lord your God," in singular form, "your God." Also, we should understand the meaning of "unto the throne."

We should interpret that "for you have failed in your iniquity" means the first iniquity that *Adam HaRishon* sinned with the tree of knowledge, where the blunder was that he heeded the serpent's advice. The Creator told him not to eat from the tree of knowledge but he listened to the advice of the serpent, that if he worked in order to bestow he was permitted to eat.

The serpent said that the Creator commanded not to eat from the tree of knowledge because in the state he was in, he was unfit to eat it. But if he mended his ways, certainly, in such a manner the Creator did not forbid him to eat from the tree of knowledge.

It follows that with *Adam HaRishon* there was a blunder and a failure. That is, he did not intend to act against His will. On the contrary, following the serpent's advice, he intended to perform a great correction, as the serpent advised him, that it was to the contrary and the Creator would enjoy this action (see "Introduction to Panim Masbirot," where he interprets the matter of the sin of the tree of knowledge).

This was the failure of *Adam HaRishon*, that he heeded the serpent's advice, who told him that this work of eating from the tree of knowledge is considered a *Mitzva* [commandment/good deed], and not a transgression. But in the end, he saw that he had sinned, as it is written, "And the eyes of both of them were opened, and they knew that they were naked."

RASHI interpreted "and they knew that they were naked": "Even a blind person knows that he is naked. So what is the meaning of 'and they knew that they were naked'? They had one *Mitzva* in their hands, and they were stripped off of it" (stripped off means naked, bare, undressed).

That is, he saw that he should not have heeded the serpent's advice, although the serpent made him think that everything he said to him was for the sake of the Creator and not for his own sake, as he told him that if he prepared to purify himself and aim for the sake of the Creator, on this, there was no commandment of the Creator (see "Introduction to Panim Masbirot," Item 17).

By this we should interpret what our sages said (Sanhedrin 38), "*Adam HaRishon* was a thief." RASHI interprets that he "leaned toward idolatry." We should understand how such a thing can be said of *Adam HaRishon*, who spoke to the Creator, that we can say he was an idolater.

According to what we learn, faith means that he believes above reason. Therefore, although he himself heard from the Creator that he must not eat from the tree of knowledge, and it cannot be said that he had to believe in the commandment of the Creator, but it means that after the serpent came to him and made him understand within reason why the Creator told him not to eat, *Adam HaRishon* should have told the serpent, "Although within reason you are correct, meaning that if I eat from the tree of knowledge with the aim to bestow, the Creator will have contentment from this eating, and I see that you are one hundred percent correct, still, I am going above reason. I want to observe the commandment of the Creator without any intellect or reason, since what you add to faith is already called 'leaning toward idol-worship.'"

But *Adam HaRishon* added to what the Creator had commanded him. It is about this that they said, "*Adam HaRishon* was an idolater." From this sin extends to us the concealment in the work, for it is hard for us to move away from self-love. Naturally, it is difficult for us to believe in His guidance in the form of good and doing good, so we will have the power to praise and thank Him for all the things that a person feels—that it is only good.

This lack of faith in His guidance, that He leads His world as the good who does good, causes us to be so far from the Creator. A person can serve and do things that are even beyond his power, if he feels for whom he is working. But as long as one is in self-love, he cannot feel His existence as is required for having permanent faith.

This is as it is written ("Introduction of The Book of Zohar," Item 138), "When one feels bad, denial ... lies upon him," meaning he cannot have faith before he has equivalence of form. "It is a law that the creature cannot receive disclosed evil from the Creator, for it is a flaw in the glory of the Creator for the creature to perceive Him as an evildoer, for this is unbecoming of the complete Operator."

By this we should interpret his expulsion from the Garden of Eden into concealment and hiding, and for which all the generations following him have much work in that they must believe that there is a leader in the world, and that He also watches over with a guidance of the good who does good. When a person does not have such faith, it causes him all the sins that he commits, since it extends from the first iniquity of Adam HaRishon that man has the quality of self-love, and naturally, he is incapable of taking upon himself the burden of faith.

It follows that everything extends from the first failure, when Adam HaRishon fell into self-love. This caused the following generations to have work of simple faith, since when a person is in self-love, the Tzimtzum [restriction] and concealment are on him, and the upper light cannot shine for him. For this reason, a person can believe in the Creator only above reason, since the will to receive causes him denial.

Thus, the failure that Adam HaRishon had with the tree of knowledge caused us absence of faith. Naturally, from this we come into all the sins. Therefore, the only counsel is to be rewarded with faith, for man to feel Godliness personally, so he will not need the general public, to have faith from the whole of Israel. Instead, a person must repent to the extent that it is "unto the Lord your God." That is, he should feel that "the Lord is your God" personally, and then the flaw of the tree of knowledge will be corrected.

By this we can interpret what is "unto the Lord your God." Because the failure was that he heeded the serpent's advice—who told him what was His intention according to the intellect—a person must repent until he is rewarded with "the Lord is your God" personally, and not be taken after anyone.

That is, he should not follow the general public when he sees in what ways, meaning with what intentions the order of the work should be, as well as the manner of the work. In other words, he should not consider the goal that a person from the general public aspires for. Rather, he must repent until he is personally rewarded with "The Lord is your God."

This is as it is written ("Introduction to The Study of the Ten Sefirot," Item 54), "When the Creator sees that one has completed one's measure of exertion and strengthening in faith in the Creator, the Creator helps him. Then, one attains open Providence, meaning the revelation of the face. Then, he is rewarded with complete repentance, meaning he clings to the Creator once more with his heart, soul, and might, as though naturally drawn to Him by the attainment of the open Providence. ...It is written, 'What is repentance like?' ... 'when He who knows all mysteries testifies that he will not turn back to folly.'" That is, when can one be certain that he has been rewarded with complete repentance? "When He who knows all mysteries testifies" to him. "This means that he will attain the revelation of the face, at which time one's own salvation will testify that he will not turn back to folly."

Accordingly, we should interpret what we asked, What is "unto the Lord your God"? It means that a person should repent, meaning do all that he can until the Creator helps him and he is rewarded with open Providence, meaning the revelation of the face. Then it is regarded as "the Lord your God," meaning that he has obtained the revelation of the face of the Creator personally. This is called "unto the Lord your God," meaning that he was rewarded personally, and this is called "the Lord your God."

Now we will explain what we asked about the meaning of what our sages said, "Great is repentance, for it reaches unto the throne" (Yoma 86). It is known that it is impossible to correct anything unless we see the corruption. For this reason, it is impossible to repent if he does not see the sin. In other words, the evil cannot be corrected if one does not see the evil in its true form.

As in corporeality, if one does not see the weight of something, one cannot lift it. Hence, when a person does not see the real form of evil within him, he cannot ask for complete help so he can overcome the evil. It is known that "Man's inclination overcomes him every day, and were it not for the help of the Creator, he would not be able to overcome it." For this reason, if a person does not see the measure of the evil, his prayer is incomplete.

If, for example, a person asks the Creator to help him with a little bit of evil, so that by this he will be rewarded with repentance, as a result, the help that comes from above is only in order to revoke a little bit of evil and not all the evil within him. This is akin to a person coming to the doctor and telling him that he has a fever and asking the doctor to give him a pill to lower his temperature. The doctor asks, "What is your temperature?" and he says, "38° (centigrade)" [100.4f]. The doctor gives him a pill but the pill does not help. So the doctor says to him, "You must have a higher temperature." So what does the doctor do? He takes his temperature himself and sees that his temperature is more than 40° (centigrade) [104f]. Then the doctor gives him a medicine suitable for someone with 40° (centigrade) temperature.

The lesson is that since a person must pray, which is the tool to receive salvation, and if a person does not pray for the real evil within him, but thinks that he has a little bit of evil, his prayer does not draw help from above, but only for someone who has a little bit of evil. Therefore, when a person begins to walk on the path of truth and asks for the Creator's help, the Creator shows him each time a little bit of the evil within him. Consequently, the person begins to think that each time he overcomes in Torah and Mitzvot [commandments/good deeds], he grows worse than before he began the work of truth.

At that time he comes to a state of "pondering the beginning." That is, he regrets having started this work. The whole reason why he started this work was in order to thereby draw closer to the Creator. But now he sees the opposite, that he is going backward instead of forward.

However, a person should believe that he is making progress in the work, except he sees that each time he is getting worse. As in the above allegory, where the doctor takes the temperature and not the patient, the Creator "takes his temperature," meaning shows him each time how he is immersed in evil to such an extent that he cannot believe that such a thing can be.

That is, a person does not understand how there can be such a state where a person begins to increase his labor in Torah and Mitzvot, and should have seen that each day he becomes better. But in reality, he sees that he is getting worse.

The answer is that when a person begins to walk on the path of truth, to the extent that he overcomes in the work, to that extent he is sown the evil in him, so he can ask the Creator for help over the actual evil. That is, at that time a person sees that unless the Creator helps him, it will be utterly impossible for him to emerge from the control of the evil, as the control of the evil within him grows more powerful each day. But all this is in order for him to need the salvation of the Creator, for specifically then he receives a desire and need for the Creator's help.

This is as it is written in the "Introduction to The Study of the Ten Sefirot" (Item 138): "The concealment is the reason for the revelation. After its correction, at the time of revelation, the concealment becomes revelation like a wick to the light that grips it. And the greater the concealment, the greater the light that will cling to it and be revealed when it is corrected."

Accordingly, we should interpret the meaning of "Great is repentance, for it reaches unto the throne." Baal HaSulam said that we should interpret Kisse [Throne] in two ways: 1) from the word Kissui [cover], that it covers, 2) from the word Kisse [chair] that is fit for the King to sit on.

It follows that by a person achieving the recognition of evil, where he sees how far he is both in mind and in heart, that everything is blocked and covered, that he sees no inlet making it possible to be rewarded with Dvekut [adhesion] with the Creator, this is called the "covering throne."

This degree is regarded as a *Kli* [vessel] and a real need for the salvation of the Creator. On this throne, the help of the Creator is later revealed, as in "He who comes to purify is aided." It follows that this throne, that was in such lowliness, meaning that he felt a state of lowliness and degradation, has been rewarded with the glory of the King being on it. It follows that that same lowliness has become the throne.

By this we can interpret, "Great is repentance, for it reaches unto the throne." That is, when does one know that he has repented? The sign is if the previous throne has been rewarded with the revelation of light. This is until the King of Glory, who sits on the throne, becomes revealed.

What It Means that the World Was Created for the Torah

Article No. 3, Tav-Shin-Nun, 1989/90

RASHI brings the words of our sages about "In the beginning [God] created," "for the Torah, which is called 'the beginning of his way,' and for Israel, who were called 'The holy of Israel, his first crop.'"

We should understand what it means that "The world was created for the Torah." "Torah," simply put, is the King's commandments, who commanded to observe them. But are the King's commandments lacking, and want to have someone following them? Do they have feelings?

We can say that the King wants His commandments followed. But this pertains to a flesh and blood king, who wants to command them and enjoys this. But we cannot say this about the Creator, that He wants to be given respect and that they will keep what He commands them.

Also, we should understand what our sages said, that the world was created for Israel, meaning not for the Torah. Therefore, we should understand if the creation of the world has two reasons or is it one reason, meaning that both point to the same thing.

It is known that the reason for the creation of the world was His desire to do good to His creations. In order to carry out the perfection of His deeds, meaning so there would not be shame, a Tzimtzum [restriction] and concealment were established, so the delight and pleasure would not shine unless the receiver has the intention to bestow. Otherwise, there is a concealment of the face of the Creator. For this reason, we were given the commandment of faith that He leads His world as The Good Who Does Good, whereby the commandment of faith in the Creator, and by observing the Torah and Mitzvot [commandments/good deeds] on the basis of faith, the matter of shame will be corrected.

However, because of the creation of the creatures, who were created with a desire to receive for themselves, the creatures cannot achieve a degree where all their actions are for the sake of the Creator and not for their own sake. This is why the will to receive is called "evil," and one who walks in the path of this evil is called "wicked." The will to receive for one's own benefit is called "evil inclination" because all it depicts for one to do is to do everything only in a manner of self-reception, and this harms a person.

This means that this is the only reason why a person cannot obtain the delight and pleasure that the Creator wishes to impart upon the creatures, since there was a correction on this quality, called "will to receive for oneself," since the will to receive is opposite from the Creator, whose desire is only to bestow, while the will to receive cannot be a giver.

In order to have equivalence of form, meaning that while a person receives he will be able to aim that the reception will be in order to bestow, this is already considered that he bestows. This is called "equivalence of form" or Dvekut [adhesion], since in spirituality, equivalence is called *Dvekut*, although in the act he is receiving. This is called "receiving in order to bestow."

However, how can one achieve equivalence of form? Since the Creator created this will to receive, how is it possible to revoke the nature that the Creator created? There was a correction on this that while it is impossible to revoke the nature of the will to receive, an intention to bestow is added on top of it. It follows that the will to receive, meaning that a person sees something from which he can enjoy, remains. In other words, a person still enjoys in the end, but with a different intention. This is called "receiving in order to bestow."

However, how can one have a different aim than to receive for his own benefit, but rather for the benefit of the Creator? Our sages said about this, "The Creator said, 'I have created the evil inclination; I have created the Torah as a spice.'" In other words, through the *Segula* [merit/virtue/remedy] of Torah and *Mitzvot*, a person can obtain the desire to bestow. This is the only way by which one can be rewarded with vessels of bestowal, and our sages said about it, "The light in it reforms him."

It follows that through the Torah, a person will obtain vessels of bestowal, and then he will be able to receive the delight and pleasure that the Creator wants to give to the created beings. In this respect, the Torah is called "613 counsels," meaning 613 tips by which one is rewarded with vessels of bestowal.

Afterward, once he is rewarded with vessels of bestowal through the Torah, he must receive the delight and pleasure that is found in the thought of the Creator. That delight and pleasure is also called "Torah," meaning that at that time, the 613 counsels become 613 deposits. This means that in each *Mitzva* [singular of *Mitzvot*] there is a special light.

This is as it is written ("Introduction of The Book of Zohar," "General Explanation for All Fourteen Commandments and How They Divide into the Seven Days of Creation," Item 1), "In Torah and *Mitzvot* there are 'We shall do' and 'We shall hear,' as our sages said, 'Doers of His word, to hear the voice of His word. In the beginning, they do, and in the end, they hear.' When observing Torah and Mitzvot as 'doers of His word,' prior to being rewarded with hearing, the Mitzvot are called '613 counsels,' and are considered Achor [back/posterior]. When rewarded with hearing 'the voice of His word,' the 613 Mitzvot become Pekudin, from the word Pikadon [deposit], for in each Mitzva, the light of a unique degree is deposited."

According to the above, we can interpret what we asked, What does it mean that the world was created for the Torah? Does the Torah have feelings, that she should feel that she needs someone to observe her? We also asked, But elsewhere, our sages said that the world was created for Israel?

The thing is that both point to the same thing—that the reason for the creation of the world was His desire to do good to His creations. It is written (Midrash Rabbah, Beresheet) that when the Creator wanted to create Adam HaRishon, the angels objected to this saying, "What is man that You should think of him? Why do You need this trouble?" The Creator replied to them that it is like a king who has a tower filled with abundance but he has no guests.

It follows that man's creation was in order to do good to His creations. This is why they said that the creation of the world was for Israel, who are called Resheet [beginning]. Yet, what is the delight and pleasure that He wanted to give them?

Our sages came and told us that the delight and pleasure is the Torah. That is, the creation of the world was for Israel to receive and enjoy the delight and pleasure found in the Torah.

It follows that when they said, "The world was created for Israel," and when they said, "The world was created for the Torah," it is the same.

However, here we are speaking of the receivers, which are Israel, and here, of what Israel receive. That is, one speaks from the perspective of the Kli [vessel], and one speaks from the perspective of the light. Yet, they are both one—light and Kli.

However, we should interpret what they said, "The world was created for the Torah," in two ways: 1) The Torah is regarded as 613 counsels, 613 tips for subduing the evil, as it is written, "I have created the evil inclination; I have created the Torah as a spice." That is, through the Torah, the evil is corrected because "the light in it reforms him."

In this way, we should interpret what our sages said (*Shabbat* 33), "Were it not for My covenant day and night, I would not place the ordinances of heaven and earth." They interpreted "day and night" to mean the Torah, as it is written, "And you shall reflect on it day and night." In other words, were it not for the Torah, the world would not exist.

We should interpret that through the Torah, whose light reforms him, the world can exist. In other words, it will be possible to receive the delight and pleasure because the Torah will correct the evil in the creatures and they will have equivalence of form by which the flaw of shame will be corrected.

Naturally, if the Torah did not reform, it would be impossible for them to receive the delight and pleasure. It follows that "I would not place the ordinances of heaven and earth," so everything would be useless.

It follows that here the Torah is regarded only as counsels, meaning tips by which to receive the good.

2) The Torah is considered 613 deposits, which are the holy names. As is said in the "Introduction of The Book of Zohar" ("General Explanation for All Fourteen Commandments and How They Divide into the Seven Days of Creation," Item 1), "In each *Mitzva*, a light of a unique degree is deposited, which corresponds to a unique organ in the 613 organs and tendons of the soul and the body. It follows that while performing the *Mitzva*, one extends to its corresponding organ in his soul and body the degree of light that belongs to that organ and tendon. This is considered the *Panim* [face/anterior] of the *Mitzvot*," which are then called *Pekudin*.

Now we can interpret what our sages said, "The world was created for the Torah," meaning that we say that the reason for the creation of the worlds was in order to do good to His creations. That delight and pleasure is found in the Torah, which is called "the names of the Creator," whose general name is The Good Who Does Good.

The names given to the Creator are only by way of "By Your actions we know You." For this reason, since they attained from the Creator delight and pleasure for themselves and for the whole world, they named Him, The Good Who Does Good, as our sages said, "Good for himself, and does good to others." This means that they perceived that they received abundance from the Creator, and also perceived that the Creator does good to others, too.

However, we cannot speak of the Creator Himself, as it is written in *The Zohar*, "There is no thought or perception in Him at all." This means that it is impossible to speak of the Creator Himself because we have no attainment in the Creator. It follows that what our sages said, that the world was created for the Torah, and what our sages said, that the world was created for Israel, are the same thing. The only difference is between the light and the *Kli*. The light is called "Torah," and the *Kli* for reception of the light is called "Israel."

This matter is explained in the book *A Sage's Fruit* (Part 1, p 118), where he explains the matter of "the Torah, Israel, and the Creator are one." These are his words: "Thus, you see that the meaning of the 620 names, being the 613 *Mitzvot* of the Torah and the seven *Mitzvot de Rabanan* [lit. commandments of our great sages], are, in fact, the five properties of the soul, meaning NRNHY. This is because the vessels of the NRNHY are from the above 620 *Mitzvot*, and the lights of NRNHY are the very light of Torah in each and every *Mitzva*. It follows that the Torah and the soul are one. However, the Creator is the light of *Ein Sof* [infinity], clothed in the light of the Torah, which is found in the above 620 *Mitzvot*."

It follows that "Israel" and the "Torah" are the same thing, except the difference is whether we speak from the perspective of the light or from the perspective of the *Kli*.

However, the order of the work is that since we were born after the sin of the tree of knowledge, we are already immersed in the will to receive for our own sake, on which there were the *Tzimtzum* and concealment. For this reason, the order of our work begins in work *Lo Lishma* [not for Her sake]. That is, when we begin to observe Torah and *Mitzvot*, we must believe even if *Lo Lishma*, since without faith, even if *Lo Lishma*, we cannot work.

Wherever the work is on the basis of faith, it is hard work. That is, only where the reward and punishment are revealed, the work is called "within reason" because we immediately see the results.

But when the reward and punishment are covered and we must only believe in reward and punishment, even *Lo Lishma* is a great effort. However, this is still not so bad because it is not against the nature of the will to receive for oneself. But if we want to achieve *Dvekut*, called "in order to bestow," the body begins to resist with all its might, and it is impossible to emerge from the control of the will to receive without help from above.

It was said about this, "Were it not for the help of the Creator, he would not overcome it." The advice for this is Torah, since "the light in it reforms him." Afterward, when he is rewarded with vessels of bestowal, he is rewarded with the quality called "the names of the Creator," which is the delight and pleasure that was in His thought to give to the created beings. This is the meaning of what they said, that the reason for the creation of the worlds was to do good to His creations.

What It Means that the Generations of the Righteous are Good Deeds, in the Work

Article No. 4, Tav-Shin-Nun, 1989/90

Our sages said about the verse, "These are the generations of Noah; Noah was a righteous man," "To teach you that the generations of the righteous are primarily good deeds." We should understand this, since our sages said (*Nedarim* 64), "One who has no sons is considered dead, as it is written, 'Give me sons, or else I die.'" It therefore follows that righteous, who have good deeds, are still considered dead. Can this be said about righteous?

In the work, father and son are called "cause and consequence." In other words, the potential is called "father," and what is later revealed in practice is called "son." The potential is like a drop in the father's brain, and the emergent result is called "birth," and a "son," which emerges from potential to actual.

For this reason, when a person thinks of doing something, he must first think what he wants to do that will give him pleasure from the act, since it is known that man likes rest. The reason for this is that our root is in a state of complete rest, so the creatures, too, desire rest and do not make a single move unless it brings them more pleasure than they have in the state of rest.

For this reason, righteous, meaning people who want to be at the degree of righteous are called righteous, although they have not achieved the degree of righteous. It is as Baal HaSulam interpreted about the verse, "Will bring wisdom to the wise." The question is, Should it not have said, "Will bring wisdom to the fools"? Why does it say "to the wise"? Indeed, one who seeks wisdom is already called "wise," whereas a fool does not want wisdom, as it is written, "The fool does not desire wisdom."

It follows that one who wants to be righteous arranges for himself in his mind what he must do, meaning what he should crave. Our sages said "good deeds," meaning that he thinks how he can come to a state where he can do good deeds. That is, when he has good deeds in his hand, he will know that he is righteous, as our sages said (*Berachot* 61), "Rabba said, 'One should know in one's heart whether he is righteous or wicked.'" For this reason, a person arranges for himself in his mind, regarded as the "potential," what he must do in order to come to a state where everything he does is a good deed.

However, we must know what is a good deed, by which to know that he is righteous. We should interpret that good deeds are interpreted in the Torah and in the prayer, as well as in the performance of *Mitzvot* [commandments/good deeds]. We should interpret that a good deed is when a person feels good during the act. For example, when a person wants to stand and pray to the Creator, the person wants to feel as though he is standing before the King, for then all of one's heart and mind are given to the King. Because of the greatness and importance of the King, it is impossible that he would be distracted from the King.

Thus, there are two things here: 1) There is no room where another thought, which does not concern the King, may enter. At that time, it is as though there is no one in the world but he and the King, due to the fear of the greatness of the King. 2) At that time, he feels that he is in a state of good feeling because he has the privilege of speaking with the King.

Likewise, when he comes to observe some Mitzva [singular of Mitzvot], he thinks that the Mitzva he will perform will be a good Mitzva. That is, while performing the Mitzva, he should feel that now he is going to bring contentment to the King. For this reason, a person should feel, while performing the Mitzva, that he has the privilege of delighting the King, meaning that now the King enjoys his observing of the King's commandment. This is called "a good deed."

When he feels this way and has no other thought during the performing of the Mitzva, since he engages in the commandments of the King, therefore, his entire thought is that he wonders if the King will truly enjoy what he is doing now. This is what he regards as "good deeds."

Also, when he learns Torah, he prepares for the learning of Torah, meaning he first thinks what Torah he is about to learn—does he intend to enjoy the wisdom in the Torah or is it to have the strength to awaken in himself that this is the Torah of the Creator, that the whole of the Torah is the names of the Creator, and that he still has not been rewarded with understanding and seeing the connection between the Torah and the Creator. Yet, at least he wants to believe what our sages said, "The Torah and Israel and the Creator are one," and this is what he regards as good deeds.

It follows that one who wants to be righteous, while preparing and reflecting that he wants to do things that will be good, he is called "righteous." That is, he wants to engender through the preparation he has in his mind, which is called a "father who begets sons," which are good deeds.

It is written, "Noah was a righteous man," which is called "These are the generations of Noah," meaning the good deeds, which are the generations of the righteous. The verse "Noah was a righteous man" means that he was rewarded with good deeds. That is, during the act, he felt that his actions were truly good, and felt contentment while performing his actions and felt the good that is in them. Because the acts are good, he was rewarded with the delight and pleasure clothed in the performance of *Mitzvot*.

According to the above, we can understand what our sages said, "One who has no sons is considered dead." We asked, From this, from Noah, it seems that only one who has good deeds is considered righteous. But it is written, "One who has no sons is considered dead," which means that even righteous, if they have no sons, are considered dead. According to the above-said, where sons are called "good deeds," the meaning of "One who has no sons is considered dead" is that he has no good deeds and is considered dead because the righteous in their lives are called "dead," since they are separated from the Life of Lives.

However, why does man need to do good deeds? That is, what causes him to want to be righteous? Also, why must one leave all the needs he has been accustomed to do for the sake of the body? He was used to enjoying eating and drinking, and handsome clothes, and so forth, and although he hears from books and from authors that there is the matter of the soul, that a person should acquire the matters of the soul, after he has been given with a body, a person begins to ask, What is a soul, for which he must toil in order to obtain? At that time, the body asks, "What will I gain from having a soul?" Moreover, it asks, "What is a soul, that I should merit attaining it?"

To this comes the answer that a person is told, "There is no soul without a body." This is why man was given a body, which is like a machine, and with the machine he can go and come to all the places he wants. Therefore, we must preserve the machine and give it everything it needs, such as oil, water, and fuel. Only after you give the machine everything it needs, it will do what it must and bring the person to the places where he needs to go. Certainly, the person does not take a machine and gives it everything it needs and then leaves it and does not drive it.

Likewise, a person must think about the body. The body is like a machine whose role is to bring a person where he needs. When a person understands that the body is an instrument by which to obtain a soul, and this is why man was created with the body. This is similar to what is presented in the book *A Sage's Fruit* (Part 1, p 117), "By this you will understand that before a soul comes into the body, it is but a tiny dot, though attached to the root as a branch to a tree. This dot is called the 'root of the soul and its world.' Had it not entered this world in a body, it would have had only its own world, meaning its own part in the root. However, the more it comes to walk in the paths of the Creator, which are the 613 ways of the Torah that return to being the actual names of the Creator, the more its stature grows, according to the level of the names it has attained, except it must increase its stature 620 times more than how it previously was in the root."

It therefore follows that if we believe in the sages, there is room to contemplate why we were born in this world with a body that includes within it many base lusts. Also, how can we say that this body, for all its lowliness, was created for a sublime matter, which the soul could not attain before she descended into the lowly body— 620 times more than what she had prior to clothing in a body?

In this regard, we must work with faith, to believe in the sages that this is so. However, it is not necessarily for this that we need faith in the sages. Rather, for every single step, we must believe that such is the way to go in this world with our bodies as they were arranged for us. Otherwise, we stumble on our way as we walk on the path of the Creator.

However, concerning faith, we also need true guides, who arrange for us how and in what way to walk in the path of the Creator, since many times a person gives all his might to something that is not the main thing in the work. As a result, he is left with no time or energy to make the effort in the right place, meaning in the most important thing he needs in order to be completed in the rungs of holiness.

Since it is impossible to learn only from books, since one person is not like another, for each has different tendencies, as the ARI says, "One person is not like another, and one day is not like another, and the *Helbona* [resin] will correct what the *Levona* [incense] will not correct," therefore, each person needs his own precise order, and the order of the work of one person does not suit another's. For this reason, each one must go with the order that suits specifically him.

It is as presented in the "Introduction to the Book, Panim Masbirot" (Item 3), "We distinguish four divisions in the speaking species. For this purpose, the Creator instilled three inclinations in the masses, called 'envy,' 'lust,' and 'honor.' Due to them, the masses develop degree by degree to elicit a face of a whole man."

We should interpret the still, vegetative, animate, and speaking according to the four degrees, where neither understands the other. In other words, each one understands how a person should behave in this world, and no one can understand the other.

For example, the still is the first phase. This kind understands only lust. Sometimes, we see two neighbors living next to one another, and the wife of one husband, who is at the second degree, the vegetative, which pertains to respect and control, goes over to the wife of the still husband and sees how the neighbor sits with his family next to the table and eats with the family, and tells his family what his workday was like and how he is resting now and enjoys sitting together with his family and eating.

When the wife of the vegetative returns home, she waits for her husband to return from the store to have dinner with the family. But when the husband comes, he says, "I have no time to eat with you now because I am invited to some meeting for the public benefit." His wife asks, "Why does your neighbor come from the store and sits and eats with the family, and does not run anywhere, but sits at ease and joyfully with the family, while you have no consideration for your family, and your mind is only given to other people? I do not even know if you know them, but you are giving the time that our family deserves and you regard others more than us!"

Then, he replies to her that his neighbor has no feeling for others. He is like a hen with its chicks, strolling with them and tending only to her chicks. "Likewise, our neighbor has no more brains than a chicken. Would you like me to be like him? Would you want a husband who is like a chicken?"

That woman returns to the neighbor and asks him, "Why are you eating with your family after work and behave like a chicken instead of being like my husband?" He replies, "I am not crazy like your husband, giving my precious time that I need for rest and to be happy with my family to other people." Certainly, both are correct, but no one understands the other.

It is likewise between the second state to the third state. Let us take as an example two neighbors. One woman visits the other and sees that the neighbor's son gets up at eight in the morning and goes to work. In the evening, he comes and behaves fine, just like all other people. Afterward, he goes to meetings to do something there for the benefit of the public, and then he returns and goes to sleep, as usual, like all other people.

When that woman returns home she asks her son, "Why do I often see that I fix you dinner, and when I get up in the morning I see that the light is still on and dinner is still in front of you, untouched, while you are sitting by your books? Why does my neighbor's son behave like a human being?"

The son replies, "I love knowledge, so I think that it is worthwhile to give up everything and acquire knowledge. Conversely, the neighbor's son has no connection to knowledge; he is like a beast, working for the public needs, meaning in whatever way is convenient for beasts like him. That is, without knowledge, I see myself as similar to a beast. But the neighbor's son, who belongs to the quality of the beast, how can he understand that a person without knowledge is called 'a beast'?"

When that woman tells her neighbor that her son says about her son that he is a beast, that son tells his mother, "I am not crazy sinking my head into knowledge. Who and what will it give me? No one will want to speak with me, and everyone will say that I have no idea about worldly matters. Conversely, when I work for the needs of the public and go to meetings, where smart people gather to do something for the public benefit, many people will respect me since I am not tending to my own needs but to the public benefit. The neighbor's son, on the other hand, cares only for his own needs, this is why he delves in the books."

It follows that each one says that the way he is walking is the path of truth, and neither understands the other.

This is even more so with the speaking level. Those who are from the animate level cannot understand the speaking level. That is, those who engage in the work of the Creator seem to the smart people who delve in books their entire lives and say that brains is what counts and only reason determines, while those who engage in the work of the Creator say that we must go above reason, they laugh at them and say, "Without reason, we are as beasts. How can they say that we must go above reason?" It follows that one does not understand the other.

This is called "the generation of Babylon," when one does not understand the other's language.

Accordingly, how can a person emerge from the tendencies that he is used to since birth? Intellectually, it is impossible to understand how it is possible that a person will think other than his inclinations. And there (in the introduction, Item 3) he says, "Because of this, we were given corrections, by which man must toil and labor. Otherwise, all creations would have been in a state of rest, since the root of the creatures, which is the Creator, is in a state of complete rest, and every branch wants to resemble its root."

These corrections, called "envy," "lust," and "honor," bring man out of the world (Avot, Chapter 4:28). He says there that through the envy and respect, it is possible to change the inclinations to lust into the degree of vegetative, where he begins to work for the sake of others for the purpose of Lo Lishma [not for Her sake]. Likewise, through envy, he can shift to the level of knowledge, as our sages said, "Authors' envy increases knowledge." And likewise, through *Lo Lishma* they can also shift from the animate level to the speaking.

Yet, how does the *Lo Lishma* help if one does not have the real inclination to the degree to which he enters? Our sages said about this, with respect to the Torah, "The light in it reforms him." It turns out that through *Lo Lishma*, we come to *Lishma* [for Her sake]. This is why they said, "One should always learn *Lo Lishma*, as from *Lo Lishma* we come to *Lishma*."

However, we must know that these four divisions, which are still, vegetative, animate, and speaking, apply to the same person. The person himself shifts from state to state, as he writes there, "Yet, those who remain without any *Segula* [remedy/virtue/power], it is because they do not have a strong desire. Hence, all three above-mentioned tendencies work within them in a mixture. At times they are lustful, at times jealous, and at times craving honors. Yet, their desire shatters into pieces and they are as children craving anything they see, but they will obtain nothing. For this reason, their value is like the straw and bran that remain after the flour."

Now we can understand how a person has three states during the work: 1) the permanent state, 2) the state of ascent, and 3) the state of descent.

That is, when a person wants to emerge from his permanent state, it is known that there is a fixed routine that a person observes Torah and *Mitzvot* like the general public. This means that we are careful to observe Torah and *Mitzvot* in practice, meaning that they do not pay attention to the aim to bestow. This is called *Lo Lishma*. At that time, he can generally be in this state permanently, since he sees that each day he is progressing in Torah and *Mitzvot*. This is so because he looks only at the act, to see whether or not it is fine, and he is more or less meticulous about observing. For this reason, each day he acquires Torah and *Mitzvot*. And there is a rule: Where a person succeeds, he enjoys and can continue. For this reason, this state is called the "permanent state."

Conversely, the second state is the time of ascent. This means that a person heard from authors and books that there is the issue of the flavors of Torah and Mitzvot that a person should attain by observing Torah and Mitzvot, that he should work on Dvekut [adhesion] with the Creator, that one must attain Godliness, which is the main thing required from the Torah and Mitzvot. The books say that in the end, every person will be rewarded with this degree.

This person begins to ascend the degrees of holiness and begins to feel that now he is in a different world, as though the state he was in compared to his current state is like the difference between day and night. However, he is not accustomed to walking in this path and falls into a descent.

When his ascents and descents increase, he sometimes despairs and says, "This path is not for me," but he cannot return to the permanent state he had. In truth, a person should learn from all three states. It is as our sages said, "I have learned much from my teachers, more from my friends, and most from my disciples." "My teachers" are the states of ascent, "my disciples" are the states of descent, and "my friends" are the permanent state.

In other words, a person should use the state of descent. That is, during the ascent, he should reflect on the thoughts and desires he had then. In other words, the learning is done primarily at the time of ascent, meaning the time of Gadlut [adulthood/greatness], which is called "my teachers," for only during an ascent does a person have the brains to think.

Then, when he begins to learn from the state of descent, this is considered that he is learning from his disciples, which is below the routine that he was used to regularly. When a person learns from that state, he learns a lot, since now he can praise and thank the Creator for delivering him from the trash and the garbage where he was lying like the rest of the animals, whose food is only the waste that people throw into the trash, and animals such as cats come and nourish themselves on this waste. Now, during the ascent, he can praise and thank the Creator for this.

Baal HaSulam said that according to the praise and gratitude that is given to the Creator, to that extent he ascends. It does not matter what he has. What matters is how much he is impressed by the nearing to the Creator. To the extent of the gratitude that a person gives, to that extent he ascends in degree.

Also, he should learn from his friend's state. That is, during the ascent, he should reflect and scrutinize on what understanding his work was built then.

It follows that if a person learns from his current state during the ascent, this is regarded as not learning much. But when he learns from the state of "his friend," he learns more than from the state of ascent. "And [I learned] most from my disciples" means the time of descent. This is called "and most from my disciples."

However, we must not forget that all the learning is specifically during the ascent. It follows that if he does not learn from the above-mentioned states during the ascent, it is considered that he did not learn much. For this reason, during the descent, a person must not decide anything, but only pray to the Creator to deliver him from the lowliness and believe that the Creator hears a prayer.

What It Means that the Land Did Not Bear Fruit before Man Was Created, in the Work

Article No. 5, Tav-Shin-Nun, 1989/90

It is written in *The Zohar* (*VaYera*, Item 1), "Rabbi Hiya started, 'The buds appeared on the earth; the time of pruning has come.' This means that when the Creator created the world, He placed in the earth all the power it deserves, and everything was in the land. Yet, it did not bear fruit in the world until man was created. When man was created, everything appeared in the world and the land revealed the fruits and forces that were deposited in it. And then it was said, 'The buds appeared on the earth, the time of pruning has come, and the voice of the turtledove was heard in our land.' This is the speaking of the Creator, which was absent in the world before man was created. Once man is present, everything is present."

We should understand why the land did not bear its fruit before man was created. What is the connection between the earth and man, where if there is no man, although the land has everything, it still does not bear its fruits before there is man? Also, what does it mean that before man was created, the speaking of the Creator was not present in the world? After all, it is written several times, "And God said, 'Let there be light.'"

We should interpret this in the work. Our sages said about the verse, "In the beginning God created," that it is for Israel, who were called *Resheet* [beginning], as it is written, "The sanctity of Israel, the *Resheet* [beginning] of its crop." This means as it is written, that the purpose of the creation of the world was to do good to His creations. That is, He created in the creatures a desire to receive delight and pleasure, and in this desire, meaning that this desire causes him to yearn to receive the delight and pleasure. By this the delight and pleasure that a person can derive from there is measured.

This is called "the work of the Creator," meaning that He created a desire to enjoy for the pleasure that He wants to give them. It turns out that nothing is missing in the world; there is abundance that belongs to the will to receive. That is, to the extent that He wanted to give delight and pleasure, to that extent He created a *Kli* [vessel] for this. This means that the will to receive is not greater than the Creator created it, so he can receive what the Creator wants to give. It follows that the delight and pleasure are present, the *Kli* to receive is present, so what else is missing?

It is known that the land is called *Malchut*. That is, the desire to receive the abundance from the Creator is called *Malchut*. This means that *Malchut* receives the abundance for the souls, as for this reason *Malchut* is called "the assembly of Israel," which is the collection of the souls. It follows that *Malchut* already received all the light for the souls. The question is, Why do the creatures not receive from *Malchut* the abundance she received for the creatures, and there is the power of concealment in the world, so the voice of the turtledove is not heard in our land, meaning that the speaking of the Creator is not heard in the world, but rather each one feels the concealment and there is a lot of work to believe in His Providence over the created beings, and the delight and pleasure are not revealed in the world?

The answer is that it is because the Creator did not want there to be shame. For this reason, there was a correction, called *Tzimtzum* [restriction] and concealment so the upper Providence will not be revealed. Instead, we must believe that the Creator leads the world as the good who does good. This causes us all the work, that we must exert and relinquish the will to receive for ourselves, although this is our entire reality.

In other words, everything that we relate to the creatures is only a will to receive. Yet, it is forbidden to use the will to receive as it emerged by nature, but we must go above nature. In other words, our nature is the will to receive for ourselves. It follows that when a person is told we must relinquish the will to receive for ourselves, there is not an organ in us that will be able to understand this. The body begins to ask the "Who" and "What" questions, meaning demands an intellectual answer if the Creator truly hears each and every one who asks of Him.

The body argues to a person, "You see that you have asked the Creator many times to help you with what you think you need. Until now, you see that you have received no answer to the prayer. Therefore, why do you say each day, 'For You hear the prayer of every mouth'? If this is so, why is He not helping you?" It follows that reason asserts that the body is right, meaning that it is making a reasonable and sensible argument.

We must answer the body about this that we are going above reason. That is, although reason asserts that the Creator does not accept the prayer of every mouth, meaning that he can explain the fact that the Creator is not answering him as because he is still unfit to receive the salvation from the Creator, but in truth, the Creator does hear the prayer of Israel. It is only to you that He does not want to answer the prayer you made, since you are not regarded as Israel.

The body asks once more, "You see that we must believe that 'You hear the prayer of every mouth,' as we say in the prayer, 'For You hear the prayer of every mouth.' Thus, the Creator should have heard your prayer, as well. Moreover, if He does not hear the prayer of every mouth, then why do you need to pray?"

Then, when a person comes to such a state, he can say that he is going above reason. That is, although reason is very important, and he sees that the body speaks with reason, but a person should say that we must go above reason. That is, we, too, see contradictions, such as that many times he prayed but received no answer for his prayer. But then, when he overcomes and goes above reason, this is called "faith above reason."

Likewise, when a person must relinquish the quality of the heart and say, "I relinquish the self-benefit and care only for the benefit of the Creator," of course this is above reason. In other words, above reason means that a person should say that to him, faith is at a higher level than reason. For this reason, he obeys the voice of faith and not the voice of reason. This is against reason, since we see that we were given reason and we measure every person according to the level of his intellect, as it is written, "A man will be praised according to his mind" (Proverbs 12), and one who has more reason is a more important person. Therefore, when we are told that we must go above reason, it is against our reason.

For this reason, when a person comes to a state where the body begins to ask the "Who" and "What" questions, then begins the real work. Then we must ask for the help of the Creator to give us the strength not to hear these questions of Pharaoh and the wicked one, which are "Who" and "What." It was said about this, "Were it not for the help of the Creator, he would not overcome it," since a person cannot emerge from their control by himself and say, "I am going above reason," since it is against nature.

According to the above, we can interpret what we asked, What is the connection between the land that did not bear its fruit before man was created? In the work, man is regarded as one who has emerged from the control of the quality of a beast. A "beast" means one who is immersed in self-benefit, like a beast, and man means one in whom there is fear of heaven and works because of fear, which *The Zohar* calls "Because He is great and ruling," where he works only because of the greatness of the Creator and does not care for his own benefit, but for the benefit of the Creator. It is as our sages said about the verse, "In the end of the matter, fear God and observe His commandments, for this is the whole of man. What is 'for this is the whole of man'? Rabbi Elazar said, 'The whole world was created only for this'" (*Berachot* 6).

It follows that man is regarded as one in whom there is the fear of heaven. And what is the fear of heaven? That is, what is fear? It is as he says ("Introduction of The Book of Zohar," Item 191), "Both the first fear and the second fear are not for his own benefit, but only for fear that he will decline in bringing contentment to his Maker."

According to the above, we already know the meaning of Adam. It is one who has fear of heaven, who is afraid that perhaps he will not be able to do everything in order to bestow. This is called "man." A "beast" is the opposite: one who cares only for one's own benefit, as it is written (Ecclesiastes 3), "Who knows the spirit of man, whether it goes upward, and the spirit of the beast, whether it goes downward to the earth?" We should interpret that "spirit of man" goes upward means that everything he does is for the sake of the Creator. This is called "upward," when his intention is that everything will be only in order to bestow. From this man derives contentment.

The "spirit of the beast" is that in everything he does, he wants it all for "downward," meaning "down to the earth," which is worldliness, for the will to receive for oneself is called "earth." When that person does things, he sees that it will be only for his own benefit. From this he derives spirit, meaning his contentment. That is, he will enjoy his actions only if it yields benefit for himself. If he sees that the will to receive cannot enjoy it, he will not have strength to work. If he must work for some reason, then he is not in a good mood at all.

Now we can understand the connection between man and earth. We asked, What does it mean that the earth did not bear its fruit in the world before man was created although all the power it deserved and everything was already in the land? The thing is that in the work, "land" is the kingdom of heaven, which is the assembly of Israel, who receives abundance for the created beings, since all the souls come from her. From the perspective of the Creator, everything is already corrected in the best possible way.

It is as he says ("Introduction to The Book of Zohar," Item 13), "The thing is that by the very thought to create the souls, His thought completed everything, for He does not need an act, as do we. Instantaneously, all the souls and all the worlds that are destined to be created emerged filled with all the delight and pleasure that the souls were intended to receive at the end of correction, after the will to receive in the souls has been fully corrected and has been turned into pure bestowal. This is so because in His eternalness, past, present, and future are as one."

By this we should interpret the connection between man and the earth, which is that if man is present, the earth bears its fruit. The "earth" means the will to receive that has been fully corrected. From the perspective of the Creator, everything has been completed in utter perfection and there is nothing to add to it, as he says, "Instantaneously, all the souls emerged filled with all the delight and pleasure." However, in order for the creatures to enjoy the fruits of *Malchut*, which she received, *Malchut*, which is called "land," does not give this to the created beings before they correct the will to receive to work in order to bestow, due to the correction that took place, so there will be in them the matter of equivalence of form.

It turns out that as long as a person has not achieved the degree of "man," which is regarded as bestowing upward, as in "the spirit of man goes upward," meaning that "man" means that everything he does is for the sake of the Creator, while the spirit of the beast "goes downward," meaning for his own benefit, *Malchut*, which is called "earth," cannot show the delight and pleasure she received for the created beings.

The Zohar says, "The buds appeared on the earth," meaning that everything was in the earth, but it did not bear fruit in the world until man was created. Before the created being achieved the quality of "man," the Creator does not see any fruits from Malchut, which is called "earth."

Now we can understand what we asked about *The Zohar* saying that "the voice of the turtle dove was heard in our land" is the speaking of the Creator, who was not present in the world before man was created, though it is written many times in the Torah, "And God said," before man was created. The meaning is that before a person achieves the degree of "man," meaning emerges from the state of a beast, the "man" is in concealment and it is impossible to hear the voice of the Creator.

This is regarded as the "speaking of the Creator was not present in the world before the quality of man was created." Only afterward, when a person achieves the degree of "man," he hears the "speaking of the Creator." The "speaking of the Creator" is called Torah, and then he is rewarded with the Torah, which is called "the names of the Creator." This is called the "speaking of the Creator." It is not that the Torah is a wisdom, as with other wisdoms. Rather, the Torah is the speaking of the Creator.

Not easily can one achieve the degree of "man" and emerge from the quality of a beast. This is so because in the work of the Creator, one is always in oppositeness of form, and only out of two extremes, a middle line is born. It is as it is written in the poem by the ARI, "Right and left, and in between them a bride." This means that through the right and the left, which are two opposites, the kingdom of heaven, called "bride," is born.

It is known that *Malchut* is called "faith." To be rewarded with faith, we must first emerge from the state of a beast, called "self-love," as was said that the spirit of the beast goes downward. Downward means decreasing in importance, which is the quality of a beast, which can only work for its own sake.

While the creature is still under the control of the will to receive for himself, he can receive only partial faith. This means that he has descents and ascents. During the descents, he loses the power of faith because the descent comes to him due to some flaw, and all the flaws come to the creature while he is immersed in self-love. For this reason, there is a correction for the creature so as not to blemish the King: He loses the faith in the existence of the King, as explained in the "Introduction of The Book of Zohar" (Item 138, beginning with the words, "It is a law").

Since there is a rule that a person cannot walk on one leg, but only on two legs, this points to spirituality, too. "Right" implies wholeness. That is, the first beginning, when the creature wants to begin the work of the Creator, is that he must believe in the Creator. It does not matter how much faith he has, but with whatever faith he has, he can already begin to observe Torah and Mitzvot [commandments/good deeds], and each day he adds as much as he can.

However, this state is not regarded as "right," but as "one line." This is called "still of Kedusha [holiness]." From this still emerge all other degrees, called "vegetative," "animate," and "speaking," as it is written (Ecclesiastes 3), "All was from the dust." The Zohar interprets, "even the wheel of the sun" (Tzav, Item 173). That is, everyone must begin in still of Kedusha.

However, we should know that as with the corporeal still, a person does not need to make efforts in order for the still to be revealed. Rather, the still develops according to the development of nature. In other words, if a person does not spoil the corporeal still, it develops. For example, if a person does not spoil the earth or takes out stones from the earth, the still develops.

It is the same with the still of Kedusha. If he does not spoil his actions, his still of Kedusha develops. However, it does not require any intention or thought in order to continue his quality of still of Kedusha.

Conversely, if he wants to acquire the quality of "vegetative," we see that in corporeality, the vegetative already requires special treatment. It needs to be given food, meaning water and sun, and to fix the still from which the vegetative will grow, namely plowing and so forth. Also, other plants, which do not belong to the plant that the person wants to grow out of the still, must be removed, so in corporeality, weeds that have intermingled are uprooted.

Likewise, in the vegetative of *Kedusha*, we must dedicate thought and desire to nursing this still, meaning plowing. That is, we must turn the will to receive in us to work in order to bestow, and then it is relevant to speak of work in "right" and "left." That which was previously one line, which is the act, a person must use it as the "right line," meaning that he should appreciate the simple act and say that he is grateful to the Creator for rewarding him with doing simple works in utter simplicity, and to say that he is not worth even this—that the Creator gave him the present of serving Him in simplicity.

At the same time, he must shift to the left line, meaning criticize himself if he is truly working for the Creator or for himself, meaning for his own benefit and not for the benefit of the Creator. He should pray for this, that he is so immersed in self-love.

Sometimes, he sees that he cannot pray that the Creator will help him and deliver him from the governance of self-love. Sometimes, he is even in a worse state—that he does not even want to pray the Creator will bring him out of self-love. On the contrary, he wants the Creator to help him satisfy his will to receive for himself with every possible satisfaction. This is called "left," since in spirituality, something that requires correction is called "left."

It follows that there are two opposites here. On one hand, a person is told that the order of the work is that a person should try to observe the one line to the fullest. That is, as when the creature was in a state of still, called "one line," and felt himself as whole and was happy and glad because he knew that he had wholeness and all he needed to add was quantity.

But the reason was that he had no idea about the vegetative. He thought that the still is the wholeness that man must do. Therefore, he felt high spirited because of the feeling of wholeness and he could not understand why all the creatures were not as smart as him.

But now that he has a notion of the quality of "vegetative," he no longer has the wholeness of the one line. For this reason, now he must make great efforts to be able to appreciate and derive vitality from the right, as he received from it while being in one line. The reason for this is that the left line makes him see that this is not wholeness.

Indeed, why do we need to walk on the right line? The answer is that this is the truth. That is, a person should indeed consider the little bit of grip he has on *Kedusha* as a great fortune, and this is the time to thank the Creator. Afterward, he should return to the left line, for this is also true, that we must work for the sake of the Creator. Out of those two, from the wholeness and importance of the right, and from the lack of the left, a person is rewarded with the middle line. This is the meaning of "Right and left, and in between the bride."

When Should One Use Pride in the Work?

Article No. 6, Tav-Shin-Nun, 1989/90

It is written (2 Chronicles 17), "His heart was proud in the ways of the Lord." And in the Mishnah, it was said (*Avot*, Chapter 4:4), "Be very, very humble." Thus, this contradicts what is written, "His heart was proud."

The Zohar (*VaYera*, Item 17) asks, "'And the Lord appeared unto him by the Oaks of Mamre.' Why in the Oaks of Mamre and not elsewhere? It is because Mamre gave him an advice about the circumcision. When the Creator told Abraham to circumcise himself, Abraham went to consult his friends. Aner told him, 'You are over ninety years old; you will torment yourself.' Marme told him, 'Remember the day when the Chaldeans threw you in the furnace, and that famine that the world endured, and those kings whom your men chased and whom you struck. The Creator saved you from all of them. Rise up and do as your Master commands.' The Creator said to Mamre: 'You advised him in favor of the circumcision, thus, I will appear to him only in your abode.'"

This is difficult to understand. If the Creator commanded him to circumcise himself, he went to ask his friends if he should obey the Creator? What if Mamre had said otherwise? He would heed the advice of Mamre and not the word of the Creator. Can we say this?

It is also difficult to understand what Mamre told him, that he should obey the Creator, that He will save you for sure, just as He saved you from the furnace. This implies that the basis for why Mamre told him to obey the Creator is because He would save him, just as He saved him from the furnace. Otherwise, you should not obey.

We see the same thing where our sages said (RASHI brings the words of our sages, Genesis 11:28), "'Terah died in the presence of his father,' during his father's life. Some say that because of him, his father died, when Terah complained to Nimrod about his son, Abram, about the breaking of his statues and throwing them into the furnace. Haran sat and said to himself, 'If Abram wins, I am with him. If Nimrod wins, I am with him.' When Abram was saved, they said to Haran, 'Who are you with?' Haran replied, 'I am with Abram.' They threw him in the furnace and he burned."

We see about Haran that since he said that he was going to take upon himself devotion on condition that the Creator would save him, he was burned. Thus, why in Abram's case, when Mamre told him, "You should obey the Creator," since He saved Abram from the furnace, meaning yesterday's Abram, for example, He would also save Abram today when he circumcises himself? This is just like Haran and Abram with the furnace. The only difference here is that they are the same thing but in the same body, meaning in two states of Abram.

In the literal, we see that with Haran and Abram and the furnace, there was the matter of gentiles, meaning that foreigners wanted both Abram and Haran not to obey the Creator. This is not so with the circumcision, which the Creator instructed him. That is, there is a difference between foreigners saying not to obey the Creator, or the Creator telling him to obey Him.

We should say that when foreigners want a person to idol-worship and detach himself from faith in the Creator, a person should give unconditional dedication. For this reason, when Haran said that he was ready to dedicate himself on condition that he survives, like Abraham, this is not regarded as dedication. This is why he was burned in the furnace.

This is not so here when the Creator told him to circumcise himself and he went to consult his friends. We should interpret this differently, that he thought that the Creator telling him to circumcise himself is a high degree and he was still unworthy of it, as he thought that if the Creator told him to circumcise himself and he was still unworthy of it, he might fall even from the state he was in at the time, since he knew that he was in lowliness, as it is written, "And I am dust and ashes." Therefore, he went to ask whether he was permitted to walk into this high degree and circumcise himself, or should he wait until he is worthy of it.

This is why Aner told him, "You are over ninety years old; you will torment yourself" beginning to ascend high degrees now, and beginning to do more work in order to qualify yourself to be worthy of the Mitzva [commandment/good deed] of circumcision. "You are too old to start making great efforts now in order to be rewarded with higher degrees. This is suitable for a young man, who has a great future, not for you, who is already over ninety. Therefore, this is not for you."

However, when he came to ask Mamre, Mamre replied to him, "You see that the Creator does not look at your lowliness; let Him say when you are worthy, and then He can help you, as our sages said, 'He who comes to purify is aided.' When you feel that you are dust and ashes, the Creator cannot help you, but you see that when you were thrown in the furnace, the Creator helped you nonetheless, since He is merciful and gracious."

This is as our sages say about the verse, "'And I will pardon whom I pardon,' although he is unfit and unworthy of it." Therefore, here, too, with the Mitzva of circumcision, the Creator wants you to enter a higher level although you are not worthy or fit. Hence, go and do your Master's commandment and do not look at your own lowliness.

This is as Baal HaSulam said about what the Creator said, "Now I know that you are God fearing." The question is, Does the Creator not know the future, that He said, "Now I know," meaning that now He knows that "you are God fearing"? That is, this means that now Abraham knew that he was God fearing.

The question is, Why did Abram need to know this? We should say that now that he knows that he is God fearing, Abraham can go to a higher level and is not afraid that it might be too high for him. Rather, he can already ascend.

Likewise, we can interpret what Rabba said (*Berachot* 61), "One should know in one's heart whether he is a complete righteous or not." We should also understand there why he needs to know this. Indeed, by this he will try to walk in higher degrees and will not think that it is too high for him. This is why Mamre advised him not to look at his lowliness that he feels, that he is dust and ashes. Rather, the Creator wants you to ascend in degrees through the *Mitzva* of circumcision? Go and do it, and do not look at anything. This is the meaning of the verse, "The Lord is high and the low will see," as it is written, "The Lord raises up the lowly."

Now we can understand what we asked, Why did Abraham consult his friends whether to obey the Creator? The meaning is that if he should wait and qualify himself to enter the high degree with which he will be rewarded following the doing of the commandment of circumcision, or should he do it right away and ignore his lowliness, where he feels that he is dust and ashes. This is what he asked his friends about, and not whether to observe the commandment of the Creator.

By this we will also understand why when he was thrown into the furnace, he did not seek his friends' advice, but agreed to be thrown into the furnace in order to sanctify the name of heaven. However, this is the quality of faith, where we must give unconditional devotion, meaning to say, "I am very low; this is why He does not want to give devotion."

But in idol-worship, the rule is "Be killed but do not breach." For this reason, when Haran wanted to sanctify the Creator with dedication only on condition that he stays alive like Abram, this is clearly not "Be killed but do not breach," since his view was that he agreed to be thrown in the furnace provided he is not killed. It follows that he did not observe at all the Mitzva that there is in idol-worship, "Be killed but do not breech." This is why Haran was burned in the furnace.

Conversely, Abram's view was in the form of "Be killed but do not breach." Therefore, thanks to the complete Mitzva, he was saved from the furnace. This is the meaning of the nations speaking to him there, demanding of him to idol-worship.

But with the commandment of the circumcision, where the Creator told him to circumcise himself, the Creator certainly demanded of Abram to ascend in degree. Once he sanctified the Creator with Nimrod, what did the Creator want from Abraham? Certainly, to ascend to a higher level. It was about this that he thought that perhaps he was still unworthy of ascending to such a high level, which is why he went to ask his friends what to do, since he felt that he was still not worthy of such Gadlut [greatness/adulthood], which he would be awarded by observing the Mitzva of circumcision. Therefore, it is a completely different matter here.

According to the above, we see that there are two states in the work: 1) faith, 2) Torah.

In the state of faith, it cannot be said that he is lowly, and therefore cannot observe the commandment of sanctifying the Creator, which is done by the general public in Israel, even among common people, that we hear that they died for the sanctification of the Creator.

Therefore, when a person begins the work of the Creator on the path of truth, he must take upon himself the burden of faith above reason even though all the nations of the world in his body laugh at him. He must sanctify the Creator before the gentiles in his body and say that he believes in the Creator and wants to serve Him with all his heart and soul. And even though they disagree with him, he can say that he takes upon himself to love the Creator. Even if he has no feeling when he utters it, a person should not be impressed with the organs disagreeing with his view. He does what he can do. That is, in speech and action he can do this by coercion. And although he feels nothing in it, he is still doing an awakening from below.

It was said about this, "And I will bless you in all that you will do." That is, the Creator will later send him blessing on what he does. Although after the overcoming he does not see that he received any blessing, meaning he does not feel any nearing to the Creator more than he was prior to the overcoming, so the body asks the person, "You told me that if you overcome your mind and reason, the Creator would give you blessing, meaning that by this you will feel the importance of spirituality. But you see that you are in the same state as before the work, when you exerted to do things by coercion."

To this comes the answer, "If I felt the blessing instantaneously, then I would have done it in order to receive reward." This is similar to Haran who said, "If I see that Abraham was saved from the furnace, I am with him." Here, too, when he says, "I am willing to bow myself and do good deeds against the body's will, but on condition that afterwards I will get a good feeling, how worthwhile it is to serve the Creator in order to receive reward, meaning a good feeling."

Hence, if a person wants to receive reward immediately after the work by coercion, it is as though he began with the coercion so that afterward he would not have to work by coercion. It follows that when accepting the faith, he sets conditions. But the faith of acceptance of the kingdom of heaven must be unconditional surrender. For this reason, where faith is concerned, it cannot be said that a person feels that he is too lowly, that it is not for him to assume the burden of the kingdom of heaven. Also, a person should not say, "Now I am not in the mood for this; I'll wait for when I am in a better mood, and then I'll try to take upon myself the burden of the kingdom of heaven." Rather, this duty lies with every person to take upon himself the burden of the kingdom of heaven, at any place and at any time.

Conversely, when speaking of the Torah, this is the time when one should feel one's lowliness. Since our sages said, "It is forbidden to teach Torah to idol-worshippers," but only to Israel, he should therefore first see if he is truly regarded as "Israel." This means that he should see whether he is worthy of learning Torah. If he sees that he is still unworthy, he must try to be worthy, and then he will be able to learn Torah.

What is the way by which one should qualify himself to be worthy? The way is as our sages said, "The Creator said, 'I have created the evil inclination; I have created the Torah as a spice.'" In other words, a person should learn Torah first, so the Torah will lead him into being regarded as "Israel." When he has the quality of "Israel," he will ascend in degree to learn Torah, which is then called "the Torah of the Creator, as in the names of the Creator." Before he is rewarded with being "Israel," he must try to engage in Torah and Mitzvot so it will make him become "Israel." Then is the time to come to wholeness, called "the purpose of creation," which is to do good to His creations.

However, when he engages in Torah and Mitzvot, since a person must walk on two lines—right and left—meaning a time of wholeness and a time of lack, on one hand we must thank the Creator, and one who feels he has received a lot of good from the Creator is more capable of giving more gratitude, so when a person engages in Torah and Mitzvot, this is the time to be in wholeness, as though the Creator has brought him close, to be among the King's servants. However, one must not lie to oneself and say that he feels that he is serving the King when he does not feel this way. Therefore, how can he be grateful to the Creator for drawing him near if he does not feel it?

Instead, at that time a person should say that although he is in utter lowliness, meaning he is still immersed in self-love, and still cannot do anything above reason, the Creator still gave him a thought and desire to engage in Torah and Mitzvot, and has also given him some strength to be able to overcome the spies who speak to him and poke his mind with their arguments. And still, he has some grip on spirituality.

At that time, a person should pay attention to this and believe that the Creator is tending to him and guides him on the track that leads to the King's palace. It follows that he should be happy that the Creator is watching over him and gives him the descents, as well. That is, a person should believe, as much as he can understand, that the Creator is giving him the ascents, since certainly, a person cannot say that he himself receives the ascents, but that the Creator wants to bring him closer; this is why He gives him the ascents.

Also, a person should believe that the Creator gives him the descents, as well, because He wants to bring him closer. Therefore, every single thing that he can do, he must do as though he is in a state of ascent. Therefore, when he overcomes a little during the descent, it is called an "awakening from below." Each act that he does, he believes that it is the Creator's will, and by this itself he is rewarded with greater nearing, meaning that the person himself begins to feel that the Creator has brought him closer.

It is as Baal HaSulam said, that when a person is happy, when he feels that he is privileged that he has some grip on spirituality, that person is called "blessed," and "The blessed clings to the Blessed." That is, the person begins to feel that the Creator is blessing him now, and he feels no lack at all. However, this is so specifically when he engages in Torah and *Mitzvot*.

Yet, one must dedicate a little bit of his time to work on the left line, as this gives him room to pray for the lacks in him. It is needed that during the wholeness, when a person is grateful to the Creator for bringing him a little closer, this is the time to receive the filling for his lacks, which he felt while working in the manner of the "left."

It follows that the answer to the prayer is not when he prays, since then he is in a state of "cursed," meaning deficient, and the complete does not connect to the deficient. Rather, when a person feels whole not because he knows that he has wholeness but because he feels himself as lowly, and regards whatever grip he has on spirituality as a great fortune, from this he derives wholeness and says that he is not even worthy of this. This is the time when he can receive the filling for what he felt while he was working in the manner of the "left."

Now we can understand what we asked, why on one hand they said, "Be very, very humble," and on the other hand, it is written, "And his heart was proud in the ways of the Lord," as they are two opposites on the same topic. The answer is that they are two opposites on the same topic, but in two times.

In other words, when he engages in the kingdom of heaven, to take upon himself faith above reason, when the body disagrees with it and gives him many excuses that now is not the time for this, and brings him evidence from other people, who do not pay attention to this work of faith in the Creator above reason, he should say about this, "And his heart was proud in the ways of the Lord." He does not look at anyone, but is determined that this is the path of truth and he should not look at anyone or hear what the body makes him understand—"Go and look at reputable people, who understand what is the work of the Creator." It is about this that they said, "And his heart was proud," to be proud that he understands better than everyone.

But when he engages in Torah and *Mitzvot* and sees that he has no idea what he is learning or what he is praying, at that time he must not be proud and say that if he does not understand, why should he look at the books in vain, if he does not understand the matters of Torah and *Mitzvot*. At that time he should be in lowliness, as our sages said, "Be very, very humble." In other words, a person should be in lowliness and say that he is happy with whatever grip he has, since he sees how many people do not have any grip on spirituality. Therefore, here he needs to feel that he is not worthy of anything, and be happy.

What Are the Times of Prayer and Gratitude in the Work?

Article No. 7, Tav-Shin-Nun, 1989/90

Our sages said (*Berachot* 32), "One should always establish the praise of the Creator, and then pray." They also said (*Rosh Hashanah* 35), "Rabbi Elazar said, 'One should always establish one's prayer, and then pray.'"

We should understand why we must first establish the praise of the Creator. When a person is in a state of deficiency and wants to pray to the Creator to satiate his lack, then he needs His help. Thus, why should one first establish the praise of the Creator?

With a flesh and blood king, we can understand that first we must show our respect for the king so the king will see that we are among those who love him, and for this reason the king will grant our wish. But how can this be said with regard to the Creator? Does the Creator need a person to show Him that he is among those who love the Creator, and then He will help him, and otherwise He will not?

After all, the Creator is merciful and gracious. Although one is unworthy, the Creator helps those who pray to Him, as Baal HaSulam explained what we say in the Eighteen Prayer, "For You hear the prayer of every mouth," meaning that it does not matter what mouth prays, but the prayer of any mouth, even if this mouth is unimportant, still, the Creator hears it. Thus, why must we first establish the praise of the Creator?

In order to interpret this, we should first present the words of *The Zohar* (*Chayei Sarah*, Item 224), "Come and see, 'And it came to pass, before he concluded speaking, that, behold, Rebecca came out.' He asks, it should have said, 'Came,' as it is written, 'Rachel his daughter comes.' Why does it say, 'came out'? He says that this indicates that the Creator took her out from among the town's people, who were all wicked, and Rebecca came out and parted from the rest of the people in the city because she was righteous."

RASHI interprets the verse (Genesis 24:39), "Suppose the woman does not walk." He writes, "It says, 'to me' [in Hebrew, "suppose" and "to me" are spelled the same]. Eliezer had a daughter. He was looking for a reason that Abraham would turn to him to marry his daughter. Abraham said to him: 'My son is blessed and you are cursed, and the cursed does not cling to the blessed.'"

We should interpret the meaning of Isaac and Rebecca, as well as the meaning of the matter of the daughter of Eliezer in the work. *The Zohar* writes (*Chayei Sarah*, Item 94), "He said to him, 'My master shall say if he heard how the authors of the Mishnah said this portion, which they interpreted concerning the soul, that Abraham is the soul and Sarah is the body.'"

In this manner, we should interpret the matter of Isaac and Rebecca, as it is written in *The Zohar* (*Chayei Sarah*, Item 249), "Rabbi Yehuda said, 'His mother Sarah,' since as the form of Isaac was as the form of Abraham, similarly, Rebecca's form was just as Sarah's. This is why it is written, 'His mother Sarah.'"

By this we should also interpret that Isaac was the soul and Rebecca the body. In the order of man's work, when he wants to achieve *Dvekut* [adhesion] with the Creator, he should always walk on two lines—right and left. "Right" means wholeness, when a person feels satisfaction in the work and praises and thanks the Creator for rewarding him with being among the King's servants. He sees that he has achieved a degree in spirituality, which is not so among the rest of the workers of the Creator. Yet, he recognizes his lowliness and does not know why the Creator chose him over other people, who have not reached this degree. For this reason, he thanks and praises the King and can observe what is written, "Serve the Lord with gladness." At that time he has nothing for which to pray to the Creator to help him, since he feels no lack in his situation.

However, later, when a person goes to work on the left line, when he criticizes the state he is in and sees that he is flawed in mind and in heart, and even worse, he sometimes sees that he is immersed in self-love more than usual, sometimes he comes to such lowliness that he does not want the Creator to help him out of his lowliness. On the contrary, he is angry that he is not receiving delight and pleasure from the corporeal life. It follows that sometimes the left does not let him even pray and ask of the Creator. Thus, how can he feel himself as a whole person and thank the Creator?

However, we must know that the work is mainly during the ascent, for only during an ascent can we speak of man's work in two lines—right and left. Conversely, during a descent, a person is considered dead. Can we say that we are speaking to the dead, or that we want something from the dead, that he will do something?

For this reason, when a person is in a state of work, it can be said that a person should work in two ways: 1) right, 2) left. "Right" means primarily that the wholeness in him is built on above reason, while the left in him is built on the reason and intellect. That is, at that time he sentences himself as he sees, as our sages said, "A judge has only what his eyes see" (*Baba Batra* 131).

It turns out that when he engages in the left and sees the truth, how lowly and immersed in self-love he is, how can he then say that he is in a state of wholeness and be grateful to the Creator for giving him such a great gift that he is in *Kedusha* [holiness]? This is the complete opposite of the truth he sees, and how can one be happy when he sees the truth?

The answer is in two ways: 1) It is written in the essay from *Tav-Shin-Gimel* (*Shamati*, Article No. 40, 1943) concerning faith in his teacher, that Baal HaSulam said that a person should go with faith in the sages, as they have arranged for us. These are his words, slightly changed: The student must believe as his teacher tells him, to walk on the path of "right" and wholeness. The student should depict to himself that he has already been rewarded with complete faith in the Creator, and already feels in his organs that the Creator leads the whole world as The Good Who Does Good. This means that the whole world receives from Him only good, and although when he looks at himself, he sees that he is bare and destitute, and when he looks at the world, he also sees that the world suffers torments— each suffering according to his own degree—he should say about this what is written, "They have eyes and see not." That is, as long as a person is in a state of "they," that "they" have two authorities, "they" cannot see the truth. For this reason, a person must believe above reason that he is in wholeness, and so is the whole world.

It follows that in this way he can and should thank the Creator for giving us abundance. This is called the "right line," which is the complete opposite of the left line. That is, in the left line, we walk within reason, as was said, that "A judge has only what his eyes see." In other words, it is specifically with the intellect and not above the intellect. But when shifting to work with the "right," the left is the cause that the right is built on the basis of above reason.

This is as our sages said, "The left pushes away and the right pulls near." In other words, the state of "left" shows a person how he is rejected and separated from the work of the Creator. "The right pulls near" means that it shows him that he is close to the work of the Creator. This means that when he engages in the left, the left should bring him to see a state of rejection, that he is rejected and separated from the work. When he engages in the right, he should come to a state where he sees that he is close to the Creator. He should thank the Creator for the "right," and pray to the Creator for the "left," for only on two legs can a person walk in corporeality. This extends from spirituality, which shows that a person should walk on two lines.

Concerning the wholeness, there is another manner. If a person comes to a state where he sees that he is bare and destitute, since he is behind both in mind and in heart, meaning sees that he is immersed in self-love and that he has not a single organ that has any desire to work for the sake of the Creator, now he sees that he has come to his true state called "recognition of evil."

He says that the fact that now he sees the recognition of evil is a gift from above that he was shown the truth. Otherwise, he would deceive himself and think that he need not change his way, since he is certainly walking on the path of truth. Thus, he could remain with his evil forever. But now, a revelation from above came to him, to see the truth.

This is as it is written in *The Zohar* about the verse, "Or make his sin known to him." It interprets that the Creator notified him that he sinned, meaning he was informed from above that he sinned. In other words, recognition of evil is a revelation from above. For this reason, he rejoices at the fact that the Creator tends to him and guides him, and shows him his true state. This gives him wholeness from being rewarded with the revelation of the truth at the hands of the Creator. This discernment, that he receives wholeness, means that he says that the Creator is bringing him closer and shows him the truth.

It follows that now he is not in a state where he says that the Creator has rejected him from *Kedusha* because he feels the bad. On the contrary, this makes him feel that the Creator is pulling him closer. This is called "the right pulls near." Naturally, in that state, when he sees that he is all bad, he can overcome and seek advice how to emerge from this bad. Hence, he thanks and praises the Creator.

It follows that now he is regarded as blessed, in that he sees that he has received awareness from above about the recognition of evil. When he thanks the Creator, he is certainly called "blessed," since he received a blessing from the Creator, and then he can come to *Dvekut* with the Creator since "the blessed clings to the blessed."

This is as Baal HaSulam interpreted what our sages said, "The world was created either for the complete wicked or for the complete righteous" (*Berachot* 61). He asked, "We can understand that it is for the complete righteous, but can it be said, 'for the complete wicked'?"

He explained that when a person knows about himself that he is wicked, he will certainly do all that he can to repent. We should interpret his words, "For the complete righteous," who then enjoy the world in that they are rewarded with the delight and pleasure that the Creator wanted to give at the time of the creation of the world, since they already have *Kelim* [vessels] to receive the light of the Creator in order to bestow, for in these *Kelim*, the purpose of creation is revealed, which is called "His desire to do good to His creations."

Likewise, when he has already been rewarded with the recognition of evil, it is *Kelim*, for he has an inner drive to do what he can to emerge from the state of wicked. But when he does not feel the bad, he has no one to awaken him to emerge from that bad state, since he does not feel so bad that he must do all that he can in order to emerge from it.

It follows that the fact that he has come to a state where he sees that he is all bad, already has a great merit to it. The evidence is that he can already say that the world was created for him, as was said, "The world was created either for the complete wicked." But before he discovered the bad state, he had no right to exist in the world, as was said, "The world was created either for the complete wicked or for the complete righteous." It follows that prior to the recognition of evil, he has no right to exist in the world.

It therefore follows that if he has achieved the recognition of evil, it is regarded that he already has a grip in the world. In that respect, it is considered that he has wholeness and he can already praise and thank the Creator for this, and he already has connection with the Creator and it can already be said that he is called "blessed," and "the blessed clings to the blessed."

At that time, he can be, and this is the time when he can ascend in degree, meaning that at the time of gladness, he can receive all the prayers he has given over his deficiencies. It is as our sages said, "The *Shechina* [Divinity] is present only out of joy," as it is written, "And he will be as a musician playing, and the spirit of the Lord shall be upon him." It follows that the primary time when one is rewarded with instilling the *Shechina* is specifically the time of wholeness, for specifically at the time of wholeness is the time when he can receive his soul.

According to the above, we can interpret what our sages said, "Eliezer had a daughter. He wanted her to be a wife for Isaac." Literally, this is difficult to understand. After all, Eliezer's daughter was the daughter of a sage, as our sages said (*Yoma* 28b), "And Abraham said to his servant, the elder of his house, who ruled over all that was his. Rabbi Eliezer said that the governor of the teaching of his master is of the household of Eliezer." They also said there, "Eliezer, Abraham's servant, was old and sat in a seminary."

Abraham did not agree to this match and replied, "The cursed does not cling to the blessed." This was not so about the match with Rebecca, who was the daughter of Betuel and the sister of wicked Lavan. Our sages said that Betuel sought to feed Eliezer the potion of death so they would be left with the wealth. In other words, he was not merely wicked; he was also a murderer. Yet, Gabriel came and replaced the bowl and gave it to Betuel, and he died.

Rebecca, too, came from an environment of wicked, yet, this match is a good match, as it is written, "And Rebecca came out." In other words, the Creator brought her out from among all the town's people, who were wicked. "Rebecca came out" because she was righteous. In the literal, if a person is offered two matches, where one is a daughter of a sage, and the other comes from the house of wicked people and a city of wicked people, of course he would choose the daughter of the sage.

But in the work, we should interpret that the state of Eliezer is a state of "left," for he was yelling all the time, "*Eli* [My God], *Ezer* [help!], since I am under the governance of the evil." It follows that this woman, the daughter of the left, who prayed to be given the quality of Isaac, who is called *Neshama* [soul] as a "wife," which is the body, in order to receive the soul, Abraham did not agree because when a person is in the left and cries out, "Lord, help me emerge from the evil," that body is in a state of "cursed." He told him that Isaac, meaning the soul, was "blessed," and "the cursed does not cling to the blessed."

It is written in *The Zohar* (*Toldot*, Item 49), Therefore, although Eliezer was a sage, he felt that he lacked the quality of truth. He was always in the state of "the left," and always had grievances, why the Creator would not hear him and give him a soul, since "the light in it reforms him." Although the left "speaks to the point," since everything is built on reason, as was said, that "the judge has only what his eyes see," but in truth, he is cursed.

This is why Abraham told him, "The cursed," meaning the body in a state of "cursed," cannot receive the instilling of the Shechina, regarded as one's personal soul. This is so because the Shechina is called *Malchut*, which is the collection of the souls. For this reason, *Malchut* is called "the assembly of Israel." Hence, in this state, the body is unfit to receive the quality of Isaac, who is called a "soul," as was said that the body is called "wife," and the soul is called "husband."

However, Rebecca, means in the work that the body sees everything that the left shows it, its true state, that all its organs are wicked, that it understands only that which concerns self-love, but with regard to the benefit of the Creator, it cannot do a thing, just as the "left" shows it.

This is the meaning of "all the town's people were wicked," since the body is called "city," as it is written (Ecclesiastes 9:14), "A small city with few people in it. A great king came to it and found in it a poor wise man, who saved the city with his wisdom." Rebecca, who was a single righteous woman, came out from among all the town's people.

Why does it say "came out"? He says that "It indicates that the Creator took her out from among all the town's people." This means that this body felt itself as whole, meaning as righteous, because the Creator notified it the truth. From this, it is glad, and this in itself is regarded as wholeness, that the Creator notified it, or, for the second above-mentioned reason, that he believes above reason that he has wholeness because he believes in faith in his teacher that we must go above reason and say, "They have eyes and see not."

In a state of wholeness, we can be rewarded with the state of Isaac, who is called a "soul." This means that the two opposites are in one body but in two times. We are told that the most important is to walk on the right line, once he has a little bit of the left line. This is the meaning of "One should always establish the praise of the Creator," which is called "right," "and then pray," regarded as "left," and then he returns to the right.

What It Means that Esau Was Called "A Man of the Field," in the Work

Article No. 8, Tav-Shin-Nun, 1989/90

The *Zohar* says (*Toldot*, Item 75), "It is written here, 'A skillful hunter, a man of the field,' and it is written there (about Nimrod), 'He was a mighty hunter before the Lord.' As there, it means that he was hunting the minds of people and misleading them to rebel against the Creator, so here, 'A man of the field' means to rob people and to kill them. Esau said that he was in the field to pray, like Isaac, as it is written, 'And Isaac went out to stroll in the field,' and hunting, and he deceived Isaac."

We should understand what are the two things said about Esau, meaning what is the difference between "a skillful hunter" and "a man of the field" in the work. We should also understand why *The Zohar* says, "a man of the field, since his lot is not in an inhabited place, but in a desolate place, in the desert, in the field, and this is why he is called 'a man of the field.'" But Noah, too, was called "a man of the earth," as it is written, "And Noah, man of the earth,

425

began." Also, it is written about Isaac himself, "And Isaac went out to stroll in the field," and it is also written that Isaac said about Jacob what is written, "And he said, 'See, the scent of my son is as the scent of the field that the Lord has blessed.'" Thus, from where is it implied that with Esau, "a man of the field" means robbing people and killing them? We should interpret this in the work.

It is written, "Which God has created to do." That is, the Creator created the world with the aim to do good to His creations. For this purpose, He created something new called a "desire to receive delight and pleasure." As we learned, in order to enjoy the delight and pleasure that He wants to give, the pleasure is according to the need and the yearning for the thing, since the yearning determines the measure of the pleasure that one can derive from the matter.

Therefore, first emerged this will to receive existence from absence. This is called "which God has created." "To do" is the correction of creation, since by this there is a difference between the Bestower and the receiver. Therefore, there is the matter of the bread of shame, namely shame. This is why we can have an aim to bestow, meaning not to receive despite the great yearning to receive the delight and pleasure. Still, in order not to feel shame, work was given to the created beings.

It is called "work" because it is against the nature with which the Creator created creation, since the matter of the purpose of creation to do good to His creations means that anything that can be said that a person receives, meaning that he has a desire to receive, comes from the Creator, who created this nature. Conversely, not receiving the delight and pleasure that the Creator wants to give, this we attribute to the creatures. For this reason, this correction not to receive the delight and pleasure unless we have the aim to bestow is called "doing," and the creatures must do this although it is against nature.

This will to receive is called *Malchut*, as it is known that the *Kli* [vessel] to receive the lights is called *Malchut*. As we learn, there was a *Tzimtzum* [restriction] and concealment on this *Malchut*, and *Malchut*, with respect to the will to receive for herself, remained without light. Only when it is possible to place on her a desire in order to bestow, to that extent the *Tzimtzum* and concealment depart and she can receive the abundance. Otherwise, *Malchut* is called a "vacant space" from light. From this, it extends that afterward, two systems were made, as in "God has made one opposite the other." In other words, just as there is ABYA of *Kedusha* [holiness], opposite it there is ABYA of *Tuma'a* [impurity].

Malchut has several names: "land," "earth," "sea," and "dust," depending on what she receives. In this *Malchut*, called "earth," the man is extended, as it is written, "And the Lord God created the man dust off the earth." This is the *Malchut* of whom it was said, "All was from the dust." It was said in *The Zohar* (*Tzav*, Item 173), "All was from the dust, even the wheel of the sun." This means that when we speak, we speak only of lights clothed in the *Kelim* [vessels], as it is known that there is no light without a *Kli*, and all the *Kelim* extend from *Malchut*, who is the will to receive.

This means that all we speak of is only of *Malchut*, who is the will to receive, which is either in *Kedusha* or in *Klipa* [shell/peel]. The only difference is that the *Kedusha* does not use the will to receive unless it can place on it a desire that works in order to bestow, or it restricts itself from using the will to receive. Conversely, the *Klipa* wants to use the will to receive in order to receive. This means that when it is said that a person is using vessels of bestowal, it does not mean that the vessels of bestowal are doing something, since there are no vessels of bestowal in the will to receive, as all of creation is regarded as only a desire to receive, as it is known that other than the will to receive, we attribute everything to the Creator.

Creation is called "existence from absence," and this pertains specifically to the lack that the Creator created. However, when we say that a person is using the desire to bestow, it means that the will to receive is not using its own quality, but the Creator's desire, Whose wish is only to bestow and not receive anything.

According to the above, we can understand the meaning of the "field" that was said about Esau, who is called "a man of the field."

We see that Isaac, too, went out to the field, and it is also written about Jacob that Isaac said, "See, the scent of my son is as the scent of the field that the Lord has blessed." This means that a "field" means *Malchut*, which is the will to receive, and there, there is the matter of the choice whether to correct it into working in order to bestow, which is called *Kedusha*. It is about this that Isaac said, "as the field that the Lord has blessed."

If we do not correct it into working in order to bestow, but engage in receiving in order to receive, this is called "a man of the field," which is a *Klipa*, as was said, "a man of the field, in order to rob people and kill them." This pertained to Esau. But concerning Isaac, it is written, "And Isaac went out to stroll in the field." He went to correct the field, which is *Malchut*, to correct so that the quality of *Malchut*, which is a desire to receive, will work in order to bestow. This is called "correcting the world with the kingdom of *Shadai*." It is known that the name *Shadai* means *Yesod*, and *Yesod* is called *Yesod Tzadik* [righteous], who is the Bestower. The intention is to correct *Malchut*, who is reception, so she becomes like the quality of *Yesod*, meaning aiming to bestow. This is the meaning of "Isaac went out to stroll in the field."

It is written likewise about Jacob, that Jacob said, "See, the scent of my son is as the scent of the field that the Lord has blessed." In other words, Isaac saw that Jacob corrected *Malchut*, so it was possible to see the blessing of the Creator on the field, which is *Malchut*.

However, we should understand why *The Zohar* speaks of the field in a reproving manner with respect to Esau. We should interpret that it is because it is written, "a skillful hunter," and then it is written, "a man of the field." It interprets that "a skillful hunter" is from Nimrod, for Nimrod was "a mighty hunter before the Lord." *The Zohar* interprets that it means that "he was hunting the minds of people and misleading them to rebel against the Creator."

We should understand the difference between a skillful hunter and a man of the field. According to what we learn, there is a difference between the mind and the heart. The mind, Baal

HaSulam explains, refers to faith above reason. The heart means the desire in the heart, which works only for its own sake. That is, for its own sake means that a person is willing to do any work in the world as long as he sees that the reward he will receive in return for his effort is worthwhile. It follows that when it says "a skillful hunter" or "a man of the field," they are two things, which in the work, are called "mind" and "heart."

Now we can understand that if the writing says about Esau that he was a skillful hunter, and we learn from Nimrod what hunting means, that he hunted the minds of people and misled them to rebel against the Creator, this is a flaw in the mind, meaning in faith. From this we know how to interpret "a man of the field." It means that as he flawed the mind, he also flawed the heart. This is why we interpret "a man of the field" to mean self-love, meaning that his field was about robbing people and killing them. He was supposed to choose the good for the field, so there would be blessing there. Yet, he did the opposite, extending death and killing into that field.

In the work, we should interpret that since man was created with a desire to receive, and must correct it into working in order to bestow, in order to be able to correct, meaning to have a choice, meaning that a person will observe Torah and Mitzvot [commandments/good deeds] in order to bestow and not for his own sake, a Tzimtzum and concealment were made, where man must begin the work in the form of faith above reason, since within reason, the concealment has been placed.

This is when the work on the choice begins, meaning that a person must accept the burden of the kingdom of heaven, which is a burden, as in, "as an ox to the burden." In other words, although the body does not agree to do anything unless it sees what is done with its work, since this is the nature with "God has created to do," that man must see what he is doing, meaning what is done with his work. He must see who enjoys the work he is doing.

Therefore, when a person engages in Torah and Mitzvot, he wants to see who received his work. Since a concealment and hiding were made, for the purpose of correction, a person does not see or feel who receives his work, and he must believe above reason that the Creator receives his work. But the body does not want to believe.

For this reason, we were given this work "as an ox to the burden." In other words, as the ox works by coercion and must obey what its owner wants, man must not ask the body if it wants to take upon itself the burden of Torah and *Mitzvot*. Rather, he must force it and believe in the sages that such is the path of truth.

Also, there is the discernment of "and as a donkey to the load," meaning it is the quality of the heart. In other words, a person must work not in order to receive reward. Therefore, when the body is told to work without any reward, this work is a load to it and the body wants to take off this load, which man wants it to suffer. In other words, the body understands that it can carry a load even for a doubtful reward for this work. But if it is told, "Work and carry loads without any reward," it wants to get rid of this work every moment. Then it was said, "as a donkey to the load." That is, a person must walk in this direction even though the body disagrees.

It follows that the labor is in two manners: 1) as an ox to the burden, 2) as a donkey to the load. If a person walks on the path of Esau, the person is called "a skillful hunter, a man of the field." That is, he lacks faith, which is called "a skillful hunter," like Nimrod, when the body wants to rebel against the faith in the Creator, which blemishes the quality of "mind." Also, he is "a man of the field," meaning he robs people. This means that he robs the "man" in him and he remains as a beast, knowing only himself and not others.

It is written, "a man of the field, to rob people and to kill them." This means that if he robs the man in him and enters the state of a "beast," which is the desire to receive for oneself, then he is in a state of "The wicked in their lives are called 'dead,'" since they are separated from the Life of Lives. This is called "heart." Baal HaSulam said that in truth, the quality of the heart is man's primary quality, meaning that this is the root, that he does not want to believe because man has more pleasure when he sees and feels. Therefore, he does not want to degrade himself and walk with his eyes shut and believe all that our sages said.

Yet, the primary basis is faith in the sages, as it is written (*Shabbat* 31), "There is a tale about a foreigner who came to Shammai and said, 'How many laws [Torah] do you have?' He replied, 'Two, the written Torah and the oral Torah.' He said to him, 'I believe you about the written Torah, and I do not believe you about the oral Torah. Convert me, so as to teach me the written Torah.' He rebuked him and ejected him with a rebuke. He came to Hillel: 'Convert me.' On the first day, he said to him, '*Aleph, Bet, Gimel, Dalet.*' The following day he reversed [them] to him (such as *Tav, Shin, Reish, Kof*). He said to him, 'But yesterday, did not say them to me thus?' He said to him: 'Do you not trust me? So trust me with the oral too.'" RASHI interprets "Do you not trust me?" as "How do you know that this is *Aleph* and this is *Bet*? But since I taught you and you trusted me, 'trust me with the oral too.'" From this we see that Hillel told him without faith in the sages there is nothing.

However, faith is an argument of the intellect. That is, a person says, "If I did not have to believe above reason, but everything would be within reason, I would progress without any breaks." But Baal HaSulam said that in truth, the will to receive—that a person wants to work only for his own sake, like a beast—is the reason why he cannot believe. This means that when a person claims that it is difficult for him to go above reason, it stems from self-love, which is the beast in man. This is all that interferes. For this reason, two forces are required, the mind and the heart, as it is written, "As an ox to the burden and as a donkey to the load."

Hence, if we correct the field, meaning *Malchut*, who is called "will to receive for oneself," whether in mind or in heart, it is called "the field that the Lord has blessed," which was said about Jacob. And likewise, it is written about Isaac, "And Isaac went out to stroll in the field," which is the correction of *Malchut*. But Esau, who is called "a man of the field," in the action, it seems as though he is going to correct the field, but in the intention, which is called "in order to bestow," which is the whole correction of *Malchut*, there is room for one to deceive oneself, since this is something that is given to the heart, and it is not apparent from the outside that it is possible to monitor.

This is not so with actions, which are revealed outwards, a person can check whether or not he is deceiving himself. This is why *The Zohar* interprets, "And Esau said that he was in the field in order to pray, like Isaac," as it is written, "And Isaac went out to stroll in the field, and hunting, and he deceived Isaac." This means that he went into the field in order to pray, meaning he entered the field in order to correct it, like Isaac, but "hunting," meaning that he hunted, like Nimrod, who misled people's minds to rebel against the Creator. By this, Esau misled himself, as well, and from this extends the robbing, too, as it says, "to rob people."

This is as our sages said about *Adam HaRishon*. They said that he was a thief in that he ate from the tree of knowledge, meaning took it out from the singular authority, meaning the authority of the Creator. In other words, everything must be for the sake of the Creator, and by eating from the tree of knowledge, he fell into his own authority, meaning wanted to receive everything for his own sake.

It is likewise with Esau, who entered the field, meaning to correct *Malchut*. Externally, it did not show that he was not working in order to bestow. Externally, Esau said as it is written, that he entered in order to pray, like Isaac, meaning to correct the field, which is *Malchut*.

Yet, he deceived himself, meaning that the intention that should have been for the singular authority, for the sake of the Creator, was "in order to rob people." That is, as *Adam HaRishon* stole and was a thief, so did Esau do everything for his own sake. This is called "robbing people."

Therefore, a person who begins to do the holy work, meaning to turn everything into *Kedusha*, must be careful with the externality, so he does not deceive himself while performing the actions, which is work *Lo Lishma* [not for Her sake]. He must tell his body, "I am engaging in Torah and *Mitzvot Lo Lishma*, and by this I want to come to aim *Lishma* [for Her sake]." He believes in the words of our sages, who said, "One should always engage in Torah and *Mitzvot Lo Lishma*, and from *Lo Lishma*," I want to come to *Lishma*. He believes with faith in the sages, who said, "The light in it reforms him," and he will be rewarded with it.

What Is, "A Ladder Is Set on the Earth, and Its Top Reaches Heaven," in the Work?

Article No. 9, Tav-Shin-Nun, 1989/90

The *Zohar* says (*VaYetze*, Item 52), "'And behold, a ladder was set up on the earth.' What is a ladder? It is a degree upon which all other degrees depend, meaning the *Nukva* [Aramaic: female], who is the gate to all the degrees. (And in Item 53), See there, "'And behold the angels of God ascending and descending on it.' Those are the appointees of all the nations, who are ascending and descending on this ladder. And when Israel sin, the ladder is lowered down and those appointees ascend. When Israel improve their actions, the ladder rises and all the appointees come down, and their governance is cancelled. Everything depends on this ladder."

We should understand all the above in the work: 1) Why does everything depend on the ladder, that if Israel sin, the ladder is lowered down, and when Israel improve their actions, the ladder ascends? 2) What does it mean when it says that the ladder ascends or descends? What does this teach us in the work?

It is known that man should try to achieve the degree of *Dvekut* [adhesion] with the Creator, which is equivalence of form. When a person is rewarded with *Dvekut* with the Creator, see in the essay "A Speech for the Completion of The Zohar," "Now we can understand the merit of one who has been rewarded with cleaving unto Him once more. It means that he has been rewarded with equivalence of form with the Creator by inverting the will to receive imprinted in him through the power in Torah and *Mitzvot* [commandments/good deeds]. This was the very thing that separated him from His Essence and turned it into a will to bestow. It follows that one is just like the organ that was once cut off from the body and has been reunited with the body: It knows the thoughts of the rest of the body once again, just as it did prior to the separation from the body. The soul is like that, too: After it has acquired equivalence with Him, it knows His thoughts once more, as it knew prior to the separation from Him. Then the verse, 'Know the God of your father' comes true in him, as then one is rewarded with the complete knowledge, which is Godly knowledge. Also, one is rewarded with all the secrets of the Torah, as His thoughts are the secrets of the Torah."

In order for a person to be able to achieve equivalence of form, and since this is a very difficult matter because it is against the nature that the Creator created, as we learned that in order for the creatures to enjoy the delight and pleasure that He wants to give them, which was the reason for the creation of the world, since He desires to do good to His creations, and without desire and yearning a person cannot enjoy, therefore, the core of creation, which He created existence from absence, is the will to receive for oneself. This is in oppositeness of form from the Creator, whose desire is to bestow upon the creatures. For this reason, the correction was *Tzimtzum* [restriction] and concealment, where a person must first believe in the Creator, and then we can speak of working for the sake of the Creator and not for one's own sake.

There are many measures in the work of faith. As he writes in the "Introduction to The Study of the Ten Sefirot" (Item 14), there is partial faith and there is complete faith. Hence, man's main work in order to be able to annul himself and accept the burden of the kingdom of heaven depends on the extent to which he appreciates the greatness of the Creator. This is as it is written in *The Zohar*, that fear should be primarily because He is great and ruling. This means that a person should observe Torah and *Mitzvot* in order to serve a great King. Hence, man's primary work is to work to be rewarded with complete faith, for only then, if one knows he has a great King, the body will annul before Him and he will have great pleasure in serving a great King.

In *The Zohar*, this work is regarded as a person having to do the holy work in order to "raise the *Shechina* [Divinity] from the dust." It is written in the *Selichot* [prayers for forgiveness], "I remember God and I weep when I see every city built on its foundation, and the city of God lowered to the netherworld." The "city of God" is the kingdom of heaven and is in utter lowliness among the creatures. Naturally, when it is lowly, how is it possible to work for a lowly king? But if the king is a great king, there is a desire, according to the importance and greatness of the king, so there are people who want to serve him and annul their self-benefit in order to benefit the king.

Now we can understand that man's work is primarily to achieve faith that he has a great King. This is regarded as the *Shechina* being in *Gadlut* [greatness/adulthood]. It follows that man's work is to "raise the *Shechina* from the dust." Then, all his actions can be in order to bestow. If a person does not work in Torah and *Mitzvot* in order to raise the *Shechina* from the dust, and the kingdom of heaven is as important as dust, the *Sitra Achra* [other side] can control the quality of Israel, and they force a person to work for a foolish old king and not for the King of all Kings.

It follows that man's primary work is on the intention and the purpose—what a person wants to gain from engaging in Torah and *Mitzvot*. The answer to this is that a person's main work with the evil inclination, which comes from the control of the *Sitra Achra*, is lack of faith in the greatness of the Creator. In the words of *The Zohar*, this is called "to raise the *Shechina* from the dust," as our sages said, "Habakkuk came and established then on one: a righteous shall live by his faith" (*Makot* 24).

In the words of *The Zohar*, faith is called *Malchut*, and *Malchut* is called "fear." This is as our sages said, "What does the Lord your God ask of you? Only to fear Him." This means that a person must know that in order to advance in the work of the Creator, he does not need anything other than fear, which is called "faith." This is as our sages said (*Berachot* 6), "Any person in whom there is fear of heaven, his words are heard."

Literally speaking, this is difficult to understand. After all, there were many righteous in Israel, so why did He not reform them? After all, he who has fear of heaven, his words are heard. But in the work we should interpret that the words were said about an individual with respect to himself, when he sees that everything he tells his body, it does not want to obey him. He does everything he can but he cannot overcome the body. Then, our sages tell him that what he needs in order to be able to take control of the body is only one thing: fear of heaven, for only when he has fear of heaven, his words will be heard by his body.

According to the above, we should interpret the words of *The Zohar*, where we asked about the meaning of the words, "What is a ladder? It is a degree upon which all other degrees depend, meaning the *Nukva* [Aramaic: female], who is the gate to all the degrees." The answer is that a ladder, which is the *Nukva*, refers to the kingdom of heaven, which is called "faith" and "fear of heaven." That is, all the degrees with which a person can be rewarded depend only on the ladder, as she is the gate to all the degrees. In other words, everything depends on the faith one has. That is, there is a difference between one who has only partial faith or complete faith. It follows that everything depends on the ladder, meaning the kingdom of heaven, which is the whole basis of *Kedusha*, and the gate to all the degrees.

This is the meaning of what he says about the verse, "'And behold the angels of God ascending and descending on it.' Those are the appointees of all the nations, who are ascending and descending on this ladder. And when Israel sin, the ladder is lowered down and those appointees ascend." This means that if *Malchut*, who is the holy *Shechina*, is lowered because of the sins—and "sins" means that they work only for their own sake and not for the sake of the Creator—they each cause separation at the root of his soul.

In other words, where they should have created unification through work in Torah and *Mitzvot*, they cause separation. That is, all those "appointees of the nations of the world," whose wish is only to receive for themselves, ascend in their importance. This is why they govern, for the important one rules.

Therefore, when the people of Israel engage in bestowal, they cause an awakening from below that the *Kedusha* will be revealed. That is, *Malchut*, in the sense that she wants to be united with the Creator, will ascend, and the *Sitra Achra*, which is reception for oneself, will naturally descend from prominence.

This is called, "All the appointees come down, and their governance is cancelled. Everything depends on this ladder." This means that everything depends on the greatness of the faith, which is called a "ladder." This is why he says, "When Israel sin, the ladder is lowered." It means that they cause the *Shechina* to be lowered, which is regarded as the ladder being lowered down, and the *Sitra Achra* and the *Klipot* [shells/peels] ascend in importance. This means that everything pertaining to self-love ascends in importance, and everything pertaining to the benefit of the Creator, a person feels as a taste of lowliness and unpleasantness, and he cannot do anything that pertains to the benefit of the Creator. This is regarded as the ladder being lowered.

"When they improve their actions, the ladder ascends." That is, through an awakening from below, they cause the rising of the

Shechina from the dust, and all the appointees descend. That is, all the thoughts, desires, and actions pertaining to the *Sitra Achra*, meaning everything that has to do with self-reception, seems to him as lowly and loathsome, and despicable to engage in such matters, which pertain to self-reception.

According to the above, it follows that the ladder is like scales: If one pan goes up, the other pan comes down. For this reason, if there are good deeds, meaning that they engage in a manner that the actions will rise up to the Creator, this is regarded as the ladder ascending, meaning that to him, the kingdom of heaven is in ascent. At that time, the other pan, which belongs to self-reception, namely the opposite of *Kedusha*, descends. That is, the appointees of the nations of the world descend. In other words, they descend from the value of being worthwhile to work for. This is considered that the quality of Israel in a person controls them, meaning the thoughts and desires of the nations of the world, which are regarded as self-reception.

At that time, all of a person's concerns are how to bring contentment to the Creator. When thoughts of self-reception come to him, the governance of faith, which is the ladder, promptly cancels them. Therefore, all of man's work is to aim what he does so that it will yield faith, to believe in the greatness of the Creator. From this he will achieve the goal, as this is the gate to all the degrees that a person wants to achieve.

It is written in *The Zohar*, in the *Idra Zuta* (Item 135), "As the actions that the lower ones do, so it appears below, for better or for worse." These are its words: "The *Eynaim* [eyes] of the ZA are Providence of reward and punishment. At times he is revealed, and at times he is concealed. When the lower ones improve their actions, they are rewarded with attaining His Providence (meaning that His Providence is in the form of good and doing good), and he is awake and will not slumber or sleep. If they worsen their actions, Providence is concealed and they say, 'The Lord will not see, and the God of Jacob will not understand.' This is regarded as sleep, as in 'Their God is asleep.' This is so because when they worsen their actions, they make the left line prevail over the right, and then the eyes are concealed from them and they say, 'The Lord will not see.' Hence, they do not keep themselves from them and they are unafraid to sin. This is the meaning of what he says, 'They are asleep and not asleep. To the wicked, they are asleep, and to the righteous, they are not asleep.'"

We see that His guidance is in a state of rest from the perspective of the upper one, as it is written (Lamentation 3), "Is it not from the mouth of the Most High that good and bad come?" Thus, everything depends on the work of the lower ones. This is why it says, "As the work that the lower ones do, so it appears below, for better or for worse." This means that a Mitzva [singular of Mitzvot] induces a Mitzva. That is, if they improve their actions, meaning if the lower ones do good deeds, meaning that their intention is to benefit the Creator, this is certainly considered a Mitzva and induces another Mitzva. Namely, they feel that the Creator bestows upon them only good. This is called "open Providence." In other words, they see the delight and pleasure they are receiving from the Creator, and then everyone stands and praises the Creator.

But if the lower ones worsen their actions, meaning that each one is concerned only with doing things that yield self-benefit, then a transgression induces a transgression. In other words, they say that Providence is not in the form of good and doing good, and feel only the concealment of the face. They say that the Creator does not hear a prayer, since they asked Him many times but were not answered. Therefore, they say "The Lord will not see, and the God of Jacob will not understand," since the transgression they committed before—wanting to do everything in order to receive for themselves—causes a concealment of the face.

But one says to oneself, "I see that I have already prayed many prayers that the Creator will give us the desire to bestow, meaning that we ask the Creator to give us a desire to want to do everything in order to bestow, so we are not asking that the Creator will help us so we can work for our own sake, but rather that we can work for the sake of the Creator. So, why is He not answering our prayer? Thus, how can we say that He hears the prayer of every mouth?"

However, we must believe above reason that the Creator does hear the prayer of every mouth. And within reason, if a person wants to understand the order of the work, he must say that from above he has been notified what is for the sake of the Creator and not for his own sake. That is, he was given from above the feeling of what is not for his own sake. When a person feels this, that he should leave nothing for himself, he sees he cannot do this, since as long as a person does not know what is not for his own sake, he asks the Creator to help so that he will be able to work for the sake of the Creator and not for his own sake.

But when he receives from above the feeling of what it means to do everything only for the Creator, the person does not want the Creator to give him this power, and he resists with all his might. Therefore, when a person begins to ask the Creator to give him the power to overcome the will to receive, a person still does not have the full power of resistance of the body, since he still does not know what is "entirely for the Creator."

Therefore, when his prayer is answered from above, what is the answer? The answer comes from above in that they show him so he will know what he is asking, as though there is no deceit here, so he will later be able to say, "I did not know what I was asking." For this reason, a person must know that the Creator does hear the prayer. And the reason he sees that now he is worse than before he prayed for the power to overcome the will to receive, this is the answer from above to his prayer.

Therefore, one should not say that his prayer is not heard. Rather, one should say that the answer that comes from above is not what one understands, but what they understand above concerning what is for his best to know. In other words, a person must know how far he is from bestowal, and that all the organs of the body object to this. The person is asking of the Creator for something that there is not one element in the body that will agree to the request that he is making of the Creator. And at that time, a person sees something new that he did not know before he began to ask of the Creator to be given strength to overcome the body, so he will be able to do things only for the sake of the Creator, and not for his own sake.

This new awareness that the person attains is that he sees that the body does not agree to such a prayer to cancel the will to receive for himself. Thus, the question is, Why does a person sometimes want to cancel the will to receive for himself? That is, many times he sees that when he asks the Creator to give him vessels of bestowal, the whole body resists, and his prayer is only lip-service, meaning only empty words. Yet, he sees that there are times when he can pray wholeheartedly. The answer is that this is already the answer to the prayer, meaning that the Creator gave him the strength to pray for this with all his heart. Therefore, a person must be hopeful that the Creator will bring him closer.

What Does It Mean that Our Sages Said, "King David Did Not Have a Life," in the Work?

Article No. 10, 1989/90

The *Zohar* says (*VaYishlach*, Items 52-54), "Rabbi Shimon says, 'We learned that before King David came to the world, he did not have a life at all, except for the seventy years that *Adam HaRishon* gave him of his own.' Another interpretation: The patriarchs gave him of their lives, each and every one. Abraham gave him of his life, and so did Jacob and Joseph. Isaac did not leave him anything, since King David came from his side."

Interpretation: "Because King David is the *Nukva* from the left side, when it is darkness and not light, hence, he did not have a life, since there is life only from the right side, which is ZA, called 'The Tree of Life.' Isaac, too, was from the left side, but he was included in Abraham, as it is written, 'Abraham begot Isaac,' and also because of the tying [of Isaac]. This is why he had life. And this was only to himself, but he could not give life to David, since he is essentially from the left line."

We should understand what is "right," where he says that "there is life only from the right side," and what is left, where "it is darkness and not light." We should also understand why Isaac, who is left, had life, but needed *Hitkalelut* [merging/mingling] with the right, which is Abraham, whereas David had no life at all, but each one had to give to David of his own life.

To understand this in the work, we must remember what we learned, that there are two things before us: 1) The purpose of creation, which is to do good to His creations. This means that all creations must achieve the goal and be rewarded with the delight and pleasure that there is in the purpose of the Creator, who created it. 2) The correction of creation, which is that there will not be the bread of shame. For this purpose, a correction called *Ohr Hozer* [Reflected Light] was established, which means that the lower ones return bestowal upon the Creator. That is, they do not want to receive the delight and pleasure for their own sake, but in order to bestow.

Those two things are opposite to one another because the Creator created in the creatures a desire to receive for themselves, meaning that the creatures will enjoy, as this was His entire purpose, as we learn. The correction is the complete opposite from the quality of the creatures, who were created with a desire to receive for themselves, so now the creatures must do something that contradicts nature, namely to bestow.

In other words, the work begins with the lower ones having to perform acts of bestowal and with the intention to bestow. Afterward begins the work where they can receive delight and pleasure with the intention to bestow.

In order to have room for work and to choose, so they can aim to bestow, a *Tzimtzum* [restriction] and concealment were made. This means that as long as one cannot aim to bestow, he is placed under the concealment. In other words, besides the fact that he is unable to aim in order to bestow and wants only to work for his own sake, through this concealment, another thing took place, and this is the hardest—that man has to do hard work in order to be rewarded with faith above reason, since because of the concealment, he cannot see within reason the delight and pleasure that the creatures receive from the Creator, though the whole purpose of creation was because of His desire to do good to His creations. Yet, he cannot see this good neither with regard to himself nor with regard to other people.

It turns out that in addition to having to work and obtain the equivalence of form, which is to have vessels of bestowal, a person has to work to be rewarded with faith that the Creator leads His world in the form of good and doing good. And who caused all this? It was all done by the *Tzimtzum* and concealment that were placed because of the correction of creation.

However, here, a serious question arises: We say that the concealment took place for the purpose of correcting creation, but as a result of this concealment, two discernments arise: 1) the matter of lack of faith, 2) the prohibition to use the will to receive for oneself, which are generally called "mind and heart." The question is, Who comes first? That is, should one first be awarded faith, and then he can be rewarded with working for the sake of the Creator and not for his own sake, or is it the other way around?

It stands to reason that first one must be awarded faith, and then it can be said that he annuls his self and does not work for his own benefit, but only for the benefit of the Creator. This matter, that a person should do everything only for the sake of the Creator, depends on the extent to which one believes in the greatness of the Creator. To that extent it can be said that he is working for Him. This means that it is impossible to make great efforts for something that is not important because it is natural that for something that is more important we make greater efforts.

This means that the labor that one can give depends on the importance of the object. Naturally, in order for one to relinquish the will to receive for himself and work only for the Creator, the more important the Creator is for a person, the easier it is to work for Him. It follows that in order for one to be able to relinquish self-pleasure and rise and work for the sake of the Creator, a person must be awarded faith in the Creator. Afterward, a person will be able to annul himself before the Creator and do everything for the sake of the Creator. This is what common sense dictates, that such should be the order of the work.

However, from is written in the *Sulam* [Ladder commentary on *The Zohar*] ("Introduction of The Book of Zohar," Item 138), it seems the opposite: Before a person is rewarded with correcting his *Kelim* [vessels] to work in order to bestow, called "equivalence of form," a person cannot have faith. He says there that since as long as one does not have vessels of bestowal, he cannot receive the delight and pleasure from the Creator and cannot believe that the Creator leads the world as The Good Who Does Good. It follows that he is slandering the Creator. Therefore, at that time he no longer believes that the Creator leads the world as The Good Who Does Good.

Worse yet, he is in denial of His Providence, as it is written, "Prior to the correction, *Malchut* is called 'the tree of knowledge of good and evil,' since *Malchut* is His guidance in this world. As long as the receivers have not been completed so they can receive His whole benevolence, which He had contemplated in our favor in the thought of creation, the guidance must be in the form of good and bad.

..."It is written, 'The Lord has made everything for His own purpose,' yet we say the complete opposite. For this reason, we taste His guidance of good and evil as guidance of reward and punishment, for they are interdependent, since because we are using the vessels of reception, we necessarily sense that the operations of Providence are bad for us. It is a law that the creature cannot receive disclosed evil from the Creator, for it is a flaw in the glory of the Creator for the creature to perceive Him as an evildoer, for this is unbecoming of the complete Operator. Hence, when one feels bad, denial of the Creator's guidance lies upon him and the superior Operator is concealed from him to that same extent. This is the greatest punishment in the world.

"Thus, the sensation of good and evil in relation to His guidance brings with it the sensation of reward and punishment, for one who exerts not to part from faith in the Creator is rewarded even when he tastes a bad taste in Providence. And if he does not exert, he will get a punishment because he has parted from faith in Him. It follows that although He alone does, is doing, and will do all the deeds, it still remains hidden from those who sense good and evil, since at the time of evil, the *Sitra Achra* [other side] is given the strength to conceal His guidance and faith. Thus, one comes to the great punishment of separation and becomes filled with heretical thoughts. And upon repentance, one receives the corresponding reward and can adhere to the Creator once again."

Thus, we see that it is impossible to have faith in the Creator before one is rewarded with vessels of bestowal, for only then does one have complete faith. So, the question is, If one has no faith, how can one do everything for the sake of the Creator before one has faith in the Creator?

The answer is that man has partial faith, meaning from what he believes from the general public. In the general public in Israel, there is faith in the form of Surrounding Light. This is the light of faith that illuminates in general in the whole of Israel, and each one receives from this faith. This is called "partial faith," and it is called "still of *Kedusha* [holiness]." Everyone begins their work in the manner of the "still."

This is as it is written ("Introduction to The Study of the Ten Sefirot," Item 14), "I once interpreted the saying of our sages, 'He whose Torah is his trade.' The measure of his faith is apparent in his practice of Torah because the letters of the word, *Emunato* [his faith]. It is like a person who trusts his friend and lends him money. He may trust him with a pound, and if he asks for two pounds he will refuse to lend him. But he may trust him with all his property without a shadow of a doubt. This last faith is considered 'whole faith,' and the previous forms are considered 'incomplete faith,' but rather as 'partial faith.'"

For this reason, a person begins his work with faith of the whole of Israel, who have faith that is as Surrounding Light. From this faith, each one receives a part of faith that is sufficient for him to begin his work, to want to begin the work of the individual, meaning that a person will be rewarded with faith in the form of Inner Light, which is called "And you shall love the Lord your God." "Your God" is an individual discernment, when his faith is not built on the general public, that he receives from this only the part called "partial faith." However, he is rewarded with individual faith, and this is called "complete faith," when he does not need the general public.

To be rewarded with complete faith, a person must first work in the form of equivalence of form, which is that all his work will be in order to bestow. Only once he has been rewarded with obtaining vessels of bestowal, he can be rewarded with complete faith, for then he can keep what is written, "And you shall love the Lord your God with all your heart."

However, when a person begins to work in the form of equivalence of form in order to be rewarded with complete faith, the work goes in two directions, called "mind" and "heart." That is, it is impossible to work in order to bestow unless we want to bestow upon a great and important person. Therefore, a person must work part of his time in the "mind" and part of his time in the "heart."

Here is where the real work begins, when he wants to work in faith in the individual manner, since here there are ups and downs, since the basis of this work is to work for the sake of the Creator, which is opposite from human nature, who was created with a desire to receive for his own sake. Hence, here begins the real war against the inclination. For this reason, there must be order in the work, or he will not be able to continue on this path, meaning achieve Dvekut [adhesion] with the Creator.

When a person sees that the work is hard because he must always go above reason, meaning that his reason always makes him think that it is not worthwhile to work unless it is for his own sake, and each time, his reason lets him see, "You see that you were born with a desire to receive for yourself, so how do you want to annul yourself and not think at all about your own benefit, but of the benefit of the Creator? What will you get out of working for the sake of the Creator?" Our reason can understand a person doing the holy work in Torah and *Mitzvot* [commandments/good deeds] in order to receive reward. This is the normal way, that we work for someone, and it does not matter who is the boss, but we always think about how much we are getting paid for the work, since the reward is what determines. This is the work of the general public.

However, when a person wants to work in order to bestow and by this to be granted with complete faith, here begin the ascents and descents, since it is impossible to work without reward. Rather, when can one work without reward? Only when he wants to bestow upon an important person. This, he regards as a reward. This is as our sages said about "the pleasure he receives from him," meaning that a person enjoys the important person accepting his gift.

This means that it is within nature that the smaller one enjoys if he can serve the King. It follows that when he wants to work in order to bestow, a person must appreciate the Creator, so as to be able to bestow upon Him, and to have the strength to work for the sake of the Creator. Therefore, when he loses the importance of the Creator—which *The Zohar* calls "*Shechina* [Divinity] in the dust," when he does not feel the importance of *Kedusha* but regards it as dust—then he is powerless to work in order to bestow. This is why the work is in both mind and heart.

However, during the work, when a person works in order to achieve the goal, which is to be rewarded with *Dvekut* with the Creator, the order is as it is in corporeality, when a person does not walk forward unless he uses both legs, right and left. This is as our sages said (*Sotah* 47), "The left should always push away, and the right should pull near." "Right" means that which brings closer to the Creator, meaning when one feels close to the Creator. Even if he still does not have this feeling, he should go above reason, as though he feels completely whole, as is said (Article No. 9, *Tav-Shin-Nun*), "And he is happy with his lot and is called 'blessed.'"

At that time, "The blessed clings to the Blessed," and from this he receives vitality, since he is close to the Creator. This is called "adhering to the tree of life," when he uses the vessels of bestowal, on which there is no *Tzimtzum* or judgment. Hence, from the right side, called "wholeness," a person extends life from the Life of Lives.

Conversely, the "left" is something that requires correction. When a person criticizes his work, he (sees) his faults. Since he has nothing in which he has wholeness, he sees that he is rejected from *Kedusha*. Naturally, he sees that he is cursed, and "the cursed does not cling to the Blessed." It follows that then he is separated from the Creator, and naturally, he has no life. It follows that in the left, when a person makes his calculation within reason, he sees that he is bare and destitute. Hence, when a person walks on the left line, he has no life.

According to the above, we can interpret what we asked about the words of *The Zohar*, that King David had no life before he came to the world. The reason is that since King David is *Malchut*, on whom there was a *Tzimtzum*, and David is regarded as "the whole of *Malchut*," which requires correction, that the whole of the will to receive that there is in the vessels of reception should be corrected, for this reason, he needed to be included with *Kelim* [vessels] in which there are vessels of bestowal. By this, the general *Malchut* will also be corrected.

This is called "the end of correction," meaning that the Messiah King is called "the end of correction." This means that the general *Malchut* will be corrected to work in order to bestow. This is why *The Zohar* said that only Abraham, Jacob, and Joseph, who are not from the quality of judgment, gave of their qualities to David so he would have life. That is, by them he would have vessels of bestowal, which belong to the "right," which is *Hesed* [mercy], the opposite of the quality of judgment, which are vessels of reception. This is why he did not receive from Isaac, who is the left, the quality of judgment, which are vessels of reception.

This is the meaning of "there is no life on the left," since when a person walks in the manner of the "left," meaning sees what he is lacking, and a deficiency is called "the quality of judgment," hence, on the left there is no life. Rather, it is on the right, when he engages in the form of "For he desires mercy" and is not lacking anything; this is when a person feels alive. But when a person is in a state where he is bare and destitute, it is considered that he has no life. When a person feels his faults and the future does not shine for him—that he will ever be able to satisfy his wants—then the person says, "I would rather die than live."

By this we should interpret what is written, "King David had no life." It means that the whole matter of the creation of the world was for the creatures to receive the delight and pleasure. Therefore, the order of the work is that first, a person must believe in the purpose of creation, that it is the Creator's will for the creatures to receive delight and pleasure. If he believes this, he should think, "What is the reason that I do not have the delight and pleasure that the Creator wants me to take?"

It follows that if he believes that he should receive, to that extent he feels the absence. When he feels the absence, he goes to search for the reason why he cannot correct his lack. At that time, we must believe in the words of our sages, who said that what we lack is *Dvekut*, which is equivalence of form, as it is written, "As He is merciful, so you are merciful."

It follows that to the extent that he believes that the Creator bestows abundance to the whole world, to that extent he should also bestow upon the Creator. Then, when one believes that the Creator gives to the entire world, from this a person should derive the importance and greatness of the Creator, like an important person in corporeality, where we see that it is a great privilege to serve important people, and from this service itself, a person derives delight and pleasure and he does not need any other reward. It follows that to the extent of the faith in the "mind," to that extent he can also work with faith.

However, since man is born as a will to receive for himself, in this manner there is no life. It follows that the quality of King David, which is the point in the heart, has no life. In other words, the light of life cannot shine there.

For this reason, "the association of the quality of mercy with judgment" took place, as it is written that *Malchut*, which is the quality of judgment, will receive life from the quality of the "right," which is bestowal, when it is associated with the quality of King David. Hence, the quality of Abraham, Jacob, and Joseph, who are the quality of *Hesed* and mercy, was placed in the quality of King David, and not from Isaac, who is the quality of the "left," which is vessels of reception.

What Placing the Hanukkah Candle on the Left Means in the Work

Article No. 11, Tav-Shin-Nun, 1989/90

Our sages said (*Shabbat*, p 22), "The Hanukkah candle is on the left, so that the Hanukkah candle will be on the left and the *Mezuzah* [a cased piece of parchment inscribed with specified verses from the Torah] on the right." RASHI interprets, "*Mezuzah* is on the right, as it is written, '*Beitecha* [your house]—*Derech Bi'atcha* [the way by which you came], when a person begins to walk, he begins to walk with the right leg.'"

In the book *Shaar Hakavanot* (p 326), he says, "But the matter of Hanukkah and Purim is different, since both are in *Hod*, even though in regard to the morning prayer, we explained that Jacob is in *Netzah* and *Malchut* is in *Hod*. Accordingly, a weekday is holier than Hanukkah and Purim, who are both in *Hod*.

But the issue is that at that time, she receives her illuminations by herself, not through her husband, since on a weekday Jacob suckles his illumination and her part of the illumination from the *Netzah* and from *Hod*. Afterward, he gives her illumination to her and it extends from *Hod* through him. But now, on Hanukkah and Purim, she suckles the share of her illuminations from *Hod* by herself and not through her husband.

We should understand what it means in the work that the *Mezuzah* is on the right and the Hanukkah candle is on the left. What does it come to teach us? Also, we should understand according to what is written in the book *Shaar HaKavanot*, that Hanukkah and Purim are both one discernment, as it is written, that both Hanukkah and Purim are a single discernment that extends from *Hod*.

Why do both suckle from the same root if on Purim there is joy, a feast, and one must eat the Purim meal, while on Hanukkah, our sages said, "These candles are holy, we have no permission to use them"? In the work, we learn that one person contains the whole world. This means that Israel and the seventy nations are in one person.

In other words, a person consists of all the bad qualities that exist in the seventy nations. It is known that the seventy nations extend from the opposite of the seven qualities of *Kedusha* [holiness], as in "God has made them one opposite the other," and each quality consists of ten.

This is the meaning of the seventy nations, meaning when the seventy nations govern the Israel in a person, it is considered that the people of Israel is in exile under the governance of the nations. This means that the desires and yearnings control the Israel in him, and the part of Israel cannot work for the sake of the Creator, but only for its own sake.

It is completely impossible to understand with reason how it will ever be possible to break free from the dominion of the nations of the world within him. This is because as much as one has toiled to emerge from their governance, it was futile. On the contrary, each time he could see more that it is impossible to come out of their exile. This is why we must always remember the exodus from Egypt, as it is written, "that you may remember the day when you came out of the land of Egypt," meaning believe what is written, "I am the Lord your God, who brought you out from the land of Egypt ... to be a God unto you."

This means that just as the Creator brought the people of Israel out of Egypt and they were rewarded with "To be a God unto you," He can deliver us, too, from the dominion of the seventy nations, to be rewarded with "To be a God unto you."

One must not say that he is worse than the people who were in Egypt, or that the Creator had the power to deliver only them out of their rule. But when a person sees his own lowliness, he despairs and says that he must be worse than those who were in Egypt.

Here we must believe the words of the ARI who says that the people of Israel prior to the exodus from Egypt were already in forty-nine gates of *Tuma'a* [impurity], until the Creator appeared to them and redeemed them. It follows that even when one sees that he is in utter lowliness, he should not escape the campaign and believe that the Creator will deliver him from exile, from being among the nations of the world.

Thus, we can see that the whole basis is founded entirely on faith, that only by faith is it possible to emerge from exile. We should not mind our reason, although a person is judged according to it. But when a person has the intellect to see his true state, it enables him to go above reason. In other words, one cannot go above reason without the help of the Creator. But if he sees that with reason, he can advance, he does not need His help.

And the main thing that is required of a person is to achieve his own completeness, meaning to be rewarded with NRNHY *de* [of] *Neshama*. This comes specifically by needing the Creator. Our sages said about it, "One who comes to purify is aided." And *The Zohar* says, "How is he aided? With a holy soul. When one is born, he is given a soul from the side of a pure beast. If he is rewarded more, he is given *Ruach*," etc.

This is why it is a great thing when a person needs the Creator to help him, since one's salvation is in being given greater powers from above. And by receiving new powers each time, meaning a new soul, in the end he will receive the whole of the *NRNHY* that belong to the root of his soul. It follows that "a miracle" implies something that a person cannot obtain. That is, it is impossible for one to obtain it unless through a miracle from above. Only in this way is it called "a miracle."

For this reason, when a person comes to a state where he already has recognition of evil, that it is impossible for him to emerge from the domination of the nations of the world in him, that Israel in him is in exile under them, and he sees no way that he can emerge from their power, when the Creator helps them and brings them out from the authority of the nations of the world and turns it around so that the people of Israel governs them, this is called "a miracle."

This is regarded as being as it was in the land of Egypt, when the Creator delivered them from the land of Egypt, meaning that the Creator brought them out from under the afflictions of Egypt. One should believe that as this miracle happened in the exodus from Egypt, every single one who is walking in the work of the Creator must believe that the Creator will deliver him, for it is truly a miracle that one exits the governance of self-love and cares only about that which belongs to the benefit of the Creator.

And when a person comes to this, it is considered that this person has achieved *Lishma* [for Her sake]. This means that he has already been rewarded with faith in the Creator and he has the power to work for the sake of the Creator, and this is called *Lishma*. It is also called "right," when one engages on the path of bestowing upon the Creator, meaning that everything he does is to benefit the Creator. That is, he wants to do *Hesed* [grace/mercy] to the Creator, meaning to give contentment to the Creator.

However, we should know that a person wanting to do everything for the sake of the Creator is only the correction of creation. It is not the purpose of creation. The purpose of creation is for man to receive delight and pleasure in the vessels of reception. However, there must be a correction on the vessels of reception, which is called "in order to bestow."

The abundance of the purpose of creation is called *Hochma* [wisdom], which is the light of life, as in, "Wisdom will give life to one who has it." Also, light of *Hochma* is called "left," since anything that requires correction is called "left," as in "the weak hand, whose strength has weakened like a female's." This is called "left."

And what is the correction that should be placed on the light of *Hochma?* It is the right, which is called *Hassadim* [mercies]. In other words, once he has already been rewarded with the purpose of creation, which is the delight and pleasure called *Hochma*, the light of *Hassadim* must be drawn once more—the abundance that comes into the vessels of bestowal—since we said that we were given the work in Torah and *Mitzvot* in the form of "We shall do and we shall hear." This means that by doing and observing Torah and *Mitzvot* in action, we will be rewarded with the state of hearing, too.

In other words, one must observe Torah and *Mitzvot* even by coercion. There is no need to wait for a time when he has a desire to observe Torah and *Mitzvot*, and then he will observe. Rather, one must overcome and observe only in action, but the doing will later bring him hearing, meaning that afterwards he will hear about the importance of Torah and *Mitzvot*. In other words, he will be rewarded with the delight and pleasure that is found in Torah and *Mitzvot*. This is the meaning of Israel's saying, "We shall do and we shall hear." Thus, in the right, which is called that he engages in *Hesed*, in vessels of bestowal, it is a keeping so that one can do everything for the sake of the Creator and not for his own sake.

It follows that according to the rule, "We shall do and we shall hear," the act affects the aim. This necessarily means that when one receives *Hochma* from above, the act must be done, so that the aim will be like the act. It follows that the act of reception affects the intention, making it in order to receive, as well. Therefore, even during the act, when he draws the light of *Hochma* with the aim to bestow, because of the rule, "We shall do and we shall hear," he must still receive abundance from the act.

This is why care is needed, to extend clothing, meaning to clothe the light of *Hochma*, where there is "We shall do." "We shall do" is the act of bestowal, and we will be rewarded with the intention being in order to bestow, as well. And also, "We shall hear," that the aim will be to bestow, as well, like the act. This will keep the vessel of reception, which receives the light of *Hochma*, so it may keep the intention to bestow upon reception of the delight and pleasure, and for it to be in the form of receiving in order to bestow.

With the above said, we should interpret the meaning of the *Mezuzah*, which must be on the right. Since the *Mezuzah* is keeping, for it guards a person, there is a hint that the *Mezuzah* is on the right. In other words, keeping belongs to the right, which is considered *Hesed*, and *Kelim* [vessels] of *Hesed* [mercy/grace] are considered right, meaning that they do not require correction. But *Hochma* is considered left because *Hochma* comes in vessels of reception, and vessels of reception require keeping.

This is why RASHI interprets "*Beitecha* [your house]—*Derech Bi'atcha* [the way by which you came]," meaning that a person begins to walk on the right. It should be interpreted that the beginning of a person's arrival at the holy work is with the right, that is, that the vessels of bestowal will be in order to bestow. Afterward, one begins to walk in the left, meaning to correct the vessels of reception to be in order to bestow.

This is why it is written that as one begins to walk in corporeality, he begins with the right leg. This points to spirituality, meaning that in the beginning of one's arrival at the work of the Creator, he should begin with the right, meaning in wholeness. In other words, for everything he does in the work, he should give thanks to the Creator for having given him some thought and desire to work in the holy work, that still, he has some grip in Torah and *Mitzvot*, in the practical part.

At that time, he still does not think about the aim, for there are two issues to be discerned in the intention, too.

1) The intention, meaning who it is who obligates the engagement in Torah and Mitzvot. Is it the environment he is in, since all the friends engage in Torah and Mitzvot, and everyone prays and keeps the Torah lessons at the synagogue, etc., or is he observing Torah and Mitzvot only because the Creator commanded us to observe Torah and Mitzvot, and he believes in everything that the sages said, and based on that he observes Torah and Mitzvot?

2) The intention for the reward, what to receive for observing Torah and Mitzvot. Some expect to be rewarded for their work, as it is written in The Zohar that there are three reasons for engaging in Torah and Mitzvot: a) to be rewarded in this world; b) to be rewarded in the next world; c) not to be rewarded, but only because of the greatness of the Creator, because He is great and ruling.

Hence, the beginning of one's work in Torah and Mitzvot is in order to be rewarded. And in that, too, we said that there are two discernments to make:

1) Sometimes a person is not yet strong in faith or able to work for the Creator, so He will reward him, since subconsciously he lacks the faith to make him able to do good deeds. However, he works because of the friends, since he does not want to be despised by them. It is not the Creator who commits him to do good deeds, but because of the shame from the friends, he does it.

One must think that this is utter lowliness that the friends commit him to work and not the Creator. However, this should not be slighted, either. For such deeds, too, a person should be thankful to the Creator—that the Creator gave the friends the power to commit him to act as they wish. It is considered that the Creator is watching over him in concealment. In other words, the Creator hides Himself in the clothing of the friends who compel him to do good deeds.

Here we should interpret what our sages said, (Avot, Chapter 3:20), "And they collect from a person knowingly and unknowingly." "Knowingly" means that a person knowingly wishes to observe Torah and Mitzvot. In other words, he says that he is doing good deeds is because it is according to the view of the Creator. In other words, the Creator is the one who commits him. "And they collect from him unknowingly" means that a person does good deeds without knowing that he is observing the Torah and Mitzvot of the Creator, since he thinks that he is observing the Torah and Mitzvot of the friends, meaning that the friends commit him.

This is considered that without one's knowledge, he is observing the Creator's will, although he thinks that he is observing the friends' will. And if he believes it—that unknowingly he is doing the Creator's will—meaning if he knew that he would not observe it because he thinks he is observing only the will of the friends, this is called "concealment of the face." In other words, the Creator hides Himself in the clothing of the friends, and in this way he does the Creator's will.

2) If he thanks the Creator for helping him through the concealment—meaning that now he has the choice to say that he is working because of the friends and he has no contact with the Creator, or that he believes that the Creator hid Himself in the clothing of the friends, and by that he engages in Torah and Mitzvot, and if he chooses and says that only the Creator helped him to be able to do good deeds by clothing in a clothing of friends, and he thanks the Creator for this—it brings upon him a great ascent: to be rewarded with the revelation of the face of the Creator. In other words, the Creator gives him a thought and desire to do the Creator's will, since now he has some illumination from above by sentencing above reason. This is why the Creator helped him, so that through the Achoraim [posterior], he will later be rewarded with the Panim [anterior/face] of the Creator. This means that he has been rewarded with being collected knowingly.

It therefore follows that the Mezuzah is keeping, which is right, called Hassadim, at the time when one is in a state of bestowing in order to bestow. This is considered the "correction of creation." But Hanukkah and Purim, says the ARI, are both considered Hod, which is left. This implies to the purpose of creation, which requires correction so as to be able to receive the delight and pleasure in a corrected manner, implied in the abundance called *Hochma*. This is why Hanukkah is on the left, to indicate to the light of *Hochma*.

However, on Hanukkah there was the state of *Hanu Koh* [parked there], which means, as Baal HaSulam explained, that it was only a pause there and not the end of the war. In other words, the light of the sun, called "left," was shining but lacked the clothing, the keeping of the *Hochma* that comes in vessels of reception, since there is a grip to the *Sitra Achra* [other side] in the vessels of reception and there was light of *Hassadim* there, called "right."

This is why the miracle was only on spirituality. It means that the light of the purpose of creation was shining, but they could not use it for lack of the clothing of *Hassadim*, since it is forbidden to use it. This is called "spirituality," when it has not yet materialized so it can be used. This is why it is written that it is forbidden to use the Hanukkah candles but only to see them, for lack of clothing.

But on Purim, they had the clothing, called *Hassadim*, as it is written (*Talmud Eser Sefirot*, end of Part 15), "Hence, since the matter has already been materialized, meaning they could use the light of *Hochma* in order to bestow, on Purim there is a feast and joy."

Why Is the Torah Called "Middle Line" in the Work?

Article No. 12, Tav-Shin-Nun, 1989/90

The Zohar writes (*Miketz*, Item 238), "Come and see, each day when the sun rises, a single bird awakens on a tree in the Garden of Eden and calls three times, and the announcer calls out loud, 'Who among you who sees and does not see, who are in the world without knowing why they exist, and do not observe the glory of their Master, the Torah stands before them and they do not delve in it, it would be better for them not to be created than to be created.'"

He interprets there in the *Sulam* [commentary on *The Zohar*] as follows: "Seeing is *Hochma*. Those who cling to the left line and not to the right, see and do not see, since the *Hochma* on the left does not shine without clothing in the light of *Hassadim* [mercies] on the right. Hence, even though there is *Hochma* there, namely that 'they see,' they still do not receive *Hochma* for lack of clothing of *Hassadim*. This is why they do not see.

"It is written, 'who are in the world without knowing why they exist.' This is said to those who cling to the right, and not to the left, who have sustenance in the world through the light of *Hassadim*. However, they do not know why they exist, meaning they lack GAR, since illumination of the 'right' without the 'left' is VAK without a *Rosh* [head]."

They do not observe the glory of their Master, the Torah stands before them, and they do not delve in it. Torah means "middle line," which is ZA, who is called "Torah," which unites the two lines with one another.

We should understand why if they advance on the right, which is *Hassadim*, when they work in order to bestow, why is this regarded as not observing the glory of their Master? After all, they are engaging only in bestowal upon the Creator because He is great and ruling, and not in order to receive reward, and their whole vitality is that they increase the glory of heaven, and this is why they do all their deeds in order to bestow.

We should also understand why those who have already been rewarded with *Hochma*, which is regarded as the purpose of creation, are regarded as not observing the glory of their Master, but only when they take upon themselves the Torah, for the Torah is called "middle line," and only they are regarded as observing the glory of their Master, for only through the Torah they come to glorify their Master.

We have spoken many times about the two matters before us: 1) The purpose of creation, which is for the lower ones to receive delight and pleasure, meaning that all the creatures will feel how the Creator behaves with them in attainment of The Good Who Does Good, as our sages interpreted, "good," since He is good to him. In other words, a person feels that he receives from the Creator only good, and doing good. "To others" means that he sees that the Creator does good to others, too.

2) The correction of creation, which is that in order not to have the bread of shame, for the creatures not to feel shame while receiving delight and pleasure, a correction was made that the pleasure and the good will not shine on the will to receive for one's

own sake, but only when the creatures can aim in order to bestow. At that time, the delight and pleasure pour onto the creatures.

But this is only in order for the world to exist before they come to the correction of being able to bestow, for the creatures to be able to exist. If they do not have delight and pleasure, they cannot exist in the world, for the need for the delight and pleasure comes to the created beings from the purpose of creation, which is to do good to His creations. The ARI says that the delight and pleasure come from the breaking of the vessels in the world of *Nekudim*, when they fell down to the *Klipot* [shells/peels], which *The Zohar* calls "a slim light," which is a very thin light compared to the delight and pleasure bestowed upon those who are in *Kedusha* [holiness], meaning compared to the delight and pleasure revealed in Torah and *Mitzvot* [commandments/good deeds], as it is written in *The Zohar*, that there are 613 *Mitzvot* opposite the 613 organs of the soul. But the sparks of *Kedusha* fell to the *Klipot* only in order to sustain them.

However, the order of the work is to begin from the right. Yet, there are many meanings to "right," and it is understood according to the context. In other words, wholeness is always called "right" compared to the incomplete. But what is complete and what is incomplete depends on the matter in discussion at the time. In other words, what we need according to the situation, this is called "right."

Therefore, when a person is far from Torah and *Mitzvot*, he is regarded as being "on the left." That is, *Kedusha* is called "right," which is man's wholeness when he observes Torah and *Mitzvot*. But when we begin to speak of *Kedusha* but we do not speak of those people who are far from observing Torah and *Mitzvot*, we do not speak at all about those who are far from religion, those secular ones.

Thus, the state in which we begin to speak is that they observe Torah and *Mitzvot* only in their actions. They are regarded as "one line." It is known that we cannot speak of "right" if there is no "left" opposite it, or vice-versa. Therefore, in this regard, those who begin the work in actions are called "one line," since here is the beginning. But compared to secular people, who have no connection to with the reason, they are considered "right," for they have wholeness, while the secular are called "leftists."

Yet, when we begin to speak of people who want to work with the aim to bestow, we must say that people who work only in actions are incomplete. At that time, we must call them "left," meaning that they have no wholeness. Conversely, those who want to work in order to bestow should be called "right."

However, if we speak in terms of the feeling of the worker himself, and not with respect to the truth about the order of degrees, we should say that this person, who works only in actions, feels his state in observing Torah and Mitzvot as whole. Therefore, to him, this state is regarded as walking on the "right," meaning wholeness.

Also, they feel the work in intentions as a lack, since they see that they cannot emerge from the governance of the receiver for oneself. It follows that he feels his deficiency. Hence, we should say that this is considered "left." That is, normally, we say that something that requires correction is called "left," as our sages said, that we put Tefillin on the left hand since it is written, "Your hand, a weak hand," since its power has waned and it needs help.

For this reason, those who want to do the holy work in a manner that has wholeness, to do everything in order to bestow, when they criticize their work and see that they are still not fine, that state is called "left" compared to the work in actions without an intention. In other words, a person must use the act, as well.

Thus, a person should say that although he cannot do something in order to bestow, he still feels himself as whole with respect to actions. He says that it is a great privilege that he can nonetheless perform acts of Kedusha [holiness], even without an intention. It is a great privilege that the Creator awarded him a thought and desire to engage in Torah and Mitzvot only in actions, without an intention.

This is called "right" because he feels that he is in wholeness, that it is worthwhile to give thanks to the Creator for this.

Therefore, afterward, when he shifts to the intention and sees that he is deficient, all he needs is to pray that the Creator will help him and give him the power to be able to work with the aim to bestow. This is called "left" compared to the previous state.

However, when he has already been rewarded with the Creator helping him, when he can already work in order to bestow, though only in acts of bestowal, for the acts of bestowal are easier to aim in order to bestow, whereas in acts of reception of pleasure he still cannot aim to bestow, this state is called "right." But it is called "right" compared to the previous state.

When he wants to work in order to bestow but does not succeed, this is called "left," and there he has a place for prayer that the Creator will help him be able to aim in order to bestow. But now that the Creator has helped him and he can aim in order to bestow with acts of bestowal, now he must give thanks for the wholeness he has now, and this is called "right." This light is called "light of Hassadim," which is considered the correction of creation, when he has the power to perform actions in order to bestow.

Yet, although with regard to the correction, this state is regarded as wholeness, with regard to the purpose of creation, that state is still not regarded as wholeness because he must achieve the purpose of creation. For this reason, it is considered "right" from the perspective of wholeness, and he must thank the Creator for being rewarded with vessels of bestowal, with aiming in order to bestow.

But with regard to the absence of correction of the purpose of creation, it is considered a lack. Therefore, if he has been rewarded with receiving the purpose of creation, called "light of Hochma," this is certainly regarded as complete wholeness compared to the state where he was rewarded with only light of Hassadim, called "light of the correction of creation." It should have been called "right," yet, that state, too, is considered incomplete. Hence, it is called "left, which requires correction," since even though they extended the light of *Hochma* in order to bestow, he still needs guarding because the act of reception of pleasure contradicts the intention, which should be in order to bestow.

For this reason, we must extend the middle line, meaning light of *Hassadim*, which now includes both: *Hochma*, as well as *Hitkalelut* [merging/mingling] of *Hassadim*.

There are two things: 1) the correction of creation, 2) the purpose of creation.

This is called "Torah" or "middle line," which is included from the right and from the left. At that time we can use the light of the purpose of creation, which is the delight and pleasure that the Creator wants to impart upon His creations, which is the purpose of creation. This means that before there is *Hitkalelut* with *Hassadim*, the light of the purpose of creation cannot shine, since the two qualities must be there together. This is called "Torah."

Now we can understand what we asked, why people who walk in the quality of the "right," whose works are only to bestow, and who have already been rewarded with the abundance called "light of *Hassadim*," are regarded as "not observing the glory of their Master." Also, those who have already emerged from the right and have already been rewarded with *Hochma*, called "left," are still considered "not observing the glory of their Master," and the Torah stands before them, yet they do not delve in it. This is very difficult to understand, if we are speaking of people who have already been rewarded with *Hassadim*, and people who have been rewarded with *Hochma*, that they are not delving in the Torah. Can we say this?

Yet, according to what we explained before, "right" means light of *Hassadim*, which is only the correction of creation. It follows that as long as they do not engage in extending the light of the purpose of creation, which is what the Creator wants to give to the created beings, the delight and pleasure where His greatness is revealed, called "the revelation of His Godliness to His creatures," at which time His glory is revealed to the created beings, it follows that they are not looking at the glory of their Master, which will be revealed to the created beings.

This is the main deficiency for which, meaning to reveal His Godliness in the world, which is the purpose of creation—to reveal His Godliness to the created beings. For the created beings to receive this goal, all the restrictions and corrections took place. It follows that those who walk only on the right, which is the correction of creation, there is certainly a key deficiency here. That is, they did everything except for what is most important, meaning the goal. This is why it is considered that they are not observing the glory of their Master.

Also, those who have already been rewarded with the light of *Hochma*, which is the purpose of creation, we asked, What else do they need? The answer is that since there is a rule that the light of *Hochma* cannot shine to the lower ones without a clothing of light of *Hassadim*, since the light of *Hochma* comes in vessels of reception, so although he drew the light in order to bestow, he still needs guarding from being drawn after the act, as he is using the vessels of reception.

For this reason, he must extend clothing that is light of *Hassadim*, which dresses in the vessels of bestowal, which is considered the correction of creation. Hence, although he extended the light of the purpose of creation, he cannot use it because it does not shine without a clothing of *Hassadim*. Naturally, he, too, is not observing. In other words, the purpose of creation does not become revealed in him, to see the revelation of His Godliness, as it is written, that those who walk on the left also do not observe the glory of their Master.

This is the meaning of what is written, "The Torah stands before them and they do not exert in it. The Torah means the middle line, ZA, called 'Torah,' which unites the two lines with one another." In other words, through the Torah, called "the middle line," where there are two qualities together, meaning the purpose of creation, namely the revelation of His Godliness to the creatures, which is called "the glory of their Master," and there is also the clothing of the correction of creation, called "light of *Hassadim*," which is considered "right." For this reason, when those two are separated, the purpose of creation cannot shine to the created beings. This is considered that they are "not observing the glory of their Master." But once they delve in Torah, the purpose of creation shines. In the words of *The Zohar*, this is called "The Torah, and Israel, and the Creator are one."

Now we can understand what we said (Article No. 11, *Tav-Shin-Nun*), that the Hanukkah candle is on the left, and its light must not be used because the left, which is *Hochma*, was already extended to the creatures, but as long as they do not extend the middle line, which is regarded as "Torah," so as to have right and left together, the light does not shine to an extent that they can use it, due to absence of clothing of *Hassadim*, which comes through light of *Hassadim*.

But on Purim, they extended the light of *Hassadim*, called "right," through their fasting and crying out, as is explained in *The Study of the Ten Sefirot* (end of Part 16). It turns out that although on Hanukkah they were complete from the right side, when they shifted to the left to extend *Hochma*, they no longer had the *Hassadim* of the right.

This means that the *Hassadim* that they extend after the extension of *Hochma*, where *Hochma* is called "left," is called "middle line." It follows that then, on Hanukkah, there was a state of *Hanu-Koh* [parked here]. That is, they had the quality of the "right." The miracle was that they had "right" in wholeness. But the quality of the "left" did not have wholeness, for they lacked the middle line, which is the Torah.

Hence, on Shabbat, which is the middle line, the candles are for use. This is called "peace at home," as in, "In *Hochma* [wisdom] is a house built." For this reason, "[between] The Shabbat [Sabbath] candle and the Hanukkah candle, the Shabbat candle precedes," since Shabbat indicates wholeness. There is the quality of *Yesod*, called "middle line," which bestows upon *Malchut*, called "house." For this reason, the Shabbat candle comes to imply wholeness. This is why Shabbat is called "Shabbat of peace," since *Yesod*, which is the middle line, makes peace between the lines, which are called "right" and "left."

It follows from the above that the miracle of Hanukkah was on the "right," called "the correction of creation," that they had wholeness. This is called that the miracle was over spirituality, since the vessels of bestowal, called "spirituality," from the perspective of the *Kelim* [vessels], and these *Kelim* pertain to the good inclination.

Conversely, the vessels of reception are attributed to corporeality, meaning to the evil inclination, as we explained, "And you shall love the Lord your God with all you heart," meaning with both your inclinations. That is, with the good inclination, which is vessels of bestowal, we should work for the sake of the Creator. But also with the vessels of reception, which belong to the evil inclination. They, too, must be used for the sake of the Creator, meaning to receive in order to bestow.

It follows that on Hanukkah, when the ARI says that Hanukkah and Purim are both regarded as "left," the Hanukkah candle is on the left. Although the right is called "wholeness" from the perspective of the vessels of bestowal, the fact that the left illuminated, meaning *Hochma* without *Hassadim*, and it is forbidden to use *Hochma* without *Hassadim*, but this in itself is a great thing, that they extended the purpose of creation. However, it is still forbidden to use its light.

Therefore, on Hanukkah, it is considered that the miracle was on spirituality because it is forbidden to use *Hochma* without *Hassadim*. This is why it is considered a spiritual miracle, which still did not come down so we can use it. In that respect, Hanukkah is considered a "spiritual miracle," both from the perspective of *Hassadim* of the right, and from the perspective of the *Hochma* of the left, since the middle line was still missing.

What Does It Mean that by the Unification of the Creator and the Shechina, All Iniquities Are Atoned?

Article No. 13, Tav-Shin-Nun, 1989/90

It is written in *The Zohar* (*Vayigash*, Item 23), "Rabbi Yehuda started and said, 'For behold, the kings assembled' refers to Judah and Joseph, for both were kings." (In Item 27) "Rabbi Yehuda says, 'When the desire and the unification are revealed, the two worlds, ZON, connect together and are assembled together. One is ZA, to open the treasure and bestow, and one is *Malchut*, to gather and collect the abundance into her. And then, 'For behold, the kings assembled.'" (And in Item 28) He says, "'Passed by together,' since all the iniquities in the world do not pass away and are not pardoned until ZON connect together, as it is written, 'And passes by the transgression.' Similarly, 'Passed by together' means the iniquities have passed away, were pardoned." (And in Item 30) He says, "As they saw, so they were puzzled. When both kings are assembled in a single desire, they saw that desire of the two worlds, ZON. 'They were puzzled, terrified, and hasted,' since all the litigants were silenced and were removed from the world, and cannot govern. Then their existence was revoked and their governance rescinded."

We should understand why the atonement of iniquities depends on the connection of two worlds, called ZA and Malchut, for he says that the kings "assembled, passed by together." We should also understand why they are not always connected, but there is a time when the judgments govern, as it is written, "As they saw, so they were puzzled, terrified, and hasted" through the atonement of iniquities, for atonement of iniquities comes by connecting ZA and Malchut. Thus, they are not always connected. Why is this so? Who is detaining them from always being connected and not letting the judgments rule?

It is known that all the iniquities come through the will to receive for oneself. That is, since all creations come from Malchut, called "will to receive," which is the core of creation, called "creation existence from absence," this lack, where the creatures yearn to receive delight and pleasure in order to satisfy their deficiency, comes from the desire in Malchut.

As we learn, since the purpose of creation is to do good to His creations, and pleasure and delight are measured by the intensity of the deficiency and yearning for the matter, to that extent they can enjoy when attaining the matter. For this reason, Malchut was created, who contains the full measure of the deficiency for the light and the abundance that the Creator wants to impart upon the creatures.

This Malchut is the general will to receive. That is, we must say that to the extent of the delight and pleasure that He wanted to impart upon the creatures, to that extent He created the desire for that light. In the words of the ARI, this is called *Ein Sof* [no end/infinity]. In order not to have the matter of the bread of shame while receiving the pleasure, there was a correction called "*Tzimtzum* [restriction] and concealment," where the delight and pleasure shine only to the extent that they can aim in order to bestow, for by this, the matter of shame will be corrected. And so was the order in *Kedusha* [holiness], that they will never receive more than the amount they can aim in order to bestow.

However, after that correction come more things. That is, something new took place, namely the breaking of the vessels, when there was a mingling of the will to receive for oneself with *Kedusha*, because of which the vessels broke. Also, there was the matter of the sin of the tree of knowledge, which caused holy sparks to fall into the *Klipot* [shells/peels]. It follows that the breaking of the vessels and the sin of the tree of knowledge caused the creatures that come after, that the will to receive receives its sustenance from *ABYA* of *Klipa* [singular of *Klipot*].

This is as it is written ("Introduction to The Book of Zohar," Items 10-11), "And in order to mend that separation, which lies on the *Kli* [vessel] of the souls, He created all the worlds and separated them into two systems, which are the four worlds *ABYA* of *Kedusha*, and opposite them the four worlds *ABYA* of *Tuma'a* [impurity]. And He imprinted the desire to bestow in the system of *ABYA* of *Kedusha*, removed the will to receive for themselves from them, and placed it in the system of the worlds, *ABYA* of *Tuma'a*. Because of this, they have become separated from the Creator and from all the worlds of *Kedusha*."

It therefore follows that as long as one has not emerged from the governance of the will to receive for himself, it makes him sin, meaning be separated from the *Kedusha*. That is, through the iniquities, a person grows farther from the *Kedusha* and is drawn into the *Klipot*. Hence, it extends from this that each of the created beings causes, through his sin, separation at the root of his soul in *Malchut* of *Atzilut*—who is the collection of all the souls, which is why *Malchut* is called "the assembly of Israel," who is the *Malchut* of *Kedusha*—to be separated from the *Kedusha*. This is regarded as a person causing through his sin, the descent of *Kedusha* into the *Klipa*.

It follows that this is regarded as causing at the root of his soul, separation between the Creator and the *Shechina* [Divinity]. This means that *Malchut* is not in equivalence of form with ZA. ZA is called the "giver," the Creator, and *Malchut* is the receiver, the opposite of the giver. That is, all the sins come only from a person wanting to satisfy his will to receive for himself. It follows that he causes separation above, at the root of his soul, which is in *Malchut*.

When a person repents, what is the repentance that a person takes upon himself? It is when a person says that from now on he will do everything for the sake of the Creator and not for his own sake, meaning that all his actions will be in order to bestow, which is called "equivalence of form." It follows that through repentance, he causes the root of his soul, *Malchut*, to also be only in bestowal, like ZA, who is the giver, called the Creator.

This is called "the unification of the Creator and the *Shechina*." That is, as the Creator is the giver, likewise, *Malchut*, who is called "the *Shechina*," works in order to bestow. Naturally, the Creator can bestow upon *Malchut*, and then the abundance extends downward. It follows that through the sin, a flaw was made above, which caused separation. Now, through the repentance, the separation has been corrected and unification was made. This is considered that through the unification, the iniquities, meaning the corruptions he caused by his actions, were corrected.

By this we can interpret what is written, "Return, O Israel, unto the Lord your God." What does "unto the Lord your God" mean? It is known that "the Lord" is called ZA, which is the quality of mercy, namely a giver. "Your God" is judgment, meaning *Malchut*, who is the will to receive on whom there was a *Tzimtzum* and judgment that it is forbidden to use the will to receive without a correction of the *Masach* [screen] called "in order to bestow."

Since Israel's sin caused *Malchut* to move away from ZA, who is called "the giver," since all the sins come only from the will to receive for himself, it follows that there is judgment on *Malchut*. Hence, we must repent to the extent that *Malchut* will draw near to ZA, which is called "equivalence of form" and *Dvekut* [adhesion].

In other words, as ZA gives, so will *Malchut* acquire such a correction, where by repenting, when we say that henceforth, all the actions will be in order to bestow, which is called *Rachamim* [mercy], like ZA, it follows that repentance causes *Malchut*, who is called "the quality of judgment" prior to the correction, to become *Rachamim* [mercy] after the correction, like ZA.

By this we can interpret "Return, O Israel," meaning that the repentance that a person should make is to make *Malchut*—who is called "your God," the quality of judgment—become "the Lord," which is mercy. This unification corrects all the corruptions that the iniquities caused, creating remoteness between the Creator and the *Shechina*. It follows that through this unification, all the iniquities have been atoned.

According to the above, we should interpret what we asked, Why does the atonement of iniquities depend on the connection of two worlds, called ZA and *Malchut*? As said above, by repenting, to the extent that "the Lord will be your God," meaning by causing unification, meaning equivalence of form between *Malchut* and ZA, the corruption that is done through the iniquities—which caused separation between *Malchut* and ZA by committing iniquities with the will to receive—will be corrected.

Because we must believe the words of our sages, who said that each one, through his iniquities, causes separation at the root of his soul, in *Malchut*, that the separation that is done means that he brings the *Kedusha* down to the *Klipot*, it follows that by correcting and repenting, and saying that henceforth everything will be in order to bestow and not to receive for oneself, now this causes what he had corrupted at his root to reconnect with the *Kedusha*, meaning it becomes a giver like ZA. It follows that through the iniquities there was a departure of the abundance, since there was a separation between the receiver and the giver, meaning between ZA and *Malchut*, and now it has reunited.

This is the meaning of the words, "When the desire and the unification are revealed, the two worlds, ZON, connect together and are assembled together. One is ZA, to open the treasure and bestow, and one is *Malchut*, to gather and collect the abundance into her. And then, 'For behold, the kings assembled.'" The meaning is that once the unification between the giver and the receiver has been done through the repentance, for the receiver to receive everything in order to bestow, it follows that through equivalence of form, the giver can give to the receiver.

According to the above, we can understand what we asked, Why are they not always connected, but there are times when the judgments govern? The reason is that while there are iniquities, the iniquities cause the separation, and naturally, there are judgments. Judgments means that since there was a judgment on the will to receive for oneself, where the abundance cannot shine there due to disparity of form, hence, when there are iniquities below, it causes disparity of form above, at the root of *Malchut*.

It follows that the judgments govern. That is, the *Sitra Achra* [other side], which extend only from the iniquities, which is the will to receive for himself, governs. In other words, the iniquities of those who engage in the will to receive for oneself cause an addition of power to the *Sitra Achra*. That is, just as when we engage in order to bestow, we cause an addition of power of the desire to bestow at the root above, which causes unification, which is equivalence of form, so it is to the contrary: When engaging in the will to receive for oneself, the *Klipot* receive the power to control.

This is the meaning of the words, that then the judgments rule. At that time, the abundance does not extend below, since all the abundance will go to the *Sitra Achra*, since *Malchut* of *Kedusha* cannot receive because of the separation and remoteness between her and ZA. This is considered that the kings do not assemble together. That is, when there is equivalence of form, called "connection," they "pass by together," meaning that the iniquities passed away and were atoned.

This is the meaning of the words, "As they saw, so they were puzzled, terrified, and hasted, since all the litigants were silenced and were removed from the world, and cannot govern." It follows that everything a person does, so he causes at the root of his soul, whether for better or for worse.

By this we can interpret what is written in the *Neila* [concluding] prayer, "You lend a hand to the transgressors, and Your right is stretched out to welcome the returning." Also, our sages said, "Anyone who stretches out his hand is given." Normally, each one closes his hand and does not want to give to the other unless he sees that he will get some reward, in which case he stretches out his hand. In other words, he opens his hand to receive the reward. For this reason, the other person also opens his hand and gives to the other. But to stretch out one's hand just like that, without a reward, a person closes his hand and cannot give anything to the other.

Therefore, when we speak of the work, meaning what a person wants to receive from above, meaning that the Creator will bestow upon him into the person's *Kelim* [vessels], called "hands," the order in the act below is that in whatever way a person does, so it awakens above, at the root of his soul.

Therefore, if a person stretches out his hand, meaning opens his hand and does not close, but wants to bestow above, it follows that at the root of his soul, *Malchut*, becomes regarded as a giver, which is called "equivalence of form." At that time he is given, since now there is equivalence of form, called "the kings assembled, passed by together." In other words, the abundance pours to *Malchut*, and from her to those who caused the unification of the kings, who are ZA and *Malchut*.

This is why they said, "Anyone who stretches out his hand is given," since he caused unification above, in his root. Hence, if a person wants to be given something from above, he must awaken in his essence, the vessels of bestowal.

However, sometimes a person wants to stretch out his hand and be a giver, but he cannot. His body disagrees with it. What can he do? His only way is prayer. Yet, he sees that he has prayed many times for the Creator to satisfy his deficiency, meaning to be able to work in order to bestow, yet the Creator did not answer him, as though He does not watch over him.

Thus, how can he pray once more? He sees that he receives no attention whatsoever. These thoughts remove him from prayer. Thus, what should he do then, when he comes to a state where these thoughts poke his mind?

The answer is as Baal HaSulam said, that a person must believe what is written, "And it came to pass that before they call, I will answer; while they speak, I will hear." He said that it means that a person should believe that the fact that now he has come to pray is because I made him see that he is deficient and should come to pray that the Creator will satisfy his deficiency.

That is, a person should not think that he started first. Rather, the Creator started by giving him a desire to pray. Thus, he cannot say that the Creator is not watching over him by him not seeing the answer to the prayer when he prays for his lack. Rather, it is the Creator who began.

This is called "I am the first and I am the last." That is, "I began the contact with you," and the person should wake up from this. However, a person does not complete the work. Rather, it is as it is written, "The Lord will finish for me." By this we should interpret, "You lend a hand to the transgressors." It means that the Creator gives the hand, meaning the power to the transgressors to pray for their deficiency, and not the person. Also, a person must trust the Creator to help with his prayer and not give up.

What Is True *Hesed* in the Work?

Article No. 14, Tav-Shin-Nun, 1989/90

RASHI interprets the verse that Jacob said to Joseph, "Do for me mercy and truth." *Hesed* [mercy/grace] that is done with the dead is true *Hesed*, for one does not expect a reward in return. This means that when he asked him the favor, "Please do not bury me in Egypt," he asked that he will perform true *Hesed*, without reward. We should understand this, since common sense dictates that if he paid him for the trouble, he would certainly be more certain that he would do this for him, as it is customary that when we want something done to the fullest, we pay a higher fee. Thus, why did he choose the other way, to do the work without any payment?

Even more perplexing, according to the words of RASHI about the verse, "And I give you one Shechem more than to your brothers" (Genesis 48:22), RASHI interprets "'I give you,' since you trouble yourself with my burial, 'one Shechem more than to your brothers.' The actual Shechem will be to you one portion more than to your brothers." Thus, this contradicts a true *Hesed*, which means without any payment, while here he pays him "one Shechem," meaning one portion more than to his brothers.

We should interpret all this in the work, that Jacob implied to Joseph the order of the work. We see that the order of the work that was given to us in Torah and Mitzvot [commandments/good deeds] also seems contradictory. On one hand, we see that our sages said that the reason for the creation of the worlds was His desire to do good to His creations, meaning for the creatures to receive from Him delight and pleasure, since the Creator is in utter wholeness and the only reason He created creation is in order to give abundance to the created beings, as it is written (Midrash Rabbah, Beresheet), "The Creator replied to the angels when He wanted to create the man. He said that it is like a king who has a tower filled with abundance but he has no guests. What pleasure does it give?" It follows that all that He created was for the creatures to receive delight and pleasure and to feel His guidance as good and doing good.

On the other hand, we see something that is the complete opposite from the purpose of creation, meaning that a Tzimtzum [restriction] and concealment were placed, that it is forbidden to receive for one's own benefit. Rather, everything we receive should be for the sake of the Creator. This means that our main work is to work for Him. This is the meaning of the words, "Blessed is our God, who created us for His glory." That is, all of creation is only for His glory and not for the created beings. This is why we were given 613 Mitzvot to observe.

As our sages said, "I have created the evil inclination; I have created the Torah as a spice," said the Creator. In other words, a person cannot work for the sake of the Creator because the evil inclination obstructs him. Hence, the Creator has given us 613 Mitzvot, which The Zohar calls "613 Eitin" (meaning counsels), by which we will be able to work for the sake of the Creator.

Ostensibly, this is the complete opposite of the purpose of creation—to do good to His creations. The thing is that we must believe what the ARI says, "When it came up in His simple will to create the worlds, emanate the emanations, and bring to light the perfection of His deeds." In The Study of the Ten Sefirot, at the beginning of the Ohr Pnimi commentary, he explains there that "perfection of His deeds" means that the delight and pleasure that He contemplated giving to the creatures, so there would be wholeness in them, so they would not feel shame while receiving the delight and pleasure, this is called "the perfection of His deeds."

It follows that the *Tzimtzum* that took place, where the light shines only when the creatures do everything for the sake of heaven, to benefit the Creator, and then they will receive the delight and pleasure and there will be no shame, this is the correction of the *Tzimtzum*, where we must do everything for the sake of the Creator and not for our own sake. It therefore follows that the only reason we must work for the sake of the Creator is only for our own benefit. By this we will receive the complete delight and pleasure without any unpleasantness of the bread of shame. This is called "to bring to light the perfection of His deeds," meaning the deed that He wants to do good to His creations will be complete when the creatures receive the delight and pleasure.

Hence, there is no contradiction between the purpose of creation, to do good to His creations, meaning that the goal is to benefit the created beings, and not that the Creator wants to be served. Rather, it is all for the created beings and not at all for the sake of the Creator, since He has no deficiency. Moreover, He would like the created beings to be so happy that they will feel good and not feel any unpleasantness upon receiving the delight and pleasure.

The rule is that anyone who eats the bread of shame is ashamed. The Creator would like to save them from this shame; hence, He made a correction called "*Tzimtzum* and concealment," where as long as they do not have the correction of doing everything for the sake of the Creator, they cannot receive the delight and pleasure because this concealment was placed, so that afterward, when they do everything for the sake of the Creator, the delight and pleasure that they want to receive and enjoy is only for the sake of the Creator, they will be saved from the shame that is present in one who receives sustenance from others as a free gift.

It follows from the above said, that there is no contradiction between the purpose of creation to do good to His creations, meaning for the sake of the created being, and the correction of creation, that we must do everything for the sake of the Creator and not for our own sake, which is also for the sake of the created beings and not that the Creator needs to be served or given anything. Rather, everything is for the sake of the created beings.

Now we can explain what we asked, Why did Jacob say to Joseph to do for him "true mercy." This refers to the matter that Jacob established the order of the work that we must do here. He implied to him the order of the correction of creation and the matter of the purpose of creation, which are both one aim—to benefit the creatures.

This is why he began to tell him that we must begin the work in a manner of "true mercy," meaning without any reward, but everything not for his own sake but for the sake of the Creator, as it is written in the book *Matan Torah* (in the beginning), that when a person works for the sake of others, it should also be because of the commandment of the Creator, meaning that everything a person does should be for the sake of the Creator, and then he will naturally be adhered to the Creator in everything he does.

Afterward, he implied to him that the fact that we must work for the sake of the Creator is in order to yield benefit for himself, meaning that if a person truly works for the sake of the Creator and does not want anything for his own benefit, he comes to a degree where he wants to give something to the Creator so He will enjoy. At that time, he sees that there is only one thing by which he can please the Creator—by receiving from Him the delight and pleasure because this is why He created creation. Hence, he wants to delight the Creator. And certainly, the more a person enjoys the King's gift, the more pleasure the King has.

This is similar to someone giving a gift to his friend. Usually, if the receiver of the gift praises the gift he received from his friend, his friend enjoys more. But if the receiver of the gift tells him, "I don't really need the gift you gave me," his friend does not enjoy this. On the contrary, the more the recipient needs the gift, the more the giver enjoys. This is expressed in the measure of the gratitude that the recipient gives to the giver. Therefore, the more a person tries to enjoy the delight and pleasure that the Creator has given him, the more contentment there is above from the lower one enjoying more.

Therefore, once Joseph took upon himself the work in order to bestow without any reward, he should receive the delight and pleasure for what he did in order to bestow. This is why it is written that Jacob told him, "And I give you one Shechem more than to your brothers." "Shechem" means one portion more than to your brothers, according to RASHI's interpretation, since you trouble yourself with my burial, meaning that because then you took upon yourself to work without any reward, now comes the time for you to receive the payment, meaning the part of the light and abundance that should be revealed on the work in order to bestow, since the work in order to bestow is primarily for this purpose—to be able to receive the delight and pleasure without shame, as one who receives free gifts.

Concerning the words "one Shechem," we should interpret the way Baal HaSulam interpreted what is written about King Saul, who was "from his Shechem [shoulder] and up, higher than all the people" (1 Samuel 9). The corporeal meaning is that he was taller by a head than the rest of the people, meaning that his head was higher than all the people. He said that in spirituality, the degrees divide into Rosh [head] and Guf [body]. Guf means that there is still no wholeness in him, and Rosh means that he already has wholeness.

We should interpret that wholeness means that he has already been rewarded with the correction of creation, called "vessels of bestowal." This means that with the actions of the vessels of bestowal, he can already aim to bestow. This is considered that he has been rewarded with the light of Hassadim [mercies], which dresses in vessels of bestowal. Also, he has been rewarded with the purpose of creation, meaning that he can use the vessels reception in order to bestow. This is considered that he has been rewarded with the light of Hochma.

It follows that "from his shoulder and up" means that he has been rewarded with wholeness, called Rosh. Similarly, we should interpret what Jacob said to Joseph, "And I give you one Shechem more than to your brothers." That is, by accepting his work as true mercy, meaning without payment, he was later rewarded with the wholeness of using the vessels of reception in order to bestow. In other words, he was awarded two things together: 1) the correction of creation, 2) the purpose of creation.

According to the above, we should interpret what is written in the Shabbat [Sabbath] song, "Anyone who sanctifies the Seventh, his reward is great, according to his work." We should understand what is the novelty in saying, "his reward is great, according to his work." Yet, this applies in the corporeal world, too, that any worker receives a salary according to the time he worked. Thus, where is the novelty that he comes to tell us, that he receives reward according to his work? Even more perplexing, we should work not in order to receive reward, but for the sake of heaven, meaning to benefit the Creator, and not to benefit ourselves, so what does it mean, "his reward is great"?

As said above, after a person worked in the correction of creation during the six workdays, in order to bestow and not for his own benefit, it follows that he has worked not in order to receive any reward. Rather, it was all for the sake of the Creator. It follows that to the extent that he worked not in order to receive reward, when Shabbat comes—which is a "similitude of the next world," the conclusion of heaven and earth—he receives reward. That is, he uses the vessels of reception and enjoys the delight and pleasure that is the purpose of creation, since now he can receive everything in order to bestow.

It follows that if he does not enjoy, it is as though the host gives food to a guest and tries to make for the guest a tower filled with abundance. But if the guest says to the host, "I did not take any pleasure in your meal," what contentment does the host have? Thus, the more the guest enjoys the meal, the happier is the host.

This is as our sages said (*Berachot* 58), "A good guest, what does he say? 'What troubles has the host troubled himself for me?!' And all that he troubled himself, he troubled himself only for me.' But a bad guest, what does he say? 'What trouble the host troubles himself is only for his wife and children.'"

We should interpret what are a good guest and a bad guest in the work. When a person has not corrected his evil, meaning his will to receive for his own sake, he is under the governance of evil. Hence, he says, "The fact that the Creator gave us the Torah and Mitzvot to observe is because He needs our work. Therefore, He commanded us to observe Torah and Mitzvot. In return, He will pay us." That is, He did not create the world in order to do good to His creations. Rather, they say that He created the world for His own sake.

However, He wants us to work for Him, and in return He will pay us. Therefore, sometimes, the bad guest says, "I do not want to work for Him, meaning to observe His Torah and Mitzvot, and I relinquish the reward." He says, "Neither they," meaning the work in Torah and Mitzvot, "nor their reward," of Torah and Mitzvot. In other words, this work that the Creator commanded us, this reward for the work is not worthwhile.

A good guest in the work is one who has already corrected the bad and has vessels of bestowal. Afterward, he is rewarded with the purpose of creation, meaning he receives the delight and pleasure because he already corrected the bad. Then he says, "All that the host has troubled Himself with was for me," and not that the Creator is the needy one, that we should work for Him. Rather, working for Him is to our benefit, so we can receive the delight and pleasure and not feel shame when receiving the pleasure.

But a bad guest, one who is still under the governance of his evil, which is the receiver in order to receive, says the complete opposite, that (the Creator) did everything for Him, and not for the sake of the created beings.

According to the above, we should interpret mercy and truth as two things: 1) Hesed means to do everything not for one's own sake, but only for the sake of the Creator. 2) "Truth" means that then we are rewarded with seeing the truth, that the reason for the creation of the worlds with all the corrections is only for the sake of the creatures, so they will receive delight and pleasure. But before they are rewarded with Hesed, the truth is not revealed—that the creation of the world was in order to do good to His creations.

What Does It Mean that Before the Egyptian Minister Fell, Their Outcry Was Not Answered, in the Work?

Article No. 15, Tav-Shin-Nun, 1989/90

*T*he *Zohar* (*Shemot* [Exodus], Item 341) says, "As long as their minister had dominion over Israel, Israel's outcry was not heard. When their minister fell, it is written, 'The king of Egypt died.' And promptly, 'And the children of Israel sighed from the work, and they cried, and their outcry went up unto God.' But until that time, their outcry was not answered."

We should understand this: If he says that before their minister fell, their outcry was not answered, who caused their minister to fall so that afterward it will be possible to hear their outcry? We should also understand why, if their minister had dominion, it is impossible for their outcry to be answered. Does their minister have the power to detain the prayers of Israel? We should also understand what is written (Exodus 5:22), "Then Moses returned to the Lord and said, 'O Lord, why have You brought harm to this people? Why did You ever send me? Ever since I came to Pharaoh to speak in Your name, he has done harm to this people, and You have not saved Your people at all.' Then the Lord said to Moses, 'Now you shall see what I will do to Pharaoh, for with a mighty hand he will send them.'"

We should understand Moses' argument when he said, "Ever since I came to Pharaoh to speak in Your name, he has done harm to this people, and You have not saved Your people at all." It appears as though Moses' complaint was true, since it implies from the Creator's reply that what Moses said was true. But the Creator said, "Now you shall see what I will do to Pharaoh." In other words, he would see what the Creator would do to Pharaoh. It seems as though it should have said, "You will see," meaning that Moses will see, meaning *Atah* [you] with an *Aleph* [which changes the meaning from "now" to "you"]. Why is it written *Atah* with an *Ayin* [which means "now"], which implies that now he will see? It means that when he came to Pharaoh previously, and he harmed this people, there could not be an exodus from Egypt. But now there will be a place for with a mighty hand he will send them and drive them out.

We should understand why specifically now is the place of the exodus from Egypt. There are two things to understand here: 1) why when he came as the Creator's messenger, the situation of the people of Israel grew worse. 2) why specifically now, after the situation has deteriorated, there can be an exodus from Egypt.

We should interpret this in the work. The ARI says that the exile in Egypt was that the view of *Kedusha* [holiness] was in exile. This means that the *Klipa* of Egypt ruled over the people of Israel. We should interpret that the people of Israel means that the whole nation wanted to work for the sake of the Creator and not for their own sake, as it is known that "Israel" means *Yashar-El* [straight to the Creator], meaning everything for the Creator.

The governance of Pharaoh is the opposite: to work only for one's own sake. For this reason, the view of *Kedusha* means that we must work for the sake of the Creator, meaning to bestow. This discernment was in exile under the rule of Pharaoh, king of Egypt, where *Mitzrayim* [Egypt] has the letters of *Metzar-Yam* [narrow sea], and it is known that "narrow" means scarce in *Hassadim* [mercies].

It is like the [Hebrew] expression, "narrow eyed" [jealous], meaning that he can only receive and not give anything. "Wide" means expansive, meaning giving much, and "narrow" is the opposite, not giving, which means that the *Klipa* [shell/peel] of Egypt was that each one could work only in order to receive in return. But without return, meaning only to bestow, he does not permit any action. This is considered that Egypt was narrowing [constraining] the quality of Israel.

By this we can interpret what our sages said, "Anyone who constrains Israel becomes a *Rosh* [head]." That is, who can control the quality of Israel? Only he who is the *Rosh*, he governs. Then he constrains the quality of Israel, not letting one work for the sake of the Creator, which is called to engage in *Hesed* [mercy], but only in reception for oneself. This is called "the *Klipa* of Egypt."

Therefore, the order of the work is as our sages said, "One should always engage in Torah and *Mitzvot* [commandments/good deeds] *Lo Lishma* [not for Her sake], and from *Lo Lishma*, we come to *Lishma* [for Her sake], since the light in it reforms him." This is so because man was born with a desire to receive for himself. Hence, if we want him to do something, to emerge from the state where he is used to working for his sustenance, meaning a person is told, "Until now you knew that all your pleasures, by which you sustain the body so it can exist, came only from corporeal things. You found pleasure only in corporeal things, and this is called 'the sustenance of the body.' Engage in Torah and *Mitzvot*, where greater pleasure is clothed, so it is better for you to engage in Torah and *Mitzvot* because by this you will have more pleasure."

It is like a person being told, "Stop working where you are used to work; there is a company where you can earn ten times more." If he believes what he is told, he will certainly leave the job he was used to doing all the time and go work at the new place, since he will receive a higher return.

This is called *Lo Lishma*. However, from *Lo Lishma* he will come to *Lishma*. Therefore, it is worthwhile to begin even in *Lo Lishma*, since in the end, he will come to *Lishma*. It is as Maimonides says, "Therefore, when teaching little ones, women, and uneducated people, it is in order to receive reward, until they gain knowledge."

All this is because the body understands only the mother tongue. That is, if the first language that the mother speaks to it is the language of reception, meaning to work only for the will to receive for oneself, meaning to act only for its own benefit, and the language of bestowal is something new to it and it does not understand it, it is very difficult to learn this language. That is, understanding this language requires help from above, so as to be able to grasp this language of the desire to bestow.

It was said about this, "He who comes to purify is aided," to understand this language. This is called "the generation of Babylon," as it is written (Genesis 7:11), "They will not hear one another's language." In other words, when they were given work of bestowal, for each to work for one's friend, the package soon fell apart.

That is, it is as it is written, "and they stopped building the city," since when they were told that each one should work for his friend, they did not know this language, and no one wanted to work for another. Hence, they immediately "stopped building the city," as they had no motivation to work for the sake of others.

For this reason, when the people of Israel were in exile in Egypt and were under the governance of Pharaoh, King of *Metzar-Yam* [Narrow Sea/Egypt], and wanted to emerge from his governance, they could not. It was still unclear to them what it means to work in order to bestow and not for one's own sake. Although they wanted to work for the sake of the Creator, they saw that they could not. Yet, they always had excuses as to why they cannot aim in order to bestow, and they did not feel that they were so far from the Creator.

However, when Moses came to the people of Israel and spoke to the quality of Pharaoh in each and every one, meaning to the will to receive in their hearts, and told them that he wanted that the quality of Pharaoh in them would not dominate the quality of Israel in them, but that it would allow working for the sake of the Creator and not for the sake of the body, when the Pharaoh in the nation heard what Moses had told them—to work only for the sake of the Creator—they understood what it means to bestow and not receive and were promptly weakened in the work, since the body resisted with all its might so they would not perform any act of *Kedusha*.

In other words, even the *Lo Lishma* now became difficult for them to do. Before Moses came, they had strength to work because they still did not know what "for the sake of the Creator" meant. But when Moses came and explained to them what it means to bestow and not receive anything, the Pharaoh of each one started asking questions: 1) As it is written, Pharaoh asked, "Who is the Lord that I should obey His voice?" 2) Then came the wicked one's question, who asked, "What is this work for you?"

It follows that once the people of Israel heard from Moses that they must work for the sake of the Creator, the real resistance of the evil in man began. This is the meaning of the words, "Then Moses returned to the Lord and said, 'O Lord, why have You brought harm to this people? Ever since I came to Pharaoh to speak in Your name, he has done harm to this people.'" In other words, the body, which is called Pharaoh, began to resist the work.

It follows that Moses' question was in order. That is, intellectually, we understand that if we observe the Torah and *Mitzvot* that the Creator commanded, the order should be that if we engage on the path of truth, the work should certainly be stronger, since we are marching on the path of truth, whereas *Lo Lishma* is not on the path of truth.

Hence, when Moses came to speak in the name of the Creator, the work should have been stronger, meaning to overcome the evil with the quality of truth. Yet, what did Moses see? It is written, "Ever since I came to Pharaoh to speak in Your name, he has done harm to this people," meaning the work to overcome the evil has become harder. In other words, not only did they not become better, meaning had more power to overcome the evil, but on the contrary, the evil gained more power.

Yet, the truth is that before we know what it means to do everything in order to bestow, the evil in man does not show its resistance all that much, since it is given a holding place while engaging in Torah and Mitzvot. Yet, when the body hears what it means to bestow upon the Creator and not receive anything for one's own sake, meaning wanting to completely uproot the evil and not give it any grip on one's Torah and Mitzvot, of course it resists with all its might and does not allow being cancelled.

It therefore follows that it is not that something new occurred in the evil. That is, it is not that now he received the evil, but that the evil that was in him had nothing to do and was virtually idle within him. But when a person wants to give all his actions to the Creator and not give anything to his body, called "will to receive for oneself," it begins to show its strength and resists being overthrown from governance over the body.

It is written in The Zohar that the evil inclination in a man is called "a foolish old king." It says, Why is it called "king"? Because it controls the body. And why is it called "old"? Because as soon as one is born, it is present in a person, whereas the good inclination comes to a person after thirteen years.

It therefore follows that as long as the evil is not revealed, there is still no one to cancel. But once its might has been exposed in full, it is possible to revoke it, since then, when he revokes it, he revokes it entirely. When the evil is not revealed, only a part of it can be cancelled, and this is not wholeness, since from above, when a person is given something, he is given a complete thing.

Otherwise, if one were to be given the power to be able to work for the sake of the Creator, if a bad part that has not been revealed remains in a person, it follows that a part that is bad and is still not revealed remains within a person and works with the intention for the sake of the Creator, and this is not considered wholeness. This is as our sages said (*Sukkah* 48), "Anyone who associates 'for the sake of the Creator' with another thing is uprooted from the world."

We should interpret this in the work. This means that if a person observes Torah and *Mitzvot* for the sake of the Creator, but does part of the work also for the sake of the body, meaning that it will yield benefit to the body, too, he is uprooted from the world, meaning from the spiritual world, since everything must be for the sake of the Creator, and not at all for one's own sake.

It follows that before the evil reveals its true form, it is impossible to give the person the power to uproot it, since he still does not have the measure of the bad that will give him the power to overcome, as it is known that there is no light without a *Kli* [vessel], meaning no filling without a lack.

According to the above, we can understand the Creator's answer when He told him, "Now you shall see what I will do to Pharaoh." We asked, it should have said *Atah* with an *Aleph* [meaning "you"], meaning that Moses would see that the Creator will do to Pharaoh. Why does it say *Atah* with an *Ayin* [meaning "now"]?

According to what we explained, it is impossible to give half a thing. Rather, first, the full evil must be disclosed, and then comes the help from above over a complete thing. Therefore, after Moses said, "Why have You brought harm to this people and did not save at all," but rather the bad manifested in all its might, now is the time when the salvation will come from above. This is why He said, "now," meaning that now you will see that I will give them the necessary help, as it is written, "For with a mighty hand he will send them, and with a mighty hand he will drive them out from his land." For only now is it the time, since all the bad has been revealed in them.

Now we can understand why when Moses came as the Creator's emissary, their situation grew worse. The reason is that this is not regarded that they grew worse, but that when Moses let them see what it means that they must work for the sake of the Creator, as it is written, "Ever since I came to Pharaoh to speak in Your name," meaning that we must work for the sake of the Creator and the quality of Pharaoh must descend from its throne, there was room for the revelation of the evil.

It follows that by Moses explaining to them the meaning of working in order to bestow, they advanced in the work and achieved the degree of truth, to know how the bad controls them. Before Moses came to them as an emissary of the Creator, they did not know the truth—how far they were from the Creator. It follows that although in action, they grew worse, in truth, they advanced, for only now do they have *Kelim* [vessels] that the Creator can fill with His help, as our sages said, "He who comes to purify is aided."

Now we can also understand the second question: Why specifically after they grew worse, the time came when the Creator gave the help. This was so because only now do they have *Kelim* that are ready to receive a complete thing. This is why it is written, "Now you will see" with an *Ayin*.

Concerning what we asked about what *The Zohar* says, that before their minister fell, the outcry of Israel was not heard, as it is written, "And the king of Egypt died," and promptly, "And their cry went up unto God." But until that time their outcry was not answered. We asked, 1) Who caused their minister to fall? 2) Why does their minister have the strength to detain their prayer?

We can understand this the way Baal HaSulam said, as is presented in the book *A Sage's Fruit* (Part 1, p 103): "The thing is that to the extent that the children of Israel thought that Egypt were enslaving them and impeding them from worshipping the Creator, they truly were in the exile in Egypt. Hence, the redeemer's only work was to reveal to them that there was no other force involved here, that 'I and not a messenger,' for there is no other force but Him. This was indeed the light of redemption."

It follows that the exile is primarily that we think that there is a minister of Egypt, meaning that their minister is given authority and he governs Israel. When a person thinks so, their minister rules. When the people of Israel want to emerge from the governance of the minister of Egypt and see that they are asking the Creator to deliver them from his dominion but the Creator does not deliver them from exile and they are under his governance, then they say that the Creator does not hear their prayer.

The evidence of this is that He does not hear their outcry, since they see that they keep regressing instead of progressing. In other words, each time, they see that they are farther from the work of bestowal, since it makes sense that according to the work and toil that a person gives and prays to the Creator, He would deliver him from Pharaoh's governance.

Yet, each day he sees the opposite. That is, each day, he sees that Pharaoh is ruling over him with more power, meaning he sees that he is more connected to the will to receive, and also more remote from the desire to bestow. For this reason, a person says that the Creator does not hear a prayer.

This is the meaning of what *The Zohar* says, that as long as their minister was given dominion over Israel, Israel's outcry was not heard. This is considered that their minister detains the prayers of Israel. That is, the people of Israel say so; otherwise, why does the Creator not hear their outcry?

And what happens in the end, meaning after the full form of the evil has been revealed to them and they did not escape the campaign in the middle of the work? At that time they are rewarded with seeing the truth, that there is no minister of theirs here, who was detaining their prayers, but the Creator Himself did everything, as it is written, "for I have hardened his heart." That is, the Creator made them see each time how far they were from *Kedusha*, meaning that the Creator revealed to them the bad "that I may set these signs of Mine." Thus, specifically by revealing all the bad, the Creator can give them the help for a complete thing.

Accordingly, it means that when they were rewarded with seeing, "And the king of Egypt died," which *The Zohar* calls "the fall of their minister," this awareness, that they thought that there was a minister to Egypt and that he had authority and was detaining their outcry so it would not be heard above, that view has fallen from the people of Israel.

Instead, now they were rewarded with seeing that there was no minister to Egypt who detained the prayers of Israel from being accepted. Rather, the Creator did hear their prayer and the Creator hardened their hearts. That is, the Creator wanted the real form of evil, called "will to receive for oneself," to be revealed.

It follows that He did hear their outcry. Were it not for the awakening from below of the people of Israel, who want to emerge from Egypt's governance, meaning when they saw that all their work was in favor of the will to receive for themselves, called "Pharaoh king of Egypt," without this awakening, the Creator would not reveal to them the form of the bad.

The Creator shows the form of the bad only to those who want to emerge from the governance of the bad. They think that they are growing worse each time, when in truth, it is common sense that everything in which we exert, we advance more or less, but we do not regress. The answer is that we are not regressing. Rather, we are advancing to the form of the truth of how much the bad can work within them. Then, when they have a complete *Kli* of evil, the Creator gives them the help, and then everyone sees that the Creator did hear the prayer the whole time.

According to the above, it is clear what they thought, that there is a minister of Egypt who detains the prayers. We asked, Why does this minister have the power to control the prayers of Israel? The answer is that this is what they thought.

The second question, Who caused their minister to fall from his authority? It is that they worked all the time and did not escape the campaign until there was room to reveal all the bad. Then, they were rewarded with the truth. Until then, there was also no minister here of theirs, but they thought so. It follows that two things came at once, which our sages call, "His divorce and his hand come as one."

According to the above, we need great strengthening and not to escape the campaign, but to believe that "The Lord hears the prayer of every mouth," and there is no other force in the world but only one force—that of the Creator, and He always hears everything that is turned to Him.

What Is "For Lack of Spirit and for Hard Work," in the Work?

Article No. 16, Tav-Shin-Nun, 1989/90

It is written in *The Zohar*, *VaEra* (Item 65), "Rabbi Shimon said, 'For lack of spirit' means that the *Yovel* [Jubilee], which is *Bina*, had not finished yet to give them rest and freedom. And the last spirit, which is *Malchut*, still did not rule the world, to instill upright laws in the world. Hence, there was lack of spirit. And which spirit is it? It is *Malchut*, who was unable to save Israel. This is the meaning of 'for lack of spirit.'"

We should understand the meaning of "hard work" and "lack of spirit." In other words, what is the connection between hard work and lack of spirit, in the work? We should also understand what Rabbi Shimon interprets about lack of spirit with regard to *Malchut*, what is the connection to hard work?

It is known that the order of the work in the work of the Creator is that a person should work to provide himself with *Kelim* [vessels] in which he will be able to receive the delight and pleasure that the

Creator contemplated giving to the creatures. It is known that the reason for the creation of the worlds was His desire to do good to His creations. Because of this, He created in the creatures a desire and yearning to receive delight and pleasure. In the desire and yearning for the pleasure, we measure the taste of the pleasure, meaning that to the extent of the yearning for something from which he thinks he will receive pleasure, so is the measure of enjoyment. For this reason, smallness or greatness of the pleasure of a person are measured by the measure of the yearning for the pleasure in that thing.

Accordingly, from where do the discernments of the recipients of the pleasure come? After all, they were all created with a desire to receive for themselves, so who makes one feel little pleasure, and another, great pleasure? That is, what fool would want to receive little pleasure where he can receive much pleasure? But because the Creator wanted "to bring to light the perfection of His deeds," meaning that doing good to His creations means complete giving, meaning that when he receives the delight and pleasure, he will not feel any unpleasantness, namely shame, as it is written, "One who eats that which is not his, is afraid to look at his face," hence, the *Tzimtzum* [restriction] and concealment on the vessels of reception was installed, which are *Kelim* [vessels] that man was created with them by nature.

In other words, there are two matters about this: 1) We cannot receive any abundance of *Kedusha* [holiness] in these *Kelim*, 2) As long as one has not acquired vessels of bestowal, he does not see the delight and pleasure found in *Kedusha*, and he cannot perceive the taste of pleasure, except the tiny illumination that was given to the *Klipot* [shells/peels] so they can exist. Out of these sparks that fell into the *Klipot* come all the corporeal pleasures.

This is revealed to all, meaning that the pleasure is revealed, namely that each one can taste these pleasures with the vessels of reception, which want to receive pleasure for their own benefit. Conversely, the delight and pleasure of *Kedusha*, where there are the majority of pleasures that He wanted to impart upon the creatures, this is hidden from the vessels of reception. This is called "*Tzimtzum* and concealment."

Therefore, two things emerged from this correction—that it is possible to receive the pleasures of *Kedusha* only to the extent that he has acquired vessels of bestowal: 1) A person must believe that the majority of delight and pleasure that the Creator wants to give to the created beings is found in *Kedusha*. 2) We must work against nature and not receive anything for our own sake, but only for the sake of the Creator.

This induces a distinction of degrees. That is, no person is like another, since with regard to what comes from the Giver, everyone is the same, as the ARI says, "Before the emanations were emanated and the creatures were created, the simple, upper light had filled the whole of reality. And there was not beginning or end, but everything was simple light." Yet, afterward, after the correction to receive only in vessels of bestowal was done, a proliferation of worlds took place, meaning many discernments according to the intention that one can aim in order to bestow. This is called proliferation of *Masachim* [screens], and by this, a distinction of degrees took place.

This is as our sages said (Shabbat 152), "Each and every righteous is given a section according to his glory." This is so because there is a difference on the part of the *Kelim* of the receiver, meaning the *Kelim* that the receiver should make, which are called "vessels of bestowal," meaning to receive in order to bestow. Vessels of reception for one's own benefit come from the Emanator. A person does not need to work on these *Kelim*, since the Creator created him with such *Kelim*. Hence, the created beings' only work is to obtain vessels of bestowal.

According to the above, we know what is man's work: It is work only to obtain vessels of bestowal. That is, a person should come to a state where everything that does not concern the benefit of the Creator does not interest him. Instead, his only desire is to come to a state where he can bring contentment to his Maker. Hence, when a person begins the work, he begins in *Lo Lishma* [not for Her sake], meaning for his own sake. Afterward, he begins to understand that the fact that he is working *Lo Lishma* is only a *Segula* [remedy/power/quality] by which to achieve *Lishma* [for Her sake], as our sages said, "From *Lo Lishma*, we come to *Lishma*, since the light in it reforms him," and he believes that in the end he will achieve *Lishma*.

Afterward, a person goes another step forward and begins to exert. He does things that will bring him to *Lishma*, meaning he begins to understand that one must take actions and intend that these actions will bring him to the level of *Lishma*, and he calculates to himself how much he has already been rewarded with the matter of *Lishma*.

At that time, he begins to see the truth—how far he is from the work of bestowal. With each time, he sees more how immersed he is only in self-love. He sees that each day he is regressing, and then his work, where he wants to work in order to bestow, is called "hard work."

This is so for two reasons: 1) Now he sees what "in order to bestow" means. A person must believe in our sages, that the fact that now he sees what is "for the sake of the Creator," he did not know its true meaning. Rather, as we explained about the words of *The Zohar* about the verse, "Or make his sin known to him," he asks, "Who made it known to him?" And he replies, "The Creator." We should interpret that when a person feels how far he is from the work of bestowal and that he is immersed in self-love, this is a revelation from above. Now, this work becomes harder, meaning that once he was notified from above the meaning of "for the sake of the Creator and not for his own sake," now his work has become harder.

However, a person thinks that now he has become worse than when he began the work in order to bestow, as though he himself has become worse now. At that time, a person must believe that this is not so. Rather, he advanced toward the truth by the Creator notifying him his real situation. It follows that through the work, when he began to do this work, which now seems to him as hard work, it is because the Creator has turned to him because now he is in a better state than when he was still not involved in work of bestowal.

However, the second reason why now it has become harder for him is that normally, when a person wants to learn a profession, he goes to a craftsman to learn the profession that he thinks is good for him. If the craftsman sees that he is not progressing after some time of learning with him, the craftsman tells him, "This profession is not for you; it is too difficult; go look for another occupation that is easier for you, and from this you will make a living."

Therefore, in the work of the Creator, when a person begins to do the work of bestowal, and thinks that according to the order of the work, each day there should be progress, he says that it is worthwhile to continue with this work of bestowal because he is certain to learn this profession of knowing how to do everything only for the sake of the Creator.

But when he sees that after some time of exerting in this job, not only did he not progress, but he even regressed, his body tells him, "You are wasting energy in this occupation; this job is not for you. This job requires special skills and a brave heart. Go and find another occupation like everyone else, and do not be an exception."

It follows that this is called "hard work," since in any work, when he wants to exert and walk on the work of bestowing, the body does not let him work by resisting him with just arguments.

And indeed, within reason, it is absolutely right. It follows that the slander he hears from his body makes the work heavy on him, which is why it is called "hard work."

However, a person should believe that in truth, he is making progress, and the reason he sees that each time he is more immersed in self-love and that now he is worse off—meaning in a state of lowliness that is worse than when he began the work of bestowal—is because "For I have hardened his heart."

In other words, the Creator shows him each time what it means not to work for one's own benefit but only for the sake of the

501

Creator, by the Creator letting a person know the meaning of not working for himself. By this one sees how this is truly against nature. Since man was created with a desire to receive for his own sake, and now he wants to do something that is against nature, this is why it is called "hard work."

Yet, the question is, Why does the Creator notify him the truth that a person is unable to work against nature? This is because, as it is written, "that I may place these signs of Mine within him." That is, by revealing all the bad within a person, the Creator can give help, as our sages said, "He who comes to purify is aided." And since what is given from above is a complete thing, a person must have a complete *Kli* [vessel], meaning a complete lack, called a "complete *Kli*" in which the whole of the light may enter.

It follows that the Creator reveals the bad to a person in order to help him. That is, since there is no light without a *Kli*, when the bad is not revealed to the fullest, he still does not have a complete *Kli*. We can interpret "complete *Kli*" to mean "complete desire for His help," since as long as the evil is not revealed, a person sometimes says that if he overcomes, he will certainly be able to achieve the work of bestowal. Also, sometimes he says that the Creator cannot help him, either. Hence, when a person exerts in the work of bestowal, the powers he has invested do not let him escape the campaign, and each time he gets a greater need for the help of the Creator. It follows that the hard work itself was the cause that he would cry out to the Creator to help him.

This is similar to what is presented in *The Zohar* (*Beresheet Bet*, Item 103), "There are two ways in the corporeal and spiritual afflictions he had prior to repenting:

1. All that the Creator does, He does for the best. He sees that were it not for the terrible pains that he had suffered for being immersed in the nature of reception for himself, he would never have been rewarded with repentance. Therefore, he blesses for the bad as he blesses for the good, since without the bad he would not have been rewarded with the good. It follows that all

that the Merciful One does, He does for the best, meaning they induce good.

2. That, too, is for the best. Not only did the evils that were done induce good, but the evils themselves have been inverted into good through very great lights that the Creator illuminated through all those evils until they were inverted into good."

Therefore, we see that specifically when all the bad is revealed, there is a complete *Kli* in which a complete light can shine. From the above, we see why the Creator hardened his heart, meaning that the heart, called "desire," resisted the work of bestowal more forcefully each time. The reason is that we need hard work, for only through the suffering of hard work, these sufferings induce an outcry to the Creator with a complete desire that He will help him emerge from the rule of Pharaoh king of Egypt. That is, specifically from the state of lowliness, when a person feels that he is worse off than all other people, it pushes him to cry out to the Creator with all his heart to help him.

However, in that state, there are many ups and downs. That is, sometimes a person cannot believe that the situation he is in comes from the Creator, meaning that the Creator has turned to him and hears his prayer, when a person asks that the Creator will help him out of the exile he is in under the rule of self-love.

Therefore, when a person has this faith, he does not escape from the campaign, meaning says that he sees that the Creator does not hear his prayer, so there is no one to pray to. Rather, he believes that the Creator does hear his prayer and the Creator has given him the awareness to know what lowliness one is in, that it never occurred to him that he would be so immersed in self-love.

Hence, each time he braces himself and does not move from praying to the Creator. He says, "The Creator must want a true desire to appear in me, which will deliver me from this exile." Then, he does not stop thanking the Creator for revealing to him his true state.

Also, he stands and prays to the Creator, since he sees that the Creator hears a prayer, in that He showed him the evil, and He will certainly also help him out of the evil, which is called "redemption." In other words, he believes that the Creator let him see that he is in exile and will certainly deliver him from exile.

However, at times there are descents where it is hard for him to believe that the Creator hears a prayer, since in the person's eyes, he thinks that he has already prayed to Him far too much, and if the Creator hears what is being asked of Him, He should have helped me. And since I have not been saved from what I have been praying about, he says that the Creator does not hear his prayer. Perhaps He hears others, but what difference does this make, since what matters is what he feels, meaning whether he is happy or sad.

These descents induce within him thoughts about escaping the campaign and to say that this is not for him. But if he does not escape, he gets another ascent and he begins to think differently and forgets about all the decisions he had made. In this way, the procession of ascents and descents continues until a true need for nearing the Creator appears within a person, meaning that the *Kli*, called "desire," has been completed in all of its correct form.

Yet, it is the Creator who knows when it is completed, and a person cannot know this. At that time, the Creator gives the help and delivers a person from exile.

Now we can understand what we asked about how *The Zohar* interprets the words "And Moses spoke thus to the children of Israel (meaning the annunciation of the redemption), but they did not listen to Moses for lack of spirit and for hard work." He says, "Lack of spirit means *Malchut*, who was unable to save Israel." We should interpret that the main work is in the *Malchut*, as the ARI says, that the exile in Egypt was that the view of *Kedusha* [holiness] was in exile. That is, the kingdom of heaven, that we must accept the burden of the kingdom of heaven because He is great and ruling, meaning not in order to receive reward, but that the work must be a great pleasure because one has been rewarded with serving the King because of the importance of the King, this was in exile.

In other words, the importance of *Kedusha* was not revealed. This is called "*Shechina* in the dust," meaning that when a person should take upon himself to work for the sake of the Creator, this work is regarded as lowliness, since he finds in this no taste of importance. It follows that by *Malchut* being in the dust, which is something that is not important, this made it hard work.

This is called "lack of spirit," meaning that *Malchut*, which is an important thing, meaning that one who serves the King is regarded as one "who sees the face of the King," who sit first in the kingdom, among these people, it is not considered that they are dwelling with the King, and they are regarded as seeing the King's face, sitting first in the kingdom, they regard it as hard work and we say that they have "lack of spirit," meaning they are not high spirited.

However, when *Malchut* is in exile under the governance of the *Klipot* [shells/peels], they regard *Malchut* as dust, unimportant. This is called "lack of spirit," when *Malchut* cannot give high spirits, as one should feel when dwelling with the King. It follows that "lack of spirit and hard work" are tied to one another. This means that if *Malchut* is in the dust, unimportant, this causes hard work, because something that is tasteless, each moment when one overcomes and works, this overcoming is very difficult, and a person cannot always overcome.

This is the meaning of what he says, "The last spirit, which is *Malchut*, still did not rule the world, to instill upright laws," meaning that *Malchut* still did not have governance, so everyone would see that all the laws that come from her are upright laws, meaning that everything will be in accord and each one will feel *Malchut*, called "Providence," as good and doing good, since the world follows Her leadership, as it is written, "And His kingship rules over all." This was still not revealed.

This is the meaning of the words, "Hence, there was lack of spirit. And which spirit is it? It is *Malchut*, who was unable to save Israel." This means that since this *Malchut* was still in exile, she could not save Israel. But when she is delivered from exile, it is to the contrary, she gives man the spirit so that he is high spirited.

Therefore, when Moses came and announced the annunciation of the redemption, they could not believe such a thing—that they would be delivered from the exile in Egypt, as it is written, "And I will bring you out from under the afflictions of Egypt, and I will save you from their work." That is, they will not only have no hard work, but they will not have any work at all. This, they could not believe, that such a thing could be.

Had they believed it, then by the power of faith they would have come out from the exile. *Malchut*, which is called "spirit," would have risen in importance, as it is written (Ecclesiastes 3), "Who knows the spirit of the sons of men, if it ascends upward? And the spirit of the beast, if it descends down to the earth?" We should interpret "the spirit of the sons of men" to mean that after he emerges from his beast and becomes a "man," as our sages said, "you are called 'man,'" the spirit, meaning *Malchut*, who is called "spirit," ascends, rises in importance.

But the quality of spirit in a beast, when a person is in a state of beastliness, for him the spirit descends in importance. Hence, the people of Israel had to reveal their evil so they would have a complete lack, for then the complete help could come. This is why the children of Israel still did not hear.

What Is the Assistance that He who Comes to Purify Receives in the Work?

Article No. 17, Tav-Shin-Nun, 1989/90

The *Zohar* asks (Exodus, Item 36), "Why is it written, 'Come unto Pharaoh?' It should have said, 'Go unto Pharaoh.' What is 'Come'? Moses was afraid of him. When the Creator saw that Moses was afraid of him, the Creator said, 'Behold, I am against you, Pharaoh king of Egypt.' The Creator, and none other, had to wage war against him, as you say, 'I the Lord,' which they explained, 'I and not another.'"

This means that the answer to why it is written, "Come," is because Moses could not defeat Pharaoh king of Egypt by himself, but the Creator waged war against him. In that case, why did He say to Moses, "Come," if Moses could not defeat him but only the Creator? How does Moses help in this, and why is it written, "Come unto Pharaoh"?

We should also understand the words, "Come unto Pharaoh, for I have hardened his heart that I may set these signs of Mine within him." All the interpreters ask, Why after the first five plagues, the Creator took from Pharaoh the choice? And if the Creator took from him the choice, why is it Pharaoh's fault that he did not obey the Creator?

The answer to this, says the writing, is "for I have hardened his heart." And why did I harden his heart? It is not because he is at fault, but for another reason, as it is written, "that I may set these signs of Mine within him." Because the Creator wanted to set His signs, He took from him the choice, so he will suffer plagues.

This is difficult to understand. Does the Creator, who created the world in order to do good to His creations, for the creatures to receive only good, can it be said that because He wants to show His signs, He hardened Pharaoh's heart, so He would have an excuse to give the signs? It seems like one who benefits from his friend's downfall.

It was said (*Sotah* 11) about the verse (Exodus), "And a new king arose, who did not know Joseph": "Rav and Shmuel, one said, 'truly a new one,' and one said, 'whose decrees were renewed.'" We should understand how this is interpreted when interpreting in the work, that Pharaoh is the evil inclination that is within man's body. How can it be said that he is actually new, if the evil inclination is called "a foolish old king"?

The Zohar said that the reason is that since the evil inclination comes to a person as soon as one is born, as it is written, "Sin crouches at the door," meaning that as soon as one is born, the evil inclination emerges along with him, whereas the good inclination comes to a person after thirteen years. Therefore, why does it say, "'And a new king arose,' truly new"? Instead, we should say that the foolish old king, who is the evil inclination, is not something new in a person. Rather, as soon as one is born, it is present, as it is written, "A wild ass's colt, a man is born." Thus, what does "truly new" mean?

To understand the above, we should know what is the work that was given to us in Torah and Mitzvot [commandments/good deeds]. That is, why do I need this work? We learned that the purpose of creation is because of His desire is to do good to His creations. Hence, why do we need to exert ourselves? Is receiving pleasure, this act of receiving pleasure, called "work"?

We see that reception of pleasure is considered a reward and not work. However, this is as we learned that in order for the creatures not to feel shame when they receive pleasure, since the branch wants to resemble its root, and as our root bestows upon the creatures, when one does something that is not in the root, he feels unpleasantness about it, so in order to correct this, so that when the creatures receive they will feel wholeness in the pleasure and there will be no flaw in the reception of the pleasure, there was a correction called Tzimtzum [restriction] and concealment. That is, as long as the creatures have not obtained vessels of bestowal, they will not receive and will not feel the pleasure that the Creator wanted to give them.

Therefore, when engaging in Torah and Mitzvot, they still do not feel the delight and pleasure clothed in Torah and Mitzvot. This is why it is considered work, since the importance of the King is not yet revealed, that it is worthwhile to serve Him because of His importance and greatness. This is regarded as the Shechina [Divinity] being in exile in each and every one. Hence, if there is no importance, it is considered that the Shechina is in the dust, meaning that there is no flavor in this whatsoever.

Through the sin of the tree of knowledge, our sages said that the serpent came to Eve and cast filth within her. Baal HaSulam interpreted that the serpent, which is the evil inclination, cast filth in her, meaning let her understand, "This-what." That is, the serpent cast a flaw in Malchut, who is called "Eve," and said, "This-what," that you are working for the kingdom of heaven.

It turns out that as a result, we must work before we obtain the vessels of bestowal, where through the vessels of bestowal we can receive the delight and pleasure that the Creator wanted to give to the created beings. It follows that when we say that there is work in observing Torah and *Mitzvot*, it does not mean that observing the Torah and *Mitzvot* is work, but that the work is while observing Torah and *Mitzvot* before we can direct them in order to bestow. Then there is work, since we are placed under the rule of the evil and the serpent, as was said, that the serpent cast filth and blemished.

For this reason, we are under the rule of the rule of the will to receive for ourselves, at which time the delight and pleasure in Torah and *Mitzvot* are not revealed. And this is all the work— to obtain vessels of bestowal, for only through vessels of bestowal are the *Tzimtzum* and concealment that were placed on Torah and *Mitzvot* removed, for the delight and pleasure are not revealed in vessels of reception.

Hence, at that time we are given the Torah and *Mitzvot* to observe as an advice and *Segula* [remedy]. That is, we must aim, while observing Torah and *Mitzvot*, while we still cannot aim, that they will be in order to bestow, that these 613 *Mitzvot* that he observes will bring him the ability to achieve *Lishma* [for Her sake]. In the words of our sages, this advance is called *Lo Lishma* [not for Her sake], meaning that by observing *Lo Lishma*, he will come to *Lishma* because "the light in it reforms him."

It follows that when a person sees that he cannot do everything in order to bestow, what should he do so as to come to be a giver? Our sages advised us that he should learn *Lo Lishma*, meaning in order to receive. This is the only advice by which he will achieve *Lishma*. There is no other advice. In the words of *The Zohar*, this is called "613 *Eitin*," meaning 613 counsels.

These are his words ("Introduction of The Book of Zohar," "General Explanation for All Fourteen Commandments and How They Divide into the Seven Days of Creation," Item 1): "The *Mitzvot* in the Torah are called *Pekudin* [Aramaic: commands/deposits], as well as 613 *Eitin* [Aramaic: counsels/tips]. The difference between them is that in all things there is *Panim* [anterior/face] and *Achor* [posterior/back]. The preparation for something is called *Achor*, and the attainment of the matter is called *Panim*. Similarly, in Torah and *Mitzvot* there are 'We shall do' and 'We shall hear.' When observing Torah and *Mitzvot* as 'doers of His word,' prior to being rewarded with 'hearing the voice of His word,' the *Mitzvot* are called '613 *Eitin*,' and are regarded as *Achor*. When rewarded with 'hearing the voice of His word,' the 613 *Mitzvot* become *Pekudin*, from the word *Pikadon* [deposit]. This is so because there are 613 *Mitzvot*, where in each *Mitzva* [singular of *Mitzvot*], the light of a unique degree is deposited."

We therefore see that there are two times in observing Torah and *Mitzvot*: 1) During the preparation, regarded as "doers of His word." At that time, it is called "work," since he has not been rewarded with hearing, as then a person is still under the governance of receiving in order to receive, the state on which there was a *Tzimtzum* and concealment where the delight and pleasure are concealed from the Torah and *Mitzvot*, and a person must observe the 613 *Mitzvot* as counsel, meaning that by this he will be able to be rewarded with vessels of bestowal.

At that time, when he has these *Kelim*, the *Tzimtzum* and concealment will depart from him, and he will obtain the delight and pleasure, which was the purpose of creation–to do good to His creations. At that time, the 613 *Mitzvot* are called "613 *Pekudin*," where in each *Mitzva*, the light that pertains to that *Mitzva* is deposited.

Then, there is no more room for work because he has already been rewarded with working for the sake of the Creator and not for his own benefit. This is as the Sayer of Duvna says, when he explained the verse, "You did not call upon Me, Jacob, for you labored in Me, Israel." He said that if a person says that he has labor in observing Torah and *Mitzvot*, it is a sign that "You are not working for Me," says the Creator. This is the meaning of "You did not call upon Me Jacob." The sign that you are not working for the sake of the Creator is that you say that you have labored in observing Torah and *Mitzvot*, since when a person works *Lishma*, the concealment and *Tzimtzum* are removed and he begins to attain the delight and pleasure that exist in Torah and *Mitzvot*, which are called "613 *Pekudin*."

By this we will understand what we asked, If the purpose of creation is to do good to His creations, from where does the work in Torah and *Mitzvot* come to us? The answer is that in order not to have shame, the concealment and *Tzimtzum* were made. It follows that the delight and pleasure are not revealed in vessels of reception.

Hence, there is work: 1) because we must work against our nature, for we were born with a desire to receive for our own sake, 2) for by making the *Tzimtzum*, we must work on what is important, meaning we must work on going above reason, and we must believe that there is a leader to the world, who watches over the world as The Good Who Does Good.

These two things cause man labor and work, and require great overcoming in order for man not to escape the campaign in the middle of the work. This is so because when a person does something, he must see progress in the matter. If he sees no progress, he says that this is not for him, since he sees that he is not succeeding. This causes him to want to escape the campaign he is in.

But the truth is that there are two kinds of assistance from above, meaning that without help from above we cannot attain it: 1) the *Kli* [vessel], meaning the lack. That is, a lack to know what is the real lack, so as to know for what to ask for help from above.

In other words, often, a person is lacking something for which he becomes sick. The doctors give him medicines but it does not help him because he is not sick with what the doctors think he is. It turns out that he comes to a doctor, who prescribes him a medicine, but the medicine does not help him, and all the doctors have already discouraged him that he may stay with the illness for the rest of his life.

But finally, a professor comes along and says that he is sick and tormented because there is a substance deficient in his body, and this is why they cannot cure him, while he says that he is suffering from something that causes him the illness and the suffering. Therefore,

I will give him a cure according to the substance that I think is deficient in his body, and he will be well right away. Afterward, they saw that he was completely healed.

It follows that first, one must know what he is missing so he can observe Torah and *Mitzvot*. A person might think of many things, and for each thing, he receives a medicine, but it does not help him because the reason why he cannot walk on the path of truth is not what a person thinks. It follows that he is praying to the Creator to help him, to give him filling what he thinks, but what he thinks is not the truth. Hence, a person is not healed from the control of the evil inclination.

For this reason, first, a person receives help from above to know the illness from which he is suffering. That is, he thinks he is deficient of something quantitative, meaning he needs more time to learn, and more brains, talent, etc., and for this he prays that He will help him. However, in truth, a person is deficient in quality, to know that the main lack within him is that he has no importance to feel that there is the Upper Guidance. In other words, he is lacking faith that the Creator leads the world in a manner of The Good Who Does Good. If he could really feel this, he would rejoice that he is receiving from the Creator delight and pleasure, and he would not want to part from the Creator for one moment, for he would know what he loses by turning his thought to other things.

So if he does not think that this is what he is lacking, but that he is lacking other things, which are not important in the work, then the first assistance that a person receives from above is to know his evil, his main obstructor for which he cannot be a true servant of the Creator. This help must come first, and afterward it is possible to make corrections, to correct them. That is, a person must come to a state where he knows that he needs only two main things, which are "mind" and "heart," that this is all he must strive to obtain. Hence, the first assistance that a person receives from above is this lack.

However, this cannot be revealed in him at once, but gradually. According to his work when he exerts in the work to achieve the truth, to that extent he receives assistance from above. Once he has obtained the real *Kli*, meaning the real lack that he needs, then is the time when he receives the real filling that is suitable for the *Kli*. It therefore follows that a person receives from above both the light and the *Kli*, meaning the need, called "lack."

In other words, what he is lacking hurts him. Yet, not everything that one does not have is considered a lack. For example, a person who has abundance and is enjoying life, when a person comes to him and asks him, "Why are you so happy? I see that my neighbor's son, whose parents are very wealthy and respected, and yet I saw him suffering. That is, I saw him walking with a tormented expression. I asked him, 'My friend, what is it you need? Your parents are very wealthy, so tell me, what is it you need? Are you unwell?' So he replied, 'I was supposed to get my doctor's diploma, for which I labored many years, but I failed the tests, and I am sad that now I do not have a doctor's diploma.'" Can it be said that any person who does not have a doctor's diploma regrets it?

Rather, as said above, not everything that one does not have is considered a lack. A lack is everything that a person wants, but does not have. This is called "a lack." For this reason, when we want to measure the intensity of the desire, we measure it according to the suffering one feels at not having what he yearns for.

It therefore follows that the first assistance that the upper one gives to the lower one is the awareness what he should obtain. The suffering from not having obtained it is regarded as the upper one giving the lower one the *Kli*. Then, when the lower one has a real need, the upper one gives him the second assistance, namely the light and the filling of the lack.

By this we will understand what we asked, If the Creator knew that Moses could not fight and defeat Pharaoh king of Egypt by himself, but the Creator Himself, as it is written, "I and not a messenger," why did he say to Him, "Come unto Pharaoh"? This implies that together with Moses, the Creator can help. But the

Creator said, "I and not a messenger," so how does Moses help us here? Why is it written, "Come unto Pharaoh"?

It means that a person must begin to walk on the path of the Creator and achieve the truth, meaning to be rewarded with *Dvekut* [adhesion] with the Creator. Then, if he advances in the walk, the person receives the first assistance—the sensation of the lack, to know what he is lacking. Subsequently, he grasps that he is lacking only two main things: "mind" and "heart." And along with it, he receives suffering at not having them. In other words, he feels the need for this. At that time, if the person does not work by himself, it cannot be said that he is suffering from not having it. Only the need for something, if one labored to obtain something, can it be said that he has a need for it to the point that he is suffering from not having it.

This is why it is written, "Come unto Pharaoh." It indicates two things: 1) The person himself should exert, such as the allegory about the doctor, who labored many years to study medicine and finally failed and did not get the doctor's diploma. Then it can be said that he is suffering from not having what he wants.

But if he did not exert, it cannot be said that he is suffering from not achieving what he wants, since the labor one puts into something awakens the desire, so he will not escape the campaign because he is sorry about all the efforts he had put into the matter, and he always thinks, "Perhaps I will finally obtain what I want." It follows that by working, even though he cannot obtain it, the labor he exerts each time invokes the yearning for the matter.

It follows that there are two forces here:

1) Man's power, who must toil not in order to obtain the matter, but in order to have a strong desire to obtain the matter. It follows that man's work is required in order to obtain the need for the Creator's help. This is called "a complete desire." In other words, it is not that man's work causes the obtainment of the matter, but rather the obtainment of the lack and need for the matter, and in order to know what he is lacking. For this, he receives help from

above, by seeing each time, that he is more deficient and cannot emerge from the governance of Pharaoh. This assistance is called "for I have hardened his heart." It follows that the hardening of the heart is required in order to have a real need for a real thing.

2) At the same time, we must have the Creator's help, to give the light, as it is written, "I and not a messenger." This means that since by nature, the will to receive for oneself—called "a foolish old king"—controls a person, and man's ability to change nature is only in the hands of the Creator, meaning that He made nature, and He can change it, and this is called "the exodus from Egypt," which was a miracle. This is why it is written, "Come," meaning both of them together, as we say, "Come together," likewise, the Creator and Moses.

Now we can understand what we asked, Why is it written, "For I have hardened his heart that I may set these signs of Mine within him"? We said that it seems as one who benefits from his friend's downfall. That is, the Creator made him wicked so He would show His signs. According to the above, the meaning of "set these signs of Mine" refers to the light, for the light is called "letters." It follows that He made him wicked, meaning deficient, so he would have a complete *Kli* to receive the light. This means that the letters are not for the sake of the Creator, but for the sake of the created being.

By this we will also understand what we asked, what is "And a new king arose," since he is an old king? The answer is that each time, his decrees are renewed. That is, each time, the evil inclination is made anew, because "I have hardened his heart." It follows that "Anyone whose desire is great, his inclination is greater than him."

Why the Speech of Shabbat Must Not Be as the Speech of a Weekday, in the Work

Article No. 18, Tav-Shin-Nun, 1989/90

It is written in *The Zohar* (*BeShalach*, Items 70-78), "'The Lord will fight for you while you keep silent.' Rabbi Aba started, 'If because of the Sabbath, you turn your foot from doing what you wish, and from speaking words, so your speech of the Sabbath will not be as the speech of a weekday.' Each day, one must show a deed and evoke awakening below, from what he should evoke. However, on Sabbath, one should awaken only in the words of the Creator and the holiness of the day, and not on anything else, since on Sabbath, there is no need for an awakening from below. Come and see, here, when Pharaoh drew near, to make war with Israel, at that time the Creator did not want Israel to evoke an awakening from below at all, since there was an awakening from above, as it is written, 'The Lord will fight for you, and you will keep silent,' since the name of

517

Rachamim [mercies] must awaken on them because an awakening from below would only activate judgment."

We should understand the adjacency of "The Lord will fight for you" and Shabbat [Sabbath], and why each day we need an awakening from below, but on Shabbat we do not need it because on Shabbat, there is only an awakening from above. We should also understand what it means that on Shabbat we should engage only in the words of the Creator and the sacredness of the day.

It is known that there are two things before us: 1) The lack, which is yearning. Without a lack, a person cannot feel pleasure, even if this thing is the most important thing in the world. If he has no lack for the matter, although he can receive it, but not enjoy it, since this depends on the measure of his yearning for it. Hence, we have a time of lack, and then it is the time to receive more lack each time.

That is, where he feels a lack, he goes to fill the lack. If it is hard for him to obtain that thing, we do not say that he tried in vain to obtain it but rather that he did obtain something: He obtained a *Kli* [vessel] called "yearning." In other words, had he obtained the filling right away, the filling would not be regarded as a filling with regard to pleasure, which is the main purpose, as we learned, that the purpose of creation was His desire to do good to His creations, meaning that they will receive delight and pleasure.

It follows that if a person receives something without effort, meaning that he did not have the time to obtain the *Kli* to receive the pleasure, called "yearning," the pleasure he should receive from it, the filling cannot yield the pleasure because he has no *Kli* to receive the pleasure, for the *Kli* to receive pleasure is called "yearning," and in order to receive yearning for something, it depends on time, meaning time for feeling the lack.

It follows that when a person prays to the Creator to satisfy his need, this, too, depends on the amount of time he has been praying for the Creator to satisfy his lack. For this reason, the Creator first helps him by the growing of the *Kli* within him, called "a *Kli* of yearning," meaning that the Creator hears his prayer. And the reason why a person does not receive the filling for his prayer right away, he should say that this is not so, but that the Creator does hear his prayer and is increasing the yearning within him so he will have a real Kli to feel the pleasure. It follows that if he were to receive what he wants right away, he would not be able to enjoy because of the lack of yearning.

By this we will understand what our sages said (Sukkah 52), "To the wicked, the evil inclination seems like a hairsbreadth, and to the righteous, like a high mountain." However, first we must understand, when we speak in terms of the work, what does "in terms of the work" mean?

The thing is that there are two manners in observing Torah and Mitzvot [commandments/good deeds]: 1) Doing, which is regarded as action. He learns Torah; he observes Mitzvot in all their details and precisions, and there is nothing to add to this. Indeed, in terms of actions, he is considered righteous. 2) Work, which is work in the heart. In the words of our sages, a prayer is usually called "work," for a prayer is called "work in the heart," which is an intention, meaning the intention of the heart. That is, a person should aim while observing Torah and Mitzvot, why he is observing the Torah and Mitzvot, whether for his own sake or does he aim for the sake of the Creator?

For this reason, we should discern between righteous and wicked in terms of the action, and righteous and wicked in terms of the intention. In terms of the actions, the righteous are the Ultra-Orthodox and the wicked are the secular. But with respect to the intention, righteous and wicked go by a completely different order. In other words, in terms of the action, both are righteous. But with regard to the intention, there is a difference: Righteous are those who work for the Creator, and wicked are those who work for themselves although in terms of the work, both are righteous.

When we want to walk in the work, meaning with the aim of the heart, to intend that all his work will be for the sake of the Creator, then begins the order of the work. That is, the wicked in his heart, which are called "will to receive for oneself," resist working for the sake of the Creator. However, "God has made them one opposite the other," meaning that to the extent that he wants to walk on the path of truth, to that extent the truth about the evil within him appears.

When one has a small desire to walk on the path of truth, meaning to do everything for the sake of the Creator, his evil is small, as well, since "one opposite the other..." In other words, to the extent of the *Kedusha* [holiness] in him, so is the resistance to *Kedusha*. It follows that the more he advances in the work, and wants to go more on the path of truth, the more the evil surfaces by not letting him cancel the evil, and the evil exerts to control more forcefully.

It follows that "Anyone who is greater than his friend, his inclination is greater than him." Therefore, it follows that one who wants to be righteous, that his actions will be for the sake of the Creator, the evil grows within him. This is why they said, "To the righteous, the evil inclination seems like a high mountain." In other words, the evil ascends each time. *Har* [mountain] means *Hirhurim* [reflections]. That is, he has bad reflections, meaning that each time, the bad thoughts increase and become a high mountain.

But to the wicked, those who do not mind the intention, to make it in order to bestow, but believe that they are working *Lo Lishma* [not for Her sake], and that from *Lo Lishma* they come to *Lishma* [for Her sake], and rely on it and say "Glory will finally come," meaning that only when they have a desire to aim for the Creator, they will certainly have the power to overcome and do everything for the sake of the Creator, since their bad seems to them like a hairsbreadth, meaning that it is not so difficult to aim.

The reason is that their bad is not so great, as was said, since their good is small, meaning the desire to do everything for the sake of the Creator is small. The proof of this is that they do not have such a need to begin this work, so the bad in them does not need to show the evil within it and resist him. Therefore, the evil inclination seems to them like a hairsbreadth. This means that none of them is lying, but each speaks according to his feeling.

Accordingly, we understand the meaning of extending the light and the meaning of extending the *Kli* [vessel]. That is, we still do not have the *Kli* for reception of delight and pleasure, called "yearning," since this depends on man's work, that specifically through the work there is development for this *Kli*, called "lack" and "yearning." This *Kli* is acquired specifically through labor, meaning without labor, it is impossible to obtain the *Kli*, meaning the need to acquire vessels of bestowal.

This means that the very obtainment of the vessels of bestowal is already called "light." That is, this is something that comes from above, called "assistance from above" for obtainment of the vessels of bestowal.

It is known that there are two discernments to make in the light: 1) To obtain vessels of bestowal, meaning the *Kelim* [vessels], namely desires, which were previously outside of *Kedusha*, meaning that these desires could not be used in order to bestow. 2) This light is named after the *Kelim*, since the light comes in order to correct the *Kelim*. This is called "light of *Achoraim* [posterior]," after the *Kelim*, for the *Kelim* are called *Achoraim*, with respect to the light, and the light is called *Panim* [face/anterior].

In the work, this is called "assistance from above," as it is said in *The Zohar*, "He who comes to purify is aided." And it asks, "With what?" The answer is "With a holy soul." That is, he is given from above a light that is called *Neshama* [soul], and this light purifies the person so he will have the strength to bestow upon the upper one, for as the light comes from the Giver, so this light gives one the strength to be able to work in order to bestow.

It follows that in the order of the work, we should discern the following:

State 1) When a person awakens to emerge from what he has from his upbringing. He feels that he cannot be drawn to the general public, who engage in Torah and *Mitzvot* with the same understanding they had when they began to observe Torah and *Mitzvot*. This understanding and feeling have been going on for them for a long time, but they are not making any progress in Torah and *Mitzvot*, except in quantity. But as for quality, meaning to have more of a feeling for the importance of Torah and *Mitzvot*, they do not have it. They wonder how is it possible that there will be no progress in the quality of Torah and *Mitzvot*, since it is written about Torah and *Mitzvot*, "For they are our lives and the length of our days." But in that sense, they are not advancing whatsoever. Therefore, they go look for a place where they can obtain the progress in terms of the greatness and importance, so they will feel that "They are our lives."

State 2) When we begin to walk on the path to achieve "For they are our lives," our sages tell us that the advice to come to feel the life that is found in Torah and *Mitzvot* is *Dvekut* [adhesion], as it is written, "and to cling unto Him." That is, "cling unto His attributes, as He is merciful, so you are merciful." This means that as the Creator wants only to bestow, so man should come to such a degree where he wants all his actions to be only to bestow, and not for his own sake.

Here, in this second state, when he wants to ascend in degree and observe Torah and *Mitzvot* in order to bestow, he receives the first assistance, when a person is notified that he is far from this quality called *Lishma*. In other words, although before he began the work of bestowal, he knew that there was the matter of having to work *Lishma*, called "for the sake of the Creator," and he believed in what our sages said, "One should always engage in Torah and *Mitzvot*, even if *Lo Lishma*, since from *Lo Lishma* he will come to *Lishma*" (*Pesachim* 50), but it never occurred to him that in order to work *Lishma*, one needs a miracle from above, or it is impossible to emerge from the control of the will to receive for oneself.

This is so because if a person has only a little bit of good, he cannot be given a lot of bad, for he will not be able to subdue it and will immediately escape from this work. But when a person begins to work with energy in order to come to work in order to bestow, he is given, according to his work, a sensation and awareness how far he is from it.

It follows that the first assistance he receives is the revelation of the evil in him. This is called "hardening of the heart," as it is written, "For I have hardened his heart." This is regarded as obtaining the *Achoraim* of *Kedusha*. *Kedusha* is called *Panim*, and *Panim* is considered something that illuminates, as he says ("Introduction to The Study of the Ten Sefirot," Item 47), "We must first understand what is the meaning of the 'face of the Creator,' about which the writing says, 'I will hide My face.' It can be thought of as a person who sees his friend's face and knows him right away. However, when he sees him from behind he is not certain of his identity. He might doubt, 'Perhaps he is another and not his friend?' So is the matter before us: Everyone knows and feels that the Creator is good and that it is the conduct of the good to do good. Hence, when the Creator generously bestows upon His creations, it is considered that His face is revealed to His creations, since then everyone knows and recognizes Him. Yet, when He behaves with His creations the opposite from the above mentioned, meaning when they suffer afflictions and torments in His world, it is considered the *Achoraim* of the Creator, for His face, meaning His complete attribute of goodness, is entirely concealed from them."

Therefore, in that state, if he can accept the *Achoraim*, which is called "exile," and does not run, but rather, "And they cried out to the Lord" to deliver him from the exile, then he accepts the *Achoraim* and says that it comes from the Creator, hence he asks Him that as He made him feel the taste of exile, so He will help him emerge from exile. This is called "the second state."

State 3) This is the second assistance, when he receives assistance to obtain vessels of bestowal, which is regarded as emerging from exile, where he was under the rule of self-love. Through the assistance from above, which is called that the Creator is giving him a soul, this light gives him the vessels of bestowal. It is as we learned, that when the light of *Hochma*, called light of AB, comes and brings out the *Kelim* of *Bina*, ZA, and *Nukva* that fell into the *Klipot* [shells/peels], having been placed under the governance of receiving in order to receive, which is called a *Klipa* [singular of *Klipot*], this light of AB brings them out of the *Klipot*, meaning it gives strength for these *Kelim* to be corrected in order to bestow. This is regarded as these *Kelim* entering the *Kedusha*, meaning that he can already use them in order to bestow. This is called "the exodus from Egypt."

State 4) When he receives the light that dresses in vessels of bestowal, at that time the 613 *Mitzvot* [commandments/good deeds], are called 613 *Pekudin* [Aramaic: deposits], meaning he obtains a different flavor in each *Mitzva* [singular of *Mitzvot*]. This is the meaning of *Pekudin*, that in each *Mitzva*, a special light is deposited, which belongs to that *Mitzva*. This is similar to corporeal pleasures, where there is a taste in meat, and there is another taste that is clothed in fish. Likewise, in each *Mitzva*, there is a unique flavor. At that time, a person comes to feel that the matter of Torah and *Mitzvot* is as in, "For they are our lives and the length of our days." This is so because he has obtained from the Creator the vessels of bestowal, called *Dvekut*, "equivalence of form," and in these *Kelim*, the delight and pleasure that was in the purpose of creation is clothed.

Now we can understand what we asked about the adjacency of "The Lord will fight for you and you will keep silent," and Shabbat. Since the work on obtaining the vessels of bestowal comes by obtaining the state of *Gadlut* [greatness/adulthood] of the evil, as it is written, "For I have hardened his heart," meaning the attainment of the bad, then, when the people of Israel came to a state where they saw that they could not escape from the bad, meaning they saw that the power of the bad was on all sides and they did not see any salvation by nature, this is considered that the *Kli* of the bad has been completed.

At that time comes State 5), when the Creator gives them the light, and this light reforms them. In other words, by this they emerge from the governance of evil, called "vessels of self-reception," and are rewarded with vessels of bestowal. This is the meaning of "Stand by and see the salvation of the Lord, which He will do for you today." This means that once the *Kli* of the bad has been completed, there is room for disclosure of light on the part of the upper one. This is considered that the Creator is giving them the vessels of bestowal.

It follows that this work of increasing the bad is work that pertains to *Hol* [non-holy/weekday]. That is, work and *Hol* are one and the same, meaning one discernment, as it is known that in *Kedusha*, there is no work, since when a person has vessels of bestowal he enjoys giving, but when he still does not have vessels of bestowal, it is a great effort when he must give something without receiving anything in return, since it is against man's will to receive.

This is why it is called *Hol* and not holy, and this is why it is forbidden to work on Shabbat, since Shabbat is a time of rest and not of work. In other words, Shabbat indicates *Kedusha*, which is the time when through the *Kedusha* of the Shabbat, light shines because of the awakening from above. For this reason, one does not need to work on increasing the bad, as in hardening of the heart, since then is the time to speak only of what the Creator gives, and not to speak about man, who must receive and think whether he is cleansed of self-love and must correct the *Kelim*.

The work on the bad pertains to *Hol* and not to holiness, since seeing the bad, the state he is in, pertains to man's work. That is, he looks at himself and wants to see his state of lowliness, and how he should pray to the Creator, and pay attention to whether he is advancing or to the contrary.

In other words, when a person works, this is the time for a person to be seen, meaning to see his deficiencies, what he lacks. But when speaking of an awakening from above, meaning what the Creator does, we must only look at the Creator, meaning what He has to give, namely to see the meaning of the holy names, for each name indicates attainment.

For example, when we look at a person and see that he is rich, the name of that person is "wealth." And if we see that the person always heals the sick, then he is called "healer of the sick." Therefore, when speaking of the Creator, sometimes He is called "who heals the sick," and sometimes "nourishing and sustaining," or "redeems the captives," etc., all according to what we see that He gives. Therefore, on Shabbat, which is a time of awakening from above, which pertains to what the Creator gives, we must see and examine the names of the Creator.

By this we will understand the adjacency of what is written, "The Lord will fight for you, and you will keep silent," and Shabbat. It is so because then, when they were already complete in terms of the evil, when they saw that it was impossible to emerge from the bad in a natural way, but only by a miracle, this is regarded as the evil being completed sufficiently. At that time, the help from above should come, to give them the light to complete the *Kelim*, meaning that the vessels of reception will acquire the form of bestowal. This does not pertain to man's work.

This is why it is written, "You will keep silent," since now is the time when the Creator gives. Also, on Shabbat, which is an awakening from above, we should speak only of what the Creator has, as he says that on Shabbat, we should speak only of the words of the Creator and the sanctity of the day, since Shabbat is an awakening from above. Conversely, on other days, meaning weekdays, there should an awakening from below, to invoke the lacks that are below, among the created beings, and to ask that the Creator will satisfy their lacks.

Now we can understand what we asked about the adjacency of "You will keep silent" and Shabbat. We will also understand why on weekdays we need an awakening from below, and on Shabbat it is only an awakening from above. Also, we will understand what is, "so your speech of the Sabbath will not be as the speech of a weekday." And we will also understand why on Shabbat we must speak only about the words of the Creator and the sanctity of the day.

Why Is the Torah Called "Middle Line" in the Work?

Article No. 19, Tav-Shin-Nun, 1989/90

It is written in *The Zohar* (*Yitro*, Item 293), "The Tanna Rabbi Yehuda says, 'The Torah was given on the side of *Gevura*.' Rabbi Yosi said, 'Thus, the Torah is on the left side.' He told him, 'She returned to the right, as it is written, 'On his right, a fiery law unto them.' And it is written, 'Your right, O Lord, glorious in power.'" Thus, we find that left is included in the right, as it is written, 'On his right, a fiery law,' and the right in the left, as it is written, 'Your right, O Lord, glorious in power.' Thus, *Gevura*, which is left, is included in the right."

It follows that the Torah is the middle line, as it includes both lines—right and left.

It is also written (Item 235), "On the third month, on this month, Uriel governs, since Nissan, Iyar, Sivan correspond to HGT—Michael governs *Hesed*, Gabriel on *Gevura*, and Uriel on *Tifferet*. And this is the meaning of "A whole man," who is called Jacob, who is *Tifferet*. Also, "Whole" is from the word "wholeness."

It is written (Item 242), "And was given on the third month, to the third people, who were included in three degrees, meaning three patriarchs, the triple Torah, which is Torah [Pentateuch], Prophets, and Hagiographa, and it is all one." Thus, the Torah is considered the middle line.

It is also written (Item 296), "'And the whole people saw the voices.' It asks, the writing says, 'Saw,' but it should have said, 'Heard.' He replies, 'So we learned. These voices were engraved in darkness, cloud, and mist, and they appear in them as a body appears.'"

We should understand what it means to us in the work that the Torah consists of right and left. Also, what does it mean that the Torah was given on the third, who is Jacob, a whole man, who is called "Wholeness." And what does it mean that they were engraved in darkness, cloud, and mist, which is the body, where the voices are engraved.

It is known that in the order of the work, first one must take upon oneself the burden of the kingdom of heaven, and then he should learn Torah. This is so because if he does not have the kingdom of heaven, we should ask, "Whose Torah is he learning?" because first, one must believe in the Giver of the Torah, and then he can observe the Torah. Thus, the kingdom of heaven is called *Assiya* [action], meaning that he takes upon himself to go above reason.

In other words, although one's reason may come to him with many questions, he answers them, "You are asking me questions within reason, and I'm going above reason, from a place where reason cannot reach, attain, or understand, which is called 'faith.' Thus, there is no place to all the questions you are asking me."

This is called "right," that he believes that the Creator watches over the world as The Good Who Does Good. Although when he looks at the world, he has many questions, he goes above reason and says, "They have eyes and see not."

Instead, he thanks and praises the King for giving everyone only good. This is called "right," *Hesed*, meaning that the guidance of the world is in *Hesed* [grace/mercy]. That is, the Creator leads the world only with *Hassadim* [mercies]. And he says about that, "I will bless You every day."

However, there is an evil *Yetzer* [inclination] in a person. Baal HaSulam interpreted it as being from the word *Tziur* [drawing]. In other words, it shows a person bad images of the guidance of the Creator, of how the Creator is behaving with the world. It also gives an image of the lowliness of the work in general, which is called "*Shechina* [Divinity] in the dust." Thus, how can one overcome and walk on the path of the "right," called "wholeness," and be able to say, "Only goodness and mercy shall follow me all the days of my life"?

Our sages said about that, "The Creator said, 'I have created the evil inclination; I have created the Torah as a spice.'" It follows that the Torah that he engages in is so it will be a spice, meaning that through the Torah, he will be able to overcome the evil and walk on the path of *Hesed*, called "right." In that regard, it can be said that the Torah was given on the right, named after the action. In other words, it qualifies a person to walk on the right path. This is called "the first discernment in the Torah," where "right" is called "wholeness," when he feels no lack at all.

The second discernment in the Torah is the left, called *Hochma* [wisdom]. This is considered the wisdom of the Torah. In other words, once he already has the right, which is *Hesed*, meaning faith above reason, and he believes in the Creator—that the Creator leads the world as The Good Who Does Good—he is rewarded with the giver of the Torah, called "the wisdom of the Torah," as it is written, "The Torah comes out of wisdom."

In other words, once he believes that there is the giver of the Torah, this is the time to be rewarded with the Torah. It is known that the Torah comes out of *Hochma*, and this discernment can be called "left," meaning it comes after a person has been rewarded with the right, which is faith above reason, called "covered *Hassadim*."

However, when speaking of a time when there is already disclosed *Hochma*, called "left," there is another issue, called "middle line," which means that the *Hochma* must be clothed in *Hassadim*. Prior to that, there is a big distance between *Hassadim*, which are called "right," and *Hochma*, regarded as "left."

It is as our sages said, "One who learns Torah *Lishma* [for Her sake]" means that he is learning Torah with the aim to be rewarded with *Lishma* through the Torah, that his intention in the Torah that he is learning is to achieve the degree of *Hesed*, meaning to have the power to do everything in order to bestow, which is called *Hesed*. It is as our sages said, "Who is a *Hassid* [pious/follower]? He who says, 'What's mine is yours and what's yours is yours,' who wants nothing for himself." Afterwards, when he is rewarded with *Hesed* through the Torah, "He is shown the secrets of the Torah" (*Avot*, Chapter 6:1).

This is already called "left." At that time, this left must be incorporated in the right. This means that the light of *Hochma*, which is left, is clothed in *Hassadim*, which is right, and this is called Torah, the middle line between the right and the left. This is why it is considered that the Torah consists of *Hesed* and *Gevura*.

It follows that the first state is when he wants to reach the degree of *Lishma*, meaning in order to bestow. This is considered that a person is in exile, governed by the evil inclination. At that time he needs the Torah. This is called "learning Torah in order to achieve *Lishma*," meaning that he believes in what our sages said, "I have created the evil inclination; I have created the Torah as a spice." It is called "Torah in the form of right," meaning *Hesed*, in order to bestow.

And when he has already attained the degree of *Lishma*, a second state arises and he is rewarded with the revelation of the secrets of the Torah. Thus, after he has been rewarded with the Giver, meaning that there is a Giver in the world, there comes a state where the Giver gives the person the Torah.

But there is more. He needs a third state, called "*Hochma* having to be included in the right," which is called *Hassadim*. This is so because the Torah comes out of *Hochma*, which means that the Torah comes out of *Hochma* and must be clothed in light of *Hassadim*. Also, *Hassadim* are called "action," and Torah is called "*Hochma*." One's Torah must not be more than one's actions. Our sages said about that (*Avot*, Chapter 3:12), "Anyone whose *Hochma* [wisdom/knowledge] is greater than his actions, his *Hochma* does not persist." It also follows that the Torah, which is called *Hochma*, illuminates as the middle line. This is considered that the Torah consists of *Hesed* and *Gevura*, that she contains both.

There are two discernments to make in regard to one who is learning Torah *Lishma*:

1) He sees that he has no connection with doing things for the sake of the Creator. Instead, he sees that he is under the governance of the evil inclination, which claims, "She is all mine." It does not let him do anything in order to bestow. Rather, where he sees that there will be self-benefit, he can work. But if he does not see any benefit for his will to receive, he has no energy to work. Put differently, he measures according to what his will to receive will gain.

When a person tries to emerge from its dominion, as it is written in the essay, "What Does It Mean that the Speaking of Shabbat Will Not Be as the Speaking of a Weekday, in the Work?" (*Beshalach*, Article No. 18, *Tav-Shin-Nun*, 1989/90), "To the extent that one tries to emerge from enslavement and exile, he sees that he is placed in darkness, cloud, and mist."

In that state, he sees the opposite of what our sages said, "I have created the evil inclination; I have created the Torah as a spice." In other words, the evil in him has grown too strong, meaning he never dreamed that if he began to work, toil, and do good deeds with the aim to achieve *Lishma*, that now he sees the opposite—that he never thought he could fall into such baseness.

Indeed, this came to him from the state of, "For I have hardened his heart." And although the reason he is now in lowliness comes from above, in the sensation of the lower one, who feels in the dark—that nothing shines for him—he is tasting the taste of exile, even though it is coming from above.

With the above said, we can interpret what we asked, "What does it mean that *The Zohar* says, 'These voices were engraved in darkness, cloud, and mist, and they appear in them.'" We should interpret that these voices are the voice of the Torah, which comes to give strength so one can act in order to bestow. This is called "the second discernment of *Lishma*," meaning darkness, cloud, and mist, which is the need and the *Kli* [vessel] to obtain the voice of Torah.

Two discernments come from above, which is called *Lishma*: 1) The *Kli*, meaning the darkness. This is the need—when he can no longer tolerate the darkness. 2) The light, meaning the power. This is the voice, the voice of Torah, which gives him the strength to aim in order to bestow, the light that reforms him. This is, "I have created the evil inclination; I have created the Torah as a spice." In other words, the voice of Torah "spices" the evil inclination with the ability to intend *Lishma*.

This is why it is written, "These voices were engraved in darkness, cloud, and mist, and they appear in them as it appears in a body." This means that if they previously had *Kelim* [vessels], which are called "darkness" and "a place of lack," then the voice of Torah could enter the darkness and illuminate.

But when there is no dark place, meaning when he still does not feel the deficiency of not being able to do anything in order to bestow, it cannot be said that the light comes and illuminates, since the light has nowhere to enter. This belongs to the discernment of right, meaning *Hesed*. That is, he has already obtained the vessels of bestowal, and *Hesed* is called "bestowal," when he acts mercifully with others. In that respect, he has already completed the *Kelim*.

Afterward begins the third discernment, when he is rewarded with the secrets of the Torah, called "left." Since this light comes in vessels of reception, it must certainly be in order to bestow. Yet, even though he has already been rewarded with being a receiver in order to bestow, it is still considered left, since the correction of clothing the *Hochma* in *Hassadim* is missing here. Otherwise, it will be, "His *Hochma* is greater than his actions."

Here begins the matter of the middle line, where *Hochma* is clothed in *Hassadim*. That is, the left, called "vessels of reception that receive *Hochma*," will be clothed in *Hassadim*. This is the meaning of what is written, "The Torah comes from the right, which is *Hesed*, and comes to the left, which is *Gevura*. This is called 'disclosure of *Hochma*.'"

However, the right must be mingled with the left, and the left with the right. This is considered that the Torah is called "middle," meaning comprising *Hochma* and deeds, as we said that his *Hochma* must not be more than his deeds.

Baal HaSulam explained the verse, "And the whole people saw the voices." It is known that "voice" means *Hesed*, which comes from "hearing," which is called *Bina*. "Seeing" is called *Hochma*, as it is written, "The eyes of the congregation are the sages of the congregation." Also, *Hochma* that shines in vessels of reception requires keeping, so as not to receive them in order to receive. Hence, clothing of *Hassadim* must be extended to it, called "voice" and "hearing."

Therefore, the words, "And the whole people saw the voices" mean that they saw that they received the light of *Hochma* when it is clothed in a voice, in *Hesed*. This is why it is written that they saw the *Hochma* when it was clothed in voices, meaning in *Hassadim*. This is called "middle line," comprising *Hochma* and *Hassadim*.

With the above said, we will understand what we asked, "What does it mean that he says that the Torah was given on the third, which is *Tifferet*, which is the meaning of "A whole man," Jacob, who is *Tifferet*, and whole means wholeness? We asked, "What is wholeness, that Jacob is called 'A whole man?'"

The answer is that the Torah is the middle line and Jacob is the middle line, comprising right and left, hence there is wholeness. In other words, there is a mingling of *Hochma* and *Hassadim*. In the work, this means that a person should consist of both actions—called *Hassadim*—and of *Hochma*, since it is forbidden for his *Hochma* to be more than his deeds.

However, one should believe that "there is none else besides Him," that the Creator does everything. In other words, as Baal HaSulam said, before each action one should say that man was given only choice, since "If I am not for me, who is for me?" Thus, everything depends on one's choice. However, after the fact, one should say that everything is private Providence, and that one does nothing on his own.

We should interpret this as the Ari writes (*Talmud Eser Sefirot*, Part 13, Item 152), "There is the matter of *Se'arot* [hairs], which cover the light, so they do not enjoy the light as long as they are unworthy, since they might blemish." The thing is that we must believe that the Creator gave us a desire and yearning to do good deeds. And as long as one is unworthy, he must not feel that the Creator compels him to do good deeds. This is why the Creator hides Himself in dresses, and this dressing is called *Lo Lishma* [not for Her sake]. In other words, sometimes the Creator hides Himself in a clothing of friends.

For example, there is a situation where a person does not want to get up and learn before dawn. So the Creator hides Himself in a dressing of friends and he gets out of bed, even though he is tired, since a thought came to his mind that it is not nice to the friends that they all come to learn, and he is not, since then everyone will look at his lowliness. Hence, he gets up and goes to the seminary and learns. It follows that he does not have the energy to get out of bed because of the commandment of the Creator, so the Creator does not force him to go to the seminary, since if this were the reason, he would be lying in bed. But the friends do obligate him.

And similar to this example are all other things when a person acts *Lo Lishma*. Although there are many degrees in *Lo Lishma*, we will speak of this example. Here we should look at the person who is going to learn and to observe *Mitzvot* [commandments/good deeds] not because the Creator commits him. In other words, if it were because of the commandment of the Creator, he would not have the strength to overcome the body and to compel it to do good deeds.

However, because of people, he does have the strength to do good deeds. Thus we see what importance there can be in the *Lo Lishma*.

Yet, one must believe as was said above, that "there is none else besides Him," meaning that it is the Creator who compels him to do the good deeds, but since he is still unworthy of knowing that it is the Creator who commits him, the Creator dresses Himself in dresses of flesh and blood, through which the Creator performs these actions. Thus, the Creator acts in the form of *Achoraim* [posterior].

In other words, the person sees people's faces but he should believe that behind the faces stands the Creator and performs these actions. That is, behind the man stands the Creator and compels him to do the deeds that the Creator wants. It follows that the Creator does everything, but the person regards what he sees and not what he should believe. For this reason, a person says that he is doing the deeds *Lo Lishma*, as with the example of the friends who commit him.

Also, it does not have to be friends. Rather, everyone has his own external clothing, which suits him. Hence, when, for instance, one comes to the synagogue because the friends committed him to come, he says, "The Creator was the reason that he went to learn, but the Creator only dressed in a clothing of friends." Thus, now he thanks the Creator for being the reason.

It follows that when a person did the deed *Lo Lishma*, when the Creator was not the reason that compelled him to perform the *Mitzva* [singular of *Mitzvot*], but he acted because, for instance, the friends ordered him and he had to obey, one must believe that he did this because the Creator commanded him to observe the *Mitzva*, and he had to obey what the Creator commanded him to do. However, the Creator hid Himself in a clothing of *Lo Lishma*, such as the friends, so that through this clothing he would think that he must obey the voice of *Lo Lishma*.

But in truth, one must believe that it was all the Creator's doing. Thus, after he performs the *Mitzva*, he should say that it was the

Creator who acted behind the clothing of *Lo Lishma*. It follows that then one should thank the Creator for giving him the desire to observe His commandments through this clothing.

With the above said we can understand the great importance of *Lo Lishma*. That is, it is not as one thinks—that he does everything for the *Lo Lishma*. Rather, he is doing everything because the Creator commanded him, except he was still not rewarded with feeling that the Creator is actually the commander. For this reason, a person thinks that the *Lo Lishma* is the commander, and hence the act is not so important in his eyes.

However, if he believes that "there is none else besides Him," as was written in previous articles in this portion, then in truth, he is observing the commandments of the Creator, and he should appreciate his actions in *Lo Lishma*. And one's imagination that he is only observing an act in *Lo Lishma* is only because he was not rewarded yet with feeling that he is observing the King's commandment and that he is serving the King.

Hence, if he believes that the *Lo Lishma* is truly the Creator committing him to engage in Torah and *Mitzvot*, then he can give thanks to the Creator for dressing in a clothing of *Lo Lishma*. And from this, one can come to appreciate the importance of Torah and *Mitzvot* even *Lo Lishma*. Our sages said about this: "And they collect from a person knowingly," meaning *Lishma*, and "Unknowingly," meaning *Lo Lishma*.

This is the meaning of what is written, that the *Se'arot* [hairs], meaning the *Lo Lishma*, cover the light, so they will not be fed by the light as long as they are unfit for it. In other words, the *Se'arot* are a clothing, and under that clothing, the light stands and shines. But in the meantime, the light is covered.

What Is
Half a Shekel
in the Work - 2?

Article No. 20, Tav-Shin-Nun, 1989/90

The verse says, "When you count the heads of the children of Israel to number them, each one of them shall give a ransom for his soul to the Lord, when you number them, and there shall be no plague among them when you count them. This is what they shall give: half a shekel in the shekel of holiness. The rich shall not give more and the poor shall not give less than half a shekel, to make a contribution to the Lord, to make atonement for your souls."

We should understand what specifically a half shekel implies to us in the work, and not a quarter or a third of a shekel, where the whole point is to know the number of Israel. What does specifically the half imply to us? Also, why does it say, "The rich shall not give more and the poor shall not give less"? Even a small child understands that if we take from someone less or more we will not know the number of Israel. And also, what is the meaning of "there shall be no plague among them"?

It is known that the purpose of the creation of the world was because He desires to do good to His creations. However, in order

537

for this doing good to be complete, meaning not to have any shame in it while receiving the delight and pleasure, a correction took place, called *Tzimtzum* [restriction] and concealment. This means that before a person can aim his actions to be in order to bestow, they will not feel the delight and pleasure unless when they engage in Torah and *Mitzvot* in order to bring contentment to the Creator.

Afterward, when he has vessels of bestowal, the delight and pleasure found as a deposit in Torah and *Mitzvot* will be revealed. At that time he will receive the delight and pleasure that was in the thought of creation, and for which He created the world.

Since man was created by nature to yearn only for his own benefit, from where can one work on the intention to bestow upon the Creator? This is regarded as a person exerting himself in all kinds of works so as to please the Creator, since then the body asks, "What will you gain if the Creator enjoys"? You should do things so you will enjoy, and why did our sages tell us, "All your works should be for the sake of the Creator?" How can we do something against nature?

The body also asks, "Why should the Creator mind if the creatures work for themselves, meaning that they will enjoy? After all, His desire is to delight His creations." It follows that on one hand, man can enjoy life, meaning work for his own sake, which is natural. On the other hand, it is said that man should not go according to the nature with which he was born, but should work for the sake of the Creator.

And as much as we may explain with all kinds of answers, the body cannot understand this. Although sometimes the body agrees that it is worthwhile to work for the sake of the Creator, in practice, when the body faces something it will enjoy and it must give it up because it will benefit only the Creator, the body chooses its own benefit and relinquishes the benefit of the Creator.

Therefore, we get two things out of this: 1) Since we must believe in the words of our sages that we must do everything for the sake of the Creator although the body does not understand it after all the explanations we give to it, our sages said, and so did Maimonides determine in practice (*Hilchot Teshuva*, Chapter 10), "Therefore, when teaching little ones, women, and uneducated people, they are taught to work only out of fear and in order to receive reward. Until they gain knowledge and acquire much wisdom, they are taught that secret little-by-little."

The question is, What is, "Until they gain knowledge and acquire much wisdom"? That is, what is "wisdom" and what is "much wisdom," so we will know how to determine when we are permitted to reveal to him that secret little-by-little.

At the beginning of man's work, we must say to the body that it is worthwhile to relinquish corporeal pleasures, which are only a "tiny light" compared to the delight and pleasure found in Torah and *Mitzvot* [commandments/good deeds]. It follows that to the extent that he believes and faith illuminates for him, the body agrees to replace a small pleasure with a big one. As in corporeality, when a person makes his effort, the reward he acquired for his work and gives it in order to obtain nourishments to sustain his household, since he has more pleasure when he buys groceries for his household with the money he earned through the labor.

Also, to the extent that faith illuminates for him and he feels that it will give him more pleasure to engage in Torah and *Mitzvot*, he can relinquish corporeal pleasures in order to obtain greater pleasures. However, sometimes a person gets a descent in the faith that he will be rewarded. At that time, it is difficult for him to concede corporeal pleasures. However, if he watches over himself and is in a good environment, the body does not resist this work because this is not considered against nature, since he says that he will receive a greater reward, meaning greater pleasure from observing Torah and *Mitzvot*. It follows that this reason is a strong reason that can compel a person to relinquish the corporeal pleasures that the Torah forbade, and all in order to receive greater pleasures.

2) Since man has to come to a state where "All your works should be for the sake of the Creator," meaning against nature, and this

is for the purpose of the correction of creation, which is for the creatures to be able to receive the delight and pleasure without shame, a correction was placed where one must aim that all his enjoyment will be only for the sake of the Creator. That is, that the Creator will enjoy the creature's pleasure, since this was the purpose of creation. However, sometimes the body feels that it is impossible that with the same intellect and understanding he had when he began to do the holy work, he is constantly in the same intellect and is making no progress, but only in quantity.

When he begins to ask about this, this is regarded as what we asked, What is "wisdom" and what is "much wisdom"? "Wisdom" means that he already observes Torah and *Mitzvot*. "Much wisdom" means that he wants to understand the meaning of Torah and *Mitzvot*, to what state it should bring a person. This is called "intention," which is to aim while observing Torah and *Mitzvot*, that it should bring him to some degree. This is called "much wisdom." At that time they begin to reveal to him this secret, meaning what is the work *Lishma* [for Her sake]. In other words, they begin to let him see that he must work not in order to receive reward, but completely for the sake of the Creator.

When he obtains "much wisdom," he begins to understand that in Torah and *Mitzvot* there is what was said, "For it is your wisdom and understanding in the eyes of the nations." However, there is concealment on it. At that time he is told that this is true, there is a concealment on it for the purpose of correction, since the purpose is for man to achieve *Dvekut* [adhesion] with the Creator, and this is obtained by equivalence of form, regarded as "all his actions should be in order to bestow."

Here is where man begins to be a servant of the Creator. In the work, "serving the Creator" means that he is working for the sake of the Creator and not for his own sake. At that time, the work he does, meaning the fact that he wants to work for the sake of the Creator and not for his own sake, is the beginning when a person begins to enter the exile, under the rule of the will to receive for himself.

Also, he has no hope of emerging from this exile unless with heaven's mercy. That is, the Creator Himself should deliver him from exile, as was in Egypt, where it is written (in the Haggadah [Passover narrative]), "And the Lord brought us out from Egypt, not by an angel, but the Lord Himself." However, the fact that a person feels that he is in exile under the rule of the will to receive for himself, a person cannot feel this at once, meaning when he begins to work to come out of its control.

Rather, this Kli is called "a lack," meaning a need to overcome his vessels of reception. A person does not acquire this at once, but it requires time and effort. Then, over time, there is room for a person to feel that he cannot emerge by himself, but time causes a person a need and suffering, to feel how good it would be if he could emerge from exile, and bad when he is in exile.

For this reason, a person is given ascents and descents, and he must believe that both the ascents and the descents come to him from above. At the same time, during the work, he should say, "If I am not for me, who is for me?" When a person comes to a state where his lack is complete, this is considered that he has a Kli [vessel] to receive the filling, to satisfy his lack. Then comes the time when the upper one fills his Kli.

It is known that there is no light without a Kli, as there is no filling without a lack. Accordingly, a complete thing is called "light and Kli," which divides into two halves: The first half is the Kli, namely the lack. The second half is the light, namely the filling.

It follows that when a person prays to the Creator to satisfy his lack, it is called "half," meaning making a lack, which is the Kli, for the Creator to satisfy his lack. This is as our sages said (VaYikra Rabbah 18), "A prayer makes half." We should interpret that a prayer is when a person prays to the Creator to satisfy his lack. This is already regarded as "half," meaning the first half, which is in one's hand. The second half is in the hands of the Creator, meaning that the Creator must give the light, and then there will be a complete thing.

However, there are many interpretations to light and Kli. If we are to define a Kli, we can say that it is a lack, and it does not matter what is lacking. For example, sometimes a person feels that he is lacking a Kli to receive abundance, since the abundance cannot reach a Kli that cannot aim in order to bestow. Since he feels that he is under the control of the will to receive for himself, it follows that he lacks a Kli that can receive abundance.

It follows that he is not praying to receive abundance. Rather, he is praying to be given a Kli called "desire to bestow." Thus, in this case, "a prayer makes half" means the prayer made half a Kli, and the Creator should give the other half of the Kli. It follows that these two halves are actually a complete Kli and not light.

On the other hand, we should say that the lack is in man's hands. This is called "the first half of the Kli." And the filling of the Kli, meaning having the desire to bestow, considered the "second half of the Kli," is regarded as light, since the desire to bestow that the upper one gives him is a filling for a lack, and any filling is called "light" with respect to the lack.

According to the above, we should interpret what we asked, What does the half a shekel imply to us? for the Torah said specifically half: "The rich shall not give more, and the poor shall not give less." The thing is that we should interpret the words "When you count the heads of the children of Israel to number them," we should interpret the meaning of "heads" as it is written, "May we be the head and not the tail," meaning that they will be regarded as Israel, which are the letters Li-Rosh [a head to me].

This is the meaning of "each one shall give a ransom for his soul." That is, a person must come out of exile, which is called "a ransom for his soul" from the hands of the Sitra Achra [other side]. This is why it is written, "This is what everyone who is numbered shall give," meaning those who feel that they are breaking the commandments of the Torah because they are placed under the governance of the will to receive. Half a shekel means that they must pray that the Creator will deliver them from exile.

"A prayer makes half" means that the *Kli* and the desire for something are regarded as half, meaning that by this they will have a complete thing, meaning that they will be rewarded with the "shekel of holiness." That is, they will have a half shekel, which is the *Kli*, and the Creator will place the light on this, at which time it is called "a complete thing." This is the meaning of the words "This is what everyone who is numbered shall give," meaning those who feel that they are breaking the commandments of the Torah and want to pay a ransom for their souls so that their souls will enter *Kedusha* [holiness], meaning that they will have the strength to do everything for the sake of the Creator.

They must give half a shekel, meaning a prayer. That is, they must pray and not stop praying until they have a complete measure of lack and desire to emerge from the exile, where they are placed under the control of the will to receive for themselves. By giving their half, they will be rewarded with the shekel of holiness, where the other half, which is the filling for the prayer, will be together the shekel of holiness, meaning it will be one complete shekel of *Kedusha*.

By this we will understand what we asked, What does it tell us when it says, "The rich shall not give more, and the poor shall not give less"? Even a small child understands that if we want to know the number of something, everyone must give the same amount. We should interpret this in the work. The Torah is telling us a great thing here: We should know that to the Creator, great and small are equal, as it is written ("All Believe"), "Who is equal and equalizes small and great."

This means that a person thinks that he is rich in good deeds, therefore he deserves the help of the Creator, and he does not need to pray so much for the Creator to satisfy his wish. Therefore, if he has prayed, to the extent of his virtues, the Creator should have promptly granted his wish. And if the Creator does not help him right away, according to his understanding, he stops praying and says that the rest of the people, who are inferior to him, must pray a lot for the Creator to help them. Therefore, he escapes the campaign.

This is why it is written, "The rich shall not give more." This means that the rich should not think that he is praying too much, according to his understanding. Rather, there is a certain measure of lack and need, and precisely by praying a lot, a person receives a greater lack than he has. That is, a great light requires a great lack, meaning to have a feeling of lack in that he is in exile under the governance of the will to receive and he cannot come out.

As long as he does not have true suffering, it is still not considered a true lack so as to be called "a prayer that counts as half a shekel." We must know that in the work, a prayer is a lack, meaning that which a person feels in his heart that he lacks, this is called "a prayer," and not what he utters with his mouth. This is as our sages said, "A prayer is work in the heart," meaning that which the heart feels it is lacking. To the extent that his heart feels a lack because of what he does not have, by this is the size of the prayer measured.

Concerning the shekel, *The Zohar* explains that this concerns the balance scales on which we weigh the deficiencies and fillings, since they are regarded as light and *Kli*. Hence, the light can come only to its proper *Kli*, since the lack for the filling is in the heart. For this reason, the light, too, comes to the feeling in the heart, and it has nothing to do with what the mouth says while he is praying.

It therefore follows that when a person gives his half in prayer, which is a sense of deficiency in the heart, the Creator will give the light, which is *Kedusha*. Out of both the lack and the light, will be one shekel of holiness. This is the meaning of the words "half a shekel," since then this half is still not holiness. But when the Creator gives him the light as in "The light in it reforms him," the two halves are shekel of holiness, as it is written, "in the shekel of holiness."

Now we can understand the words, "And the poor shall not give less." That is, one who feels that he is poor in virtues and good qualities, and he is poor in the sense that he has a weak character, when he prays for the Creator to help him and give him the power to overcome the bad in him and to be able to work in order to bestow, he sentences the Creator to the side of merit when the Creator does not grant his prayer, since he is poor.

Thus, what should he do? Only escape the campaign and say that this path is only for the rich. The writing warns us about this, "The poor shall not do less." Rather, "Each one of them shall give a ransom for his soul," to emerge from the exile and be rewarded with redemption. To the Creator, everyone is equal, as it is written, "And all believe that he is easy to please, equal and equalizes small and great."

In other words, for the part of the Creator, there is no discrimination. Rather, He answers everyone. However, everyone should come to feel the lack, to know what they are lacking and to pray for this. And the prayer itself increases the lack and the pain at being far from the Creator. When a person does all the prayers he should do, he receives the other half of the shekel, which at that time is all holiness, as it is written, "in the shekel of the holiness."

Then "there shall be no plague among them." This means as it is written, "The wicked in their lives are called 'dead,'" as presented in *The Study of the Ten Sefirot*, that it is because the will to receive is in disparity of form from the Creator, and disparity of form creates separation. Hence, they are separated from the Life of Lives. This is why they are called "dead." It follows that through the prayer, which is the half shekel that a person must give, if the giving is complete the Creator gives the other half, meaning the light. By this, a person can already work in order to bestow. This is regarded as being rewarded with *Dvekut* with the Creator, to adhere to the Life of Lives.

It therefore follows that there are two manners that cause a person to escape the campaign even when he enters the work of being adhered to the Creator. Once a person begins to walk on the path of truth, he is shown from above his lowliness, meaning that the more he overcomes, the more hardening of the heart he receives from above, because as it is written, "That I may set these signs of Mine within him." This means that by this, there will be room for the revelation of the light of Torah, called "letters," and this reforms him. That is, since there is no light without a *Kli*, through the hardening of the heart, the lack appears sufficiently, and the Creator knows when the measure is sufficient, when the *Kli* is completed.

Therefore, sometimes a person escapes the campaign when he sees that he has already prayed a lot in his opinion, but the Creator does not notice him. At that time, sometimes a person sentences the Creator to the side of merit for not granting his prayer, and says that it is because he has a poor character in every way, in virtues, and in good qualities, etc.

It was said about this, "The poor shall not give less," meaning that a person should not belittle himself and say that the Creator cannot help a lowly person such as him, for it was said about this, "The Lord is high and the low will see."

And sometimes, a person leaves the campaign because he knows that he is rich, meaning he has much Torah and many good deeds, and he knows that he is superior to others. Therefore, when he asks the Creator to help him be able to do everything in order to bestow, why is the Creator not granting him, for he knows that he has already given many prayers for it. Therefore, he says that the Creator does not want to answer him, and therefore he runs.

And yet, a person must always overcome.

What Is, "As I Am for Nothing, so You Are for Nothing," in the Work?

Article No. 21, Tav-Shin-Nun, 1989/90

It is written in *The Zohar*, *Truma* (Item 34), "'And they shall take a donation for Me.' 'They shall take for Me' indicates that one who wishes to exert in a *Mitzva* [commandment/good deed] and exert in the Creator must not exert in it futilely and for nothing. Rather, one should exert in it properly, according to one's strength, as it is written, 'Every man shall give as he is able, according to the blessing of the Lord your God which He has given you.' If you say, 'But it is written, 'Come, buy and eat, and come buy for no money and at no cost wine and milk,' it means that it is free, since wine and milk mean the Torah.' He replies, 'But with exertion in the Torah, anyone who wishes is granted with it. The exertion in the Creator, to know Him, anyone who wishes is rewarded with Him without any pay at all. But the exertion in the Creator that stands in an act must not be taken for nothing and futilely, for he will not be rewarded by this act at all, to extend on it the spirit of

Kedusha [holiness], but at full cost." The matter of "for nothing" is also brought (in *Masechet Hagigah*, p 7) as follows, "As I am for nothing, so you are for nothing."

We should understand the following:

1) What is exertion in the Torah?

2) What is exertion in the Creator, to know Him?

3) What is exertion in the Creator, which stands in an act?

4) What is the meaning of "for nothing or for a cost"? Whom should we pay? We see that one who works should be paid, which means that the person who is working should pay. Who has heard of such a thing? We see that there are people who work for no pay, but to work and pay to those for whom we work? Where do we see such a thing?

First, what is the meaning of "exertion"? That is, we see that normally, when someone wants something that is difficult to obtain, the person must exert and make great efforts to obtain that thing. But with something that is abundant, you cannot speak of exertion. Rather, anyone who wants that thing takes it, or pays for what he wants, but you cannot speak of exertion.

For example, a person does not say, "Today I made great efforts to buy bread and milk for the kids," when bread and milk are in stores for anyone who wants. But sometimes, during war, when there were no bread or milk in the stores and he made great efforts to obtain them, while other people were not as successful in obtaining them, in such a state you can speak of exertion.

But concerning Torah and *Mitzvot* [commandments/good deeds], how can we speak of exertion? That is, how can we say that observing Torah and *Mitzvot* is so difficult that it requires exertion? After all, the verse says, "For this commandment that I command you today is not too difficult for you, nor is it far, nor is it in heaven or beyond the sea, for the matter is very close to you." Thus, we should understand what is exertion in Torah and *Mitzvot*.

It is known that the purpose of creation is to do good to His creations. For this reason, He created creatures that have the desire to receive delight and pleasure. This is called a *Kli* [vessel] that the Creator created for the creatures, and in this *Kli* they will receive the delight and pleasure. This *Kli* is regarded as coming from the Creator; hence, this *Kli* is complete in the created beings. When the created beings want to use this *Kli*, they have no work at all to obtain the *Kli* because the Creator created that *Kli*, so there is complete wholeness in this *Kli*.

From this we see that wherever the created beings feel that they can obtain pleasure from something, they immediately use that *Kli*, called "will to receive for oneself," meaning for one's own benefit. There is no need to awaken the person to want to receive pleasure, but rather to the extent of the pleasure clothed in the thing, that pleasure attracts a person and he chases the pleasure in order to obtain it. This means that to the extent of the pleasure in that thing, so it awakens yearning in a person, and it does not let him sit until he makes every effort to obtain the pleasure.

But later, when the correction of the *Tzimtzum* [restriction] took place, which is the matter called "the wholeness of His works," meaning when they receive the delight and pleasure from the Creator, in order for them not to feel shame, a correction was done, called "concealment." That is, before the person obtains a vessel of bestowal, he does not see the delight and pleasure that will be revealed, that the delight and pleasure will give him an awakening to receive the good.

This is in order to have room for choice. In the work, choice is in order to be able to observe Torah and *Mitzvot* not in order to receive reward, since when the pleasure is revealed while performing the *Mitzva*, a person cannot say that he is observing the Torah and *Mitzvot* because he wants to delight the Creator, meaning that for himself, he would relinquish the pleasure he is tasting, but because the Creator wants the creatures to enjoy, only for this reason does he accept the pleasure.

This is impossible, since man was born with a nature of wanting to receive for himself. Therefore, how can he say that for himself, he relinquishes the pleasure? How can a person relinquish the great pleasure that is found in Torah and *Mitzvot*?

Because of this, sparks of light, called "tiny light," were placed in the *Klipot* [shells/peels], on which all of creation feeds before they are rewarded with vessels of bestowal. Since this is only a very thin light, a person begins to do the work of giving small pleasures in return for great pleasures, meaning to receive reward in return for relinquishing small pleasures that have nothing more than a tiny light in them.

It is like commerce—where we gain more, this is where we trade. It is likewise in the work, where only later, when a person is used to relinquishing pleasures, although they are small compared to the pleasures found in Torah and *Mitzvot*, it is still considered that he is accustomed to the work and there is room for choice.

However, accordingly, we should understand, if a person engages in Torah and *Mitzvot* in order to receive reward for his work, why is observing Torah and *Mitzvot* regarded as an effort? After all, this is also the conduct in corporeality: to relinquish small pleasures in order to obtain great pleasure. The answer is that in corporeality, the pleasure one receives for one's work is revealed in this world. Therefore, it cannot be regarded as an effort. But in Torah and *Mitzvot*, he must believe that he will have a reward in the next world, and since it depends on faith, there is already labor, since he must believe, and the body cannot believe because by nature, it needs to see and to know. But when we must believe, there are already ascents and descents.

It follows that the effort one should make in Torah and *Mitzvot* is one discernment. But there is another discernment, which is to exert in the Creator, to know Him. We should try to observe both in order to receive reward for the labor. That is, we must believe that we will receive reward both in this world and in the next world. This is as it is written in *The Zohar* ("Introduction of the Book of

Zohar," Item 190), "Fear is interpreted in three discernments. There is a person who fears the Creator so that his sons will live and not die, or fears a bodily punishment, or a punishment to one's money. It follows that the fear he fears of the Creator is not placed as the root, for his own benefit is the root, and the fear is the result of it. And there is a person who fears the Creator because he fears the punishment of that world and the punishment of Hell. Those two kinds of fear are not the essence of the fear. The fear that is the most important is when one fears one's Master because He is great and ruling," meaning both exertion in Torah and Mitzvot and exertion in the Creator.

But the main meaning of knowing Him is to know that He leads the world in a guidance of The Good Who Does Good, and we must strive to know Him in this respect. We should interpret that knowing Him is when a person prays to the Creator or thanks the Creator, he should know to what name he is praying, or to what name he is giving thanks. That is, when a person prays to the Creator for someone who is sick to get better, he should know that he is praying to the name, Healer of the Sick. At that time, it cannot be said that he is praying to the name, Redeemer of the Captive, etc. Or, when he thanks the Creator for delivering him from imprisonment, he should thank the name, Redeemer of the Captive, and it cannot be said that he is thanking the name, Dresses the Naked. He says that both the exertion in Torah and Mitzvot and in the Creator, to know Him, in them, a person can be rewarded, if he exerts, for nothing, for no money and at no cost.

Conversely, exertion in the Creator that is in action (is) for a complete reward. We should understand what "stands in action" means. The writing says, "which God has created to do." This means that the Creator created the world in order to do. That is, over that which the Creator created, man must act. This is called "the six workdays," which is the time of work, which is called "action."

We find likewise in the words of The Zohar, in the words ("Introduction of the Book of Zohar," Item 67), "'And to say to Zion, 'You are My people." Do not pronounce 'You are My people

[Ami]' with a *Patach* in the *Ayin*, but 'You are with Me [Imi],' with a *Hirik* in the *Ayin*, which means partnering with Me. As I made heaven and earth with My speech, as it is written, 'By the word of the Lord the heavens were made,' so did you." They also said (*Avot*, Chapter 1), "It is not the learning that is most important, but the deed," and also, "Great is the learning of Torah, for it yields action" (*Kidushin* 40).

We should understand what deed they are talking about as being the most important. We should interpret this in the work, that the wholeness is mainly for the created beings to receive the goal for which the world was created, namely His desire to do good to His creations, meaning for the lower ones to receive from Him delight and pleasure. In order for the creatures to receive delight and pleasure, He created in the creatures yearning, meaning to have a desire and yearning to receive the delight and pleasure.

As was said, this *Kli* comes from the Creator. However, afterward, there was a correction where this *Kli* became half a *Kli*. In other words, after there was a correction so there would not be the matter of shame, a *Tzimtzum* and concealment were placed on this *Kli*, called "will to receive for oneself." For this reason, this *Kli*, called "will to receive," is considered as only half a *Kli*, meaning that as long as we cannot make the will to receive for ourselves work in order to bestow, we cannot use this *Kli*. But after we place on it the desire to bestow, the *Kli* can receive the abundance.

It therefore follows that the Creator made the first half *Kli*, called "will to receive." The other half, meaning the aim to bestow, pertains only to the creatures—to place the *Masach* [screen] on the will to receive, and from this emerges the other half. When both of these halves are present, they become one *Kli*, which is suitable to receive the delight and pleasure.

It follows that man's work is to make the second half of the *Kli*. This is called "action," and this is the meaning of "which God has created," meaning the first half, the will to receive for oneself, on which man does not need to do. But the second half, which is in order to bestow, which pertains to the created beings, here there is work, since it is against nature. Hence, there is a lot of work here to obtain it. This is called "action," which a person must do, and which is not done by the Creator because we attribute to the Creator what He gives. That is, every bestowing, meaning giving, pertains to the Creator, but the second half of the *Kli*, which is what the lower one wants to give, this belongs to the lower one.

Now we can interpret what we asked, What is exertion in the Creator, which stands in an act? Which act are we speaking of? We should interpret that when a person exerts in the Creator in action, meaning in bestowing upon the Creator, this act belongs to the lower one, namely that a person has to work to have this *Kli* called "desire to bestow."

As in corporeality, when a person needs to learn the trade of making tools to sell to people, and making the tools is a profession, meaning a craft that must be learned not at once, and not in one month. Likewise, here in the work, a person must learn the trade of making vessels of bestowal. A person cannot do it as soon as he wants to have these *Kelim* [vessels]. Rather, it is a craft that must be learned over a long period of time until he has such *Kelim*, meaning the ability to observe Torah and *Mitzvot* in order to bestow.

Our sages said, "The Creator said, 'I have created the evil inclination; I have created the Torah as a spice'" (*Kidushin* 30). This means that the Creator created the will to receive, which is considered the first part of the *Kli*, namely the yearning for pleasure, "and I created the Torah as a spice," which spices the evil inclination into a good inclination, making the will to receive work in order to bestow.

Therefore, this means that the Creator gives the second part of the *Kli*, as well. According to what our sages said about the verse, "And to say unto Zion, 'You are My people,'" and they explained, "Do not pronounce 'My people [Ami]' but 'with Me [Imi],' which means partnering with Me." This means that the creatures also make. We should interpret about the second half of the *Kli*, that it is not all done by the Creator, but that there is man's work here, too.

However, we should interpret about the second half of the *Kli*, which we attribute to man, that in this *Kli*, called "desire to bestow," we also discern the matter of light and *Kli*. Hence, the *Kli* in the *Kli* belongs to man, meaning that which the Creator gives is called "light," and that which man gives is called "a *Kli*," since a *Kli* is called "a lack," and light is called "the filling of the lack."

Since the Creator is the Giver, and abundance is called "light," we attribute the light to the Creator, and the *Kli*, called "a lack," belongs to the created beings, as this is their whole root—only a lack—and the Creator fills the lack.

Hence, when speaking of the vessels of bestowal, this *Kli* also divides into two parts, as said above. 1) A lack, meaning that one must feel that he is lacking vessels of bestowal. That is, he feels that everything he does is for his own benefit, and believes that a person should adhere to the Creator, as it is written, "And to cleave unto Him," where *Dvekut* [adhesion] is called "equivalence of form." It pains him that he is far from *Dvekut* with the Creator, and he sees that for himself, he has no way to emerge from the domination of the will to receive. This is called "a lack," and this pertains to man, meaning that man must feel the lack. This is regarded as an act, meaning work in vessels of bestowal.

The light of the *Kli*, meaning in the *Kli*, which is the lack, will be the filling that is clothed, meaning the power that he can bestow. This is called "the light in the *Kli*," and the Creator gives this. By this we can interpret what we asked, "Our sages said, 'I have created the Torah as a spice,'" meaning that the Creator also gives the *Kli* called "desire to bestow," and not man. Thus, why is the *Kli* called "action," which pertains to man's work in action?

The answer is that the *Kli*, called "lack," when it pains him that he cannot do anything for the sake of the Creator, we attribute this to the creature. That is, the lack belongs to the creature, and the filling of the lack belongs to the Creator. This is why they said, "I have created the evil inclination; I have created the Torah as a spice," meaning the light spices the evil inclination. In other words, the Creator gives the power to want to do everything for the sake of the Creator.

But the lack in the *Kli*, this a person has to feel within his body. This means that the person must do all that he can in order to achieve *Dvekut* with the Creator, and making that lack is called "a lack," and this is regarded as what we asked, What is the exertion in the Creator that stands in an act, meaning that a person exerts in the Creator, to be able to delight the Creator, meaning to bring Him contentment. This desire is called "an act," meaning "making the lack." This is when he can bring contentment to the Creator, and this is the light in the *Kli*.

Now we will explain what we asked, What is the meaning of the reward, and what is the meaning of "for nothing"? Ostensibly, it should have been the opposite. That is, the exertion in the Creator should be for nothing, and exertion in Torah and *Mitzvot* and exertion in the Creator, to know Him, should be for a reward. That is, those who exert will be rewarded. However, it implies that those who exert in action pay a fee!

This is hard to understand for two reasons: 1) Where do we see such a thing that the one who works is the one who pays? There are people who work for no pay, as volunteers. We do see this. But to pay in order to be allowed to work? This we do not see. 2) The question is, Whom must we pay this fee? We should say that it is to the Creator, but how can it be said that the Creator receives reward, called "profit"? That is, how can we say that if a person does not think that the Creator will benefit, then his effort, called "action," this act that the person does will not yield that person any results?

However, we should interpret this according to our way: There is the matter of *Lo Lishma* [not for Her sake], which means that a person engages in Torah and *Mitzvot* in order to receive reward. Naturally, one who works in order to receive reward always looks at what he will gain from exerting and following the orders of the landlord, and does not think at all about what the landlord will gain from his work. Sometimes, when the worker thinks that the landlord should profit, too, it is not because he is concerned with the benefit of the landlord, but because the worker knows that if this business does not yield profits to the landlord, the business will shut down and he will have no work. Other than that, he does not think about the landlord whatsoever.

That is, the worker does not need to think that the Creator should profit, unless for nothing, meaning that he is not interested in the Creator making a profit. This is called "for nothing." But one who wants to work in action, which is making a *Kli* to bestow contentment upon the Creator, it is explicitly for a reward, meaning that the Creator will enjoy his work. In other words, a person is not concerned with his profits, but with the profit of the Creator. This is the meaning of the prohibition to take it for nothing, meaning without a profit. In other words, a person should aim all his actions that the Creator will enjoy. This is regarded that work in action should be for a reward, meaning that this will reward the Creator.

What Is the Order in Blotting Out Amalek?

Article No. 22, Tav-Shin-Nun, 1989/90

The *Zohar* says in the portion *BeShalach* (Item 471), "Rabbi Yitzhak said, 'It is written, 'For I will surely blot out,' which means that the Creator will blot out. It is also written, 'Blot out the memory of Amalek,' meaning that we should blot it out? He replies, 'However, the Creator said, 'You will blot out the memory of Amalek below, and I will blot out the memory of Amalek above.'''"

We should understand what is "Amalek below" and what is "Amalek above" in the work. It means that there is the matter of blotting out two Amaleks here—above and below. Also, this implies that first we must blot out Amalek below, and then the Creator will blot out Amalek above? We should understand why we were not given a complete thing, as we learn, "The awakening from below awakens the doing above." This means that the things we do below cause changes to occur above, as well, meaning the revelation of the abundance and annulment of the *Sitra Achra* [other side]. Thus, why with the blotting out of Amalek, our actions cannot blot out

Amalek above? Why were we given only half the work, and the Creator does the other half? Why this partnership?

Concerning Amalek, we should also understand what his name implies. Generally, Amalek is called the "evil inclination." However, specifically, the evil inclination has many names. Our sages said (*Masechet Sukkah*, p 52), "The evil inclination has seven names: Evil, Uncircumcised, Impure, Enemy, Obstacle, North Stone. It also has other names such as Pharaoh King of Egypt and Amalek."

It is known that in everything, we discern two discernments: light and *Kli* [vessel]. Even in corporeal things, we discern internality and externality in everything. The externality is called the *Kli*, and the internality is called the "light." For example, when a person yearns for bread, or for meat and fish, etc., a person does not yearn for the *Kli*, meaning the external part, which he sees. Rather, he yearns for the interior, which is not seen, meaning to the taste of bread, or meat, or fish.

Moreover, we see that enjoying the pleasure dressed in the *Kli* requires preparation. To the extent of one's preparation, so one can enjoy the light of pleasure clothed in the *Kli*, which is regarded as the externality. In other words, a person who comes to drink water when he is thirsty is not like one who drinks water when he is not thirsty, since the *Kli* for reception of pleasure is measured by the level of yearning for the pleasure.

For this reason, we see that when a person wants to enjoy drinks, he first eats acrid and salty foods in order to invoke in him the desire to drink. It is likewise in everything: Without yearning, it is impossible to enjoy anything. This stems from the beginning of creation, as we learn that the purpose of creation, which is His desire to do good to His creations, created a desire to receive delight and pleasure. Before the fourth phase—which is yearning—is revealed, it is still not regarded as a *Kli* that is fit to receive the light and pleasure.

Now we will return to the light and *Kli* in spirituality, meaning that the same order that applies in corporeality, applies also in spirituality. In truth, it is to the contrary: That which applies in corporeality, extends from spirituality. However, there is one difference between corporeality and spirituality. In corporeality, the pleasure, meaning the light, which is the internality, is revealed, as it is written, "The eye sees and the heart covets." Therefore, when looking at something corporeal, we can more or less feel that there is an inner taste there. The pleasure clothed in the externality of the *Kli* attracts us and invokes within us the desire.

Conversely, in spiritual pleasures, which are clothed in the externality of the *Kelim* [vessels], which are called Torah and *Mitzvot* [commandments/good deeds], they are under *Tzimtzum* [restriction] and concealment. Therefore, we cannot say that the pleasure and light clothed in the *Mitzva* [singular of *Mitzvot*] of *Tzitzit* [prayer shawl] attracts him and this is why he wears a *Tzitzit*. It is likewise with the rest of the *Mitzvot*. As we learned, the *Tzimtzum* was for the purpose of the correction of creation. It follows that in this, there is a big difference between corporeal pleasures clothed in external matters, and spiritual pleasures, clothed in external matters, which are Torah and *Mitzvot*.

Hence, because of the *Tzimtzum*, there is the matter of *Lo Lishma* [not for Her sake] and *Lishma* [for Her sake] here. This is so because of the concealment that was done on spiritual pleasures. That is, a person cannot be told, "Try to wear a *Tzitzit* and you will see how good it feels to wear a *Tzitzit*." Therefore, we must say, "Wear a *Tzitzit* and in return you will receive pleasure that is not clothed in the *Mitzva* of *Tzitzit*, for in this, you cannot feel any flavor."

Therefore, a person asks, "Why do I need to wear a *Tzitzit*?" Then, the person who asks should be told, "You will receive great pleasure in return for this." "What pleasure will I receive?" Then he is told, "You can choose worldly pleasures in return for work in Torah and *Mitzvot*, as it is written in *The Zohar*, such as provision, health, and long life, or you will also receive a reward in the next world, as Maimonides says at the end of *Hilchot Teshuva*."

It follows that *Lo Lishma* means not as it is in corporeality, where there is some pleasure of meat or fish is clothed there in the interior of the *Kli*. That is, the light that is clothed inside the *Kli* draws him to observe Torah and *Mitzvot*. Rather, there is a different pleasure there, which is not clothed in these *Kelim* that he will receive, and this draws him to observe Torah and *Mitzvot*.

This is called *Lo Lishma*, meaning that the intention in the *Mitzva* does not draw him, meaning what is clothed inside the *Mitzva*. Rather, the *Lo Lishma* draws him, meaning that which is not clothed in the *Mitzva*, this is what draws him. However, the pleasure that is not clothed in the *Mitzva* and is outside the *Kelim*, which are called Torah and *Mitzvot*, this is what draws him.

This is called *Lo Lishma*. That is, when he engages in Torah and *Mitzvot*, he receives the strength to work because he will receive reward later. This means that if he could receive greater pleasures elsewhere, he could relinquish Torah and *Mitzvot*. But since he has faith in reward and punishment, he must therefore observe Torah and *Mitzvot*. Yet, he would be happier if he did not have to observe so many *Mitzvot* and would receive the same reward.

This means that observing *Mitzvot* does not interest him, but rather the reception of the reward. As in corporeality, every person wants to work fewer hours and receive a higher salary. Likewise, all those whose work is *Lo Lishma* are not concerned with observing more Torah and *Mitzvot*, but are concerned with the opposite—why they must observe so many Torah and *Mitzvot*, since the Creator could have given us fewer Torah and *Mitzvot*, and more reward. This is regarded as the *Lo Lishma* forcing him to engage in Torah and *Mitzvot*.

It is not so with those who want to work *Lishma*, meaning that they want the Torah and *Mitzvot* themselves to be the causes compelling them to engage in Torah and *Mitzvot*. As with corporeal pleasures, the internality clothed in the externality is what invokes them to use the externality. This means that they yearn to eat meat or fish not so that in return for the labor of eating meat and fish and so forth, they will receive a reward. Rather, they yearn for the pleasure found inside the meat and the fish, and there is no one in the world who is angry at the Creator for creating so much externality, meaning many things where in each one, a different pleasure is clothed, and a person says, I am content with bread and water and I do not want to have more pleasures dressed in more things.

On the contrary, we see that each one tries as hard as he can to increase external things, meaning of several kinds. Even when he eats meat, he tries to get the best meat, meaning he is meticulous about eating meat. In other words, he exerts in the light, in the pleasure clothed in the externality, so as to feel a better taste.

In the same manner, a person behaves when he works Lishma. That is, he is not angry that he has so many Mitzvot, meaning he has no grievances why there are 613 Mitzvot, and he would settle for less, since a person believes that in each Mitzva there is a different flavor, as in corporeality. When he wants to walk in the path of Lishma, although he does not feel the interior of the pleasure clothed in each Mitzva, he believes in the sages that this is so, as it is written in The Zohar, that there are 613 deposits, where in each Mitzva, a special light is deposited, which belongs to that Mitzva.

And although he does not feel, he believes that this is so because there was concealment and Tzimtzum so they would not feel the pleasure, regarded as the internality clothed in Torah and Mitzvot, which is for the sake of the lower ones. In other words, as long as they were not rewarded with the aim to bestow, which is called "Dvekut [adhesion] with the Creator," if the pleasure is revealed, they will certainly receive it in order to receive, which will separate them from the Life of Lives, and this is regarded as death in spirituality.

For this reason, they want to work only in order to bestow. That is, they want to serve the King, as it says in The Zohar, that "the essence of fear is that a person serves the Creator because He is great and ruling," namely because of the greatness of the King. It is also within nature for a person to enjoy when serving a great one.

For this reason, a person who wants to work in order to bestow needs to have a great King to serve. Then, the person does not want a reward, meaning to receive the pleasure clothed in the externality of Torah and Mitzvot, but wants to take upon himself to work only to maintain the externality of Torah and *Mitzvot*, and does not want the internality because he believes in the sages that if he yearns to receive the internality, it will cause him separation.

For this reason, he wants to work only to observe the externality of Torah and *Mitzvot*. But what is his pleasure? According to the rule, "Without pleasure, a person cannot work," because of His desire to do good to His creations, a person must enjoy the work. Yet, the difference is that sometimes a person works in order to receive the reward of one day's work, as it is written, "In the evening, you will give his reward," or he will receive his reward each week. Also, there are people who are merchants and receive their reward with each and every transaction, but without reward, it is impossible to work.

For this reason, those who want to work in order to bestow, meaning with the intention to serve the great King, enjoy instantaneously. That is, in everything they do, they already enjoy and they have no need to receive reward later because they receive the reward instantaneously, like the merchants.

However, there is great work here, meaning that the main work in the engagement in Torah and *Mitzvot* begins here. If the whole of man's basis is that his pleasure is in that he is serving a great King, if His greatness were to be revealed in the world, it would not be difficult to serve the King. But we learned that there was a *Tzimtzum* [restriction] and concealment on the delight and pleasure clothed in Torah and *Mitzvot*, and there was also concealment on the Creator Himself so that we must believe in His guidance, that He is good and does good and that the *Shechina* [Divinity] is in the dust and that the *Shechina* is in exile, meaning that His glory is not revealed to the lower ones.

However, we have much work to overcome our bodies, since the body argues that we see that the Creator created in us an intellectual power, and we go with our intellect. That is, we heed what our intellect tells us. Therefore, when we come to the body and say to it that we do not need to look at what the intellect tells us, but go above the intellect and believe in the Creator above reason, the body rejects to this.

Therefore, when the greatness and importance of the King are not revealed, how can we work and observe Torah and *Mitzvot* because of the greatness of the King, since the *Sitra Achra* [other side] is covering His greatness? Thus, how can we work because of the greatness and importance of the King?

This is the meaning of the *Klipa* [shell/peel] of Amalek, as it is written (Portion *Ki Tetze*), "Remember that which Amalek did unto you, which occurred to you along the way when you were tired and weary and not fearing God." RASHI interpreted the meaning of "which occurred to you along the way" to mean heat and cold: "He cooled you and chilled your boiling, for all the nations feared you, but he began and showed a way for others." He interprets there in *Siftey Hachamim*, "He wanted to say with a hot matter that everyone fears it. So were the nations of the world afraid of you, but Amalek chilled you and made you lukewarm, as in tepid water."

It follows that Amalek is a *Klipa*. When a person overcomes and begins to walk on the path of truth, he comes and weakens the person and says, "Do not fear departing from the path of bestowal." And the more a person overcomes with greatness of the Creator, saying it is worthwhile to work only for the Creator and not for himself, (Amalek comes) and makes a person understand, "You see that you are tired and weary from this work, and you are not fearing God," meaning that the fear of heaven that Israel had, when they said that it is worthwhile to work and serve a great King, he instilled his view in this, meaning that there is no importance to the King. Thus, "Why do you want to work for no reward, but only for the sake of the Creator, because of His greatness?" He spoiled this fear, meaning that his whole purpose was only to revoke the importance of the fear of heaven called "the essence of fear is that it is because He is great and ruling."

It turns out that he instilled in the people of Israel a cancellation of the importance of fearing God, for his entire war was to weaken them from the work of serving a great King, that for this, meaning for the importance of the greatness of the Creator, it is worthwhile to work and serve Him.

This is the meaning of "which occurred to you along the way," meaning on this path when we want no reward but this, namely to serve the King. This importance, he spoiled.

This means that when Amalek sees that a person becomes excited and heated up in the work, and a person is delighted that he has been rewarded with some importance, that it is worthwhile to serve a great King, he comes and slanders, and takes this importance away from the person. Naturally, a person loses the warmth he had in the little bit of sensation he had, that he was connected to a great King.

This is the meaning of the words, "And you are tired and weary." That is, during the work, when a person believes that he is serving a great King, a person lives without feeling any fatigue. But when Amalek instills in him the cancellation of the greatness of the Creator, a person immediately grows tired from the work. This is as *The Zohar* says, "Where there is effort, there is the *Sitra Achra*. This means that a person should know that if he does the holy work and feels this work as a burden and a load, it is a sign that the *Sitra Achra* is there and weakens a person so he will not feel that he is serving a great King.

It follows that the *Klipa* of Amalek aims primarily against the greatness of the Creator, meaning that the foundation of Judaism is built primarily on fear, "because He is great and ruling." Precisely on this was the war of Amalek, meaning that a person will not work on the quality of "fear of God." This is the meaning of the words, "and not fearing God."

According to the above we can understand what we asked about the meaning of what *The Zohar* says, that "There is Amalek below and there is Amalek above." "Amalek below" refers to the *Kli*, and "Amalek above" refers to the light. That is, Amalek not letting him work for the sake of the Creator is called a *Kli*, meaning the desire to work for the sake of the Creator, although Amalek interferes with his arguments.

In other words, "Amalek below" means that a person wants to work for the sake of the Creator but Amalek does not let him work. He recognizes and feels that this is the *Klipa* that brings him these thoughts that revoke the glory of heaven, and it pains him. This is called "man's work," meaning that the person wants to revoke all the arguments of Amalek, and a person comes to feel that by himself, he does not see how he can cancel the slander that Amalek speaks to him every time he wants to work only because of the greatness and importance of the King. The person sees that more than a prayer, to pray to the Creator not to be impressed by his slander, there is nothing he can do. This is regarded as a person wanting to blot out the Amalek in his heart and mind.

This completes the *Kli* for blotting out Amalek, where with this desire and lack that a person has, he feels in it the losses that this Amalek causes him in life, and yet he cannot overcome by himself. At that time, a person feels that all he needs is the help of the Creator, that the Creator will help him, and he believes in our sages, who said, "He who comes to purify is aided," and then the Creator revokes his Amalek.

According to the above, we can interpret what we asked about what *The Zohar* says, that there is Amalek above and there is Amalek below, and that the Creator said about the Amalek above, "I will surely blot out," meaning that the Creator will blot him out above, and about Amalek below, the Creator said, "Blot out the memory of Amalek," meaning that man must blot out. We asked why the two Amaleks, and why does the Creator not blot out both, or that man will have the power to blot out both? Why this partnership?

The meaning is that there are light and *Kli*, and there is no light without a *Kli*, as it is known that there is no filling without a lack. We also asked, What is the quality of Amalek that we must blot out more than the rest of the names of the evil inclination? The answer is that the evil inclination slanders the Creator, that it is not worthwhile to engage in Torah and *Mitzvot*. Since according to the rule that one cannot make a single move without a reason that compels him to do so, *The Zohar* says that there are three reasons for which man observes Torah and *Mitzvot* ("Introduction of The Book of Zohar," Item 190): "Fear is interpreted in three discernments, two of which do not contain a proper root, and one is the root of fear. There is a person who fears the Creator so that his sons may live and not die, or fears a bodily punishment, or a punishment to one's money. Hence, he always fears Him. It follows that the fear he fears of the Creator is not placed as the root, for his own benefit is the root, and the fear is its offshoot. Then there is a person who fears the Creator because he fears the punishment of that world and the punishment of Hell. Those two kinds of fear are not the essence of fear or its root. Fear, which is the most important, is when one fears one's Master because He is great and ruling, the essence and the root of all the worlds, and everything is considered nothing compared to Him. And he will place his will in that place, which is called 'fear.'"

Accordingly, we see that although there is the evil inclination, which does not let one observe Torah and *Mitzvot*, they are not the opposite of the essence of fear, called "because He is great and ruling." This is the essence of the fear for which a person wants to serve the King because of the greatness and importance of the King. Amalek wants to weaken specifically this, meaning he argues that the person himself sees that there is no importance to the Creator that He should be served because of His greatness, for you see what great concealment there is on His guidance, that we can say that He leads the world as the good who does good.

He argues that this is not concealment, but that as we can see with our eyes, this is really so, and not as the people of Israel say, that in truth, the Creator leads the world as the good who does good, but we have not yet been rewarded with seeing how His Providence is in the manner of good and doing good. Thus, instead, we must believe above reason and say, "They have eyes, and see not."

Accordingly, we see that this *Klipa* is truly against the essence of the fear. But with the rest of the *Klipot*, they are not so specific against faith that He is good and does good. It follows that the *Klipa* of Amalek is truly the opposite of the true fear.

This is the meaning of what is written about Amalek, "and he was not fearing God." That is, he slandered the fear of the glory of heaven, meaning the fear because of the glory of heaven, that we should walk on that line. This was all of Amalek's resistance, since this is truly against the real work that a person should be rewarded with attaining.

By this we can understand why we must blot out this *Klipa*. The reason is that we should say that there is no truth in her words that there is no concealment here. Rather, as we see, so it is. This discernment must be blotted out, meaning to say that there is no truth in her words.

However, how can a person blot out when there is concealment on His guidance, when Amalek stands strong against the person? The Creator says about this, "You must give the *Kli*," meaning the lack, namely that which you need, so you must pay attention to what it is you lack.

This is why the Creator says, "Blot out the memory of Amalek," meaning He says that you do not need to do anything, meaning any tips so you can work for Me, but only blot out what Amalek says to you and believe above reason, meaning above Amalek's reason, who is slandering Me, that it is not worthwhile to work for Me.

If you want to work above reason because, as it is written, "What does the Lord your God ask of you but to fear Me?" it is specifically this quality that he resists, and you want to blot him out. If your desire is true but you cannot blot him out, this is regarded as blotting him out from below.

With what will you blot him out? Answer, with the desire—that you want to go above reason. Then, I will blot him out above, meaning I will give you the strength to blot out.

We understand this in two discernments, meaning that you will be rewarded with the revelation of the face. It follows that everything that Amalek said was blotted out. That is, his words were not true. And 2) you will have the strength to go and accept the concealment of the face

However, the revelation of the face will come later, as it is written about Moses, that our sages said, "In return for 'And Moses hid his face for he was afraid to look,' he was rewarded with 'The image of the Lord he beheld.'" It follows that he blotted him out above, meaning that there is already revelation of the face.

The question we asked, Why does the Creator not let a person do everything? is simple: Concerning the revelation of the face, only the Creator can reveal His face. It cannot be said that we attribute this to the person. Also, concerning a person having to work during the concealment, and the Creator not giving the strength right away, why must man begin, or he will not have the *Kli*? It is because first a person must acquire a lack, and then it can be said that the Creator satisfies the lack.

It follows that "Amalek below" means that a person feels that this is Amalek and wants to blot him out because he does not want to hear his slander. This work belongs to man.

Amalek above means that his entire grip is in the concealment, and afterward the Creator gives the revelation of the face. This is considered that Amalek has been blotted out above, and this work belongs to the Creator.

What Does It Mean that Moses Was Perplexed about the Birth of the Moon, in the Work?

Article No. 23, Tav-Shin-Nun, 1989/90

RASHI brings the words of our sages who said about the words, "This month." These are his words: "Moses was perplexed about the birth of the moon, at what measure should it be seen so it is worthy of sanctifying. He showed him with a finger the moon in the firmament and said, "Such as this, see and sanctify."

We should understand what it implies to us in the work, that Moses was perplexed about the birth of the moon, and what it implies to us that the Creator showed Moses with His finger. Also, we should understand what our sages said (*Sukkah* 29), "Israel count by the moon, and idol-worshippers by the sun." What does the difference between counting by the moon and counting by the sun imply to us in the work?

It is known that the purpose of creation is His desire to do good to His creations. However, in order to bring to light the perfection of His deeds, there was a *Tzimtzum* [restriction] and concealment both on the Torah and *Mitzvot*, for in the Torah and *Mitzvot*, the delight and pleasure are clothed, and on the fact that He placed a *Tzimtzum* and concealment on the Creator Himself, as it is written, "Indeed You are a God who hides." This means that the Creator is concealed from us and we were given the commandment of faith, to believe in the Creator, that He leads the world with a guidance of good and doing good.

Although when a person begins to look at creation, it is full of flaws, meaning that The Good Who Does Good is not revealed in the world, one must believe above reason that His guidance is in a manner of good and doing good. Although he does not see this, he should say, "They have eyes and see not."

Therefore, when a person begins to take upon himself the burden of the kingdom of heaven, he immediately gets foreign thoughts that remove a person from the work of the Creator. And the more a person overcomes the thoughts, these thoughts of separation poke his mind and heart, and he thinks, "Although now I cannot overcome the foreign thoughts, I am waiting for an opportunity when I have more importance for Torah and *Mitzvot*, and then I will have the strength to overcome." And in the meantime, he leaves the campaign.

Concerning faith, Baal HaSulam said that to man, it is of little importance, since man wants to understand and to know everything. Therefore, when a person takes upon himself faith, which is against reason, meaning that the reason does not attain this, the body does not want to take upon itself such work, especially since this is not just any work, but on the basis of above the intellect, he must work "with all his heart and with all his soul," as our sages said, "even if he takes your soul."

Therefore, because of the concealment that occurred, there are ascents and descents here. That is, the matter of faith does not always illuminate to a person. But most important, a person must believe in reward and punishment. And concerning reward and punishment, we said many times that faith in reward and punishment apply in every discernment that a person is in, but the difference among people is in the *Kelim* [vessels].

There are people for whom reward and punishment are dressed in vessels of reception. That is, what the vessels of reception of a person can receive is considered a reward, and they do not speak at all about the reward that cannot clothe in vessels of reception, since reward that does not dress in the will to receive for oneself does not interest them.

Then, there are people for whom reward and punishment are called "reward and punishment" specifically when they dress in vessels of bestowal. That is, if they can be rewarded with bestowing contentment upon the Creator through their work, they regard this as a reward. For this purpose, they say that it is worthwhile to work and to come to this, that He will have good taste and pleasure in being able to perform acts of bestowal upon the Creator.

If they see that they do not have this feeling, they consider this a punishment, meaning that the Creator is pushing them away and does not want to accept them as servants of the King, since the Creator looks at them as indecent people. Hence, He cannot permit them to enter the King's palace and they are outside the King's palace. They understand why they deserve punishment, since they are still immersed in self-love.

Therefore, all of their work is for the Creator to help them be able to emerge from self-love. It follows that in general, everyone must work with reward and punishment, and in this there is no difference among people. The difference is which reward and which punishment we speak of.

Therefore, when a person is promised reward and punishment clothed in vessels of self-love, the body does not resist it so much, since to the extent that one believes in reward and punishment, he has fuel that enables him to overcome the foreign thoughts that come to him and do not let him believe in reward and punishment.

But those for whom the reward and punishment is what dresses in vessels of bestowal, the body resists this with all its might. The body says, "If I agree to what you are saying, that you believe in reward and punishment, then what reward do you promise me if I do not resist engaging in Torah and *Mitzvot*? The reward will be that you will revoke me altogether, so I, meaning the will to receive, will have no right at all. You want to have a reward such as that of King David, of whom our sages said about what David said, 'My heart is slain within me,' where 'slain,' means that they killed the evil inclination by fasting. Thus, if I believe you, that you will be rewarded with killing me, in return for observing Torah and *Mitzvot*, this reward that you hope for is actual death to me, so how can I help you kill me?'"

Therefore, one who wants the reward and punishment to be in vessels of bestowal, where if he is rewarded, this will be his reward, the body certainly objects. Hence, in this work begins the matter of ascents and descents, to such a point where a person often decides that this path of being rewarded with vessels of bestowal, that this will be his reward, this work is not for him, and he wants to escape from this campaign.

In this work, the reward and punishment—that he wants to be rewarded with vessels of bestowal—there must be a concealment of the face on Providence, or it will be utterly impossible that one will be able to do anything for the sake of the Creator.

Hence, when a person wants to take upon himself the kingdom of heaven, in a state of the time of concealment, *Malchut* is regarded as "the moon, which receives its light from the sun." However, in *Malchut* herself, no light is revealed on her own self, as it is written in *The Zohar*, "*Malchut* has nothing of her own, except that which her husband gives her."

That is, for the part of the lower one, one who takes upon himself the burden of the kingdom of heaven does not taste any flavor of importance from himself. "From himself" means that he does not want any flavor, but if the upper one gives, the lower one receives. This is considered that she has nothing of herself except that which her husband gives her. This she has. But for herself, she does not want anything.

Rather, a person agrees unconditionally to be a servant of the Creator, meaning whether he feels the flavor of importance or does not feel any flavor in the work. He says, "If I want to bring contentment to the Creator, why should I mind whether I take pleasure in my work? I must only believe that the Creator enjoys my work. And although I see that the work I am doing is not with all my heart, and I do not have the feeling that I am observing the King's commandment, since for now, everything is hidden from me, and in my view," says the person, "there is no value in what I do, and how can I say that the Creator enjoys such an act, and if at least such faith would illuminate for me, that the Creator enjoys this, then I, too, would feel some pleasure."

The answer is as Baal HaSulam said, that one must believe that when he does something and wants the Creator to enjoy what he is doing, He already feels pleasure above. The form of the act does not matter; it is enough that the person wants, even when a person sees that this act is in utter lowliness, the lowest that can be.

This is considered that he is walking on the straight path, meaning that the person does not say that his work is perfect; he does not lie to himself. Instead, he says that the work he is doing could not be more flawed, and this is true, but he believes in the sages, who tell us to believe in what is written, "The Lord is high and the low will see." For this reason, he believes that the Creator does enjoy this work.

Now we should interpret what we asked, What is the meaning of Moses being perplexed about the birth of the moon, to what extent should it be seen and be fit for sanctification? We should interpret that the birth of the moon implies that when a person begins to take upon himself the burden of the kingdom of heaven, and "begins" means the beginning of man's birth, at that time, the question is, To what extent is the acceptance of the kingdom of heaven, meaning the faith that one takes upon oneself.

On this measure of faith he performs actions," and the "birth of the moon" means that the faith in the Creator is still not felt in all his organs. However, he already wants to assume the kingship, but the body disagrees with it, and he works with his body through compulsion. In other words, on one hand, he wants to believe in the Creator and love Him, and on the other hand, the body resists this and he feels his lowliness.

We can say about such a person that he is in a state of "concealment of the face." But those people who have no connection to faith in the Creator are not in a state of concealment of the face. That is, they do not believe that the Creator is hidden from them, meaning that the Creator has covered Himself so they would not feel Him for the purpose of the correction of creation.

For this reason, we do not speak of them at all. Rather, the beginning of the speaking in the work is from the time when a person begins to take upon himself the burden of the kingdom of heaven, and based on this faith he observes Torah and Mitzvot. With respect to him, we begin to speak of the matter of the birth of the moon, to what extent should it be seen and become worthy of sanctification. In other words, at what level of faith can we say that he already has Kedusha [holiness] and can say that the Creator enjoys what he is doing because his actions are of Kedusha. Even though the things he does are compulsory, since the whole body resists what he wants, so how can it be said that the Creator enjoys such actions, when "his heart is not with him"?

For example, if a person gives a gift to his friend, and his friend knows that although he is giving him the gift, it is not with all his heart, since he still does not love him. That person would not receive the gift from him. But in reality, we see that if someone invites his friend to a meal, and the guest knows that this invitation is not from the bottom of the heart, but is compulsory, if the guest knew this, he would decline the offer. So, how can a person say about a state of concealment, when he is doing his work in a compulsory manner, that the Creator accepts his work and enjoys it?

However, we must believe in the sages, who tell us that all our work, however we work, if the person attributes the work to the Creator, even if it is in utter lowliness, the Creator enjoys it. The person should be happy that he can do things while in a state of lowliness.

The person should tell himself that He enjoys this work, which is entirely above reason. Reasonably thinking, this work is not considered "work," meaning an important act that the Creator enjoys. Yet, he believes in the sages, who told us that the Creator does enjoy, but this is above reason.

By this we should interpret why Moses was perplexed about the birth of the moon: How can it be that about such work during the birth, which is a state of concealment, can we say that it is *Kedusha* and that the Creator enjoys such actions?

It is written, "Moses was perplexed about the birth of the moon. The Creator showed him with a finger the moon in the firmament and said to him: 'Such as this, see and sanctify.'"

We asked, What does it imply that He showed him with a finger? This is as Baal HaSulam said about what our sages said (End of *Taanit*): "Rabbi Elazar said, 'The Creator is destined to pardon the righteous, and dwell among them, and each one will point with his finger.'" He said that "point with his finger" implies the light of *Hochma*, called "seeing," meaning that everyone will be rewarded with the revelation of *Hochma* [wisdom].

Accordingly, we can interpret here "the Creator showed Moses with a finger and said, 'Such as this, see and sanctify,'" as it is written, "showed him the moon in the firmament," meaning that the birth of the moon is seen in the firmament. The "firmament" is the "separating *Masach* [screen]," as our sages said, "And God made the firmament, and it divided between water and water," and the lower water cries, "We want to be before the King."

The moon that is in the firmament at the time of the birth is in concealment of the face. The Creator said, "This measure that you see during the birth, such as this, see and sanctify. Although this is utter lowliness, which is completely above reason, since all his actions are still compulsory, still, if you attribute this work to My name, I enjoy it as though he were pointing with a finger."

As is said in the words of our sages, "The Creator is destined to pardon the righteous, and each one will point with his finger." That is, I enjoy this as though they have already been rewarded with Hochma. For this reason, if a person overcomes in this, and believes with faith in the sages, he can ascend, since he says to the Creator, "I want to subjugate myself unconditionally, so You do not need to give me a good taste in the work."

That is, a person says to the Creator, "If You see that I am enjoying, then I can work in order to bestow, so You will enjoy, too. Otherwise, I cannot work in order to bestow." It follows that he dictates to the Creator how He should behave with him, meaning according to man's mind. We should say about this that the Creator said, "For My thoughts are not your thoughts."

Rather, the person says, "I do not mind how much I understand about appreciating the importance of observing Torah and Mitzvot, that I will receive from this such great inspiration that the whole body will surrender to the Creator and do everything with love and joy. Rather, by this, I see that I can do the holy work only by coercion. It follows that I still do not have the knowledge to understand and appreciate whom I am serving, meaning to feel that I am serving a great King. Thus, how can I say that I am working in Kedusha? After all, I have foreign thoughts against the work of the Creator, to such an extent that I must do everything coercively." And yet, he believes with faith in the sages.

The answer to this is that the Creator said, "Such as this, see and sanctify." That is, although he still does not see the measure of importance of the moon, where "moon" implies the kingdom of heaven, and the moon, the Creator showed with a finger in the firmament that it is concealment toward the lower ones, as said in the interpretation to, "And God made the firmament, and divided between the water that is below the firmament."

In other words, the lower ones cannot look up, since there is a firmament that hides and divides from the lower ones. This was the Creator's answer to Moses, who was perplexed, to what extent it should be seen and be worthy of sanctification, meaning so he can say, "This is *Kedusha*, and this *Kedusha* ascends before Me and I accept it as *Kedusha*."

He showed him with a finger. That is, "Such as this, see and sanctify." In other words, as the moon in the firmament is in utter concealment, and the person sanctifies it and says, "Whatever grip I have in spirituality, I accept it with love, even though my work is compulsory, this, too, is important, that I have some faith in the Creator, that I can nonetheless bend myself and do something by coercion in order to please the Creator, and this is the least that I have." The person should say that it is as important in his eyes as if He is pointing with a finger.

This is the meaning of "Israel count by the moon, and idol-worshippers count by the sun." We asked, What does this come to teach us in the work? We should interpret that since man is a small world, which comprises the quality of "Israel" and the quality of "the nations of the world," Israel count by the moon, and idol-worshippers count by the sun." Something important is called "something that is counted."

Among the nations of the world in a person, it is when the work of the Creator shines for him like the sun. As the sun is called "day," as our sages said, "If the matter is as clear to you as light, meaning as light that shines" (*Pesachim* 2b). In other words, the matter of work shines throughout his body. At that time he can work and engage in Torah and *Mitzvot*.

But if it does not shine for him throughout his body, he cannot do the holy work. This discernment is called "the nations of the world," who serve only the sun, meaning specifically when it illuminates for them, and they cannot overcome and work coercively.

But the Israel in a person count by the moon. That is, they sanctify their work during the birth of the moon, when the light she should receive from the sun is still not seen. Rather, "Such as this, see and sanctify." He does not wait until some illumination from above shines for him, and then he will begin to work. Rather, for whatever grip he has on spirituality, he thanks the Creator. This is called "the quality of Israel," and specifically by this is one rewarded with ascending on the rungs of holiness, as was said, "In return for 'And Moses hid his face for he was afraid to look,' he was rewarded with, 'The image of the Lord does he behold.'" In other words, specifically by taking upon oneself to do the work of holiness unconditionally, a person is rewarded with achieving the purpose of creation, which is His desire to do good to His creations.

Such as this we see presented in *The Zohar* (*Beresheet Bet*, Item 14), "Within that palace are all those who suffered torments and illnesses in this world to be corrected in complete repentance, who thanked and praised their Master each day, and never cancelled their prayer. That is, it is the nature of a man who is concerned before Him to see himself as full of deficiencies. This enables him to always pray for complementing his deficiencies. However, he cannot thank and praise the Creator because in his mind, he has nothing for which to thank and praise. On the other hand, if he overcomes and always thanks and praises the Creator each day for the great kindness toward him, he necessarily feels satisfaction in his state, and again he cannot pray and complain to the Creator about his deficiencies." *The Zohar* says that "the merit of those righteous is that they are complete on both sides. Therefore, they were rewarded with entering the palace of *Hod* in the Garden of Eden."

It therefore follows that a person should walk on both lines, although they contradict one another, for specifically by this are we rewarded with entering the King's palace.

What Does, "Everything that Comes to Be a Burnt Offering Is Male," Mean in the Work?

Article No. 24, Tav-Shin-Nun, 1989/90

It is written in *The Zohar* (*VaYikra*, Item 70), "'If his offering is a burnt offering.' Rabbi Hiya started, 'For My thoughts are not your thoughts.' The thought of the Creator is superior and the beginning of everything. From that thought, ways and paths extend to devise the holy name. And from that thought emanate the written Torah and the oral Torah, which is *Malchut*. Man's thought is the beginning of everything. Ways and paths extend from that thought to divert one's ways in this world and in the next world, and from that thought emerges the filth of the evil inclination to harm oneself and all others. Also, transgressions, sins, and evil doing come from that thought, as well as idolatry, incest, and bloodshed. It is written about that, 'For My thoughts are not your thoughts.'"

In Item 73, it says, "Everything that comes to be a burnt offering is male and not female, since the burnt offering rises ["rises" is spelled the same as "offering" in Hebrew] over the heart, meaning on the thought, which is above the heart, since the thought, which is *Hochma* [wisdom], is regarded as male and the heart as female, meaning *Bina* [understanding], as in 'the heart understands.'"

We should understand what is "the thought of the Creator" in the work, and what is "the thought of man" in the work, of which the writing says, according to what is written in *The Zohar*, "for My thoughts are not your thoughts." We should also understand what it implies to us when he says, "a burnt offering is male," since it atones for the thought, which is male. What does this imply to us in the work, so we will know how to behave?

It is known that although the purpose of creation is to do good to His creations, for the creatures to receive delight and pleasure, in order to bring to light the perfection of His deeds, a correction was done, called "*Tzimtzum* [restriction] and concealment," on the delight and pleasure. Since all creations were created with a desire to receive delight and pleasure, it follows that man cannot do anything unless he knows he can receive delight and pleasure from that thing. Otherwise, he cannot make a single move, since it will contradict the root of the creatures.

Sometimes, when a person does act, although he derives no pleasure from these actions, it is because he knows that by this he will receive delight and pleasure later, which he will be given in return for his work, meaning for the actions he took and in which he took no pleasure. Only because of the pleasure he will receive after the work, it gives him strength to do the work from which he does not enjoy at the moment, but will in the future.

Yet, if the reward is not certain, he has no power to work when he does not enjoy it. For example, a mother feeds her children. Although it is work to buy the groceries and prepare them for eating, and she also feeds them, we should discern two actions here: 1) actions she would give up, 2) actions she does not intend to give up.

Buying groceries and preparing them for eating, she would give up. We see that among the rich, there are people who buy the groceries and there is a cook. This shows that the mother can do without them. But the mother looking at the children eating, although while looking at the children eat, the mother does not eat, in that state she gives up on herself but she enjoys seeing the children eat. It will never occur to the mother to think, "What do I get out of watching the little children eat?"

She does not want "the next world" for this, or "this world," since she derives pleasure from this act, so she needs no reward. Hence, if the taste in Torah and Mitzvot [commandments/good deeds] were revealed, as our sages said, that the 613 Mitzvot are called "613 Pekudin [Aramaic: deposits]," as is explained in the Sulam [Ladder commentary on The Zohar], in each Mitzva [singular of Mitzvot] there is a special light that shines in it, if this were revealed and they would not have to believe it, the whole world would engage only in Torah and Mitzvot.

However, since a concealment was placed on the delight and pleasure, and it is not revealed before a person is rewarded with vessels of bestowal, there are disturbances from the body, which cry out, "Why do you want to go against the nature with which the Creator created man, to receive delight and pleasure? You want to give this up?" Although a person promises the body that it will be rewarded, in that it observes the commandments of the Torah, meaning it will be rewarded, the body seemingly asks, "In what Kelim [vessels] will I receive reward, in vessels of reception or in vessels of bestowal?"

At that time, if the person says to it, "You will receive the reward in vessels of reception," the body asks, "Why did the Creator give us so many commandments? After all, He is a merciful Father and is good and does good, so why does He not give us all the reward He wants to give for observing all 613 *Mitzvot* in return for observing half of the 613 *Mitzvot?* Why does He mind if He gives the full reward for observing a small part of the Torah and *Mitzvot?* Also, why do we need to work so hard to observe the full 613 *Mitzvot?*"

This is similar to the allegory about the mother who feeds her children with food and drink, but she must buy the groceries and cook them and so forth, which she would forego. What she does not forego is that she sees and looks at how her children eat. The little children, she herself feeds and enjoys it. She does not want to relinquish this work, since she enjoys the work itself and does not need any reward for this work.

We therefore have two things:

1) It is not so far from the intellect. That is, one who wants to receive reward in vessels of reception but asks why the Creator wants us to observe so many *Mitzvot*, meaning that He should have given all the reward He wants to give for observing half of the 613 *Mitzvot*, since there is no pleasure in the work he is doing, but rather in the reward he will receive afterward, this is regarded as "receiving reward in the next world." That is, during the work, he feels no pleasure, and the only reason he wants to work is for the reward that will come later.

2) We can discern in the reward that he wants to receive the reward in vessels of bestowal, meaning to have love of the Creator and to feel that he is serving the King. It follows that he hopes to receive a reward, and he will receive this reward later, in *Kelim* [vessels] that are in this world, meaning in the present. Then, when he is rewarded with 613 *Pekudin*, when he receives each *Mitzva* in the manner of "this world," he does not say, "Why were we given so many *Mitzvot?*"

Likewise, in the corporeal world there is no one who is angry at the Creator for preparing for us so many corporeal pleasures. In the same way, when he is rewarded with 613 *Pekudin*, at that time he feels in each *Mitzva* a different taste and does not intend to relinquish it.

But there is a big flaw here while working in the form of 613 *Eitin* [Aramaic: counsels], meaning when the Torah and *Mitzvot* are only "tips" that concern how to receive the vessels of bestowal, since the body's resistance is intense because it is completely against his will to receive with which man was born.

It follows that they (work and reward) are two separate discernments. When the reward is in vessels of reception, he has fuel because he can receive reward. However, he always has exertion since the reward he receives is in "the next world," meaning not now but some other time, when he comes, he will receive reward. In other words, he looks at the reward he will receive later.

It follows that he would be happier if he received a greater reward for less work, since he is looking at the reward. It turns out that he always has exertion because to him, the reward is the reason that compels him to engage in Torah and *Mitzvot*. This is similar to the corporeal world: When we are paid for the work, the work is only a means. If he could receive the reward for less work, certainly, each one would choose a place that gives more reward for less work.

Conversely, when a person is rewarded with vessels of bestowal, the concealment and *Tzimtzum* that were placed on the Torah and *Mitzvot* are lifted from him and he is rewarded with 613 *Pekudin*. That is, in each *Mitzva* that he performs, he obtains the taste in the *Mitzva*. It follows that the reward is in this world, meaning in the present state that a person is in. Certainly, it cannot be said that a person should relinquish the work, since the work itself is the place to receive the reward. It follows that in "vessels of bestowal," the 613 *Mitzvot* are considered "rest," and not "work and labor."

According to the above, we should interpret what *The Zohar* says about the verse, "for My thoughts are not your thoughts." We asked, What does this imply to us in the work when it says that ways and paths extend from the thought of the Creator "to devise the holy name," whereas from the thought of man extend "the filth of the evil inclination to harm oneself and all others. Also, transgressions, sins, and evil doing come from that thought, as well as idolatry, incest, and bloodshed."

The text says about this, "for My thoughts are not your thoughts." The "thought of the Creator" refers to the thought of creation, which is to do good to His creations. That is, He wants only to bestow abundance upon the creatures. For this reason, the Torah and *Mitzvot* that He has given us to do, we must say that His intention is not that we will give Him this work and He will accept it. After all, His desire is only to bestow. This is why he says that from the thought of the Creator "ways and paths extend to devise the holy name."

We should understand the meaning of "to devise the holy name." According to what we learn, the purpose of creation is to do good to His creations. It follows that the "holy name" of the Creator is The Good Who Does Good. Because that name is hidden from the creatures as long as they do not have vessels of bestowal, we were given the Torah and *Mitzvot* as *Eitin*, meaning counsels by which to obtain the vessels of bestowal, as our sages said, "The light in it reforms him."

It follows that our work in Torah and *Mitzvot* is not because He needs us to observe His *Mitzva*. Rather, the created beings observe His *Mitzvot*, for by this the created beings correct themselves so they can be rewarded with vessels of bestowal. This is the meaning of what is written, "to devise the holy name," for by this, each one will feel that the name of the Creator is The Good Who Does Good.

But (from) man's thoughts extend "the filth of the evil inclination" because man, who is a "created being," existence from absence, thinks only about how to receive and not bestow. Although this is the root of man, concealment and *Tzimtzum* were placed on that will to receive, which is why the evil inclination extends from this thought in man. In other words, when a person must perform acts of bestowal in order to have *Dvekut* [adhesion] with the Creator, called "equivalence of form," that desire depicts to a person depictions that he will suffer by giving of his strength to others.

Therefore, when a person wants to observe Torah and Mitzvot with the aim to bestow and not receive anything that concerns his own benefit, this thought depicts to him how he will suffer. With that power of depiction, it prevents a person from achieving Dvekut with the Creator.

This is the meaning of the words "From that thought emerges the filth of the evil inclination," as Baal HaSulam said about what our sages said, "The serpent came over Eve and cast filth within her." He said that Zuhama [filth] is Zu-Ma [what is this?], meaning that in every matter of Kedusha [holiness], the serpent, which is the evil inclination, comes and says to a person, "What is this?" meaning "What will you get out of wanting to work and do everything for the sake of the Creator and not for your own sake?" It follows that "for My thoughts are not your thoughts" means that the thought of the Creator is to bestow, while the thought of man is only to receive.

Now we can understand what we asked, What does it imply to us when The Zohar says, "a burnt offering is male," since it atones for the thought, which is male, since a thought is Hochma and is considered male, and the heart, which is Bina [understanding], is female, as in "the heart understands."

Our sages said, "The eye sees and the heart covets." We should understand what the "eye" implies. It is known that eyes are called Hochma [wisdom], meaning thought, and the thought is considered male. It is said about it in The Zohar that when a person must take upon himself the burden of the kingdom of heaven, this faith that a person believes is called "mind." That thought impacts the heart, and then the heart begins to covet this thing that came as a thought in his mind. In that sense, the eye is called "a thought." The wisdom, what he sees and likes, is what he gives to the heart; hence, the heart covets the thing that is in the mind.

According to the above, the thought of the Creator is to bestow. We should interpret about this as our sages said (Avot, Chapter 2:1), "Know what is above you; an eye that sees." We should interpret that man should know what is above him, meaning what is above his thought, that there is the thought of the Creator there, which is called "an eye that sees." It is as *The Zohar* says, that "eye" is called "thought," and thought is called "wisdom," which is male.

As we learned, the light of *Hochma* comes from the Giver to the receiver. Hence, man must resemble the "eye" of above and be a giver to the Creator. This is called "equivalence of form," and it is called "faith in the Creator." It is called "mind," meaning a thought that man should be in equivalence of form with the Creator.

This is as it is written in the essay, "A Speech for the Completion of The Zohar": "Similarly, all your actions will be to bestow and to benefit others. Thus, you will equalize your form with the form of the qualities of the Creator, and this is spiritual *Dvekut*. There is a discernment of 'mind' and a discernment of 'heart' in the above-mentioned equivalence of form. The engagement in Torah and *Mitzvot* in order to bestow contentment upon one's Maker is equivalence of form in the mind. This is because the Creator does not think of Himself—whether He exists or whether He watches over His creations, and other such doubts. Similarly, one who wishes to achieve equivalence of form must not think of these things, as well, when it is clear that the Creator does not think of them, since there is no greater disparity of form than that. Hence, anyone who thinks of such matters is certainly separated from Him."

It therefore follows that if a person believes in "Know what is above you; the eye sees," "know" means *Daat* [knowledge], and *Daat* means connection and *Dvekut*. "What is above you, an eye that sees," meaning that the eye of the Creator, which is *Hochma* [wisdom], and "know" refers to *Dvekut*, when a person adheres to "above you," which is the "mind," meaning faith.

According to the rule, "The eye sees and the heart covets," meaning that the thought, which is "male," gives to the heart, which is "coveting and desire," then as the thought, which is "faith," has equivalence with the Creator, the heart, too, which is the will to receive, does not want to use its own quality, which is reception, but rather to be influenced by the thought and wants to be a giver like the thought. It follows that if a person is complete with equivalence of form in the "mind," it influences the heart, so the heart, too, will be as in "All your works will be for the sake of the Creator."

This is as we explained about what our sages said, "Anyone in whom there is fear of heaven, his words are heard." This means that anyone who assumes the burden of the kingdom of heaven, which is faith, the body hears his words, meaning that the whole body obeys his voice for the above reason that if the thought is faith above reason, equivalence of form, then the thought, which is male, influences the heart, which is female, as it is written, "The heart understands." This is the meaning of what The Zohar says, "Bina is the heart," and she is female.

Therefore, if it is a burnt offering, it is male. He says that the reason is that a burnt offering comes to atone for the thought, which is male, Hochma. That is, if a person sinned, meaning blemished his thought, which is faith above reason, he must correct what he has blemished. Since faith is discerned as "the eye sees," which is "wisdom of above," meaning that the thought of the Creator is His desire to do good to His creations, meaning to bestow upon the lower ones, and that person blemished this, meaning he does not believe that there is a leader to the world, who watches over the creations as The Good Who Does Good, and man must praise and thank the Creator, if a person does not believe that the Creator is the Giver, called "male," the person must bring a male offering, which is its corresponding discernment, which he blemished. For this reason, the blemish of the thought is very serious, since this is the whole matter of the purpose of creation. When a person does not believe this, it is regarded that he sinned and blemished the thought, and must make the correction in the same discernment.

According to the above, we should interpret what The Zohar says about the words, "If his offering is a burnt offering," "for My thoughts are not your thoughts." He says, "Also, the written Torah and the oral Torah, which is Malchut, were emanated from that thought." We should interpret that in the work, Malchut means "the kingdom of heaven," which is faith, while "Oral Torah" is called Torah. In other words, it is impossible to be rewarded with the Torah if one has not been rewarded with faith, as our sages said, "It is forbidden to teach idol-worshippers the Torah."

But once he has been rewarded with faith, he can be rewarded with the Torah. This is the meaning of the words, "from that thought," meaning from the thought of creation, which is to do good to His creations, extend faith and Torah. That is, the fact that we were given faith, where everyone asks why He placed a concealment on His guidance and we need faith for this, the answer is that this, too, is in order to do good to His creations, called "in order to bring to light the perfection of His deeds." It follows that when we are adhered to His thought, we have everything. This is unlike what man's thought says, but from that thought emerge transgressions, sins, and evil deeds, as it is written, "for My thoughts are not your thoughts."

Therefore, man must exert to focus all his work on being only in *Dvekut* with His thought, and believe that He watches over the world as The Good Who Does Good. When he has this faith, he will be rewarded with everything.

What Is, "Praise the Lord, All Nations," in the Work?

Article No. 25, Tav-Shin-Nun, 1989/90

The writing says (Psalms 117), "Praise the Lord, all nations; laud Him, all the peoples, for His mercy has prevailed over us, and the truth of the Lord is everlasting, Hallelujah." We should understand why all the nations must praise the Creator, since it is written, "for His mercy has prevailed over us." It would seem that it should be to the contrary, that by being merciful with the people of Israel, the nations should be angry with the Creator. Yet, here the writing says, "Laud Him, all the peoples, for His mercy has prevailed over us." Can this be?

We should interpret this according to the work. When we speak of one person, since every person is a small world, as it is written in *The Zohar*, there is the quality of the "nations of the world" in a person, and there is the quality of "Israel," and the Israel in a person is in exile under the rule of the nations of the world.

In other words, it is known that Israel means *Yashar-El* [straight to the Creator], that he wants all his actions to be directly to the Creator, meaning that everything will be for the sake of the Creator.

However, the thoughts of the nations of the world are only about their own benefit, as it is known that each nation has its own lust. They govern the Israel within him and do not let Israel do what Israel must do. Instead, each time, each and every nation imposes its lust on a person so he will do as it wishes. This is called "the people of Israel being in exile."

However, we should know and believe that everything that a person can receive in vessels of reception is not more than a tiny light compared to the light of the pleasure that is clothed in spirituality, which is received in vessels of bestowal. And yet, our sages said a rule: "One does not die with half one's wishes in one's hand."

That is, there is not a person in the world who can say that he is the happiest person in the world, according to the rule, "One who has one hundred wants two hundred." Hence, there is not a person in the world who is carefree, at rest, or at peace. Rather, each and every one has his own deficiency, as it is written, "Envy, lust, and honor bring one out of the world."

It follows that in the end, every person suffers because he cannot satisfy his deficiencies. But one who is rewarded and receives from the Creator vessels of bestowal, in these *Kelim* [vessels] he receives the delight and pleasure that the Creator has prepared for the created beings, and then a person lives in a world that is all good. It is as our sages said (*Avot*, Chapter 6:1), "Rabbi Meir says, 'Anyone who engage in Torah *Lishma* [for Her sake] is rewarded with many things. Moreover, the whole world is worthwhile for him.'"

In other words, he sees how the world is worthwhile for him, since when a person receives everything in vessels of bestowal, which is equivalence of form, called *Dvekut* [adhesion], which is called *Lishma*, the delight and pleasure that is found in the thought of creation called "His desire to do good to His creations" is imparted upon him to the extent of His ability.

This is as described in the essay *Matan Torah* ["The Giving of the Torah"] (Item 6), "Our sages tell us that the world had not been created but for the purpose of observing Torah and *Mitzvot*. That is, the aim of the Creator from the time He created His creation is to reveal His Godliness to others. This is because the revelation of His Godliness reaches the creature as pleasant bounty that is ever growing until it reaches the desired measure. And by that, the lowly rise with true recognition and become a chariot to Him, and to cleave unto Him, until they achieve their final completion."

It therefore follows that when a person is rewarded with vessels of bestowal, he is rewarded with the delight and pleasure that were in the thought of creation. This is called, "When the Lord favors a man's ways, even his enemies make peace with him." Rabbi Yehoshua Ben Levi interprets, "This is the serpent" (Jerusalem Talmud, *Terumot* 8:3). The serpent is the evil inclination, who is the appointee of the seventy nations. As was said, the quality of the nations of the world in one's body cause him not to be able to be rewarded with the delight and pleasure.

It therefore follows that when a person receives delight and pleasure, the vessels of reception are also mitigated by his using the vessels of reception in order to bestow. Therefore, they, too, receive the delight and pleasure. This is called "When the Lord favors a man's ways," which is when he works only for the sake of the Creator, called "engaging *Lishma*." Then, he is rewarded with many things, as said in the words of Rabbi Meir.

For this reason, the nations of the world in a person's body must also praise the Creator because they are now receiving delight and pleasure by a person being rewarded with vessels of bestowal, called "*Kelim* of *Hesed* [mercy]." This is the meaning of the words, "Praise the Lord, all nations; laud Him, all the peoples." But why should they praise the Creator? "for His mercy has prevailed over us."

That is, it is because the *Kelim* of *Hesed* overcame the vessels of reception. And who gave the power to make the *Hesed* prevail? Only the Creator gave this, as our sages said, "Man's inclination overcomes him every day. Unless the Creator helps him, he cannot overcome it."

It follows that the nations, too, should praise the Creator "for His mercy has prevailed over us." We have been rewarded with the Creator's mercy, and by this we now see "the truth of the Lord," meaning the truth that the Creator watches over the world with a guidance of good and doing good, which is now revealed to all the nations.

It follows that man's enemies, which is the evil inclination, called "enemy," as it is written, "If your enemy is hungry, feed him bread," referring to the evil inclination, as our sages said, that King Solomon would call the evil inclination by the name "enemy," so he, too, will make peace with him. This is called, "And you shall love the Lord your God with all your heart, with both your inclinations," namely with the good inclination and with the evil inclination. When a person's vessels of reception obtain the force to receive in order to bestow, at that time he serves the Creator with the evil inclination, too. That is, the evil inclination also loves the Creator, for it, too, receives delight and pleasure.

This is why it is written, "and the truth of the Lord," as he interprets in *The Study of the Ten Sefirot* about the seventh correction of the thirteen corrections of *Dikna*, called "and truth," that it is called "and truth" because in this correction it becomes revealed to all that this is the truth, that such was the purpose of creation: to do good to His creations.

It therefore follows that in the work, we should interpret what *The Zohar* says, that all the nations have a minister over them, but as for the people of Israel, only the Creator governs them, for the people of Israel are the portion of the Lord, since the nations of the world receive for themselves, as it is written in *The Zohar* about the verse, "The grace of the nations is a sin, for all the good that they do, they do for themselves." That is, everything they do is only for their own benefit.

This is called "seventy nations," meaning "seventy rulers," where each nation has a special lust. This is generally called "the evil inclination," since it causes man to become separated from the Creator. This is regarded as the ministers ruling over the nations of the world. In other words, they do not feel that there is a Creator who leads the world.

Conversely, the quality of Israel, which means *Yashar-El* [straight to the Creator], feel that they are in the portion of the Creator, since all their actions are for the sake of the Creator and not for their own sake. This is considered that the Creator took the people of Israel to His portion, and no minister governs them. In other words, one who enters the quality of Israel says that only the Creator governs him, and no other force.

This means that both ascents and descents, the Creator does everything. This is as is said (in the Shabbat [Sabbath] Morning Prayer), "God, Master of all the deeds." That is, everything that a person does, the Creator is the Operator. As Baal HaSulam said, before the fact, a person should say that it is all up to him, as our sages said, "If I am not for me, who is for me?" meaning that man does everything. But after the fact, he should say that the Creator does everything, for He is the Master of all the deeds.

According to the above, we should interpret what is written (Psalms 89), "The heavens will praise Your wonders, O Lord; Your faithfulness also in the assembly of the holy ones. For who in the skies is comparable to the Lord? Who among the sons of gods is like the Lord?" We should understand how this concerns us that the heavens are thankful for the work of the Creator, since the main thing we need to know is what we must do.

In the work, we should interpret that "heaven" and "earth" are two states in which man is: 1) In a state of ascent, it is considered that a person is in "heaven." That is, as heaven is called "giver," if a person is in a state of ascent, it means that then he wants to bestow upon the Creator. This is considered that all his works are for the sake of the Creator. 2) When a person is in a descent and falls to the earth, "earth" is the quality of reception. In other words, a person has fallen into a state where he cannot do anything unless it satisfies his will to receive. This is called "earth."

According to the above, a person should believe that the Creator does everything. That is, once a person has overcome his will to receive and works only for the sake of the Creator, it is said, "The heavens will praise Your wonders, O Lord." That is, this act is truly a wondrous act, since by nature, man cannot do anything that is not for his own benefit. But now the Creator has raised him to heaven.

It is written, "And those people will thank," those who are now in a state of "heaven," will thank the Creator, since this work is done only by the Creator and not by man, for man is incapable of doing anything that does not concern his own benefit, since he was created with such a nature.

"Your faithfulness also in the assembly of the holy ones." This means that faith, which is in the assembly, who now feel that they are holy, as it written, "You will be holy, for I am holy." That is, as the Creator wants to bestow, so man should have a desire only to bestow, as it is written, "Your faithfulness also in the assembly of the holy ones," that this, too, comes from the wonders of the Creator—that they have been rewarded with faith, and because of this they are regarded as an assembly of holy ones. There is a double meaning [in Hebrew].

It is written, "For who in the skies." That is, one who is in the skies, who was rewarded with being in the heavens, meaning with the desire to bestow, called "heaven," "is comparable to You?" This seems perplexing, because according to the literal meaning, the verse should say, "For who in the skies is comparable to the Lord." Is there anyone who can make a mistake and say that someone will value himself similar to the Creator?

In the work, we should interpret that the writing tells us that one should not think that the overcoming, the work and labor that he has given, by this he became the quality of heaven—a giver. However, the person had nothing to do with it, that he helped the Creator be able to pull a person out of self-love into the desire to bestow for the sake of the Creator.

Afterward, the verse says about this: "Who among the sons of the gods is like the Lord?" In other words, those strong and mighty people should not think that the fact that they had the power to overcome their evil was by their own strength. Rather, everything came from the power of the Creator, as it is written, "Who is like the Lord?" able to overcome the evil without the Creator's help.

Yet, it is written, "He who comes to purify is aided," which implies that man's work did help the Creator, creating a place to give help, so why is it said that everything is done by the Creator? We should interpret what our sages said, "He who comes to purify." That is, if we see that the person came on his own to purify, which is an awakening from below, the answer to this is "He is being aided."

That is, the fact that he has come to purify comes by assistance from above. Otherwise, he would not come to purify. It follows that the fact came to purify also comes from the Creator and not from the created being. This contradicts human reason, that on one hand, we say, "He who comes to purify," which means that man can choose to do, and on the other hand, we say that the Creator does everything, so they contradict one another.

Maimonides writes in his interpretation on the Mishnah (Avot, Chapter 3:15), "Everything is expected; everything is revealed and known to the Creator in advance, and the permission is given. Nevertheless, man has the authority to choose the good or the bad. In other words, man has free choice. Knowing the Creator, that He knows everything in advance, does not obligate a person in any way. Although this is impossible according to our attainment and understanding, but the Creator's knowing is not the same as our knowing. There is no similarity between them whatsoever, since He and His knowing are one. As we do not attain the existence of the Creator with our limited mind, so we do not attain His knowing."

Thus, we see in the words of Maimonides that it is not in our attainment to understand the two above matters, which contradict one another. Baal HaSulam said that although they contradict one another, it is before a person is rewarded with private Providence. However, after he has been rewarded with private Providence, he can understand that this is not a contradiction. But with the external mind, it is impossible to understand this.

This means that there is a contradiction between reward and punishment and private Providence, but with regard to everything, we must go above reason and do both. As we see in the words of *The Zohar* (*Tazria*, Item 6), "'For her price is far above pearls.' He asks, 'It should have said 'worth,' that it is harder to buy her than pearls, why does it say 'her price'? He replies, 'All those who do not adhere to her completely and are not whole with her, she sells them and turns them over to other nations. It is as you say, 'And the children of Israel abandoned the Lord,' and He sold them to the hand of Sisera. And then they are all far from those high and holy pearls, which are the secrets and the internality of the Torah, for they will have no share in them.'"

It follows that here he speaks of reward and punishment. That is, in the work, we should interpret that when a person receives some awakening from above and does not know how to maintain that state of ascent, since he does not appreciate it as he should when the King calls on him to enter a little bit into *Kedusha* [holiness], at that time the *Kedusha* sells the person to other nations. That is, the thoughts and desires of other nations control him. It follows that on one hand, a person should say, "Everything is under Providence," and on the other hand, there is reward and punishment. However, it is as in the words of Maimonides.

What Is, "There Is None as Holy as the Lord, for There Is None Besides You," in the Work?

Article No. 26, Tav-Shin-Nun, 1989/90

The Zohar says (*Tazria*, Item 37), "'If a woman inseminates, she delivers a male child.' Rabbi Yehuda started, 'There is none as holy as the Lord, for there is none besides You, and there is no rock like our God.' This verse is perplexing. It is written, 'There is none as holy as the Lord.' This implies that there is another one who is holy, though a little worse than the Creator. Also, 'There is no rock like our God' implies that there is another rock, but is a little worse than the Creator. He replies that there are many holy ones. There are holy ones above, meaning angels, and Israel are also holy, but there are none as holy as the Creator. And what is the reason? 'For there is none besides You.' Rather, the holiness of the Creator is without their holiness, of the angels and of Israel, for He does not need their holiness. However, they are not holy without You. 'And there is no rock like our God' means that the Creator forms a form within a form, meaning the form of the *Ubar* [embryo] within the form of its mother."

We should understand the connection between "If a woman inseminates, she delivers a male child" and the verse, "There is none as holy as the Lord, and there is no rock like our God." Also, how did you think of saying that the people of Israel impart *Kedusha* [holiness] upon the Creator, for which the text should tell us, "There is none as holy as the Lord"? And also, what is the meaning in the work, that he interprets "There is no rock like our God," as the Creator forming a form within a form?

It is known that the order of the work is that we must achieve *Dvekut* [adhesion] with the Creator, as it is written, "You will be holy, for I am holy." This means that as the Creator is holy and separated from reception, for the Creator only bestows and does not receive, we must also be holy and separated from reception, and all our actions must be only in order to bestow upon the Creator.

However, since we were born with a nature of self-reception, how can we be rewarded with *Kedusha* and be separated from self-love? This quality of the will to receive for oneself is called "evil inclination," and our sages said about it, "The Creator said, 'I have created the evil inclination; I have created the Torah as a spice.'" In other words, by engaging in Torah and *Mitzvot* [commandments/good deeds] in order to achieve *Lishma* [for Her sake], the light in the Torah will reform him. This means that he will emerge from the governance of evil and will do good. That is, he will be able to do good deeds, which are called "acts of bestowal."

It therefore follows that only man's actions when he engages in Torah and *Mitzvot* cause him to be rewarded with *Kedusha*, meaning to be holy and separated from acts of self-reception, and will be in a state of "As He is merciful, so you are merciful," regarded as equivalence of form. This is called "You will be holy, for I am holy."

It therefore follows that a person has been rewarded with *Kedusha* by himself, as our sages said, "If I am not for me, who is for me?"

That is, "According to the sorrow, so is the reward." This means that according to the labor that one gives in order to be awarded with the reward, to that extent he is rewarded, as our sages said, "He who comes to purify is aided."

Therefore, this means that the Creator does not give assistance from above, meaning *Kedusha* from above, before a person gives *Kedusha* from below. That is, when a person sanctifies himself and comes to purify, the Creator can give him *Kedusha* from above. It therefore follows that the Creator cannot give *Kedusha* from above until the creatures give *Kedusha* from below.

Now we can interpret what we asked about how *The Zohar* answers the question, "There is none as holy as the Lord," implying that there is another one who is holy, but is a little worse than the Creator. He replies that the fact that it is written, "There is none as holy as the Lord," is because "There is none besides You." However, the *Kedusha* of the Creator is without their *Kedusha*, for He does not need their *Kedusha*. "However, they are not holy without You."

We asked, How can you think of saying that the Creator takes the *Kedusha* that He has from below, from Israel, can we say this? However, when it concerns the work, although it is implied in all the places in the words of our sages that the fact that the Creator gave *Kedusha* to the people of Israel, is because He needed them, hence, first there must be an awakening on the part of man, meaning that he should have a desire for *Kedusha*, then the Creator can give *Kedusha*.

It follows that the Creator needs the *Kedusha* from below, and then he can give them *Kedusha*. *The Zohar* tells us about this, "There is none as holy as the Lord." This means that man has no *Kedusha* at all, meaning that the *Kedusha* that the Creator gives, He does not need man's *Kedusha*. In other words, first a person should be in the form of "He who comes to purify," and then the Creator can give him *Kedusha*.

He says about this, "For there is none besides You," for there is no one to assist You, to give of their *Kedusha*, meaning that they will give You *Kedusha* from below, since "There is none besides You," there is no other force in the world but the Creator. In other words, we must believe in private Providence, as it is written (in Thirteen Tenets, presented in the prayer book after "On us"), "I believe in complete faith, that the Creator, blessed be His name, creates and leads all creations, and He alone does, is doing, and will do all the deeds."

This means that after a person has done good deeds, by which he will be rewarded with *Kedusha*, with being holy, meaning that all his actions will be only to bestow, it implies as though man helps the Creator. *The Zohar* says about this, "For there is none besides You." Rather, the Creator does everything, and He does not need man's *Kedusha* to help Him. Instead, "He alone does, is doing, and will do all the deeds," and man has no part in this.

Thus, what is the meaning of "He who comes to purify is aided"? It seems as though man does do! We should interpret that this means that man must believe that now he has come to purify and not before. This action, when a person comes now to purify, comes from the assistance from above. In other words, previously, there was an awakening from above, which gave him a desire and yearning to come purify and sanctify himself. It follows that his coming to purify now is not by man's power, but rather comes from above.

In this way, we should interpret what our sages said (*Avot*, Chapter 5:27), "Ben Heh Heh says, 'The reward is according to the sorrow.'" This means that to the extent of the sorrow that a person suffers while observing Torah and *Mitzvot*, so will his reward increase. This implies that a person does do something, and for doing it, he is rewarded. However, this, too, we should interpret in the above manner, that man must believe that the sorrow and labor that a person has in feeling that he is far from *Dvekut* with the Creator and that he is immersed in self-love, this sorrow is called "reward."

In other words, the Creator gave him an awakening not to want to remain in the state of the general public, who go with the flow of the world and do not reflect on what makes them higher in degree than any other animal. That is, they feed on the same things that animals feed, and do not feel that they were created in God's image, meaning that they have any connection to Godliness and that they must receive nourishment from spirituality, which is suitable for the speaking level and not for the animate level.

This is a reward. That is, the labor and sorrow that they feel is that actual reward that the Creator gives them. We should not think that this is labor that comes by itself when a person exerts. Rather, this is a reward that the Creator calls them to the work of the Creator, whereas others, He does not call. Thus, along with the sorrow and suffering they feel, they should be happy that the Creator wants to connect with them.

According to the above, we should interpret "According to the sorrow, so is the reward," meaning to what extent should one appreciate the Creator rewarding him? The answer is that according to the sorrow and labor he can feel from being far from the Creator, this is the measure of the reward.

This means that when we want to know how much was the profit of the reward, a person should evaluate how much suffering and sorrow he had had from being far from the work of the Creator. This is the measure of the reward. In other words, it is impossible to appreciate the lack of spirituality before one feels the importance of spirituality. To the extent of the importance of spirituality, to that extent a person can feel the need for it.

It follows that the sensation of the lack is already a reward. Hence, we should interpret the words of Ben Heh Heh, who says, "According to the sorrow." When a person regrets being far from the Creator, it does not come from the person, but the Creator gave him this feeling, and not the person by himself.

This means that by the Creator illuminating for him the importance of spirituality, to that extent he is sorry that he is far from spirituality. For this reason, we must not say that what a person comes to purify is work that comes from a person. Rather, the Creator gave him a thought and desire to come and purify.

It follows that this is not out of man's work that we can say that the Kedusha that the Creator has given him, Kedusha from above, the person helped Him, too. Rather, "There is none besides You." As in the words of The Zohar, the Creator does not need any Kedusha of theirs, meaning of the lower ones, but He does everything.

In this manner, we should interpret the words of our sages about the verse (Exodus 32:10), "And now leave Me alone." RASHI interpreted that "We still did not hear that Moses prayed for them, and He says, 'And now leave Me alone.' However, here He opened for him an opening and notified him that the matter was up to him, that if he prayed for them, He would not destroy them" (Gate of the Words of Our Sages).

We should interpret the words of our sages, who said, "Here He opened for him an opening and notified him that the matter was up to him, that if he prayed for them, He would not destroy them." It means that the Creator notified him, meaning gave him a desire to pray for Israel that He will forgive them the sin of the calf. It follows that the fact that the Creator told him to pray means that He gave him the strength to pray. That is, unless the Creator gives the strength to pray, a person cannot pray.

It therefore follows that the fact that a person prays to the Creator to forgive his sins, that, too, comes from the Creator, for the Creator gives him the strength and desire to pray. It follows that the Creator does everything. In other words, even when a person prays to the Creator to forgive his sins, they implied about this too, "There is none as holy as the Lord," since "There is none besides You," to have power of Kedusha. Rather, everything comes from the Creator.

However, we must not forget that although we say, "Everything comes from the Creator," a person should say, "If I am not for me, who is for me?" Rather, everything depends on the acts of people. Although this is in contradiction to the above-said, we must believe that so it is, as Maimonides says (as said in Article No. 25, *Tav-Shin-Nun*).

According to the above, we should interpret what is said on Shabbat [Sabbath] in the song, "Anyone who sanctifies the seventh properly, anyone who observes Shabbat according to the law, so as not to desecrate it, his reward is great, according to his work." This is difficult to understand. What is the novelty in saying, "His reward is great, according to his work"? This is a straightforward matter; it is customary that one is paid according to the value of one's work. So, what is he telling us by saying, "His reward is great, according to his work"? Can it be otherwise?

If he had said that one who observes Torah and *Mitzvot*, even though he transgresses a little, receives a great reward, if this were so then there would be a novelty to hear. But if he does not receive reward more than he works, this is natural and so it is in corporeality.

However, the novelty is that when Shabbat comes, when a person is rewarded with the quality of Shabbat, he feels the truth, that the work itself is the reward that the Creator gives to a person, meaning that He gives a person a thought and desire to observe Torah and *Mitzvot* and to come and purify himself, as it is written, "He who comes to purify." The question is, Why did he come to purify now, at this time, and not before? When a person receives assistance from above, the person comes to purify and not before. It follows that the meaning of "His reward is great according to his work" is that the fact that a person works and labors in Torah and *Mitzvot* is his reward.

It turns out that if he works a lot, this is the reward that the Creator has given him. That is, He gave a thought and desire to do the holy work. Thus, this is not as it is in corporeality, where to the extent that a person works, any worker receives a salary, meaning a reward in return for his work. Rather, here the innovation is that the reward is the work.

Accordingly, the meaning of "His reward is great," is that how much is the reward? There is no matter here of giving him more reward or less reward. This can be said when a person works in order to receive reward in return for his work, where there is the matter of surpluses and deficits. But if the reward is the work itself, there is no issue of being rewarded for the work. Therefore, to imply this, he says, "His reward is great," specifically "according to his work," since only the work is the reward.

By this we should interpret what is written (Deuteronomy 4:2), "You shall not add to the thing which I command you, nor will you take away from it, to keep the commandments of the Lord your God that I command you." In the work, we should interpret what he says. We understand "Nor will you take away," but why is it forbidden to add?

In the work, we should interpret that if a person wants to receive more reward, his way can be by adding more Torah and Mitzvot. But rather, "Do not add and do not take away," since the reward is the work itself that the Creator gives to a person a place to serve the King. And that power is the reward. Hence, there is the intimation, "Do not add and do not take away," meaning that it is impossible to add more, to receive more reward, but that it is precise, meaning the work and the reward are as two drops in a pond.

This is so particularly in the work. That is, when a person wants to work on the path of truth, which is work in order to bestow, although the literal meaning pertains to practical Mitzvot, that in practice, it means you should not add or take away, but in terms of the intention, meaning when a person works in order to bestow, there is also the matter of "Do not add." In other words, it is impossible to add to the reward more than he works, since what he wants to receive more from the work is that he wants a reward, meaning that besides the work, he will be given a reward. It follows that he is working Lo Lishma [not for Her sake]. But as said above, the reward and the work are equal, and it is impossible to receive more reward, but only according to the work.

According to the above, we should interpret what The Zohar explains about the verse, "There is no rock like our God." It means that the Creator forms a form within a form, meaning the form of the *Ubar* [embryo] within the form of its mother. What is "forms a form within a form" in the work? It is that a person sanctifies himself, meaning wants to work in order to bestow. This *Kedusha* does not come from man, so that man helps the Creator in any way, for the Creator to impart *Kedusha* upon him, as it is written, "He who comes to purify is aided." Rather, the Creator does everything, for "He alone does, is doing, and will do all the deeds."

This is the meaning of what is written, "forms a form within a form," meaning the form of the *Ubar* within the form of its mother. This means that the form of the mother is the basis, and with this form, the man is born. This is called "the form of its mother." Afterward, when a person begins the work and wants to walk on the path of bestowal, he begins with the first degree of *Kedusha*.

It is known that there are three discernments called 1) *Ibur*, 2) *Yenika*, 3) *Mochin*.

The first beginning, when a person enters the *Kedusha*, is the *Ubar*. This is the meaning of the Creator forming a form of bestowal within the previous form, which is the mother, who is called "vessels of reception." In the vessels of reception, the man is born. Afterward, the man shifts to *Kedusha*, which is that all his actions are for the sake of the Creator.

Thus, who gave him the vessels of bestowal? It is as we learn, that *Aviut* [thickness] *de Keter* is called *Aviut de Shoresh*, and is called *Aviut* of the *Ubar*. The *Shoresh* [root] is the Creator, whose desire is to do good to His creations. When a person receives the first quality of *Kedusha*, he receives vessels of bestowal, meaning he can aim to bestow in vessels of bestowal.

This is called that the Creator "forms a form," meaning the form of bestowal, which is that He gives him the power to be able to bestow within the form of his mother, who is the previous state, before he came to connect with the *Kedusha*. The previous state is called "mother," and the next state is called *Ibur*.

After the *Ubar* there is birth, until the newborn grows and through corrections becomes *Gadol* [big/grownup], regarded as having been rewarded with *Mochin* of *Kedusha*. We should interpret *Ubar* from the word *Over* [passing], which is the first state, when he passes from using the vessels of reception into the degree of *Kedusha*, where he uses only *Kelim* [vessels] that can aim to bestow. Otherwise, the *Kelim* are not used.

It follows that *Ibur* is the most important. As in corporeality, when a woman conceives, she is certain to also deliver. Thus, all the concern is for the woman to conceive. Afterward, the woman will usually deliver, too. However, sometimes there are exceptions and the woman has a miscarriage due to some corruption.

Likewise, in the work, the main thing that is hard for us is to enter the *Ubar*, meaning that the will to receive will receive within it a different desire called "desire to bestow." When a person is rewarded with the state of *Ubar*, meaning that within the desire to receive enters a desire to bestow, this is considered that the Creator forms a form within a form.

We should understand this wonder of forming a form within a form. According to what we interpreted, this is a great novelty, a real miracle, since it is against nature, for only the Creator can change nature, and it is out of man's hands. This is the novelty, that the Creator forms the form of bestowal within the form of the mother, which is the form of reception. This is called the *Kedusha* that the Creator gives.

It is said, "There is none as holy as the Lord, for there is none besides You," as there is no one in the world who can change nature and make within the *Kli* [vessel] that comes to a person by nature, the desire to receive, that it will later have a different nature, called "desire to bestow." This is all the innovation of forming a form within a form.

Now we should interpret the meaning of the proximity of "If a woman inseminates, she delivers a male child." Rabbi Yehuda started with what is written, "There is none as holy as the Lord, for there is none besides You." It is known that sowing is like, for instance, taking wheat or barley and so forth, and placing them in the ground until they decay. Afterward, the grain that we need comes out of them.

In the work, a woman is considered the one who works, the one who should deliver. For this reason, if the woman, who is a female, meaning a vessel of reception, if one sows the quality of a "woman," meaning a female—which is the will to receive—in the ground, to decay, this will later yield a male. In other words, if a person sows his female in the ground, meaning the vessels of reception, it will yield vessels of bestowal, called "male."

And if the man inseminates first, meaning that he wants the vessels of bestowal in him to decay in the earth, meaning that when he engages in Torah and Mitzvot, his intention is that by bestowing and engaging in Torah and Mitzvot, his aim is for the acts of bestowal to come into the earth and decay, then she delivers a female. That is, his will to receive grows. This is the meaning of delivering a female. In other words, the acts of bestowal will bring him self-benefit, called "female."

What Is, "Every Blade of Grass Has an Appointee Above, Who Strikes It and Tells It, Grow!" in the Work?

Article No. 27, Tav-Shin-Nun, 1989/90

O ur sages said, "You have not a single blade of grass below that does not have an appointee above, which keeps it, and strikes it, and tells it, Grow!" It is said (*The Zohar*, and *Beresheet Rabbah* 10), "Rabbi Simon said, 'You have not a single blade of grass that does not have a force in the firmament that strikes it and tells it, Grow!'"

We should understand what these words mean to us in the work. We see that in our world, all the creatures like rest, as it is written (*The Study of the Ten Sefirot*, Part 1, *Histaklut Pnimit*, Item 19), "It is known that the nature of every branch is equal to its root. Therefore, every conduct in the root is desired and loved and

608

coveted by the branch, as well, and any matter that is not in the root, the branch, too, removes itself from them, does not tolerate them, and hates them. Therefore, all the matters that are included in Him and extend to us from Him directly are pleasant to us. That is, we love rest because our root is motionless."

Accordingly, the question is, Why do we do things that we do not like? Who forces us to exert? The answer is that there is an appointee above with a cane in his hand, who beats the created beings with torments. And since they cannot tolerate the suffering, it causes them to leave the rest and go to work. It follows that this work is called "compulsory work," where a person is compelled to go to work by the suffering that the appointee beats. Therefore, we act, "and tells it, Grow!" Otherwise, when as a person is born, he would lie in his place and there would be no development at all, both physically and emotionally. Hence, this cane in the hand of the appointee who beats the creatures, causes the development of the creatures.

It follows that the cause of receiving the pleasures, which comes by the development of creation, is because there is an appointee above, who strikes and says, "Grow!" meaning that each and every blade of grass will grow. It follows that people in the world are as blades of grass, and each blade must grow.

In the work, we should interpret that the appointee strikes the created beings, and when the created beings suffer the torments, they must move forward and cannot remain restful, as man is by nature, which extends from his root, which is in a state of complete rest. It follows that the whole drive for the work is only that the suffering caused it.

However, we should understand who is the appointee with a cane in his hand who beats all creations so they do not remain restful, but each one, which is called "every blade of grass," which strikes it and tells it, "Grow!" This is the second discernment we must make in our root.

In other words, the Creator, who is our root, is full of pleasure. Hence, this begets in us suffering if we have no pleasure, since that which exists in the root, the branches want to resemble, as was said (ibid.), "Every conduct in the root is desired and loved and coveted by the branch, as well."

Therefore, the fact that the creatures yearn for pleasure and it is impossible to live without it is because pleasure is in the root; this is the appointee that strikes and says, "Grow!" This is as it is written (Item 21), "However, it is also impossible to remain devoid of possessions and good. Hence, we choose the torment of movement in order to acquire the fulfillment of possessions." Thus, this is the suffering that a person receives from the appointee who strikes and says, "Grow!"

This matter applies in corporeal matters as well as in spiritual matters. The difference is that in corporeal matters, there is no concealment, meaning that in corporeal pleasures there is the matter of "The eye sees and the heart covets." It follows that what the eye sees causes man suffering, since what he sees, whether in the eyes or in the mind, he yearns to obtain. The yearning for the matter, as long as one has not obtained the matter, afflicts a person.

The suffering is measured by the yearning for the matter. It is as we see in corporeality, that sometimes unrequited love can cause a person to take his life because of his suffering at seeing that he will not be able to obtain the matter. Therefore, he says, "I'd rather die than live," and commits suicide. However, this pertains only to corporeality.

In spiritual matters, for the purpose of correction, a *Tzimtzum* [restriction] and concealment were placed, so that one does not see the delight and pleasure clothed in Torah and *Mitzvot*. This was done on purpose, so as to have room for work for the sake of the Creator. Otherwise, it would be impossible to choose, so that one will have the strength to work in order to bestow, due to the above-mentioned reason, since when the eye sees, the heart covets. He would be compelled to do, meaning to observe Torah and *Mitzvot*, because the revealed pleasure would force him to receive in order to calm his pains of coveting, as is done with corporeal lusts.

But now that he must do everything with faith above reason and say that the Torah and Mitzvot are in manner of "for they are our lives," and as it is written, "Who are nicer than gold, than much fine gold, and sweeter also than honey and the honeycomb," if everything were revealed, the will to receive would yearn for the pleasure and it would be utterly impossible that someone will not observe Torah and Mitzvot. But since in order to be rewarded with Dvekut [adhesion] with the Creator, we must work in order to bestow, there are concealment and hiding on the Torah and Mitzvot. Hence, we cannot say here, "The eye sees and the heart covets."

It follows that in spirituality, where we first need to work on faith, meaning believe in reward and punishment, it cannot be said, "You have not a blade of grass below that does not have an appointee above that strikes and tells it, 'Grow!'" Thus, the matter of "strikes it and tells it, 'Grow!'" is the suffering that a person feels, that he is far from the Creator, and that he wants and yearns to adhere to the Creator, but is unsuccessful. From this he suffers, and these sufferings push him to do all that he can only to have Dvekut with the Creator.

It therefore follows that since it is impossible for man to suffer because of something that he craves, except according to the importance of the matter, the question is, Since man does not progress at all without suffering, for the above reason that he wants rest, from where will man take importance to work for the sake of the Creator? meaning yearn to bring contentment to the Creator, that he will suffer if he sees that he cannot bring contentment to the Creator. These sufferings push him to do everything he can do if only to be rewarded with true Dvekut with the Creator. The verse says about that (Psalms 94), "Happy is the man whom You chasten, Lord, And whom You teach out of Your law [Torah]."

We should understand why he is "happy" when the Creator afflicts him. We should interpret that it means that the Creator is imparting upon him the importance of Torah, and he begins to feel that Torah is as in, "The Torah, and the Creator are one." That is, the Torah is the names of the Creator. To the extent of the importance that the Creator imparts upon him, the person begins to feel suffering at being remote from the whole spiritual matter.

In other words, he begins to yearn to be rewarded with spirituality, and each time he sees that he is far, he begins to suffer, and the pain pushes him to do everything he can, since he begins to feel that without spirituality, there is no meaning to life.

It follows that in spirituality, too, there is the appointee above who strikes him, meaning afflicts him. But concerning these afflictions, not everyone is rewarded with the Creator imparting him with the importance that there is in Torah, so that this will afflict him. By this we can understand the meaning of the words, "Happy is the man whom You chasten, Lord." That is, the Creator bestows upon him this importance so he will crave it. This is the above-mentioned suffering, where the appointee above strikes and says, "Grow!" This applies to both corporeality and spirituality.

This is the meaning of what is written in *The Zohar* (*Kedoshim*, Item 108): "There is not even a tiny blade of grass in the land on which there is no higher force above in the upper worlds. All that they do in each one, and everything that each one does is all by prevailing of the upper force that is appointed over it above. And all the conducts in them derive from the judgment; on judgment they journey, and on judgment they exist, and there is not one who emerges outside of one's own existence."

We should interpret according to the above, that everything is conducted by private Providence, and the lower ones have no free choice to emerge from the laws that Providence has imposed upon them. It follows that when speaking of the work, where each person is a small world, "You have not a blade of grass that does not have an appointee over it from above." This means that there is not a single desire or thought that comes to a person that does not follow these rules of above. Hence, all the heaviness there is in the work of the Creator is the contradictions that we find. In other words, on one hand, we say that everything depends on man's work, as our sages said, that man should say, "If I am not for me, who is for me?" This means that everything depends on man, which is the meaning of reward and punishment.

On the other hand, we should say, "Everything comes from above," as in the words of *The Zohar*, which says, "There is not even a tiny blade of grass in the land on which there is no higher force above," implying that everything follows the upper Providence and the lower ones have no ability to change. The answer to both matters, which contradict one another, is as was said in the words of Maimonides (presented in Article No. 25, *Tav-Shin-Nun* [1989/90]), who says that we cannot understand it, but we must believe that this is so.

The order of advancement in the work, which we said comes by obtaining the importance of the goal, is as our sages said, it comes by the Torah. This is so because even when he sees that he is learning *Lo Lishma* [not for Her sake], still, the light in the Torah reforms him, meaning that through the light, he receives the importance of the Torah.

At that time, a person comes to a state of "appointee over each blade of grass, which strikes it and tells it, 'Grow!'" In other words, he begins to feel suffering because he is remote from *Dvekut* with the Creator. These afflictions cause him to do all that he can in order to obtain *Dvekut* with the Creator.

It follows that a person should begin in *Lo Lishma*, although he sees that he cannot work *Lishma* [for Her sake]. However, if he learns *Lo Lishma* because he believes that by this he will achieve *Lishma*, then he receives the light of Torah, and from this he is rewarded with achieving *Lishma*.

Concerning the suffering, I will bring here what is written in *The Zohar* (*Beresheet Bet*, Item 103), for our sages said, "There has never been such joy before the Creator as on the day when heaven and earth were created." However, a person cannot take part in His great joy unless he has made complete repentance from love.

"Before this, he will not rejoice at all with himself or with the people of the world. On the contrary, he feels before him a world full of sorrow and pain, both pains of the body and pains of the soul, which are the transgressions he commits. All of this has come to him because the world was created only in bestowal, to engage in Torah and good deeds in order to bestow contentment upon one's Maker, and not for one's own pleasure.

"But in the beginning, 'A man is born a wild ass' colt,' meaning that his sole interest is his own delight. Hence, the Creator has imprinted bitter and harsh afflictions in self-reception, instilled in man from the moment of his birth—bodily pains and pains of the soul—so that if he engages in Torah and *Mitzvot* even for his own pleasure, through the light in it he will feel the lowliness and the terrible corruptness in the nature of receiving for oneself. At that time he will resolve to retire from that nature of reception and completely devote himself to working only in order to bestow contentment upon his Maker. Then the Creator will open his eyes to see before him a world filled with utter perfection.

"There are two ways in the corporeal and spiritual afflictions he suffered prior to repenting:

1) "'All that the Creator does, He does for the best.' He sees that were it not for those terrible pains that he had suffered for being immersed in the nature of reception for himself, he would never have been rewarded with repentance. Therefore, he blesses for the bad as he blesses for the good, meaning that the bad causes the good.

2) "'That, too, is for the best.' That is, not only did the evils that were done cause good, but the evils themselves have been inverted to good through very great lights that the Creator illuminated through all those evils until they were inverted into good."

It turns out that all of man's progress is specifically if he suffers in the situation he is in, as this gives him a thrust forward.

According to the above, we should interpret what the ARI says, that no degree ascends unless through the ascent of *Mayin Nukvin* [Aramaic: female water, MAN], for *Nukvin* [Aramaic: females] means lack. "Water" means *Bina* that received within her the quality of

Malchut, where *Malchut* is called "a lack," from the [Hebrew] word, "hole." Hence, the upper one must give to the lower one what it needs.

Since "There is no new light in the world except from *Ein Sof* [infinity/no end], hence, the upper one ascends in degree in order to receive abundance for the lower one. In the work, we should interpret that upper and lower mean that the first state is called "upper" and the second state is called "lower." This means that if in the state one is in, he does not feel any lack and he is satisfied, clearly, he has no need to advance in the work, since he sees no deficiency that will push him to go forward.

For this reason, if a person is successful, he elicits a lack in the state he is in. There is a rule: "Each and every state is called 'upper and lower.'" It follows that while he has found a lack in the state he is in, in the second state, called "a state of lack," that lack is now called "the lower one," and causes him to leave the previous state and try to correct the lack that he is feeling now.

In the work, this is regarded as the *Mayin Nukvin* of the lower one causing an ascent in degree to the upper one, meaning to the previous state. This is the meaning of what the ARI said, that through his MAN, the lower one induces an ascent to the upper one. It follows that only the lacks, which are called "suffering," induce the ascents by which they always rise to go forward.

According to the above, we can interpret what our sages said (*Beresheet Rabbah* 92a), "Rabbi Yehoshua Ben Levi said, 'Every suffering, when it comes upon a person and distract him from words of Torah, are afflictions of admonition. But sufferings that come to a person and do not distract him from words of Torah are pains of love, as it is written, 'He whom the Lord loves, He admonishes.'"

This is seemingly difficult to understand. Should the Creator afflict him because He loves him? It stands to reason that as we see in life, if a person loves another, he gives him gifts, and not that one who loves another makes him suffer. But according to the above, since without suffering, a person wants to remain in a state of rest, since our root is in a state of complete rest, and only by the appointee who strikes and tells him, "Grow!" meaning only the suffering make us cancel the pleasure of rest and try to acquire new possessions.

But if he does not suffer, he remains in his present state. For example, a person who lives in a single-room apartment gets married, but he is lazy, meaning likes the rest more than others, so he agrees to live in one room. Although when he was single, he lived in one room, he continues to live this way even after he has married.

But if he has a few children, then he, too, feels the crowdedness in the house, and he, too, begins to feel the suffering of living in one room. Then, the suffering forces him to work overtime, meaning to exert more than he is used to, in order to move to an apartment with several rooms.

It is the same in the work. When a person is educated, and his father brought him up to engage in Torah and *Mitzvot*, and as much as his father let him see what is spirituality and what is for the sake of the Creator, this was enough for him to continue with the work and observe Torah and *Mitzvot*. But when he grew up, married, and became his own man, with children, and he knows that he must educate them and give them the matter of fear of heaven, he reflects on how much understanding and sensation he has now more than he did when he was a nine-year-old child who had begun his education, or when he had his Bar-Mitzvah [at age thirteen].

Then he sees that he has made no progress so as to say, "Now I understand the importance of Torah and *Mitzvot*, which I did not know when I was a child." And if he begins to feel suffering because of this, meaning sees himself as retarded, that he is already a grownup but his mind is as that of a child, meaning that now he has the same understanding that he had then in Torah and *Mitzvot* and he did not advance as one should advance. It follows that he feels himself like a little boy, and these sufferings push him to exert to find a guide who can instruct him so he grows and becomes a man, and does not remain as a child in the work.

Now we can understand what we asked, What is the meaning of what our sages said about suffering that does not distract from the Torah, that they are called "pains of love"? It means as it is written, "He whom the Lord loves, He admonishes." That is, these sufferings bring a person the need to advance in Torah and Mitzvot, meaning to understand the Torah and Mitzvot not as when he was a child, but as is suitable for an adult.

It follows that the suffering caused him to learn and engage in Torah and Mitzvot as is suitable for the state of "man" and not for the state of "child," as our sages said, "You are called 'man,' and the nations of the world are not called 'man.'" "Man" means that he is regarded as "speaking," meaning he does not take for himself the nourishments of "animals," but nourishments that are suitable for the "speaking." This is called "pains of love that do not distract from the Torah," but on the contrary, for attainment of Torah and Mitzvot.

What Is, "Warn the Great about the Small," in the Work?

Article No. 28, Tav-Shin-Nun, 1989/90

Our sages said (*Yevamot* 114a), "Say, and you said, to warn the great about the small." RASHI interprets this as follows, "Say to the priests, sons of Aaron, and you said these two sayings, 'Why warn the great about the small? So they will not be defiled.'"

We should understand the novelty about warning the great about the small. When speaking of the work, at which time we speak of one body, what does warning the great about the small imply? That is, who is the small when we learn within one body, and who is the great when it comes to tell us that we must warn the great about the small?

It is known that the labor and the work that we must give in Torah and *Mitzvot* is because we are born with a nature that we want to receive for ourselves. Therefore, in everything we do, and which the will to receive enjoys, we cannot speak of labor. It is as we see in our world, that a person is never unhappy when he is hungry but has a nice-smelling meal, and say that now he is going to do hard work and great labor in that now he is going to eat, since where there is pleasure, we cannot speak of work and labor.

Accordingly, we should understand this, since the Torah is called "For they are our lives and the length of our days." So, why is it said that a person must labor in the Torah? Is there anyone who does not want to live and enjoy life? It is written about it, "Who are nicer than gold and from much fine gold, and sweeter also than honey and the honeycomb." Therefore, why is it considered "labor" when we observe Torah and Mitzvot?

The answer is that if the pleasure in Torah and Mitzvot were revealed to all, the whole world would certainly observe Torah and Mitzvot. This is as it is written in the "Introduction to The Study of the Ten Sefirot" (Item 43), "If, for example, the Creator were to establish open Providence with His creations in that, for instance, anyone who eats a forbidden thing would immediately choke, and anyone who performed a commandment would discover wonderful pleasures in it, similar to the finest delights in this corporeal world. Then, what fool would even think of tasting a forbidden thing, knowing that he would immediately lose his life because of it, just as one does not consider jumping into a fire? Also, what fool would leave any commandment without performing it as quickly as possible, as one who cannot retire from or linger with a great corporeal pleasure that comes into his hand, without receiving it as quickly as he can? Thus, if Providence were open before us, all the people in the world would be complete righteous."

We should therefore ask, Why is Providence not revealed, but we must believe in reward and punishment? Would it not be better if everything were revealed? The answer is that since we must achieve Dvekut [adhesion] with the Creator, which is equivalence of form, because of it, we must do everything for the sake of the Creator, meaning in order to bestow contentment upon the Maker. If the reward and punishment in Torah and Mitzvot were revealed, it would be impossible to work for the sake of the Creator, since the pleasure would force a person to observe Torah and Mitzvot.

We see that when a pleasure is revealed in corporeality, although it is only a pleasure that is a "tiny light" compared to the pleasure in Torah and *Mitzvot*, how difficult it is for a person to say that everything he does is in order to bestow, or he would relinquish the corporeal pleasures if he could not aim in order to bestow upon the Creator.

Therefore, with the great pleasures found in Torah and *Mitzvot*, it would certainly be impossible to be able to say that if he cannot aim in order to bestow, he gives them up. Hence, this correction was done that before a person can say about the small pleasures in corporeal things that he accepts them only on condition that he can aim to bestow, he is placed under *Tzimtzum* [restriction] and concealment where he does not see any pleasure. Rather, he must believe that this is so. That is, a person must believe that the Creator leads all creations with a guidance of The Good Who Does Good.

This is as it is written in the article (*Shamati*, No. 40, "Faith in the Rav, What Is the Measure," 1943), "One should depict to oneself as if one has already been rewarded with whole faith in the Creator, and already feels in his organs that the Creator leads the whole world in the form of 'The Good Who Does Good,' meaning that the whole world receives from Him only good."

According to the above, it follows that when a person engages in faith in the Creator, he should dedicate some time to depicting how he would feel if he were rewarded with being near the Creator, and he would see with his own eyes the delight and pleasure extending to him and to all creations, how high spirited and elated he would be.

This depiction requires continuation—that his faith will be as knowing and seeing, meaning that the measure of the faith should be like seeing and knowing. This is a lot of work because this is a path of truth, and it is as it is written, "truth and faith," meaning that for his faith to be true, it is specifically like this depiction, that he must believe in the measure of the greatness of the faith as though he saw it, that he was believing with his eyes.

In other words, to the same extent that he was inspired when he saw, so should be his excitement when he does not see, but only believes that this is so. This is why it is called "faith in the path of truth." That is, his faith is true as though he knew this. This is called "true faith," or as it is written, "truth and faith."

And since the whole basis should be built on faith, and at the same time we were given intellect and reason to understand everything with the intellect we have, it follows that faith is against our nature, for we can follow the intellect and not be stupid, doing things mindlessly. It follows that on one hand, we teach a person to walk according to the intellect and behave this way with one another, but when a person begins to observe Torah and Mitzvot, he is told that although he should follow the intellect, between man and the Creator we were given faith. That is, we must believe in the sages and follow this path, although it contradicts the intellect, as it is written, "And they believed in the Lord, and in his servant Moses." In other words, we must believe what the sages said to us and not look at our intellect.

But since this contradicts our reason, we have ups and downs. That is, at times we can believe the words of the sages and depict before us the depiction of truth and faith, meaning that his faith is truly faith, namely that there is no intellect there but everything is against our reason, what we understand. This is why it is called "true faith" or "simple faith," since there is nothing to understand there but everything is above reason.

Hence, it is beyond man's power to always be on the same degree. Rather, he ascends and descends, as our Baal HaSulam said, Why is assuming the burden of the kingdom of heaven called Emuna [faith]? It comes from the word Oman [craftsman], Omenet [nanny], who raises the child slowly until she rears him. Therefore, when working on the basis of faith, until we are rewarded with permanent faith, there is the matter of "partial faith."

For this reason, during the work there are ups and down. That is, sometimes a person might depict the greatness and importance of Torah and *Mitzvot*, and of the greatness and importance of the Giver of the Torah. In other words, when he can depict to himself the greatness and importance of the Giver of the Torah, he feels that he is in a state of ascent. In other words, he feels that he is above the corporeal world. He sees people who follow corporeal things as beasts and animals who settle for nourishments that suffice for the animate level. But for himself, he feels that he can receive sustenance only from what suits the "speaking" level. As is written in the introductions, the whole merit of the speaking level in man is that he is fit to receive the sensation of Godliness, and this does not pertain to the animate level.

However, afterward, he descends once more from his state and falls into the multiple authorities. That is, now he is in his own authority, and not as before. Therefore, during the ascent, when he feels that there is no one in the world but the authority of the Creator, and he himself does not merit a name, since he wants to annul before Him unconditionally, therefore, during the ascent, a person is in the singular authority, and during the descent, he is in multiple authorities, meaning he already has two authorities.

However, sometimes when a person falls into a state where he is worse than two authorities, since when a person says that there are two authorities, at least he believes that there is a Creator to the world, which is one authority. That is, the Creator is the host, and He does what He wants, but there is another authority, meaning that man, too, is a landlord and does in the world what he wants. At that time, the person wants the Creator to serve the person according to his wish, meaning that the Creator should be at man's service and the Creator will serve man according to man's command.

However, even worse is when one does not believe that there is a Creator and a leader to the world, at all. It follows that for this person, there is nothing more than his own, singular authority. However, a person sees that many people have this view, and they all say that they are their own landlords. In other words, each one does what he needs and does not care about other people. If sometimes someone does something good for another, it is because he expects his friend to return him a favor and not be ungrateful.

This is as it is written in *The Zohar* and in the "Preface" [to the Wisdom of Kabbalah] (Item 57) about the verse, "The mercy of the nations is a sin," "Since all that they do, they do for themselves." In other words, they will probably receive something in return for the favor. At that time, "authority of many" means "many individuals."

It follows that this is not regarded as "two authorities," meaning the Creator's authority and man's authority, and the person still believes in the authority of the Creator. But when a person falls into the authority of many, of many individuals, he does not incorporate the Creator at all, and this is certainly the worst state.

It follows that before one is rewarded with permanent faith, which is a gift of God, and not within man's hands, he is always in ascents and descents. At that time a person needs heaven's mercy in order not to escape the campaign. At that time, the order of the work can be only during an ascent, meaning when he is in the domain of *Kedusha* [holiness].

At that time, a person must work and pay attention to the state he was in during the descent. That is, during the ascent, he can calculate and see the difference between light and darkness, as it is written, "As the advantage of the light from within the darkness." In other words, at that time he can observe what our sages said (*Avot*, Chapter 2:1), "Consider the cost of a *Mitzva* [commandment/good deed] compared to its reward, and the reward for a transgression compared to its cost."

In other words, during an ascent, a person understands that reception for oneself is considered a transgression, meaning it removes him from the Creator, and there is no transgression greater than this. But during a descent, a person cannot understand that if he does not aim to bestow, it is considered a transgression and that he should have the strength to believe that we must do everything for the sake of the Creator. Rather, he only believes what is written, that a person should observe the 613 *Mitzvot* that the Creator commanded us through Moses to do. But he will certainly not commit a transgression, breaking what is written in the Torah.

Rather, sometimes a person is angry at why the Creator treated us this way, forbidding us so many things. That is, a person says that if the Creator had asked him about observing the Mitzvot [plural of Mitzva], he would have asked Him not to be so strict and forbid so many things that he covets. Nevertheless, he observes the Mitzvot.

But during the ascent, a person is angry at the opposite: Why did the Creator make us do such things that are necessary, like eating and drinking? It would be better if He did not create them at all and we would not have to do them.

It follows that during the ascent, he wants to have fewer pleasures in the world, and during the descent, he is angry that the Creator forbade us many things that we would enjoy had the Torah not forbade them. We therefore see that there are ascents and descents when a person wants to be rewarded with Dvekut with the Creator. Therefore, we should call the time of descent, a "state of Katnut [smallness/infancy]," and the state of ascent, a "state of Gadlut [greatness/adulthood]."

By this we can interpret what we asked about the meaning of what our sages said, "Say, and you said, to warn the great about the small." We asked, How can we speak within one person about "great" and "small"? According to the above, we should interpret that "great" or "small" does not refer to two bodies, since in the work we learn everything within one body. Rather, "great" and "small" should be interpreted in two times in a single subject, meaning one person at two times: 1) During the ascent, it is called "great." 2) During a descent, it is called "small."

By this we should interpret that when a person is in a state of ascent, he must pay attention and consider that he might come into a descent. And what is a descent? That is, who says that a descent is so bad? After all, he sees that there are many people who live and enjoy life although they are in a state of descent. Therefore, when he himself is in a state of descent, he is taken after them, and then he, too, enjoys life like they do.

However, we can say about the state of descent that this person had a road accident and he was hurt and he is unconscious. That is, he does not feel that he is in a state of descent. Rather, he enjoys the state he is in and does not feel a descent, since he has completely forgotten that there is spirituality in the world and we must strive to achieve *Dvekut* with the Creator. He forgot everything because of the accident he had, and therefore does not ache because he is in descent.

Therefore, when a person is in a state of ascent, he can think and fear that he might have a road accident. That is, now that he is exerting to advance to spirituality, that he will not fall from his degree in the middle.

But during a descent, he no longer remembers because he has no sensation of spirituality. He can know all this only at the time of *Gadlut*. Hence, the text tells us: "Say, and you said, to warn the great about the small." In other words, during the *Gadlut*, which is the time of ascent, this is the time to be careful with *Katnut*, meaning not to come into a descent, called "small," for only during an ascent can one think about the matter of *Katnut*, meaning about the reason he has come into *Katnut*, for one should know that there must be something that causes the descent.

This is as I had heard from Baal HaSulam (written in *Shamati*, No. 35, "Concerning the Vitality of *Kedusha*," *Tav-Shin-Hey*), "Yet, we must also know that if one could sustain any luminescence, even a small one, but if it were permanent, one would already be considered whole. In other words, one would have been able to advance with this illumination. Hence, if one loses the luminescence, one should regret it. This is similar to a person who placed a seed in the ground so that a big tree would grow from it, but took the seed out of the ground right away. Thus, what is the benefit in the work of putting the seed in the ground? Moreover, we can say that he dug out a tree with ripe fruits out of the ground and corrupted them. That is, had he not dug out the seed, a tree with fruits would have grown out of the seed. Likewise, if one had not lost this tiny luminescence, a great light would have grown out of it. Therefore, he should regret having lost a great light."

We therefore see that a person should keep himself with all kinds of precautions during the ascent. Then, even if he feels that he has a small sensation, if he does all that he can not to lose it, he will march forward every time.

This is the meaning of the words, "Say, and you said, to warn the great about the small." That is, during the *Gadlut*, which is a time of ascent, he must make every calculation so as not to come into *Katnut*, meaning a descent. He must calculate what is the importance he has now, even a small connection to spirituality.

He must work with himself to believe that this feeling comes from above, meaning that at that time, the Creator is calling him, and to think how important it is that the Creator is calling him, and also, that if he can keep this small sensation permanently, he will certainly go forward, as in the allegory, that this ascent is regarded as only a seed that is placed in the ground, but that a big, fruit bearing tree will emerge from that seed.

It turns out that he must appreciate the state of ascent and depict to himself as though this is how he is looking at the purpose. That is, as though he already has a big fruit bearing tree—in what way would he guard the tree so people would not spoil this big tree? In this way, he should continue until he feels in his organs that he must always watch over the tree, and he even does things to hide the tree from people so they cannot cast an evil-eye on the tree.

Likewise, a person should keep this feeling that he has now in a state of ascent, so that strangers will not cast the evil eye on him.

Thus far, we have been talking about the importance of the ascent. However, this is only one side.

However, we should also think about the state of lowliness during the descent. This is called "looking at the other side that there is to think about." In other words, only during an ascent can a person think about the lowliness of the state of descent. This is called "Warning the great," meaning a state of *Gadlut*, "about the small," the time of *Katnut*, meaning what he might lose if he comes to a state of descent, for only during an ascent can he calculate "as the advantage of the light from within the darkness." This can be precisely when he has light. At that time, he can compare between light and darkness, but not while he is in the dark.

This is as our sages said (*Avot*, Chapter 5:1), "The world was created in ten utterances. But it could have been created with one utterance! However, in order to avenge the wicked, who are destroying the world, it was created in ten utterances, and to give a good reward to the righteous, who are sustaining the world, which was created in ten utterances."

This is seemingly perplexing. We can understand "to reward the righteous," so they will have a great reward. But "to avenge the wicked"? Why did He do so? After all, the Creator does not complain against His own creations! Why did He make it so there would be much suffering?

We should interpret that in the work, this means that a person should think what is the good that he might lose, and what is the bad that he might suffer, and from those whom he will come to need to keep the *Gadlut*, meaning the time of ascent. Otherwise, he will see what he can suffer from the state of descent. This is the meaning of "to warn the great about the small."

What Is, "The Torah Exhausts a Person's Strength," in the Work?

Article No. 29, Tav-Shin-Nun, 1989/90

Our sages said (Sanhedrin 26b), "Rabbi Hanin said, 'Why is the name of the Torah *Tushia* [gumption/resourcefulness]? It is because she *Mateshet* [exhausts] a person's strength.'" We should understand this. After all, our sages said (*Avot*, Chapter 6:7), "Great is the Torah, for she gives life to those who make her, as it was said, 'For they are life to those who find them, and a healing to all his flesh.'" They also said (*Iruvin* 54), "If his head aches, let him engage in Torah; if his throat aches, let him engage in Torah; if his stomach aches, let him engage in Torah, as was said, 'a healing to all his flesh.'" Thus, this contradicts the above said.

To understand this, we must first understand what is the Torah. That is, for what purpose did the Creator give us the Torah? Our sages said (*Kidushin* 30), "I have created the evil inclination; I have created for it the Torah as a spice." This seems to mean that if there were no evil inclination, He would not create the Torah, as it is written, "I have created the Torah as a spice." Can it be said that the Torah was created for the evil inclination?

The Zohar says ("Introduction of The Book of Zohar," "General Explanation for All Fourteen Commandments and How They Divide into the Seven Days of Creation," Item 1): "The *Mitzvot* in the Torah are called *Pekudin* [Aramaic: commands/deposits], as well as 613 *Eitin* [Aramaic: counsels/tips]. The difference between them is that in all things there is *Panim* [anterior/face] and *Achor* [posterior/back]. The preparation for something is called *Achor*, and the attainment of the matter is called *Panim*. Similarly, in Torah and *Mitzvot* [commandments/good deeds] there are 'We shall do' and 'We shall hear.' When observing Torah and *Mitzvot* as 'doers of His word,' prior to being rewarded with 'hearing the voice of His word,' the *Mitzvot* are called '613 *Eitin*,' and are regarded as *Achor*. When rewarded with 'hearing the voice of His word,' the 613 *Mitzvot* become *Pekudin*, from the word *Pikadon* [deposit]. This is so because there are 613 *Mitzvot*, where in each *Mitzva* [singular of *Mitzvot*], the light of a unique degree is deposited, opposite a unique organ in the 613 organs and tendons of the soul and of the body."

According to the above, it means that the Torah and *Mitzvot* are discerned in two degrees: 1) An advice, as it is written, "613 *Eitin*." That is, by observing Torah and *Mitzvot*, they will have the strength to cancel the evil inclination. By this we should interpret what is written, "I have created the evil inclination; I have created the Torah as a spice." That is, the Torah is considered a spice for the evil inclination. In *The Zohar*, this is called "613 *Eitin*." 2) Torah for the sake of Torah, which are regarded as 613 *Pekudin*. This Torah is the names of the Creator. We attain this Torah after we have corrected our actions and can work in order to bestow and not for our own sake.

However, when beginning to walk toward attainment of the vessels of bestowal, we said that for this we need the Torah as *Eitin*, called 613 *Eitin*. There is also work before this, namely the first manner in which we begin to observe Torah and *Mitzvot*. This is called *Lo Lishma* [not for Her sake], and this is the first discernment.

The second manner is when we want to work *Lishma* [for Her sake]. At that time, we must do everything we can in order to achieve *Lishma*, meaning to be able to come to do everything in order to bestow.

Afterward, we arrive at the third manner, when we are rewarded with the Torah, called "the names of the Creator," which *The Zohar* calls "613 *Pekudin*."

Therefore, when beginning to observe Torah and *Mitzvot* in the first manner, meaning in *Lo Lishma* and in order to receive reward, as it is written in *The Zohar* ("Introduction of The Book of Zohar," "General Explanation for All Fourteen Commandments and How They Divide into the Seven Days of Creation"), The beginning of man's work in Torah and *Mitzvot* is because of reward and punishment in this world, or reward and punishment in the next world. In this state, he still does not need the Torah and *Mitzvot* as *Eitin*. Rather, to the extent that he believes in reward and punishment, the reward and punishment obligate him to observe Torah and *Mitzvot*, and not because of the advice, "I have created the evil inclination; I have created the Torah as a spice," where the Torah is the counsel against the evil inclination within man, and the man wants to emerge from its control. That is, a person wants to emerge from self-love and do everything for the sake of the Creator, and this is why he observes Torah and *Mitzvot*. Instead, the will to receive for himself obligates him to observe Torah and *Mitzvot*.

Thus, what does "From *Lo Lishma* we come to *Lishma*" mean? since we see no connection between a person observing Torah and *Mitzvot* in order to receive reward, that should make it a springboard for him to shift from *Lo Lishma* to *Lishma*. Our sages said, "because the light in it reforms him." That is, the light in the Torah shines to a person so he will feel that he is not regarded as human, but that he is like any other animal, as it is written (*Yevamot* 61), "You are called 'man,' and the idol-worshippers are not called 'man.'"

By this we should interpret what we asked, What does it mean that they said, "Why is the Torah called *Tushia*?" It is because she exhausts a person's strength. But they said the opposite: "a healing to all his flesh."

The meaning is that when a person learns *Lo Lishma*, the Torah makes him feel that the quality of "man" in him is very weak. That is, the "man" power within him is very weak and he is like all other animals. But what is the form that the man sees? It is that the "man" in him is very weak.

We know that the main difference between man and beast is that a beast has no sensation of the other. This is called "will to receive only for one's own sake." This is also called "evil." In other words, the will to receive for oneself is called "evil' because the *Tzimtzum* [restriction] and concealment were on it, so that no light of *Kedusha* [holiness] may reach into this will to receive.

Since this will to receive is all that interferes, so we cannot receive the delight and pleasure that He wished to give to the created beings, this is why it is called "evil," or "evil inclination." However, it is difficult to understand why when a person observes Torah and *Mitzvot* with the aim, "I have created the evil inclination; I have created the Torah as a spice," it bring a person the feeling that there is evil in him, meaning that he was happy at the time of ascent, and then he suffered a descent and feels the bad in him, and why does he have many descents?

It is because the Torah is the spice for the evil inclination. Thus, why do we not see that the evil inclination loses its power? Instead, each time, the evil appears anew. We see that there are many descents when we begin to walk on the path of doing everything in order to bestow. That is, each time, the evil is renewed with greater forcefulness than before he began the work with the aim to achieve a state where all his actions are for the sake of the Creator.

The thing is that the part of the will to receive for himself that is called "evil" has already been cancelled in him, yet there are other parts that he has not cancelled through the light in the Torah.

We can understand this through an allegory. Let us say that the will to receive contains 100 kilograms of pleasure. Yet, a person cannot cancel 100 kilograms of pleasure all at once. If he were to see the size of the evil within him, he would immediately escape the campaign. Therefore, this takes place gradually.

In other words, in the beginning, a person feels that he can receive one kilogram of the corporeal pleasures. When he receives an ascent, the power of the evil is cancelled in him, meaning he can overcome the one kilogram of pleasure that he felt in corporeal things. But since he must receive the strength to cancel all 100 kilograms of pleasure that there is in corporeality, and he cannot overcome 100 kilograms of pleasure right away, he is given one more kilogram of flavor for corporeality.

Consequently, he suffers a descent, since he had the power to overcome only one kilo of pleasure. When he is given a feeling of greater pleasure, he suffers a descent as a result, since he surrenders under a great pleasure. When he overcomes, which is called "an ascent," he is made to feel three kilograms of pleasure in corporeality, until he completes all the overcoming that there is in work in order to bestow in corporeal pleasures.

Assume he can already overcome all the corporeal pleasures and work with them in order to bestow. Certainly, this requires constant help from above; otherwise, one cannot overcome even the smallest pleasure, as it is written, "Man's inclination overcomes him every day. Were it not for the help of the Creator, he would not overcome it."

However, a person must always seek help. If he were to be shown the measure of the lust in the will to receive, he would immediately see that this work is not for him. Hence, in the beginning, he is shown small flavors in corporeal lusts. But afterward, once he has received the power to overcome all the corporeal lusts, a person is rewarded with receiving spiritual lusts, where there is the matter of Masachim [screens], which is about overcoming the light of spiritual pleasures.

But there, too, it follows an order. That is, we begin, for example, from a small degree, meaning light of Nefesh. When he can receive this in order to bestow, he is given the light of Ruach, until he is rewarded with all the NRNHY, as it is written in *The Zohar*, "When he is born, he is given *Nefesh*. If he is rewarded further, he is given *Ruach*."

This is as our sages said (*Sukkah* 52), "Anyone who is greater than his friend, his inclination is greater than him." "Great" means that he has been granted an ascent in spirituality, meaning that he can already overcome a certain measure of pleasure and receive it in order to bestow. Then he is given pleasure once again, and on that measure of pleasure he is still unable to overcome.

When he is rewarded with overcoming this pleasure and becomes great again, meaning achieves *Gadlut* [greatness/adulthood], which is called "an ascent," he is given an even higher degree, which he has never overcome. Therefore, now he sees that he is worse. That is, he is unable to overcome this degree.

Now, too, the same sequence takes place, where he asks the Creator to give him the strength from above to be able to overcome this great measure of will to receive, as well. This is regarded as the lower one ascending to the upper one to seek the power of the *Masach* [screen].

By this we should interpret what our sages said, "Why is her name *Tushia*? It is because she *Mateshet* [exhausts] a person's strength." That is, each time, according to his greatness, he receives a greater measure of evil. In other words, the greater the pleasure, the harder it is to overcome it. It follows that "man" means "a giver," as it is known that "man" in *Gematria* is MA, and MA is called ZA, a Giver. BON is called *Malchut*, the receiver. MA is the male, "man," a giver, whereas *Behema* [beast], which is BON in *Gematria*, means female, receiving and not giving.

It follows that in *Gadlut*, which is the greater light, it is harder to overcome. Thus, the quality of "man" grows weaker every time because each time, he has a greater light.

By this we should interpret what we asked, "If his head aches, let him engage in Torah." According to what Baal HaSulam said, "If his head aches" means that his thoughts are not in order. "If his stomach aches" means that everything that comes into his stomach is for his will to receive. "Let him engage in Torah," as was said,

"It is a healing to all his flesh." That is, through the Torah, he is rewarded with *Gadlut* because "The light in it reforms him" and he is rewarded with being great.

Afterward, he is rewarded with a higher degree on which he still did not have the power to overcome, and he must ask the Creator to be given help to be able to overcome this, as well. It follows that each time, we should speak of two opposite things.

We should always discern two sides in each degree:

1) The lower one ascending to *Gadlut*, which is called "an ascent" in degree. He begins to appreciate what it means to be close to the Creator. Now he understands that he should be concerned only with the benefit of the Creator, and he himself should not merit a name. That is, he does not need anything for himself and he can relinquish both corporeality and spirituality. Where it concerns his own benefit, he relinquishes, and all his actions will be only to bring contentment to his Maker. This is considered that the Torah gives life to all, as it is written, "Great is the Torah, for she gives life to who make her, and a healing to all his flesh."

2) "Anyone who is greater than his friend, his inclination is greater than him." That is, afterward, he receives a greater pleasure. In other words, as long as he has not been rewarded with vessels of bestowal, he is still attached to corporeal pleasures. Then, each time, he receives a greater taste for corporeal things so he will have to overcome the will to receive for himself, for a person is not shown the measure of the pleasure that is found in corporeality because he will not be able to overcome. Rather, there is a certain measure that each one feels in corporeal pleasures.

But when a person begins to walk on the path toward doing everything in order to bestow and not for his own benefit, he is given from above more sweetness in self-love. It follows that when he begins to enter the *Gadlut* of the work, meaning that he wants to be among those who work in order to bestow, then each time, he is given more taste for self-love, so naturally, each time, he sees that he has more evil.

According to the above, we see that even during the preparation, when a person wants to begin to work in order to bestow, although he was still not rewarded with this, the matter of "Anyone who is greater than his friend, his inclination is greater than him" already begins. That is, when a person wants to begin the work of great ones, who engage in order to bestow, he receives many ascents in the form of "the light in it reforms him." At that time, he is regarded as "great."

Afterward, he is given more evil to taste, so he will ask the Creator to help him. It follows that we should make two discernments here: 1) The Torah gives him life and he becomes great. 2) Afterward, he is given bad, as said above, that "Anyone who is greater than his friend, his inclination is greater than him."

It follows that then he is in a state where through the Torah, he has become great. He came to see the truth, that the strength of the quality of "man" in him has exhausted its strength and he is like a beast, in the sense that the will to receive for himself in him grows stronger in him every time, to the extent of the good that he received from the Torah, which reforms him.

Therefore, we should explain why the name of the Torah is *Tushia*. It is because through the Torah, he sees that the "man" power within him is weak, and only his "beast" power has strengthened.

It is the same in spirituality. That is, once a person has been rewarded with vessels of bestowal, there is constant overcoming of his *Aviut* [thickness]. Each time, he must ascend to his upper one and ask for the power to overcome the will to receive, which is now greater than his strength to overcome that he has from what he received before, since now he received greater *Aviut*. Hence, there, too, meaning after he has been rewarded with vessels of bestowal, he must always go forward in order to correct the will to receive, each according to his degree.

It therefore follows that when a person wants to begin the work of bestowal, he sees that he has only a little bit of evil. That is, he knows about himself that he has a little bit of evil. It follows, that the bad he has comes from what he knows about himself. For this reason, a person understands that he has the power to overcome by himself. Therefore, as was said, "Anyone who is greater than his friend, his inclination is greater than him."

It follows that from above, he is given the awareness of the evil, meaning that the evil that has now been revealed to him comes from above. At that time a person stands and thinks, "From where did this evil come to me? since, according to the rule, 'The light in it reforms him,' in the beginning, I already felt that I received an ascent in spirituality. Thus, what is the reason that now I have more bad?"

He regards this bad that he received now as coming to him from above reason. That is, the reason cannot understand how he fell to a state of lowliness, called "evil," meaning that now he received a feeling for all the corporeal things that before he began the work of bestowal, he was already far from them, but now he received greater closeness to self-love.

This is as it is written in the book *Panim Meirot*: "The meaning of 'a good reward for the righteous' is their own attainment of those degrees that through their good deeds, they returned the lights to the upper ZON. The punishment of the wicked is the meaning of the words, 'One opposite the other.' To the same extent that a person is rejected from attaining the eternal light, he descends into the pleasures of the filthy *Klipot* [shells/peels], which are called *Sheol* [netherworld] and *Avadon* [oblivion], since a certain attitude has emerged within him that enables him to tolerate them."

It follows that the bad that appears in a person does not come from himself. Rather, he sees as though this bad has come to him above his own reason. At that time, a person sees that there is no way he can overcome this bad that has been added to him now by giving work and labor. But what was the result? He received more bad. Thus, he asks, "What will be the end?" since no work and labor help him out of the governance of evil, which is self-love.

The answer is that a person must know that as the bad came to him from above, so his emergence from the bad will come to him through help from above. Therefore, a person should not be impressed with the fact that he sees that he is utterly incapable of emerging from the governance of evil by himself. Instead, he must know that as the evil in him has been added to him each time not by his own strength, since he did not labor in order to get more bad, but it came from above, namely above reason, which a person does not understand, likewise, he should believe that he will also receive from above the strength to emerge from the evil.

In other words, everything that comes from above reason is cancelled above reason, and we can say that the fact that a person is in exile, under the governance of reason, did not come to a person by his own doing. Rather, it is from above. Likewise, redemption, too, comes from above.

It therefore follows that when a person begins the work of bestowal and knows that he has a little bit of evil, he still does not find such great flavor in self-love. However, when he wants to cancel his self-love and work in order to bestow, he receives from above more passion for self-love. That is, he is shown what was hidden from him, the size and power of control that exist in self-love.

At that time, a person sees that he is on the complete opposite end of the Creator, for the Creator is all to bestow, and man is all to receive. When the Creator helps him, a person feels the greatness of the Creator, how the Creator is treating him in order to deliver him from the governance of evil. Then, each time more bad appears in a person, meaning that a person is lowlier, he sees that the Creator is tending to a lowlier person.

By this we should interpret what our sages said, "Rabbi Yonatan said, 'Wherever you see the greatness of the Creator, there you find His humbleness.'" This means that wherever a person sees the greatness of the Creator, he sees that the Creator is humble, tending to him personally, in private Providence. Therefore, when the Creator becomes greater, the person sees that the Creator is more humble.

What It Means that "Law and Ordinance" Is the Name of the Creator in the Work

Article No. 30, Tav-Shin-Nun, 1989/90

The *Zohar* says (*BeHukotai*, Items 16-18), "*Malchut* is called 'law.' The decrees of the Torah are included in her. 'My ordinances shall you keep.' An ordinance, which is ZA, to which that statute, which is *Malchut*, grips. Thus, upper and lower conjoin, meaning the statutes in *Malchut* are in the ordinances in ZA. And this is the rule of the holy name, since 'law and ordinance' is the name of the Creator. 'And do them.' He asks, 'Since he already said 'walk' and 'keep,' why the 'do,' as well?' He answers that one who performs the *Mitzvot* [commandments/good deeds] of the Torah and walks in His ways, it is as though he made Him above. The Creator said, 'as if he made Me.' And they determined it. Hence, 'And do them,' as a law and ordinance, which are ZA and *Malchut*."

We should understand what it means when he says, "One who performs the Mitzvot of the Torah and walks in His ways, it is as though he made Him." We should also understand the difference between saying, "one who performs the Mitzvot of the Torah" and what he adds, "and walks in His ways," for it seems like they are two things. That is, it seems as though although he observes the Mitzvot of the Torah, if he does not walk in His ways, it is not said that he made the Creator. Thus, what is the meaning of "and walks in His ways"?

We should also understand what is written (Item 19), "Similarly, Rabbi Shimon said, 'And David made Him a name.' But did David make it for Him? He replies, 'Rather, because David went in the ways of Torah and kept the Mitzvot of the Torah, it is as though he actually made a name there.' For this reason, it was said, 'And do them.' That is, if you try to do them, to correct the holy name as it should be, all those blessings above will be properly corrected in you."

We should also ask, What does it mean that David made a name for the Creator? With respect to whom did he make the name? Does the Creator need someone to make for Him a good name among the created beings, so that by the Creator having a good name, they will respect Him? This would befit the creatures, where one person can respect another person like him, but how can we say that the Creator needs to have a good name among the creatures? Also, we should understand how is it that when a person walks in the ways of Torah and performs the commandments of the Torah, the Creator gets a good name.

To understand all this, we must first present the whole matter of creation, meaning for what purpose did the Creator create creation. The answer is, it is known that His desire is to do good to His creations. It follows that the Creator received the name of "a Giver," who gives delight and pleasure to creation, where creation is called "receiver," and the receiver must be deficient; otherwise, it is impossible to receive. For this reason, the will to receive delight and pleasure is called "lacking."

There is no lack in the Creator, for the Creator is perfectly complete. Hence, creation is called "existence from absence," after this lack when something was created, which did not exist before He created it. And since there is no lack in the Creator, when a person feels lacking, he is already in disparity of form from the Creator. When he satisfies the lack, although he has some measure of equivalence, for now he is not deficient, but by being the receiver while the Creator is the giver, it follows that there is no equivalence of form, since by this disparity of form he becomes separated from the Creator.

In order to correct this, meaning where a person is called "created being," who is deficient, in order to have equivalence, he must be in wholeness, meaning receive from the Creator abundance. When he receives from the Creator, he is once again in disparity of form, and then this correction called "receiving in order to bestow" is done. That is, although by nature, he has a desire and yearning to receive from something that he can enjoy, he overcomes and does not want to receive the pleasure, unless because he wants to bestow contentment upon his Maker.

Any pleasure that he can say that the Creator enjoys, meaning by observing His thought and will, which is to do good to His creations, meaning that all the pleasures we can say that the Creator enjoys when we receive from Him, only in this manner do we receive. Hence, when a person achieves this degree, which is to bring contentment to his Maker, he can delight Him by receiving from Him delight and pleasure.

Thus, now we have equivalence of form from two sides: 1) There is no longer a lack in the lower one, since he receives delight and pleasure from the Creator. 2) Now he bestows like the Creator. That is, the fact that he receives pleasure now is not for his own benefit, but only for the sake of the Creator. But for his own sake, he is willing to relinquish any pleasure. It follows that now there are two things together—the correction of creation and the purpose of creation.

This is called *Zivug de Hakaa* [coupling by striking], where by the *Hakaa* [striking], a unification occurs. In spirituality, *Hakaa* means two conflicting things, where everything that one rejects, the other wants. In other words, the Creator wants the lower one to receive delight and pleasure, meaning to bestow upon the lower one, and the lower one wants equivalence of form, meaning to bestow upon the upper one.

It follows that they are in conflict. Yet, by this they come to unification. In other words, each one takes the view of the other, meaning that the upper one wants the lower one to receive. The lower one receives only to the extent that he knows that everything that he receives is only because the upper one wants. It follows that now he receives like the upper one wants, and he gives as he wants, and there is no separation here. Rather, now, both are of the same view.

By the creature having vessels of bestowal, he receives in them delight and pleasure, and then it is evident to all that the name of the Creator is The Good Who Does Good. Before the delight and pleasure were revealed, He was called "Shechina [Divinity] in the dust," meaning that everyone suffers in the world because there are no Kelim [vessels] suitable to receive the delight and pleasure.

Hence, the lower ones must believe that the Creator leads the world as The Good Who Does Good, which is why the name of the Creator, The Good Who Does Good, is not revealed. But when the lower ones receive the vessels of bestowal, the name of the Creator, The Good Who Does Good, can be revealed.

But here comes the toughest question: How can a person receive these Kelim? By nature, he is completely opposite, for man is born only with vessels of reception, meaning that a person cannot do anything unless it yields benefit to himself. So how can he do something that is against nature, meaning to bestow and not receive anything for his own benefit?

Our sages said about this, that the Creator said, "I have created the evil inclination; I have created the Torah as a spice." There are two things to note about observing Torah and Mitzvot: 1) the practice of Torah and Mitzvot, 2) the intention, meaning what he wants for observing Torah and Mitzvot.

The reward that one should ask of the Creator is to walk in His ways, meaning in the ways of the Creator. And what is the way of the Creator? We should say that His way is to bestow upon the creatures delight and pleasure. Also, all of one's concerns should be about bestowal upon the Creator, that He will enjoy, and not to be concerned with his own benefit, but only with the benefit of the Creator, like the Creator, whose wish is to do good to His creations.

Since man was born with a nature of receiving for himself, it is known that by the Creator wanting to delight His creatures, the receiver must have a desire and yearning for the matter. Otherwise, it is impossible to enjoy. Hence, the Creator created the creatures with a yearning to satisfy their lack. But how can the creatures walk in His ways, so that the creatures will bestow like the Creator, which is called "cling to His attributes"?

To correct this, the Creator said, "I have created the evil inclination," meaning the will to receive only for oneself, "I have created the Torah as a spice." That is, through the merit of the Torah, we will receive the power to overcome the bad, and we will be able to work only in order to bestow pleasure upon the Creator.

It therefore follows that it is not enough to observe Torah and Mitzvot. Rather, one must also direct the aim, why is he observing Torah and Mitzvot. That is, what is the reward he wants the Creator to pay him for observing Torah and Mitzvot? There are many intentions in this regard. It is written in The Zohar about it, that some want, in return for observing Torah and Mitzvot, reward in this world, and some want reward in the next world. But the main thing a person needs is to receive a reason to compel him to observe Torah and Mitzvot, which is "because He is great and ruling." That is, he engages in Torah and Mitzvot because he has great pleasure in that he is serving a great King.

This implies that the reason why a person observes Torah and Mitzvot is in order for the Creator to give him the power to bestow, which he does not have by nature. The Torah and Mitzvot are a Segula [remedy/virtue/quality] to obtain this, as it is written, "I have created the evil inclination." Thus, what is the advice so we can go against nature? The answer is that for this, we were given the Torah as a spice. That is, through the Torah we will obtain the power of bestowal. It follows that a person should aim while engaging in Torah and Mitzvot for only one thing: to walk in His ways. That is, as the Creator's way is to bestow, likewise, in return for his work, man wants the Creator to give him this force.

By this we should interpret what we asked about the words of The Zohar, "One who performs the Mitzvot of the Torah and walks in His ways." We asked, What does it add to us that it says, "walks in His ways," since a person is already observing the commandments of the Torah? According to the above, it means that it is not enough to observe the Mitzvot of the Torah; he must also aim that he wants reward in return for observing the Mitzvot of the Torah. And what type of reward does he want? to be able to walk in the way of the Creator. Just as the way of the Creator is to bestow upon the creatures so the creatures will enjoy, likewise, man wants to have a desire and yearning to bestow contentment upon his Maker and to ask the Creator to reward him for his work. This should be as in corporeality, where a person works and looks, during the work, at when he will receive his salary. Likewise, in the work of the Creator in observing Torah and Mitzvot, one should look forward to the time when he receives the salary for his labor, meaning when he is rewarded with vessels of bestowal.

According to the above, we can interpret what we asked about what The Zohar says about the verse, "And David made Him a name." It says that because David went in the ways of the Torah, it is as though he actually worked there. This is why it was said, "And do them," to properly correct the holy name. We asked, Does the Creator need to make for Himself a name with the created beings? This is appropriate for a person. With respect to a person, you can say that he wants to have a good name, but not when it comes to the Creator with regard to the creatures. Can it be said that a person who walks into a henhouse wants to have a good name among the roosters, so they will respect him because of his importance? It is even more so with regard to the Creator and the creatures. What value do the creatures have compared to the Creator, that we can say that the Creator wants to have a good name so they will respect Him? Thus, what is the meaning of "And David made Him a name" by walking in the ways of Torah, meaning that man should make a good name for the Creator?

But since the Creator wants to give delight and pleasure to the creatures, so they will enjoy, if the creatures enjoy the Creator giving them abundance, then the creatures give Him a good name, meaning they say that the Creator is good and does good. This means that the name that the Creator will receive from the creatures, that He is good and does good, He does not need this name so they will respect Him by this. Rather, He wants them to feel this name, meaning that this name is not for the Creator, since He needs this name, but rather for the creatures. That is, the Creator wants the creatures to perceive Him in this way. In other words, it is a sign that they are enjoying their lives, and the evidence of this is that they are saying that the Creator is called The Good Who Does Good.

Therefore, there is a difference between man and the rest of the created beings. Man wants to have a name in order to be rewarded for it. His reward is that 1) The created beings respect him for doing good to others, 2) Sometimes a person does good to others in return for a reward in the next world.

But the name that the Creator wants to be given, The Good Who Does Good, is for the sake of the creatures. That is, when the creatures call Him The Good Who Does Good, the creatures are enjoying Him. Otherwise, they would not call Him The Good Who Does Good.

However, from the perspective of the correction of creation, in order for the creatures to have *Dvekut* [adhesion] when they receive the delight and pleasure, a person must receive everything in order to bestow. But since man is born by nature with a desire only to receive, we were given the Torah and *Mitzvot* by which we can emerge from the control of the will to receive for ourselves and do everything in order to bestow.

This is the meaning of what he says, "Because David walked in the ways of the Torah," meaning that through the Torah, he corrected himself and was rewarded with vessels of bestowal. In these vessels, the abundance is poured from above and a person is rewarded with The Good Who Does Good, meaning that then he attains the real name of the Creator—The Good Who Does Good—because he received the good by correcting himself through the ways of the Torah. This is the meaning of "And David made Him a name," meaning that David was rewarded with attaining the name of the Creator, called The Good Who Does Good.

However, concerning what it says, "Law is *Malchut*, ordinance is ZA," this is the rule of the holy name, since "law and ordinance" is the name of the Creator. This is the meaning of "And do them." We should understand this, since he says that law is regarded as *Malchut*, and ordinance is regarded as ZA. Therefore, they are two separate names, so how does he say that law and ordinance is the name of the Creator? They are two names! ZA is called "The Creator," and *Malchut* is called *Shechina* [Divinity]. Thus, what does it mean that he says, "Law and order is the name of the Creator"?

It is known that there is no light without a *Kli* [vessel]. That is, the purpose of creation, to do good to His creations, created in the creatures a desire to receive delight. This desire is called *Malchut*, as he writes in *The Study of the Ten Sefirot* (Part 2, Answer 39), "She is called *Malchut* because from her extend a guidance of assertiveness and utter control," like the fear of the kingship. It follows that the abundance that the Creator wants to give to the created beings is called *Malchut*, and the *Sefira Malchut* is the *Kli* that receives the light in each and every degree.

Baal HaSulam said that in general, the light is called "the Creator," and the *Kli* that receives the light is called *Malchut*, or *Shechina*. This *Kli* is called *Shechina* because the light dwells inside the *Kli*. He said that this is the meaning of what *The Zohar* says, "He is *Shochen* [dweller]; she is *Shechina* [dwelling place]," meaning that they are one thing: light and *Kli*.

However, there is disparity of form between the light and the *Kli*, between the giver and the receiver, and disparity of form is called "separation." Since all the creatures extend from *Malchut*, and *Malchut* is called "the assembly of Israel," which is the collection of all the souls, in order for *Malchut* to be able to receive abundance for the creatures, *Malchut* must be united so as to be in equivalence of form with the light.

Because of this, we were given Torah and *Mitzvot* by which we can achieve equivalence of form with the Creator. That is, all those who engage in Torah and *Mitzvot* and intend to thereby receive desire and yearning to do everything with the intention to bestow contentment upon the Maker, meaning that as the Creator bestows upon the creatures, the creatures want to bestow upon the Creator, and by this each one corrects the root of his soul, which is *Malchut*, to work in order to bestow, which is called "unification," meaning uniting the light and the *Kli* to be in equivalence of form, at that time the abundance pours out to the creatures, namely the delight and pleasure.

According to the above, we should interpret what we asked, Why does *The Zohar* say that law and ordinance is the name of the Creator? After all, they are two names, ZA and *Malchut*, which is "law" and "ordinance." But as said above, ZA, who is called "ordinance," is the light that is revealed. This is the abundance. *Malchut* is the receiver who should receive everything in order to bestow. This is called "law," meaning that although man sees that he was born with a desire to receive for himself, and was born with mind and reason, and a person should weigh everything he wants to do with his reason, but here, in the work of the Creator, he is told that he should not look at what his mind tells him. Rather, he must accept this as a law, above reason.

Thus, although he was created by nature with a desire to receive, he should nonetheless believe in the words of our sages, who said that man should cling to the attributes of the Creator, as it is written, "As He is merciful, so you are merciful." It follows that by accepting the Torah and *Mitzvot* as a law, although it is above reason, meaning that the body does not understand it, through faith above reason, a person can achieve equivalence of form.

That is, each person who engages in Torah and *Mitzvot* with the aim to bestow, by doing so, he unites ZA, who is called "ordinance," meaning the light and abundance, with *Malchut*, who is the *Kli* that must receive the light, so its intention will also be to bestow, like the light. This is called "the unification of the Creator and His *Shechina*." At that time, the name "One" is made, meaning that the two names, ZA, called "ordinance," meaning *HaVaYaH*, and His Name, called *Malchut*, become one.

According to this, we should interpret what is written, "One who performs the *Mitzvot* of the Torah and walks in His ways, it is as though he made Him above. The Creator said, 'as if he made Me.' And they determined it. Hence, 'And do them,' as a law and ordinance, which are ZA and *Malchut*." This means that by performing the *Mitzvot* of the Torah and walking in His ways, a person causes at the root of his soul that *Malchut* above will work in order to bestow, like ZA. This is called "unification." It follows that the meaning of "and do them," is the intention to make this unification of ZA and *Malchut*, called "law" and "ordinance." And that, too, is called "the unification of the Creator and His *Shechina*." This is the work that the created beings should do.

It follows that the meaning is that since they are two names, the creatures must make the unification, so it becomes one. When all creations achieve their wholeness, meaning when all are corrected at the root of their souls, the verse "On that day will be the Lord is one and His name, One," will come true. This is the work of which it is written, "And do them."

647

What "There Is No Blessing in That Which Is Counted" Means in the Work

Article No. 31, Tav-Shin-Nun, 1989/90

It is written in *The Zohar* (*Bamidbar*, Item 13), "Come and see, they said that there is no blessing of above on something that is counted. But should you say, 'How were Israel counted? How was ransom taken from them?' First, they would bless Israel, then count the ransom, and then bless Israel again. Thus, Israel were blessed in the beginning and in the end, and there was no death among them. He asks, 'Why is there death because of the counting?' He replies, 'It is because there is no blessing in counting, and when the blessing is gone, the *Sitra Achra* [other side] is on him.'"

RASHI brings the reason why He counts Israel. He says, "Out of His fondness for them, He counts them every hour." This means that RASHI wishes to explain that if we say that there is danger in something that is counted, that there could be death there, why did the Creator say to count Israel and place them in a place of danger? This is why RASHI explains, "Out of His fondness for them, He counts them every hour, despite the danger in it. But for the love that He has for Israel, and for His wish to know their number, He said that He would count Israel."

Outwardly, it is hard to understand it, meaning to say that since the Creator wants to know their number, He said that they need to be counted through a correction so there will not be a hindrance among them, so He will count them through ransom. We should understand how it is possible to say that because the Creator wishes to know their number, they need to be counted and give the amount of Israel, and then the Creator knows, for otherwise He does not know the number of the children of Israel in advance but needs the creatures to inform Him. Can this be? Also, we must understand what a blessing is in the work, what a count is in the work, and why it causes death when there is no blessing on the count. And we should also understand why there cannot be a blessing on something that is counted.

It is known that there are two matters in the work of the Creator: 1) the purpose of creation; 2) the correction of creation. The purpose of creation means is that the creatures will receive delight and pleasure, as it is written, "His desire to do good to His creations." The correction of creation is for the creatures to walk on the path of the Creator, meaning equivalence of form. Therefore, as the Creator gives to His creations, the creatures, too, should give to the Creator. Otherwise, there is disparity of form, and in spirituality, disparity of form causes separation, meaning causes separation from the Life of Lives.

It is written about it in *The Zohar* (presented in *Talmud Eser Sefirot*, Part 1, *Histaklut Pnimit*, Item 17), "Hence, the wicked, in their lives they are called 'dead,' since out of their disparity of form—being completely at the other end from their root, where they have nothing in the form of bestowal—they are severed from Him, and are actually dead." However, it was already said about them in *The Zohar*, "'All the grace that they do, they do for themselves,' meaning that their aim is primarily for themselves and for their own glory."

In other words, what we ascribe to the Creator, meaning everything that the Creator does, is in a state of wholeness. This means that the Creator wishes for the creatures to receive delight and pleasure, hence He created in them a desire to receive and a great craving to receive pleasure. By this, He is certain that they will want to receive pleasure. But the correction of creation, the *Kli* [vessel] and the desire that the creatures should make—the desire with which they will be able to receive delight and pleasure—this desire is called "the will to bestow." Obtaining that desire happens gradually because the lower one does not have the strength to go against the will of the upper one—the will to receive for oneself that the Creator created.

Thus, we see that there are two kinds of *Kelim* [vessels]:

1. Vessels of reception. However, a correction is placed on them, meaning that on the vessels of reception there is the opposite intention from the *Kli*. In other words, a person is actually receiving, but in the intention, he is now giving. It follows that the aim is the very opposite of the act, and the light that is received in those *Kelim* is now called "receiving in order to bestow."

The name of this light is *Hochma* [wisdom], and this is the light of the purpose of creation. Also, it is sometimes referred to as "mitigation of the *Dinim* [judgments]." That is, there were *Dinim* on the vessel of reception, meaning that there was a *Din* [judgment] that it is forbidden to use this *Kli* because it creates disparity of form and separation, and now it has been mitigated. And what is the mitigation? It is placing on the *Kli* the intention called "in order to bestow."

This means that before one places the aim to bestow on the will to receive, that desire caused him bitterness. Anything spiritual that he wanted to touch tasted bitter because there were *Tzimtzum* [restriction] and concealment on the will to receive for himself, so it was impossible to taste a good flavor in spirituality. In other words, anything holy felt remote, inaccessible, and impossible for the will to receive to enjoy. This is called "bitter."

However, if he places the aim to bestow over this desire, he sees and feels that there is sweetness in everything in holiness. But in matters that do not belong to holiness, he must turn away from them, meaning that he cannot tolerate them.

It follows that after he corrects himself so he can now aim in order to bestow, we should discern a light and a *Kli* here, which consists of *Aviut* [thickness] and *Masach* [screen]. The *Aviut* is called *Dinim*, where there are *Tzimtzum* and concealment, and the light does not shine there. This is why *Aviut* is called "darkness."

In other words, wanting to receive for himself is called "being *Av* [thick]," and wanting to bestow is called *Zach* [pure/clean/immaculate]. Afterwards, when he places the will to bestow over this *Av*, the *Din* is mitigated and what was previously dark becomes a place where the light shines in the *Kli*. This is called "mitigation of the *Dinim*."

2) We should also note that there are vessels of bestowal in a person, things that a person gives to his friend so his friend will enjoy. The giving itself is called "bestowal." A person who is *Zach* is one who tries to make people happy, to make them feel good. On these *Kelim*, it cannot be said that there is *Din* in these actions, meaning that there is a judgment that prohibits using *Kelim* that wish to bestow.

However, here, too, there is a matter of intention, meaning whether he is sincere. That is, when he gives, is his aim that others will enjoy it without a care for himself, for he cares only about others? This quality is called "bestowing in order to bestow," when the act and the aim are both in order to bestow.

Sometimes, everything he does is for the good of others, but the aim is to obtain respect or similar things. It is as *The Zohar* writes about the wicked, that all the good that they do, they do for their own benefit, "All the good that they do, they do for themselves." And here, there is no *Din* from the perspective of the *Kli*, meaning no deficiency. In other words, in terms of the act, there is nothing to correct.

However, in the intention there needs to be a correction. That is, from the perspective of the aim, there is no difference whether the act is bestowal or the act is reception. Both actions need correction so the aim, too, will be in order to bestow.

This is so because the work is primarily in the heart. That is, a person should reach the degree of love of the Creator, as it is written, "And you shall love the Lord your God with all your heart and with all your soul." Everything we do in Torah and *Mitzvot* [commandments] is to correct the heart. It is written about it ("Introduction to the Book, Panim Meirot uMasbirot," Item 10), "Come and see the words of the sage, Rabbi Abraham ibn Ezra ... 'Know that all the *Mitzvot* that are written in the Torah or the conventions that the fathers have established ... are all in order to correct the heart, 'For the Lord searches all hearts.'"

With the above said, we can generally detect the two matters—the purpose of creation, to do good to His creations; this light is called *Hochma*, and "seeing," which means that he sees what he has in his hand, meaning he can already count how much he has obtained, since the purpose of creation is to do good, and then one should feel and attain what he has in his hand.

For example, let us say that there are two brothers, one of whom is rich and lives in the United States, and the other is poor and lives in Israel. The rich brother deposits a million dollars in the bank under the name of the poor brother. However, he did not let the poor brother know about it, nor did the bank inform the poor brother that he has money in his name. So this brother remains poor because he does not know about it.

It is the same here with the purpose of creation to do good to His creations. If they do not know and do not feel the delight and pleasure, what benefit is it? This is why this light is called *Hochma* [wisdom] and "seeing," and is named "light of *Panim* [face/anterior]," as in, "A man's wisdom illuminates his face."

In the work, this is called "something that is counted," meaning something that is received in the vessels of reception. This means that if he receives it, he will see what he has received and will be able to count what he has.

It is also called "a gift." Usually, when someone gives his friend a gift, he wants his friend to count and appreciate the value of the present for the simple reason that he gives the present to his friend because he wants to show his love for him. According to the value of the gift, a person can appreciate the measure of the love. It follows that if one does not look at the gift, to see the greatness of the gift, he blemishes the measure of the love.

Therefore, when a person receives a gift, if he does not see or does not try to see the importance of the gift, he blemishes the measure of love that the giver wants to show by it. For instance, our sages said, "Buy yourself a friend." And that person wants to buy his friend by sending him gifts. If that person does not see or appreciate the greatness and importance of the gift that he receives from him, how can he come to a state of "Buy yourself a friend"? It follows that with the gift, one should count and measure what he has received from his friend.

Therefore, if the creatures cannot count and measure what the Creator gives them, then the purpose of the Creator does not reach a state where the creatures attain that He created creation with the aim to do good to His creations.

This is called "light of Hochma," and this light is received in the vessels of reception. However, one must also use it with the correction that was placed on the vessels of reception, called "receiving in order to bestow." This means that one should put an aim to bestow on the vessel of reception. And if he does not place the aim to bestow, he becomes separated from the Life of Lives, since disparity of form causes separation. Thus, by becoming a receiver, it causes him spiritual death, as was said above, "The wicked, in their lives they are called 'dead.'"

However, the light that is received in the vessels of bestowal is called "light of Hassadim [mercy]." Hesed [mercy/grace] means that he is giving, like a person who performs an act of mercy or grace toward his friend. This is called "covered Hassadim," meaning that the Hassadim—what he receives in vessels of bestowal, meaning what he gives—the light has the same value as the Kli.

In other words, it is known that there is charity and there is a gift. With a gift, we explained above that a person must see what he received and not simply receive a gift from his friend. If a person says, "It doesn't matter what he gave me," he is blemishing his friend's gift. Thus, the purpose for which he sent him the gift is not realized. The gift was meant to buy him a friend, as was said above, "Buy yourself a friend," but if he does not see the importance of the gift, he cannot buy him as a friend. Hence, he must count and measure the gift.

But when a person sends charity to his friend, the giver should try—if he truly wants to give charity—for the receiver of the charity not to know who sent him the charity. And the receiver of the charity will also be very happy if he knew that the giver of the charity did not know to whom he gave.

Similarly, sometimes people collect money for an important person and they do not want the receiver of the charity to be ashamed. Those who collect the money say, "We are collecting for someone anonymously." Thus, with charity, when neither knows—the giver or the receiver—it is considered true charity, and there is no unpleasantness on the part of the receiver of the charity.

It follows that in *Hesed*, we speak from the perspective of the giver, meaning the lower one. At that time, a person is in a state where he acts above reason, meaning he gives but does not know to whom he gives, but he believes that everything he gives goes to its purpose. This is called "charity in concealment."

Charity is considered *Hassadim*, that he gives. That is, we speak of a time when a person is working with the vessels of bestowal, meaning we are only speaking of a person who is bestowing upon the Creator. This is called "a blessing," like a person blessing another, speaking to him in a favorable manner, meaning blesses [greets] him. He does not actually give him, but it is still considered that he blesses him verbally. This is already regarded as a blessing in the heart. In other words, what he cannot give in actual fact, he gives with the heart, and he shows him verbally what is in his heart.

It follows that blessing means giving, bestowal. That is, at that time, he engages in vessels of bestowal. This means that a blessing is when he wants his friend to have more than he can actually give. Hence, when a person engages in bestowal, he wants to give contentment to his Maker, so he says to the Creator, "More than the good deeds that I can give You, I bless You that I will be able to give You more than good deeds." In other words, one should always bless the Creator, which means that he wants to be able to give more contentment to the Creator than he is actually giving Him.

This is why there is no issue of counting on a blessing, since vessels of bestowal are called "charity," and charity should be giving in concealment, meaning that the giver does not know to whom he is giving and the receiver does not know from whom he is receiving. Thus, there is no issue of counting here, for counting brings the excitement and a bond of love, as is said regarding a gift.

With the gift, our sages said, it is completely the opposite: "He who gives a present to his friend must let him know." This is so because the result of the gift should be love, which connects the two, unlike charity, where he must be entirely to bestow. This means that in charity, it is best if one does not know the other, making counting irrelevant.

Therefore, when speaking in the work, charity means vessels of bestowal, when the *Kli* wishes to do *Hesed*, and the light that is poured into the *Kli* is called "light of *Hassadim*." This is called "the correction of creation," when everything is in order to bestow.

But the purpose of creation is for the *Kelim* to receive delight and pleasure, and here they must certainly see what they are receiving because one speaks about the purpose of creation, that it is good and to do good, according to what he receives. If he cannot count what he received, it means that he still did not receive in a way that the delight and pleasure are felt in him. Thus, he still cannot say that now he sees that he received from the Creator only delight and pleasure. This is why light of *Hochma*—the purpose of creation—is also called "seeing," since the purpose of creation is considered seeing.

But it is to the contrary with the correction of creation. It is called "covered *Hassadim*," meaning that he still does not see everything that he is receiving and it is still covered from him. In the work, it is called "desiring mercy [*Hesed*]," meaning only to bestow. It is of no interest to him if he is receiving anything from above. It is considered that he is content with his share, meaning that he is happy that he can do something in the work of the Creator.

In other words, he is content with his share of being able to say that he is doing something that is not for the needs of his material body, as our sages said, "He who walks and does not do, the reward for walking is in his hand" (*Avot*, Chapter 5:14).

The interpreters explain, "The reward for walking is in his hand." Even though he is not doing, he still has the reward of walking, for even going to the seminary is a *Mitzva* [commandment/good deed] in itself, since there he is in an atmosphere of Torah. It follows that it should be noted if a person engages in vessels of bestowal—called *Hesed*, where there is no issue of counting because he wants to work in charity—it is regarded as "the correction of creation."

With the above said, we will understand what we asked, why they said, "Out of His fondness for them, He counts them every hour." We asked, If the Creator wants to know the number of Israel, does He have to wait until Israel count and then submit the sum to the Creator, and only then He will know Israel's number?

Indeed, "Out of His fondness" means that He sees that they are doing everything in order to bestow. This means that they have already made the correction of creation, and this is why He wants to give them the purpose of creation, which is light of *Hochma*, called "light of seeing." In other words, they should already be counting what they have because this light is received in vessels of reception.

However, they should receive it in order to bestow, and according to the rule that the act follows the aim, while one is engaged in acts of reception of pleasure, the act of reception might cause the aim not to be in order to bestow but in order to receive. And reception for oneself causes separation from the Life of Lives, which is considered death, as it is written, "The wicked, in their lives they are called 'dead.'"

It was written, "Why does death increase because of the counting?" The answer is that since something that is counted is called "light of *Hochma*," which is received in vessels of reception, the act might govern the aim and he will not be able to aim in order to bestow. Thus, naturally, it will be death.

And it was written, "He replies, 'It is because there is no blessing in counting, and when the blessing is gone, the *Sitra Achra* is on him.'" In other words, there is the matter of the middle line, when *Hochma* shines in the vessels of reception, which is called "left." They need correction so that one is not drawn after the act of reception. In that state, the light of *Hassadim*—which works with the vessels of bestowal—must be drawn, and we have said above that acts of bestowal affect the thought to be like the act.

This is the keeping over the light of *Hochma* that is received in the *Kelim* of the left line, which requires correction. However, one cannot be rewarded with the light of *Hochma* before one has been rewarded with the degree of *Lishma*, meaning that everything one does is *Lishma*. In other words, the order of the work is that first, one is rewarded with *Katnut* [smallness/infancy], considered that he can only aim the vessels of bestowal to be in order to bestow. Afterward, one is rewarded with *Gadlut* [greatness/adulthood], which means that he can aim in order to bestow in vessels of reception, too, where the light of *Hochma* shines—the light of the purpose of creation.

It follows that before one is rewarded with the light in the count, one must be rewarded with the light of *Hassadim*, called "blessing," meaning that he blesses the Creator and does not want to receive anything from Him. Instead, he is all about bestowal and does not want to receive anything for himself. Afterward, he is rewarded with the light of *Hochma*, which is a light of counting. This means that this light comes in vessels of reception, at which time the light in the counting requires keeping so he will not be drawn after the act. Because it is an act of reception, a light of blessing must be drawn once more, meaning light of *Hassadim*, which is the keeping.

Now we can interpret what we asked:

1) Did the Creator want to know the number of the children of Israel, and this is why He wished to count the children of Israel, so that the people of Israel would tell Him the number, and the Creator did not know by Himself? The answer is that since He loves them, He wanted the people of Israel to know their number. In other words, the Creator wants them to obtain the light of *Hochma*. It follows that He wants to know, that they will know and attain the light that is in counting, meaning that they themselves will count and see what they have attained, for this is called "the light of seeing," which comes to the vessels of reception. He does not need to know for Himself, but so that the people of Israel will know.

2) Why is there death where there is no blessing? The answer is that something that is counted is light of *Hochma*, which comes into vessels of reception. When using vessels of reception, one might be drawn after the act of reception and thus be separated from the Life of Lives. This is called "death," and this is why keeping is required. The keeping is the blessing, meaning extension of light of *Hassadim*, which is an act of bestowal that keeps the act of reception from straying from the aim to bestow.

3) Why is there a need for a blessing before and after? The order of the work begins with a need to achieve *Lishma* [for Her sake]. Our sages said about it, "He who learns Torah *Lishma*, the secrets of Torah are revealed to him." Also, *Lishma* means that all his actions are in order to bestow, which is called a "blessing." When he gives, this is the meaning of a blessing, meaning oral blessing. That is, since he cannot add in action, he tries to give a blessing with the mouth, which indicates that what he is giving is with all his heart. This is called "light of *Hassadim*."

Thus, the order is as follows:

1) A blessing before, which is called "right line," *Hesed*.

2) He is rewarded with the secrets of Torah, called *Hochma* [wisdom], which is a gift, as it is known that Torah is called "a gift" that is received in vessels of reception. For this reason, it is called "a

count." In other words, he looks at what he received so as to know he should thank Him.

This is called "left line," since here is a place where he can come into death, called "separation," such as there was in the death of the seven kings in the world of *Nekudim*. For this reason, there is a need to extend *Hassadim*, and these *Hassadim* are the keeping so there will not be death in them, meaning separation from the Life of Lives.

This is why it is written that there is a need for a blessing at the end. It follows that Israel were blessed in the beginning and in the end, and there was no death in them.

In general, this is called "correction of lines," which are called "correction of the world," since by that the world exists.

4) What is a blessing in the work? It is light of *Hassadim*, when a person is in a state of giving.

5) What is counting in the work? It is the light that comes in vessels of reception. At that time, one needs to see what he has received and count them. This is considered "a gift."

6) Why is there no blessing in something that is counted? Something that is counted means the light and abundance that come into vessels of reception, and blessing is the abundance that comes into vessels of bestowal, and they are opposites. In *The Zohar*, it is considered that the two lines are in dispute, since the right line, called *Hesed*, is only to bestow and does not wish to use the vessels of reception; but the left line is the opposite—it wishes to use specifically the vessels of reception, since it says, "But the purpose of creation is to receive!" However, there should be a correction to be in order to bestow. For this reason, afterward comes the middle line, which makes peace between them. This is why there is a need for a blessing in the beginning, and a blessing at the end.

What "Israel Do the Creator's Will" Means in the Work

Article No. 32, Tav-Shin-Nun, 1989/90

Our sages said (*Midrash Rabbah*, *Nasso*, Portion 11:7), One verse says, "The Lord will favor you," and another verse says, "who will not be biased." How do these two verses coexist? When Israel do the Creator's will, He favors them. When they do not do the Creator's will, He "will not be biased."

This is perplexing: 1) If they do the Creator's will, why do they need partiality? After all, they are fine, so what else do they need to do in order to be fine? 2) The verse says (Deuteronomy 10), "who will not be biased and will not take a bribe." But if we do the Creator's will, there is no greater bribe than this. It is the same as among people, when someone wants the judge to be on his side in a trial, he does what the judge wants and in return the judge leans toward him in the trial and acquits him. So what is the answer that if they do the Creator's will, He will be biased, as though He would take a bribe?

To understand these two questions, we need to understand the following:

1. What is "the face of the Creator" [in Hebrew, "turning the face to someone" means being biased toward him], and what is "will not turn lift up the face [be biased]"?

2. What is doing the Creator's will and what is not doing the Creator's will?

3. Our sages said, "The Creator said, 'I have created the evil inclination; I have created the Torah as a spice.'" We should understand what is the evil inclination and what is the spice.

4. Our sages also said, "I labored and found, believe; I did not labor but found; do not believe." We should understand what is the meaning of labor. That is, why did they say that there is labor specifically in Torah and Mitzvot [commandments/good deeds], and without labor, nothing is given. Where is the novelty here? After all, in the corporeal world, where there is no connection to the work of the Creator, nothing is given without work and labor, too. As we can see, the custom is that a person goes to work, as it is written, "One should leave for one's toil and labor until evening." Thus, where is the novelty in that Torah and Mitzvot require labor, and without labor no reward is given, to the point that they say, "I found but did not labor, do not believe"? After all, in corporeality, too, there is no such thing as a person obtaining something without labor. Therefore, we should understand why they said, "I did not labor but found, do not believe."

We know that there are two matters before us: 1) the purpose of creation, 2) the correction of creation.

The purpose of creation is for the creatures to receive delight, to feel contentment. The correction of creation is for the Creator to have contentment. That is, there must be equivalence of form, where as the Creator wants the creatures to enjoy, as it is written, that the creation of the world was because of His desire to do good to His creations, and since the Creator is the giver and the creatures the receivers, the creatures should also bestow contentment upon the Creator. Then it is considered that the creatures seemingly give and the Creator receives, as our sages said, "Israel furnish their father in heaven." This is called "correction." That is, in order to have equivalence of form with the Creator, there must be "Cling unto His attributes."

However, how does one achieve a state where he wants to do everything for the sake of the Creator and not for his own sake, while man is born with a desire to receive for his own sake? As we learned, this desire—that the Creator wants to delight the creatures—the Creator created in the creatures this desire, a desire to receive, to want and to yearn to satisfy their deficiencies. That is, the Creator created in the creatures a lack. This lack demands its satisfaction, or this lack yields in us suffering, which forces a person to do everything he can to satisfy his lack.

Thus, when a person has a desire and a yearning to satisfy his lack, how can he relinquish the satisfaction of his lack and say that he receives the filling because he wants to satisfy the Creator's will? That is, since the Creator wants the creatures to enjoy abundance, therefore, he receives only for this reason. This is against the way that the Creator created nature!

To this comes the answer, "The Creator said, 'I have created the evil inclination; I have created the Torah as a spice.'" This means that the will to receive for oneself is called the "evil inclination," since it obstructs us from achieving *Dvekut* [adhesion] with the Creator, called "equivalence of form." Through the Torah, there is the light of Torah that reforms him so as to have the power to overcome the will to receive for himself and do everything for the sake of the Creator.

It therefore follows that the reason that should compel a person to engage in Torah and *Mitzvot* is in order to obtain vessels of bestowal, which is called the "correction of creation." When a person engages in Torah and *Mitzvot* with this intention, it is regarded as "working *Lishma* [for Her sake]." That is, he works and labors in order to obtain something that does not exist in nature. For this reason, he needs the *Segula* [remedy/virtue] of Torah and *Mitzvot* to make him obtain these *Kelim* [vessels], which he cannot obtain by himself unless with the help of the Creator. This *Segula* is found in Torah and *Mitzvot*, and this is called the "light of Torah," as was said, "the light in it reforms him."

However, our sages said, "One should always engage in Torah and *Mitzvot*, even if *Lo Lishma* [not for Her sake], since from *Lo Lishma* he comes to *Lishma* [for Her sake]." That is, the beginning of man's work is *Lo Lishma*, meaning to receive reward, as it is written in *The Zohar*, "either for a reward in this world, or a reward in the next world." When a person works for a reward, he must believe in reward and punishment. If he believes in this, his work is regarded as "according to nature," meaning that the body does not resist his work in Torah and *Mitzvot* because at that time he is working for his own sake.

This is called "the natural way," as in corporeal affairs, when we work we get reward. Yet, in corporeality, he sees the reward in the same place, so the reward mandates the work, while in Torah and *Mitzvot* he must believe in the reward, so there is work to believe in reward and punishment. But when he believes in reward and punishment, the body can do the holy work.

However, when a person wants to engage in Torah and *Mitzvot* not in order to receive reward, the body objects to this, as it is against nature. By nature, a person can work only for his own sake. Therefore, when he wants to work for the sake of the Creator, the body objects to this.

Here begins the labor, as our sages said, "I labored but did not find, do not believe; I did not labor but found, do not believe." Indeed, it is difficult to understand how a person can deceive himself and say, "I did not labor but found." After all, in corporeality, we do not see that a person finds provision without labor. And here, in the work, where our sages said, "A thousand walk into a room and one comes out to teach," we see that acquiring Torah is harder than obtaining corporeality. And in corporeality, we do not obtain anything without labor, so how can a person say that he has obtained something without labor?

We should also understand what they said, "I labored but did not find." Does one lie when he says, "I did not find," of which they said, "do not believe"? After all, we are speaking of a person who wants to obtain something in the Torah, would he lie?

The thing is that when a person wants to work and achieve the degree of *Dvekut*, which is equivalence of form, as the Creator wants to bestow upon the creatures, man, too, wants to come to be able to do the Creator's will. That is, as the Creator wants to bestow, so man wants to do everything in order to bestow. But since bestowing is against nature, man cannot obtain this desire, as it contradicts human nature, for the Creator created man with a desire to receive, so how can man go against the nature with which the Creator created him? Only the Creator can change nature, but not man, as our sages said (*Taanit* 25), "He who said to the oil, 'Burn!' will say to the vinegar, 'Burn!'"

Therefore, here, too, in work matters, we must say, "He who created in the creatures the desire to receive for oneself will give the creatures the desire to bestow." That is, only the Creator can change nature, and not man. This is why it is called "a miracle from above," as it is above nature. This is called "the miracle of the exodus from Egypt," when the Creator delivered them from control of the Egyptians, which is the control of the will to receive.

Accordingly, "I labored but did not find" means that I have made great efforts to be rewarded with the desire to bestow, meaning I have done everything I could but did not find within me the desire to bestow and I remained with the will to receive for myself even more than when I began the work on obtaining the desire to bestow, which is the Creator's will, whose desire is only to bestow. When I began to labor, I saw that each time I found myself immersed deeper in the will to receive for myself. Then, I decided that it is true that I labored but did not find, but the Creator helped me find in me the desire to bestow. This is as *The Zohar* says, "He who comes to purify is aided." And it asks, "With what?" It replies, "With a holy soul. When he is born, he is given a soul. He is rewarded more..."

It follows that the Creator gives him the soul, each time a higher degree, and this is called the "face of the Creator," meaning the light of the Creator, called when it is a complete degree by the name NRNHY. This is the assistance he receives from above.

It therefore follows that when a person says, "I did not labor," it means that the labor did not help him at all, so as to be able to say that through the labor he has found within him the desire to bestow. If the Creator had not given him the light of His face, called a "holy soul," he would remain in the will to receive for himself, and nothing more. It follows that when he says, "I labored but did not find," he is telling the truth, meaning that his labor did not help him whatsoever.

Here we should ask, If he is right when he says "I did not labor," why did they say, "Do not believe"? The answer is that one is not given something for which he has no need, since one who has a need and asks the Creator to satisfy his need receives from above a filling for his need. Therefore, the person's labor and desire to be rewarded with vessels of bestowal, and his labor and toil for this, for obtaining the desire of the Creator, called "desire to bestow," this is the Kli [vessel], and the light is called "The desire to bestow." Only the Creator can give this desire. That is, just as He has given to man the desire to receive when he was born, He can later give him the desire to bestow. But if a person does not labor in order to obtain the desire to bestow, then he has no need. And the evidence that it is not worth his while to exert and toil in order to be rewarded with it is that he cannot receive from above this desire that will change the workings of nature.

By this we can interpret what our sages said (Avot, Chapter 2:21), "It is not for you to finish the work, nor are you free to idle away from it." We should interpret that if a person knows that he cannot obtain the desire to bestow, but only the Creator can give it to him, then why does he need to labor in vain, since he cannot obtain it?

Therefore, we should ask, Why do I need this work? since in any case, he cannot obtain this by himself.

Our sages said about this, "You are not free to rid yourself of it." This is so because man's labor is required not because man can obtain the desire to bestow, since the desire to bestow is called "light," as it is written, "He who comes to purify is aided," and the aid, says *The Zohar*, is the light of *Neshama*, as it is written that he is assisted by giving him a holy *Neshama* [soul]. Rather, we need the labor for the *Kli*, meaning to obtain the lack—how much he needs the Creator's help, to help him and give him the light of *Neshama*.

However, when a person begins to work in order to obtain the desire of the Creator, which is the desire to bestow, just as the Creator wants to bestow, and a person thinks that he must obtain this by himself, during the work, he sees that each time he becomes more immersed in self-love. At that time, a person escapes the campaign because he sees that he is not advancing. Then the person tells himself that this work of obtaining the desire of the Creator is not for him. Why? Because he sees that each time he becomes worse.

Yet, if a person believes that only the Creator gives the desire to bestow, then why should he escape the campaign and say that it is for more gifted people? After all, the Creator helps with this, so why is it important to the Creator to differentiate one person from other people?

It is known that to the Creator, small and great are equal. Hence, when a person says that working only to bestow is only for a chosen few and not for ordinary people, it is a sign that he thinks that it is within man's hands to obtain the desire to bestow. For this reason, a person must be strong-minded and believe that he is not required to achieve this desire. Rather, he is required to have a need to achieve the desire to bestow. And when he has a true desire and need to achieve this, the Creator will help him, as it is written, "He who comes to purify is aided." All the labor that one should give is only to obtain the need and desire to bestow, and nothing else.

Yet, there is a question: When a person feels the bad, to the extent that the will to receive obstructs him from achieving *Dvekut*, and he prays to the Creator to help him and give him the desire to bestow, why after several efforts that a person has given in order to obtain the desire to bestow, it makes sense that the Creator should give him the desire to bestow? But in the end, what does one receive? Not only did he not get help by the Creator giving him the desire to bestow, but instead, in return for the effort he made, he receives an even stronger desire. That is, each time, he sees that his will to receive has grown more excessive. Therefore, he sees here the opposite work of what should have happened.

The answer is that a person cannot be shown how much evil there is in him, meaning the full measure of evil with which one is born, as it is written in *The Zohar* about the verse "Sin crouches at the door," that as soon as one comes out of the womb, the evil, called "sin," comes along with it. If one were to see all the evil in him, he would immediately say that this work of doing everything for the sake of the Creator is not for him, and he would not even want to begin the work. He would give up in advance.

For this reason, only a little bit of evil is shown to a person, and for the little bit of evil, a person begins to ask the Creator to help him. At that time, some more evil is revealed to a person and he begins to ask the Creator for help once more. Therefore, after every request for help, he can be shown a little more evil, and so he adds requests, and more revelation of evil within him is added to him. Finally, a person gives all the prayers about all the evil that is in him, and then he receives the good he asks for, meaning the desire to bestow, for which he begins to work in order to obtain this desire, which is the will of the Creator, whose desire is only to bestow.

It follows that if a person receives the desire to bestow on a little bit of evil, he will think that this is enough for him. If he is satisfied in the work, then all the evil that is left in him, for which he did not receive the correction of a desire to bestow, this bad will stay within him uncorrected. Conversely, when they see above that each time he asks for help over the bad that is revealed in him each day, then all the bad within him, meaning which was revealed to him, he asks for help from above, and the help he receives through his prayers now is that evil is revealed to him so that in this way, all the evil will be revealed in him.

Afterward, when he receives the help from above, all the bad will be corrected into work in order to bestow. Because he did not receive the desire to bestow in the middle of the work, he does not have anything from which to derive satisfaction. For this reason, he prays each time to be given the desire to bestow. Then, through his prayers, when he asks the Creator to give him the help, there is room for the evil to be revealed in him because he is standing and crying out to be given the help he needs.

This is similar to an expert physician who comes to the country, who heals all of man's sicknesses in the world. However, a person can only see him once. Any patient who comes to him, whatever illnesses the patient tells him, he heals. One patient came to him with stomach problems, and the doctor healed him. Afterward, the patient learned he had a heart disease, for example, and wanted to go see the doctor. But since he has already been to the doctor and the doctor does not see patients twice, then he was left with a heart disease for the rest of his life. Another patient went in and said, "I have a heart disease and arthritis, and my gallbladder is also troubling me," since other doctors told him he was suffering from this illness, too. He went to the expert doctor, who healed everything at once. But other patients, who did not know their illnesses, remained with the illnesses they had.

Then, all the patients who did not know their illnesses came to consult with the doctor about how they might know all their illnesses when he gives them the medicine, so it will cure all their sicknesses. Then, the doctor said that anyone who wants to see him, while he makes an appointment, he will give him a pill, and this pill that the doctor gives them will show them all their illnesses. Afterward, when they come to him, he will cure them. Thus, all the illnesses that each one has will be cured at once.

But the patients did not understand what the doctor told them. When they took the pill that the doctor gave them when they made an appointment with him. Therefore, each one saw that he was a little sick, and the doctor gave them a cure and they were healed. Now he sees the doctor's expertise, that now he has become sicker than before. Previously, he suffered from one disease, and now he sees that each time his situation worsens. That is, sometimes he had headaches, but now he has heartaches, or stomachaches, and so on. Everyone yells at the mediators for advising them to go to this doctor, since they have become worse since they went to the doctor, and still the doctor himself did not treat them, only the doctor's secretary when he made an appointment to see the doctor. She gave him a pill and his situation has worsened each day.

The lesson is that when a person signs up to do the holy work, which is to achieve the desire of the Creator, the desire to bestow, he is told that the doctor heals all the illnesses at once, and our illness is called "will to receive for ourselves." In order for the desire to receive to be revealed within man to its full meanness, otherwise, if he asks the Creator to be given help to be able to overcome the will to receive and perform actions in order to bestow, then that person will be satisfied with the work of the desire to bestow.

Thus, the bad will remain in him but will not be revealed, as in corporeality when a person is sick but does not know his illness and must take tests to know the illness. Likewise, a person who wants to work and labor in order to be able to do the Creator's will, the person does not know his illness, and only through Torah and work can we know his illness.

This is as our sages said, "If his head aches, let him engage in Torah." Baal HaSulam interpreted that it means he has foreign thoughts. "If his stomach aches," this means that the will to receive in his guts controls him, and so forth. Hence, first, all the evil in a person must be revealed, and he does not receive the desire to bestow immediately after he has labored. Rather, it is until all the evil in him is revealed. Then, when he receives the desire to bestow, it is over all the evil in him.

It follows that the fact that one sees that he is growing worse each time is a sign that he is walking on the path of truth. The evidence is that the way he is walking on is doing its thing. It is like a person giving a medicine to the sick person once, and he comes to the doctor and tells him, "Now, through your medicine, the illness has become worse." Then the doctor tells him, "On the contrary, now I see that my medicine has begun to work. It is simply that first it works in one way, and then it works in another way until he regains his health."

According to the above, we will understand what we asked, What is "doing the Creator's will"? We should interpret, a desire to bestow, meaning that His will is to do good to His creations, and He wants the created beings to enjoy. Likewise, man wants to obtain that desire because he wants adhesion with the Creator, which is the meaning of equivalence of form. Since man was created with an opposite desire—a desire only to receive and not to bestow—he therefore has much labor to obtain it.

Conversely, when a person works and receives reward in corporeality, it is not regarded as "labor," since it is not against nature, since everything he does is for his own benefit.

This is not so in the work to obtain the will of the Creator, namely the desire to bestow, where one does only that which yields benefit to the Creator and not to himself. This is labor, since it is against nature. Such a person cannot obtain this desire by himself, but needs the Creator to give it to him. This is called the Creator "favoring him," since it is impossible to obtain this unless miraculously, above nature.

It follows that there is no other way to obtain this desire unless by being favored. This is the meaning of the words, "The Lord will favor you." The Midrash explains that when they do the Creator's will, when they work on obtaining this desire, the Creator must give man the *Panim* [face/anterior] of the Creator, called a *Neshama* [soul]. That is, he is assisted by giving him a holy soul, which is the face of the Creator, as there is no other way to be rewarded with the will of the Creator unless through the Creator's face [favor]. This is the meaning of "The Lord will favor you."

This is not so with people who do not engage in Torah and Mitzvot in order to be rewarded with the will of the Creator, but engage in Torah and Mitzvot for a reward. They do not need the face of the Creator, called a "soul," since they are not going against nature. Hence, to the extent that they believe in reward and punishment, they can engage in Torah and Mitzvot, since the reward awakens them to work. It follows that when they do not do the Creator's will, meaning engage in Torah and Mitzvot, they do not want reward for their work—that the Creator will give them the desire to bestow, but rather a reward for the will to receive. It is written about them that He "will not be biased," since they do not need a soul, that He would give them, for the face of the Creator is the light of the Creator, called a "holy soul," which a person receives in order to reform him, and which is called "help from above."

It therefore follows that what they said, that when they do not do the Creator's will, the Creator will not favor them, it is because they do not need the Creator to give them the soul that will reform them, since they feel that they are good, that they are observing Torah and Mitzvot in all its details and intricacies. And what is the reason for which they engage in Torah and Mitzvot? It is the reward. To the extent that they believe in reward and punishment, they can do the holy work, since this does not contradict the desire to receive.

Therefore, precisely when they do the Creator's will, meaning when their work in Torah and Mitzvot is because "I have created the evil inclination; I have created the Torah as a spice," then they are learning Torah in order to emerge from the control of the will to receive, which is called the "evil inclination." They need the light of Torah, for by this they will be rewarded with the desire of the Creator, which is the desire to bestow. By this we will understand what we asked, What is the "face of the Creator"? The answer is that it is a light, the holy soul that the Creator gives to a person in order to reform him.

Now we can also understand what we asked, What is "who ... will not take a bribe"? After all, doing the Creator's will seems to be a bribery in itself. The answer is that he wants the Creator to favor him, meaning give him a holy soul, not for his own sake. On the contrary, he wants the Creator to favor him so he can emerge from self-benefit and be able to work only for the sake of the Creator, and not for his own sake.

Thus, he does not want the Creator to give him something for his own sake, that we can say that the person is bribing the Creator the way one bribes by giving someone a gift with the aim that the receiver of the gift will give the giver of the gift something for his own sake. Conversely, here, a person doing the Creator's will means that he wants to be able to do the Creator's will and asks Him to favor him so he can do all that he does for the sake of the Creator.

By this we understand that the "evil inclination" is the will to receive, and the "spice" is the power to emerge from the control of the will to receive, and the Torah is called "the light of Torah," which is the interior of the Torah, the soul of the Torah.

What Is "The Earth Feared and Was Still," in the Work?

Article No. 33, Tav-Shin-Nun, 1989/90

Our sages wrote in *Masechet Shabbat* (p 88a), "Rabbi Hizkiya said, 'Why is it written, 'From heaven You sounded judgment, the earth feared and was still'? If it feared, why was it still? And if it was still, why did it fear? Indeed, first it feared and in the end it was still. And why did it fear? As Rish Lakish said, 'Why is it written, 'And there was evening and there was morning, the sixth day'? Why the extra *Hey* [in Hebrew]? It shows that the Creator set a condition along with the work of creation and told them, 'If Israel receive the Torah, you exist. If they do not, I send you back to *Tohu ve Bohu* [chaos].'''"

We should understand why the Creator set a condition along with the work of creation, that it depends: If Israel accept the Torah, very well. If not, He will return them to *Tohu ve Bohu*. First we should understand what is the work of creation. We see that we refer to the whole of the work of creation by the name "Earth," as it is written, "The earth feared and was still." Therefore, we should understand what the word "earth" implies. The verse says, "In the beginning, God created the heaven and the earth." Thus, why does it call the work of creation only by the name "earth," as it is written, "The earth feared and was still"?

We should interpret that "the work of creation" pertains to the beginning of the thought. This means that the beginning of the thought of the work of the creation of the world is as it is written, "The purpose of creation was because of His desire to do good to His creations. This is the meaning of 'the work of creation.'" In other words, this is the purpose of the act, that the created beings will receive delight and pleasure.

However, in order for the pleasure that they receive to be complete, meaning that they will not feel shame upon the reception of the pleasures, there was a correction called *Tzimtzum* [restriction], where the light does not shine where there is a desire to receive for one's own sake, meaning that the light of pleasure does not reach there, but rather after the created beings correct themselves so as to have the intention to bestow.

It follows that if there is no intention to bestow, they will have no abundance. Naturally, the whole of the work of creation, meaning the purpose of creation to do good, there will be no one to receive it, and naturally, the whole purpose of the work of creation will be cancelled. We therefore understand that if there is no one with the aim to bestow, this is called "the return of the work of creation to *Tohu ve Bohu*."

However, we should understand the connection to Israel, that if Israel receive the Torah, the work of creation will persist, and if they do not, it will be cancelled. According to the above-said, that the Creator wants to give them delight and pleasure, and they also need to correct their will to receive so as to work in order to bestow, what is the connection between the correction to work in order to bestow, that because of this they must receive the Torah?

The answer is as our sages said, "The Creator said, 'I have created the evil inclination; I have created the Torah as a spice.' Through the Torah, its light reforms him," and he will achieve the intention to bestow. It follows that without Torah, there are *Tzimtzum* and concealment on creation, which is called "existence from absence," namely the vessels of reception, and the light of the Creator cannot come into the vessels of reception.

It follows that the work of creation, which is the matter of doing good to His creations, is cancelled if there are no *Kelim* [vessels] that can receive the purpose of creation, which is the delight and pleasure, due to the correction of the *Tzimtzum*. This correction comes by observing the Torah, and then instead of the *Tzimtzum*, the abundance appears once more.

However, according to this, it means that if a person has already achieved the correction of his *Kelim*, meaning that he already has *Kelim* that are called "receiving in order to bestow," why does he need the Torah? After all, he has already accepted all the counsels how to do everything for the sake of the Creator.

The answer is that it is known that *The Zohar* calls the 613 *Mitzvot* [commandments/good deeds] by the name "613 counsels" and by the name "613 deposits" ("Introduction of The Book of Zohar," "General Explanation for All Fourteen Commandments and How They Divide into the Seven Days of Creation," Item 1). These are tips by which to achieve the correction of creation, which is to obtain the desire to bestow, by which we acquire equivalence of form and the *Tzimtzum* and concealment are removed. This is the correction that our sages said, "I have created the evil inclination; I have created the Torah as a spice."

Once he has obtained the spice, the 613 *Mitzvot* are called "613 deposits," for in each *Mitzva* [singular of *Mitzvot*] there is a special light that is there as a deposit, waiting for man to have the suitable *Kli* [vessel] for it. At that time, a person is given what was there as a deposit, which he could not take out because the *Tzimtzum* and concealment governed it.

It follows that the purpose of creation is the 613 deposits, which are deposited there until the creatures correct the creation, and only then will they receive the purpose of creation. And the way by which to obtain the correction of creation—that everyone will have *Kelim* that can aim to bestow—is through the 613 *Mitzvot*, which are as counsels, meaning tips.

What are the counsels? It is as it is written, "The light in the Torah reforms him." We should know that in the 613 *Mitzvot*, which are called "counsels," a counsel is given when a person desires to obtain something but does not know how. That person seeks advice how to obtain that something.

Therefore, when a person observes Torah and *Mitzvot*, the body asks a person, "Why are you observing Torah and *Mitzvot*?" Then the person replies, "I believe in reward and punishment. Therefore, in order to receive reward and not to be punished, I observe Torah and *Mitzvot*." However, we cannot refer to reward and punishment as an advice, for an advice is a means to obtain something. It follows that counsels are one thing, and what one receives through the counsels is another thing.

Thus, one who observes Torah and *Mitzvot* in order receive reward, it cannot be said that they are tips how to receive reward. Rather, the work is called "labor," and the reward is called "return." It is not that we say that the work is the counsel for the reward. Rather, it is like an exchange, where the employee gives the employer the work, and in return, the employer pays him.

Thus, what is the meaning of the 613 counsels? We should interpret that counsels apply when a person wants to be rewarded with *Dvekut* [adhesion] with the Creator, meaning that he wants all his actions to be in order to bestow contentment upon his Maker and not to work for his own sake. Since man is born with a nature that he cannot understand doing anything other than for oneself, and a person wants to emerge from the governance of nature, but sees that he cannot do anything not for his own sake, then a person seeks advice how to obtain this desire.

Since the body claims that it is customary that one who does something for another receives reward, here, when a person begins to work for the sake of the Creator and not for his own sake, the body's resistance to the work grows stronger every time because the person wants to annul self-benefit through Torah and Mitzvot, meaning that he will not work for the sake of the body. How can the body give him energy to work on annulling it?

This is similar to one person assisting another person, who wants to kill him. Is it normal for a person to help the murderer kill him? Rather, as hard as one can, he resists him.

Therefore, when a person comes and says to the body, "I want to kill you," of course the body resists. It is as our sages said about the verse that King David said, "My heart is slain within me, that they killed the evil inclination through fasting."

Thus, the body certainly resists with all its might if he wants to work only in order to bestow. At that time, a person seeks advice how to emerge from the control of the evil inclination, called "will to receive for himself." It follows that only in this state, when he wants to work in order to bestow, he needs advice. It was said about this that the 613 Mitzvot are 613 counsels, meaning tips how to emerge from the control of the evil.

Thus, when a person learns Torah, he must intend that the Torah and Mitzvot he is doing will help him emerge from the control of the evil, and he will have the strength to do everything with the aim to bestow. Then, when he learns Torah, he wants the light in the Torah to reform him, and then he needs what they said, that the Creator said, "I have created the evil inclination; I have created the Torah as a spice." It follows that the Torah and Mitzvot that he engages in are to him in this state only as tips.

Now we can understand why after he was rewarded with vessels of bestowal through the tips of the Torah and Mitzvot, what should he do next in observing Torah and Mitzvot? That is, he no longer needs the Torah and Mitzvot as tips. It is known that the tips only cause to achieve the goal that he wants to achieve, and that until he found the counsels, he could not obtain what he wanted to obtain. The question is, What does he want? That is, What is the purpose he should achieve?

There is a simple answer to this: The purpose is that a person seeks advice how to achieve the goal. What is the purpose he must achieve? We should say that since a person does not work for his own sake, but has already been rewarded with emerging from the control of self-love, now he wants to achieve the purpose of the Creator, whose desire is to do good to His creations, for the created beings to receive delight and pleasure.

It follows that through the 613 counsels he has reached the goal of the Creator, meaning the Creator's desire for the creatures to receive delight and pleasure. *The Zohar* tells us about this that the delight and pleasure are as 613 deposits, that in each *Mitzva* there is a special light deposited, which waits for the time when it can return the deposit that is in the *Mitzva*, as was said, that in each *Mitzva* there is a special light that implies the *Mitzva* as a branch and root.

It follows that once a person has achieved 613 counsels, he observes the 613 deposits. For this reason, afterward there is a new order, and then the Torah is called "the names of the Creator." This discernment is called "the Torah, Israel, and the Creator are one."

It follows that we can detect many discernments in Torah and *Mitzvot*, but in general, they divide into three discernments: 1) *Lo Lishma* [not for Her sake], 2) *Lishma* [for Her sake], when all his actions are in order to bestow. At that time the 613 *Mitzvot* are to him as 613 counsels. 3) When one is rewarded with achieving the purpose of creation, for His desire is to do good to His creations. At that time, the 613 *Mitzvot* are to him as 613 deposits.

The 613 counsels are how to achieve *Lishma*, and the 613 deposits are called "revealing the secrets of Torah."

In *Lo Lishma*, there are also several discernments to make: 1) One who learns in order to complain. On this manner, it was said, "His Torah becomes to him a potion of death." 2) One who learns in order to be called "Rabbi" [great one/teacher]. Those two, he does only for the sake of people, and not for the sake of the Creator.

3) To be rewarded in this world. 4) To be rewarded in the next world. Those two, he does for the sake of the Creator and wants

the Creator to pay his reward. In the first two discernments, his reward is what he wants to receive from people like him. That is, one who learns in order to complain, his pleasure is from what he receives from his friend. Likewise, one who learns in order to be called Rabbis demands this of people and not of the Creator.

Now we can explain what we asked: 1) Why is the work of creation called specifically "earth"? After all, it is written, "In the beginning, God created the heaven and the earth." The answer is that "earth" is called *Malchut*, and our sages said, "Why was her name 'earth'? Because she wanted to do her Maker's will."

Generally, we speak of only two discernments: light and *Kli*. The abundance and all the lights are called "heaven," and all that receives them is called "earth." This is why it is written, "The earth feared and was still." When we speak in the work about "The earth feared and was still," we should interpret that *Eretz* [earth] means *Ratzon* [desire]. That is, the desire is in man's heart, fear. What is the fear? Since the *Kli* that receives the abundance is called "earth," and in man, his heart is called "earth," and since the purpose of creation to do good to His creations should appear within man's heart, since man's heart is called "will to receive," and since there was a *Tzimtzum* and concealment on the will to receive, the upper light does not reach there.

Thus, how can the purpose of creation, to do good to His creations, come to the creatures when all of creation is a desire to receive for oneself? It is through the Torah, as was said, "I have created the evil inclination; I have created the Torah as a spice," when they engage in Torah and *Mitzvot* with the aim to thereby be rewarded with vessels of bestowal.

However, there is fear on this, since the desire to bestow is against nature. Therefore, here the fear is because he is afraid that he might not be able to do everything in order to bestow, and the work of creation—which is the purpose of creation that must be revealed to the lower ones—will be cancelled.

That is, there are two things here: 1) Perhaps he will not be able to aim the learning of Torah to bring him the desire to bestow, since the body will do everything it can and will not let him aim that the Torah and *Mitzvot* he does will be with the aim to bring him the spice. Rather, he will have other thoughts: Why should he engage in Torah and *Mitzvot*? All this is because the body objects to it.

2) Fear that all the work of creation, namely the intention of the Creator to do good to His creations, will be cancelled and there will be no one to receive. Thus, the purpose of creation would not be carried out. This is why "the earth feared," meaning the general desire, called *Eretz* [earth], and every person's desire is also called "earth," since man's heart is called *Ratzon* [desire].

Accordingly, what is the condition that the Creator set along with the work of creation? If Israel accept the Torah, you persist. That is, only by observing the Torah, which is the spice that yields equivalence of form, there is room for the delight and pleasure, which is the work of creation, to persist, meaning that it can be revealed to the lower ones.

Also, why was specifically the earth afraid and not the heaven? It is because fear pertains only to the receivers, perhaps they will not be able to receive. But as for the light, called "heaven," fear does not pertain to the Creator. He certainly knows that what He wants will be carried out. Thus, all the fears pertain only to the receivers, called "earth."

We should interpret that thanks to fear, which is that he might not be able to be rewarded with the desire to bestow, thanks to fear they were rewarded with the desire to bestow through the Torah. This is why it was still.

What Are "A Layperson's Vessels," in the Work?

Article No. 34, Tav-Shin-Nun, 1989/90

The Midrash writes (*BeHaalotcha* 15:8), "'Even the darkness is not dark to You, and the night is as bright as the day; darkness and light are alike.' To us, it says, *BeHaalotcha* [when you mount] (the candles), what is this like? Like a king who had a man who loved him. The king said to him, 'Know that I will be dining at your place; go and set it up for me.' The man who loved him went and set up a layperson's bed, a layperson's lamp, and a layperson's table. When the king came, his servants came with him, surrounding him from here and from here, and a lamp of gold in front of him. When the man who loved him saw all the glory, he was ashamed and hid everything he had prepared for him, for it was all of laypeople. The king said to him: 'Did I not tell you that I would be dining at your place? Why have you not prepared anything for me?' The man who loved him replied, 'I saw all this glory that came with you and I was ashamed, so I hid everything that I had prepared for you, for they were laypeople's vessels.' The king said to him: 'By your life, I suspend all the vessels

I have brought, and because of your love, I use only yours. And He said to Israel, 'Prepare for Me a lampstand and candles.'"

We should understand what the Midrash is saying, that it is an answer to what the Creator commanded about the lampstand and the candles. After all, He has everything, as it is written, "Even the darkness is not dark to You," so the question is, Why does He need the lampstand and the candles?

The answer is that although the Creator has everything, He still wants the *Kelim* [vessels] of the lower one. He calls the *Kelim* of the lower one, "vessels of laypeople." Hence, we should understand what are the vessels of laypeople that the Creator wants specifically them.

It is known that the desire is called *Kli* [vessel]. We should interpret that His desire was to do good to His creations. This is called "the *Kli* of the Creator," meaning a desire to bestow. The Creator's desire to bestow created a desire to receive delight and pleasure, everything that the Creator wants the creatures to enjoy. This is called "vessels of the lower one."

This means that the will to receive is called "layperson and not *Kedusha* [holiness]," and the desire to bestow is called "a *Kli* of holiness." It is as our sages said about the verse, "You will be holy." "Can he be like Me?" This is why it is written, "For I am holy, for My holiness is above your holiness." They asked, would anyone think of saying that man is as holy as the Creator, that you must bring evidence from the text that this is not so? Can this be? However, the meaning of "Can he be like Me?" is "As I use only the desire to bestow."

For this reason, we can say that the people of Israel should also use only the desire to bestow, and not use the will to receive at all, as it is written, "Can he be like Me? Rather, My holiness is above your holiness," and you cannot stay with only the desire to bestow, for you also need to use the vessels of reception, except you must place on the *Kli* an aim to bestow.

According to the above, we should interpret that the *Kelim* of the Creator are vessels of bestowal, and there is no reception there whatsoever. Rather, His only wish is to bestow. But in order not to have the bread of shame, a *Tzimtzum* [restriction] and concealment were placed, by which the light shines only when there is the correction there that everything is in order to bestow. At that time, the Creator shines His light there.

By this we will understand the allegory that the king said that he wanted to dine at the place of the man who loved him and said to him, "Go and set it up for me," meaning do the work of receiving in order to bestow, and he went and set it up. Afterward, when the light came as a desire to bestow upon the lower ones, and the receiving person, although it is in order to bestow, the *Kli* with which he works is the desire to receive and not to bestow. Hence, now he was ashamed that he was using the *Kelim* of a layperson. Although he had the intention, the act was of reception.

Therefore, the person is ashamed and does not want to engage then in receiving in order to bestow. Instead, he wants to work only with vessels of bestowal, which are the King's *Kelim*. All the work that he did in order to make the intention to bestow, he concealed these *Kelim*, since now he was ashamed to use the *Kelim* of laypeople. The reason is that now he was awarded seeing the greatness and importance of the King, so he wants to work only because "He is great and ruling," meaning that the greatness of the King makes serving a great king the most important thing.

This is the meaning of the words, "When the king came, his servants came with him. When the man who loved him saw all the glory, he was ashamed." It follows that because of the greatness and importance of the King, he was ashamed to use laypeople's *Kelim*, which are vessels of reception.

This is the meaning of the words, "The king said to him: 'Did I not tell you that I would be dining at your place?'" We should understand what it means that the Creator dines at a person's place. However, we should understand in general, what it means that a person should do everything for the sake of the Creator, which is in order to bring contentment to his Maker. Our sages told us that we must believe in reward and punishment, as it is written, "You can trust your landlord to reward you for your work." This means that since the Creator needs someone to observe the Torah and Mitzvot [commandments/good deeds], and they are observing the Torah and Mitzvot in order to please Him, in return, the Creator pays reward.

We can understand this among people, where one needs the other to give to him, since his friend is deficient. At that time, we can speak of giving. And when his friend gives him a gift that the recipient enjoys, the recipient pays him as he deserves.

Yet, how can we say this about the Creator? Is He deficient and the lower ones can give Him something? Therefore, what does it mean that the people of Israel give work, and in return for the work, He gives reward? Also, we should understand what our sages said, "Israel provide for their Father in heaven." What provision do they give Him by which He is sustained?

It is known that that which gives a person joy, this sustains a person, giving him satisfaction in life. A person may be making a lot of money and has enough to eat and drink, but if he has no satisfaction in life, that person is considered as having nothing to sustain him, nothing to live on, meaning some pleasure for which it is worth living, for the joy he receives.

Therefore, there are people whose satisfaction in life is only from lust. They already have provision, meaning something to sustain them, that makes living worthwhile. That is, that which gives a person satisfaction, gives him meaning to life. For this reason, there are people in the world who are rich and have no lack of money, yet are fed up with life if they have nothing in life that satisfies them. It follows that "provision" does not necessarily mean food and drink. Rather, "provision" means that which sustains a person and from which he derives satisfaction in life.

According to the above, we should interpret what our sages said, "Israel provide for their Father in heaven." That is, they give the Creator a place to carry out His will, which was to do good to His creations, a place where the Creator can give to the created beings delight and pleasure, and which the creatures enjoy and say, "We feel the delight and pleasure that He contemplated giving, that He wants to give; we are receiving the delight and pleasure."

In other words, before we obtained the vessels of bestowal, so we can receive in order to bestow, the light of doing good to His creations could not come to the lower ones because the *Tzimtzum* and concealment were placed on the *Kelim* that were meant to receive the abundance. Hence, the thought of the Creator could not be realized. But when the people of Israel correct themselves with vessels of bestowal so they can receive in order to bestow, it is possible to carry out His will, meaning that the Creator enjoys His will having a place to be revealed.

This is called "Israel provide for their Father in heaven," since the pleasure of the creatures from receiving delight and pleasure is the Creator's provision. That is, the Creator enjoys His goal being carried out, and the realization of His desire to do good to His creations.

Now we can understand what we asked, What does it mean that the king said that he wants to dine and the place of the one who loves him? In corporeality, we can say that the king is dining at the place of a person who loves him, but how can we say that the Creator dines with the created beings?

The answer is that since the creatures enjoy the delight and pleasure that the Creator gives them, this is the Creator's meal, meaning His provision, for the King's meal, His provision, is only that the creatures receive from Him abundance. This is the meaning of "Israel provide for their Father in heaven."

Now we will also understand the meaning of what the king told him, "I will be dining at your place; go and set it up for me. The man who loved him went and set up a layperson's bed." "Layperson" means vessels of reception. He corrected them so as to work in order to bestow, as it is written, "When the king came and he saw all the glory," meaning he was rewarded with attaining the greatness of the king, he was ashamed to use the vessels of reception, even though they worked in order to bestow.

Now we will explain what the Midrash asks, "It is written, 'Even the darkness is not dark to You, and the night is as bright as the day,' etc. Thus, why did He say to Israel, 'Prepare for me a lampstand and candles'"? He answers this with the allegory. But we should understand the question, and then we will be able to understand the answer that we gave with the allegory.

In the literal meaning, it is difficult to understand what is the question that the Creator said to Israel, "Prepare for Me a lampstand and candles." Would anyone think that the lampstand and the candles are in order to illuminate for the Creator? So, what is the question that they answered with the allegory?

We should interpret that this is as it was at the time of the giving of the Torah. Our sages said (*Shabbat* 88), "When Moses went up to heaven, the ministering angels said to the Creator, 'Master of the world, what is a woman-born doing among us?' He replied to them, 'He has come to receive the Torah.' They said to Him: 'Concealed delight, You wish to give it to a flesh and blood? What is man, that You should remember him? The Lord our Master, how great is Your name in all the earth, place Your majesty on the heavens.' The Creator said to Moses, 'Answer them.' He said to them, 'Did you go down to Egypt? Is there evil inclination within you?' Promptly, they admitted to the Creator, as it was said (Psalms 8:10), "'The Lord our Master, how great is Your name in all the earth.' But it does not say, 'Place Your majesty on the heavens.' But before that (Psalms 8:2), it does write, 'Place Your majesty on the heavens.'"

We see that the complaint of the angels was about the inferiority of the people of Israel because they have *Kelim* of the will to receive, called "evil inclination." For this reason, the Torah belongs to those who are not so materialized, but to angels, who have only vessels of bestowal, as it is written ("Introduction of The Book of Zohar," The Seventh Commandment, Item 225), "Elijah flew with four wings, whereas the angels with six wings." He interprets there, in the *Sulam* [Ladder commentary on *The Zohar*] that the angels are discerned as above the *Chazeh*, namely that they are from the *Chazeh* and above, settling for covered *Hassadim*, since they have only vessels of bestowal.

Conversely, the souls come from *Malchut*, who is from the *Chazeh* and below, which is the place of revealed *Hassadim*, since there it is the place of the construction of *Malchut*, which is the collection of all the souls. They have *Kelim* of NHY, namely vessels of reception. Therefore, the souls need light of *Hochma*, which is poured only into vessels of reception.

Also, the ARI says that only the souls that ascend to MAN raise ZON to AVI to draw additional *Mochin*, since the souls require the light of *Hochma* because they have vessels of reception.

But the angels, who are regarded as from the *Chazeh* and above, vessels of bestowal, need only *Hassadim*. Therefore, when they rise to MAN to ZA to ask for fulfillment, which are only *Hassadim*, and ZA always has *Hassadim*, they do not induce any ascent in ZON. Only the souls, which need *Hochma*, which is drawn by the vessels of reception, and which ZA does not have permanently, therefore the souls cause the ascent of the worlds in order to draw the light of *Hochma*. Hence, when ZON ascend, all the worlds ascend up to *Ein Sof* [no end/infinity].

According to the above, we can interpret the complaint of the angels, who complained that the holy Torah, which is regarded as the names of the Creator, the internality of the Torah, which is clothed in corporeal dresses, that all of it is the revelation of Godliness to the created beings, so how can such a great thing be given to people, who are of inferior degree? Clearly, there must be equivalence with the light of the Creator in order to be able to receive it. And the light of the Creator, which is the abundance poured onto the lower ones, so the angels understood that only they have connection to the light, which is the giver, since they, too, have vessels of bestowal, and not a woman-born, where "woman" means *Nukva* [Aramaic: female], which means that Israel were born out of the quality of *Nukva*, meaning from vessels of reception, since the souls come from *Malchut*, who is called "the assembly of Israel."

We should interpret what the angels asked, "What is a woman-born doing among us?" meaning after all, he comes from the quality of *Malchut*, which is a vessel of reception, in oppositeness of form from the Torah, which is the light of abundance. And what did Moses reply to them? "Is there evil inclination within you?" Promptly, the angels admitted to the Creator and said, "Lord, our Master, place Your majesty on the earth."

That answer that Moses replied to the angels, "Is there evil inclination within you?" requires explanation. Did the angels not know that it speaks there about observing *Mitzvot* in corporeality? Do angels have bodies, that they demanded to be given, for example, a *Talit* [prayer shawl] and a *Tzitzit* [a fringed piece of garment worn under the clothes] to cover their bodies, until Moses came and told them that the Torah speaks of corporeal matters, and that the Torah can be only in those who have corporal bodies?

The angels certainly understood it, but they probably demanded that the internality of the Torah, which is the names of the Creator, be given to them. Indeed, this is difficult to understand. If the Torah is given to Israel, why can it not be given also to angels? Is it a material thing, that if you give it to one, you can no longer give it to another?

Here it is implied that the angels saw and understood that if the Torah is given to Israel, it means that the Torah can be given specifically to Israel, and not to them, meaning that they are unworthy of receiving the inner Torah, but only Israel. Otherwise, they would have to be given, too.

In other words, the revealed Torah certainly belongs only to those who have corporeal bodies. But when they heard that Moses went up to receive the Torah from the Creator, they asked, "What is a woman-born doing among us?" He told them, "He has come to receive the Torah," and they did not know about the giving of the Torah at all, and were puzzled.

They said to Him: "'Concealed delight, You wish to give it to a flesh and blood?' And You did not notify us, so we, too, would receive the concealed delight." They must have been thinking about the internality of the Torah, for "internality" means that which is concealed inside, which is considered a "concealed delight."

This is why they complained, since they saw that the Torah, with regard to the internality of the Torah, belongs to them and not to a woman-born. In other words, they made correct arguments in their view. That is, the revealed Torah certainly belongs to Israel, but why can they not be given the inner Torah, too? And since they did not know about it, about the giving of the Torah, which shows that they have no relation, then they are right.

What did Moses reply to them? "Is there evil inclination within you?" And since you have no evil inclination, did you go down to Egypt? We should understand Moses' reply, that if they demanded the internality of the Torah, what is the answer that Moses gave them?

The answer is that the internality of the Torah divides into two lights, called "light of *Hassadim*," and "light of *Hochma*." Light of *Hassadim* is poured in vessels of bestowal, since it extends from the *Ohr Yashar* [Direct Light], as we learned, *Hochma* at its end, after receiving the light of *Hochma*, which is the purpose of creation, to do good to His creations, since this delight and pleasure that He wants to impart must have someone to receive this abundance, but this did not exist yet. Therefore, He created this will to receive existence from absence, which is called *Aviut* [thickness] of *Behina Aleph* [first discernment]. That is, this is the first *Behina* [discernment/phase] that emerged and was revealed existence from absence, where there was no root of reception in reality.

It follows that the *Kli* of *Hochma* is a vessel of reception on the light of the purpose of creation, meaning that for this *Kli*, the heaven and earth were created. In other words, the whole purpose of the creation of the worlds was for this *Kli* to receive the delight and pleasure.

It follows that without this *Kli*, called "will to receive," there is no room for the creation of the worlds. But afterward, meaning *Hochma* at its end, having received the light, felt that she was opposite in form from the Giver, and wanted equivalence of form. Hence, she overcame the will to receive in her and said, "I want to bestow."

This is the root of the light of *Hassadim* that there is in the worlds, which is regarded as the light of the correction of creation. Afterward, *Bina*, at its end, saw that since the purpose of creation is for the lower ones to receive and not to give, she made a sort of compromise, to receive *Hassadim* with a little bit of *Hochma*, meaning to receive *Hochma* as *Zeir Anpin* [Aramaic: small face], called "light of *Hassadim* in illumination of *Hochma*."

Afterward, we learn that at its end, ZA saw that the purpose of creation was not that the upper abundance, which is considered good and doing good, will illuminate in *Zeir Anpin*, but expansively. This is called the *Sefira Malchut*, which is the real *Kli* for reception of the abundance. In other words, the *Kli* of *Malchut* is the *Kli* in which the light of the purpose of creation can shine, and which the Creator wants to give to the created beings.

By this we can understand Moses' reply when he said, "Did you go down to Egypt? Is there evil inclination within you?" Therefore, you cannot receive the inner Torah, which is the names of the Creator, since this light of the purpose of creation was only for a woman-born, meaning only for those who have a desire to receive, which is *Malchut*, called "female," "a woman," and not for angels, who have no vessels of reception, and who belong to the discernment of "from the *Chazeh* and above," which are *Kelim* of *Bina*, vessels of bestowal, and not vessels of reception.

This is the meaning of the words, "Did you go down to Egypt?" That is, since there were *Tzimtzum* [restriction] and concealment on *Malchut*, a correction must be done on this *Kli*. As long as there is no correction, it is considered that the *Klipa* [shell/peel] of Egypt controls the will to receive. Since you do not have the will to receive, how can it be said that you need to make a correction to work in order to bestow? After all, you have no vessels of reception for the light of the purpose of creation!

By this we understand the allegory, that this is the answer, that although He has angels above, which are pure *Kelim*, without vessels of reception, called "vessels of a layperson," but are all holy, all pure," still the Creator chose specifically the lower ones, who have *Kelim* of laypeople, for only in those *Kelim* is it possible to receive the Torah with regard to the holy names, whereas angels pertain to the correction of creation. For this reason the angels are the servants of the soul, and this is why He said to the people of Israel, "Prepare for Me a lampstand."

What Is "He Who Enjoys at a Groom's Meal," in the Work?

Article No. 35, Tav-Shin-Nun, 1989/90

Our sages said (*Berachot* 72), "He who enjoys at a groom's meal and does not delight him transgresses in five voices. And if he delights him, what is his reward? Rabbi Yehoshua Ben Levi said, 'He is rewarded with the Torah, which was given in five voices.'"

We should understand what it means that if he enjoys at a groom's meal he must delight him. If he does not enjoy at a groom's meal, should he not delight him? Also, what does it mean that he must delight him? Is the groom sad that he became a groom, that he should try to delight him? We should also understand with what can we delight the groom, so that by delighting him, we will be rewarded with the Torah.

It makes sense that if a person is told to perform some commandment, he is promised the next world as a reward. But here they said that his reward will be the Torah. Is this a reward that obligates one to delight the groom? How should we understand all this in the work?

Also, we must understand why it is not required to delight the bride, but only the groom. Concerning the bride, we find another requirement. Concerning the bride, it was said (*Ketubot* 16b), "How does one dance before the bride? The House of Shammai say, 'the bride as she is.' The House of Hillel say, 'a fair and graceful bride.' The House of Shammai said to the House of Hillel, 'What if she is lame or blind, is she told, 'a fair and graceful bride'? But the Torah said, 'Stay far from false words.' The House of Hillel said to the House of Shammai, 'According to you, one who makes a bad bargain in the market, should one praise it before him or criticize it before him? That is, he should praise it before him. Consequently, the sages said, 'One's view should always be mingled with people.''"

We should understand why concerning the bride, we are speaking only of dancing, and it was not said that the bride should be made happy only during the dance, and what name should be given to the bride, whether as she is, or a handsome name, even if it is not the truth.

Shabbat [Sabbath] is also called "bride," as it is written, "Go my beloved, toward the bride." Before Shabbat there are six workdays. During those six days, we must toil in order to prepare everything for Shabbat, and we also eat the Shabbat meal.

Shabbat is called *Malchut*, "bride" is called *Malchut*, and the "land of Israel" is also called *Malchut*. Also, "creation" is generally called *Malchut*. This means that in general, we should speak of two subjects: 1) Creator, 2) created beings.

The Creator is called the "groom," and the created beings are called the "bride." A *Hatan* [groom] is named after being *Nahut Darga* [of inferior degree], as our sages said, "Descend in degree and take a wife." It means that the Creator can be called a "groom" only when He has a bride. It is as in corporeality, when we say that some person is a groom, it means he has a bride. But what does this imply to us in spirituality?

Since it is impossible to speak of a Creator without created beings, one who says that there is a Creator, it is after He has created creatures and they attain Him, that He created them. Then the creatures say that there is a Creator. But if there is no one to attain Him, then there is no one to speak of Him. Therefore, when He created the creatures, it was by restricting Himself several times, after which it was possible for created beings to emerge. They are the receivers, and they are far from Him in terms of oppositeness of form, since His desire is only to bestow, and the creatures want only to receive, and disparity of form in spirituality creates remoteness and separation.

It follows that precisely by lowering Himself so that the creatures would attain Him, it is possible to say that the Creator is called a "groom," for He lowered Himself so as to be attained.

Those who attain are called "bride," who knows that there is a "groom," and if the creatures would not attain Him, He would certainly not be called a "groom," and those who attain would not be called a "bride."

When we speak about the worlds in general, we distinguish everything into two discernments: 1) The bestowing light, called a "groom," which shines into the worlds though *Tzimtzum* [restriction] and *Masach* [screen]. This is called a "groom." 2) The *Kli* [vessel] that receives the light and abundance, which is called the "general *Malchut* of the worlds."

However, in person, there are many discernments in the light, and the proliferation comes because of the *Kli* that receives them. That is, concerning the light, we say that there are no changes in the light, but all the changes are in the *Kli*. This is so because the light shines only through restrictions, and to the extent that there is equivalence between the light and the *Kli*.

For this reason, it depends on the work of the receiver, how much he can correct himself so as to have equivalence with the light. Hence, from the perspective of the receiver, who is called a *Kli*, we can discern many discernments in the light. For this reason, although we have many details, it is still generally one light and one *Kli*, as we learn that at the end of correction "the Lord will be one and His name, One."

Shabbat is called a "bride," and there are six workdays before her, which is the time of labor, as it is written, "For six days, the Lord made the heaven and the earth, and on the seventh day, He *Shavat* [rested]." Thus, Shabbat means the completion of the work, and "bride" also means the completion of the work, as it is written, "Moses finished" [in Hebrew, *Klot* (finished) is similar to *Kalah* (bride)], that the work was completed.

We should understand the meaning of "labor," and the meaning of "the completion of the work," which is called "Shabbat" in the work. The writing says, "Which God has created to do." As it is explained in the *Sulam* [Ladder Commentary on *The Zohar*], the six workdays are the correction of the six qualities called HGT NHY, since the Creator created the world with a desire to receive for oneself. This is called "created," meaning existence from absence.

Since it is of different form, which causes remoteness and separation, this *Kli*, which the Creator created, was given for the lower ones to do, meaning to correct, namely to place on the act of reception, the aim to bestow. This is called *Dvekut* [adhesion], "equivalence of form," by which creation, called "receiving for himself" and "separation," was corrected with a correction of *Dvekut*, where reception acquires the form of bestowal.

When the lower ones give this *Kli*, the light can reach the lower ones. That is, at that time comes the thought of creation, which is "His desire to do good to His creations," into practice. This is called "the completion of the work" of the *Kli* that is fit to receive the abundance that belongs to the *Kli*.

It follows that the six workdays are regarded as work to do the intention to bestow, and Shabbat means that the *Kli* that will work in order to bestow has been prepared. Therefore, "the coming of Shabbat" implies that the light has come to a *Kli* that is ready for the light. Then it is called "Shabbat," meaning that He already *Shavat* [rested] from His work of making the *Kli*, since He already corrected the *Kli*.

When the light shines in the *Kelim* [vessels], the *Kli* has nothing to do but only to enjoy the light, as this is the purpose of creation, "to do good to His creations." This is the meaning of what our sages said, "When Shabbat comes, rest comes." This is so because when the light shines in the *Kelim*, there is no more room for work. Rather, this is called "enjoying the meal of Shabbat." This is what our sages said, "He who did not toil on the eve of Shabbat (to make *Kelim*), what will he eat on Shabbat?"

In other words, Shabbat is called "a meal," which is a time of reception of delight and pleasure. If he has no *Kelim* that have been prepared on the eve of Shabbat, when the light comes, he hasn't the *Kelim* in which to receive the meal. This is why Shabbat is called *Kallah* [bride/finished], from the words "concluded," "ending," "completion." It is as it is written, "And on the seventh day, God concluded the work that He had done." This means that the meal is already prepared, since the *Kelim* for reception of the meal have already been completed, and it is known that it cannot be said that the light is missing, as it is written, "The whole earth is full of His glory." Rather, when there are *Kelim* that are ready, we see the light, meaning the light is revealed inside the *Kelim*.

The land of Israel is also called a "bride," since she has a groom, as it is written, "A land that the eyes of the Lord your God are upon it from the beginning of the year to the end of the year." This is seemingly difficult to understand why specifically the land of Israel is like that. After all, it is written, "The eyes of the Lord roam in everything," and not specifically in the land of Israel.

We should interpret that the Torah gives us a sign, to those who work for the Creator and want to know if they have already been rewarded with the quality of the "land of Israel." The sign is that the person feels that "the eyes of the Lord," meaning His Providence, is in the form of good and doing good. This is regarded as a person being in the land of Israel. At that time, the land of Israel is called "bride," since she knows she has a groom.

Likewise, in whom is there a groom? That is, who knows that there is a groom? It is the one who attains the groom. This degree is called "bride," meaning one who has attained Godliness. The light is considered Godliness, and the receiver of the light is the one who attains. For this reason, the "land of Israel" is called a "bride," meaning that the groom is revealed in her, that the Creator is the Overseer.

In order to attain the land of Israel, called "a land that is regarded as a bride," it is customary that as in corporeality, we go to look for a bride in whom there are no flaws, as it is written about the spies, who slandered the land of Israel saying that the bride, meaning the land, is not worth taking for many reasons.

Some said that she was proud and had many demands from a person, meaning that one should annul his reason and will before her, and only those who can walk with eyes shut and obey all her demands, with him she can speak. And if he wants to understand what she is saying within reason, she promptly runs away from him.

Therefore, they say, how can one annul his entire being for her? That is, she is so firm-minded that if he disobeys what she tells him once, she will immediately run away from him. In other words, the "land of Israel" is the kingdom of heaven, and one must accept the kingdom above reason, and not wait for the body to agree to assume the burden of the kingdom of heaven. Acceptance of the kingdom of heaven must be so that a person comes to love the Creator "with all your heart, and with all your soul, and with all your might," and all on the basis of above reason, meaning unconditional surrender, namely that the body, too, does not understand.

The person must go and assume the land with his eyes shut, meaning above reason. If, in the middle of the work, when he is awarded some ascent in spirituality, a person feels a good taste in the work and says, "Now I do not have to believe in faith in the Creator because I already feel a good taste in the work, and I take the taste I feel in the work as a basis," at that time it is as in the allegory, that the minute he wants to understand faith above reason, "Why should I?" and says, "Now I already have a basis for believing in the

Creator," she immediately runs away from him. In other words, the whole ascent that he is feeling, he immediately descends from his state. This is regarded as *Malchut*, called the "land of Israel," runs away from him, and he remains in a state of "abroad."

This is as our sages said, "The land of the nations, their air is impure." This means that during a decline, a person descends from the land of Israel and enters the "land of the nations," whose air is impure, meaning that all the thoughts of the "nations of the world" enter his mind and heart, and the desires of "Israel," called "desire *Yashar-El* [straight to the Creator]," depart from him, and instead comes the desire of the "nations of the world," which are the opposite of *Kedusha* [holiness].

It turns out that in a state of descent, a person says, "What have I gained from all the efforts I made in order to obtain *Kedusha*? Now I see that not only did I gain nothing, I am even worse than before I began the work of obtaining the aim for the sake of the Creator." In other words, he says, "Not only do I not have the aim to bestow, but even in practice, the situation has become harder to observe, meaning in the act without an intention. Conversely, before I wanted to come into the 'land of Israel,' I could easily observe Torah and *Mitzvot*."

This is as it is written in *The Zohar* (Shlach, Item 63), "It is written, 'And they returned from touring the land.' 'And they returned' means that they returned to the side of evil, and returned from the path of truth. They said, 'What have we gained? To this day, we have not seen good in the world. We have toiled in the Torah but the house is empty. And who will be rewarded with that world? Who will come into it? It would be better if we did not toil so. We toiled and learned in order to know the part of that world, as you advised us, and it is also flowing with milk and honey. That upper world is good, as we know from the Torah, but who can be rewarded with it?' The faithful ones, what did they say? 'If the Lord desires us, He will give it to us.' When a man exerts with the desire in the heart for the Creator, he will be rewarded with it, for all He wants of us is the heart."

Thus, we see that the "land of Israel" is *Malchut*, meaning a bride. People are sent to see if the bride is good or if she is proud.

Also, Shabbat is called a "bride," with respect to the completion of the work. Therefore, before Shabbat there are the six workdays, where the work and toil are in order to adjust to the terms that the bride presents, if we want to accept her. The labor during the six workdays is as it was with the spies: Sometimes they think that the bride is good, and the one who takes her is the happiest man in the world, and it is worth doing anything, meaning accept all the terms that she demands.

But what does she say? Only after a person says that he annuls all his needs, which a person's body demands, meaning his desires that are for his own sake—he relinquishes them and cares only for the benefit of the "bride," who is called *Malchut*, the "bride," which is the kingdom of heaven, only then, when he cancels his self, as our sages said, "The Torah exists only in one who puts himself to death over it," this means that all the thoughts and desires pertaining to his own needs, he puts to death and cares only for the sake of the Creator.

Likewise, during the six workdays, a person has ascents and descents. In other words, sometimes a person says that the spies are right in saying that we should escape the campaign, that this is not for us. Sometimes, they overcome and say that Joshua and Caleb, who said, "If the Lord desires us, He will give it to us," are right.

After we complete the work, when a person agrees to all of the bride's terms, a person is rewarded with Shabbat being called "Shabbat the Queen." That is, she gives to the man who annuls himself before her all the delight and pleasure she receives from the groom. These are the demands she presents—that specifically after he accepts all of her terms, she shows what a person gains in his life if he can accept her as a "bride." And then the "bride" gets a name, which is "the King's daughter," and nothing is missing in the King's house.

Now we can interpret what we asked, Why is it required to delight the groom? The answer is that since from the perspective of branch and root, the "groom" is the Creator and the "bride" is the created beings, who should receive from the Creator, and since the Creator created the world in order to do good to His creations, when the creatures receive delight and pleasure, this is called "the groom's joy." It is as our sages said, "There has never been joy before Him as in the day when heaven and earth were created."

It follows that every person enjoys a groom's meal, meaning that all the pleasures in the world come from the Creator, which is called "a groom's meal." "Not delighting Him" means that he slanders the "bride," meaning says that the "bride" is not fair and is full of flaws. The "bride" is the created beings, who should receive the delight and pleasure from the Creator. They say that the bride, called *Malchut*, who contains all the soul, does not give to the created beings delight and pleasure.

It follows that it is as though the Creator does not give her anything. Thus, if a person says that *Malchut* has nothing to give to the created beings, he is slandering the bride—that she is poor and meager—as well as slanders the Creator because the Creator is not giving her anything so she has what to give to the created beings.

For this reason, any person "who enjoys at a groom's meal and does not delight him transgresses in five voices." Concerning "five," it is known that in spirituality, anything complete is called "five *Sefirot*," "five worlds." This is why he is called *Ubar* [embryo], meaning *Over* [passing over] them and does not receive them. "If he delights him," asks the Gemara, "What is his reward? Rabbi Yehoshua Ben Levi says, 'He is rewarded with the Torah, which was given in five voices.'"

We should understand why he is not promised to be rewarded with the next world, as is promised in all the places. The answer is that it is because he delights the groom, meaning he believes in the kingdom of heaven, who is the "bride." He says that she is a fair and good bride, and he believes with faith that she has a groom, and we can already see that He is with the bride.

This is called a "Shabbat meal." It means that then, on Shabbat, *Malchut*, which is the collection of the souls, already has what the Creator, who is called the "groom," wants to give to the souls. This is the meaning of Shabbat being a "similitude of the next world," for then is the time when we enjoy the groom's meal.

Now we can understand what we asked, Why does he say that the reward of one who delights the groom is the Torah, and does not say that he is rewarded with the next world, as it is written in many places? The answer is, With what can a person delight the groom in the work, when the groom is the Creator? It is when a person says that the bride is beautiful and flawless.

From this, the groom enjoys, meaning that the bride is called *Malchut* from the perspective of faith above reason. He says that *Malchut*, who leads the world with her governance, leads in the form of good and doing good. This is as it is written (Song of Songs, 4), "You are all beautiful, my wife; there is not a flaw in you." At that time, a person is rewarded with the Torah, which is called "the king's meal," which is the Torah, with respect to the names of the Creator. This Torah does not appear before a person is rewarded with "faith," called "kingdom of heaven."

However, before one is rewarded with faith, called *Malchut*, a "bride," there are ascents and descents there. This is called a "dance." There is where all the work to be rewarded with taking upon himself the kingdom of heaven is found, so he will not do anything that concerns his own benefit, but all his actions will be for the sake of the Creator.

Our sages said about this, "How does one dance before the bride?" meaning in order to be rewarded with the quality of "bride."

In this there is a dispute between the House of Shammai and the House of Hillel. The House of Shammai say "A bride as she is." That is, however a person feels, whether he feels good or bad. About everything, he should believe above reason that all his sensations are for his sake. This is very difficult.

But the House of Hillel says that a person should say that what he feels in the state he is in, that he does not feel good, he should believe that it is good, but he cannot see the good because he is still unworthy of seeing. Therefore, what he feels is untrue because "They have eyes and see not."

But everyone says that a person should go above reason and delight the groom. Therefore, there are two kinds of work: 1) during the six workdays, which is the time of work, and 2) during Shabbat, which is the time of the meal (see Article No. 12, *Tav-Shin-Mem-Tet*).

What Is, "The Children of Esau and Ishmael Did Not Want to Receive the Torah," in the Work?

Article No. 36, Tav-Shin-Nun, 1989/90

It is written in *The Zohar* (Balak, Item 138), "When the Creator wanted to give the Torah to Israel, He went and invited the children of Esau, and they did not accept it, as it is written, 'The Lord came from Sinai, and dawned on them from Seir,' meaning that they did not want to receive it. He went to the children of Ishmael, and they did not want to receive it, as it is written, 'appeared from Mount Paran.' Since they did not want, He returned to Israel."

It is said in *The Zohar* (Balak, Item 140), "Rabbi Shimon said to him: 'This question is settled. The Lord came from Sinai, and from Sinai He came and was revealed to them. 'And dawned on them from Seir' means that from what the dwellers of Seir said, that they did not want to receive, from this it shown for Israel and added to them much light and love. Likewise, He appeared and shown to

Israel from Mount Paran, from what the dwellers of Paran said, that they did not want to receive, from this, extra love and illumination were added to Israel, as it should be.'"

We should understand why it says that because the children of Esau and Ishmael declined to receive the Torah, it added extra love and illumination to Israel. It seems as though no one wanted to receive the Torah, and only Israel saved the day, and this is why He shown for Israel and added more light to them. It seems that otherwise, the additional love and illumination would be missing from Israel.

In the corporeal world, we can say that sometimes a person wants to give to someone something nice, but there is no one who wants to receive, and this pains the person. Therefore, someone feels sorry for him and accepts it, and then the person loves the person who did him a favor by accepting that thing. But how can such a thing be said with regard to the Creator, that the extra love and illumination that the Creator gives to Israel is because the children of Esau and Ishmael did not want to receive the Torah, while Israel did receive it?

To understand this in the work, we must remember that in the work, man himself is a small world, as it is written in *The Zohar*, that "Man consists of all seventy nations and contains the quality of Esau, the quality of Ishmael, as well as the quality of Israel." As we learn, the quality of Israel is in exile under the governance of the seventy nations of the world, which are generally called "will to receive for oneself," while Israel are called "desire to bestow upon the Creator."

It is known that there are two discernments:

1) The purpose of creation, which is to do good to His creations, namely for the creatures to receive delight and pleasure. The Creator's desire to bestow created in the creatures a desire to receive delight and pleasure, meaning that wherever the created being sees that there is something to enjoy, it immediately yearns to receive the pleasure. This is called "the Kli [vessel] that the Creator created," as it is written, "Which God has created."

2) The correction of creation. However, there is the matter of the correction of creation, meaning that in order to prevent the shame, a correction took place, where it is impossible to receive with the Kli that the Creator created, and which is called "will to receive for oneself." Rather, man must make a new Kli, called "desire to bestow," like the Creator, whose desire is to bestow upon His creations. Likewise, the creatures must make this Kli, or the delight and pleasure that the Creator wants to impart upon His creations lie under concealment and hiding. This is the meaning of the words, "which God has created," meaning the will to receive, "to do," meaning what the creatures must do, which is the desire to bestow, which is absent in the creatures and they must make it, so they will have a desire to bestow.

We should ask, How is it possible to do the opposite of what the Creator created, which is the will to receive for oneself? How is it possible to revoke the work of the Creator, called "will to receive," and do the opposite? It seems as though a person is acting against the Creator?

The answer is that man cannot revoke the will to receive that the Creator created. Thus, why is it required of us to do everything for the sake of the Creator, since it is against our nature?!

However, there is the matter of light and Kli. A Kli is called "desire," and desire is called "a lack," and "light" is the filling of the lack. The rule is, "There is no light without a Kli." Hence, the creatures must provide for themselves a Kli, meaning a lack, for there is a rule that any lack pertains specifically to the creatures, and not to the Creator.

It follows that the creatures must perform actions and seek ways to find in themselves a lack, which is that they want all their actions to be for the sake of the Creator, but they cannot, so the creatures see and feel this lack of a desire to bestow, which they cannot obtain by themselves.

However, in order for it to be clear that they cannot obtain the desire to bestow, the creatures must first exert on their own. Otherwise, how will they know that they cannot obtain that lack by themselves? However, we should ask, Who needs this awareness that man is incapable of obtaining the desire to bestow by himself?

The answer is that man himself needs this awareness. Otherwise, he will not ask the Creator to help him, since he will think that he has time to do everything in order to bestow, since it is within his power to do everything in order to bestow whenever he wants.

For this reason, man must first work by himself to obtain the desire to bestow, and only then can he make an earnest, heartfelt prayer, meaning have a real need for the salvation of the Creator, that He will give him this desire to do everything for the sake of the Creator.

By this we can interpret what is written (Psalms 119), "Happy are those who treasure His testimonies, who demand of Him with all their heart." We must understand the connection between his saying, "Happy are those who treasure His testimonies," meaning that they observe the Mitzvot [commandments/good deeds] of the Torah, and "who demand of Him with all their heart." As said above, we must obtain a need to feel that we are lacking the desire to bestow. Before we obtain this, meaning before we obtain the desire to bestow, we are unfit to receive the delight and pleasure, that the Creator wants to give to the created beings.

However, how can one obtain that lack? We are told that observing the Mitzvot of the Torah, this can bring one this awareness that he must obtain the desire to bestow. That is, by observing Torah and Mitzvot, when a person aims—by observing the Torah and Mitzvot—to come closer to the Creator, meaning to achieve Dvekut [adhesion], called "equivalence of form," this can bring him to feel the lack of the desire to bestow. It is written, "Happy are those who treasure His testimonies," meaning that this will give him a lack, after which he will be able to ask the Creator to give him this lack.

This is the meaning of the words, "who demand of Him with all their heart," meaning that afterward, he can demand of the Creator to give him wholeheartedly, meaning to give him the desire to bestow, so that everything he does for the Creator will be with all his heart. It follows that then, by observing Torah and Mitzvot, he will come to a state where he can demand of the Creator to give him the quality of "with all his heart," meaning that it will be for the Creator. In other words, he demands that the Creator will give him the desire to bestow, called "with all his heart," since this is the only reward he demands in return for observing Torah and Mitzvot.

It follows that man's work is to obtain a lack and a need that the Creator will give him a desire to bestow instead of the desire to receive that He has given him upon creation, for by this he will be rewarded with Dvekut with the Creator. Hence, although he asks for a different desire than the one that the Creator gave him, the Creator wants this. Baal HaSulam said about this that the Creator said, "My sons defeated Me," in that they want a different desire than the one that the Creator gave them, meaning that they demand of the Creator to give them a different desire from the one He originally gave them.

Yet, the will to receive that the Creator gave, which is called "existence from absence," is the axis of the whole of creation. However, the will to receive must undergo correction, which is called "the correction of creation." That is, creation is called "will to receive for oneself," and on it, an intention to bestow is placed. It follows that in the end, the will to receive remains, but has acquired a correction of the aim to bestow.

It follows that we should ask, According to the above, when a person begins to ask of the Creator to give him the desire to bestow, meaning to be able to do all his deeds for the sake of the Creator, why does the Creator not give him the desire to bestow as the person demands and asks? In the order of the work, we see that when a person wants to walk on the path toward obtaining the desire to bestow, he sees that he is going backward instead of forward. That is, the evil appears in him more intensely than it was disclosed in him while he was working in order to receive reward.

The thing is that we must know that the desire to bestow is only the correction of creation and not the purpose of creation, for the purpose of creation is that His desire is to do good to His creations, meaning for the creatures to receive delight and pleasure. Hence, if He gave them what they want right away, meaning the desire to bestow, they would be satisfied with the work in that they are bestowing upon the Creator and have *Dvekut* with the Creator, so what else do they need? For themselves, they need nothing, which is called "desiring mercy," and they have no need to receive anything from the Creator, so the matter of the purpose of creation, which is His desire to give to them, would remain untouched.

But the purpose of creation, which is the objective, as it is known that everything is calculated according to the goal and not according to the means, for the desire to bestow is only a means by which to achieve the goal, so if he were to receive the desire to bestow, he would be satisfied with it and the goal would remain as an unturned stone, since no one would need it because they would already be satisfied in the work.

This is as it is written in the book *A Sage's Fruit* (Vol. 1, p 118): "From all the above, you find that the soul is destined to acquire all 620 holy names, its entire stature, which is 620 times more than it had before it came. Its stature appears in the 620 *Mitzvot* where the light of the Torah is clothed, and the Creator in the collective light of the Torah. Thus you see that 'the Torah, the Creator, and Israel' are one."

This means that this is the purpose of creation—that a person must achieve his completion and be rewarded with the Torah in the manner of the names of the Creator. It is not enough that He wants to bestow upon the Creator. Although this is a great thing, it is not the goal. Rather, man must achieve 620 times the amount that his soul had had before it clothed in a body. However, if he were to receive the desire to bestow immediately after a few prayers and litanies, he would have no need to obtain the goal for which he was created. This is the reason why a person does not receive the desire to bestow, and moreover, sees that he is receiving an even more excessive desire to receive than he had before he began the work on bestowal.

However, we should understand why after a person makes efforts to come closer to the Creator, which means equivalence of form, called *Dvekut*, as it is written, "And to cleave on to Him," and they explained, "Cleave unto His attributes, as He is merciful, so you are merciful," it was enough that a person did not receive what he asked for, meaning the desire to bestow. But why is he now getting an excessive amount of the will to receive, each time more than he had before he prayed to be given the desire to bestow? It seems as though it is a mistake from above, as though it is thought above that he is asking for a desire to receive, and is therefore given a greater will to receive. But he asked for a desire to bestow, so why is he given from above a greater will to receive?

The answer is that in order for him to need to receive the purpose of creation, to be rewarded with the Torah, called "the names of the Creator," he is given a bigger will to receive each time. That is, to the extent that he does things in order to achieve the desire to bestow, he receives from above a desire to receive. And since when he asks for help from above, since he sees that he cannot emerge from its control, what is the help? It is as it is said in *The Zohar* about the words, "He who comes to purify is aided." He asks, "How is he aided?" He replies, "with a holy soul. If he is rewarded more, he is given *Ruach*." That is, through the help he receives from above, he is rewarded with assistance until he obtains his NRNHY. It follows that each time, he sees that he has more bad, and must ask for greater help each time.

This is as I heard from Baal HaSulam, who said about what is written regarding Abraham (Genesis 15), "And He said unto him, 'I am the Lord, to give you this land to inherit it.' And he said, 'How will I know that I will inherit it?' And He said unto Abraham, 'Know for certain that your descendants will be strangers in a land that is not theirs, and they will be enslaved and tormented four hundred years, and afterward, they will come out with many possessions.'"

He asked about the answer that the Creator gave him, "How will I know," that the people of Israel will be in exile in Egypt. That is, this is the guarantee by which Abraham could know that after this act of being in a land that is not theirs, from this Abraham knew for certain that they would inherit the land. He asked, What is the answer? meaning that Abraham understood that this was the right answer. As we see, Abraham could argue with the Creator in Sodom, where Abraham kept asking, "Perhaps?" But here it is implied that he understood that this was the right answer and asked no further.

He said that the answer was to the question that Abraham had asked. This is perplexing. There is a question about Abraham, of whom it is written, "And he believed in the Lord," so why did he suddenly ask such a question as "How will I know that I will inherit it?" He said that Abraham saw what inheritance the Creator wanted to give him, namely the inheritance of the land, and the whole purpose of creation is included in this land. But since there is a rule that there is no light without a Kli, meaning no filling without a lack, he therefore asked how it was possible that they would inherit the land when they have no need for it. As soon as they would receive some spiritual illumination they will be satisfied and serve the Creator with gladness and will not worry about anything, since they do not need more. Thus, they will have no need to inherit this land, which is the purpose of creation. Therefore, the question was that he did not see that they would have any need, and without a need, nothing is given, especially something as serious as the inheritance of the land.

To this the Creator replied, "Know for certain that your descendants will be strangers in a land that is not theirs." Eretz [Land] means Ratzon [desire]. That is, they will be under the rule of the will to receive, which does not belong to the people of Israel but to Egypt, and this is called "a land that is not theirs." And they will be tormented four hundred years. "Four" is a complete degree, which the four Behinot [discernments/qualities] of HaVaYaH, which are from Bina, who is regarded as vessels of bestowal. It follows that "tormented" means that the Egyptians did not let them work with vessels of bestowal. "They will be enslaved and tormented," in what? in "four hundred years," meaning in the Sefirot of Bina.

It is known from the book of *Sefirot* that *Malchut* is called "units," ZA is tens, and *Bina* is hundreds. This is the meaning of "four hundred," that they were not permitted to work. When they prevailed and worked in the quality of *Bina*, which are vessels of bestowal, they had a big war with the Egyptians. It follows that Egypt enslaved Israel when the people of Israel worked in a manner of bestowal, and then they felt that they were in exile. But when we do not work with vessels of bestowal, we do not know that the Egyptians resist this work.

This is the meaning of what he says (Exodus 2:23), "And the children of Israel sighed from the work, and they cried out, and their cry went up to God from the work." That is, by asking for help, they had to be given new lights each time, as he says in *The Zohar*, that the help that is given from above is regarded as a "holy soul," and by this, the people of Israel will need the great lights because otherwise, they cannot emerge from the control of the Egyptians.

It follows that the Creator's reply was that He would give them the need to ask for help, which is that each time, He will show them more bad, so they will constantly need to ask for bigger help. By this, the light of the purpose of creation will be revealed to them. This is called "this land to inherit it." It follows that had they received from above the desire to bestow when they asked for it, they would have been content and would have no need to inherit the land. But since He gave them the will to receive and not the will to bestow, they received a need for the Creator's help, by which it became certain that they would not be satisfied, but would receive the inheritance of the land.

It follows that specifically by being in a lowly state, it caused them to receive the great lights. This explains why when they wanted a desire to bestow, they were given a desire to receive, meaning that the will to receive grows where the lower ones should have received the desire to bestow when they asked for it. Hence, a person cannot say that he sees that his prayer is not heard above, and the evidence of this is that he is not given the desire to bestow. Instead, he must know that his prayer is being considered, and the evidence of this is that he is given an answer from above by being given what is good for him now, since now he will have a need for wholeness.

According to the above, we should interpret what we asked, Why does *The Zohar* say, "and dawned on them from Seir," meaning that because the dwellers of Seir said that they did not want to receive, it illuminated to Israel and added to them much light and love? Likewise, "He appeared and shown to Israel from Mount Paran," from the dwellers of Paran saying that they did not want to receive, this added extra love and illumination to Israel, as it should be.

We asked, Can such a thing pertain to the Creator, meaning that in truth, the children of Israel did not deserve to be given much light and love? Because they did not want to receive the Torah, for this reason He gave to Israel, meaning added to them. Otherwise, He would not be able to add to Israel much light and love.

When we speak of the work, we speak of one person. That is, if the children of Esau in a person and the children of Ishmael in a person did not resist the Torah but would agree to take upon themselves the desire to bestow, the quality of Israel in a person would be content and would not need the purpose of creation, as mentioned in the Creator's reply to Abraham, saying, "Know for certain that [your descendants will be] strangers." Specifically by being enslaved under the governance of Egypt, they will have a need to ask to be given help. And through the help, it will be possible to reveal to them the purpose of creation. It follows that precisely when there is resistance in the body, when we do not want to receive the Torah, it enables the Creator to add to them much light and love.

What Is, "The *Shechina* Is a Testimony to Israel," in the Work?

Article No. 37, Tav-Shin-Nun, 1989/90

The *Zohar* says (Pinhas, Item 491), "'For the Leader on Shoshan Edut.' Moses said, 'Shoshan Edut,' the *Edut* [testimony] of the *Shechina* [Divinity], who is called 'Shoshan Edut' because it is a testimony standing over us and testifying about us before the King. It is holy help for us to praise in praises. This is why it is called 'Shoshan Edut.' Moses said, 'It is called 'Shoshan Edut' because the *Shechina* is a testimony to Israel, who are her organs, and she is a soul upon them. She is help from heaven, as it is written about her, 'And you will hear the heaven.' She is holy assistance.'"

We should understand why the *Shechina* is called *Shoshan*. What does this color [*Shoshan* is a rose] of the *Shechina* imply to us? We should also understand what it means that the *Shechina* testifies to us before the King. We know that *Edut* [testimony] should be by seeing and not by hearing. Therefore, we should understand what seeing is there here, to say that the *Shechina* testifies to us with respect to seeing.

It is known that we have two opposite discernments in the work of the Creator: 1) On one hand, we learn that the purpose of creation is because His desire is to do good to His creations. For this reason, He created in the creatures a desire to receive delight and pleasure, since to the extent of the yearning for something, so is the measure of the pleasure. It follows that the purpose of creation was that the creatures will enjoy the world. In other words, He created a desire to receive pleasure for the creatures to enjoy, meaning that the whole purpose was for the creatures to enjoy. 2) On the other hand, we are told that it is forbidden to receive for ourselves. That is, a person must not do something in thought, speech, or action for his own benefit. Rather, one should be concerned with doing everything for the sake of the Creator and not for his own sake, as it is truly against the purpose of creation.

The answer is that a person needs to work for the sake of the Creator not because the Creator needs that others will work for Him or to be given something. Rather, it is a correction for the creatures. It is as the ARI says, that in order to bring to light the perfection of His deeds, meaning for this act, called "to do good to His creations," for the creatures to enjoy and so that there will be wholeness in this pleasure, meaning so they would not feel shame in this, a *Tzimtzum* [restriction] and concealment were placed on the delight and pleasure that the Creator wants to give.

Yet, this is only when they have the intention for the sake of the Creator, meaning that because the Creator enjoys His will being followed and receiving the good from Him because He wants this, this naturally removes the issue of shame that the disparity of form causes because there is a rule that every branch wants to resemble its root. As the Creator bestows, likewise, when the lower one bestows, he enjoys.

When the lower one must receive, he is ashamed. Hence, this correction was placed on the will to receive for one's own sake, which comes from creation, that a person should place on the will to receive an intention to bestow.

However, when a person wants to observe Torah and Mitzvot [commandments/good deeds] with the intention that this will bring him a desire to do everything in order to bestow contentment upon his Maker, and since this desire contradicts human nature, which was created as a desire to receive only for one's own benefit, so when a person says, "I want to do good deeds so that through them I will be able to aim everything for the sake of the Creator and not for myself," the will to receive for oneself within one's body, which is called "wicked," yells, "What is this work for you?"

And what is the answer we should give to its question? The answer is brought in the Passover Haggadah [narrative]: "A wicked one, what does he say? 'What is this work for you?' For you, and not for him. And since he excluded himself from the public, he denied the most important. And you, too, blunt his teeth."

This answer is very difficult to understand. He is asking a question; he wants to understand why we are going to cancel the will to receive, which is the desire that the Creator created. We must answer him, since he is asking according to his view, that he is correct. Thus, why did they say, "Blunt his teeth"?

Baal HaSulam said about this that since he asks, "What is this work?" meaning "Why must we work for the sake of the Creator and not for ourselves?" There is nothing to answer to this. In other words, a person is given an answer to his question so he would understand with his mind. Yet, here it is impossible to make it understand because he is asking, What will the will to receive have if he works in order to bestow? If he were to receive later, after he wants to bestow, meaning if we could say, "Bestow, and in return you will later be able to be a receiver," that would be bestowing in order to receive. This is called Lo Lishma [not for Her sake].

Therefore, when a person wants to work Lishma [for Her sake], meaning to bestow in order to bestow, there is nothing to answer it. This is called "Blunt his teeth." In other words, the answer is that we must go with force, meaning above reason, since within reason, the wicked is right. This is called "Blunt his teeth." He said that a person cannot defeat the evil at once, but that this work is in ascents and descents until a person is rewarded with winning it and taking upon himself the burden of the kingdom of heaven as faith above reason.

This is why *Malchut* is called *Shoshanah* [rose] or *Shoshanim* [roses] or *Shoshan* [another name for a rose], for the name is always given after the event, since we are not rewarded with the kingdom of heaven without the matter of blunting his teeth. This is why *Malchut* is called *Shoshanah*, after the act.

It follows that the meaning of *Shoshan* is "Blunt his teeth," since there is nothing to answer to his question and we have to go by force, by coercion, although the wicked one, meaning the will to receive for oneself, disagrees. This is called *Hakaa* [striking], meaning that he fights with himself. When a person says to his wicked one, "It is worthwhile to serve a great King and we do not need anything in return, but only because He is great and ruling, meaning because of His greatness, a person should be satisfied when serving a great King," the wicked one says to him, "How do you want to serve a great King? Do you feel His greatness, for which you are saying that it is worthwhile to serve Him?"

In these states, a person is sometimes unable to depict to himself any greatness of the Creator. Instead, he feels the lowliness in *Kedusha* [holiness]. This is regarded as "*Shechina* [Divinity] in exile" or "*Shechina* in the dust." In other words, he does not feel any importance in the King. On the contrary, depictions come to him that push him away from the work of the Creator to the point that sometimes he even wants to forget about the work of the Creator, for while he remembers that he should work for the Creator and not receive any reward for the work, but the work itself should be his goal, this can be said when a person feels a taste in the work. At that time, the taste he feels commits him to continue the work and he does not need any reward.

But what can one do if when he comes to do the holy work and says that he does not want any reward for his work, then he has no reward that will obligate him and will be the reason for which he can work, and work gladly, for afterward he will receive a great reward because he is working not in order to receive reward.

Also, he does not feel that he will be working for a great King, so how can one work without any joy? He is told to work coercively, meaning without the body's consent. This is called "Blunt his teeth."

But from where can one derive powers to be able to force himself to work in order to bestow? And even if he overcomes himself, he cannot do such work gladly. That is, the work he does at that time is like that of a captive person who is forced to work. Each time, he says, "Perhaps there is a way I can escape from here so I would not have to work for others?" The only joy he has then is when he looks at the clock and sees that soon he will rid himself of the work.

It follows that when the work if full of sorrow and agony from having to work for others instead of for himself, can the owner look at how his employees are working for him, crying as they work, and saying, "When will I be able to rid myself of the work?"

The person asks himself: "Does the Creator want us working for Him compulsively?"

That is, they feel that man is far from the Creator, that he does not feel the love of the Creator, meaning that during the work, that he will love the Creator. He looks at himself and does not know what happened to the person. That is, where the work is for the sake of the Creator, the person should have felt closeness to the Creator during his work, meaning to have more desire each time to draw closer to the Creator.

But now it is the complete opposite. That is, he feels each time that he is drawing farther from the Creator, that the acts he does push him away. He feels each action as though he is pushed out, meaning that he is not permitted to approach and feel the importance of Torah and *Mitzvot*, and to feel some flavor in these actions. On the contrary, it is as though a distance has been created between them. It seems to him as though no one can stand the other, and all his actions, which he does by force, are to him as a burden and a load. He always contemplates escaping from these states, but he has nowhere to run except by sleep, meaning that he finds flavor only in sleep.

However, at that time, the question is, Why is it really so? That is, a person should ask, Why do I deserve this? Is this the Torah and is this its reward? Is it because I began to work on the path of truth—which is to come to do the holy work so it is all for the sake of the Creator—that I am being pushed out of the holy work?

Why is it that when the work was like the general public, meaning to do good deeds, and I did not think at all about the intention for the sake of the Creator, and I relied my work entirely on the general public, who think only about actions and not about intentions, I had a good taste in the work and in the prayer? I knew that I was praying to the Creator and that He hears my prayer, and I had the strength to continue with the prayer, and I never looked, when I was praying, whether the Creator hears my prayer. That is, I had no criticism over my actions and I was certain that everything was fine.

But now that I need to rise in the degrees of holiness, since I want to work for the sake of the Creator, in order to approach the Creator, what have I now? I am only growing farther where I should have been growing closer.

The truth is that we must believe in faith in the sages and not follow what human intellect dictates, but rely completely on what the sages told us. Baal HaSulam said that a person should believe that this is so although he does not see. Yet, a person must believe that the Creator does hear the prayer, as it is written, "for You hear the prayer of every mouth." Since a person asks the Creator to bring him closer, the Creator wants to give him real closeness, meaning to give the person the delight and pleasure that the Creator wants to give. This is called "the purpose of creation." For this reason, the Creator prepares for him *Kelim* [vessels] for this, and *Kelim* are called "need" and "lack."

We see that there are only three things: 1) A person understands that if he wants to be a servant of the Creator, he must be abstinent and not enjoy anything, and then he will be a servant of the Creator. That is, in return for this, he will receive reward in this world and in the next world. 2) He understands that he must achieve the degree where he can work for the sake of the Creator, meaning that all his actions will be for the sake of the Creator, and he settles for this. 3) A person must achieve the purpose of creation, which is for the creatures to receive delight and pleasure, and not that they will give, since giving—which is that we must bring contentment to the Maker—is only the correction of creation.

According to the above, we can understand what we asked, Why when a person asks the Creator to give him vessels of bestowal, he receives from above bigger vessels of reception than he had before he asked the Creator to be given vessels of bestowal?

The answer is, as we said in previous articles, that if a person receives a desire to bestow right away, meaning that he will be able to overcome the small will to receive, he would settle for this, and the will to receive within him would remain uncorrected because it would not be revealed to a person so he could ask for the strength to overcome it.

This means that the fact that a person sees, when he asks to be given the power to overcome the small will to receive, and in return for the prayer he is given a big will to receive, it is not as the person thinks, that initially, his will to receive was small, and then from above he was given a big will to receive.

Rather, it is as *The Zohar* says about what is written, "Or make his sin known to him." He asked, "Who made it known to him?" And he said, "The Creator made it known to him." This means that the Creator made him see each time to a greater extent how big was the power of the will to receive with which he was born, as it is written, "Sin crouches at the door." That is, as soon as he was born, it was born with all its might. This is why it is called "a foolish old king."

However, a person need not know the full extent of the will to receive. Rather, this revelation of the power of the will to receive is gradual. That is, the evil should be balanced according to the good that he has. In other words, to the extent that a person exerts to cancel the will to receive, to that extent it is revealed to him from above.

As we explained concerning, "To the wicked, it seems like a hairsbreadth, and to the righteous, the evil inclination seems like a high mountain," we said that since the good and the bad must be balanced, as our sages said, "One should always see oneself half good and half bad," since they always go together so as to have a choice what to decide.

It follows that the bad is within man. However, the bad is revealed according to the measure of the good in a person. Hence, when one begins to walk on a line of truth, the bad appears in him each time. However, for each bad state that he feels, he cannot do anything except ask the Creator to help him, as it is written, "Man's inclination overcomes him every day. Were it not for the help of the Creator, he would not overcome it." It follows that man is powerless to overcome the evil, but the Creator must help him.

However, we should know that this, too, is a correction. That is, the fact that a person cannot overcome the bad without help from above is deliberate. This is so because if a person has the ability to work for the sake of the Creator by himself, he will remain in a state of Katnut [smallness/infancy]. That is, he will not need to rise in the degrees of Kedusha, where a person should come to attain the Torah, where the delight and pleasure that the Creator wanted to give to the creatures are concealed.

If a person feels that he is fine, he has no need for the Torah. But if a person cannot overcome the bad, and in that respect, a person cannot be satisfied, since he sees how the evil governs him, so he sees that he has no grip on holiness, so how can he be satisfied?

At that time, according to the measure of his overcoming, he sees the truth more clearly—that there is no chance he will be able to emerge from the governance of evil. At that time, when he asks the Creator to help him, he asks with all his heart. Moreover, often he despairs and needs extra overcoming to have the strength to go above reason, that the Creator can help him.

It follows that by overcoming and asking for the Creator's help, in what is he helped? It is as *The Zohar* says, "with a holy soul." That is, each time, the help is with a greater illumination. This is why a person cannot emerge from the governance of evil by himself, but rather needs the Creator to help him. By this, he will reveal his *NRNHY* of *Neshama* [soul].

According to the above, we should interpret what we asked: 1) Why is the *Shechina* called *Shoshan* [rose]? 2) Why does the *Shechina* testify to us before the King? That is, what should she testify? 3) What does it mean when he says that the *Shechina* is called "Help from above," as it is written, "And you will hear the heaven"?

She is called *Shoshan* because it is impossible to acquire the kingdom of heaven, which is faith above reason unless when the wicked comes and asks, "What is this work for you?" and wants to know within reason what he will have by working for the sake of the Creator and not for himself.

At that time, there is nothing to answer within reason, since within reason, he is right, as it is written, "And since he excluded himself from the public, he denied the most important." That is, since he denied the essence of the correction, which was in order not to have shame upon reception of the delight and pleasure, it follows that the Creator does not need to be served. Rather, the fact that we should work for the benefit of the Creator is for our own benefit.

That is, through this correction there will not be the matter of shame. This is what he denied. Hence, it will not help him to understand anything, and instead, we must go by force, meaning by coercion, which is called "Blunt his teeth." And since this work is ceaseless, it is called "Blunt his teeth a lot." This is why the kingdom of heaven is called *Shoshan* or *Shoshanah* [both mean "rose"], from the words, "Blunt his *Shinaim* [teeth]."

And what does the *Shechina* testify to us? that we are fine. We asked, Where does she see this?

The answer is that it is because she helps us. *Malchut* is called "Assistance of heaven." This means that *Malchut* herself gives the help. This is as it is written, "He who comes to purify is aided." Thus, she can testify that we are fine because she helped us in this.

Also, we asked, Why must she testify? We should interpret that once a person has been rewarded with the kingdom of heaven, when he can work for the sake of the Creator, he needs to be rewarded with the Torah, called ZA, a "King." This is what she must testify, that he already has the kingdom of heaven, and is therefore worthy of the Torah, called "the names of the Creator," which is the purpose of creation.

What Is, "A Cup of Blessing Must Be Full," in the Work?

Article No. 38, Tav-Shin-Nun, 1989/90

It is written in *The Zohar* (Pinhas, Item 630), "'Full,' which is said regarding a cup of blessing, is as it is written, 'A cup full of the blessing of the Lord.' So a man should be whole, as it is written, 'And Jacob came whole.' There must not be any flaw in it, for 'all that has a blemish will not approach.' Likewise, the letters *Aleph-Lamed-Mem* [mute] with *Yod-Hey* are the letters of *Elokim* [God], are as the count of 'cup,' namely eighty-six [in *Gematria*]. For this reason, the cup must be full, for if you reverse the word *Ilem* [*Aleph-Lamed-Mem*, mute], you will find *Maleh* [full], for the [word] 'cup,' in *Gematria*, is 'full,' *Yod-Hey*."

We should understand the following:

1) What does it imply that when wine is poured into a cup and it is full, it is called "a cup full of the blessing of the Creator"? This means that if the cup is not filled with wine, the blessing of the Creator cannot be?

2) Why does it say, "So a man should be whole," like the cup with the wine? What does it add to us by this? After all, if the cup

is already filled with the blessing of the Creator, why does man also need to be like that, implying that otherwise he cannot receive the blessing? Therefore, with regard to whom is the cup called "blessing of the Creator"? Does the cup need the blessing?

3) The most perplexing is what he says, that man should be whole, as it is written, "All that has a blemish will not approach." This implies that one who has a flaw can no longer approach the Creator. This means that one who is missing a limb can no longer approach the Creator and must stay far from the Creator and has no freedom of choice.

4) What does it imply that he says *Ilem* [mute] and *Maleh* [full] are the same letters, that a cup in *Gematria* is *Maleh Yod-Hey* [filled with the Creator]?

To understand all the above, we must remember the whole order of the work that we were given to do, as it is written, "Which God has created to do." We said several times that there are two opposite discernments before us, which are called 1) the purpose of creation, which is His desire to do good to His creations, meaning for the creatures to receive delight and pleasure, 2) the correction of creation, for the creatures to strive to bestow upon the Creator, so He will enjoy. That is, the will to receive for oneself wants to enjoy, and the Creator gave him this desire, but he relinquishes this desire and wants only for the Creator to enjoy.

It follows that the two are opposites. Hence, it is hard work to achieve such a desire called "desire to bestow contentment upon one's Maker," and relinquish the desire for self-benefit.

In order to be able to emerge from the control of the will to receive, we must begin in *Lo Lishma* [not for Her sake], meaning for our own benefit. In other words, by observing Torah and *Mitzvot* [commandments/good deeds], he will be rewarded in this world, as it is written in *The Zohar*, that he will have life, health, and sustenance. Otherwise, he will not be able to enjoy the corporeal life in this world. When a person believes this, he has someone who compels him to observe the Torah and *Mitzvot*. This is called "believing in reward and punishment, meaning that he observes Torah and Mitzvot because he is afraid of punishment and expects to receive reward.

Sometimes the reward and punishment are expressed in a person as reward and punishment in the next world, where there are the Garden of Eden and Hell, and this is the reason compelling him to observe Torah and Mitzvot. And since from Lo Lishma we come to Lishma [for Her sake], meaning that the light in the Torah illuminates to him that there is a different manner of reward and punishment—where the reward is to be rewarded with Dvekut [adhesion] with the Creator. At that time, he can feel the greatness of the King, that this is the reward he expects, and he regards as punishment when he sees and feels that he is separated from the Life of Lives and that he is far from the Creator. This, to him, is the biggest punishment.

It follows that even when a person already has some sensation of Torah and Mitzvot, which the Lo Lishma has caused him, when sometimes he begins to feel a little bit of the greatness of the Creator, this causes him to want to annul before Him as a candle before a torch. At that time, a person cannot understand why he wants to annul before Him now, and annul all of his own reality before the Creator. Rather, this comes to him as though it is a natural thing, meaning that even though he does not understand what is being done with him now—that he wants to annul—but in reality, so it is. This is called "an awakening from above," where a person's hand does not reach. "Hand" means attainment, from the words "When a hand attains," meaning that a person does not understand why he wants to completely annul before Him.

However, later, when the awakening departs from him, a person begins to yearn to achieve annulment before the Creator, and wants to obtain the feeling he had while in ascent, but now he begins to see how far he is from this, and all his organs resist such ideas as annulling self-benefit and that all his concerns will be how to bring contentment to his Maker.

At that time, he sees that the world has grown dark on him. He cannot find a place from which to receive vitality, and then he sees that he is in a state of descent and lowliness. When he comes to such a descent, he sees that no one has such bad thoughts. However, one should believe in the sages that such thoughts come from above, meaning that from above, they want this person who now wants to approach the Creator to suffer descents because by having descents, he will feel the need for the Creator to lift him.

This is as it is written, "He lifts the indigent from the trash." That is, precisely when he feels that he is in the trash, meaning that all those things that he regarded as trash, as animal food, who eat the waste that people throw in the trash, and of which they say that it is food that is unfit for human consumption, as he himself says during an ascent.

But now that the Creator wants to bring him closer, a person should feel his lack, and then he can receive a filling for the lack. It follows that precisely when a person is in the trash and from there searches for his food, when he sees to what state he has come after all the labor he has given in order to obtain the desire to bestow contentment upon his Maker, then he can make an earnest prayer. Yet, a person does not always have the strength to believe.

However, when a person is already standing near the place from which he will receive the help from above, and "near" means that the *Kli* [vessel], meaning the desire to bestow, is far away from him, then he sees that only the Creator can save him. As Baal HaSulam said, this is the most important point in man's work, for then he has close contact with the Creator because he sees one hundred percent that nothing can help him but the Creator Himself.

Although he believes this, still, this faith does not always illuminate for him that specifically now is the best time to receive the salvation of the Creator, that specifically now he can be saved and the Creator will bring him closer, meaning give him the desire to bestow and emerge from the control of self-love, which is called "exodus from Egypt." In other words, he comes out of the control of the Egyptians, who afflicted Israel and did not let them do the holy work. "And the children of Israel sighed from the work, and their cry rose up to God," and then the Creator brought them out from the exile in Egypt.

In other words, since the people of Israel felt the enslavement and wanted to escape from this exile that the Egyptians were enslaving them, when they came to this important point of feeling their lowliness, the Creator brought them out of Egypt. This is as the ARI says, that when the people of Israel were in Egypt, they were already in forty-nine gates of *Tuma'a* [impurity], and then the Creator brought them out from Egypt.

This means that they already came to the worst lowliness, the lowest that can be, and then the Creator brought them out.

It follows that when a person sees that he is in utter lowliness, he should believe that specifically now is the time when the Creator will bring him closer. And if the faith does not shine for him then, on the spot, he escapes the campaign.

It follows that the whole order of the labor that He has given is seemingly for nothing. But later, he is given another awakening from above, and once again he forgets what he had during the descent, and thinks once more that he will no longer have descents, and so on repeatedly. A person needs great mercy in order not to escape the campaign. Although he uses the counsels that our sages said, "I have created the evil inclination; I have created the Torah as a spice," but the person says that he has already used this advice several times to no avail.

He also says that he has already used the advice "He who comes to purify is aided," and it is as though all the counsels are not for him. Thus, he does not know what to do. This is the worst state for a person, meaning he wants to escape from these states but has nowhere to run. At that time he suffers torments at being between despair and confidence. But then a person says, "Where will I turn?"

At that time, the only advice is prayer. Yet, this prayer is also without any guarantee, so it follows that then he must pray to believe that the Creator does hear a prayer, and everything that one feels in these states is to his benefit. But this can be only above reason, meaning although the mind tells him, "After all the calculations, you see that nothing can help you," he should believe this, too, above reason, that the Creator can deliver him from the will to receive for himself, in return for which he will receive the desire to bestow. Then, when a person receives from the Creator the desire to bestow, he becomes whole with the Creator, meaning he has been rewarded with equivalence of form, which is called "unification."

At that time, a person is considered "unblemished," since all of man's blemishes are that he has bad thoughts about spirituality. That is, instead of feeling the importance of *Kedusha* [holiness], that it is something very important, when he wants to annul before Him, when he has love of the Creator because of the yearning for the Creator, to him it is the opposite. That is, he feels the resistance of the body.

All this comes for lack of faith in the greatness of the Creator, and how can he approach the Creator with the blemishes he has within him? This is the meaning of what we asked, How did they say that one who has a blemish shall not approach? for it means that he no longer has any choice to be able to approach the Creator. In other words, the verse, "therefore choose life," was not said about him. Can this be said?

However, in the work, we should say that a "blemish" means a lack, meaning lack of faith in the Creator. Thus, "all that has a blemish will not approach," meaning cannot approach the Creator. Instead, first he must correct his blemishes, meaning do good deeds with the aim to be rewarded with faith in the Creator, that He watches over the world as The Good Who Does Good.

Now we will explain what we asked why it is implied that "a cup of blessing should be filled with wine," otherwise it is not regarded as a cup of blessing. And he says, "So a man should be whole." But what is the connection between the cup and the man, that if the cup must be full, so should man be whole?

The answer is that the cup is the *Kli* in which wine is placed. A *Kli* is called "a lack," and in the lack enters the filling. Wine is called "abundance," and with respect to the abundance, there is never a lack, since "Nothing is missing in the King's house," and as it is written, "I the Lord do not change," meaning that there is never a deficit in the light. Rather, everything depends on the receiving *Kelim* [vessels], so they are complete *Kelim* and not broken ones.

As we learned, there was the matter of the breaking of the vessels, where from the breaking of the vessels emerged the *Klipot* [shells/peels]. The breaking of the vessels means that just as when a physical vessel breaks, if you place a liquid in the *Kli*, it all spills out, so it is in spirituality: If the cup, called a *Kli*, is not full, but the *Kli* is deficient with the Creator, the abundance exits to the outer ones, namely to the *Klipot*.

The intimation that the cup must be full means that the cup should be in equivalence of form with the abundance that comes from the Giver. Then the cup can be full and the abundance will not go to the external ones. In order to understand the intimation, they added and said, "so a man should be whole" and there will be no flaw in him. This is when the cup is called "a cup of blessing."

In other words, man, who is the *Kli* that should receive the abundance of blessing, should be whole with the Creator. This means that all of man's concerns should be only about the benefit of the Creator and not about his own benefit. This is called "a complete cup," implying that man should be complete, and then the cup can be full.

In other words, if the *Kli*, called "cup," implying to the receiving individual, the blessing can be full in the *Kli*, and it does not spill over from the blessing, meaning the *Kli*, to the outer ones, who are the *Klipot*. Rather, everything stays in *Kedusha*, since man has no blemish, for a blemish in spirituality means that there is a mixture of will to receive. If a person has corrected himself from all the flaws, which is the will to receive for himself, what remains is a cup full of the blessing of the Creator and no abundance flows out to the external ones.

Now we will explain what he says, *Ilem* [mute] with *Yod-Hey* is the letters *Elokim* [God], and it is the same number as "cup" [in *Gematria*]; hence, a cup must be full, for if you invert the [letters of the] word *Ilem* you will find *Maleh* [full]. We should understand what this implies to us.

The ARI explains the Lord, God [*Elokim*] after the name of the *Kli* that is fit to receive the abundance, called "light." He says that the order of scrutinies is that the sparks and *Kelim* must be raised from BYA to *Atzilut* for *Ibur* [impregnation] in *Ima*. At that time, 320 sparks ascend, comprising thirty-two *Behinot* [discernments], where each *Behina* [singular of *Behinot*] comprises ten, thus 320 *Behinot*.

The breaking occurred because of *Malchut* of the quality of judgment that was in each *Malchut* in each of the thirty-two paths. Hence, the first correction was that *Abba*, called *Hochma*, sorted and removed the *Malchut* of each *Behina*. This is regarded as removing the *Malchut* in each path, which is called *Peh* [mouth], which is *Malchut*, from which the degree is revealed and shines.

This is as he says in *The Study of the Ten Sefirot* (Part 12, Item 246): "The *Ubar* [embryo] does not speak at all, for it is *Ilem*, from *Elokim*. Hence, it is mute, devoid of speech. This is the meaning of 'Or who makes him mute.'" And it is written (*The Study of the Ten Sefirot*, Part 12, Item 221), "Now (at the time of *Yenika* [nursing]), they will be filled with the letters *Yod-Hey* and become complete *Elokim*."

We should discern between speech and mute in the work. Speech means revealing, when a person already has *Yenika* in spirituality, and he feels that he is nursing from *Kedusha*, for nursing on milk indicates *Hassadim*, for the quality of *Hesed* [mercy] is bestowal, when a person is rewarded with vessels of bestowal and all his actions are for the sake of the Creator and he has no concerns for his own benefit. This is regarded as the quality of *Hesed*.

However, before the *Yenika* there is *Ibur*, meaning that the upper one corrects him. This can be when a person is like an embryo in its mother's womb, where the embryo annuls before the mother and has no view of its own, but as our sages said, "An embryo is its mother's thigh, eats what its mother eats," and has no authority of its own to ask any questions. Rather, it does not merit a name. This is called "mute," when he has no mouth to ask questions.

This is so when a person can go with his eyes shut, above reason, and believe in the sages and go all the way. This is called *Ibur*, when he has no mouth. *Ibur* means as it is written (*The Study of the Ten Sefirot*, Part 8, Item 17), "The level of *Malchut*, which is the most restricted *Katnut* [smallness/infancy] possible, is called *Ibur*. It comes from the words *Evra* [anger] and *Dinin* [Aramaic: judgments], as it is written, 'And the Lord was impregnated in me for your sake.'"

We should interpret the meaning of "anger and judgments." When a person must go with this eyes shut, above reason, the body resists this work. Hence, the fact that a person always has to overcome, this is called "anger, wrath, and trouble," since it is hard work to always overcome and annul before the upper one, for the upper one to do with him what the upper one wants. This is called *Ibur*, which is the most restricted *Katnut* possible.

The correction is as our sages said, "*Abba*, who is *Hochma*, gives the white," meaning he whitens the lower one from its will to receive, so a person begins to feel that the will to receive is waste, as it is written, "Though your sins are as scarlet, they will be as white as snow." At that time, it is considered that "His mother gives the red," meaning that *Bina* is called "light of *Hassadim*," which is the light that comes into vessels of bestowal. That is, once a person has come to know that the will to receive is called "waste," he receives the desire to bestow. All this is considered that the upper one works and the lower one annuls itself without any criticism. This is regarded as having no "mouth," and this is called "mute," which means he has no mouth.

Afterward come the states of "birth" and *Yenika* [nursing]. At that time, he already has a mouth, meaning that he has his own authority and he already knows what he is doing. He already has permission to make his own choices, which is regarded as being on his own. This is regarded as receiving *Ruach*, which illuminates when he already has his own authority in *Kedusha*. But in *Ibur*, he had only *Nefesh*, from the word *Nefisha* [rest/stillness], meaning still, which has no independent movement but the upper one moves it in every action.

At that time, he receives a complete name from *Elokim*, meaning that being in *Ibur*, *Ilem* [mute] from *Elokim* [God], meaning that he did not have his own authority, that he owned the work, but rather everything was attributed to the upper one. When he was born and has his own *Yenika* in *Kedusha*, he is a full name of *Elokim*. This is the intimation that that which was mute from its own perspective, has now become full. That is, he has been rewarded with *Yod-Hey* from *Elokim*, which implies a complete name, "cup" in *Gematria*, which is the number four—*Elokim*, which is 86—and then the cup is full.

In other words, when a person has corrected himself into the domain of *Kedusha*, it is called "a complete *Kli*," and this is called "a cup of blessing," meaning that the blessing can already be in it, since the *Kli* is corrected so that everything that it receives will remain in *Kedusha*.

By this we understand what it implies that the cup should be filled with wine. It implies to us that the abundance will remain in the *Kli* and nothing will spill out from there to the outer ones. Rather, everything will be in order to bestow. It follows that when speaking of the *Mitzvot*, it all pertains to branch and root. This is why a cup of blessing must be full, which implies to spirituality, meaning the order of man's work to achieve the purpose of creation.

What Is, "Anyone Who Mourns for Jerusalem Is Rewarded with Seeing Its Joy," in the Work?

Article No. 39, Tav-Shin-Nun, 1989/90

Our sages said (*Taanit*, p 30b), "Anyone who mourns for Jerusalem is rewarded with seeing its joy." Taken literally, this is hard to understand. Certainly, there were many righteous who mourned for Jerusalem, yet Jerusalem was still not built, so how were they rewarded with seeing its joy? In the literal explanation, there are probably many answers to this, but we should interpret it in the work.

It is known that *Malchut* is called "Jerusalem." Hence, when we say, "the ruin of the Jerusalem," it refers to the ruin of the Temple. This is called "*Shechina* [Divinity] in the dust" or "*Shechina* in exile." In other words, a person should take upon himself the burden of the kingdom of heaven and believe that the Creator leads the world with a guidance of The Good Who Does Good, since it is hidden from us.

Malchut is the one who gives to the souls and to *BYA*. Everything that comes from above to the creatures is considered *Malchut*. Thus, *Malchut* is not respected by the creatures because they do not see her importance, meaning what she gives to us. This is called "Jerusalem in its ruin." In other words, where she should have been giving delight and pleasure to the creatures, and where everyone should have seen her merit, they see that everything is ruined in her and she has nothing to give, instead. It is said about it (in the *Nachem* [comfort] prayer on the 9th of *Av*), "The mourners for Jerusalem, and the lamenting, ruined, degraded, and desolate city." In other words, everything is ruined and destroyed, and this is called "*Shechina* in the dust." Hence, when a person should take upon himself the burden of the kingdom of heaven, the body resists vigorously.

Thus, if a person overcomes and takes upon himself the burden of the kingdom of heaven although he sees no importance, and mourns for the importance of Jerusalem being so hidden from us, and prays about why *Malchut* has no importance, and asks of the Creator to raise Jerusalem from the dust it is in, to the extent that one regrets its ruin, he is rewarded with the Creator hearing his prayer.

And that man is rewarded with seeing its joy, meaning that it does bestow upon him delight and pleasure. It follows that the meaning will be that he who regrets and mourns for Jerusalem, for the *Shechina* being in the dust, that person is rewarded with seeing its joy, since there is no light without a *Kli* [vessel]. Since he has the *Kli*, meaning the lack—his regret that *Shechina* is in the dust—he is therefore rewarded with seeing the comfort of Jerusalem.

According to the above-said, we should interpret what is written (Isaiah 1), "The ox knows its owner, and the donkey its master's crib; Israel does not know; My people does not understand." We should understand the difference between an ox and a donkey in the work, as well as the difference between Israel and My people in the work, Baal HaSulam said that the difference between an ox and a donkey is that an ox is considered "mind," which is faith above reason. This is the meaning of "The ox knows its owner." A donkey is considered "heart," meaning the will to receive, which is "And the donkey, its master's crib."

Thus, there are two discernments to make here:

1) Those who work for a reward, who observe Torah and Mitzvot [commandments/good deeds] in order to receive reward. Their question is primarily "How much reward will I receive, and what will be the reward, meaning is this reward worth the labor in Torah and Mitzvot?"

2) Those who want to work in order to bestow because, as it is written in The Zohar, "He is great and ruling." In other words, they work only because of the greatness of the Creator. That is, they feel very privileged serving a great King. It follows that those who work in order to bestow need to know who they are serving, that He is truly a great and important King, worth serving.

However, when they begin to work in order to bestow, and the whole reason that they have the strength to work is the importance of the Creator, then begins the work in the form of "Shechina in the dust." In other words, where spirituality, meaning working to benefit the Creator, should have been more important each time, a person gets such thoughts that demonstrate the opposite. And instead of a person going forward and working more gladly because he is serving a great and important King, he gets pictures of insignificance. In other words, he does not feel His greatness, and this causes him constant descents.

This means that even when he overcomes the descents he cannot always endure and fight against these thoughts. And what these thoughts show him is that the Shechina is in the dust. He wishes to work with joy for serving a great and important King, and this should bring him joy, but he feels the complete opposite—rejection. It is as though he is being repelled from the work.

This is called "*Shechina* in the dust"—this feeling that he is being pushed outside. In other words, he feels that while wishing to take upon himself the burden of the kingdom of heaven, Pharaoh's questions come to him, asking "Who is the Lord that I should obey His voice?" This is considered that *Malchut*, meaning the *Shechina*, is in exile with Pharaoh, King of Egypt, who shows the lowliness of the kingdom of heaven.

At that time, one can only ask for *Malchut* [kingdom] to be built, meaning that *Malchut* will not remain in a form of lowliness, since one cannot receive joy from this lowliness when he sees that it has no importance. This is considered that one should pray for the ruin of the Temple, for the world not being able to see the receiving of the kingdom of heaven as a good thing, meaning consider working for the Creator a respectable, dignified work.

Hence, when one prays for the exile of the *Shechina*, he should not pray that it is in the dust only for him. Rather, one should pray about its lowliness in the whole world, that the whole world gives no thought to spirituality. And he prays for the whole world, as we pray, "And build Jerusalem soon in our days," so it will be glorified in the whole world, as it is said in the *Rosh Hashanah* [the beginning of the year] prayer, "Be King over all the whole world with Your glory." But since the general public does not feel the lack, how can they pray?

However, such a person, who was rewarded with obtaining the need, who has attained the exile, he can ask for redemption. But those who do not feel that there is an exile, how can they ask that He will deliver them from exile? It follows that a person's feeling of being in exile is already considered an ascent in degree, and he must ask for fulfillment for the general public.

As was mentioned above, "Anyone who mourns for Jerusalem is rewarded with seeing its joy." In other words, the one who feels the exile of the *Shechina* and mourns is the one who is rewarded with seeing its joy, since in terms of *Kelim* [vessels], only he has *Kelim* that are ready for redemption because *Kelim* are a desire for fulfillment.

Hence, he mourns when he feels how the *Shechina* is in exile and her greatness is not seen. But one who wishes to take upon himself the burden of the kingdom of heaven because He is great and ruling gets thoughts and imaginations, and these thoughts repel him outside of *Kedusha* [holiness], and only by overcoming and coercion above reason can he endure.

And each time he wishes to believe that His Providence is in the manner of good and doing good, he gets thoughts that slander the Creator and it pains him that he must hear slander. He believes that it is only because the nations of the world rule over the *Kedusha*, meaning that there is concealment, and for those who wish to enter the holy work, the *Sitra Achra* [other side] hides the importance of *Kedusha*. It follows that it is precisely the one who mourns who needs heaven's mercy, to be able to overcome the evil in him, and he mourns and cries for the Creator to help him.

But he should certainly pray for the whole public, or it is considered that he is praying only for his own sake, that is, that only he will be delivered from exile. And if one truly asks for the sake of the Creator, to have the glory of heaven revealed in the world, how can he ask only for himself? Thus, one should ask for the glory of heaven to be revealed to the whole world, as our sages said (*Baba Kamah* 92), "Anyone who pleads mercy for his friend, and needs the same, is granted first."

In the work, we should understand why a person is answered first if he pleads mercy for his friend. It seems as though the mercy he is asking is not because he wishes to evoke mercy on his friend. It seems like deceit. Because our sages said that he will be answered first, he is pleading mercy for his friend.

And yet, we should understand why he is answered first. Can't the prayer be granted for both of them together? Must it be one at a time and not both at once? We should understand what is it about him being answered first.

We should interpret that when a person asks for mercy for his friend in the work—when one begins to walk on the path of achieving *Dvekut* [adhesion] with the Creator through observing Torah and *Mitzvot*, considered that all his actions will be for the Creator and not for himself—the body begins to resist this work. It brings him thoughts of how this work is not for him, since the nature of the body is for its own sake, while he wishes to work for the sake of the Creator. Thus, the body, called "will to receive," always shows him that it is not worthwhile to work for the Creator. And since one cannot make a single move without pleasure—for this is the nature of creation, since He wishes to delight His creatures, which is the reason for creation—hence, one cannot work unless he receives pleasure from the work.

Thus, everything that a man does is only to enjoy, meaning receive reward for the exertion he is making. Therefore, in *Lo Lishma* [not for Her sake], when one believes in reward and punishment, one has fuel for work during the labor because he is looking at the reward he will receive. But when one works in order to bestow, meaning he does not wish to receive any reward for the labor, how can he work without pleasure?

The Zohar says about this that we must work because the Creator is great and ruling, meaning because of the greatness of the Creator. This is so because we see that in nature, the smaller one receives pleasure when serving the greater one, since naturally, one has strength to work in service of an important person. Especially, it is a great pleasure to serve a great king. One does not need to work on it; it is in the nature of creation. What one should work on is to know and to feel that he is an important person, and then he will be able to serve him.

Therefore, particularly when one wishes to work because of the greatness of the Creator, bad thoughts come to him and do not let him feel the greatness of the Creator, but actually show him the opposite. Indeed, this concealment governs the whole public. But for those who do not work because of the greatness of the Creator, the body does not need to hide the greatness of the Creator from them, since as long as they do not make the greatness of the Creator the reason for the work, the body is not working for free because it considers the reward, not the giver of the reward.

It follows that particularly for people who wish to work only because of the greatness of the Creator, there is resistance and the nations of the world cover and hide the Israel in man. Thus, naturally, the majority of slander against the greatness of the Creator is in those who wish to achieve *Dvekut* with the Creator. Those who feel that discernment called "*Shechina* in the dust" are the ones who feel the need to ask of the Creator to deliver her from exile, from being among the nations, meaning that the nations rule over her and hide the greatness and importance of the holy *Shechina*.

Therefore, those who feel that the *Shechina* is in the dust should pray for the glory of heaven to be revealed throughout the world. However, it is not the whole world that needs it—to raise the *Shechina* from the dust—and so he is answered first, since he needs the same thing. But afterward this brings disclosure to the whole generation. And yet, as long as they do not have the proper *Kelim* for it, it cannot be so disclosed in them. It is as our sages said, "If he performs one *Mitzva* [commandment/good deed], happy is he, for he has sentenced himself and the entire world to the side of merit."

Thus, only that person—who feels the concealment over spirituality, over the desire to bestow because of the greatness of the Creator—must ask for mercy for the whole generation. And since he needs the same thing, he will be answered first. This is why it is said about him, "Anyone who mourns for Jerusalem is rewarded with seeing its joy." And the reason is, as we said above, that he needs the same thing, and not the public. This is why he who pleads mercy for his friend, they cannot both receive the granting of the prayer at once because only he needs that thing, meaning that salvation—to feel the greatness of *Kedusha* [holiness] called "raising the *Shechina* from the dust."

But those who work in the first above-mentioned manner, who work for a reward, they consider the reward. There is a rule: The one who gives is important. It follows that if they believe that they will receive reward, that the Creator will pay their reward, then He is already important to them. But those who are not working for a reward should now feel His greatness, and on that there is the concealment that is placed on the *Kedusha*—its greatness is unseen. For that, we were given the request from the Creator to remove the concealment, as it is written, "Hide not Your face from me."

Now we can understand what we asked about what is "Israel does not know," and what is "My people does not understand." Israel are those who work with the aim to achieve *Dvekut* with the Creator, to be rewarded with achieving the degree *Yashar-El* [straight to the Creator], and not for their own benefit. They belong to the intention called "knowing," since they need to come to clear knowledge that they must achieve the greatness of the Creator. This knowledge comes specifically through faith above reason, since the reason is dominated by the nations of the world, who hide the greatness of the *Kedusha* and degrade the kingdom of heaven to the dust.

And particularly by overcoming with faith above reason, when one carries out his actions by coercion, when bad thoughts of the *Sitra Achra* come to him, which slander and say that it is not worthwhile to work for the sake of the Creator, that the reason for this work is only the greatness of the Creator, then there is nothing one can do except believe in the sages, who tell us that it is specifically this work that a person does above reason that the Creator enjoys. It is as Baal HaSulam said, that the majority of the work is when a person gives something to the Creator precisely when he goes above reason.

This means that reason tells him that it is not worth it to do things in order to bestow. But one overcomes it and works above reason. This is considered that a person gave something to the Creator. But when the Creator gives him an awakening from above, there is nothing that one can do, about which he can say that he is giving something to the Creator, since then a man is annulled before the Creator as a candle before a torch, without any choice.

In that state, one is giving nothing because he has no choice. But when he must go above reason, since reason states otherwise, he can say that he is giving something to the Creator. And he said that we must believe that this work is more important to the Creator than the rest of the works.

The prophet said, "The ox knows its owner." This belongs to the quality of Israel, who are considered the heads of the people. Israel means *Li Rosh* [The head is mine]. Knowledge belongs to them, and this is why he said, "Israel does not know," since they were not engaging in labor in order to come to know the Creator, as it is written, "Know this day, and lay it to your heart, that the Lord, He is God."

And the prophet said that they were not engaged in this. Also, the prophet spoke to the public, meaning to the populace, whose work is only to receive reward and this is why they engage in Torah and Mitzvot. They did not consider the matter of "And the donkey, its master's crib." The donkey, as we said above, is the will to receive called "only self-love." And then the prophet told them that the donkey, meaning he who looks at his master's crib—the reward—did not consider that the Creator is giving them the reward, meaning that by considering, they will receive the love of the Creator, just as there is love for one who gives presents to people. But they did not notice the Giver; they only thought that they would have reward.

It follows that what they did, they did for reward were without love and fear, meaning they did not give any thought to "His master's crib," meaning to the landlord—that the Creator is the Giver. Instead, they cut the Mitzvot from the giver of Torah and Mitzvot and did not think of the Giver of the work during the work. Also, when they thought about the reward, they were not thinking of who was the Giver of the reward.

This means that the prophet stands and warns both Israel—who work on the intention but do not give sufficient heed to achieving *Dvekut* with the Creator—and those who work only in action and their aim is only to receive reward, and they do not consider who it is who gives the reward. This is why "My people does not understand." And naturally, they lack the love of the Creator.

It follows that a man should reflect on what to pray for before he comes to pray. This is why Baal HaSulam said that one should pray for only one thing, and this includes many things: It is that he asks of the Creator to give him a desire to work in order to bestow and not for his own sake. This is so because to have a desire to bestow, he must have faith in the Creator and believe in the greatness of the Creator. But the prayer that he wishes for the Creator to give him the desire to bestow means that a person tells the Creator, "I want that while I engage in Torah and Mitzvot, the intention will be that I will believe that the Creator takes pleasure in my actions."

In other words, even though one does not taste or feel anything during his labor, he will have the strength to say to his body—while the body argues, "You see that the study of Torah and the prayer are tasteless to you," a person wishes to have the strength to tell the body, "since I am working only for the Creator's pleasure, why should I care if it feels tasteless to me or not? If I were working for my own benefit, you would be right in what you are telling me, that you are tasting nothing in your work. Likewise, a person who does not enjoy his food does not eat. I, however, am working to benefit the Creator, so it makes no difference to me what flavor I am tasting." This is what he asks of the Creator, and this is called unconditional surrender.

What Is, "For You Are the Least of All the Peoples," in the Work?

Article No. 40, Tav-Shin-Nun, 1989/90

I t is written (Deuteronomy 7:7-8), "It is not because you are more in number than any of the peoples that the Lord desired you, for you are the least of all the peoples. Because the Lord loves you, and because He keeps the oath that He swore to your forefathers, the Lord brought you out with a mighty hand and redeemed you from the house of slavery, from the hand of Pharaoh king of Egypt." Our sages said (*Hulin* 89), "'It is not because you are more in number,' said the Creator to Israel, 'that I desire you, for even when I bestow upon you greatness, you diminish yourselves before Me.'"

We should understand what this comes to teach us, that our sages said that the Creator said to Israel, "I desire you, for even when I bestow upon you greatness, you diminish yourselves before Me." If the Creator said, "Although I bestow upon you greatness, you diminish yourselves before flesh and blood," I would understand this. But our sages said, "You diminish yourselves before Me,"

743

meaning before the Creator. What degree is it, that if the Creator gives a person greatness, he does not pride himself before the Creator because the Creator gave him greatness?

If the king gives greatness to a person and extols him before the ministers, does the person pride himself before the king, as well? Can this be? If so, why is it important that they do not pride themselves before the Creator but diminish themselves before Him? In other words, before whom do they diminish themselves? It stands to reason that when a person understands the greatness of the King, he lowers himself even more before the king.

In order to understand this, we must remember the order of the work, which is the correction of creation. That is, in order to achieve Dvekut [adhesion], called "equivalence of form," meaning in order to be rewarded with vessels of bestowal, a correction took place, which is called "Tzimtzum [restriction] and concealment on the Kedusha [holiness]." That is, the taste of Torah and Mitzvot [commandments/good deeds], where the delight and pleasure that He wished to give to the created beings became concealed. This is called "His desire to do good to His creations," where everything He wanted to give to the creatures is clothed in Torah and Mitzvot, which The Zohar calls "613 Pekudin [Aramaic: deposits]."

It is as it is said in the Sulam ["Ladder" commentary on The Zohar], that Pekudin comes from the word Pikadon [Hebrew: deposit], for in each Mitzva [singular of Mitzvot] there is a special light clothed in that Mitzva. But because of the Tzimtzum and the concealment over them because of the correction of creation, in order to reach the light that is clothed in them, and for a person to receive the delight and pleasure clothed in them, he must first acquire the suitable Kelim [vessels] for the light, since there must be equivalence of form with the light—as the light gives, so the Kli [vessel] should work in order to bestow.

However, by nature, man has a desire to receive for himself, and not a desire to bestow. Thus, how can a person change his nature, which the Creator created? Our sages said about this, "The Creator said, 'I have created the evil inclination; I have created the Torah as a spice.'" In other words, the Torah advises a person how to emerge from self-love and acquire the desire to bestow. *The Zohar* says that in that state, the 613 *Mitzvot* are called "613 *Eitin* [Aramaic: counsels]," meaning 613 counsels by which to acquire the desire to bestow, for only in the desire to bestow can the light, which is called "good and does good," clothe.

Our sages said about this, "One should always engage in Torah and *Mitzvot*, even *Lo Lishma* [not for Her sake], since from *Lo Lishma*, he will come to *Lishma* [for Her sake]." Because the light in it reforms him, by this he will achieve the degree of *Lishma*.

Concerning *Lo Lishma*, there are many discernments:

1) Learning in order to provoke. This manner is the worst. Our sages said about this (*Berachot* 17), "Anyone who engages in Torah *Lo Lishma* would be better off not being born."

2) Learning in order to be called "Rabbi."

In those two discernments, he wants reward from people, and does not want the Creator to reward him for his work.

3) Learning in order for the Creator to reward him in this world—to have life, provision, health, etc.

4) Learning so the Creator will reward him in the next world.

5) He engages in Torah and *Mitzvot* because he feels that he is serving a great King. Therefore, he derives pleasure from engaging in Torah and *Mitzvot*. That is, because of this joy that he feels, that he is serving a great King, it is worthwhile for him to work. It follows that one who works because he is serving a great King also cannot be regarded as pure *Lishma*, although he is working for the sake of the Creator, meaning that he does not want any reward for his work. Yet, he does yearn to feel a good taste in this work because he is feeling a great King.

So, we must know that this is still not considered pure *Lishma*, since in the end, he yearns for the pleasure he will feel during the work. The pleasure he feels during the work is the reason he wants to be a servant of the Creator. It follows that the pleasure that the desire feels during the work is the only thing that makes him engage in Torah and *Mitzvot*. Hence, this, too, is considered *Lo Lishma*. However, this *Lo Lishma* brings him to *Lishma*, since the light in it reforms him.

This is as it is written in the "Introduction to The Book of Zohar" (Items 30-31), "The second division is from thirteen years and on. At that point, the point in his heart—which is the *Achoraim* [posterior] of *Nefesh* of *Kedusha* [holiness] dressed in his will to receive—is given strength. At that time one begins to enter the system of the worlds of *Kedusha*, to the extent that one observes Torah and *Mitzvot*. The primary aim is to obtain and intensify the spiritual will to receive. Yet, it is a much more important degree than the first; this is the degree that brings one to *Lishma*, as our sages said, 'One should always engage in Torah and *Mitzvot Lo Lishma*, as from *Lo Lishma*, one comes to *Lishma*.'

"This is considered the maidservant of *Kedusha* who serves her mistress, which is the Holy *Shechina* [Divinity]. The maidservant brings one to *Lishma*, and he is rewarded with the instilling of the *Shechina*. Yet, one should take every measure suited to bring one to *Lishma*. And the final degree in this division is to become infatuated with the Creator just as one becomes infatuated in corporeal love, until the object of infatuation remains before one's eyes all day and all night, as the poet said, 'When I remember Him, He does not let me sleep.'"

After all this, begins the order of *Lishma*, called "desire to bestow." And here, a person cannot bring himself to work entirely in order to bestow, meaning to want only to bestow upon the Creator "because He is great and ruling." Man has no idea how to achieve this. This is regarded as the desire to bestow being in exile in Egypt. A person can understand this desire only above reason, since within reason, there is no grip on understanding this.

In other words, a person cannot understand how it is possible to do something from which one does not enjoy. It follows that even if a person does not require any reward for his work, what compels him to work is that the Creator will enjoy. From this he derives his pleasure. Hence, there is already a matter of pleasure here, meaning that he enjoys serving the King; this is his pleasure. But how can it be otherwise, that he will work without pleasure?

Therefore, when it is said that man must work in order to bestow, this is called "above reason." Anything that is above reason, the will to receive for oneself is absent there. In other words, a person is told that he must work only so the Creator will enjoy this work. At that time, it is said that the person should be happy that he is serving a great King.

However, if the great King were to reveal His greatness and importance, the pleasure would be within reason. That is, the mind understands that it is worthwhile to serve a great King. But when a person must have faith in the greatness and importance of the King, he feels that he is serving a small king. Therefore, when he says above reason that He is a great King, there is no room for the will to receive to agree to this work, since all the pleasure is built on above reason.

Thus, it is clear why the body does not want to work when it does not see the importance of the King. Rather, it is told, although the mind necessitates, if the greatness of the King is not revealed, there is no more room there for the will to receive for himself. Thus, how can one work "because He is great and ruling"? This would be good if it were revealed, but Pharaoh king of Egypt, who said, "Who is the Lord, that I should obey His voice," governs this discernment of the greatness of the Creator.

Hence, the work is mainly in this place, meaning that here begins the matter of *Lishma*, meaning that he wants to work so the Creator will enjoy his work, and it does not matter to him what taste he feels. In other words, the work he does is to him as though he felt that the King is great, while in fact, he feels that the "*Shechina* [Divinity] is in the dust." That is, he does not feel any importance, but tastes the taste of dust. And yet, he overcomes and says, "It is as important to me, as though I felt that I was serving a great King." At that time, the will to receive certainly enjoys, as well, since he does not need to believe in the greatness and importance of the King.

However, how can one muster the strength to overcome the body when he feels that the *Shechina* is in the dust? What joy can he receive from this work? Even more perplexing, how can one need and want to work when he feels no taste in it? This would be understandable if he had no choice; we can understand when a person is forced to work. But how is it possible to want such a work, which feels tasteless? And since he does not have the strength to overcome and feel joy in such a work, how can he serve the King in such a lowly state, when he feels the taste of dust while serving the King?

Hence, in this regard, he does not ask the Creator to give him the revelation of His greatness, so he will feel a good taste in it. Rather, he asks the Creator to give him strength to be able to overcome the body and work gladly because now he can work only for the Creator, since the will to receive does not enjoy work that tastes like dust. Therefore, why is he working? Certainly, only for the sake of the Creator. There is no room for such work within reason, and in this work, a person sees that it is inherently impossible that he will want to work in such a manner.

In this work, in such a state, a person sees that there is no way that he will be able to work with the desire to bestow and not for his own sake. Such a thing can happen only through a miracle from above. And indeed, this is called "the exodus from Egypt," meaning to emerge from the mind he has by nature, where it is possible to move unless he enjoys it. Conversely, here he is asking the Creator to give him the strength to work where he has no feeling or flavor, but to believe that the Creator enjoys this work, since it is all in order to bestow.

For this reason, this prayer is an honest prayer, since a person sees that he cannot hope to ever be able to do anything in order to bestow. It follows that a person feels that he is lost. At that time he has close contact with the Creator, and this is something that a person should appreciate—that he is asking the Creator to help him and there is no one in the world who can save him.

Yet, here comes the most difficult question: Who told the person that the Creator derives contentment from this work, which tastes like dust, and that this is the work that one should ask of the Creator because he wants to do everything only so that the Creator will enjoy?

The answer to this is "faith in the sages." We must believe their words. It follows that this prayer that a person prays that the Creator will help him so he can work in a state of lowliness, and the taste is only the taste of dust, this can be only on the basis of faith in the sages, to believe them that only in this way can we achieve a state of *Lishma*, and not for our own benefit. In other words, only they know what is *Lishma* and how to achieve it.

According to the above, we can interpret what we asked about what our sages said about the verse, "It is not because you are more in number." "The Creator said to Israel, 'I desire you, for even when I bestow upon you greatness, you diminish yourselves before Me.'" We asked, Is it customary that one whom the king extols prides himself before the king? Thus, why do they tell us that Israel diminish themselves before the Creator?

We explained above that there are two discernments in the work: 1) When the Creator shines for him while he engages in Torah and *Mitzvot* and feels a good taste in the work, and feels the greatness of the Creator, that he is serving a great King and has already achieved the degree of "When I remember Him, it does not let me sleep." 2) The work *Lishma*, meaning to bestow and not in order to receive reward. At that time, a person's body resists because he does not feel any flavor in the work. However, he does not want any feeling of the greatness of the Creator because then this feeling gives him a reason that because of this feeling that he feels when engaging in Torah and *Mitzvot*, it compels him to engage in Torah and *Mitzvot*. It follows that it is no longer only for the sake of the Creator, but his own pleasure is included in it, too.

749

And since this work is entirely above reason, since there is no intellect in the world that can understand such a thing, and this discernment is called "*Shechina* in the dust," and a person must believe that specifically from this work the Creator derives contentment, this is called work in the manner of "You diminish yourselves before Me."

That is, when the Creator let them feel the greatness of the Creator, they do not say, "Now we do not need to work above reason, since the body, too, when it feels the greatness of the Creator, annuls "as a candle before a torch." Instead, they say, "We want to work in the manner for, 'for you are the least of all the peoples,'" meaning that all the peoples in a person say that this work is contemptible, inferior, and lowly, meaning that it is "*Shechina* in the dust."

As our sages said, "'It is not because you are more in number,' said the Creator to Israel, 'that I desire you, for even when I bestow upon you greatness, you diminish yourselves before Me.'" "I gave greatness to Abraham." Certainly, at that time, he should be happy because he already feels the greatness of the Creator and he will no longer have resistance from the body. Yet, he diminishes himself and says, "And I am dust and ashes."

In other words, he said to the Creator, "I yearn for the state of the work that was in a manner of, "I am the Lord your God," in the manner of dust and ashes, meaning to the time when the work was to him "*Shechina* in the dust." At that time, he was certain that his work was entirely to bestow, that the will to receive has no part in this. It follows that this does not mean that he diminishes himself before the Creator, meaning that he does not pride himself before the Creator. Rather, it means that he is diminishing himself in order to work in a state of lowliness, although the Creator is giving him greatness.

Likewise, the Creator gave greatness to Moses and to Aaron, and they said, "What about us?" In other words, they yearned for work, for a time when to them the *Shechina* was in the dust. At that time, when they feel no flavor in the work, the wicked comes and asks the

"What" question, meaning "What is this work for you?" that you want to work specifically in this contemptible work? The wicked asks, "What is this work for you?" because then they were certain that their work was completely to bestow, and the will to receive had no part in it.

It is the same with David. The Creator gave him greatness, and he said, "And I," meaning "I am the Lord your God." This work was to him—when he wanted to take upon himself the burden of the kingdom of heaven, called "I am the Lord your God"—to his body, it was in the manner of "And I am a worm and not a man."

The Even Ezra asks about the words, "And I am a worm and not a man." He says, "It is unlikely that one will say about himself that he is not a man. He only speaks against the enemies, that they despise him and he is not regarded as anything in their eyes."

Here, too, the meaning is that when the Creator gave him greatness, he did not say, "Now I no longer need to wage war against the body, since the body will annul before the Creator as a candle before a torch." Instead, he said, "I yearn for a state of lowliness, so that my enemies, meaning the nations of the world within my body, will despise my work, since they said, "to work only in order to bestow," and he would have no feeling in the work. This is a sign that he is not a man at all—when they despise the order of his work. This is regarded as "Israel diminishing yourselves before Me."

What Are the Light Mitzvot that a Person Tramples with His Heels, in the Work?

Article No. 41, Tav-Shin-Nun, 1989/90

About the verse "And it shall come to pass, because you listen, and keep and do them, and the Lord your God will keep with you the covenant and the mercy that He swore to your forefathers," RASHI interpreted as follows, "If the *Mitzvot* [commandments/ good deeds] are light, which a person tramples with his feet, listen, and the Lord will keep, keep with you His promise."

We should understand what it means to us that if a person observes the light *Mitzvot* then the Creator will keep with you the oath. We should understand this condition, which implies that otherwise, it is as though He cannot keep the oath he swore to your forefathers. We should also understand what the interpreters ask, Why does he begin with plural form [in Hebrew], "keep and do," and ends in singular form [in Hebrew], "will keep with you."

To understand this, we first need to understand the meaning of the 613 *Mitzvot* that we were given. In the "Introduction of The Book of Zohar" ("General Explanation for All Fourteen Commandments and How They Divide into the Seven Days of Creation," Item 1), "The *Mitzvot* in the Torah are called *Pekudin* [Aramaic: commands/deposits], as well as 613 *Eitin* [Aramaic: counsels/tips]. The difference between them is that in all things there is *Panim* [anterior/face] and *Achor* [posterior/back]. The preparation for something is called *Achor*, and the attainment of the matter is called *Panim*. Similarly, in Torah and *Mitzvot* there are 'We shall do' and 'We shall hear.' When observing Torah and *Mitzvot* as 'doers of His word,' prior to being rewarded with hearing, the *Mitzvot* are called '613 *Eitin*' and are regarded as *Achor*. When rewarded with 'hearing the voice of His word,' the 613 *Mitzvot* become *Pekudin*, from the word *Pikadon* [deposit]. This is so because there are 613 *Mitzvot*, where in each *Mitzva* [singular of *Mitzvot*], the light of a unique degree is deposited, corresponding to a specific organ in the 613 organs and tendons of the soul, etc., and this is regarded as the *Panim* of the *Mitzvot*."

"Doers of His word" is during the preparation, before a person is rewarded with "Hearing the voice of his word," for "hearing" is when a person has been rewarded with vessels of bestowal, for only then is there a receptacle for the abundance to clothe in vessels of bestowal. At that time, he has "ears" to hear the voice of the Creator.

But while he is still immersed in vessels of reception, a person must work in "doing," called "action," although the body disagrees to work for the sake of the Creator. Rather, he must believe that although he is in a state of lowliness, meaning that the body disagrees with this work—to work for the sake of the Creator—still, the Creator enjoys this because in a state of lowliness, a person feels that he needs the Creator's help. Hence, at that time he has close contact with the Creator, since he feels that he has no other way and only the Creator can save him and deliver him from this lowliness.

However, a person asks himself, "Where are the Creator's justice and integrity?" He labors and observes Torah and *Mitzvot*, and he wants no reward for this. Rather, he wants to work for the sake of the Creator, as it is written in *The Zohar*, to work because he wants to serve a great King, meaning because He is great and ruling. When he asks the Creator to let him feel His greatness, and the person believes that the Creator hears the prayer of every mouth, each day he stands and waits to have more feeling of the greatness of the Creator, but in the end he sees that he has come to greater lowliness. In other words, he feels that people on the street are not as immersed in self-love.

So, the person asks, "How come people on the street, who have no prayer that the Creator will deliver them from self-love, are fine?" He sees that they feel the order of the work as utter completeness, meaning they know that each day they are advancing, meaning that their possessions are growing. It is as I said once, that each of them has a log where he sees how many *Mitzvot* were registered to his name each day, and how many pages of Gemara he can write in his log. He, on the contrary, sees the opposite, that each day he is worse than the day before.

When a person introspects, he sees that he has several ascents each day until he sometimes thinks, "Now I am certain that I have reached my goal, not as it was until now." But suddenly, thoughts that confuse him come to him and he forgets everything, meaning he completely forgets even about the ascents and feels nothing but lowliness. Now, after all the work he has done, he has become worse than ever. He begins to look at himself and finds not one good deed, and he feels as though he never observed Torah and *Mitzvot*.

The question is, How can a person explain these feelings to himself? Are they true or false? That is, with respect to reality, and reality cannot be erased, he certainly exerted and observed Torah and *Mitzvot*. But according to his feeling, it all disappeared. The question is, Where did they go, meaning who took them, since he does not feel them? He cannot say that he is suffering from amnesia and this is why he has forgotten everything. After all, he sees that he does remember the bad things he did.

The answer is that we must believe in the sages, as it is said in *The Zohar*, which interprets what is written, "Or make it known to him that he has sinned." He asks, "Who makes it known to him?" And he explains, "The Torah." As we once explained, by learning Torah with the intention to achieve the truth, meaning to really be a servant of the Creator, meaning that by observing Torah and Mitzvot, he does not mean to work for himself, meaning that he will receive reward. Rather, he wants to observe Torah and Mitzvot as our sages said, "I have created the evil inclination; I have created the Torah as a spice." That is, he learns Torah as an advice by which to truly become a servant of the Creator, meaning that he wants to work for the sake of the Creator, so the Torah notifies him that he has sinned.

This means that the order of "the Torah as a spice" is that first, it lets him know that "he has sinned," meaning how immersed he is in self-love. This is regarded as the Torah, which is the spice, gives him the Kli [vessel], meaning the lack, so he will need the Creator's help. It follows that the Torah notifies him that his faith in the Creator is something foreign to him. Put differently, he feels how far he is from the Creator, that the Creator to him is like a stranger. As Baal HaSulam said about the verse "There shall be no strange God within you," "God" means that the Creator should not be to you like something foreign with which you have no connection.

A person is immersed in self-love, which is disparity of form from the Creator, since the Creator wants only to bestow while a person by nature wants only to receive. For this reason, "He and I cannot dwell in the same abode." It follows that where one should have felt close to the Creator, he feels remoteness from the Creator. This is what the Torah makes him know, meaning one who learns Torah, since he believes in the words of our sages, who said, "The Creator said, 'I have created the evil inclination; I have created the Torah as a spice.'" This spice is given to a person so he will feel how far he is from the Creator.

It follows that the Torah gives man the Kli, meaning the lack, for man to ask the Creator to deliver him from exile, called "exile in Egypt." It is known that Metzar-Yam [Mitzraim (Egypt)] means Tzar-Ayin [lit. narrow-eyed, meaning "jealous"]. That is, a person has no power to bestow, but only to receive. Although he sees that it is impossible to approach the Creator before all his actions are in order to bestow, he nonetheless sees that there is no way he will be able to achieve this without His help.

We already said many times why the Creator did this, meaning that there will be no option for a person to emerge from Pharaoh's control. The answer is as Baal HaSulam said about what Abraham asked the Creator when He promised him the inheritance of the land, "How will I know that I will inherit it? And He said to Abram, 'Know that your descendants will be strangers in a land that is not theirs.'"

He said that Abraham's question was that he saw what would be the inheritance of the land, which is *Malchut* that carries the upper abundance, which contains the five *Behinot* [qualities] NRNHY of *Kedusha* [holiness]. Also, it is known that there is no light without a *Kli* [vessel], meaning no filling without a need. Yet, Abraham saw that Israel have no need to obtain the completion of the degree. Rather, if they attain a little bit of illumination from above, they will be satisfied. Naturally, they would have no need to obtain the NRNHY of *Neshama* that is included in *Malchut*, which is called "the inheritance of the land."

"So how," said Abraham, "will they receive the light, when they have no *Kelim* [vessels], called 'need'?" At that time, the Creator told him, "Know for certain that your descendants will be strangers in a land that is not theirs." In other words, the people of Israel will be in an *Eretz* [land], meaning a *Ratzon* [desire] that does not belong to the people of Israel. They will be under the governance of the will to receive, which belongs to Pharaoh, King of Egypt.

"They will be tormented," meaning that the people of Israel will suffer because they are unable to work in order to bestow, which would bring them *Dvekut* [adhesion] with the Creator. At that time they will need the Creator's help, as it is written, "And their cry rose up to God from the work, and God heard their groaning, and God remembered His covenant with Abraham."

Our sages said, "He who comes to purify is aided." *The Zohar* asks, "How is he aided?" and it replies, "with a holy soul." In other words, first one is given *Nefesh*. If he is rewarded more, he is given *Ruach*. This means that to the extent that one comes to purify himself and demands help, the help he receives from above is considered part of the inheritance of the land.

According to the above, we should interpret what we asked, Why when a person begins to learn Torah for the reason that the Torah is called "a spice," when one begins to walk on the path of truth, where the Torah is as *Eitin*, meaning counsels how to conquer the evil inclination, the person begins to see how each time, instead of feeling closer to the Creator, he feels that he has become farther?

We asked, "Is this the way of Torah, by which one becomes farther from the Creator?" The answer was that the Torah first gives him a *Kli*, meaning the lack, to see how far he is from the Creator. This is why *The Zohar* says that the Torah notifies him that he has sinned.

It follows that one should not say that he is learning Torah in truth, so why does the Torah not help him as a spice? The answer is that one should believe in the sages that the Torah does help him by revealing to him that he has sinned, meaning how far he is from the Creator, and because of it, he can pray from the bottom of the heart, since he feels that he is worse than other people.

Although if he asks himself, he will see that he makes more efforts to observe Torah and *Mitzvot*, so why does he feel that he is worse? A person cannot answer this, but he says that as far as feeling, he feels that now he is worse than when he engaged in Torah and *Mitzvot* before he began to walk on the path of truth. In other words, in everything he does, he sees that it is all halfheartedly, and not as before.

This is as Baal HaSulam said, that the Creator said to Abraham, "Know for certain that your descendants will be strangers in a land that is not theirs, and they will be tormented." By this they will have a need to inherit the land. That is, by the lack that they will have when they are bare and destitute, they will be in a state of "And the

757

children of Israel sighed from the work, and their cry rose up to God from the work."

In other words, the work itself, the fact that they are not progressing in the work, but on the contrary, will create their need, and then the Creator will help them each time they want to be purer. By this they will have Kelim [vessels] to receive the inheritance of the land.

According to the above, we should interpret what we asked, "And it came to pass, because you listen, that the Lord your God will keep with you the covenant and the mercy that He swore to your forefathers." RASHI interpreted, "If the light Mitzvot, which a person tramples with his feet, listen, and the Lord will keep, keep with you His promise." We should understand this condition, that if you keep the light ones, the Creator will keep His promise; otherwise, He will not keep the oath.

The thing is that "light Mitzvot" means things that people belittle, referring to the mind and the heart. That is, all the Mitzvot, when observing them in order to receive reward, a person does not belittle these Mitzvot. Instead, all of these Mitzvot are called "serious," since they might cause the loss of the reward. Therefore, the reward they expect to receive in return for them makes the Mitzvot important. In other words, the reward makes them valuable.

But when a person should work for the sake of the Creator, which is to him above reason, a person has no regard for this, since the body resists working for no reward. Therefore, when we say to the body that we must work only in order to bestow upon the Creator, the body says that this is far from the mind and it is not worth straining for such work. Then, the person sees that he cannot overcome the body. As Baal HaSulam explained, the fact that it is not within man's power to emerge from the control of the will to receive for himself, the Creator did this on purpose, so that by this a person will acquire a need for the Creator's help, for otherwise he is lost.

Hence, when a person asks the Creator to help him, by this he receives help from above. This is the light of the Torah, which "reforms him," as said in *The Zohar*, that by this he receives *Kelim* and a need to attain the NRNHY of *Neshama*. This was the Creator's answer to Abram's question, "How will I know that I will inherit it?"

It follows that precisely when a person wants to observe the light *Mitzvot*, he needs the Creator's help. Otherwise, if a person has no need to observe the light *Mitzvot*, which are contemptible *Mitzvot*, then he does not need the Creator's help. And since he has no need for the Creator to help him by giving him NRNHY of *Neshama*, since he has no need for this, so Abram's question, "How will I now that I will inherit it?" returns, since he has no need to obtain the inheritance of the land.

It therefore follows that the Creator cannot keep the oath concerning the inheritance of the land. For this reason, RASHI's interpretation, where he says that if you keep the light *Mitzvot*, the Creator will be able to keep, "And the Lord will keep," meaning that the Creator will keep His promise; otherwise, it is impossible to keep His promise.

Accordingly, we should interpret what we asked, Why does it begin in plural form, "do" and "keep," and ends in singular form? The answer is that when a person begins to work, he has two authorities: his own authority, namely the will to receive, and he also wants to work for the Creator. When a person sees that he has two authorities, he asks the Creator to help him cancel his authority and leave only the singular authority, meaning the authority of the Creator. Then, the Creator helps him annul the authority and leaves man with only the singular authority. This is why it is written in singular form, "And the Lord your God will keep with you," meaning that the Creator will keep him so he will have only the singular authority.

According to the above, we can understand what is written (Deuteronomy 9:5), "It is not for your righteousness or the integrity of your heart that you are going to inherit their land, but it is because of the wickedness of these nations that the Lord your God is driving them out before you, and in order to confirm the oath which the Lord swore to your forefathers, to Abraham."

We should understand this. If the Creator wants to give the inheritance of the land to Israel because He swore to "your forefathers, to Abraham," it means that the reason He gave the inheritance of the land to the people of Israel was that He promised to Abraham the inheritance of the land. But here the verse says that the reason He gave the inheritance to Israel was the wickedness of the nations. This implies that were it not for the wickedness of the nations, He would not be able to keep His promise to the forefathers. We should understand why it is that if there is the wickedness of the nations, the Creator can keep the oath, and because of "your righteousness or the integrity of your heart," the Creator cannot keep the oath.

According to the above, in the work, the wickedness of the nations means the evil within man's heart. A person cannot defeat it and must cry out to the Creator to help him and liberate him from the governance of Pharaoh, King of Egypt. How does He help him? It is as it is said in *The Zohar*, "with a holy soul." This means that each time he asks for help, he receives a holy soul. By being in exile and wanting to emerge from exile, meaning when a person feels that he has the wickedness of the nations, who are not letting him work for the sake of the Creator, but only for himself, this is regarded as having to work for the sake of the nations of the world within his body.

This is as it is written (Exodus 1:11), "And they built for Pharaoh cities of affliction, Pithom and Rameses." Baal HaSulam interpreted that when they wanted to work for the sake of the Creator and overcame the control of the Egyptians, this is the meaning of Rameses, meaning that they overcame the self-love, like *Ra'am* [thunder] *Sus* [horse], meaning with great power, like a horse. They thought they had already emerged from the governance of self-love, but then they came to *Pi-Tehom* [mouth of the abyss], meaning that all the buildings they had built sank and were swallowed in the abyss, and not a remnant was left of the work. This is called "Pithom."

In other words, each time, they had work in the manner of "Pithom and Rameses," meaning that each day they had to work anew. That is, each day they felt that as though today they began the work of holiness, and felt as though until now, they had never engaged in the work. They ask themselves, Where did the work and labor they had done thus far vanish? But they do not know what to answer. As was said, it all sank and was swallowed in the ground.

They could not tell their bodies, "Why do you not want to exert today? After all, yesterday, you saw that when you labored, you received the strength to work. You cannot receive something from yesterday," since he does not feel that yesterday he did something, for it was all swallowed in the ground. Indeed, why is this so? This is a correction.

It follows that if a person looks at himself and he has good deeds, he has no need to ask the Creator to help him, since anyhow, he has no place in which to receive help from the Creator, as there is no filling without a lack. Thus, the Creator cannot keep the oath concerning the inheritance of the land, since they have no need that He will give to them the inheritance of the land as help.

This is why he says, "It is not for your righteousness or the integrity of your heart that you are going to inherit their land." Why? Because if they are fine, they have no need. This is the meaning of the words "It is because of the wickedness of these nations that the Lord your God is driving them out," since because of the evil in his body, there is a need for help.

What Are a Blessing and a Curse, in the Work?

Article No. 42, Tav-Shin-Nun, 1989/90

The interpreters of the Torah ask about the verse, "Behold, I set before you today a blessing and a curse. The blessing, if you obey the commandments of the Lord your God, which I am commanding you today. And the curse, if you do not obey." The question is, Why does it begin in singular form [in Hebrew], "Behold"? And they also ask, why is it written specifically "today"?

It is known that the purpose of creation is His desire to do good to His creations, meaning that all created beings will feel that they are receiving delight and pleasure from the Creator. This is called "Blessed is our God, who created us for His glory," meaning that the creatures receive delight and pleasure from the Creator, and it glorifies the Creator that the creatures receive from Him delight and pleasure.

It follows that each one respects the Creator, and from this, the Creator is honored. Conversely, if the creatures do not receive from Him delight and pleasure, it does not glorify the Creator. That is, by creating creatures that do not feel that the Creator gives them delight and pleasure, but rather that they are tormented and suffer in the world, this does not glorify the Creator.

This is as it is written (Psalms 50), "Call upon Me in the day of trouble; I shall rescue you, and you will honor Me." RASHI interpreted "and you will honor Me" as "Honor Me, as this is My honor, that I save those who trust in Me." We should understand this: Does the Creator need respect, that the creatures will respect him? After all, His desire is only to bestow, to impart delight and pleasure. Why is it said that the Creator receives honors by saving those who trust Him?

The answer is that the Creator knows that the creatures know that He created the world in order to give to the created beings delight and pleasure only when the created beings respect the Creator for giving them delight and pleasure. It follows that the matter of "Blessed is our God, who created us for His glory" applies when the creatures respect the Creator because we received delight and pleasure.

It follows that the creatures thank the Creator for receiving delight and pleasure, and this feeling, from the pleasure that the creatures receive this pleasure, emerges from the hearts of the receivers and is revealed outward through gratitude. That is, to the extent of the reception of pleasure, the glory of the giver is revealed. We see in corporeality how a person respects his friend when he gives him a great gift, and how he respects him when he gives him a small gift. This means that the honor that the recipient of the gift gives to the giver of the gift establishes the measure of the size of the gift, meaning the measure of the recipient's sensation.

For example, a person whom the Creator brings closer, meaning gives him a thought and desire to serve the King, there is certainly a difference in how he feels if he is serving a great King: He is certainly happy day and night that he has been rewarded with serving a great King.

That is, if a person prays to the Creator and imagines that he is standing before a great King, how impressed he is? Or if he is speaking to a small king, what is his impression? In other words, according to a person's sensation to whom he speaks and prays is his joy and elation, as our sages said, "Know before whom you stand," meaning before a great or a small king.

It turns out that to the extent that a person respects the Creator, to that extent he can see to which King he is praying, a great or a small King. It follows that honoring the Creator is not for the sake of the Creator. The Creator does not need to be respected. Rather, this respect is for man's sake. That is, a person needs to know before what King he stands—small or great.

However, in order for the Creator's will to be carried out with the completeness of the goal, meaning so there would not be shame, there was a correction called "Tzimtzum [restriction] and concealment," meaning that there was a Tzimtzum and concealment on two actions: 1) The Creator Himself is hidden from us and we must believe that He is treating us with private Providence over all creations. 2) The real delight and pleasure is in the 613 Mitzvot [commandments/good deeds], which The Zohar calls "613 deposits," as is explained in the Sulam [Ladder Commentary on The Zohar] ("Introduction of The Book of Zohar," "General Explanation for All Fourteen Commandments and How They Divide into the Seven Days of Creation," Item 1) that in each Mitzva [singular of Mitzvot], a special light is deposited. However, this, too, is concealed and we must believe that there is where we will find the delight and pleasure. Yet, this concealment was only for the sake of the created beings, so there would not be shame upon the reception of the delight and pleasure, meaning in order not to have shame by the creatures receiving the delight and pleasure because they feel like it, as this is opposite from the Creator. According to the rule that each branch wants to resemble its root, when the creatures receive the delight and pleasure, they will feel unpleasantness.

Therefore, the creatures must try to do everything for the sake of the Creator, meaning in order to bestow contentment upon the Creator, and then there is equivalence of form between them, meaning that the creatures, too, will do everything in order to bestow, like the Creator. Then there will be no place for shame, which is called "the perfection of His deeds,"

Yet, how can a person achieve this degree of doing everything for the sake of the Creator? After all, by nature, man is born with a desire to receive in order to receive. Our sages said about this, "He who comes to purify is aided." That is, when a person sees that he is far from all his actions being for the sake of the Creator, he tries in everything he does. When he sees that on every act that he performs there is no intention to bestow, he asks of the Creator to give him the intention to bestow on the act that he performs.

In other words, he asks the Creator that thanks to the act that he performs, the act will be as an awakening from below, meaning a prayer that the Creator will send him the intention to bestow. It follows that the awakening from below is the Kli [vessel] that the Creator can fill. But when he has no actions over which to ask that the Creator will send him the intention to bestow for them, this is as is written, "There is no light without a Kli," meaning no intention without an action.

For this reason, a person must do many actions, and the actions should be as a lack, that he will ask the Creator to satisfy their need. However, it is human nature that when he knows that the most important is that we must do everything for the sake of the Creator, and he sees that his actions are in utter lowliness, he becomes contemptuous of his actions.

He says that in any case, his work is worthless, so why bother exert so hard to do them? Therefore, when it is not difficult for him to work, he works. But when it is hard for him, he does not have the strength to exert himself and work because thoughts come to him from the world that there is no need to engage in Torah and Mitzvot because secular people do not believe in reward and punishment. Also, when he sees that his actions are lowly, he says about his actions that they are incomplete.

He says that he knows for certain that no reward should be given for such actions. It turns out that in this state, when he sees that his actions are so lowly that they merit no reward, it follows that then he is in a state where he does not believe in reward and punishment.

Since he cannot fool himself and say that he has a desire "for the sake of the Creator," since he sees that the whole body objects to this, so when he says to himself, "If you do not aim for the sake of the Creator, you will be punished," he does not understand this because he does not see how he will ever be able to say that he is working for the sake of the Creator.

Therefore, this is called "not believing in punishment," meaning to say that because he will be punished, he will aim for the sake of the Creator. He cannot understand this because how can one be punished for something that is impossible? As for reward, at that time he says that he does not deserve reward for such actions. It follows that at that time he does not believe in reward and punishment, like secular people, who do not believe in reward and punishment. Therefore, he snubs them.

However, without faith in the sages, we cannot go forward. Rather, we must believe in the sages, who said that the order of the work is that there is no light without a Kli. For this reason, a person must believe that when he sees that his actions are not for the sake of heaven, it is a revelation from above, that he is shown the truth, how the will to receive governs a person, and he cannot do anything if it does not yield self-benefit.

A person can see this only when he wishes to walk on the path of truth, meaning to achieve Dvekut [adhesion] with the Creator. This knowledge is given to a person in order for him to need the Creator to help him and give him the desire to bestow. This desire attaches a person to the Creator, meaning that once he is rewarded with receiving the desire to bestow, the Creator can bestow upon him the delight and pleasure that was in the intention of creation to do good to His creations.

It follows that we should make three discernments here: 1) The person begins to feel that he is lacking the Kli called "desire to bestow," but is immersed entirely in self-love. This deficiency does not come from the person himself. Rather, one must believe that this deficiency, that he cannot do anything in order to bestow, is help that comes to a person from above, and the help is that he feels a lack.

2) To ask of the Creator to give him a blessing, which is the desire to bestow, called "*Kli* of *Hesed* [mercy]," where he wants only to work in order to bestow contentment upon his Maker. This is as it is written ("Introduction of The Book of Zohar," "*Otiot de Rav Hamnuna Saba* [The Letters of Rav Hamnuna Saba]," Items 37-38), "[*Hesed*] is a blessing, as it is written, 'And I will pour out a blessing for you.' This is the meaning of 'I said, a world of mercy shall be built.' The words *Yibanne* [shall be built] mean construction and understanding [in Hebrew], since He established it as sufficient distinction to distinguish those who adhere to *Kedusha* [holiness] from those who veer off from following the Creator to cling unto another God, as it is written, 'And test Me now in this,' says the Lord of hosts, 'if I will not open for you the windows of heaven and pour out for you a blessing until it overflows.'"

This means that before they receive the *Kelim* of the blessing, meaning vessels of bestowal, there are no *Kelim* to receive the delight and pleasure for which the world was created. This is so because everything will go to the *Klipot* and not to *Kedusha*, and the whole basis of the *Kedusha* is built on the desire to bestow.

3) When his 613 *Mitzvot* are as 613 deposits. This is the time when he obtains the 613 lights that are clothed within the 613 deposits. This is considered the delight and pleasure that is clothed in them.

However, the main work is in the first state, where the 613 are called "613 counsels," meaning tips how to ask the Creator to give him vessels of bestowal. In that state, there are ups and downs because a person often decides that this work of ever receiving help from above, vessels of bestowal, is impossible, since concerning asking the Creator to give him these vessels, he sees that complete opposite—where the Creator should have helped him acquire vessels of bestowal, he sees that after each effort he makes, he receives an even bigger desire.

Therefore, a person thinks that there is no point asking for it, since it is as though there is no attention from above watching over him. As a results, he often decides that it is not worthwhile to work pointlessly.

Here a person needs great strengthening so as not to escape the campaign and say once and for all, "This work is not for me." In that state a person needs heaven's mercy. Here, a person must go only above reason because he sees that the reason is correct. That is, reasonably thinking, when he makes his calculation, he sees that he should escape the campaign, and he should thank the Creator for not running, for not being thrown from above outside the path that leads to the King's palace.

That is, a person should be grateful and always thank the Creator that he did not accept the slander that the body always tells him, "This is not for you." The body says to him: "You see that as much as you have labored, you are still standing in the same place as when you began the work." It tells him, "If you want to know if you succeeded at all, you see that you regressed rather than progressed." This is the reason [view] that separates him from *Kedusha*, since within reason, the body is correct.

It follows that the fact that a person does not escape from the campaign is also not by his own powers. Rather, he should say that it is only power that he is given from above so as not to run. In other words, a person should believe that on one hand, he is allowed to see how far he is from working in order to bestow, meaning that he is regressing. On the other hand, he must believe that the fact that he is not escaping the campaign and often believes above reason that he will be brought closer and will be rewarded with nearing the Creator, it follows that everything he does in the work is built only on faith above reason.

Now we can understand the verse "Behold, I set before you today." "Today" means that each and every day a person must begin anew and say that today he will be rewarded with "Behold, I," meaning with "I am the Lord your God," and he will not escape the campaign.

That is, he should not say, "I have already prayed many times for the Creator to give me the vessels of bestowal and to emerge from the control of the will to receive for myself, but I receive no answer to my prayer. Thus, what is the point of praying once again?"

It follows that the word "today" implies that "each day they should be as new in your eyes." That is, a person must know that every beginning in the work is called a "day," and the prayer that a person makes for the Creator to bring him closer to the work, that prayer is called a "day."

Yes, since the prayer for nearing the Creator makes a person's *Kli*, which is the need and desire, and the desire makes a person suffer because the Creator is not bringing him closer, therefore, each day it creates in a person one hole. Yet, there must be a deep deficiency, and to be recognized as a big deficiency so as to suit a big filling.

For this reason, each day we must begin a new overcoming. This means that each overcoming creates a new lack, until from each and every day it becomes one long day, when there is the ability for the Creator to impart the filling there, called "desire to bestow," which is that he receives the blessing, which is the quality of *Hesed*, called "vessels of bestowal."

By this we can interpret the meaning of "we will do and we will hear." "We will do" pertains to the lower one. That is, the lower one must make the deficiency, meaning to need the Creator to help him obtain the vessels of bestowal, for all those who first say, "We will hear," meaning that the body must first hear if it is worthwhile to do everything for the sake of the Creator, then he will agree to work, meaning to the work for the sake of the Creator. But if he does not see that it is worthwhile to work for the sake of the Creator, how can he work for the sake of the Creator?

For this reason, the people of Israel—those who want to be *Yashar-El* [straight to God], meaning directly to the Creator and not for their own sake—see that the body will never agree to work for the sake of the Creator. Then they say, "We will perform actions with the intention for the sake of the Creator." Although we see that we are not succeeding, as it is against nature, we believe that if we ask the Creator to hear our prayer, He will certainly hear the prayer. Then we will hear, meaning we will be rewarded with seeing that the Creator does hear the prayer, and He will give us the power of a desire to bestow.

This is the meaning of the people of Israel—although the evil inclination in the people of Israel also does not agree to work for the sake of the Creator and not for one's own sake—still believed that the Creator hears a prayer, and if we ask Him to give us this power, that we do want to work for the sake of the Creator except the evil inclination in us objects to this, and certainly the Creator hears a prayer. We will certainly be rewarded with the Creator hearing our prayer, by receiving from Him the desire to bestow. Then we will certainly be able to say that the Creator hears.

We can interpret what Israel said, "For our part, we will do what we can do, and we will ask of Him to hear what we are asking of Him, and then we will be rewarded with 'We will hear,' meaning that the Creator will give us the vessels of bestowal, which are vessels of the blessing. That is, the upper abundance that the Creator wants to give, which is the delight and pleasure, can clothe in these *Kelim* because there is equivalence between the light and the *Kli*."

It follows that first we must receive a lack, meaning for a person to receive a real need for the desire to bestow. In other words, he should feel that the deficiency is so great that no one in the world can satiate the need but the Creator Himself. At that time he is considered "needy of the Creator." At that time, a person needs heaven's mercy so as not to escape the campaign, for usually, when a person works and sees that he is not advancing, he escapes the work. Therefore, a person must ask the Creator to help him not flee in the middle of the work.

We can say about this that the person is making efforts to obtain the desire to bestow. The feeling that he has made great exertions is called "old age," meaning that he has been a long time in this work. Therefore, we must pray to the Creator, "Do not cast us off in the time of old age; do not forsake us when our strength fails." "When our strength fails" means that "We have run out of patience, that after all the prayers that we have given, that You will give us the desire to bestow, we have still not been rewarded with receiving it. Do not cast us off midway; give us the strength to endure and not to escape the campaign, and give us more strength to pray to You to give us the desire to bestow."

We should know that in the work, "old age" does not pertain to years. Rather, "old age" means that a person has come to a state where he says, "I see that I have made great efforts in order to obtain something in spirituality, and I see that I am not succeeding." Therefore, he accepts the situation he is in and says, "Perhaps younger people will come instead of me, who have more energy. I see that I am unfit." This is called "old" in the work.

However, in the corporeal world we also see that sometimes people are old in age, meaning old in years, but are as energetic as young people. There could be a person who is already more than eighty years old but with more energy and works more than others who are younger than him, and still has desire and yearning to achieve something in the corporeal world. But in the work of the Creator, "old age" is certainly not about years. Rather, "old age" means that his aspiration to achieve the goal has ceased.

Now we can understand what they ask, why does it say "Behold" in singular form [in Hebrew] and then says, "I set before you," in plural form [in Hebrew]? The meaning is as said (in Article No. 41 from *Tav-Shin-Nun*), that the Creator said "Behold" in singular form, "I set before you," meaning that "before you" there is the authority of the many, meaning two authorities. "And I will give you the 'Behold,' meaning that you will be rewarded with seeing that there is not more than one authority. In other words, all your actions will be only to bestow upon the Creator, and the authority of the will to receive will be cancelled."

By this we should interpret what our sages said about "It is carved on the tablets," that they became free from the angel of death. We should understand what is freedom from the angel of death in the work. We must know that the will to receive for oneself is the angel of death. It is as our sages said, "The wicked in their lives are called 'dead,'" since they are separated from the Life of Lives due to disparity of form, which is the will to receive.

In other words, the will to receive for oneself separates one from the Life of Lives. Thus, who is the angel of kills a person? It is the will to receive. It therefore follows that when a person is rewarded with the Creator giving him the desire to bestow, with which we are rewarded by observing Torah and *Mitzvot*, when the singular authority is made and the will to receive for oneself enters the singular authority, which is the authority of the Creator, he is liberated from the angel of death, since the will to receive for oneself does not operate in him because the Creator has given him the singular authority. This is the meaning of "Behold, I set before you," as in, "I am the Lord your God," "I set before you" that at that time there will be only the singular authority.

Afterward, the verse interprets more, to know what is a blessing and what is a curse. It says, "The blessing, if you obey the commandments of the Lord your God." In other words, "What is the blessing that I give? It is that you can obey the commandments of the Lord your God." This is done specifically by being rewarded with vessels of bestowal. This is the blessing, as it is written, "the blessing that you will hear."

"And the curse," meaning that if a person sees that he cannot hear, he must know that he is under the authority of the *Sitra Achra* [other side], which is the opposite of *Kedusha*, as it is written, "A blessing is called 'bestowal' and a curse is called 'reception.'"

It therefore follows that a person should exert every day with a new beginning so as not to appear as an old man. He should try to acquire the singular authority, for then he will be rewarded with receiving the delight and pleasure, which is the purpose of creation.

What Is, "You Shall Not Plant for Yourself an Asherah by the Altar," in the Work?

Article No. 43, Tav-Shin-Nun, 1989/90

The verse says, "You shall appoint for yourself judges and officers in all your gates, which the Lord your God is giving you. You shall not plant for yourself an Asherah, any tree by the altar of the Lord your God." Our sages said (Sanhedrin 7), "Rish Lakish said, 'Anyone who appoints an unworthy judge, it is as though he plants an Asherah in Israel.' Rav Ashi said, 'Instead of a wise disciple, it is as though he planted it by the altar.'"

We should also understand what is "judges and officers" in the work, and what is "in all your gates" in the work. It is known that "work" means the work that a person gives in order to achieve *Dvekut* [adhesion] with the Creator, which is that a person should achieve equivalence of form, called "cleave unto His attributes; as He is merciful, so you are merciful." That is, a person should come to seeing only to the benefit of the Creator, and not to his own benefit. In this way, we learn the whole Torah on the individual level. That is, we learn both the quality of Israel and the quality of the nations of the world within one body. In other words, a person consists of the seventy nations of the world, from wicked and from righteous. For this reason, litigants, who come to judge in courthouses, we learn that they are also—both the litigants and the courthouse—in the same body.

We should understand why if a person wants to observe Torah and *Mitzvot* [commandments/good deeds] only for the sake of the Creator, it is considered "work," and without the aim for the sake of the Creator it is not considered "work and labor." After all, the fact that a person likes the rest, we learned that the reason is that our root is in a state of complete rest. Hence, when we make any movement, we must receive more pleasure than the rest. Hence, when the reward and punishment are revealed, it is not considered that a person is complaining that he must work, since during the work, he is considering the reward.

It follows that the reward sweetens the work so he does not feel the labor during the work. For this reason, we see that a person does not tell his friend, "Poor me, I got a job at a famous company where the work conditions are great." Because the reward sweetens the work, the work and the labor are insignificant.

Therefore, when engaging in Torah and *Mitzvot* in order to receive reward in the work of holiness, although his aim is the reward, because the reward and punishment are not revealed, it is still regarded as exerting in Torah and *Mitzvot* although it is in order to receive reward, and he is careful not to transgress against the Torah and *Mitzvot* in order not to be punished. And since the main work is in practice, and "practicing" means that which is revealed, this work is called "the revealed Torah."

We learn this Torah in the general public. Hence, we learn this not in one body, but in the world in general. In other words, in general, we discern many people in the same world, and there are many people in the world. As their faces are not similar to one another, so their views are not similar to one another. In that state, we learn the Torah between man and man, in two bodies. The same applies to wicked and righteous, and everything is likewise.

But in the work on the level of intentions, which is called "work in the heart," none of this work is revealed outside. This work is called "the hidden part," meaning that which is not revealed outside. It is even hidden from the man himself, for precisely through the work of Mitzvot, when the act is revealed outward, the Mitzva [commandment/good deed] is regarded as revealed to a person. That is, a person sees that he is observing the Mitzva in practice, and it cannot be said there that the person is deceiving himself during the performance of the Mitzva.

Conversely, in work on the intention, a person cannot see the truth by himself. He may think that all his intentions are for the sake of the Creator, and he cannot tell if there is a mixture of self-benefit there.

This is as Baal HaSulam said about the words, "Walk humbly with the Lord your God." Although the literal meaning of "walk humbly" refers to another body, in the work, "walk humbly with the Lord your God" refers to his own body. That is, when a person works with "faith above reason," this is called "walk humbly." That is, a person's reason cannot come to work above reason. Only above reason, a person walks without a gauge by which to see, monitor, and measure his work, whether he is walking on the right path or not.

When a person wants to see if this is true, he examines it with his mind and reason. Since he is going above reason, he has no one to tell him if he is fine or not, since man's reason, which is his monitor, which should see if this is fine or not, cannot see anything because his work is above his mind, and the mind cannot see this. This is why this work is called "Walk humbly with the Lord your God," when his body does not see this work.

It therefore follows that when a person works in order to achieve Dvekut [adhesion], which is to come to a state where all his actions are in order to bestow, the will to receive comes and resists it. At that time, a person comes to his litigant and establishes the arguments of the will to receive and the arguments of the desire to bestow. Each one claims that he is right, and then this judge must decide which is right.

Certainly, the will to receive, with reason and intellect, says, "What's to decide here about 'who is right'? Let's go and see what everyone does, meaning how the world behaves, if the whole world works for the desire bestow or for the will to receive. The rule is that we follow the majority, and the majority of the world use only the will to receive, as our sages said, 'I saw the ascended ones, and they are few.' Hence, the quality of 'Israel' is one among seventy nations, so we must follow the majority."

Indeed, this is regarded as the "people of Israel being in exile among the nations." Because they are the majority, they control the quality of Israel. But with argument does not conclude the arguments of the will to receive. He comes and argues like one who is clever, whose arguments are all clear and there is nothing to reply to them. The verse says about this, "You shall not take a bribe, for a bribe blinds the eyes of the wise." In other words, since the will to receive argues only in its own favor, he is biased. Hence, he can no longer see the truth, since the eyes of his mind see only his self-benefit.

Therefore, when one wants to take upon himself the burden of the kingdom of heaven, the body asks, "In whose favor do you want to work in Torah and *Mitzvot?*" If he tells him, "For the sake of the Creator," the dispute promptly begins. That is, the dispute begins primarily during the work on intention, when determining with what intention he wants to observe Torah and *Mitzvot*. Hence, a person should see that this judge rules justly. And since the will to receive argues for its own benefit, it is impossible to listen to it, since it is biased. For this reason, all his clever arguments are incorrect, since "a bribe blinds the eyes of the wise."

We should also interpret that when a person begins to determine who is right, the question is, When should one decide? The answer is, "In all your gates." This is as it is written in *The Zohar* about the verse, "Her husband is known at the gates." They said, "Each one according to what he assumes in his heart." "Gates" means "measures." That is, in each Behina [discernment/quality] where a person begins to work in holiness, he must determine there with "judges," to see for whose favor he should work—for himself or for the Creator. That is, in everything a person does, he must first contemplate what he wants from this act, meaning for what purpose is he doing this act.

If he sees that his intention is improper, meaning that he sees that he cannot aim in order to bestow, then he has room for prayer. That is, the bad he finds within him through the calculation that he does with his litigant, he sees that the litigant is sentencing justly, except he cannot uphold the verdict.

Therefore, the question is, Where is the benefit in sentencing justly if he cannot follow what the judge says? It is written about this, "judges and officers." "Judges" is only the verdict. That is, he sees the truth about what he must do. But when it comes to the execution, which is the "officers," he sees that he cannot follow through.

At that time, a person says, "Now I can pray to the Creator" because I see that I will never be able to work for the sake of the Creator. Hence, then a person can make a heartfelt prayer that the Creator will help him. Put differently, at that time he has a Kli [vessel] called "lack," which needs the Creator's help to give him the desire to bestow, since without His help, he is helpless.

By this we should interpret what is written (Psalms 119), "Your commandments make me wiser than my enemies, for it is ever mine." We should interpret "my enemies" to mean "the bad within me." I see that they interrupt me from doing Your will, for the Creator's will is to bestow, and I am immersed in the desire to receive, which separates me from the Life of Lives. Hence, although I observe Your Mitzvot, they are still only an act, without the wisdom, for "wisdom" means that the light of Hochma [wisdom] is clothed in the Mitzvot, and the "light of Hochma" is called "the light of doing good to His creations," which is the purpose of creation.

However, it is impossible to receive the light of the purpose of creation, called *Hochma*, before a person has the light of the correction of creation, called "light of *Hassadim* [mercies]," which are vessels of bestowal. Since a person sees how his enemies, meaning his will to receive, is in full control and they cannot emerge from its governance, he therefore prays to the Creator to be given the desire to bestow. By this he can later receive the *Hochma*, as well.

This is the meaning of what he says, "Your commandments make me wiser than my enemies." That is, the enemies caused him to be rewarded with *Hochma*. "Your commandments make me wiser" means that the enemies were the reason to be rewarded with delight and pleasure since the help he received from above brought him each time a higher degree than the one he had. Had he not felt that he had bad, he would have settled for what he had and would not have cried out to the Creator to bring him closer and reward him with vessels of bestowal, for only the vessels of bestowal are fit to receive *Hochma*. It follows that the meaning of "Your commandments make me wiser than my enemies" is that in order for the *Mitzvot* to have *Hochma*, only those enemies caused me all this.

This is the meaning of the words, "for it is ever mine." "It is mine" refers to the enemies, which are always my causes that the *Mitzvot* will not be without *Hochma*, but rather dry *Mitzvot*. Instead, I have been rewarded through the enemies. "It is mine" means that I do not have the choice to follow the ways of the Creator like the rest of the people, since my enemies are worse than those of other people. For this reason, I must stand and ask the Creator to help me, since I am worse than the general public.

From this we can understand the meaning of trials in the work: For whose sake should we know if a person has endured a trial or not? Clearly, the Creator knows everything. Thus, why does the trial come to a person? Many times during an ascent, a person says, "I do not need the Creator's help anymore," since I have something on which to base my faith, for I feel the Creator to some degree, so henceforth I will be able to adhere to *Kedusha* [holiness], and I will be able to observe Torah and *Mitzvot* once and for all.

What happens from above? Since they want the person to advance and mount the trail that leads to the King's palace, where everyone works only in order to bestow upon the Creator, and during the ascent, that person built the foundation of his Judaism on the basis of feeling a good taste in the work, which is a basis of Lo Lishma [not for Her sake], for this reason, the person is given some foreign thought. At that time, a person is tried, to see if specifically when the Creator gives him some flavor that the will to receive feels, he will be able to be a servant of the Creator. But above reason just like that, when he has no sensation at all, how can he do something? This is called "sending a person some trial," so he will see that all his work is based on the will to receive, and then he will feel that he is deceiving himself in the work of the Creator. At that time, he has room to pray that the Creator will give him the strength to be able to work only in order to bestow, and not for his own sake.

Hence, every descent is a trial. If a person can endure the trial, meaning that the thought that comes to a person causes him to see if he is under the governance of Kedusha or not, during the descent, a person can see that at the time of ascent, his whole structure was built on the will to receive for oneself.

During the descent, a person cannot make any calculations. But afterward, when he receives nearing from above once more, which comes to a person by what is written, "I am the Lord, who dwells with them in the midst of their impurity," meaning that even though a person is still in the authority of self-love, still, an illumination comes to him from above, called "an awakening from above." At that time, he must awaken the state of descent that he had by himself, and think what was the reason he received the descent, and what he must correct so as not to come into a descent once more. A person must believe that the fact that he suffered a descent is because he was thrown from above. This is why he fell into such lowliness. At that time, he can work on himself, correct corrections so he does not fall again, since he must believe that the descent is a correction for him.

According to the above, we can understand what is written, "You shall not plant for yourself an Asherah." They interpreted, "Anyone who appoints an unworthy judge, it is as though he plants an Asherah in Israel." We should understand what is an Asherah in the work. Asherah is as it is written, "*Ashreihem* [happy are they] every green tree." "Happy are they" means that they are happy when they work for their own sake, that he feels that he is happy. This is called "Happy are they," meaning when a person works for his own sake, meaning that only when he feels good in the work can he work in Torah and *Mitzvot*.

But when he does not feel good, he says, "It is true that if I worked for the sake of the Creator I could say that I can serve the Creator under any condition, and not necessarily when I feel good. But I am working in the holy work because I was told that in the work of observing Torah and *Mitzvot* there is more flavor to feel than in corporeal work." Hence, if he does not feel a good taste in the work, why should he work in Torah and *Mitzvot*? After all, his entire basis is only self-love.

Thus, what should one do when he wants to appoint a worthy judge? At that time, a person must look at the intention, meaning the reason why he wants to work on the path of truth. Certainly, he had an awakening from above that we should work for the sake of the Creator. And what is "for the sake of the Creator"? At that time, a person begins to work on the goal that the Creator will enjoy his work, meaning not as in corporeality, where if the owner enjoys the employee's work, he gives him a raise to his salary. Rather, his reward is that he is delighting the Creator and he does not consider his own benefit. It follows that the judge he is appointing now is in order to see that he follows the right path, which is for the sake of the Creator. This is called "an altar." That is, the judge lets him see that a person should sacrifice himself on the altar, meaning that we must observe as our sages said, "The Torah exists only in those who put themselves to death over it."

If he is an unworthy judge, he lets him think that a person should provide for himself things that pertain to his own benefit. This is called "Asherah," as was said, Ashrei-Hem [happy are they], meaning that the idol-worship of Asherah was that they would always look at what the body could enjoy, and were not interested to know if the Creator would derive from this contentment, but always looked at their own benefit.

However, there is a difference between Asherah and the general public. For those whose work is in practice, who do not think at all about the matter of Lishma [for Her sake], but as Maimonides says, "Women, little ones, and uneducated people are taught only to work out of fear and in order to receive reward. Until they gain knowledge and acquire much wisdom, they are taught that secret little by little."

It is about those people that we should interpret, "Anyone who appoints an unworthy judge, it is as though he plants an Asherah in Israel." In other words, the judge, meaning when he wants to do something and asks the judge in his heart, a person should be careful that his judge will not be biased. Otherwise, he will not give him a just verdict. This is called "It is as though he plants an Asherah in Israel," meaning idol-worship.

If the judge is biased, he might permit any transgression, that it is permitted to do them, "for a bribe blinds the eyes of the wise." This is called, "It is as though he planted an Asherah in Israel." That is, pertaining to the whole of Israel, who engage only in the practice of the Mitzvot but not in the intention in the Mitzvot, meaning concerning the need to aim for the sake of the Creator, they have no interest in dealing with this and say that this work belongs to a chosen few.

Now we can understand why he says there, "Rav Ashi said, 'Instead of a wise disciple, it is as though he planted an Asherah by the altar.'" We should understand what Rav Ashi adds to us by saying, "Instead of a wise disciple, it is as though he planted an Asherah by the altar," whereas if he is not a wise disciple, "it is as though he planted an Asherah in Israel." We should understand the difference.

We should interpret the difference between those who work in the manner of the general public. He said about them, "as though he planted an Asherah in Israel," referring to the general public in Israel. But concerning a wise disciple, meaning those who want to be "wise disciples," as Baal HaSulam interpreted, a "wise disciple" is one who wants to be a disciple of the Creator, who is called "Wise," who bestows upon the whole world, and that person also wants to be rewarded with being a giver, meaning to work with the aim to come to work in order to bestow. If his judge is worthy, the judge advises him to sacrifice himself on the altar. If he is unworthy, he advises him only for his own benefit, which is "Happy are they." This is why he says, "Instead of a wise disciple, it is as though he planted an Asherah by the altar."

What Is
an Optional War,
in the work - 2?

Article No. 44, Tav-Shin-Nun, 1989/90

R ASHI interprets the verse "If you go to war against your enemies," that the verse speaks of optional war. We should understand the meaning of "If you go to war against your enemies" in an optional war. What is an "optional war" in the work, and what is a "non-optional war"?

It is known that there are 248 commandments to do, and 365 not to do. These are called 613 Mitzvot [commandments/good deeds]. These must be observed in every detail and precision; otherwise, it is regarded as a "transgression." It is said about them, "Do not add and do not take away." This obligation pertains to actions, meaning that as far as actions are concerned, a person must do, or not do what is forbidden.

This is not so concerning the intention. Thus, to aim to work in order to bestow, this war is optional. In other words, it cannot be said that this work pertains to everyone, but rather to those who have an inner drive, who feel that observing Mitzvot in the way that they are observing has nothing to do with Dvekut [adhesion] with the Creator. They see that instead of where a person should achieve love of the Creator, they see that in all that they do, they have no other intention other than their own benefit. This work, called "in order to bestow," belongs to them.

But the general public was not given this thing. This is why the work of bestowal is called "optional war," and not mandatory. This is as Maimonides says at the end of *Hilchot Teshuva*: "Therefore, when teaching little ones, women, and uneducated people, they are taught to work only out of fear and to be rewarded. Until they gain knowledge and acquire much wisdom, they are taught this secret bit by bit."

This means that the matter of *Lishma* [for Her sake], called "in order to bestow," does not belong to the general public but to people who have acquired much knowledge. Thus, it means that the work of bestowal is specifically for those who have gained much knowledge. This is why the work of bestowal is called "optional war," and not "mandatory war," since this is not required of the general public, but of those "who have gained knowledge and acquired much wisdom. Then they are taught that secret bit by bit."

We should also add about the optional war, since the matter of *Dvekut* with the Creator is annulment of one's own authority. By nature, man is born feeling only his own authority, that he is the landlord and does what he wants. In order for him to know that there is the authority of the Creator, that He is the leader of the world, a person must believe this, that the Creator is the King of the world.

A person must believe that this concealment, where a person does not feel that there is a King to the world, the Creator did this, and this is called "the correction of the *Tzimtzum* [restriction]." However, one must believe and make great efforts until he feels in his organs that the Creator is the leader of the world. And not just a leader! Rather, one must believe that His guidance is in the manner of good and doing good. A person must do all that he can to be able to attain this, as this is expressed in two manners:

1) A person should work on having a desire and yearning to want to annul his authority, as our sages said about the verse "If a man dies in a tent," since the Torah exists only in one who puts

himself to death over it." This means that he wants to annul his self, meaning he must achieve a state where he has but one authority—the authority of the Creator. In other words, a person does not do anything for his own benefit, but sees only to the benefit of the Creator. This is called "singular authority," and it is called "optional war." In other words, he is fighting against himself to obtain this singular authority, and this is called "optional war" in the work.

2) After all the efforts that a person makes in order to achieve this authority, regarded as a person acquiring a second nature, where he previously had only a desire to receive for his own benefit, he wanted to annul that authority and receive a new one: the desire to bestow upon the Creator. This is the meaning of *Dvekut*. In other words, as the Creator is the Giver, so a person wants to bestow upon the Creator.

However, a person cannot receive this authority, but only the Creator. As He previously gave him the authority of the will to receive for his own benefit, the Creator can give him a different authority, meaning the singular authority of the Creator. This is regarded as the Creator giving him a second nature, which is the desire to bestow upon the Creator.

It follows that when a person is born, he has only one authority, his own. Afterward, when he takes upon himself the kingdom of heaven, to observe the Torah and *Mitzvot*, he comes into two authorities. In other words, he works in order to receive reward, as Maimonides says, "When teaching little ones, women, and uneducated people in order to receive reward."

Afterward begins the work in the optional war, meaning to annul his own authority, which is called "self-benefit," and to yearn for the Creator to give him the singular authority, meaning the authority of the Creator. This is regarded as a person having to acquire a second nature, called "desire to bestow," to have a desire to bring contentment to his Maker.

This is the meaning of what is written, "If you go to war against your enemies," meaning in the optional war. It is impossible to conquer the enemy, called "will to receive for oneself," meaning annul this authority. Rather, the text promises us, "and the Lord your God delivers him into your hand." In other words, the Creator will give you this power, this authority called "singular authority." Put differently, the Creator will give you a second nature.

In order for a person to be ready to ask for this authority, there needs to be a prayer from the bottom of the heart. In other words, a person should feel how much he needs this power, called "desire to bestow." For this, we were given the 613 Mitzvot in the form of Eitin [Aramaic: counsels], called "613 counsels." Through them, a person takes the lack, to feel how much he needs the desire to bestow, since this is all that detains him from achieving the completion of the goal.

Also, in that regard, meaning about the fact that he does not feel the real lack, that he does not have a real need to bestow, a person should pray for this, as well, that the Creator will give him the lack over not having a lack to obtain the desire to bestow.

In truth, when a person has faith in the Creator and believes that He is a great King, a person must annul "as a candle before a torch." At that time, there is no question of choice because he naturally annuls. But when a person begins to work in order to bestow, foreign thoughts come to him, which weaken his faith. It follows that the fact that a person cannot work in order to bestow is for lack of faith.

This is as it is written (Psalms 42), "My tear has been my bread day and night, while they say to me all day long, 'Where is your God?'" In other words, thoughts of Pharaoh come to him, who said, "Who is the Lord that I should obey His voice?" It follows that at that time, a person should pray for two things together: 1) for faith that the Creator will not hide Himself from him, as it is written, "Do not hide Your face from me," 2) to bring him closer, meaning to give him the power of the desire to bestow. Through this desire, a person comes closer to the Creator, which is called "equivalence of form."

The reason why when a person wants to work in order to bestow, foreign thoughts come to him, is that as long as one is working for himself, the body does not resist him so much, since he promises the body that it will receive a great reward, that it is worthwhile to observe Torah and Mitzvot, since the reward sweetens the labor, as in physical work and labor. Hence, the body does not ask any questions about its work in Torah and Mitzvot, and a person lives in peace. He is content with his work, since he believes that his reward is growing every day. For this reason, he leads a peaceful life and feels tranquility in his life. And if he can also observe the Mitzva [singular of Mitzvot], "Reprimand your neighbor," he is certainly pleased.

But when a person says to his body, "Until now I have been working in your favor, meaning everything I did, both corporeal things and in Torah and Mitzvot, was all in order to make you happy. That is, all my concerns were only for the will to receive for oneself, which is called 'self-love' or 'self-benefit.'

"But now, meaning henceforth, I do not want to work for the benefit of the body any longer, but only for the benefit of the Creator." At that time, the body begins to resist, why is he throwing it away. It does all that it can, bringing him questions from all over the world, meaning the argument of Pharaoh, who asked, "Who is the Lord that I should obey His voice?" and the argument of the wicked one, who asks, "What is this work for you?" These thoughts burden one's work so much that often, the descents and ascents that a person has cause him to see that this is endless and he wants to escape the campaign.

And all that one can tell the body is that he wants to work in real fear, which is called in *The Zohar*, "Because He is great and ruling," meaning for it to be a great privilege to him that he is serving a great King, and he wants to bring contentment to his Maker, and that this will be his only concern, and he does not want to worry about himself anymore.

Now we can understand what is written (Deuteronomy 26:16), "This day the Lord your God commands you to do these laws and judgments, and keep and do them with all your heart and with all your soul." RASHI interprets "This day" as "Each day, they will be as new in your eyes, as though on this day you were commanded them." We should understand what it adds to us, meaning what we gain by needing to exert to make each day as though on that day we were commanded. The thing is that there are two discernments before us in the work: 1) in order to receive reward, 2) not in order to receive reward, but because of the greatness of the Creator.

Those whose work is in order to receive reward do not need "Each day they will be as new." Rather, when a person believes that he will be rewarded for his work, he has the power to work since the reward causes him to observe Torah and Mitzvot. Thus, there is no difference whether he believes in the reward that the Torah promises us, and he does not need to renew the imperative each day, for what will this add to him?

Conversely, those who want to work because "He is great and ruling," meaning because of the greatness of the Creator, for this reason there is a need "as though on that day you were commanded," since when a person engages in Torah and Mitzvot in order to bestow, each day he should discern how much he assumes the greatness of the Creator, for whom it is worthwhile to exert in order to serve Him.

It is as it is written in *The Zohar*, "Her husband is known at the gates," that "Each one according to what he assumes in his heart." This means that in the work of bestowal, there is the matter of ascents and descents. It follows that "no day is like another," for sometimes he assumes he has a great King, and sometimes to the contrary. It follows that each they should be "new," "as though on that day you were commanded them."

In other words, the strength to exert is according to which King he serves at that time, great or small. In other words, if yesterday he thought that He is a great King, and today he does not think so, then he does not make the same effort as yesterday, but according to his faith today. This is why the verse tells us, "This day the Lord your God commands you." That is, a person must know that each day, he has a different measure of faith in Him.

Therefore, one should not be alarmed if sometimes during a descent, there is a small king. This means that the person's faith is small, and cannot obligate him so he can overcome his body. Instead he surrenders to his body and is contemplating leaving the campaign.

But one must believe that this descent he has received, and he does not have the power to overcome, to believe in the Creator that He will help him and deliver him from this lowliness where a person is, and he will later acquire greater faith in the Creator, and then he will certainly have powers to work, since each day is new, meaning new faith. This is why he says, "As though today you were commanded them." Thus, everything is according to the faith he has on that day, to that extent a person works.

We should know that when a person begins to work in order to bestow and the body objects to it, the body brings him down to the worst lowliness. That is, the will to receive overcomes him and brings him down to sordid lusts. Sometimes he gets thoughts and desires he had never thought of. They come to him like uninvited guests, and the person is surprised and says, "How is today different from other days? That is, who caused me these thoughts and desires? Is it by thinking that one needs to work only for the sake of the Creator that these thoughts threw me into such baseness?" He asks, "But it is known that a Mitzva induces a Mitzva, so why does the desire to obtain vessels of bestowal cause a person to receive such thoughts in return for it? And also, what can one do in such states?"

However, a person must know, as Baal HaSulam says (Shamati, Article No. 1, "There Is None Else Besides Him") that the Creator sends these thoughts to a person so he will not be able to tolerate such lowliness, so it will cause him to pray to the Creator from the bottom of the heart to give him the strength to come closer instead of the thoughts that cause separation and remoteness from the Creator. At that time, a person must pray and cry out to the Creator, "Do not cast us from before You, and do not take away from us the spirit of Your holiness," but rather that the Creator will give him the second nature, the desire to bestow, meaning to have only a desire to bestow contentment upon the Maker, and no concern for himself. Then all these thoughts and desires that the will to receive brings him will naturally move away from him.

In other words, since a person should believe that all those thoughts that the will to receive brings him are sent to him from above because he wants to walk on the path of bestowal, and in the meantime he is idle in the work, because he prayed for the Creator to bring him closer to being in *Dvekut* with the Creator, which is equivalence of form, when it is apparent that the person is idle in the work, he is sent the foreign thoughts that a person cannot agree to be under such a control. This, in turn, gives a person a push that he must overcome the state he is in.

It therefore follows that from this bad, when a person feels that he is in such a lowly state that he never imagined that he could be under such governance, for this reason, he should not be alarmed and escape the campaign. On the contrary, he should believe that the Creator is taking care of him now, and He is bringing him closer through a state of *Achoraim* [posterior].

This is as it is written in the book *A Sage's Fruit* (Vol. 1, p 139), "About the verse, 'My beloved is like a gazelle,' our sages said, 'As the gazelle looks back when he runs, when the Creator leaves Israel, He turns back His face.' Then the face returns to being in the *Achoraim*, meaning craving and longing to cling to Israel once more. This begets in Israel longing and craving to cling to the Creator, too, and the measure of the longing and craving is actually the face itself."

We should interpret that he means that when a person is in a state of lowliness, it is considered that the Creator has moved away from him, and he has no desire or yearning for the work, this is regarded as the Creator giving a person a shape of tastelessness about spirituality. Moreover, a person wants to escape and forget about the work altogether. This is regarded as the Creator showing him the *Achoraim*.

The *Panim* [face/anterior] of the Creator is His desire to do good to His creations, and the *Achoraim* is the complete opposite. Why does the Creator show a person the *Achoraim*? It is on purpose, for by this a person gets a thrust toward *Dvekut* with the Creator, for he cannot remain in a state of lowliness. It follows that here, within the *Achoraim* is the discernment of *Panim*.

What Is, "The Concealed Things Belong to the Lord Our God," in the work?

Article No. 45, Tav-Shin-Nun, 1989/90

It known that in observing Torah and Mitzvot [commandments/ good deeds], there is the act, and there is the intention. An "act" means that a person should observe Torah and Mitzvot with all its details and precisions, in return for which a person should believe that he will be rewarded. It is as Maimonides says at the end of *Hilchot Teshuva*, "Hence, when teaching little ones, women, and uneducated people, they are taught to work only out of fear and in order to receive reward. Until they gain knowledge and acquire much wisdom, they are taught that secret little by little."

It follows that they are looking at the practice of Mitzvot as being for sake of those engaging in them. This is called "the revealed part of the work." It means that a person can see if his actions are in order, and when another person looks at how he observes

Torah and Mitzvot, he, too, can see. This is called the "revealed part," since the actions that a person does are revealed to him, as well as to others.

This is not so with the intention, meaning to aim that these actions will be for the sake of the Creator. With the intention, a person does not see the truth. He might deceive himself because a person cannot see the truth. Because one does not find fault in oneself, it follows that the intention is called the "concealed part." That is, it is concealed from the person himself. He cannot know the truth.

And especially, the intention is concealed from his friend, for one cannot see what his friend intends when he performs Mitzvot. This is why this part is called the "hidden part" of the work.

Accordingly, in our work, we should discern a revealed part, which is called "actions," a concealed part, which is called the "intention for the sake of the Creator," and we should discern between the work of the general public and the work of the individual. In the work of the general public, a person sees that he is making progress. That is, each time, he acquires more Torah, more Mitzvot, and therefore has motivation to work and is always happy. He cannot understand why all people do not connect to Torah and Mitzvot, since he feels a good taste in Torah and work.

This taste shines to the general public as Surrounding Light, and it is called "still of Kedusha [holiness]." In other words, as in corporeality, all the plants emerge from the still, so in the work, every "vegetative" in the work comes from the "still of Kedusha." Without the "still," there is no "vegetative." This Surrounding Light shines in the general public if they take upon themselves the burden of Torah and Mitzvot.

But the main point is that they have no intentions that go against the "body," called "self-benefit," since with the general public we should learn as Maimonides says, "in order to receive reward." To the extent that they believe in reward and punishment, they already have fuel to advance in the work happily and willingly.

This is not so when a person wants to walk on the path of meriting to work in order to bestow, which is against the body's nature. At that time, the body immediately begins to resist his path. Then, the faith that illuminated for him as Surrounding Light is not enough for him, and he sees that he is lacking faith in the greatness of the Creator, to have the strength to overcome the body's questions.

Then begins a procession of ascents and descents, and the person thinks that he is not worthy of being a worker of the Creator with the aim to be able to do everything for the sake of the Creator. He sees that foreign thoughts keep coming to him, which he cannot overcome.

However, according to what Baal HaSulam said, we must believe that the Creator sends us these thoughts so that by this we will receive a desire to pray to Him from the bottom of the heart, as it is written in the article "Other Gods," from the year *Tav-Shin-Hey*. Thus, we must only increase our prayers to the Creator to give us the desire to bestow, and we cannot obtain that desire by ourselves.

We must only seek advice in two manners: 1) to seek advice how to feel that all that we are missing is the power to bestow, 2) to ask Him to give us this power. This is called "613 *Eitin* [Aramaic: counsels]," meaning 613 counsels how to come to have a *Kli* [vessel], called "lack," and the filling, which is called "light."

In other words, the Creator gives the desire to bestow. This is called "Whatever you can do with your hand and strength, that do." At that time, the Creator gives him the second nature, called "desire to bestow." Only once we achieve the desire to bestow can we be rewarded with 613 *Pekudin* [Aramaic: deposits], which is the light that is clothed in the 613 *Mitzvot*.

According to the above, we should interpret the verse, "The concealed things belong to the Lord our God." This pertains to the intention, which is to aim that all his actions will be for the sake of the Creator. This belongs to the Creator. In other words, it is not within man's power to obtain this force by himself. For this reason, a person needs to know, when he sees that he will never be able to come to work for the sake of the Creator, at that time a person wants to escape the campaign because he sees that he will never achieve it. This is why the verse says, "The concealed things belong to the Lord our God." This means that the concealed part, the aim to bestow, is out of one's hands, but in the hands of the Creator to give the second nature, called "desire to bestow." This is why it is written, "concealed," and it belongs to the Creator, as He should give this.

However, when a person is rewarded with the desire to bestow, he should not pray for the will to receive to die, since then, if the will to receive dies, the person will not be able to see the lowliness of the will to receive. It follows that the will to receive within him will die without repentance, but the person wants the will to receive to repent, for by this he takes vengeance against the will to receive.

That is, a person sees how the will to receive must work according to the will of the desire to bestow, for "repentance" means that the will to receive surrenders to the desire to bestow, and the will to receive must now work in a manner of receiving in order to bestow. But if the will to receive were to die before a person could subdue it, so it receives in order to bestow, it follows that the person did not correct the will to receive.

According to the above, we should interpret what is written (Psalms 59:11), "The God of my mercy shall meet me." RASHI interprets, "Will help me before the hand of my enemies governs me. 'Will see me in my victory,' Which I crave to see. 'Do not kill them,' as this is not an apparent vengeance, 'lest my people forget,' for all the dead are forgotten. 'Move them with Your power and bring them down,' Rather, move them from their assets so they become poor. This is a vengeance that will be remembered for many days."

We should understand who David cursed like that, telling the Creator not to kill his enemies but leave them alive and poor, whereas if He kills them, they will not suffer, so he asks Him to keep them alive but poor. Only in this manner will he be able to take revenge from them, by bringing them down from their governance, as it is written, "Bring them down."

How is this matter interpreted in the work? First, we must understand who is David. David is called *Malchut*, which is the kingdom of heaven. *Malchut* of *Kedusha* is the desire to bestow, and its opposite is the desire to receive for oneself, which is called *Sitra Achra* [other side]. This is the opposite of *Kedusha* and is the enemy of *Kedusha*, as it is written, "The wicked watches the righteous and seeks to put him to death." That is, the will to receive wants to kill the desire to bestow.

David, who is the *Merkava* [chariot/structure] for *Malchut* of *Kedusha*, prayed that his enemy, the will to receive—who wants to kill the desire to bestow, which is *Kedusha*—that the Creator will hurry His salvation so that the will to receive, meaning the enemy, will not be able to govern him.

This is the meaning of "The God of my mercy will meet me," meaning that the Creator will deal mercy with me first. In other words, the desire to bestow, called *Hesed* [mercy/grace], will govern the will to receive. However, "Do not kill them," for this is not an apparent vengeance, "lest my people forget," since the dead are all forgotten. "Move them with Your power and bring them down," meaning move them from their assets and make them poor. This is vengeance that will be remembered for many days.

To understand these curses in the work, we should interpret that he was cursing the enemy, the will to receive for himself, that it would not die. That is, if the will to receive were to be cancelled, the will to receive would not witness the domination of the desire to bestow. In other words, "vengeance" means that the other one sees how he must be subdued. Here, it means that the wholeness is the sweetening of the judgments, which is called "delighting *Gevurot*."

For this reason, if the will to receive is cancelled and only the desire to bestow governs, this will not complete the purpose, since the purpose of creation was to do good to His creations, and not for the creations to bestow upon the Creator delight and pleasure. It is known that the reason why the creatures must bestow contentment upon the Maker is only a correction for the creatures, so there is no apparent vengeance here, since the will to receive does not surrender to the desire to bestow, since the will to receive is no longer in existence.

But when the will to receive is alive and must accept the governance of the desire to bestow, this is called "apparent vengeance." In other words, it is apparent to all that the will to receive is now working only thanks to it, meaning by taking upon itself the desire to bestow. This is called "receiving in order to bestow." That is, it accepted the purpose of creation to do good to His creations, and at the same time, he is in *Dvekut* [adhesion] with the Creator, for he wants to give contentment to his Maker. At that time, he feels what he can give to the Creator so He will enjoy. He sees that only by receiving from the Creator delight and pleasure the Creator enjoys, as this was the purpose of creation.

According to the above, we should understand the meaning of the sweetening of the *Gevurot*. *Gevurot* means *Hitgabrut* [overcoming], which pertains primarily to when a person works and uses the vessels of reception. Normally, we learn that the acts impact the intention. Therefore, when he uses the vessels of reception and wants to aim the opposite of the act, meaning to bestow, this requires extra overcoming. Usually, the *Gevurot* are called "judgments" because there were *Tzimtzum* [restriction] and judgment over the vessels of reception, that it is forbidden to use them without the aim to bestow.

Hence, when a person is placed under the rule of the desire to receive, these desires cause him a state of bitterness and he wants to get rid of them. He always thinks, "How can I get rid of them?" They poke his mind and if he could kill them so they would vanish from the horizon, he would be so happy!

But this is what David says, "Do not kill them, lest my people forget. Move them with Your power and bring them down."

"Move them" means move them from place to place and bring them down from the height of their wealth so they are poor. That is, let them not receive anything in their vessels of reception but be poor without any abundance. His vengeance will be that the will to receive will surrender and take upon itself the control of the aim to bestow. His curse will be that they will all come into the *Kedusha*, called "reception in order to bestow." This is called "sweetened *Gevurot*."

This is the meaning of *Rosh Hashanah* [beginning of the year], called "terrible days." The ARI says that *Rosh Hashanah* is the building of *Malchut*, called "the quality of judgment." *Malchut* [kingship] means that the whole world follows her quality, since *Malchut* is called "the assembly of Israel," in which all 600,000 souls of Israel are included, and the whole work of *Rosh Hashanah* is to accept the burden of the kingdom. This is why we pray, "Reign over the whole world with Your glory."

In other words, *Malchut* means that we must accept and crown His kingship over us, so it does not have the form of *Shechina* [Divinity] in the dust, but a form of glory. This is why on *Rosh Hashanah*, we pray, "And give glory to Your people." That is, we ask that the Creator will let us feel, so we will feel the glory of heaven. Since *Rosh Hashanah* is the kingdom of heaven, which is in a state of *Shechina* in the dust, therefore, *Rosh Hashanah* is the time when we must ask the Creator to feel the glory of heaven, meaning that the kingdom of heaven will be glorified in our eyes.

And since when we want to ask the kingdom of heaven to be revealed throughout the world, meaning that "the whole earth is full of His glory" will be sensed the world over, as it is written, "And will bring everything to Your servants," this prayer applies to both the general public and the individual. That is, since "Man is a small world," it means that he is included with the whole world. At that time, we ask that within our bodies, there will be no residue of desire to work for our own sake. And likewise in the whole world, meaning that it will be "The whole earth is full of the knowledge of the Lord." In this manner, all the prayers on *Rosh Hashanah* are general prayers.

The order of the blowing [of the *Shofar*] is also according to the order of the work, which is in three lines. That is, when we begin with the work of the Creator, we begin with one line, since we can speak of "right" and "left" only when we have two lines. One line is called "wholeness," and this is regarded as beginning with action.

That is, a person must say that since it is written, "This day, the Lord your God commands you," and our sages said, "Each day, they should be as new in your eyes, as though today you were commanded them," it follows that each day is a new beginning. Hence, when he begins with one line, he should be happy that he has the privilege of observing the law of the Creator.

Afterward, he shifts to the intention, meaning to criticize how much he needs to do everything for the sake of the Creator. At that time begins the real work, since then he sees that he has not a single organ that wants to do anything for the sake of the Creator. This is already called "left line," as our sages said, "the left rejects." That is, he sees how far he is from the Creator, and he must believe that the Creator pushed him away so that by this he will exert to make more efforts.

Afterward, he returns to one line, called "wholeness." But now the one line is called "right line," since the left line makes the one line become "right." Then the person is rewarded with the middle line, called "the Creator gives the soul."

The Order of the Work, from Baal HaSulam

Article No. 46, Tav-Shin-Nun, 1989/90

1) To believe that there is an Overseer to the world.

2) To know that faith is of inferior importance, yet he chooses to walk in this path.

3) His faith should be in a manner of bestowal, and not in order to receive.

4) When attributing the work to the Creator, he should believe that the Creator accepts our work, regardless of how the work seems.

5) There are two discernments to make concerning faith above reason: 1) He is going above reason because he has no choice. 2) Even should he be given reason, and he will no longer have to go above reason, he will still choose to walk in the path of above reason.

6) One should know that when his work is in self-love, after all the successes that a person depicts to himself that he can achieve, he will be able to benefit only himself. Conversely, with love of the Creator, he benefits the general public.

7) We must give thanks and praise for the past because on this depends the future. That is, to the extent that we give thanks, to that extent we appreciate everything that we receive from above and know how to keep the help we receive from above so as not to lose it.

8) The heart of the work is to walk on the right line, meaning wholeness. That is, whatever grip we have on spirituality, we should be happy that the Creator has given us a thought and desire to do something in spirituality.

9) We should also walk on the left line. But for this, half an hour a day is enough, meaning to calculate how much he prefers the love of the Creator over self-love. To the extent that he sees the deficiencies, he will pray that the Creator will truly bring him closer, for specifically on two lines can one advance.

We should make three discernments in the order of the work (*A Sage's Fruit*, Vol. 1, p 115):

1) To yearn to complement one's soul and return it to its root. This is called "the quality of Israel."

2) To understand the ways of the Creator and the secrets of Torah, for "One who does not know the commandment of the upper one, how will he serve Him?" This is regarded as the Torah.

3) To yearn to attain the Creator, meaning to cling unto Him with complete recognition, which is regarded as the Creator.

It is best to strive for the commandment of the upper one, which is the middle line.